THE MAI

Latin and especially Greek texts of the imperial period contain a wealth of references to 'India'. *The Making of Roman India* offers a survey of such texts, read against a wide range of other sources, both archaeological and documentary. It emphasises the social processes whereby the notion of India gained its exotic features, including the role of the Persian empire and of Alexander's expedition. Three kinds of social context receive special attention: the trade in luxury commodities; the political discourse of empire and its limits; and India's status as a place of special knowledge, embodied in 'naked philosophers'. Roman ideas about India ranged from the specific and concrete to the wildly fantastic: it is necessary to account for such variety. The afterlife of such ideas into late antiquity and beyond also receives consideration.

GRANT PARKER is Assistant Professor of Classics at Stanford University.

GREEK CULTURE IN THE ROMAN WORLD

The Greek culture of the Roman Empire offers a rich field of study. Extraordinary insights can be gained into processes of multicultural contact and exchange, political and ideological conflict, and the creativity of a changing, polyglot empire. During this period, many fundamental elements of Western society were being set in place: from the rise of Christianity, to an influential system of education, to long-lived artistic canons. This series is the first to focus on the response of Greek culture to its Roman imperial setting as a significant phenomenon in its own right. To this end, it will publish original and innovative research in the art, archaeology, epigraphy, history, philosophy, religion, and literature of the empire, with an emphasis on Greek material.

Titles in series:

Athletics and Literature in the Roman Empire
Jason König

Describing Greece: Landscape and Literature in the Periegesis *of Pausanias*
William Hutton

Reading the Self in the Ancient Greek Novel
Tim Whitmarsh

Hellenism in Byzantium
Anthony Kaldellis

The Making of Roman India
Grant Parker

THE MAKING OF ROMAN INDIA

BY

GRANT PARKER

CAMBRIDGE UNIVERSITY PRESS
Cambridge, New York, Melbourne, Madrid, Cape Town,
Singapore, São Paulo, Delhi, Tokyo, Mexico City

Cambridge University Press
The Edinburgh Building, Cambridge CB2 8RU, UK

Published in the United States of America by Cambridge University Press, New York

www.cambridge.org
Information on this title: www.cambridge.org/9780521175364

First published 2008
First paperback edition 2011

A catalogue record for this publication is available from the British Library

ISBN 978-0-521-85834-2 Hardback
ISBN 978-0-521-17536-4 Paperback

Dedicated to my family,
especially Brendah Gaine, Milly and Dave Parker, Joan Subhani
and, of course, Mavis and Dick Parker

Contents

Figures

Maps

Preface

What did India mean to Romans of the empire? Between these covers I outline some possible answers, sifting through a variety of literary and to some degree material and documentary evidence, and paying heed to the different contexts of Roman information about India. The book is aimed not merely at classicists but also at those interested in ancient India or the history of orientalism. As a result, I have not assumed specialist knowledge. If a reader finds a particular discussion or explanation unnecessary, I hope he or she will bear in mind that others will, I trust, come to the book from different backgrounds.

Long ago it became clear to me that a study on this theme cannot be exhaustive, and that no two persons tackling it will produce the same kind of result. This realisation has brought consolation amid the appearance, in recent years, of many works of relevance. As in any work of synthesis, any one topic covered or piece of evidence deployed inevitably leaves room for greater depth of discussion. I have had to make extensive use of the researches of others, particularly archaeologists and other South Asianists. While my own background is in the study of ancient Greek and Roman societies, and particularly Latin literature, I can merely hope that this work contributes to broader debates.

During the late stages of revision, Dominique Lenfant's Budé edition, *Ctésias de Cnide*, and Pierre Schneider's *L'Éthiopie et l'Inde* came into my hands. I have tried to take account of them where possible, but have not been able to engage with them as fully as they deserve. Years ago, two books played a more formative role than their current place in the notes suggests: Arnaldo Momigliano's *Alien Wisdom: The Limits of Hellenization* and James S. Romm's *The Edges of the Earth in Ancient Thought*. Elsewhere I have delved into material that is touched on here: 'Hellenism in an Afghan context' in *Memory as History: The Legacy of Alexander in Asia*, ed. Himanshu Prabha Ray and Daniel T. Potts (Delhi: Aryan International, 2007).

An earlier version of chapter 3 has appeared in *Ancient India in its Wider World*, ed. Grant Parker and Carla Sinopoli (Ann Arbor: University of Michigan Centers for South and Southeast Asian Studies, 2008); and of chapter 4 in the *Journal of the Economic and Social History of the Orient* 45.1 (2002) 40–95. In each case I thank the publishers for permission to reprint.

This book took its current shape at the University of Michigan (thanks to a generous fellowship of the Michigan Society of Fellows) and at Duke University. The reworking process has been much helped by a UNC/Duke graduate seminar jointly taught with Richard Talbert, and earlier by a Michigan symposium co-organised with Carla Sinopoli and Tom Trautmann, as well as a graduate seminar jointly taught with Sue Alcock. Several teachers at Princeton University guided my initial efforts, and continued to take an interest: Peter Brown, Elaine Fantham, Anthony Grafton and Brent Shaw; my debt to Kathleen Coleman goes back to undergraduate days. At a crucial stage, Dieter Harlfinger was my academic host for half a year in the stimulating environment of the Graduiertenkolleg Textüberlieferung und Wissenschaftsgeschichte at the University of Hamburg. A seminar organised by John Hilton at the University of KwaZulu-Natal (Durban) helped me clarify my thoughts early on.

My research was supported by the wonderful libraries of Princeton, Hamburg, Michigan, Duke and UNC-Chapel Hill, and for substantial periods also by those of the universities of Cape Town and Sydney.

In this project I have received help of so many kinds from so many people over such a long period that I must avoid naming names: any list would be absurdly long yet unavoidably incomplete. I learned much from the referees' reports, and enjoyed working with the editorial team at Cambridge University Press. In the final stages, Tom Elliott of UNC's Ancient World Mapping Center kindly produced the maps; Marie-Louise Catsalis, Kay Ebel and Alka Patel helped secure images; Richard Parker and Fred Porta helped with proofreading.

To all, my heartfelt thanks; of course, they cannot be blamed for the deficiencies that remain. And how can I fail to mention the support of my family, when they have so long endured my efforts and made them worthwhile?

Map 1 Eastern Mediterranean and western Indian Ocean

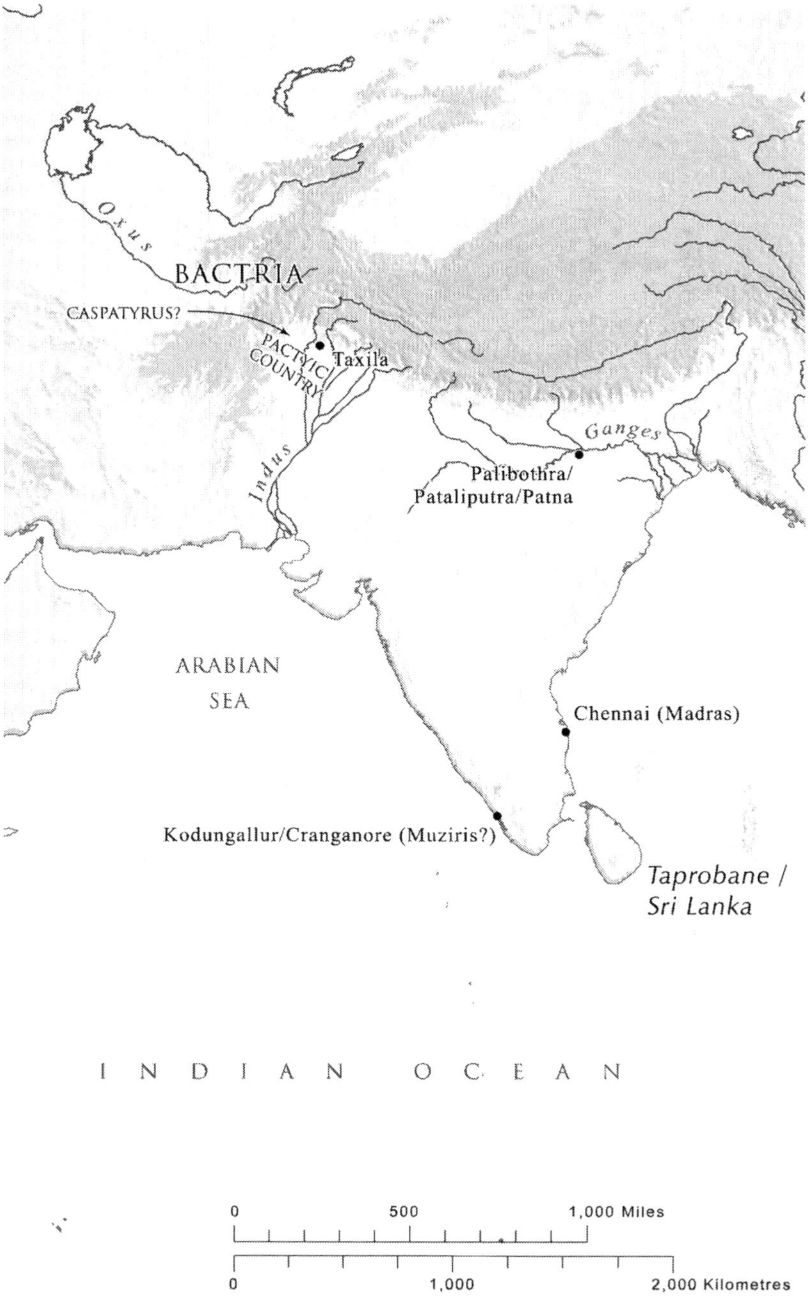

Oxus
BACTRIA
CASPATYRUS?
PACTYIC COUNTRY
Taxila
Indus
Ganges
Palibothra/
Pataliputra/Patna
ARABIAN
SEA
Chennai (Madras)
Kodungallur/Cranganore (Muziris?)
Taprobane /
Sri Lanka
INDIAN OCEAN
0
500
1,000 Miles
0
1,000
2,000 Kilometres

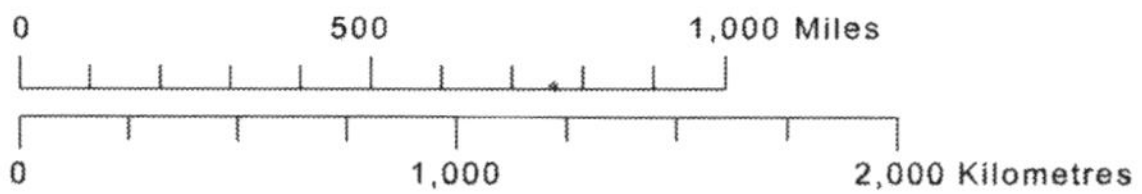

Introduction

On a journey from the eastern Mediterranean to India, the Greek sage Apollonius of Tyana encountered a Roman official at the town of Zeugma on the Euphrates:

> When they entered Mesopotamia, the tax-collector in charge of Zeugma led them to the notice-board and asked them what they were exporting. Apollonius answered, 'I am taking moderation, righteousness, virtue, self-control, courage and discipline,' thereby mentioning several feminine nouns. The tax-collector, already contemplating his own gain, said, 'Then you must declare these female slaves.' Apollonius answered, 'That is not possible, for these are not female slaves I'm taking out, but so many royal ladies.' (1.20)[1]

The setting is significant: Zeugma ('bridge'), corresponding to modern Balkis in Syria, lies at a strategic position straddling the east Roman colonies of Seleucia and Apamea, and thereby controlled a major east–west trade route.[2] More significant for our purposes, however, is the characterisation of the pious sage. Add to this the comical misunderstanding whereby his philosophical quest appears as a commercial venture, and thus subject to tax – at least in the eyes of a rapacious official. Philostratus' *Life of Apollonius of Tyana*, the hagiography of this polytheist holy man, was written in the third century AD, but it purports to tell of a journey undertaken in the first century AD. It is, in an important sense, the world of Philostratus, around

[1] παριόντας δὲ αὐτοὺς ἐς τὴν μέσην τῶν ποταμῶν ὁ τελώνης ὁ ἐπιβεβλημένος τῷ Ζεύγματι πρὸς τὸ πινάκιον ἦγε καὶ ἠρώτα, ὅ τι ἀπάγοιεν, ὁ δὲ Ἀπολλώνιος ἀπάγω, ἔφη, σωφροσύνην δικαιοσύνην ἀρετὴν ἐγκράτειαν ἀνδρείαν ἄσκησιν, πολλὰ καὶ οὕτω θήλεα εἴρας ὀνόματα. ὁ δ' ἤδη βλέπων τὸ ἑαυτοῦ κέρδος ἀπόγραψαι οὖν ἔφη τὰς δούλας. ὁ δὲ οὐκ ἔξεστιν, εἶπεν, οὐ γὰρ δούλας ἀπάγω ταύτας, ἀλλὰ δεσποίνας.

[2] Anthony Comfort, Catherine Abadie-Reynal and Rifat Ergeç, 'Crossing the Euphrates in antiquity: Zeugma seen from space', *Anatolian Studies* 50 (2000), 99–126; Anthony Comfort and Rifat Ergeç, 'Following the Euphrates in antiquity: north–south routes around Zeugma', *Anatolian Studies* 51 (2001), 19–49. Recent dam-building has necessitated rescue excavation and attracted much attention: see esp. David Kennedy *et al.*, *The twin towns of Zeugma on the Euphrates: rescue work and historical studies* (Portsmouth, RI: JRA supplement 27, 1998), with C. S. Lightfoot, 'Trying to rescue Zeugma', *JRA* 14 (2001), 643–8

AD 222–35, that most clearly emerges from the text. Yet it would be wrong to overlook the dramatic setting: Apollonius was, according to this account and others, an eminent figure of the first century AD. Journeys such as his inform *The making of Roman India*, not so much for their own historicity as for the images of India with which they are connected.

India emerges in Philostratus' work as a place of special knowledge, its religious specialists themselves the objects of pilgrimage. There are many indications that Apollonius, in this guise, is re-enacting Alexander's expedition that reached as far as the Indus valley before his troops forced him to return (327–325 BC). For it was with Alexander's invasion that this image of India entered Greek thinking; his interview with Indian sages inspired several accounts from the earliest Alexander histories into the Middle Ages. But the implicit contrast between the military expedition and the holy man's quest could not be more pointed, as the anecdote of Apollonius shows. It is mainly in connection with Alexander that we encounter the mythical figures of Dionysus and Heracles – themselves pan-Mediterranean travellers *par excellence* but in several accounts linked with India. In one way or another, the memory of Alexander will be a key motif throughout this book.[3]

Apollonius is not the only person who is supposed to have travelled from the Mediterranean to India in the first century AD. The apostle Thomas travelled from Jerusalem to India as a missionary, sent by Jesus. Here he preached a message of bodily purity and enacted various miracles until dying a martyr's death at the behest of an Indian ruler. This story, recounted in the apocryphal *Acts of Thomas*, a Syriac text composed in the early third century AD, was translated into Greek, Latin and many other languages, and widely diffused in late antiquity.

Both Apollonius and Thomas travel along routes that correspond demonstrably with networks of commodity exchange. One particularly valuable witness to the long-distance exchange is the anonymously written *Periplus of the Erythraean Sea*. This text, which dates to the years AD 40–70, is a sea-captain's manual, without literary embellishment, listing specific commodities, ports and other practical matters related to sea-borne trade between Egypt, via the Red Sea, following the seasonal monsoon winds

[3] W. J. Aerts, 'Alexander the Great and ancient travel stories', in *Travel fact and travel fiction*, ed. Zweder von Martels (Leiden: Brill, 1994), pp. 30–8, esp. 35 n. 24 on those mythical travellers; cf. François Hartog, *Memories of Odysseus: frontier tales from ancient Greece* (University of Chicago Press, 2001). It is as well to bear in mind, from a classicist's point of view, the comment of Diana Spencer, *The Roman Alexander: reading a cultural myth* (University of Exeter Press, 2002), p. xv: 'The Alexander we know and reinterpret is himself a "Roman" construct, a product of Roman sensibilities and worldview; it was the Romans who made him "the Great".'

south of the Arabian peninsula to India. Yet even this text, functional rather than literary, refers to 'evidence of Alexander's expedition' (ch. 41).

These three travellers – Apollonius the sage, Thomas the apostle and the anonymous *Periplus* author – seem, at first glance, readily open to investigation for the concrete details of their journeys. Notably different motives took them to India, and indeed it is tempting to define travellers by their motives.[4] Yet, in the first two cases, when we consider the time-lapse between event and account, it soon becomes clear that such investigation cannot proceed without due consideration of the textual complexities involved. The emphasis here will be more on travel texts than travellers themselves. Armchair travellers are no less important in this study, for it is particularly on their account that imagination comes to the forefront.

It is in the imaginative realm that the goal of this book is most readily articulated: to analyse the literary presentation of India in texts of the Roman empire. What visions of India do they harbour?[5] Consideration of these texts will be, in part, in relation to different kinds of physical travel, of lived practice, that linked India and the Mediterranean. For current purposes, the historicity of actual journeys is of some consequence, but less so than the responses they inspire. In this respect we will need to inquire where, on a modern map, these visions would be located, even as we consider mental maps.

*

What, then, did India mean to Romans of the empire? The book-ends framing this study are Augustus on the one hand and Cosmas Indicopleustes and Isidore of Seville on the other, roughly the late first century BC and early seventh AD. Its aims are to sketch the features of this 'Roman India' and to account for them by analysing the processes that brought them into being. It focuses primarily, but not exclusively, on Greek and Latin literary texts.

The term 'Roman India' is unexpected, even paradoxical. No Roman commander ever conquered India, though many were conscious of someone who had done so, in their view: Alexander III of Macedon. At least one emperor, Trajan (reigned AD 98–117), entertained fantasies of emulating

[4] Tzvetan Todorov, *On human diversity: nationalism, racism and exoticism in French thought* (Cambridge, MA: Harvard University Press, 1993), pp. 341–52; compare the framework sketched Roxanne L. Euben, 'The comparative politics of travel', *Parallax* 9.4 (2003), 18–28.

[5] Some of the Latin texts under discussion have been translated and annotated by Jacques André and Jean Filliozat, *L'Inde vue de Rome* (Paris: Belles Lettres, 1986). Greek texts have fared less well, but note Ramesh Chandra Majumdar, *The classical accounts of India* (Calcutta: Mukhopadhyay, 1960).

him.[6] Most importantly, India gained a place in Roman minds as the ultimate exotic, a sense consciously expressed in artifacts and historical texts but also, even more tellingly perhaps, in passing references in a wide variety of texts. It is this range of exotic imaginings that the book adumbrates.

The work falls into three parts. The first, 'Creation of a discourse', lends time-depth by presenting the earliest relevant texts and identifying the processes that gave rise to Roman Indography. It analyses material up to the late Republic, with special attention to the figure of Alexander. Certainly his expedition generated an enormous amount of geographic, ethnographic and other natural historical writing in the Hellenistic world. Foremost among these are the account of the naval commander, Nearchus, which underlies Arrian's *Indica* (second century AD). Megasthenes' *Indica* comes from less than a generation after Alexander's campaign, and follows directly in its wake.[7] Now accounts by Megasthenes, Nearchus and others linked with Alexander's campaign survive merely in fragments embedded in later works; here it is necessary to recreate the original works to the extent possible, and with a critical awareness of their fragmentary character.[8]

The centrality of Alexander notwithstanding, it is important to scratch below the surface in identifying the origins of this process. Special prominence in this chapter goes to the Achaemenid empire as the source of Greek Indography.[9] The most substantial pre-Alexander writers on India, namely Herodotus and Ctesias (mid- and late-fifth century BC respectively), discuss India in the context of Achaemenid Persia, of which it was a satrapy or province. This opening chapter explores, in part, the impact of Achaemenid India on the making of Hellenistic (and beyond that Roman) Indography. Indeed, it can be argued, Alexander's military achievement can be seen as a performance of Persian kingship, in its fullest geographic extent. It would be wrong, by this reckoning, to take at face value the prominence later writers attribute to Alexander in this regard.[10]

6 Dio Cassius, *Roman history* 68.29.1: cf. Chapter 5, section I.5 below.

7 Albrecht Dihle, in an important article, has shown that the figure of Alexander lent a degree of authority to these early Hellenistic accounts of India – with the result that a canon of Indography was formed at an early stage, to the exclusion of information that later came to hand: 'The conception of India in Hellenistic and Roman literature', *PCPhS* 10 (1964), 15–23, reprinted in *Antike und Orient. Gesammelte Aufsätze* (Heidelberg: Winter, 1984), pp. 89–97. Indeed, Dihle's wide-ranging work is central to most aspects of the current project; however, with the partial exception of an encyclopaedia article ('Indien', *RAC*), he has not ventured an overview of the topics discussed here.

8 Especially useful in this respect is Glenn W. Most (ed.), *Collecting fragments – Fragmente sammeln* (Göttingen: Vandenhoeck and Ruprecht, 1997).

9 This has previously been suggested, e.g., R. D. Milns, 'Greek writers on India before Alexander,' *Australian Journal of Politics and History* 35 (1989), 353–63, but its implications hardly explored.

10 Spencer, *Roman Alexander*, emphasises the variety of responses, though restricting her purview to Latin texts up to Trajan. Words of caution against overestimating the role of Alexander among

Against this background, Part II, 'Features of a discourse', moves the focus to the imperial period as it puts India in a context of Roman ethnography and geography. What are the features of India as it appears in writers such as Strabo, Pliny the elder and Arrian? How do these features compare with the profile of other lands, e.g., Egypt, Arabia and China? This inquiry rests mostly on literary sources (Chapter 2).[11] Several of these writers may be linked with the Second Sophistic, to use the modern term for a cultural movement of Greek speakers under Roman rule (around AD 60–230).[12] The literature of this period is characterised by the importance of rhetoric – particularly as practised by professional orators or 'sophists' – and by nostalgia for the classical Greek past that preceded Roman domination. Less familiar than the literary texts but no less significant is a group of images representing India, including the Great Hunt mosaic at Piazza Armerina (early fourth century AD), which deserve investigation of their own (Chapter 3).[13]

Part III, 'Contexts of a discourse', constitutes the most direct answer to the central question of this book. Following the description of Roman Indography above, this substantial section offers three specific lines of analysis. First (Chapter 4), India was the source of commodities, including spices, fabrics and precious stones. Anxieties about *luxuria* inform many of the literary texts. While it is not possible to present all archaeological and documentary evidence for Roman trade with South Asia, it is necessary and feasible to outline the kinds of objects exchanged, routes and personnel, and in particular, to indicate ways in which these informed Roman ideas about India.

Second (Chapter 5), India constituted the end of empire, and, by implication, the end of the earth. When Augustus spoke in the *Res gestae*

Roman commanders and rulers come from Peter Green, 'Caesar and Alexander: *aemulatio, imitatio, comparatio*', *AJAH* 3 (1978), 1–26; and E. S. Gruen, 'Rome and the myth of Alexander', in *Ancient history in a modern university*, ed. T. W. Hillard *et al.* (North Ryde, NSW: Macquarie University, 1998), pp. 178–91.

[11] Indographic texts are analysed within traditions of Hellenistic ethnography by James S. Romm, *The edges of the earth in ancient thought* (Princeton University Press, 1992), chapter 3. There is now a fundamental new discussion of Strabo by Katherine Clarke, *Between geography and history* (Oxford: Clarendon, 1999), pp. 193–336; notable also is Trevor Murphy, *Pliny the Elder's* Natural history: *the empire in the encyclopedia* (Oxford University Press, 2004).

[12] Amid an extensive and fast-growing bibliography, note especially the surveys of Graham Anderson, *The Second Sophistic: a cultural phenomenon in the Roman Empire* (London: Routledge, 1993), and Simon Swain, *Hellenism and empire: language, classicism and power in the Greek world, AD 50–250* (Oxford: Clarendon, 1996).

[13] The only synthesis available of these artifacts is by Hans Graeven, 'Darstellung der Inder in antiken Kunstweken', *JDAI(B)* 15 (1900), 195–218; see now also C. R. Whittaker, 'Sex on the frontiers', in a volume that bears on many of the interests addressed here: *Rome and its frontiers: the dynamics of empire* (London: Routledge, 2004).

(AD 14) of Indian ambassadors coming from India, 'which no Roman ruler had ever seen before', he was implying Roman rule over the farthest expanse of land – something that emerges from the context of that inscription. The hyperbolic language of Augustan poetry, suggesting Roman military dominance as far as India, deserves comparison here. Over time, this elision of *orbis terrarum* and empire takes on a different character, when for example the Christian geographies of Orosius and Isidore present India as marking the end of God's kingdom. (Such Christian conceptions of India from late antiquity show a high degree of continuity with maps of the later Middle Ages, e.g., the thirteenth-century Ebstorf world map, where ethnographic traditions are visually represented.) The focus on changing geographies of India thus provides an opportunity to trace changing conceptions of empire between Augustus and the early Middle Ages.[14]

Third (Chapter 6), India was a source of special knowledge. This was embodied especially in the 'naked philosophers' (*Gymnosophistae*), who featured in accounts of Alexander's expedition (e.g., Arrian's *Anabasis* and Plutarch's *Life of Alexander*, both of the second century AD). Alexander's interview with the 'naked philosophers' forms the basis of this vision of India. It was by no means limited to historiography, since it became a central theme in the Alexander legend in its many other forms. In particular, this chapter suggests why India continued to appeal, over several centuries, as a source of wisdom (*sophia*). Apollonius of Tyana, the philosophic holy man of the first century AD whose life is described in Philostratus' hagiography of him (late second or early third century AD), is one significant traveller to India, invoking as he does the memory of Pythagoras and archaic Greek traditions about eastern wisdom. Philostratus' *Life of Apollonius* is very much a text of the Second Sophistic. Another, rather different traveller is the apostle Thomas, also linked with the first century AD: the apocryphal *Acts of Thomas* present an India that is the ultimate target of Christian mission. The purpose of visiting India could thus be either to learn or to teach, and here Apollonius is a figure of special complexity.[15]

By way of conclusion, there follows an attempt to bring together these various strands. This fourth part is entitled 'Intersections of a discourse'. If different Roman Indias have emerged from the foregoing discussion, it is

[14] Anna-Dorothee von den Brincken, *Kartographische Quellen* (Turnhout: Brepols, 1988); N. Lozovsky, *'The earth is our book:' geographical knowledge in the Latin West* ca. *400–1000* (Ann Arbor: University of Michigan Press, 2000).

[15] John Elsner, 'Hagiographic geography: travel and allegory in the *Life of Apollonius of Tyana*', *JHS* 117 (1997), 22–37; more generally, Arnaldo Momigliano, *Alien wisdom: the limits of Hellenization* (Cambridge University Press, 1975).

necessary to look into the ways in which they were realised in lived practice, and how they related to each other. It will be clear by now that there were different registers of geographic and topographic knowledge, some more scholarly and scientific (e.g., Claudius Ptolemy's *Geography*, second century AD), others more popular and generalized (e.g. the *Alexander Romance*, third century AD), yet others practical (*Periplus of the Erythraean Sea*, mid-first century AD). But to what extent do they constitute a single, integrated Roman conception of India? To what extent are Roman ideas about India extrapolations of their ideas about western Asia? What conclusions emerge about the nature and place of the exotic in Roman imperial culture? In particular, this epilogue is an opportunity to evaluate the memory of Alexander as a unifying figure for Roman discourses about India: in various ways, it plays a part in ideas about India as a place of commodities, empire or wisdom.

*

The present work is a history of representations that is concerned with social context. As such, it is emphatically not a study of 'contacts' between India and the Mediterranean. (Whether it would be possible to write such a book is doubtful, though some studies do at least point in that direction.)[16] By the same token, this is not a book about the 'influence' of India on the Mediterranean world or vice versa.[17] Rather, the approach adopted here is to identify Roman responses to India, analysed with reference to the concept of discourse. Responses, in this sense, place the focus squarely in the Mediterranean, without claiming to speak in equal measure for all the cultural traditions spanned. The concept of a discourse thus refers to representations, conceived in terms of power relations within Roman society.[18] In this way India provides a vantage point from which to examine

16 For one attempt, see Jean W. Sedlar, *India and the Greek world* (Totowa, NJ: Rowman and Littlefield, 1980), which focuses on philosophy. A multi-volume project by Klaus Kartunnen traces common features between South Asian and Greco-Roman literary traditions: thus far *India in early Greek literature* (Helsinki: Finnish Oriental Society, 1989) and *India and the Hellenistic world* (Helsinki: Finnish Oriental Society, 1997) have appeared. Especially valuable is Himanshu Prabha Ray's *The archaeology of seafaring in ancient South Asia* (Cambridge University Press, 2003).

17 Comparison between Buddhism and Christianity has usually been considered in terms of influence one way or the other: Zacharias P. Thundy, *Buddha and Christ: nativity stories and Indian traditions* (Leiden: Brill, 1993), pp. 1–17, reviews earlier scholarship. Such 'influence-research' is defended by J. Duncan M. Derrett, 'An Indian metaphor in St. John's Gospel', *JRAS*, series III. 9 (1999), 271–86, esp. 271–3. In the sphere of material culture, see now the massive work of Warwick Ball, *Rome in the east: the transformation of an empire* (London: Routledge, 2000).

18 Michel Foucault, *Discipline and punish: the birth of the prison*, tr. Alan Sheridan, 2nd edn (New York: Vintage, 1995). For a more recent survey, Paul A. Bové, 'Discourse', in *Critical terms for literary study*, ed. Frank Lentricchia and Thomas McLaughlin, 2nd edn (Chicago: University of Chicago Press, 1995), pp. 50–65.

Roman worldviews. To focus on Roman responses rather than contacts or influence is perhaps to err on the side of caution. But the limitations bring with them a major advantage, namely, that it is thereby possible to avoid an essentialised view of timeless India. It is the contexts of Indography that we seek especially to understand. In examining Roman thinking, it is as much the *why* as the *how* that will concern us.

In so far as this study is concerned with empire as a context of knowledge, it shares an aim with a highly influential and controversial study of representations of eastern lands and peoples: Edward Said's *Orientalism*.[19] Said's insistence on the constructed quality of the 'Orient', on the political implications of scholarship, has become an orthodoxy of sorts, despite the prodigious critique it has received.[20] In principle, I share that sense. Hence the emphasis on the political and generic contexts of Indography discussed in Chapters 1 and 2 below. However, I do not imagine that Said's model of orientalism applies without further ado to this very different period of history – one that is separated from modern colonialism by the Industrial Revolution, and is thereby part of very different technological systems, and a different economy of knowledge. It would be unfortunate if lip-service to Said denied our temporal framework the measure of specificity due to any period of historical inquiry. Roman thinking about India may have had a very powerful context of empire, as Chapters 1 and 4 variously explore; but that does not mean that the conditions of Roman contact with India resembled those of British imperialism. It is certainly possible and even necessary to draw comparisons between modern and premodern versions of orientalism, but it would be much better for those to proceed from the material itself, appropriately delimited and contextualised, rather than a priori. To this question of comparison we shall return in individual chapters and in the conclusion. The paradigm of Said's *Orientalism* continues to be an important one, providing a critical problem rather than an easy formula.

19 Edward W. Said, *Orientalism* (New York: Pantheon, 1978); in a 1995 reprint, Said responds to his critics.

20 For a recent dossier, Alexander Lyon Macfie (ed.), *Orientalism: a reader* (New York University Press, 2000). Among discussions of its relevance to the ancient Mediterranean, Phiroze Vasunia, 'Hellenism and empire: reading Edward Said', *Parallax* 9 (2003), 88–97, offers a spirited defence, while several Roman historians and archaeologists are favourably inclined: *Dialogues in Roman imperialism: power, discourse and discrepant experience in the Roman empire*, ed. D. J. Mattingly (Portsmouth, RI: JRA, 1997). Note also M. J. Versluys, *Aegyptiaca Romana: Nilotic scenes and the Roman views of Egypt* (Leiden: Brill, 2002).

PART I

Creation of a discourse

CHAPTER I

Achaemenid India and Alexander

By way of introducing the book as a whole, this chapter strives to outline the features of Greek Indography, from the earliest texts up to the late Hellenistic world of the first century BC, and as far as possible to account for those features. What were the historical moments at which these ideas were formulated, and what were their sources? An earlier rendition of this story offers a three-part chronology: (1) Greek writings from Asia Minor from the later sixth to the early fourth century BC; (2) works based on Alexander's campaign, which brought thousands of Greek troops to the Indus Valley around 327–325 BC; and (3) writing produced by Greek ambassadors sent by Hellenistic states in the third century.[1] This periodisation provides a plausible starting point, but one that we shall reconsider in the course of the chapter. Even though several scholars have perceived continuity over time, the importance of Alexander's campaign in the production of images is a familiar fact, so familiar indeed that we may well ask to what extent it tends to be overstated.[2] This question can only be considered by sifting through Greek accounts before and after the campaign. One of the tasks of this chapter is thus to assess the campaign as an ethnographic moment, that is to say, as a defining point in the generation of knowledge about India and its inhabitants. Throughout these pages we shall be attentive to the contexts in which India is mentioned, whether in its own right, as part of a larger schema, or as a passing reference.

[1] E. R. Bevan, 'India in early Greek and Latin literature', in *The Cambridge history of India*, ed. E. J. Rapson, rev. Indian repr. edn (Delhi: Chand, 1962), vol. I, pp. 351–83, at 353.

[2] On the question of continuity and change, see especially Dihle, 'Conception'; elsewhere, Dihle has emphasised the role of Poseidonius in that continuity (*Antike und Orient*, pp. 21–6). Also Klaus Karttunen, 'The country of fabulous beasts and naked philosophers: India in classical and medieval literature', *Arctos* 21 (1987), 43–52.

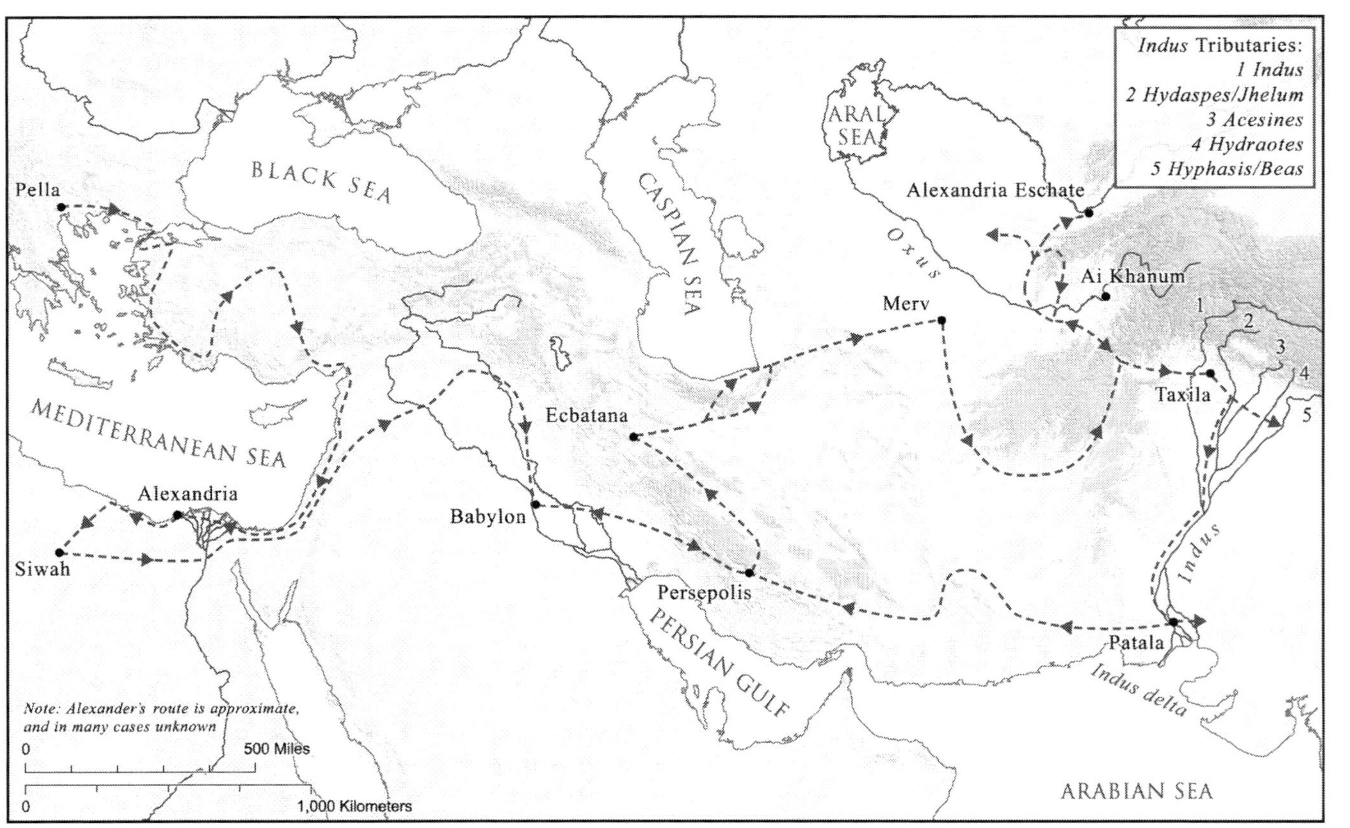

Map 2 Alexander's route

I. THE EXTENT OF ACHAEMENID POWER

Darius I's rise to power in the Iranian world in 522 was a violent and perhaps illegitimate one: after crushing the forces of Gaumata, the Magian (Median) priest known to the Greeks as Smerdis, he quashed a series of uprisings which allowed him to 're-establish [] the people on its foundation, both Persia, Media and other provinces', as he was later to say on the Behistun inscription (DB 1.66–7).[3] While this lengthy inscription, dating from the early years of Darius' reign, makes no mention of India, the King of Kings does mention India among the lands he controls in a slightly later inscription, at Persepolis (c. 518–513):

> Darius the Great King, King of Kings, King of countries, son of Hystaspes, an Achaemenian. Saith Darius the King: This is the kingdom which I hold, from the Scythians who are beyond Sogdiana, thence unto Aethiopia; from Sind, thence unto Sardis which Ahuramazda the greatest of the gods bestowed upon me. May Ahuramazda protect me and my royal house. (DPh 1–7: Kent, *Old Persian*, 136–37, adapted)

On the strength of this apparent change, and at the same time on the evidence of Herodotus (discussed below), it has been supposed that Darius conquered India some time before 513.[4] It is clear that India, 'Sind' in the inscription, is not merely the easternmost of his provinces; it is specifically, in Darius' rhetoric of power, a marker of the extent of his kingdom. In the Old Persian of the inscription, a language which Darius may in fact have had created for that purpose, the name of the province is a direct loanword from the contemporary Sanskrit: the Indian name for the river Indus and its valley is *Sindhu*, whereas the *Mahabharata* uses a different appellation for the south Asian peninsula, namely *Bharat*.[5] The royal complex at Persepolis

[3] Pierre Briant, *From Cyrus to Alexander: a history of the Persian empire* (Winona, IN: Eisenbrauns, 2002), pp. 107–14. On the lists of provinces, Roland G. Kent, *Old Persian*, 2nd edn (New Haven: AOS, 1953), e.g., pp. 119 and 136; Willem Vogelsang, 'The Achaemenids and India', *Achaemenid History Workshop* 4 (1990), 93–110. For the place of India within an Achaemenid (and Zoroastrian) worldview consisting of 'seven regions', see A. Sh. Shabazi, 'Darius Haft Kisvar', in *Kunst, Kultur und Geschichte der Achämenidenzeit und ihr Fortleben*, ed. Heidemarie Koch and D. N. Mackenzie (Berlin: Reimer, 1983), pp. 239–46. The recent survey by Bruno Jacobs, *Die Satrapienverwaltung im Perserreich zur Zeit Darius III* (Wiesbaden: Steiner, 1994), gives Herodotus little credence in reconstructing the satrapies, privileging instead the retrospective evidence of the Alexander historians; on India esp. pp. 243–7 and 261–72.

[4] M. A. Dandamaev, *A political history of the Achaemenid empire* (Leiden: Brill, 1989), p. 144; Dominique Lenfant, 'L'Inde de Ctésias', *Topoi* 5 (1990), 309–36, at 309 n. 2.

[5] Kent, *Old Persian*, p. 214; David Neiman, 'Ethiopia and Kush: Biblical and ancient Greek geography', *Ancient World* 3 (1980), 35–42, at 38, with further references. When the author of the *Periplus of the Erythraean Sea* speaks of the Indus as Σίνθος (34) he appears to be translating directly from the Sanskrit. Cf. Plin. *HN* 6.71: *Indus incolis Sindus appellatus*. Hebrew *Hoddu* (e.g., *Esther* 1:1) and Aramaic *Henda*.

Figure 1 Indian contingent in tribute procession at the Apadana complex in Persepolis, sixth century BC. Courtesy of the Oriental Institute, University of Chicago.

also offers visual representations of Indians among the many tribute-bearers and throne-bearers. On the stairway of the Apadana or audience-hall, each of the Indians wears a short skirt, baring his chest and legs; they carry jar-shaped objects, which may correspond to the containers for the gold-dust mentioned by Herodotus (section I.3 below).[6]

I.1. Scylax and the King of Kings

It is with Scylax of Caryanda that the history of Greek Indography concretely begins, for it is in connection with him that we find the first explicit reference to India.[7] Herodotus records that Darius sent Scylax, a sea-captain

[6] Erich F. Schmidt, *Persepolis*, 3 vols. (Chicago: Oriental Institute, 1953–70), vol. I, pp. 70–90 and vol. III, p. 152. See also Ernst Badian, 'The King's Indians', in *Alexander der Grosse*, ed. Wolfgang Will (Bonn: Habelt, 1998), pp. 205–24.

[7] See *FGrH* 709, esp. F1–7. For modern discussions see esp. F. Gisinger, 'Skylax', *RE* IIIA1 (1929), 619–46; cf. also Wilhelm Reese, *Die griechischen Nachrichten über Indien* (Leipzig: Teubner, 1914), pp. 2–3 and 39–52; Milns, 'Greek writers', at 353–5; Dihle, 'Indien', *RAC*, 2–3. Rudolf Güngerich, *Die Küstenbeschreibung in der griechischen Literatur* (Münster: Aschendorff, 1950), pp. 9–10, and Pietro Janni, *La Mappa e il Periplo* (Rome: Bretschneider, 1984), p. 47, underline his importance in the literary history of the *periplus*.

from Ionia, on a mission to explore the sea-route down the Indus and then from its mouth towards the Arabian peninsula, up to the Suez, i.e. to the northwest corner of the Red Sea:

> Darius was the discoverer of the greater part of Asia. Wishing to know where the Indus (the only river with crocodiles, save one) ran into the sea, he sent a number of men, on whose trustworthiness he could rely, and among them Scylax of Caryanda, to sail down the river. They set out from the city of Caspatyrus, in the region called Pactyica, and sailed downstream in an easterly direction to the sea. Here they turned westward, and after a voyage of thirty months, reached the place from which the Egyptian king . . . sent the Phoenicians to sail round Libya. Once the voyage was completed, Darius conquered the Indians, and made use of the sea in those parts. Thus all Asia, except the eastern section, has been found to exhibit the same features as Libya. (Herodotus, *Histories* 4.44)[8]

This event has been dated to the early years of Darius' reign, perhaps around 519. On this analysis the voyage made possible the conquest of 'Sind'.[9] From the basis of a modern map it is not clear how Scylax can have sailed 'in an easterly direction' towards the sea, when the Indus runs in a southwesterly direction. Further, it may well be asked how Scylax was able to assemble a fleet on the waters of the Panjab in Gandara country.[10] On such questions of detail the available sources leave us in the lurch. At all events, the route Scylax took allowed him to discover the shape and position of Arabia.[11]

It is the lack of plausible details that caused an earlier generation of modern scholars to doubt the veracity of Scylax' expedition. The extended duration of the journey, thirty months, and the apparent lack of information

[8] Τῆς δὲ Ἀσίης τὰ πολλὰ ὑπὸ Δαρείου ἐξευρέθη, ὃς βουλόμενος Ἰνδὸν ποταμόν, ὃς κροκοδείλους δεύτερος οὗτος ποταμῶν πάντων παρέχεται, τοῦτον τὸν ποταμὸν εἰδέναι τῇ ἐς θάλασσαν ἐκδιδοῖ, πέμπει πλοίοισι ἄλλους τε τοῖσι ἐπίστευε τὴν ἀληθείην ἐρέειν καὶ δὴ καὶ Σκύλακα ἄνδρα Καρυανδέα. Οἱ δὲ ὁρμηθέντες ἐκ Κασπατύρου τε πόλιος καὶ τῆς Πακτυϊκῆς γῆς ἔπλεον κατὰ ποταμὸν πρὸς ἠῶ τε καὶ ἡλίου ἀνατολὰς ἐς θάλασσαν, διὰ θαλάσσης δὲ πρὸς ἑσπέρην πλέοντες τριηκοστῷ μηνὶ ἀπικνέονται ἐς τοῦτον τὸν χῶρον ὅθεν ὁ Αἰγυπτίων βασιλεὺς τοὺς Φοίνικας τοὺς πρότερον εἶπα ἀπέστειλε περιπλέειν Λιβύην. Μετὰ δὲ τούτους περιπλώσαντας Ἰνδούς τε κατεστρέψατο Δαρεῖος καὶ τῇ θαλάσσῃ ταύτῃ ἐχρᾶτο. Οὕτω καὶ τῆς Ἀσίης, πλὴν τὰ πρὸς ἥλιον ἀνίσχοντα, τὰ ἄλλα ἀνεύρηται ὅμοια παρεχομένη τῇ Λιβύῃ.

Herodotus presents geographical curiosity as a feature of foreign kings, particularly when they plan conquest: Matthew R. Christ, 'Herodotean kings and historical inquiry', *Cl. Ant.* 13 (1994), 167–202, at 175–82. This constitutes, prima facie, an imperial context of knowledge.

[9] E.g., Dandamaev, *Political history*, p. 147; Lenfant, 'L'Inde', 309.

[10] Vincent A. Smith, *The early history of India from 600 BC to the Muhammadan conquest*, 4th edn (Oxford: Clarendon, 1957), p. 40.

[11] See further Albrecht Dihle, 'Arabien und Indien', in *Hérodote et les peuples non grecs*, Entretiens 35 (Vandoeuvres: Fondation Hardt, 1990), pp. 41–61, at 42.

about the Persian Gulf have compounded misgivings.[12] But these doubts have largely been laid to rest with the discovery, during excavations at Suez, of inscriptions which would seem to corroborate Scylax' journey and Darius' acquisition of control over India.[13]

To judge from the paucity of direct references to him, it appears that he was more known about than known. There are strong indications that among classical authors he was displaced as a source and authority at an early stage. Certainly, Aristotle's single passing refence to Scylax (*Politics* 1332b24) is so vague that it could have been at second hand. By the same token, when Strabo mentions him as 'the ancient writer' it seems that he implies a venerable authority of the distant past, vaguely known by reputation rather than specifically referred to by chapter and verse.[14]

Aristotle gives the impression that Scylax was concerned with India's political conditions:

> Clearly, it is best that the same persons should always be rulers and ruled for all time. But since it is not easy to attain this, and since there is nothing to match the difference prevailing among Indians between rulers and ruled, according to Scylax, it is obviously necessary, for several reasons, for all persons to share equally in ruling and being ruled in turn. (*Politics* 1332b21–27)[15]

This appears to prefigure the model of 'oriental despotism', to use a phrase coined in nineteenth-century political theory: for Aristotle, India is the touchstone whereby to measure social relations prevailing in the Greek world, and Scylax is merely a source guaranteeing the truth value of his information. Within Aristotle's framework, this is a dystopian view of society, and it suggests an extrapolation of Greek views about Persian kingship. But it is also important to emphasise that this is merely a passing reference to India, and arguably says more about Aristotle than it does about Scylax.

By contrast to this supposedly political element of Scylax, most surviving fragments suggest that monstrous creatures formed the significant

[12] Duration: Hdt. 4.44.2; defended by Reese, *Nachrichten*, p. 39 n. 1. Gulf: Milns, 'Greek writers', 354; C. Müller (ed.), *Geographi Graeci Minores* (Paris: Didot, 1882), I xxxv is indicative of earlier scholarship on the issue.

[13] Walther Hinz, 'Darius und der Suezkanal', *Archäologische Mitteilungen aus Iran* 8 (1975), 115–21; more skeptical about a link between the inscriptions and Scylax' journey is Christopher Tuplin, 'Darius' Suez canal and Persian imperialism', *Achaemenid History Workshop* 6 (1991), 237–81, esp. 242.

[14] ὁ παλαιὸς συγγραφεύς (14.2.20 C658 = *FGrH* T2a, cf. Steph. Byz. at T2b). The noun and its related verb sometimes carry the implication of composing a text or document, as Thuc. 1.1.

[15] δῆλον ὅτι βέλτιον ἀεὶ τοὺς αὐτοὺς τοὺς μὲν ἄρχειν τοὺς δ' ἄρχεσθαι καθάπαξ· ἐπεὶ δὲ τοῦτ' οὐ ῥᾴδιον λαβεῖν οὐδ' ἔστιν ὥσπερ ἐν Ἰνδοῖς φησι Σκύλαξ εἶναι τοὺς βασιλέας τοσοῦτον διαφέροντας τῶν ἀρχομένων, φανερὸν ὅτι διὰ πολλὰς αἰτίας ἀναγκαῖον πάντας ὁμοίως κοινωνεῖν τοῦ κατὰ μέρος ἄρχειν καὶ ἄρχεσθαι.

part of Scylax' account. The longest of the fragments mentions Skyapods (shadow-feet), Otoliknoi (winnowing fan-ears), Monophthalmoi (single-eyes), Henotiknoi (single-child-bearers), Ektrapeloi (monstrous creatures): thus Tzetzes, *Chiliades* 7.629–39 (F7b). To this list Philostratus (*VA* 3.47 = F7a) adds Makrokephaloi (big-heads). Lists of this kind are open-ended, as Tzetzes reminds us when he ends his list by speaking of 'thousands of other marvellous phenomena'.[16]

In another such fragment, we have the hint of a context for such creatures, as, for example, in Harpocration, s. v. ὑπὸ γῆν οἰκοῦντες (F6). The striking thing here is that Scylax and Hesiod are mentioned in the same breath, itself a reminder of the occurrence of fabulous creatures in archaic Greek poetry. For example, Hesiod also talks about Makrokephaloi (fr. 153 M-W).[17] The question, to what extent correspondences between Indian and Greek marvellous creatures can be explained by common Indo-European roots is a difficult one at many levels, and is beyond the scope of this study. Suffice it to note that the marvellous creatures in Greek Indography from Scylax onward have some precedent in both archaic Greek poetry and in Sanskrit epic, which reaches even further back in time.[18]

Implicit in this problem is the question of Scylax' sources. While it is possible that Indian epic was among his sources,[19] there is no direct evidence of any Greek or Roman learning local languages or reading Indian literature through interpreters.[20] If anything, this may well reflect local

[16] . . . καὶ ἐκτραπέλων ἄλλων δε μυρίων θεαμάτων (Tzetz., *Chil.* 7.144, line 631 = F7b).

[17] Gisinger, 'Skylax', *RE* III A1 (1929), 627–9. To what extent the Indian Monophthalmoi really invite comparison with the Cyclopes of *Od.* 6.5 and book 9, as Gisinger claims with confidence, may well be questioned. On the slippery history of the Makrokephaloi, whose location is mapped to the west of Colchis, and once given to the cranial deformation of infants: Hippoc. *Aer* 14, with Herrmann, *RE* XIV.1 (1928) 815; and Rosalind Thomas, *Herodotus in context* (Cambridge University Press, 2000), p. 88.

[18] Folklore theory circumvents the need to recover historically the origins of such phenomena, and explains them instead in terms of common story-telling elements, which may be common even to societies with no apparent historical link. Given the complicated and largely irretrievable origins of both the early Greek and Indian verse traditions, and given the common ancestry of Indo-European roots, the approach has much to offer in a case such as this. Stith Thompson, *Motif-index of folk-literature*, 6 vols. (Bloomington: Indiana University Press, 1955–8), abounds with examples of strange animals; on gold-digging ants, B756.

[19] Milns, 'Greek writers', 354: 'old Indian books'.

[20] In general, there is very little evidence concerning the ancient equivalents of Dolmetsch-translation: see, e.g., J. P. V. D. Balsdon, *Romans and aliens* (Chapel Hill: University of North Carolina Press, 1979), pp. 137–8; Dihle, 'Indien und die hellenistisch-römische Welt in der neueren Forschung', *Geographia antiqua* 1 (1992), 151–9 at 156. Claims that Herodotus knew no language other than Greek, and was therefore reliant on interpreters, merely underline the degree to which the mechanics of ethnography were of little interest to the ancient authors: e.g. Josef Vogt, 'Herodot in Ägypten', in *Herodot. Eine Auswahl aus der neueren Forschung*, ed. Walter Marg (Darmstadt: Wissenschaftliche Buchgesellschaft, 1962 [1929]), pp. 412–33 at 420.

information, from either written or oral sources of mythology.[21] At all events, it is important to note that the rhetoric of strange animals is fully present in the very first Greek description of India, and would remain an integral part of it throughout antiquity and beyond.

There is a further question of language: did Scylax write in Greek, and, if so, why? Herodotus' description would suggest that he wrote specifically with Persian military purposes in mind. Certainly none of the fragments would encourage us to assume that he wrote in anything but Greek. There is no hint of translation, nor do the sources suggest that he knew Persian. Once again, ancient writers tend to gloss over the issue of inter-linguistic understanding, along with other questions about the means of information gathering.

What, indeed, are we to make of the work as a whole?[22] On the basis of historiographic tradition, it would be easier to conceive of Scylax' work as a bald topography than a literary treatment; by the same token, the marvellous creatures are hard to account for.[23] Indeed, it is impossible to know how closely the surviving Greek fragments reflect the information he provided to the King of Kings.

For all the questions they leave unanswered, the fragments of Scylax do make clear one important fact about the evolution of an image of India. At the point when India shades into Hellenic consciousness it is in fact the Indus valley, namely Iranian India as it had been annexed by Darius. Thus it was to remain for considerable time to come, as subsequent discussion will show.

I.2. Hecataeus' cosmos

Among the three hundred or so fragments of Hecataeus of Miletus, only eight relate to India, and most of these are merely toponyms and ethnic appellations preserved in the dictionary of Stephanus of Byzantium.[24] The second book of Hecataeus' *Periegesis* or *Periodos ges* was devoted to Asia as a whole, and included Africa as well. Thus we hear of Gandarai and Gandroi (F294), Kaspapyrus (F295), Aegante (F297), Callatiae (F298), Opiae

21 Karttunen's attempts to identify Ctesias' dog-heads as a neighbouring people are inconclusive: *Early Greek literature*, pp. 180–5.

22 There seems to be no particular reason to suppose, with Güngerich, *Küstenbeschreibung*, p. 10, that Scylax wrote his narrative in the first person.

23 Gisinger's claim, 'Skylax', 624, of a literary work is hard to sustain.

24 *FGrH* 1, with Jacoby's own commentary ad loc. Equally fundamental is Jacoby's own article, 'Hekatios', *RE* VII.2 (1912) 2667–769. Note also Reese, *Nachrichten*, pp. 57–71; Milns, 'Greek writers', 356–8; Dihle, *RAC*, 3–5.

(F299).[25] In the last of these, after mentioning the Opiae who live along the Indus, Hecataeus places a desert (*erêmiê*) just beyond the habitation of Indians. As we shall see, this conception of India as being at the easternmost end of the *oikoumenê* is continued by Herodotus, and is to become an issue in Alexander's campaign. None of the fragments concerning India makes any reference to monstrous races, a fact that may reflect an emerging rationalism in historical writing.[26] If these fragments give an accurate reflection of the original text, Hecataeus' India seems to have been largely restricted to the listing of peoples and places: the question of naming is one that will engage us later.

More puzzling is Aelian's statement that Hecataeus tells of Amphiaraus' falling asleep while guarding the Indian king (*HA* 13.22 = F33).[27] Amphiaraus was perhaps part of an aetiological myth about the foundation or civilising of India, inviting comparison with Heracles and Dionysus in that respect. In the absence of detailed evidence, this seems to be the most plausible conjecture.

Hecataeus mentioned inland towns and people in a work more comprehensive and larger in scale than that of Scylax: the *Periegesis* represented a kind of compendium of Ionian geography.[28] Further, Hecataeus' work may be seen as a move towards a critical, rationalising historiography, departing from earlier, more myth-based attempts to make sense of the past.[29] Whereas the *periplus* form in its strictest sense is well suited to sailing in and observing the Mediterranean basin, it is less well suited to the geography of

[25] Note the question of common identity here, with Herodotus' Kaspatyrus (3.102; 4.44) and Kallistiae (3.97).

[26] This element of Hecataeus is evident from the very first fragment attributed to him by Jacoby *FGrH* F1a. See further Marcel Detienne, *The creation of mythology* (University of Chicago Press, 1986 [1981]), pp. 70–9; Peter Derow, 'Historical explanation: Polybius and his predecessors', in *Greek historiography*, ed. Simon Hornblower (Oxford: Clarendon, 1994), pp. 73–90, at 74; Momigliano, 'Historiography on written tradition and historiography on oral tradition', in his *Studies in historiography* (London: Weidenfeld and Nicolson, 1966 [1961]), pp. 211–20, at 212; John Marincola, *Authority and tradition in ancient historiography* (Cambridge University Press, 1997), p. 225.

[27] Jacoby in his commentary admits puzzlement concerning context and relevance. Likewise, Bethe, *RE* I.2 (1894) 1886–93, offers no clue as to a possible link between Amphiaraus and India, nor is there any help in O. Wolff, *Ausführliches Lexikon der griechischen und römischen Mythologie*, ed. W. H. Roscher (Leipzig: Teubner, 1884–6).

[28] Jacoby, 'Hekataios', 2688, 2699, 2718; Pierre Schneider, *L'Éthiopie et l'Inde. Interférences et confusions aux extrémités du monde antique* (Rome: MEFRA, 2004).

[29] Momigliano, 'Fattori orientali della storiografia ebraica post-esilica e della storiografia greca', *Terzo Contributo alla Storia degli Studi classici e del Mondo antico* (Rome: Edizioni di Storia e Letteratura, 1966 [1965]), vol. II, pp. 807–18, sees in Hecataeus (as in Herodotus) the crystallising of Greek tradition at the point when confronted by other traditions of the near East: by this reckoning the Persians' westward thrust to the Aegean provided the catalyst for the formation of Greek historiography. See also his 'Il razionalismo di Ecateo di Mileto', *Atene et Roma* n.s. 12 (1931), 15–44. Hecataeus' methods are in any case hard to reconstruct: Marincola, *Authority*, p. 166.

Asia.[30] But from the evidence of Hecataeus' work that we do have, there is no reason to assume that at this stage of our story India is already a unitary whole; indeed Indians are merely one people among many in the region around the Indus.[31]

While we know Hecataeus visited Egypt (Hdt. 2.143), there is no indication that he travelled to India, and this suggests that he gained his information second-hand.[32] Equally, there is no hint that he observed other marginal people in the course of his sea-voyages, namely, the Ethiopians in the south, the Celts in the west and the Scythians in the north.[33] It is certainly possible that Hecataeus used Scylax as a source, and then in turn provided Herodotus with his material; but such possibilities cannot be proven in light of the available evidence.[34] It would be wrong, however, to exclude oral sources of information about India, stories circulating in learned circles, of which Hesiod's fantastic creatures are examples. When Athenaeus says that both Scylax and Hecataeus compared the shape of the Indus with an artichoke (*kunara*), there is a faint suggestion that Hecataeus used Scylax as a source.[35]

It is with Hecataeus that the earliest Greek map can be reconstructed, and it is within this overall worldview that we should locate India. The fragments suggest that Hecataeus conceived of the inhabited world in a disk-shape in two parts, Europe and Asia/Africa, above and below the Mediterranean respectively, and surrounded by Okeanos. By this scheme India and the Indus River are in the farthest east. Even if one admits the dangers and difficulties of making such a reconstruction, there can be no doubt that Hecataeus set India into a larger, abstracted scheme of the world.[36] The cartographic significance of Hecataeus' India is immense, when the only earlier Greek map of which we can speak, that of Anaximander (*c.* 610–546 BC),

30 Jacoby, 'Hekataios', 2718; cf. Güngerich, *Küstenbeschreibung*; Janni, *Mappa*.

31 Dihle (*RAC*, 3) suggests it was Herodotus who was the first to see India as a unit.

32 Jacoby, *FGrH* comm. ad frr. 294–99; 'Hekataios', 2689–90.

33 Jacoby, 'Hekataios', 2708.

34 The main difficulty in making such an inference is that it is Herodotus himself that gives us our strongest impression of Hecataeus. It has been suggested that Herodotus' image of Hecataeus owes more to his imagination than to Hecataeus' own writings or to oral tradition, as an imaginative reconstruction: Stephanie West, 'Herodotus' portrait of Hecataeus', *JHS* 111 (1991), 144–60.

35 Athen. 2.82 p. 70 = 709 F4, cf. Hecat. F296. Jacoby, 'Hekataios', 2729–34, discusses this and other parallels.

36 J. B. Harley and David Woodward, 'The foundations of theoretical cartography in archaic and classical Greece', in *History of cartography*, ed. Harley and Woodward (Chicago: University of Chicago Press, 1987), vol. I, pp. 130–47 at 134–5. The much reproduced image purporting to be a 'reconstruction of the world according to Hecataeus' (p. 135) should be regarded with special caution, given the fragmentary nature of the evidence.

seems more concerned with celestial than terrestrial mapping, and thus to have no ostensible interest in India.[37]

I.3. Herodotus and the satrapies

With Herodotus' *Histories*, Indography takes a new turn.[38] The monstrous races of Scylax and the toponyms of Hecataeus give way to a more discursive type of ethnographic observation and to a specific focus on Indian gold. In fact, the question of Herodotus' reliance on Scylax and Hecataeus on the subject of India is one that must remain open.[39] At all events, the *Histories* do afford the rare opportunity of seeing these features in the context of a larger work. There is no Indian *logos* (excursus) in the full sense that there is an Egyptian or a Persian *logos*, for example. Yet as the discussion below will show, Herodotus' comments, most substantially at 3.97–106, cover much the same topics as the fuller *logoi*, namely, a mixture of physical and human geography, as if following a standard questionnaire.[40] Embedded within this passage, chapter 103 constitutes a kind of sub-subdigression, on the subject of camels. But even here the emphasis on India's natural resources is maintained, for the camels are used by Indians in their search for gold in the desert: as we shall see, gold is at the centre of Herodotus' conception of India.

Again, the Persian framework is all-important. Following the narrative of Cambyses' death and Darius' accession (3.61–87) comes a description of the reorganisation of the Persian empire undertaken by Darius (3.89–117). Among the twenty tribute-paying satrapies, beginning with Ionia in the west, eastern-lying India is the last to be mentioned (3.94).[41] This division does not include the Paricanii or the Aethiopians of Asia, who are included in the seventeenth satrapy (also 3.94). The Indians pay

[37] Harley and Woodward, 'Foundations', pp. 132–4.

[38] On India in Herodotus see esp. Dihle, 'Arabien und Indien'; cf. Reese, *Nachrichten*, pp. 57–71; Klaus Karttunen, 'The ethnography of the fringes', in *Brill's companion to Herodotus*, ed. Egbert J. Bakker *et al.* (Leiden: Brill, 2002), pp. 457–74; cf. the commentary, *Erodoto. Le storie*, ed. David Asheri *et al.* (Milan: Mondadori, 1990), vol. III, pp. 324–9.

[39] Questions over whether Herodotus' work is complete or not cast a certain amount of doubt over this point; I assume here that the *Histories* as we now have them represent something like a complete whole as envisaged by Herodotus. For a recent consideration of Herodotus' place in the history of historical writing, see Robert Fowler, 'Herodotus and his contemporaries', *JHS* 116 (1996), 62–87. Still important is Momigliano's essay, 'The place of Herodotus in the history of historiography', reprinted in his *Studies in historiography*, ch. 8.

[40] On the standard ethnographic 'questionnaire', see Chapter 2, section II below.

[41] Asheri *et al.*, *Erodoto*, p. 305; Smith, *Early history*, pp. 40–1.

more tribute than any province, namely 360 talents of gold per year, which amounts to approximately one-third of the total tribute of the empire:

> The Indians, who are more numerous than any other nation we know, paid a tribute beyond that of every other people, namely 360 talents of gold-dust. This was the twentieth satrapy. (3.94.2a)[42]

An important feature of this passage is the implication that the wealth of India can be measured, specifically in this Achaemenid context. Measuring recurs in Herodotus' description of Persia, contrasted with Greek virtue (*aretê*), which resists quantification.[43] Measurement will demand attention in later Indography as well, for example in Pliny's idea of India as a source of commodities (Chapter 3 below).

If the Persian empire provides the main context for Herodotus' comments, then the acquisition of gold provides its main focus. As if inspired by this, Herodotus proceeds to give a brief ethnographic description of India (3.97–106).[44] Indian gold is mentioned several times within these descriptions.[45] Thus we hear of Indians living near the town Caspatyrus and in the Pactyic country, north of the other Indians, in what is now northeastern Afghanistan.[46] These, the most warlike of the Indians, live like Bactrians and get gold from the nearby desert with the help of gold-digging ants (3.102).[47] Herodotus goes on to describe how this gold is obtained in the

42 Ἰνδῶν δὲ πλῆθός τε πολλῷ πλεῖστόν ἐστι πάντων τῶν ἡμεῖς ἴδμεν ἀνθρώπων καὶ φόρον ἀπαγίνεον πρὸς πάντας τοὺς ἄλλους ἑξήκοντα καὶ τριηκόσια τάλαντα ψήγματος· νομὸς εἰκοστὸς οὗτος.

43 David Konstan, 'Persians, Greeks and empire', *Arethusa* 20.1–2 (1987), 59–73.

44 Within this passage, paragraph 103 constitutes a still further level of digression, concerning the physiology of the camel supposedly used in the acquisition of gold.

45 To a degree that some moderns, esp. in the nineteenth century, have found hard to understand. Gregory L. Possehl, *Indus age: the beginnings* (Philadelphia: University of Pennsylvania Press, 1999), p. 232, offers a map of gold deposits in ancient India. He makes the following suggestion while speaking of the alluvial deposits in Afghanistan, Pakistan and northwest India, as opposed to the deep reefs and veins of southern India: 'That it is in somewhat short supply today might simply reflect the fact that the lode deposits were worked out by the peoples of the Indus Age and their descendants who sent so much of their wealth to the Persian kings' (p. 234). The shallower types of gold-working are much harder to trace archaeologically: F. R. Allchin, 'Upon the antiquity and methods of gold mining in ancient India', *JESHO* 5 (1962), 195–211.

46 Possehl, *Indus age*, 234, identifies Caspatyrus (or Caspapyrus) as Kabul and the Pactyic country as Paktun country, i.e. the land of Pushtus; cf. *Barrington atlas of the Greek and Roman world*, ed. J. A. Talbert, (Princeton University Press, 2000) map 6 C3.

47 These gold-digging ants have long been a puzzle, admitting no conclusive solution. Several have invoked the *Mahabharata*, with its references to *pipillika* ('ant-gold'): see, e.g., Bevan, 'India', p. 356; A. B. Bosworth, 'Aristotle, India, and the Alexander historians', *Topoi* 3 (1993), 407–24 at 412 n. 24; Asheri, *Erodoto*, ad loc.

desert and how it is transported on camels (3.104–5).[48] The Persians are the source of this information:

Such, according to the Persians, is the manner in which the Indians get the greater part of their gold, some is dug out of the earth, but of this the supply is more scanty. (3.105.3)[49]

The designation of the Persians as the source, repeated in the same paragraph,[50] is in keeping with a common Herodotean formula: a less distant group is cited as a source of information about a more familiar one. This is seen, for example, when the Thracians are mentioned as a source for ethnographic information for the area beyond the Danube (5.10).

What are we to make of the gold-digging ants? For a long time they have troubled those concerned with their historicity. Among the many attempts to explain them, the marmot (*marmota Himalayana*) has been perhaps the most plausible candidate.[51] More significant to note here is that Herodotus' discussion suggests that these gold-digging ants, whatever actual animal they may indicate, are not of the same order of marvel as the Makrokephaloi and other strange creatures of Scylax. Since the fragments do not mention them in the same breath it is reasonable to assume that they derive from a different source of information.

The other specifically Achaemenid context in which Indians appear is the list of national contingents comprising Xerxes' army and fleet (7.61–99). Like the satrapy list above, this catalogue, complete with the names of

[48] Between the two passages quoted above there is an inconsistency, in that at 3.94 Herodotus talks about ψῆγμα (from ψήχω, the frequentative of ψάω, hence 'scrapings' or 'gold-dust'), whereas at 102 and 104–5 he uses the more normal term χρυσός.

[49] Τὸν μὲν δὴ πλέω τοῦ χρυσοῦ οὕτω οἱ Ἰνδοὶ κτῶνται, ὡς Πέρσαι φασί· ἄλλος δὲ σπανιώτερός ἐστι ἐν τῇ χώρῃ ὀρυσσόμενος.

[50] 'As the Persians say': ὡς Πέρσαι φασί (3.105.2). For Detlev Fehling, *Herodotus and his 'sources'*, tr. J. G. Howie (Leeds: Cairns, 1989), e.g., p. 152, such authenticating formulae are key parts of Herodotus' 'source-fiction'; on this passage, pp. 97–8. However, the argument for radical skepsis concerning Herodotus' use of sources has been directly answered by several scholars, e.g., Fowler, 'Herodotus'; W. Kendrick Pritchett, *The liar school of Herodotus* (Amsterdam: Gieben, 1993). François Hartog, *The mirror of Herodotus: the representation of the other and the writing of history*, tr. Janet Lloyd (Berkeley: University of California Press, 1988), and Phiroze Vasunia, *The gift of the Nile: hellenizing Egypt from Aeschylus to Alexander* (Berkeley: University of California Press, 2001), have shifted the emphasis from empiricism to representations.

[51] The suggestion goes back, in modern classical scholarship, to Christian Lassen's compendious *Indische Alterthumskunde*, 5 vols. (Leipzig: Kittler, 1856–62), vol. III, pp. 314–15. Among more recent supporters of this identification of *Murmeltiere*: Reinhold Bichler, *Herodots Welt* (Berlin: Akademie, 2000), pp. 25–6; Heinz-Günther Nesselrath, 'Herodot und die Enden der Erde', *MH* 52 (1995), 20–44. Dihle, *RAC*, 4; Andrea Zambrini, 'Gli Indika di Megastene (I)', *ASNP* 12 (1982), 71–149, at 121. There have been many. The issue is usually linked to Herodotus' reliability. W. Tarn's suggestion, *The Greeks in Bactria and India* (Chicago: Ares, 1997) pp. 104–8, that they were a false intelligence to cover up the real sources of gold, identified as Siberia, has not worn well. For detailed discussion see Lenfant, 'L'Inde', 311.

commanders and descriptions of armour, also offers insights into the composition of the empire. It is organised in such a way that after Persians and Medes come the eastern nations from Tigris to Indus (7.62–68), then the southern (7.69–71), then those of Asia Minor (7.72–79) and finally those from the Levant (7.89–95). This comes to a total of sixty-three ethnic groups, divided into infantry (7.61–83), cavalry (7.84–88) and sailors (7.89–99). The Indians are light-armed foot soldiers, and in this respect they match some of the other outermost peoples, namely the African Aethiopians (7.69) and Libyans (7.71):

> The Indians wore garments made of cotton and carried bows and arrows of reed. In addition they had iron weapons. They were arranged to march under the command of Pharnazathres son of Artabas. (7.65)[52]

The term *xulon* usually indicates wood, but is used at 3.47.2 to indicate cotton-producing trees.

Apart from these geographical features, there is no mistaking the human focus of Herodotus' Indography. And here the description is qualitatively different than other authors' descriptions of marvellous races. The types of topic he broaches are in keeping with those on the Egyptians, so that we might speak here of a kind of compacted *logos*.[53]

At two different points, cannibalism is a feature of Herodotus' description of India. One of these occurs in the passage under discussion. Among the Padaei, a nomadic group of the easternmost region, the sickly are killed by their friends, so that they do not succumb slowly to disease:

> If one of their number, whether man or woman, is ill, his closest male friends kill him (in the case of a man), on the grounds that if he wasted away in sickness his flesh would spoil. (3.99.1)[54]

Likewise the aged are sacrificed and eaten, not that many reach an advanced age.[55] In the very next paragraph, Herodotus goes on to describe the custom of other Indians who kill no living creature, nor do they sow or live in houses; the sickly go instead into the desert in order to die. The obvious juxtaposition of opposites here may be taken as an example of antinomy

[52] Ἰνδοὶ δὲ εἵματα μὲν ἐνδεδυκότες ἀπὸ ξύλων πεποιημένα, τόξα δὲ καλάμινα εἶχον καὶ ὀϊστοὺς καλαμίνους· ἐπὶ δὲ σίδηρος ἦν· ἐσταλμένοι μὲν δὴ ἦσαν οὕτω Ἰνδοί, προσετετάχατο δὲ συστρατευόμενοι Φαρναζάθρῃ τῷ Ἀρταβάτεω.

[53] Cf. Dihle, 'Arabien und Indien'.

[54] Ὃς ἂν κάμῃ τῶν ἀστῶν, ἤν τε γυνὴ ἤν τε ἀνήρ, τὸν μὲν ἄνδρα ἄνδρες οἱ μάλιστά οἱ ὁμιλέοντες κτείνουσι, φάμενοι αὐτὸν τηκόμενον τῇ νούσῳ τὰ κρέα σφίσι διαφθείρεσθαι·

[55] Τὸν γὰρ δὴ ἐς γῆρας ἀπικόμενον θύσαντες κατευωχέονται (3.99.1). The theme of the cannibalism of the Padaei is picked up at [Tib.] 4.1.144–45 (=3.7.144–45 *impia . . . conuiuia*). Cf. Chapter 2, section II.5.

or polarity, a principle that takes on particular force in the description of foreign peoples.[56] In this case, it is at the very eastern fringes of the inhabited world, immediately adjacent to the eastern desert, that cannibalism is practised. This is in keeping with the Herodotean scheme of a 'world in which things become progressively more strange as one moves outward from (Greek) normality at the centre'.[57] Even so, it has a religious context (θύσαντες). In fact, Herodotus gives remarkably little attention to Indian religious practices, if one compares his other ethnographic digressions.[58]

Earlier, by way of illustrating the madness of Cambyses, Herodotus tells a story to illustrate the loyalty each society shows towards its accepted practices. Darius summons the Callatiae, who eat their parents after they have died, and asks them what possesses them to do such a deed. The fact that they flinch at conscious reflection on this custom is for Herodotus a sign that 'custom (*nomos*) is king of all'.[59] This instance of cannibalism differs from that at 3.99, and indeed from that of the Massagetae (4.26), in that here people who are already dead are eaten, whereas in the other cases death is anticipated.[60]

If Herodotus' Indians are a means of discussing cultural difference, the more somatic considerations of race come to the fore as well. This we see in the description of the 'non-cannibalistic' Indians mentioned above (3.101). Their skin and their semen are black, and in both respects they resemble the Ethiopians. The dual mention here of Ethiopians in this short paragraph suggests that a somewhat familiar people render an unfamiliar one less strange; certainly the blackness of the Ethiopians is a well-established

56 Polarity is an organising principle in Herodotus' writing, e.g., A. B. Lloyd, *Herodotus, Book II: introduction* (Leiden: Brill, 1975), pp. 149–53; more generally, G. E. R. Lloyd, *Polarity and analogy: two types of argumentation in early Greek thought* (Cambridge University Press, 1966), e.g. pp. 342–5 on the course of the Nile. Thomas, *Herodotus in context*, pp. 77–9, aptly warns of the dangers of extrapolating supposed antitheses between Greeks and barbarians into geographical symmetry (as presented, e.g., on reconstructed maps of older scholarship).

57 John Gould, 'Herodotus and religion', in *Greek historiography*, ed. Simon Hornblower (Oxford: Clarendon, 1994), pp. 91–106, at 97–9.

58 Dihle, 'Arabien und Indien'.

59 νόμον πάντων βασιλέα (3.38.4), in which Herodotus quotes Pindar (fr. 169.1 S-M). The rich concept of *nomos* is glossed by Sally Humphreys, 'Law, custom and culture in Herodotus', *Arethusa* 20 (1987), 211–20; its ethnographic implications explored by Thomas, *Herodotus in context*, pp. 122–33.

60 W. W. How and J. Wells, *A commentary on Herodotus*, 2 vols. (Oxford: Clarendon, 1912), vol. I, p. 311 on 4.26. For E. M. Murphy and J. P. Mallory, 'Herodotus and the cannibals', *Antiquity* 74.284 (2000), 388–94, Herodotus' comments reflect the 'misunderstanding of a funerary ritual' of defleshing or dismemberment. Among the many general discussions of cannibalism, two deserve special mention: both William Arens, *The man-eating myth: anthropology and anthropophagy* (Oxford University Press, 1979), and Frank Lestringant, *Cannibals* (Oxford: Polity, 1997), show the dual tendency of imputing the practice to *other* societies (however that otherness might be determined) while denying its presence in one's *own*.

commonplace by Herodotus' time. Again, people at the farthest edges of the earth are the most unusual. When Herodotus comments that these people live far from the Persians in a southerly direction, and were not Darius' subjects, there is the implication that they do not merit discussion in an Achaemenid context:

These Indians live far south, far from Persia, and they were never under King Darius' sway. (3.101.2)[61]

As in so many descriptions of the blackness of the Aethiopians, the focus is purely somatic, and is not ostensibly accompanied by any moralising comment.[62]

As if the tenor of Herodotus' Indographic excursus were not clear enough, he concludes it with some striking comments of a generalising nature. For Herodotus, India has specific interest for being at the very edges of the earth (3.106.1), a sentiment he repeats in the very next sentence for emphasis. This remark emerges as the key to Herodotus' fascination with India, just as his famous comment that Egypt has the most marvels (*thômasia*) in the world may be regarded as the key to his obvious fascination with that land:

It seems as if the extreme regions of the earth were blessed by nature with the most excellent phenomena, in the same way as Greece enjoys a climate more excellently tempered than any other country. (3.106.1)[63]

Implicit in this comment is a particular kind of fascination about the edges of the earth, one by which they have a certain advantage over the Hellas; but then Hellas is blessed with a degree of moderation unique to itself.[64] The fascination is thus offset. If we compare this passage with those describing the amount of tribute paid by Indians, then we see in India a coming together of two central Herodotean concerns: that with marvel (*thôma*) in the broader sense and, more specifically, that with the grandeur of the Persian empire. In this way India has a specific role to play in telling of the 'great and wonderful actions of both Greeks and barbarians' he mentions

[61] Οὗτοι μὲν τῶν Ἰνδῶν ἑκαστέρω τῶν Περσέων οἰκέουσι καὶ πρὸς νότου ἀνέμου καὶ Δαρείου βασιλέος οὐδαμὰ ὑπήκουσαν.

[62] By the same token, Aristotle (*Soph. el.* 167a7–8) contrasts white teeth with black skin, in ways completely comparable with Greek descriptions of Ethiopians: Lloyd A. Thompson, *Romans and blacks* (Routledge: London, 1989), esp. p. 63; Frank M. Snowden, Jr, *Blacks in antiquity: Ethiopians in the Greco-Roman experience* (Cambridge, MA: Harvard University Press, 1970), p. 258; and cf. Chapter 2, section II.6.

[63] Αἱ δ' ἐσχατιαί κως τῆς οἰκεομένης τὰ κάλλιστα ἔλαχον, κατά περ ἡ Ἑλλὰς τὰς ὥρας πολλόν τι κάλλιστα κεκρημένας ἔλαχε.

[64] The balance of the idea is of course stressed in the repetition of κάλλιστα. On India itself as utopia, see Chapter 2, section III.3 below.

in the proem to the first book:[65] it is simultaneously a vivid marker of the edges of the inhabited world and an indication of the magnitude of the Achaemenid empire.

When Herodotus goes on to describe Arabia, he begins by saying that it is the southernmost part of the inhabited world.[66] And he proceeds in the next sentence to mention Arabia's wealth in spices, which constitute an equivalent to Indian gold, just as the Arabian flying snakes and the bat-like creatures which attack people's eyes are a parallel to the gold-digging ants. Again, this is an ethnographic vision centred on commodities.

There is no suggestion that Herodotus' travels took him as far east as India. He may have been the first Greek historian to use autopsy, *opsis*, in a systematic fashion, but the principle did not apply to his comments on India.[67] It is in his second book that Herodotus most frequently invokes his own experience, as a way of counteracting the marvellous element which was so much part of it.[68] For India, then, it is Scylax, who himself sailed down the Indus, who provides the authority that Herodotus' own autopsy would otherwise have lent. At all events, it may be that this less direct authority is one reason why Herodotus' description of India is relatively toned down, and less fully worked out than his other *logoi*.[69]

Herodotus talks of Scylax in such a way as to set him up as the sort of authority to which he could appeal, in the absence of his own travels to India. But what of his actual Greek sources? He mentions none explicitly as such. Most but not all scholars agree that Herodotus did in fact make use of Scylax.[70] Hecataeus too has been suggested as a direct source.[71] Now given Herodotus' obvious reliance on Hecataeus in the Egyptian *logos*, it would be reasonable to assume that he used Hecataeus on India too, though there

[65] ἔργα μεγάλα τε καὶ θωμαστά, τὰ μὲν Ἕλλησι, τὰ δὲ βαρβάροισι.

[66] Πρὸς δ' αὖ μεσαμβρίης ἐσχάτη Ἀραβίη τῶν οἰκεομένων χωρέων ἐστί (3.107.1). The overlap in diction with 3.106.1, quoted above, is striking.

[67] Gruido Schepens, *L'Autopsie dans la méthode des historiens grecs du Ve siècle avant J.-C.* (Brussels: AWLSK, 1980), pp. 56–70; Marincola, *Authority*, p. 63. Thomas, *Herodotus in context*, pp. 200–11, stands back from the question of historicity with regard to Herodotus' supposed observation, and stresses instead the link evident between his language and that of scientific writers; cf. pp. 235–48.

[68] Thomas, *Herodotus in context*, esp. pp. 213–48, argues that controversy and polemic underly the work as a whole, including the digressions and use of the first person.

[69] Bichler, *Herodots Welt*, p. 61, rightly identifies the restrained quality of Herodotus' India.

[70] Jacoby, Reese *pro*; Milns, 'Greek writers', 356, *contra*.

[71] For an assessment of Herodotus' debt to Hecataeus, both through ancient statements on the subject and through inference, see A. B. Lloyd, *Commentary* vol. I, pp. 127–9. With the partial exception of Scylax, mentioned as a traveller not a writer (4.44.1), Hecataeus is the only literary source Herodotus mentions by name. Cf. Dihle, *RAC*, 1996.

is no direct evidence to that effect; and no overlap in content other than the reference to Kaspaturos.[72]

It is clear, on the one hand, that Herodotus has a scholar's and ethnologist's eye for the customs of foreign peoples; yet it is impossible to divorce the focus of his comments entirely from practical interests. This is a problem for the larger structure of the work: in the earlier books, ethnography is pursued on a big scale and seems an end in itself, whereas later it has a much lesser role to play. Even in the first four books, the excursuses serve as explanation for the themes of the work as a whole, both broader and more specific, and it is in this sense that Herodotus' ethnographic habit has been well characterised as a certain 'access to history'.[73] When Herodotus focuses on the military capacity of the Indians, we see hints of not only Achaemenid information, and even of Achaemenid interests. This same principle would then be true when he begins his description of Arabia by speaking of its spices in detail at 3.107.1. As in the case of Arabia, Herodotus' strong emphasis on commodities is a reminder of the extent to which the Persian empire provided Greeks with a lens through which to view India.

I.4. Marvels and lies of Ctesias

It is with Ctesias, a Cnidian physician and contemporary of Herodotus, that the fullest point of pre-Alexander Indography is reached.[74] Despite the relative profusion of Indographic texts linked with his name, Ctesias is a shady figure, whose life cannot easily be reconstructed.[75] Diodorus Siculus tells us that Ctesias went to Persia as a prisoner of war (2.32.4). At the Persian court his medical skills were utilised by Artaxerxes II Memnon (reigned 405/4–359/8 BC): here he treated the royal family and won the confidence of the king's mother. Having remained at the Persian court for

[72] Assuming that the same place is being referred to in each case: see the cautious location by M. Erdosy in *Barrington atlas*, ed. Talbert, map 6 at C3, with Directory.

[73] Donald Lateiner, *The historical method of Herodotus* (Toronto: University of Toronto Press, 1989), pp. 145–62; cf. Hartmut Erbse, *Fiktion und Wahrheit im Werke Herodots* (Göttingen: Vandenhoeck & Ruprecht, 1991), pp. 158–9.

[74] Janick Auberger has depicted Ctesias as an intermediate figure between the older Indography of Scylax, Hecataeus and Herodotus on the one hand, and the new generation of Alexander historians on the other: 'Ctésias et l'Orient', *Topoi* 5.2 (1995), 337–52. Jacoby's edition of Ctesias, *FGrH* 688, should now be read together with the commentary by Dominique Lenfant, *Ctésias de Cnide, La Perse, L'Inde* (Paris: Belles Lettres, 2004).

[75] See esp. the discussions by Truesdell S. Brown, 'Suggestions for a vita of Ctesias of Cnidos', *Historia* 27 (1978), 1–19, and B. Eck, 'Sur la vie de Ctésias', *REG* 103 (1990), 409–34; and compare now the concise survey by Rüdiger Schmitt, 'Ctesias', in *Encyclopaedia Iranica*, ed. Ehsan Yarshatar (1993), vol. VI, pp. 441–6. These efforts owe much to Jacoby's *RE* article, 'Ktesias' (1922).

sixteen or seventeen years, he departed in 398/7.[76] In the preceding year he had served as an intermediary between the Persian king and Conon of Athens.

These circumstances suggest that Ctesias had privileged knowledge of the Achaemenid empire. Given what we know about the presence of Greeks in Persia, we can safely assume that language was no obstacle to communication, especially in light of Ctesias' apparently lengthy sojourn at the court. Even if Ctesias did not himself learn to speak Persian during this time,[77] he would likely have had contact with merchants and other travellers passing through the capital at Persepolis, and perhaps even access to royal documents.[78]

In his capacity as a medical doctor, Ctesias was not unique. We hear of one Apollonides of Cos at the court of Artaxerxes I (ruled 465–424; Ctesias F14 para. 14, from Photius), and at the court of Artaxerxes II there was also Polykritos of Mende (Ctesias T7d = Plut. *Art.* 21.2). That travelling doctors were in general a well-known phenomenon can be inferred from the opening paragraph of Hippocratic *Airs waters places*, for one. Ctesias was in fact a contemporary of the historical Hippocrates. The biographies of various learned persons, not merely doctors, include travel.[79]

The medical connection may be taken further. Ctesias' apparent emphasis on natural history as opposed to ethnographic description is in keeping with medical interests, but again it must be asked whether the provenance of the fragments does not distort the picture, particularly in Aelian. Certainly, there is a tendency in Ctesias to focus on unfamiliar birds and animals, rather than on the social practices of humans.[80] On the other hand, geography is neglected, and the fragments offer no reference to the major city of Taxila. It may be no accident that, with the exception of Photius, it is principally zoologists and paradoxographers that preserve his fragments.[81]

[76] On the timing of Ctesias' stay and departure: Xen. *An.* 1.8.26–27; Diod. Sic. 2.32; with Eck, 'Vie de Ctésias', 427–32, and Schmitt, 'Ctesias', p. 442.

[77] Eck, 'Vie de Ctésias', 413, assumes he did but this is pure speculation. Klaus E. Müller, *Geschichte der antiken Ethnographie und ethnographischen Theoriebildung* (Wiesbaden: Steiner, 1972–80), vol. II, p. 145 n. 313, castigates Ctesias for failing to use this unique opportunity, and instead producing a version which is virtually worthless; likewise A. R. Burn, *Persia and the Greeks*, 2nd edn (London: Duckworth, 1984), pp. 11–13. In fairness, it must be said that such dismissals are specifically of non-contemporary Assyrian and Median history.

[78] Romm, *Edges*, p. 86; A. T. Olmstead, *History of the Persian empire* (University of Chicago Press, 1948), pp. 380–1.

[79] Jean-Marie André and Marie-Françoise Baslez, *Voyager dans l'antiquité* (Paris: Fayard, 1993), pp. 229–30; Lenfant, *Ctésias*, p. xi.

[80] Joan M. Bigwood, 'Ctesias' parrot', *CQ* 43 (1993), 321–7, at 323.

[81] See Jacoby, 'Ktesias', 2037, for details.

Whereas the *Persika* consisted of twenty-three books, one book only was devoted to the *Indika*.[82] The remaining fragments are only eight in number, but one of them is the fifty-one-section summary by Photius, amounting to more than twenty-two pages in Jacoby's edition (F45, from Photius).[83] The use of the Ionic dialect suggests continuity with the ethnographic tradition of Hecataeus and Herodotus. This fragment may be taken as typical of Ctesias' methods and concerns.[84]

The main passage is devoted mostly to a description of India itself: these are preserved at *Bibl.* 72 p. 45a21–46a37 and p. 46b25–47b4, the two passages being interrupted by an excursus on the Pygmies.[85] There follows a description of the Cynocephali and their territory (p. 47b5–49b19), and then of three marvellous peoples of India (p. 49b20–38). Photius adds a postscript on the credibility of Ctesias (p. 49b39–50a4).

The circumstances of Ctesias' life are one thing, and the historical value of his writing is another: its veracity was challenged from as early as Aristotle's time. The tone with which Lucian scorns Ctesias, referred to in the same breath as Herodotus, shows that his name was already a byword for mendacity by the second century AD.[86] The reception of Ctesias is a matter in its own right. However, it appears that Ctesias himself made a point of challenging Herodotus' authority. Now Herodotus himself was much criticised as a liar,[87] and Ctesias' criticism is, apart from anything else, a testimony to Herodotus' importance for the evolution of Greek historiography. As regards India, this is a matter of rival claims to authority. By now marvels are a severe challenge to historical writing: it is particularly at the edges of the earth that Herodotus is open to criticism for lying.

The marvel, so important to Ctesias' ethnography with its tendencies towards natural history, became an embarrassment to the development of a

82 Phot. 45a20; Aelian 16.31; Paus. 9.21.4.

83 This may be regarded as one of Photius' many 'book-reviews', to use the term of N. G. Wilson, *Scholars of Byzantium* (Baltimore: Johns Hopkins University Press, 1983), p. 93.

84 J. M. Bigwood, 'Ctesias' *Indica* and Photius', *Phoenix* 43 (1989), 302–16. On the other hand Eck, 'Vie de Ctésias', 425, is more sceptical about the extent to which Photius remains true to Ctesias' original.

85 A schematic survey of the relevant fragments is given by Reese, *Nachrichten*, pp. 73–6.

86 Lucian *Ver. hist.* 1.3 and 2.31 combines Herodotus and Ctesias as targets of scorn. (Jacoby does not include Lucian among the testimonia on Ctesias.) See esp. J. R. Morgan, 'Make-believe and make believe: the fictionality of the Greek novels', in *Lies and fiction in the ancient world*, ed. Christopher Gill and T. P. Wiseman (Austin: University of Texas Press, 1994), pp. 175–229.

87 Most famously Thuc. 1.22, where he is not named, and Plutarch's *de malignitate Herodoti* (though in neither critique do the ends of the earth feature); for a survey of his reception see Momigliano, 'Place of Herodotus', in *Studies in historiography*.

new kind of historiography that was beginning to emerge.[88] This is one possible reason why Ctesias became so vilified by the writers of self-consciously serious history. When the Indography of Ctesias is so different in character to that of the earlier writers discussed above, it is perhaps useful at this point to invoke a passage attributed to Herodotus' younger contemporary, Hellanicus of Lesbos (*c.* 480–395 BC): according to a later mythographer, 'Hellanicus says that there is a spring called Sille, in which not even the lightest objects can float.'[89] Now we know that Hellanicus wrote extensively on ethnography and geography, but this is his only reference to India, and the circumstances of its survival are such that we have no context for it. But it does suggest that by the later fifth century there was talk of the wonders of India beyond the strange creatures of the kind mentioned in Scylax. On the strength of this, it appears that Ctesias was not the first to produce the kind of Indography for which he would later become notorious.

Despite references to a Persian sojourn, Ctesias at no point claims to have visited India. Among many attempts to defend him from ancient and modern criticism,[90] some have claimed that Ctesias did not see India itself, yet saw Indian animals, plants and other objects at the Persian court. This claim should be taken seriously as a way of refining the concept of autopsy or personal observation, one that is so important to classical historiography. Various studies of the phenomenon have shown that even some small aspect of autopsy in a tradition can result in elaborate claims about truthfulness: i.e. if an earlier author saw something, then those using his work could themselves claim authenticity.[91] It follows that Ctesias' claims to having seen 'Indian things' himself, may mean that he had himself seen Indian objects and perhaps people at the Persian court.

By way of assessing the character of his Indology, it is worthwhile to distinguish between Ctesias as a source and Ctesias as a historical figure, between writer and traveller. To make this distinction is to go against the grain of an ancient tendency to tend to conflate the two: in many cases, it seems, to question the veracity of a writer's travels is a way of questioning his authority as a source.

88 Momigliano, 'Tradizione e invenzione in Ctesia', in his *Quarto Contributo* (Rome: Edizione di Storia e Letteratura, 1969 [1931]), pp. 181–212 at 211; cf. Emilio Gabba, 'True history and false history in classical antiquity', *JRS* 71 (1981), 50–62.

89 'Ἑλλάνικος ἐν Ἰνδοῖς εἶναί φησι κρήνην Σίλαν καλουμένην, ἐφ' ἧς καὶ τὰ ἐλαφρότατα καταποντίζεται (*Paradoxogr. Vatic. Rohde* 36 = *FGrH* 4 F190).

90 The many articles of Bigwood and Karttunen deserve mention here among modern discussions of Ctesias. Typically of earlier writers, Bevan ('India', p. 356) accuses him both of being a 'deliberate liar' and of plundering the material of others, provided it was 'sufficiently sensational'.

91 Autopsy was not so absolute as it might initially seem: Thomas, *Herodotus in context*, pp. 235–47.

How are we to understand the intentions lying behind the work? Little is gained by claiming that 'Ctesias, again like Scylax, seems to have composed his *Indica* primarily to entertain rather than inform his Greek audience'.[92] For one thing, broader trends in fourth-century historiography make the fantastic elements in Ctesias seem rather like 'an important step in the development toward a kind of historiography distinguished by pathos or melodrama'.[93] To be sure, it has been claimed with justification that Ctesias was an originator of the historical romance, at the very least that certain types of prose narrative may be traced back to his work.[94] Yet, as soon as we cease to retroject modern notions about truth and fiction, it becomes clear that such claims minimise the historical value, if not historiographical aims, of the work in favour of supposed entertainment value. Recent work on the novel has made it clear that 'historical' and 'fictional' elements can coexist in the same work.[95] In fact, it is a feature of the Greek novel, being the latecomer that it was, to be receptive to elements usually linked with other genres.[96] An eastern setting is common to many novels, though sometimes the eastern connection is little more than a title; it implies nothing necessarily about any possible eastern origins of the story involved. It is indeed possible that the novel's own concern with truthfulness and fictionality has some bearing on the reception of Ctesias. At any rate it would be wrong, on the basis of such considerations, to rule out the possibility of a political role played by the circulation of a work such as Ctesias', on similar lines to those which have been suggested for Megasthenes.[97]

What of Ctesias' sources? A recent scholar, perhaps with a sense of apology for the marvellous character of his tale, points to 'intermediaries who were not necessarily well-informed'.[98] Such a suggestion merely adds an additional tier of speculation, and as such achieves little. Ctesias claims to have seen a manticore (*martikhora*) at the Persian court, brought there as a royal gift:

92 Romm, *Edges*, p. 86. 93 Schmitt, 'Ctesias', 444.

94 E.g., Jacoby, 'Ktesias', 2045; Schmitt, 'Ctesias', 442.

95 Tomas Hägg, 'Callirhoe and Parthenope: the beginnings of the historical novel', *Cl. Ant.* 6 (1985), 184–204; cf. Momigliano, 'The historians of the ancient world and their audiences: some suggestions', *ASNP* 8 (1978), 59–75, at 74; Oswyn Murray, 'Herodotus and Hellenistic culture', *Classical Quarterly* 22 (1972), 200–13, at 212.

96 B. P. Reardon, *The form of Greek romance* (Princeton: Princeton University Press, 1991); Tomas Hägg, *The novel in antiquity* (Berkeley: University of California Press, 1983).

97 Susan Sherwin-White and Amélie Kuhrt, *From Samarkhand to Sardis; a new approach to the Seleucid empire* (London: Duckworth, 1993); see section II.2 below.

98 Joan M. Bigwood, 'Ctesias, his royal patrons and Indian swords', *JHS* 115 (1995), 135–40, at 140.

Ctesias states that he has indeed seen this animal in Persia, after it had been brought as a gift to the king of the Persians – if in fact Ctesias has credibility in matters of this kind. (F45dβ = Aelian, *Historia animalium* 4.21)[99]

In the same paragraph, Aelian states that Ctesias himself appealed to local knowledge to substantiate his claims: 'so states Ctesias, and he says that Indians [writers?] agree with him'.[100] Whatever may be the historical reality behind this creature, the tale may offer an important pointer. To be sure, a great many of the Indian things Ctesias mentions he could have seen at the Persian court: wine and cheese (Photius 49b3), oil (49a26), light-coloured Indians (46a26) and rare animals. These are the kinds of object the King of Kings received as presents and tribute from his subjects.[101]

The above account makes clear that Ctesias was important in the integration of the truth/falsity distinction into historical writing. This same distinction, and with it the figure of Ctesias, is important to the different genesis of the Greek novel. Though only one of the twenty-three books of Ctesias' *Persika* concerned India, it was India more than anything that determined Ctesias' subsequent reputation among later authors. In this way, India itself was central to the development of Greek historiography. What is more, India's very marginality gave it a privileged position in the early history of Greek map-making, as a marker of the edges of the world, in the cosmologies of Hecataeus and Herodotus. When Alexander III of Macedon succeeded his father Philip II in 336 BC there was thus already a vivid Greek notion of India.

II. ALEXANDER AND AFTERMATH

II.1. A conqueror and his historians

It is with Alexander's eastern expedition that the body of information about India reached new levels of complexity. To judge from the profusion of Alexander histories, there can be no doubt that the campaign marked a period when suddenly a great deal more information about India was available. However, specific questions posed here are whether this was a retrojection of later times, and whether the influx of new information was one

99 λέγει δὲ καὶ ἑορακέναι τόδε τὸ ζῷον ἐν Πέρσαις Κτησίας ἐξ Ἰνδῶν κομισθὲν δῶρον τῷ Περσῶν βασιλεῖ, εἰ δή τῳ ἱκανὸς τεκμηριῶσαι ὑπὲρ τῶν τοιούτων Κτησίας. For discussion of this passage, Lenfant, 'L'Inde', 315–16, and Christopher Tuplin, 'Parks and gardens' *Achaemenid studies* (Stuttgart: Steinev, 1996), p. 109.

100 λέγει δὲ ἄρα Κτησίας καί φησιν ὁμολογεῖν αὐτῷ τοὺς Ἰνδούς. The manticore is further discussed in Chapter 3 below.

101 Aelian 4.21, 46; cf. Jacoby, 'Ktesias', 2037.

of quantity more than quality. As we try to reconstruct Alexander's Indian expedition historically, the problems encountered are in many ways typical of the problems of Alexander history in general. Major difficulties stem from the fact that the earliest extant histories come some three centuries after the fact, however faithfully they might have reflected the contemporary accounts of Callisthenes, Onesicritus, Aristobulus and Nearchus; and even then there are serious questions about bias in the earlier sources, as far as they can be reconstructed. Nonetheless a substantial historical record exists, which has been subject to extensive source criticism.[102]

Alexander's campaign in India (summer 327 to autumn 325 BC) itself deserves consideration, as perhaps antiquity's most celebrated journey of discovery. The basic story can be found most fully in Arrian's *Anabasis* 5–6, where the campaign is marked as a major episode in its own right.[103] The most important of the other ancient accounts are those of Curtius Rufus' *History of Alexander the Great* 8.9–9.10 and Plutarch's *Life of Alexander* 57–66.[104] Since so many modern historians have already crafted a narrative on these lines, here it is necessary to rehearse only the barest outline of the campaign, so as to be able to consider selected features.[105]

Alexander, having moved through what is now Afghanistan, is well received at the city of Taxila.[106] The ruler Taxiles allies himself with Alexander in the hope of gaining support against his neighbours, Abisares and Porus. Abisares submits to Alexander but Porus resists. Alexander cannot remain in Taxila but is sufficiently interested in what he sees there to send his

102 Of the major contributions to source criticism embracing more than one author, the studies of Jacoby and Lionel Pearson, *The lost histories of Alexander the Great* (Philadelphia: APA, 1960), has yet to be replaced, despite being somewhat outdated; cf. more recently A. B. Bosworth, *From Arrian to Alexander: studies in historical interpretation* (Oxford: Clarendon, 1988). On the general problems concerning sources in Alexander history see, e.g., Simon Hornblower, 'Sources and their uses', *CAH* 2nd edn (1994), vol. VI, pp. 1–23; and Pearson, *Lost histories*, 1–21.

103 A. B. Bosworth, *A historical commentary on Arrian's* History of Alexander (Oxford: Clarendon, 1995), vol. II, p. 9, compares Herodotus' style of digressing.

104 Diod. 17.84–105 and Justin 12.7.4–12.10.7 should also be compared.

105 Among recent narrative histories the following are significant: Jakob Seibert, *Alexander der Grosse* (Darmstadt: Wissenschaftliche Buchgesellschaft, 1972), pp. 155–70, with his particularly detailed maps, esp. no. 26; P. H. L. Eggermont, *Alexander's campaigns in Sind and Baluchistan* (Leuven: Peeters, 1975), and *Alexander's campaigns in Southern Punjab* (Leuven: Peeters, 1993); E. Badian, 'Alexander in Iran', in *Cambridge history of Iran* (Cambridge University Press, 1985), vol. II, pp. 420–501, at 461–75; Badian, 'Alexander at Peucelaotis', *CQ* 37 (1987), 117–38; A. B. Bosworth, *Conquest and empire* (Cambridge University Press, 1988), pp. 119–39. See now also Frank L. Holt, *Into the land of bones: Alexander the Great in Afghanistan* (Berkeley: University of California Press, 2005).

106 Ahmad Hasan Dani, *The historic city of Taxila* (Tokyo: Centre for East Asian Cultural Studies, 1986). This updates the three-volume report of excavations undertaken in 1913–14: Sir John Marshall, *Taxila: an illustrated account of archaeological excavations . . .* (Cambridge University Press, 1951); cf. P. M. Fraser, *Cities of Alexander the Great* (Oxford: Clarendon, 1996), pp. 159–60.

officer Onesicritus to find out more about its sages. One of these 'philosophers' attaches himself to Alexander's entourage for some time, and later, upon becoming ill at Persis, freely goes to his own death on a burning pyre. The battle with Porus at the Hydaspes (Jhelum) brings the campaign to a climax. Once the troops are lined up on opposite sides of the river, Alexander uses a ruse to distract the enemy, and deploys his cavalry, which proves more effective than Porus' elephants. King Porus is captured in battle but Alexander, impressed by his bravery and imposing physique, spares him, and gives him the status of a vassal potentate. In the battle Alexander loses his horse, Bucephalus. It is buried with pomp, and the newly established settlement of Alexandria Bucephala is named in its honor.[107]

A definitive moment is reached at the river Hyphasis (Beas), at which point Alexander's troops refuse to go any farther, whereas he himself still has a burning desire to press on till the Eastern Ocean.[108] The long-festering grievances of the soldiers are expressed first in informal meetings, and then to Alexander by Coenus, the senior phalanx commander. At a second meeting Alexander finds that he cannot persuade his troops or officers to venture farther east with him. After three days spent alone he finally accepts the decision to turn back, thereby reaching reconciliation with his men.

When he returns to the Hydaspes in late September he finds that a fleet is already being built at the newly founded cities of Bucephala and Nicaea, both located in the vicinity of the encounter with Porus. This fleet consists in the main of light transport craft, which were to carry horses, troops and provisions down to the southern ocean, under the command of Nearchus, assisted by Onescritus.[109] While the ships carry most of the cavalry, hypaspists and archers, the rest of the troops and some 200 elephants move on foot under the leadership of Craterus and Hephaestion. Alexander's own activities at this time are directed against the Oxydracae (Ksudrakas) and Malli (Malavas), located on the lower reaches of the Hydraotes. Indigenous resistance is concentrated in a number of strongholds and met with a particularly ferocious response.[110] It is during an assault on the citadel of the Malli that Alexander is impaled by an arrow in the chest, and only narrowly escapes death thanks to surgery performed by Critobulus of Cos.

107 Fraser, *Cities of Alexander*, pp. 161–2.

108 The troublesome but important question of Alexander's aims will be discussed below.

109 The question of the relative roles of Nearchus and Onesicritus is assessed by Waldemar Heckel, *The marshals of Alexander's empire* (London: Routledge, 1992), pp. 228–30.

110 A. B. Bosworth, *Alexander and the East: the tragedy of triumph* (Oxford: Clarendon, 1996), esp. pp. 133–41, stresses the ferocity of the campaign in general and this encounter in particular.

To what degree can we reconstruct Alexander's intentions as he moved eastward? How far did he plan to go?[111] If the historical reconstruction of intentions is a questionable exercise at the best of times, and one of the least plausible aspects of 'great man' historiography, then the character of the sources makes it all the more so in this case. Yet this is a topic we must consider, because of its prominence in the Greek and Roman texts, and because those texts give geographical knowledge itself a role in the question. According to Arrian (*Anabasis* 5.26), Alexander tries to encourage his troops at the Hyphasis by claiming that their goal, the Eastern Sea, is not far away. In Arrian's account, the military discourse of encouragement is mixed with a scientific theorem, one involving the geography of the east.[112]

If anyone wishes to hear what will be the limit of the fighting, he should know that there remains no great expanse of land before us up to the river Ganges and the eastern sea. This sea, I tell you, will prove to be joined to the Hyrcanian sea; for the great sea encircles all the land. And it will be for me to show both Macedonians and allies that the Arabian Sea forms a continuous stretch of water with the Persian Gulf, and the Hyrcanian Sea with the Arabian Sea. From the Persian Gulf our fleet shall sail round to Libya, as far as the Pillars of Heracles; from the Pillars all the interior of Libya then becomes ours, just as all of Asia is in fact becoming ours, and the boundaries of our empire here are becoming those which the god set for the entire continent. (5.26.1–2)[113]

If we are to take this passage seriously, there might be a point in thinking of the famous marvels of India in an early context: that of soldiers on the campaign. Certainly fear is a major part of the campaign narratives. River-crossings and battles provide several moments at which this factor reaches crisis-point. At many stages the solders' fear is contrasted with Alexander's

111 A recent review of the scholarly literature on this subject stresses the early months of 330 BC, and esp. the death of Darius as the conspiracy of Bessus, as the turning point in Alexander's objectives: M. B. Hatzopoulos, 'Alexandre en Perse: la revanche et l'empire', *ZPE* 116 (1997), 41–52.

112 Cf. Curt. 9.2.26. Bosworth aptly points out the persuasive force of this argument over Alexander's soldiers: 'Aristotle', 422. There are good reasons to doubt the extent of Alexander's knowledge about the Ganges: T. R. Robinson, 'Alexander and the Ganges: the text of Diodorus 18.6.2', *AHB* 7 (1993), 84–99; cf. Bosworth, *Alexander and the East*, 186–200.

113 εἰ δέ τις καὶ αὐτῷ τῷ πολεμεῖν ποθεῖ ἀκοῦσαι ὅ τι περ ἔσται πέρας, μαθέτω ὅτι οὐ πολλὴ ἔτι ἡμῖν ἡ λοιπή ἐστιν ἔστε ἐπὶ ποταμόν τε Γάγγην καὶ τὴν ἑῴαν θάλασσαν· ταύτῃ δὲ, λέγω ὑμῖν, ξυναφὴς φανεῖται ἡ Ὑρκανία θάλασσα· ἐκπεριέρχεται γὰρ γῆν πέρι πᾶσαν ἡ μεγάλη θάλασσα. καὶ ἐγὼ ἐπιδείξω Μακεδόσι τε καὶ τοῖς ξυμμάχοις τὸν μὲν Ἰνδικὸν κόλπον ξύρρουν ὄντα τῷ Περσικῷ, τὴν δὲ Ὑρκανίαν <θάλασσαν> τῷ Ἰνδικῷ· ἀπὸ δὲ τοῦ Περσικοῦ εἰς Λιβύην περιπλευσθήσεται στόλῳ ἡμετέρῳ τὰ μέχρι Ἡρακλέους Στηλῶν· ἀπὸ δὲ Στηλῶν ἡ ἐντὸς Λιβύη πᾶσα ἡμετέρα γίγνεται καὶ ἡ Ἀσία δὴ οὕτω πᾶσα, καὶ ὅροι τῆς ταύτῃ ἀρχῆς οὕσπερ καὶ τῆς γῆς Λιβύη πᾶσα ἡμετέρα γίγνεται καὶ ἡ Ἀσία δὴ οὕτω πᾶσα, καὶ ὅροι τῆς ταύτῃ ἀρχῆς οὕσπερ καὶ τῆς γῆς ὅρους ὁ θεὸς ἐποίησε. On the significance of this passage see esp. Bosworth, 'Aristotle', 422.

bravery. If fear of unknown terrors lying ahead was indeed a factor among soldiers on the campaign, we can merely speculate how this might have impacted on the stories about the campaign told in the Greek world. Pre-existing tales about marvellous creatures at the ends of the earth will have been in the minds of soldiers, as indeed they would have been in the minds of the audiences of the Alexander histories.

To be sure, Alexander was encouraged by Indian potentates who were under pressure as a result of conflict with their neighbours. His intervention was brief, and had the net effect of changing the balance of power between these potentates. These 'invitations' at least gave Alexander a pretext by which to intervene, much as revenge earlier provided a pretext for his initial incursion into Persia. This is less a matter of real motive than of legitimisation and propaganda.

Emulation counted for a great deal in the sphere of propaganda. Stories about Heracles and Dionysus had a certain validating function in Alexander's own self-presentation. The question of emulation is one that merits later discussion in other contexts, namely emulation *of* Alexander. If this was to prove a major theme in the self-presentation of Roman leaders later,[114] then we shall have to consider the role of India in those processes of self-presentation.

But, again, how far did Alexander really intend to go? Curtius' comment, for example, that Alexander intended to make for India and from there for Ocean, is not necessarily of great value in historical reconstruction.[115] Given the temporal distance between the surviving Alexander historians and their subject, and given Alexander's own charisma, this is exactly the kind of issue that will have been most prone to distortion. Alexander did receive reports that the Ganges lay twelve days' march beyond the Hyphasis, and these reports could have encouraged him,[116] despite the fact that he could expect grim going all the way, and then the Ganges' east bank to be densely populated with hostile groups. This information was awkward enough for him to disbelieve or dissimulate to his troops.[117] It is very likely that geographical misconceptions (or even conscious misrepresentations) played a part in Alexander's strategy: whatever Alexander might have thought, his assertion that Ocean was nearby seems to have had the effect of revitalising his exhausted troops. In principle, there would have been every reason for

[114] On problems surrounding Alexander's exemplary status, see Pierre Vidal-Naquet, 'Flavius Arrien entre deux mondes', in Pierre Savinel (tr.), *Arrien, Histoire d'Alexandre* (Paris: Minuit, 1984), esp. pp. 330–43.

[115] *ceterum Indiam et inde Oceanum petiturus* (8.5.1).

[116] Curt. 9.2.5.

[117] Plut. 62.2; Arr. 5.25.2; Just. 12.8.10–15.

Alexander to think of India as the eastern edge of the world, in keeping with the Hecataean and Herodotean conceptions mentioned above. It was only after Alexander's expedition that India was no longer thought to lie on the eastern edge; now glimmers of knowledge about the Ganges appeared.[118] To what extent that is the product of retrospective fabulation on the part of later historians is unclear, yet it seems likely that it reflects the situation of the campaign itself. In the *Romance* tradition this desire of Alexander to proceed beyond the Hyphasis is transformed into the supposed fact of his actually having done so.[119]

In this narrative, rivers hold an ambiguous position. Significantly, the Hyphasis (Beas) is presented as a border of knowledge. Arrian discusses the pre-eminence of the Indian rivers among all those of Asia, and ends his description by keeping open the possibility that says that there might be even greater rivers in India, unknown to him. This passage is remarkable both for the role of the Hyphasis and for the fact that Arrian suspends his own authority:

> It is possible that also many other greater rivers run through India. But I can make no accurate assertions about territory on the other side of the Hyphasis, because Alexander did not get beyond the Hyphasis. (*Indica* 3.10–4.1)[120]

This sentiment is matched at 6.1 and Strabo 15.1.37 C702, the latter being particularly interesting since it states explicitly that India's remoteness and the consequent ignorance of writers leads to exaggeration and marvel-mongering. (Strabo goes on to instance gold-digging ants.) On the other hand rivers are also a rationalisation of space, in this case articulated in retrospect, in such a way that the narrative easily focuses on these points.[121] The military story of Alexander's campaign is punctuated and segmented by the rivers crossed, particularly in Arrian's account.

One river, the Hydaspes, is also the path of travel, and likewise the Acesines, another tributary of the Indus. In the narrative of Nearchus' voyage, which begins with the river journey down to the Indus delta, these two rivers fulfil a very different role (chapters 18–19).[122] As Arrian hastens to remind us, the bulk of his story concerns Nearchus' voyage from the mouths

[118] Dihle, *RAC*, 6, with reference to earlier writing.

[119] E.g., *Alexander Romance* (rec. γ) 2.35a.15; cf. the Byzantine poetic version (cod. Marc. 408), lines 4811, 4840 and 4858.

[120] καὶ τυχὸν καὶ ἄλλοι πολλοὶ μέζονες ποταμοὶ ἐν τῇ Ἰνδῶν γῇ ῥέουσιν. ἀλλὰ οὔ μοι ἀτρεκὲς ὑπὲρ τῶν ἐπέκεινα Ὑφάσιος ποταμοῦ ἰσχυρίσασθαι, ὅτι οὐ πρόσω τοῦ Ὑφάσιος ἦλθεν Ἀλέξανδρος.

[121] On Herodotus' keen sense of the limits of knowledge see, e.g., Lateiner, *Historical method*, pp. 146–7.

[122] On rivers as boundaries or connectors of people, Franz Schön, 'Fluss', in *Mensch und Landschaft in der Antike. Lexikon der historischen Geographie*, ed. Holger Sonnabend (Stuttgart: Metzler, 1999),

of Indus to the Persian Gulf (19.9), and it is Nearchus' own account that forms its factual basis (20.1).

Asceticism is one feature that impressed Alexander's entourage. The rigorous discipline and self-sacrificing ways of the Indian philosophers struck a chord for Onesicritus, who claimed to find in their lifestyle an analogue and model for Cynic philosophy.[123] This episode predicts the fascination that Christians would come to have with the Brahmans and Gymnosophists, as will be discussed in Chapter 6. Important for current purposes is Calanus, who is a key to the formation of this image, creating as a he did a model of both self-mortification and social criticism, as Strabo 15.1.64 C715, for one, reveals. The angles of self-control and criticism point in the direction of an emerging concept of ascetic practice, one that would later come to have philosophical and religious implications in the world of early Christian asceticism.[124]

Onesicritus was instructed to meet with the philosophers. They would not themselves be summoned, and Alexander wished neither to go himself nor to force them. At a distance of fifteen stadia from the city Onescritus found fifteen of them, sitting naked in various postures on the stones. He spoke to Calanus, one of them, and is told also to sit naked on the stones so that he can hear the teaching of the wise men. When Onesicritus says that he was sent to learn about wisdom and report back to Alexander, Calanus proceeds to rail against gluttony and luxury. In a kind of Golden Age legend he tells of an earlier time when the world produced goods in abundance; now people had lost self-control and returned to satiety and arrogance, and as a result the world had declined. Another sage, Mandanis (also referred to in the sources as Dandamis), is more conciliatory at first in his attitude to the Greeks, and rebukes Calanus as arrogant for having made Onesicritus undress and be seated in discomfort.

pp. 145–50; on later antiquity, C. R. Whittaker, *Frontiers of the Roman empire: a socio-economic study* (Baltimore: Johns Hopkins University Press, 1994), pp. 26 and 61.

[123] See further Truesdell S. Brown, *Onescritus* (Berkeley: University of California Press, 1949); Dihle, *RAC*, 7; James S. Romm, 'Dog heads and noble savages: Cynicism before the Cynics?', *The Cynics: the Cynic movement in antiquity and its legacy*, ed. R. Bracht Branham and Marie-Odile Goulet-Cazé (Berkeley: University of California Press, 1996), pp. 121–35, at 122. On Onesicritus as historian see esp. Pearson, *Lost histories*, pp. 83–111, who stresses his link with Xenophon, and Paul Pédech, *Historiens compagnons d'Alexandre* (Paris: Belles Lettres, 1984), pp. 71–158. Apparently he is the first Greek to mention Taprobane, modern-day Sri Lanka (*FGrH* 134 F12–13 = Strabo 15.1.15 C690 and Pliny *HN* 6.81; cf. Meg. F26): D. P. M. Weerakkody, *Taprobane: ancient Sri Lanka as known to Greeks and Romans* (Turnhout: Brepols, 1997), pp. 27–9, and Stefan Faller, *Taprobane im Wandel der Zeit* (Stuttgart: Steiner, 2000), pp. 29–34.

[124] Note esp. Derek Krueger, 'The bawdy and society: the shamelessness of Diogenes in Roman imperial culture', in *The Cynics*, ed. Branham and Goulet-Cazé, pp. 222–39; A. Brian Bosworth, 'Calanus and the Brahman opposition', in *Alexander der Grosse*, ed. Wolfgang Will (1998), pp. 173–204

The very name of Calanus is an act of translation.[125] Plutarch tells us that he received that name from the Greeks because he greeted them with *kalyam*, the Sanskrit form of the greeting *khaire* (*Alex.* 65.5). Since this supposed Sanskrit greeting makes no sense as it stands, it has been understood instead as *kalyanam*, hence the proximity to the name as it occurs in the Greek and Roman sources.[126] Sphines, his real name according to Plutarch, cannot be linked to any known Indian name.

Names are not the only problem in making sense of Calanus. For example, how are we to square Calanus' own eulogising of the king (e.g., Strabo 15.1.68 C717) with the frequent criticism by the later historians that the contemporary writers would flatter Alexander?[127] In this passage Strabo accuses the sages themselves of impetuosity and lack of self-control, which is after all what they most profess to teach. But it is clear that Calanus, through his link with Onescritus and thence Diogenes and ultimately Socrates, stands at a particular moment in the history of social criticism and of asceticism, representing a special kind of 'alien wisdom'.

Stepping back a moment from the narrative, we should consider the sources used by the Alexander historians. Two writers who stand out for having dealt with this most easterly part of the campaign are Nearchus and Onesicritus, these two being identified as admiral and helmsman of the fleet respectively (Arrian, *Indica* 18.9–10). This has been taken to mean that Nearchus was in overall command, Onescritus in charge of navigation.[128] It is Nearchus who is cited by Arrian as the main source for the narrative section of his *Indica*.[129]

To consider the question of sources at a further remove: from whom did Callisthenes and other contemporary historians glean their information on India? In a provocative recent study, Bosworth has suggested some complicity between indigenous priests and the Macedonians gleaning information from them.[130] This raises several questions of methodology, and is a helpful

[125] The codices of Diodorus, e.g., 17.107.1, consistently refer to him as Κάρανος instead.

[126] Jean Filliozat, 'La valeur des connaissances gréco-romaines sur l'Inde', *Journ. sav.* (1965), 97–136, at 109. J. W. de Jong, 'The discovery of India by the Greeks', *Asiatische Studien* 27 (1973), 115–43 at 120.

[127] Cf. Pearson, *Lost histories*, pp. 22–49, on Callisthenes. For Bosworth, 'Calanus', the divided literary representation of Calanus stems from divisions between Brahmans at the time of Megasthenes' visit to India.

[128] E. Badian, 'Nearchus the Cretan', *YClS* 24 (1975), 147–70 at 159.

[129] Ch. 20.1. Nearchus and Megasthenes, 'men worthy of credit', δοκίμω ἄνδρε (17.6) are together cited as the sources for the first, ethnographic section of the work. Note the remarks of P. A. Brunt, 'On historical fragments and epitomes', *CQ* 30 (1980), 477–94, at 482, on the difficulties of reconstructing Nearchus from Arrian and Strabo, his main repositories.

[130] *Alexander and the east*, 98–132.

corrective to the tendency of ancient texts to emphasise matters of factual accuracy over those of sources. Bosworth's inquiry is informed by a relatively new trend in social anthropology to concentrate on the process whereby information is assembled – a process characterised by contingencies and problems of translation – rather than the static object of earlier ethnographic writing.[131]

Tantalisingly, Strabo mentions in passing that Mandanis is speaking through the medium of three interpreters (who know, apart from language, no more than the masses, says Mandanis).[132] He mentions this to underline how hard it is for anything he himself says to have an impact, whereas Alexander would have the power to force people, where necessary, to learn to exercise self-control (*sôphronein*). The matter of interpreters is, however, not developed in ways that would be interesting to modern ethnographic studies, with their emphasis on methodology.

Among Strabo's considerable criticism, 'flattery' is a particular point, one made in connection with Callisthenes particularly. Strabo's allegations of flattery resonate with the rhetoric of bigness surrounding the contents of the description itself. As we have seen above, the idea of abundance, if not bigness, is present in Herodotus' India. This is something pre-existing that the context of Alexander seems to have magnified.

Finally, what role did Aristotle himself play? Only in the eastern tradition, much of it dating to the later period, is he said to have accompanied Alexander's expedition.[133] Even if we make allowances for the vagaries of biographical tradition, there are strong indications that Aristotle was the teacher of the young Alexander: we can therefore infer that he was a major source of Alexander's geographical knowledge, and hence of the assumptions informing his strategies. On the other hand, as we have seen above, the extant works of Aristotle contain little engagement with geography or

[131] Edmund Carpenter, *Oh, what a blow that phantom gave me!* (New York: Holt, Rinehart and Winston, 1973), pointed ahead to later studies such as those in *Writing culture: the poetics and politics of ethnography*, ed. James Clifford and George E. Marcus (Berkeley: University of California Press, 1986). For the semiotic approach to the concept of culture, Clifford Geertz, *The interpretation of cultures*, 2nd edn (New York: Basic, 2000), remains seminal well after its original publication in 1973.

[132] 15.1.64 C716; cf. B. C. J. Timmer, *Megasthenes en de Indische maatschappij* (Amsterdam: H. J. Paris, 1930), p. 45; de Jong, 'Discovery', 119.

[133] Ingemar Düring, *Aristotle in the ancient biographical tradition* (Göteborg University Press, 1957); Max Brocker, *Aristoteles als Alexanders Lehrer in der Legende* (diss. Bonn 1965). For two attempts to reconstruct historically the possible involvement of Aristotle, see James S. Romm, 'Aristotle's elephant and the myth of Alexander's scientific patronage', *AJPhil.* 110 (1989), 566–75, and Bosworth, 'Aristotle'.

in fact with India; as a result there is no reason to believe that this is an issue in which Aristotle influenced him directly.[134]

II.2. Megasthenes and Chandragupta's court

It comes as something of a surprise that a writer who is subsequently accorded greater credibility than others was not part of Alexander's campaign but visited India in its aftermath. Like Scylax and Ctesias before him, Megasthenes was attached to a royal court,[135] in his case to that of Seleucus I Nicator (c. 358–281 BC). He visited the court of the Maurya emperor Chandragupta, known to the Greeks as Sandrakottos, as an ambassador either of Seleucus himself or of Sibyrtios, satrap of Arachosia.[136] This court was based in Palibothra, known in Sanskrit as Pataliputra, near modern-day Patna.[137] Megasthenes' account seems from its fragments to have been the fullest account of India that the Greco-Roman world ever had.[138] From the point of view of ancient Indian history, Megasthenes' Indography does in fact appear to offer particularly valuable evidence, especially with regard to elephants and other military matters.[139] What is important, for our purposes, was the perception that Megasthenes' account deserved some credibility by virtue of its author's own travels.

Arrian mentions him as an example when speaking of 'those who took part in Alexander's campaign' (6.1–2). According to the usual chronology, this is an apparent error. If so, it would be interesting to account for. Possibly, it reflects the intertextual relation between the various Alexander histories by Arrian's time, in a kind of echo chamber. Or it might be considered testimony to the power of autopsy, in ways which might even have pre-empted medieval ideas about Alexander himself as scholar and explorer. Or it could be that the early loss of the contemporary Alexander historians gave Megasthenes added significance, *faute de mieux*. More radically, a recent study would take Arrian at his word, and consequently place Megasthenes' journeys as early as 320–318 BC, that is, before Chandragupta's power stretched as far as the Indus valley.[140]

134 Bosworth, 'Aristotle', 423.

135 Cf. Romm, *Edges*, pp. 83–4.

136 On Chandragupta and Sibyrtios see the texts given by Jacoby at T2, esp. Arr. *Anab.* 5.6.2; cf. Stein, 'Megasthenes', *RE* XV.1 (1931) 230–326, at 230–1. Among modern accounts John D. Grainger, *Seleukos Nikator: constructing a Hellenistic kingdom* (London: Routledge, 1990), p. 154, is particularly skeptical of Megasthenes.

137 Talbert, *Barrington atlas* 6 F4.

138 Bevan, 'India', p. 400.

139 Thomas R. Trautmann, 'Elephants and the Mauryas', in *India: history and thought*, ed. S. N. Mukherjee (Calcutta: Subarnarekha, 1982), pp. 254–81.

140 A. B. Bosworth, 'The historical setting of Megasthenes' *Indica*', *Cl. Phil.* 91 (1996), 113–27: by Bosworth's dating, Megasthenes belongs to the same world as the Alexander historians, and his visit to the Mauryan court perhaps as early as 319/318.

If the doxographic problem casts a shadow over this chapter as a whole, then Megasthenes presents an extreme case. The longest of the fragments given by Jacoby at no point names Megasthenes as source.[141] Now it is true that the degree of overlap with similar material in Strabo, Pliny and Arrian points to a common source, most likely Megasthenes. It is also true that Diodorus generally tends not to name his sources,[142] certainly less frequently than do the other writers. But this is hardly conclusive, and as things stand the identification of Megasthenes as the direct source is less secure than Jacoby would lead his readers to believe.[143]

Whatever the specifics of this passage and others like it, there is no denying the importance of Megasthenes to the later tradition. Any survey of the later, Roman-period Indographers makes clear that Megasthenes more than anyone else tends to be cited as an authority. And what is more, while he too is liable to criticism, it is he who is most often praised as accurate.[144] The thesis that the reliability of an ancient Indographer is in direct proportion to his dependence on Megasthenes is today easily dismissed as an editor's enthusiasm for his author.[145] It might be said that within the competitive context of an emerging tradition, it is Megasthenes' text as much as any that becomes an object of struggle over veracity. Whereas Diodorus, as we saw, says little about his sources, Strabo and Pliny are very doxographic, in that their mode for recounting information about India (and indeed about other distant places) is couched in the competitive language of rival authorities, of truth and fiction. For these later writers then, it is Megasthenes' *Indica* that takes on the role of the key text that needs to be proven or disproven on any given point.[146]

Given the sheer bulk of fragments of Megasthenes and given the ancient critical debate around them, we have to pose the question: what are the features of Megasthenes' description, and to what extent does it differ from earlier ones? One aspect of his Indography, absent in earlier Greek texts, is the description of an Indian city, namely Palibothra. It is no coincidence that its founding is ascribed to Herakles (Diodorus 2.39), in view of his role

[141] *FGrH* 715 F4 = Diod. 2.35.1–2.42.4, the contents of which are discussed below.

[142] Kenneth S. Sacks, *Diodorus Siculus and the first century* (Princeton University Press, 1990), argues for Diodorus' *Bibliothêkê* to be seen in its own right, as a product of its own times, rather than the product of a mere copyist.

[143] The text of Megasthenes is reconstructed by Jacoby as *FGrH* 715.

[144] Truesdell S. Brown is one of his most avid modern apologists: see esp. 'The reliability of Megasthenes', *AJPhil.* 76 (1955), 18–33.

[145] For Brown, 'Reliability', Megasthenes deserves credit for rejecting Ctesias' account and 'his ability to give a straightforward account of what he had seen' – hints of special pleading on Megasthenes' behalf.

[146] See, e.g., Brown, 'Reliability', as well as his 'The merits and weaknesses of Megasthenes', *Phoenix* 11 (1957), 12–24.

as a culture hero.[147] Megasthenes thus represents a move beyond the Indus valley *per se*, eastward toward the Ganges valley. There is no indication in the fragments that this was somehow a different region; rather, Palibothra is part of the same geographic entity, 'India'.

Perhaps the most striking feature of Megasthenes' India is its abundance. This means, in Diodorus' breathless description, a hypertrophe of the natural realm: animal (e.g., elephants, monkeys and snakes), vegetable (a double harvest) and mineral (supplies of gold and silver) all occur. It should be stressed that these are not monsters, in the style of Ctesias, but more realistic animals that are great in size and number. The excess of its scale makes Diodorus compare Libya. In size and number, India's elephants exceed even Libya's.[148] The key to this general principle of plenty, verging even on beauty, is clearly articulated by Diodorus at an earlier passage:[149]

> For India is a land of exceptional beauty, and since it is crossed by many rivers it is supplied with water over its whole area and produces two harvests each year. As a result it has such an abundance of the necessities of life that at all times it blesses its inhabitants with plentiful enjoyment of them. People say that because of the favorable climate in those parts the country has never endured famine or the destruction of crops. Also, it has an unbelievable profusion of elephants, which both in courage and bodily strength far surpass those of Libya, and likewise gold, silver, iron and copper; further, one can find within its borders great quantities of precious stones of every kind and of almost all other objects which contribute to luxury and wealth. (Diodorus 2.16.3–4)[150]

There is a certain amount of internal comparison too:[151] e.g., Gandaridae produces the largest elephants (2.37.2) and this is why it was long able to evade capture. Diodorus claims that it is on account of their consequent military power that Alexander refrained from attacking the Gandaridae

147 Among the many celebrations of Heracles as a culture hero, Isocrates' praise of his *psyche* (spirit) is noteworthy, especially when it is addressed to Philip in 346 BC (*Oration* 5.109–10); cf. G. Karl Galinsky, *The Herakles theme: the adaptations of the hero in literature from Homer to the twentieth century* (Totowa: Rowman and Littlefield, 1972), pp. 101–25.

148 F4 = Diod. 2.35.3–4.

149 This passage Jacoby has not specifically attributed to Megasthenes, though it has all the features of F4, which he does see as Megasthenes'.

150 ἡ γὰρ Ἰνδικὴ χώρα διάφορος οὖσα τῷ κάλλει καὶ πολλοῖς διειλημμένη ποταμοῖς ἀρδεύεταί τε πολλαχοῦ καὶ διττοὺς καθ' ἕκαστον ἐνιαυτὸν ἐκφέρει καρπούς· διὸ καὶ τῶν πρὸς τὸ ζῆν ἐπιτηδείων τοσοῦτον ἔχει πλῆθος ὥστε διὰ παντὸς ἄφθονον ἀπόλαυσιν τοῖς ἐγχωρίοις παρέχεσθαι. λέγεται δὲ μηδέποτε κατ' αὐτὴν γεγονέναι σιτοδείαν ἢ φθορὰν καρπῶν διὰ τὴν εὐκρασίαν τῶν τόπων. ἔχει δὲ καὶ τῶν ἐλεφάντων ἄπιστον πλῆθος, οἳ ταῖς τε ἀλκαῖς καὶ ταῖς τοῦ σώματος ῥώμαις πολὺ προέχουσι τῶν ἐν τῇ Λιβύῃ γινομένων, ὁμοίως δὲ χρυσόν, ἄργυρον, σίδηρον, χαλκόν· πρὸς δὲ τούτοις λίθων παντοίων καὶ πολυτελῶν ἔστιν ἐν αὐτῇ πλῆθος, ἔτι δὲ τῶν ἄλλων ἁπάντων σχεδὸν τῶν πρὸς τρυφὴν καὶ πλοῦτον διατεινόντων.

151 Such comparisons make it necessary to question Romm's contrast between Libya and India as mysteries of internal and external space respectively (*Edges*, p. 83).

even when he had conquered other Indian tribes: he heard of their 4,000 elephants in military service and of their readiness to withstand his attack (2.37.3). This we can dismiss as a misunderstanding on the part of Diodorus or his sources, given that Alexander never did reach the Ganges.[152] Yet even this comment is testimony both to the influence of geographical information, of 'news' as a factor within the military strategy of this campaign; and military value of elephants.[153] It is indeed with the elephant that we find a significant overlap of natural history and military interests.

Rivers are another important feature to suggest both scientific and military interests. Certainly, the big rivers bulk large in three of the major texts preserving Megasthenes' fragments: Diodorus, Strabo and Arrian.[154] As a testimony to their scale, the Indian rivers are said to surpass those of Asia, even if the Danube and Nile were to unite (Arrian, *Indica* 3.9). Arrian in fact goes on to discuss, with reference to Megasthenes, the huge proportions of the Ganges and its tributaries (4.2–16). It is bigger than the Indus. Both of them far surpass the Nile and Danube in volume, since the latter two have no tributaries (4.13). This comparison is not only a matter of establishing what is 'bigger and better', but illustrates the principle that has also been shown in Theophrastus' botany, also in the wake of Alexander's expedition: the known is used to explain the unknown.[155]

In keeping with the line of thought expressed in the Hippocratic *Airs waters places* we encounter the principle of environmental determinism involving the inhabitants of India.[156] Just as Indian elephants, living in this plenteous land, are strong (in fact stronger than Libyan) and well trained for war, so India's inhabitants are of unusually large stature. They are skilled as a result of breathing pure air and drinking fresh water (Diodorus 2.36.1).

We have now seen, in various parts of the natural sphere, a great deal of the marvellous. How did readers understand this? According to a provocative recent study, marvels carried the sense of the disturbing and threatening: by this interpretation, marvels in post-Alexander accounts of India served as a justification for the failure of the Seleucids to conquer what had by now become the Mauryan kingdom.[157] This suggestion is attractive, but it

152 Bosworth, *Arrian to Alexander*, p. 131.

153 Note Bosworth 'Aristotle', 413, on Persian elephants (e.g., Curt. 5.2.10). See further Trautmann, 'Elephants and Mauryas', and Chapter 4 below.

154 Diod. 2.37.1–7 = F4; Arr. *Ind.* 4.2–12 = F9; Strabo 15.1.35 C702 = F9 also.

155 P. M. Fraser, 'The world of Theophrastus', in *Greek historiography*, ed. Simon Hornblower, pp. 167–92 at 173.

156 Thomas, *Herodotus in context*, esp. pp. 86–98, explores the complexities of this text in relation to historical writing; also Benjamin H. Isaac, *The invention of racism in classical antiquity* (Princeton University Press, 2004).

157 Sherwin-White and Kuhrt, *Samarkhand to Sardis*, p. 97.

has weight only if it can be proven that the marvellous carried the sense of threat, and that seems something of a stretch.[158]

Megasthenes gives considerable attention to social stratification, in what has tended to be described as the caste system.[159] In the longest continuous passages Jacoby attributes to him, Megasthenes discusses the hierarchy of Indian society.[160] His description of the seven groups begins with the philosophers, who are first in prominence though smallest in number. They are exempt from state service, except in so far as they fulfil priestly duties on behalf of private citizens, including funerals and foretelling the future that do not seem far from those of a priest of the Roman state. The term in Diodorus and Strabo usually translated as 'caste' is *meros*, whereas Arrian uses *genos*.[161] Each writer goes on to describe the other six groups, which are, in order: farmers; cowherds and shepherds; artisans; the military; inspectors; and councillors. In each case, as with the philosophers, the description of the class includes their occupation, their numbers and their relation to the power of the state.

What are we to make of this careful attention to social structure? On the one hand, Herodotus speaks of a seven-fold division of Egyptian society, so perhaps Megasthenes' comments are a Herodotean projection, not to be taken seriously. Herodotus says: 'There are in Egypt seven classes (*genea*), which are called respectively, priests, warriors, cowherds, swineherds, shopkeepers, interpreters, and pilots' (2.164). These are the classes of the Egyptians, and their names are given them from their crafts. He then proceeds to subdivide the warriors into the groups Hermotybies and Calasiries, according to region (2.165–66). On the other hand, these passages have received detailed attention from historians of Indian society, and

158 Gabba's article, 'True history', and the substantial new discussion of paradoxography by Guido Schepens and Kris Delcroix, 'Ancient paradoxography: origin, evolution, production and reception', in *La letteratura di consumo nel mondo Greco-latino*, ed. Oronzo Pecere and Antonio Stramaglia (Cassino: Università degli Studi di Cassino, 1996), pp. 373–460, have much more to say about credibility than about any possible fear that might be engendered. Nor is fear prominent in Caroline W. Bynum's compelling discussion of marvel in the western Middle Ages: 'Wonder', *AHR* 102 (1997), 1–26.

159 Given the controversy over the term and concept of caste in modern Indian historiography, it would seem incautious to talk about caste in the period under discussion. At one extreme, Nicholas B. Dirks has argued for discontinuity between precolonial and colonial notions of caste: *Castes of mind: colonialism and the making of modern India* (Princeton University Press, 2001). Certainly Megasthenes' discussion has received censure from Bernard S. Cohn, 'Notes on the history of the study of Indian society and culture', in his *An anthropologist among the historians and other essays* (Oxford University Press, 1987), pp. 136–71, at 138–9; see also Donald F. Lach, *Asia in the making of Europe* (University of Chicago Press, 1965), vol. I, p. 10.

160 F4 = Diod. 2.40.1–2.41.4, which overlaps considerably with the lengthy F19 = Arr. *Ind.* 11 and Strabo 15.1.39–49 C703–7 (interrupted).

161 Cf. Diod. 2.40.6 φῦλον.

especially of Indian law.[162] Megasthenes' account has often been compared on particular points with an Indian treatise on statecraft, the *Arthasastra*. However, the comparison is a difficult one since this text, traditionally linked with Chandragupta's minister Chanakya, is most likely a later creation.[163]

What makes Megasthenes' account stand out from others, as best we can reconstruct them, are his statements concerning India's antiquity.[164] Again, the main source is Diodorus' rich but troublesome passage (2.38–39 = F4). The stories about Dionysus and Heracles are important for the time-depth they confer on India. They are presented as civilizing divinities, who come to a nomadic people and bestow on them the accoutrements of culture.[165] Diodorus seldom names his sources, but in this case he twice attributes these stories to Indian wise men, thereby implying a certain critical distance (2.38.3, cf. 2.39.1). Like the issue of the antiquity of the Jews relative to that of the Egyptians, it is contentious: Arrian, for one, dismisses it as a Macedonian boast, but not without recounting it first.[166]

Needless to say, many issues are at stake when origins are perceived across cultural boundaries.[167] Given the Greek identities of the two divinities, this may be taken as an assertion of Greek cultural priority. At the same time, *qua* charter myth, this is a way of accounting for Hellenism in the far eastern corner of the inhabited world. Given what we know from epigraphy, and especially the well-known bilingual edicts of Ashoka with their finely carved Greek and Aramaic,[168] it is remarkable that there are so few literary

[162] See esp. Bernhard Breloer, *Kautaliya-Studien*, 2 vols. (Bonn: Schroeder, 1927–8); O. Stein, *RE*; Timmer, *Megasthenes en de Indische*; and Allan Dahlquist, *Megasthenes and Indian religion: a study in motives and types* (Stockholm: Almqvist and Wiksell, 1962).

[163] Detailed textual analysis shows that the work is the product of multiple authors, compiled perhaps as late as the mid-second century AD: Thomas R. Trautmann, *Kautilya and the Arthasastra: a statistical investigation of the authorship and evolution of the text* (Leiden: Brill, 1971). Hardly contemporary with Chandragupta, it nonetheless claims continuity with that period, though in a normative rather than descriptive fashion: Romila Thapar, *Early India: from the origins to AD 1300* (Berkeley: University of California Press, 2002), pp. 184–6.

[164] On the particularity of this in ancient ethnography see, e.g., Karl Trüdinger, *Studien zur Geschichte der griechisch-römischen Ethnographie* (Basel: Birkhäuser, 1911), p. 75.

[165] On nomadism as an ethnographic trope see Brent D. Shaw, '"Eaters of flesh and drinkers of milk": the Mediterranean ideology of the pastoral nomad', *Anc. Soc.* 13–14 (1982–3), 5–31; Hartog, *Mirror of Herodotus*.

[166] *Ind.* 5.10; cf. 5.3.1–4, where he takes issue with Eratosthenes.

[167] E. J. Bickerman's essay, 'Origines gentium', *Cl. Phil.* 47 (1952), 65–81, remains an important articulation of this principle; cf. *Time: histories and ethnographies*, ed. Diane Owen Hughes and Thomas R. Trautmann (Ann Arbor: University of Michigan Press, 1995).

[168] First published by Daniel Schlumberger *et al.*, 'Une bilingue gréco-araméene d'Asoka', *Journal Asiatique* 246 (1958), 1–48; cf. Sherwin-White and Kuhrt, *Samarkhand to Sardis*, pp. 100–3, and Thapar, *Asoka and the decline of the Mauryas*, rev. edn (Oxford University Press, 1997).

references to the diffusion of Greek culture. This must count as a major absence from the literary tradition discussed here.

Apart from this, there does not appear to be any significant indication of the passage of time in Greek Indography. Significantly, most of the verbs used in the fragments quoted are in the present tense, what has been called the ethnographic present.[169] Just how typical of ethnographic writing is this account of early Indian history? To be sure, Greeks had a very definite notion of the antiquity of Near Eastern civilisations, particularly those with traditions of writing much older than their own, for example Babylonians, Egyptians and Jews.[170] But it is not clear to what extent Indians were thought to share the same features as these other ancient, learned societies of the east, and it deserves to be noted that we have not encountered any Greek ideas about Indian writing: these questions will have to be discussed below in relation to ethnographic traditions generally (Chapter 2) and to 'alien wisdom' specifically (Chapter 6). For the present, it is sufficient to note that the notion of Indian antiquity is a highly qualified one, contingent even on the antiquity of the Greeks themselves. Even if it was not a fiction of Alexander's own propaganda to the degree Bosworth has claimed, then it certainly does imply the cultural priority of Greeks, and, as such, seems like an invented tradition par excellence.[171]

II.3. Bactrians and 'Indo-Greeks'

From a Greek point of view, South Asia did at one point constitute an empire in its own right, in the sense of governance, albeit for only a brief period. It is necessary here to shift the focus away from the military aspect of Alexander's expedition, to consider instead what effect that expedition had

[169] If we stress the Greek context of this supposed Indian history, we might, with an important scholar of modern anthropology, see it as a case of the following phenomenon: 'Whenever marginal peoples come into a historical or ethnographic space that has been defined by the Western imagination' their own histories are quickly lost. Thus James Clifford, *The predicament of culture: twentieth-century ethnography, literature and art* (Cambridge, MA: Harvard University Press, 1988), p. 5; cf. Cohn, *Anthropologist*. But if we are to view ancient ethnographic modes in their own right, a passage such as this could be argued in opposite directions: on the one it is *an* ethnographic history, and a rarity as such; on the other hand it is a *limited* one, and one which is predicated on the idea of Greek cultural priority. See further Chapter 2, section II.2 below.

[170] Note for example F3 Clement of Alexandria (*Strom.* 1.72.4) who, asserting that wisdom begins with particular 'barbarian' peoples by virtue of their antiquity, compares the status of Brahmans relative to Indian society with that of the Jews relative to Syrian. Herodotus' emphasis on Egyptian antiquity forms a tacit contrast with forward-looking Greek temporalities: Vasunia, *Gift of the Nile*, pp. 110–35.

[171] To use the resonant term of E. J. Hobsbawm, in his introduction to *The invention of tradition*, ed. Hobsbawm and Terence Ranger (Cambridge University Press, 1983).

on the lands it traversed. This raises questions about the diffusion of Greek culture and language. Here we are on less firm ground, both in relation to the material at hand and to the concepts implicit in the scholarship on the subject. In assessing the 'Indo-Greek' or 'Greco-Bactrian' empire there exist few literary sources but many coins.[172] The phenomenon we are examining is the establishment in the third and second centuries of a Central Asian empire whose leadership expressed its power in Greek terms, and made use of the Greek language. If these comments sound like a minimalist definition with which to approach the topic, they are thus conceived as a conscious antidote to the highly reified notion of Hellenism that characterises the Alexander biographies by Droysen and Tarn, in which an almost missionary aspect of Greek culture is evident.[173] Contrary to the anachronisms and exaggerations of these studies, not entirely expunged from more recent accounts, it is best for us here to take a minimalist approach, and in fact the current context requires no more than that.[174]

The settlement of Greco-Macedonian soldiers in Bactria and Sogdiana, and intermarriage with east Iranian people, brought about a Central Asian centre in which the élite inhabitants expressed themselves in terms of Greek culture. Certainly Strabo stresses the Greekness of its rulers (15.1.3 C686).[175] A passage in Trogus-Justin implies that their sovereignty stretched well into the Ganges valley (41.1.8).

This has made little impact on literary texts, but archaeological work has produced some spectacular and unexpected results. Foremost among them were the discoveries at Ai Khanum at the confluence of the Oxus (Amu Darya) and the Kowkcheh.[176] The palace, theatre, gymnasium and inscriptions found there all testify to some degree of Greek presence,[177] even if domestic architecture does not tell anything like so dramatic a story. In general, coins have played a major part in the recovery of this history

[172] E.g., Frank L. Holt, *Thundering Zeus: the making of Hellenistic Bactria* (Berkeley: University of California Press, 1999), pp. 174–84.

[173] Peter Green, *Alexander to Actium* (Berkeley: University of California Press, 1990), p. 312; cf. Hartog, *Memories of Odysseus*, pp. 158–60; and Arnaldo Momigliano, 'J. G. Droysen between Greeks and Jews', in his *Essays in ancient and modern historiography* (Oxford: Blackwell, 1977 [1970]), pp. 307–23.

[174] For recent synthetic histories, see Domenico Musti, 'Syria and the East', in *CAH*, 2nd edn, vol. VII.1 (1984) pp. 175–220, esp. 210–16, and Paul Bernard, 'The Greek kingdoms of central Asia', in *History of civilizations of Central Asia*, vol. II, ed. János Harmatta (Paris: UNESCO, 1994), pp. 99–130.

[175] Further references are given by Stanley M. Burstein, *The Hellenistic age* (Cambridge University Press, 1985), p. 71.

[176] See further Musti, 'Syria', p. 214 n. 67; for an archaeologist's account, Paul Bernard, 'Aï Khanoum en Afghanistan hier (1964–1978) et aujourd'hui (2001): un site en péril. Perspectives d'avenir', *CRAI* (2001), 971–1029.

[177] On the inscription linked with Clearchus of Soli, compare also Chapter 6, section II.3 below

(in so far as it can be recovered). The recurrence of Heracles in artifacts from here is merely one reminder of the importance of Alexander to the self-presentation of the Indo-Greek rulers.

With the rise of the Greco-Bactrian empire in mid-third century, the Indus valley became separated, in the political sphere at least, from Seleucid control. Antiochus III did indeed reach the outer reaches of the valley at a later point, but his expedition failed to reconquer the area in any sense for the Seleucids.[178] It was around the start of the second century, when first Demetrius I and then Menander conquered parts of the valley, i.e. northwest India, that the Greco-Bactrians themselves reached the height of their power. A number of small states sprang up in this vicinity, each of them having some link with Greek language and customs, but they were later to be absorbed by nomadic groups of Parthians, Sacae and Indoscythians from further east.

Two shadowy but intriguing figures deserve some mention here. Demetrius I (*c.* 200–185 BC) of Bactria annexed Arachosia and Drangiana to his kingdom. There is some debate over whether coins supposedly issued by him were not rather issued by a later Demetrius contemporary with Eucratides I. His silver coins show him wearing an elephant cap on the obverse, with Heracles standing on the reverse.

But it was Menander, known in Indian sources as Milinda (ruled *c.* 155–130 BC) who was probably the greatest of the Indo-Greek kings. According to Indian tradition he led an expedition to Pataliputra in the Ganges valley but returned without having annexed anything; he embraced Buddhism following a conversation with the Buddhist scholar-priest Nagasena. Surviving coins issued by him present him as a Hellenistic king on the obverse, with Athena of Pella on the reverse, complete with the Greek inscription, 'Menander the Saviour king'.[179] This Menander has been identified with the Pali work, 'The questions of King Milinda', which has been dated to around 150–100 BC.[180] The rise of the Parthian empire interrupted contact between these Indo-Greeks and the (rest of the) Greek world, till they were blotted out or absorbed by invaders from Central Asia around

[178] On Antiochus III's campaigns against the Bactrians under Euthydemus, narrated in Polybius 11.39, see A. K. Narain, 'The Greeks of Bactria and India', *CAH*, 2nd edn (1989), vol. VIII.2, pp. 388–421 at 397–8.

[179] Green, *Alexander to Actium*, pp. 320–2 (see fig. 104 for the silver tetradrachm); George Woodcock, *The Greeks in India* (London: Faber, 1966), ch. 6. Among older works, Tarn, *The Greeks in Bactria and India*, and A. K. Narain, *The Indo-Greeks* (Oxford: Clarendon, 1957), remain important, but require caution.

[180] T. W. Rhys Davids (tr.), *The questions of King Milinda*, 2 vols. (Oxford: Clarendon, 1890–4).

80–30 BC. At all events, there is no evidence of this group after this period of invasion.

One fascinating area of evidence concerns 'Gandharan' art, which we might define as Hellenistic-Buddhist style of the western Indus Valley and Central Asia. It is widely agreed that Alexander's invasion was followed by a radical change in northwest Indian artistic styles.[181] Sculptures of the Bodhisatva, representing the young Gautama or alternatively any young man on the way to salvation, show strong features of Greek art, notably the series of folds in the garment worn, and the less-rounded presentation of the face. This is a classic instance in which material evidence encourages speculation about cultural identity. On the one hand it provides inviting source material for the study of cultural interaction;[182] on the other hand, it leaves us at the level of speculation, given that the literary sources do little to round out the historical picture. In a word, then, the Indo-Greeks are a problem of indeterminate proportions for this study: hard as it is to know about them historically, it is even harder to detect any impact they might have had on the Greco-Roman ethnographic imagination.

II.4. Mapping India: from the bematists to Eratosthenes

In the case of both Hecataeus and Herodotus we have seen how India was used to conceive the *oikoumenê* on a large scale. This is what we have called the 'cosmological India' of Greek thought. To these writers may be added the historian Ephorus (*c.* 405 and 330 BC), who was deeply interested in geographic questions and appears to have devised a novel cartographic system. India was one of the peripheral areas he incorporated into his conception of the inhabited world: by this view, according to Strabo (1.2.28 C34), the Indians occupied one of the world's four parts, the others being inhabited by Ethiopians, Celts and Scythians. These people represent the east, south, west and north respectively, defined by the direction of the winds.[183] This line of thought is visible also in Aristotle's system of winds, as described in

[181] Elizabeth Errington *et al.* (eds.), *The crossroads of Asia: transformations in image and symbol in the art of ancient Afghanistan and Pakistan* (Cambridge: Cambridge India and Iran Trust, 1992). John Boardman, *The diffusion of classical art in antiquity* (Princeton University Press, 1994), offers important analysis but grounds for caution emerge in the following note and in the introduction to Chapter 3 below.

[182] For an assessment of colonial contexts and other methodological issues (regarding Vincent Smith, Aurel Stein and others), see Stanley K. Abe, 'Inside the wonder house: Buddhist art and the west', in *Curators of the Buddha: the study of Buddhism under colonialism* (University of Chicago Press, 1995), pp. 63–106.

[183] Harley and Woodward, 'Foundations', in *History of Cartography*, pp. 143–4.

his *Meteorologica* 2.6. Some decades later Timosthenes of Rhodes (fl. 270 BC) refined the system of wind directions in a way that foreshadowed the modern compass points. According to Agathemerus (*Geographiae informatio* 2.7), Timosthenes explicitly identified the twelve winds with distant peoples or places: India is linked with the Eurus wind, being placed in the east-southeast, between the Apeliotes (linked with Bactriana) and Euronotus (the Red Sea and Ethiopia).

But this cosmological sense of India is merely one aspect of cartographic developments: the other concerns measuring, and it is here that Alexander's expedition played a major and concrete part. We have already seen that the campaign included a number of scholars. The bematists ('measurers') made up one group whose specialised skills were part of the campaign. Their task was to measure the distances between points of rest, and to describe natural features of the lands they traversed. Only two of these writers are known by name, Diognetus and Baiton, and nothing survives intact from their accounts.[184] They wrote monographs called *stathmoi* ('stages'), which went beyond mere lists of places to have a literary frame. These were mentioned and used by later writers, including notably Pliny (6.61–62); most of the fragments linked with their names concern distances between parts of the area covered by Alexander's campaign.

Though the reports of the bematists were, inevitably, subjected to criticisms of exaggeration, they did provide a basis for the subsequent work of Eratosthenes, polymath librarian of Alexandria (*c.* 234–196 BC).[185] If Eratosthenes is today considered the most important geographer of the Hellenistic age – both for his measuring of the circumference of the earth and for constructing a world map on a grid of meridians and latitudes – the first of these bears indirectly on India and the second directly. It was on a north–south axis that Eratosthenes calculated the earth's circumference, using Alexandria and Syene (Aswan) as his points of measurement.[186] The assumption that the earth is spherical made it possible to convert the angles, measured by an instrument called the gnomon, into stades, and ultimately to map the entire inhabited world (*oikoumenê*). He calculated the distance from the farthest points of India to those of Iberia at around 74,000 stades,

184 For the texts, see *FGrH* 119–122. For the authors, see Helmut Berve, *Das Alexanderreich auf prosopographischer Grundlage* (Munich: Beck, 1926), vol. II, nos. 198, 800; Fraser, *Cities of Alexander*, pp. 75–80.

185 Fraser, *Cities of Alexander*, pp. 80–2; now Klaus Geus, *Eratosthenes von Kyrene. Studien zur hellenistischen Kultur- und Wissenschaftsgeschichte* (Munich: Beck, 2002), pp. 231 and 236.

186 On Alexandria as a 'centre of calculation', see Roy MacLeod, 'Introduction: Alexandria in history and myth', in Roy MacLeod (ed.), *The Library of Alexandria: centre of learning in the ancient world* (London: Tauris, 2000), pp. 1–15, at 3.

but then, relying on the accepted knowledge that the length of the *oikoumenê* was more than double its breadth, added a further 2,000 stades to both east and west to reach an adjusted total of 78,000. This distance was measured at the latitude of Athens:

> if the enormity of the Atlantic Ocean did not prevent it, we would be able to sail from Iberia to India along the very same parallel over the remainder of the circle, that is, the remainder once you have subtracted the aforementioned distance, which is more than a third of the entire circle. (Eratosthenes in Strabo 1.4.6 C64–65)[187]

This scheme, with its effective omission of the Americas, would ultimately influence geographic knowledge at the time of Columbus' voyages.[188]

Again, India is a useful point at which to mark the farthest extent of the earth, just as Iberia marks the farthest point on the other side of the east–west axis running through Athens. According to the passage in Strabo which is the basis of our knowledge of his work, Eratosthenes included a number of distances, both north–south and east–west, all of them rounded off to the thousands: these include the distance between the far eastern capes and eastern India (3,000 stades), between eastern India and the river Indus (16,000), and between the Indus and the Caspian gates (14,000). The purpose of these distances was to allow the reader to draw his own map; to this end, 'seals' (*sphragides*) or irregular geometric shapes by which the map of the world could be put together, in the manner of a jigsaw puzzle. India was represented by a diamond-shaped quadrilateral, simpler and therefore more conceptually useful shape than that of other countries. The fact that India was now, in Eratosthenes' scheme, firmly and clearly mapped made it possible to visualise space *from* the farthest east in a westerly direction. This alone is of enormous significance to our topic. Whereas so much of ancient Greek mapping can be understood on the model of centre of periphery, Eratosthenes' worldwide grid offers a theory which allows any part of the inhabited world to be represented in its own right, with its own co-ordinates. This is a more decentred model than, say, those of Hecataeus or Herodotus, and something taken further by Strabo and especially Ptolemy.[189]

187 ὥστ᾽ εἰ μὴ τὸ μέγεθος τοῦ Ἀτλαντικοῦ πελάγους ἐκώλυε, κἂν πλεῖν ἡμᾶς ἐκ τῆς Ἰβηρίας εἰς τὴν Ἰνδικὴν διὰ τοῦ αὐτοῦ παραλλήλου, τὸ λοιπὸν μέρος παρὰ τὸ λεχθὲν διάστημα ὑπὲρ τὸ τρίτον μέρος ο]ν τοῦ ὅλου κύκλου·.

188 David Woodward, 'Medieval *Mappaemundi*', in *History of cartography*, ed. Harley and Woodward, vol. I, pp. 353–4, with reference to intermediary medieval figures, including Roger Bacon and Pierre d'Ailly; cf. Geus, *Eratosthenes*, pp. 270–1.

189 On Eratosthenes see esp. Geus, *Eratosthenes*, pp. 260–88.

III. ORIGINS AND PROCESS IN THE MAKING OF ROMAN INDIA

From the material surveyed here, a number of features may be brought out by way of concluding this chapter, and at the same time by way of introducing the rest of this book. Much here remains uncertain, and there are question marks over the sources used by many of these writers and even over the original form of their work. The doxographic problem has been a major issue throughout this chapter, but it is a problem we shall in subsequent chapters turn to our advantage when we come to examine the later contexts of reference in their own right. What is, however, both certain and obvious is something that deserves to be mentioned here: a sense of India's radical otherness, one which goes hand in hand with a sense of India's sheer distance from the Mediterranean world. The Hippocratic *Airs waters places*, to take an example of an important text of early Greek ethnography, covers a geographical span which is not restricted to, but certainly centred on the eastern Mediterranean world. India is not mentioned there, and is in fact considerably to the east of the easternmost area mentioned, that of the Scythians. In this text it is therefore not conceived as an area that an ordinary Greek, and specifically a Greek doctor, might expect to visit. In this sense India is not part of the geographic consciousness reflected in Greek ethnography, certainly up to Alexander: it is 'off the map'.

But India in ancient maps is an issue that deserves consideration in its own right. Broadly speaking, the period discussed is one in which India emerges from its conflation with Aethiopia to become a definite object in its own right. In a sense this development would never be completed, given the degree to which features of 'India' and 'Aethiopia' continued to be exchanged well into the Roman imperial and medieval periods.[190] By the same token, one might speak of the movement from the *cosmological* conception of India in Hecataeus and Herodotus, with their emphasis on the shape of the world, to the *topographic* concerns of the Alexander historians, with their greater specificity of place and the concern for measuring that comes in their wake in Eratosthenes, for one. There is some value to this overall characterisation of change, yet Hecataeus' *Periegesis* certainly contained many toponyms; and later scholars such as Aristotle and Timosthenes undoubtedly still used India to construct their cosmos, for example the wind directions.[191] And it is not least for these reasons that

[190] Schneider, *L'Éthiopie et L'Inde*.

[191] Harley and Woodward, 'Foundations', in *History of cartography*, 144–6 and 152–3; Schneider, *L'Éthiope et L'Inde*.

the Whiggish idea of history-as-progress must be avoided: rather this story should be seen as one of ever-changing contexts, of continual reinvention for ever-changing needs and circumstances of contact. Yet, it is true that a process of distinguishing India and Aethiopia does begin to develop in this period, if one distinguishes the Homeric and Aeschylean references with those in Scylax, Hecataeus and certainly Herodotus. From the time it becomes an entity in itself India is essentially the Indus valley, today's Pakistani provinces of Panjab and Sindh, the land of rivers. The few references to the Ganges Valley, including Palibothra in Megasthenes, is essentially an extension of this area. None of the writers described makes any reference to the southern Indian peninsula, and indeed is something we do not encounter until the *Periplus of the Erythraean Sea* in the mid-first century AD. The period surveyed here reveals a gradual refinement of the idea that India is the edge of the earth: one early step in this direction comes with Herodotus' idea that there is a desert to its east, and is thus the farthest part of the *inhabited* world. As a way to characterise these changes, it is useful to invoke the distinction between space and place made in recent cartographic studies: on this model, it is space that humans encounter, and place that is created mentally, specifically in the process of naming.[192] What we see in this chapter are the very beginnings of the creation of place: on balance, there is much more about the exotic, generalised space of India than about specific, articulated places within it. As plentiful as the Alexander histories are in describing Alexander's campaign in the Indus Valley, they tell us relatively little about the details of Indian topography: there are areas, to be sure, usually defined by their inhabitants (e.g., 'the Malli'), and there are rivers. But even by the time of Megasthenes we can speak of only two urban centres, namely Taxila and Pataliputra, that had acquired the specificity of names within Greek thinking.

The Achaemenid empire has emerged in this survey as both a generator of and a vehicle for Indography, and may thus be seen as a key factor in the development of a more specific Greek notion of India. From Herodotus onward, a Persian concern with India's gold-supply can be detected in Greek accounts, a feature that is easily understood in terms of Darius' conception of his empire as expressed in the Persepolis inscription (DPh). Throughout the Achaemenid period there were Indians living in the Iranian-Mesopotamian area, in close proximity to Greeks.[193] The

[192] Raymond Craib, 'Cartography and power in the conquest and creation of New Spain', *Latin American Research Review* 35.1 (2000), 7–36, at 16; still seminal is Yi-Fu Tuan, *Space and place: the perspective of experience* (Minneapolis: University of Minnesota Press, 1977), e.g. pp. 199–200.

[193] Dihle, 'Arabien und Indien', p. 51.

presence of Indian troops in Xerxes' catalogue presented just one case in which Greeks might have met Indians outside of the Indus Valley itself (Herodotus 7.65, 70, 86). The possibility that some Indians, including those captured at Plataea, may have been present in Athens as slaves is a real one, however speculative it must remain in the absence of evidence to that effect.[194] This is entirely an argument from historical probability. In all these ways it is necessary to read between the lines of Greek accounts, in order to locate Greek responses to Indian people, animals and objects outside of the Indus Valley itself. This possibility is one way in which the seemingly monolithic concept of autopsy may be questioned.

The Persians thus emerge as a key to Greek Indography: long before the use of the monsoon route from the Mediterranean to India, much travelling was done overland, and thus perforce via the Achaemenid empire. However, Persian knowledge of India in its own right is hard to reconstruct, in the absence of a tradition of narrative historical writing, at least in the Greek sense.[195] In this respect, Alexander's campaign did have a major, long-term impact, in that now Persian knowledge could be more freely circulated. Later, when sea-routes allowed more direct access to India from the Mediterranean, this Achaemenid framework remained, for by then Indography had already crystallised as a canon of information, largely resistant to new additions.

From the earliest Greek account we can reconstruct, marvel emerges as a key theme. This it was to remain, more or less, throughout antiquity, and well beyond. When Herodotus plays down the marvellous aspect and emphasises social groupings instead, that is more the exception than the rule, and should be seen as part of Herodotus' own ethnographic interests. Yet even Herodotus, who says virtually nothing about fantastic creatures in his comments on India, uses an ethnographic framework similar to that he uses to describe the Egyptians, one focused on *thômasia*. Even the death of Calanus on the funeral pyre is described by Diodorus as a marvel.[196]

Whatever its origins, the marvel goes far back in the history of Greek literature. Of the period here covered, it is the Hellenistic age which saw a profusion of both marvellous creatures generally and the metamorphosis in particular. When marvel writing comes to have life of its own, most obviously with the pseudo-Aristotelian text *On wonderful things heard* (*De mirabilibus auscultationibus*), 'India' is a venue par excellence for strange

[194] Milns, 'Greek writers', 356.

[195] Momigliano, *Alien wisdom*, p. 126: 'Perhaps the three elements of Persian education – to ride a horse, to shoot straight and to tell the truth – were not favourable to the formation of a historian.'

[196] τὸ δὲ πλῆθος κατήντησεν ἐπὶ τὴν παράδοξον θέαν (17.107.4).

occurrences. If we examine that text we see that by far the majority of its marvels are located on the fringes of the world, a feature that helps explain the conflation of features between India and Ethiopia. Tellingly, one passage mentioning India presents it as a source of wealth for the Persian empire:

> They say that among the Indians the copper is so bright, pure, and rust-free that in colour it cannot be distinguished from gold; further, that among Darius' drinking vessels there are certain goblets, many in number, of which one could not decide other than by smell whether they are copper or gold. (ch. 49 = 834a1–5)[197]

The explosion in the Hellenistic period in the amount of information circulated about India may be seen as part of Greek responses to a rapidly expanded world. It is in this sense that we can talk about the 'shock of discovery' with the conquests of Alexander and their immediate aftermath in the eastern Hellenistic world. It is in such circumstances that canonical texts and ideas are placed under new pressure, in this case Herodotus' *Histories* more than any other.[198] This is also a period which sees special developments in prose writing, both in historiography and more so in the romance: now the usual intellectual methods are rejected, and such genres as the novel, paradoxography and the fable all follow different approaches to reality.[199] The case of India is indicative of new developments: its distinctive features can be traced to an earlier period of Greek culture, yet it is in the Hellenistic period itself that they come together with a new intensity. In particular, Megasthenes is the key figure in an account that leads ultimately towards Roman perceptions: many of the elements of his Indography can be seen in earlier versions, but his text becomes a focus of Greek and even later Roman Indography. It is Megasthenes that answers Roman needs for an 'author function', a figure of authority, even if that figure turned out to be highly contested.[200]

Together with marvel emerges the discourse about truth and fiction, and here it is as well to remember that we are talking about the origins of

[197] Φασὶ δὲ καὶ ἐν Ἰνδοῖς τὸν χαλκὸν οὕτως εἶναι λαμπρὸν καὶ καθαρὸν καὶ ἀνίωτον, ὥστε μὴ διαγινώσκεσθαι τῇ χρόᾳ πρὸς τὸν χρυσόν, ἀλλ' ἐν τοῖς Δαρείου ποτηρίοις βατιακὰς εἶναί τινας καὶ πλείους, ἃς εἰ μὴ τῇ ὀσμῇ, ἄλλως οὐκ ἦν διαγνῶναι πότερόν εἰσι χαλκαῖ ἢ χρυσαῖ.

[198] Oswyn Murray, 'Herodotus and hellenistic culture', *CQ* 22 (1972), 200–13; in a New World context J. H. Elliott, *The Old world and the new, 1492–1650* (Cambridge University Press, 1970) and Anthony Grafton, *New worlds, ancient texts: the power of tradition and the shock of discovery* (Harvard: Belknap, 1992).

[199] Gabba, 'True history', 55. In terms that now seem somewhat exaggerated, E. R. Dodds, *The Greeks and the irrational* (Berkeley: University of California Press, 1951), pp. 236–69, has presented the third century BC in terms of a contest between reason and unreason.

[200] Term from Michel Foucault, 'What is an author?' in *Modern criticism and theory*, ed. David Lodge (London: Longman, 1988), pp. 197–210, at 202.

historical writing, and perhaps also the origins of the novel.[201] The question of veracity emerges from the very earliest Greek account of India: Ctesias is a key figure here, a kind of 'fall guy' in the self-conscious construction of this discourse on the part of historians and other writers. In other words, the rejection of Ctesias allowed Megasthenes to be accepted as a source.[202] It is no accident that the fourth century has been identified as the 'first real heyday of the forger and the critic'.[203] And it is no accident that the wonders of India emerged as a 'package deal' that includes the rhetoric about size and distance, and about truth and lies. This may be regarded as a function of the unfamiliarity of the edges of the earth. From the archaic period of Greek literature this was identified with fabulous creatures such as Arimaspians. Whether this shares common roots with Indian mythology is unclear, but at the very least it is clear that an archaic Greek tendency to map out the edges of the earth by 'identifying them with strange creatures, a way of filling cultural space, was reinforced by Indian mythology about marvellous beings. The importance of such creatures lies not in the question of what exactly they were or from what origins they came, but the fact that they marked the edges of the earth'.[204]

Is it happenstance that so many of the early Indographic texts are preserved as fragments? I would suggest not, if we bear in mind their marvellous quality described above. To be sure, modern theorists have shown that ethnographic information on any given groups of people tends to be conveyed in fragments, and is never complete.[205] As marvel texts go, *On wonderful things heard* is a prime example: the fact that it was composed in layers serves to remind us of the ways in which marvels can be added to and removed from texts. In most cases marvel texts tend to get broken up into pieces, and are infinitely extendable. (In its surviving form, it thus represents the reverse of the usual process.) Recognition of this fact puts fragments firmly on the agenda for the pages that follow: information is put together and divided up by a variety of forces and processes over the passage of time. The task of later chapters, in part, will be to identify and analyse some moments within those processes.

Concretely, there is no denying the significance of Alexander's expedition to the acquisition of knowledge. At the same time, we must recognise that it

[201] On the ultimate fruitlessness of trying to contemplate the origins of the novel, the warnings of Ewen L. Bowie and Stephen J. Harrison are well taken: 'The romance of the novel', *JRS* 83 (1993), 159–78, at 173. Nonetheless, nobody would deny that a concern with veracity is shared by the historical and romance genres.

[202] See especially Arrian, *Ind.* 3.6 (= *FGrH* 715 F6b = *FGrH* 688 F49).

[203] Anthony Grafton, *Forgers and critics: creativity and duplicity in western scholarship* (Princeton University Press, 1990), p. 10.

[204] Dihle, 'Arabien und Indien', 56; cf. Romm, *Edges*.

[205] Particularly Clifford, *Predicament*.

was overstated in retrospect. Alexander's own legendary status played some part in this exaggeration, indeed from his own time.[206] From this chapter we can conclude that one reason why Alexander's role was exaggerated is simply that it did provide an historical figure with whom to link now increased interest in and knowledge of India, if not a founder (*ktistês*).[207] While this is not stated explicitly, it may be inferred from the fact that most of the post-Alexander references to India here discussed tend to be in a context of the campaign and its aftermath. As we have seen, this is a role Alexander somewhat surprisingly shares with Megasthenes. On the other hand, any more systematic modern attempt at historical reconstruction must recognise that there were continuities before and after Alexander. Is it merely an optical illusion, or at most a difference of quantity? It does seem an overstatement to claim that it was with Alexander that 'the western world begins to acquire genuine knowledge of the real marvels of the land of the Indus'; indeed there is a contradiction implicit in the phrase 'genuine knowledge of the real marvels'.[208]

These continuities stem in part from a certain intransigence in the establishment of geographic knowledge.[209] Indeed, the surviving Alexander histories show that new geographical information was slow to be absorbed:[210] the more ancient writers emphasised Alexander's expedition as an ethnographic moment, the less likely they were to adopt information subsequently acquired.

In retrospect it is easy to overestimate the part played by Alexander. This may be due in part to the later image of Alexander as a scholar, an image not in the Alexander histories but in the *Romance* tradition and later developed in medieval times.[211] But in reality, knowledge was slow to filter through, and slow to have any marked effect. Alexander's campaign will certainly have had a big effect on Greek access to knowledge about India, but that may have been more indirectly than directly. In cartography,

206 Among many references to flattery (*kolakeia*) of Alexander, e.g., Aeschin. *In Ctes.* 162; Agathacides *Mar. Eryth.* 21; Callisthenes in *FGrH* 124 F14a l. 14 = Strabo 17.1.43; Aelian 6.25; Arr. *Anab.* 4.8.3–4; Josephus *BJ* 7.1.470; [Longinus] *Subl.* 32.2.

207 Due in part to the urban foundations of Alexander and his successors, the Hellenistic authors showed considerable interest in the founding of cities: P. M. Fraser, *Ptolemaic Alexandria*, 3 vols. (Oxford: Clarendon, 1972), vol. I, pp. 513–14 and pp. 775–6, with further references; more recently *DNP* s.v. 'Ktisis' and 'Ktistes'.

208 Milns, 'Greek writers', 361.

209 See Dihle, 'Arabien und Indien', p. 41, on the outdatedness of Herodotus' information.

210 Dihle, 'Conception'.

211 Fraser's comments on the textual genealogy of the *Alexander romance* (*Cities of Alexander*, pp. 205–26) provide a starting point on this topic; in general, George Cary, *The medieval Alexander* (Cambridge University Press, 1956); W. Will and J. Heinrichs (eds.), *Zu Alexander dem Grossen. Festschrift G. Wirth* (Amsterdam: Hakkert, 1988), vol. II; Margaret Bridges and J. Christoph Bürgel (eds.), *The problematics of power: eastern and western representations of Alexander the Great* (Bern: Lang, 1996).

Alexander's expedition was remarkably slow in having any effect. This may mean that it did not make much of an impact on geography after all. Though Megasthenes was not actually part of the expedition, he came in its aftermath, even its immediate aftermath if we are to follow Bosworth's dating.[212] Arrian's conflation of Megasthenes with the Alexander historians is a way of placing him at the head of the canon, and conferring on him the authority that could come only from autopsy, and particularly autopsy of a celebrated historical moment. The status he gains in this way is borne out by the relative credibility he wins in later tradition, often at the expense of Ctesias. If Megasthenes seemed the best authority on India to authors such as Strabo and Pliny, it might be that he was by their time fuller and more complete compared with others available.

Once autopsy became part of the Indographic tradition, it gained an importance that it was never to lose. From the time of Herodotus it became a major focus of claims to historiographic credibility.[213] From the point of view of authors it is something that may be called a strategy of authentication: a literary trope that comes increasingly to serve as a guarantee for the truth-value of its larger context. In broader terms, it may be seen as a part of a process of rationalisation that takes place in the early development of Greek historiography. Thus it is no accident that the above account is largely an account of individual *travellers to* India, rather than *writers about* India. If we accept, a priori, that there must have been other travellers whom we do not know about, including commercial travellers, it would be more realistic to view individual authors as landmarks in a changing body of information. For various reasons, then, a modern analysis of this material must be careful to keep autopsy in its place, and not to take it too seriously as a guarantee of anything at all. Certainly, it would be inappropriate to view autopsy as a strict antithesis to other kinds of knowledge, gained in a supposedly less direct manner. Furthermore, talk about autopsy tends to lose focus of the fact that representative objects (in this case Indian goods) could be seen outside of their original contexts. From what we know of the Achaemenid court, it is very likely that various goods and people from India would have found their way there, as tribute, as taxes and as gifts. Seen in this light, the autopsy of Megasthenes and others should be seen in broader terms. To be sure it does not ensure the truth-value of any report, however much it might overshadow other questions about reliability. In historical terms this is unjustified, though, given that there must have been other visitors to India (especially traders who don't show up in

212 'Historical setting'.
213 Schepens, *Autopsie*; Thomas, *Herodotus in context*, pp. 235–47.

the literary record), and there may even have been other accounts. From what Strabo tells us, Deimachus was another Megasthenes *qua* traveller and writer (and liar), but one who happens not to have survived.[214] The same can be said later for Dionysius; and for Patrokles, who is cited by Strabo in seven substantial fragments on India, his authority deriving from his circumnavigation of the Caspian and Hyrcanian Seas (T3).[215] Awareness of the Persian court as a place where people and objects from India could be seen, and a place where a number of Greeks could be found, in fact, is one step in the direction of breaking up autopsy as an absolute criterion of credibility.

Another effect of the emphasis on autopsy is to make this a history of successive 'discoverers'. This may well have been appropriate up to a point, but it obscures the possibility that other travellers may have contributed to the sum of knowledge about India. In other words, the natural dangers of the 'big man' approach to history are here compounded by uncritical acceptance of autopsy as a guarantee of accuracy.[216] In general, this story gives ample evidence of a tendency to elide the historical personages of particular authors with their reliability as historical writers. The history of the *periplus* as a literary form makes a certain amount of room for first-person narration, yet it does not demand it. From Hecataeus the *periplus* is a key means of making sense of the land, but one that has obvious limitations in covering the hinterland. What it does provide is a neat, sequential structure for viewing and describing foreign lands. Nowhere is this more clearly shown than in Nearchus' work, as far as we can judge from Arrian's *Indica*, itself a late instance but one that exhibits the deep structure of the *periplus*.[217]

One of the larger questions to arise may be simply stated: should we speak of Greek information about India as if it were conveyed or created? The tendency in previous accounts, and to some degree in this one, has been to operate from the assumption that information about places and people, of something concretely 'out there', is passively collected and transmitted in good faith. There is much to recommend such an approach in the historical

[214] 2.1.9 C70, after Eratosthenes; cf. 2.1.19 C76. For the fragments of Deimachus see *FGrH* 716.

[215] *FGrH* 717 and 712 respectively.

[216] It is one thing to focus on individual authors *per se*; however, to focus expressly on individual travellers is to present ancient geographical knowledge through the framework of 'discoverers', with its connotations of nineteenth-century colonial travel. Notable examples are Daniel J. Boorstin, *The discoverers* (New York: Random, 1983), and, in ancient studies, M. Cary, *The ancient explorers*, rev. E. H. Warmington (Baltimore: Penguin, 1963).

[217] Grant Parker, 'Porous connections: the Mediterranean and the Red Sea', *Thesis Eleven* 67 (2001), 59–79.

reconstruction of a body of knowledge such as this: it engages with the geographic and ethnographic realities described, and, where appropriate, gives the sources due credit for doing so. This is an historically productive method which makes the best of such evidence as there is for reconstructing a regional history of this period. On the other hand, however, if we bear in mind the intrinsic scarcity of information about an area so far from its Mediterranean points of articulation, a different picture might emerge. A little 'real' information must go a long way, and so in practice there is much scope for embroidery.[218] The process of embroidery can involve the transposing of features from one edge of the earth to another, as, for example, in the case of Ethiopia.[219] It achieves little to ascribe this creative aspect to 'entertainment literature', in itself an unhelpful appellation, implying that entertainment was the province of one particular branch of literature, for among early Ionian historians particularly it might represent a perfectly serious attempt to conceptualise the ends of the earth. The role of geographical writing in the development of Greek historiography is well known.[220]

We have seen here the beginnings of a process by which knowledge is canonised, amid competing claims for authority in the historical, geographic or specifically ethnographic spheres: the dynamics of that canon are typically shaped by questions of the writer's truthfulness, frequently related to that of autopsy.[221] It is in the name of authority that Indographers compete with one another, or others fight battles on behalf of authors. The marvellous quality of much of this information is apparent from its very beginnings, and is both an inspiration and a challenge to the emerging canon of Greek prose writing.

To put the above analysis into perspective, we might take a moment to consider what is absent from the Indian image outlined here. For one thing, there is no evidence of Greek attempts to make sense of Indian religious or

[218] In the study of Roman historiography it has been claimed that a certain degree of 'embroidery' was an intrinsic part of the literary genre of history: A. J. Woodman, *Rhetoric in classical historiography* (London: Croom Helm, 1988). By the same token, ancient views of accuracy were narrower than modern, and applied more to contemporary than early history: T. J. Luce, 'Ancient views on the causes of bias in historical writing', *Cl. Phil.* 84 (1989), 16–31. A more traditional view is reasserted by A. Brian Bosworth, '*Plus ça change* . . . Ancient historians and their sources', *Cl. Ant.* 22 (2003), 167–97. It should be noted that this debate concerns only historiographic texts, rather than the fuller range discussed in the current chapter.

[219] Romm, *Edges*.

[220] See e.g. Hornblower, 'Introduction', in *Greek historiography*, ed. Hornblower, pp. 1–72, at 14–15, following Jacoby.

[221] Marincola, *Authority and tradition*, esp. pp. 128–74; more generally Bruce Lincoln, *Authority: construction and corrosion* (Chicago: University of Chicago Press, 1994).

literary texts, an absence that is all the more striking in comparison with British colonialism and the scholarship it produced.[222] The same can be said for Indian language. As we have seen, Indian holy people certainly did make an impression on Greeks, but they seem to be a late arrival to Greek Indography. In terms of Momigliano's analysis, we might say that Greeks knew about India before they knew about Indian wisdom.[223] Exactly why this should have been so cannot easily be explained, but it must have to do with the fact that the earliest Greek ideas about India were formed in the Achaemenid empire.[224] It appears as if Achaemenid notions of India concerned commodities more than holy persons. In any case, the Iranian world has its own traditions of religious virtuosi, so that Indian holy persons would not have struck Persian observers to the degree they impressed Greeks.

'For all their denunciations the early Hellenistic writers saw the world through Herodotean eyes.'[225] It has even been claimed that the *Historics* were used in the planning of Alexander's expedition.[226] The Egyptian *logos* constituting book 2 is the most obvious case in point. At the very least we can say that Herodotus' work came to offer later generations a body of geographical and ethnographic knowledge which was not soon surpassed, and that in this he was important even for the many writers who criticised him. It does appear, though, that Herodotus' description of India in itself never gained the canonical status that those of Ctesias, Megasthenes and others would do later. Indeed, Herodotus' passages on India are no more than digressions, of no great importance in their own terms.

As we try to assess whether India in Greek thinking was either a particular space or a place-marker with transferable features, we are faced with a paradox. On the one hand, the story told in this chapter is one of increasing knowledge of India as a specific, particular place, subject to specific descriptions and scholarly controversies. Both Ctesias and Megasthenes are subject to extensive critique of detail. On the other hand, the elements of that image were fixed at an early stage, its elements having much in common with other distant parts of the world, particularly Aethiopia. This

222 Dihle, 'Indien und die hellenistisch-römische Welt', 156; contrast, on the modern period, Thomas R. Trautmann, *Aryans and British India* (Berkeley: University of California Press, 1997).

223 *Alien wisdom*: see further Chapter 6 below.

224 By this reckoning, the vivid image of India as a place of special knowledge (explored in Chapter 6) is a later, retrospective phenomenon, dating to the Hellenistic and Roman periods, by which time there was already a certain conception of India in the Greek world (a conception stemming literally from the Achaemenid empire).

225 Murray, 'Herodotus', 205.

226 Murray, 'Herodotus', 206 n. 1; further developed by G. W. Bowersock, 'Herodotus, Alexander, and Rome', *The American Scholar* 58 (1989), 407–14.

was an image that would never be completely shaken off, even much later under the Roman empire, despite substantial increments of detail resulting from commercial contact.

As to the purposes we might reconstruct for early Greek accounts of India, it is unhelpful to try to make a rigid distinction between strategic information and propaganda on one hand and entertainment on the other.[227] The discourse about India has all these elements, which emerge at different points with greater or lesser clarity. Such elements take on different proportions between one author and another in which they are found. And they take on different degrees of importance depending whether we are considering, say, the use of Scylax' reports at Darius' court, or the reception of Ctesias in the elder Pliny. Therefore analyses of purpose must remain speculative, and are in any case seriously jeopardised by the indirectness of textual transmission. The fragmentary quality of the texts is as clear a reflection as any that such information could be infinitely paraphrased, reorganised and recontextualised: this in itself reflects the kinds of information involved.

In the broader terms of Hellenistic history, these texts are a response to an expanding world, and as such respond to 'the shock of discovery'. But this shock was the less sudden for having been pre-empted by Persian knowledge of Sindh. So if this was a shock at all, it was a slow one, much slower than ancient Alexander historiography allowed: the actual content of Greek writings, focusing on marvellous creatures. At least some such objects, or rather a kernel of historical fact lying behind them, must have been available to Greeks at the Persian court. While it is hard for us to reconstruct Persian ideas about India, we can be sure that there was some considerable degree of contact between Indians and the Achaemenid empire, both in Persia itself and in India; we have also considered Greeks present in the Persian court, particularly Scylax and Ctesias. Writings about Alexander himself reveal an intensified emphasis on exaggeration, as we see for example in Strabo's comments on 'flattery': the greatness of the man is linked with the greatness of the world conquered by him.

*

Despite its marginal position, or because of it, India had a threefold impact on Greek intellectual history. First, with regard to maps: in the early days of cartography, we see that India served as a place-marker, initially by constituting part of the schematic continental structures (Hecataeus), later

[227] Both Zambrini, 'Indika', and Sherwin-White and Kuhrt, *Samarkhand to Sardis*, pp. 93–101, stress military-political contexts in their studies of Megasthenes, whereas Romm, *Edges*, pp. 86–8 (on Ctesias) emphasises the entertainment value of marvellous tales.

by defining the direction of winds and filling out the shape of the continents; and yet later, by the time of Eratosthenes, in making it possible to measure the extent of the inhabited world. Secondly, carried by similar momentum initially, India played a role in the development of historiography. It was in critical discussions of Ctesias that the issue of veracity became especially urgent in the early fourth century. As we have seen, this was often related to autopsy and thus to the self-conscious development of historiography. Some of the same issues would be important, in different ways, to the evolution of the novel. Thirdly, the sense of India's fertility and profusion gave it a prominent place in natural history, particularly in the work of Theophrastus. This would have an enormous impact on later writers such as Pliny and Aelian, for whom nature came to mean something different to what it had meant to Aristotle: in an important sense, Pliny's idea of nature is a direct response to the Indus Valley as a geographical space. In other words, very broadly speaking, this idea of nature is a way of making sense of a palpably non-Mediterranean ecology.

To end this chapter, it is fitting to revisit Bevan's tripartite division with which it began. It will be apparent that the supposed three phases – (1) pre-Alexandrian, mostly Ionian from the later sixth century BC to the fourth; (2) Alexander's expedition itself; and (3) the aftermath of Alexander – cannot be sustained, given the high degree of overlap between the second and third. What is more, Herodotus stands out among the first group for his focus on human customs and his omission of monstrous people and animals, in which respects he looks forward to later writers on India. Yet it is not Herodotus' own account of India which becomes *canonical* but those of later authors, notably Megasthenes, if we look at texts such as those of Strabo and Pliny, in which this tradition is subject to detailed critique and re-establishment of authority. A related question concerns the extent to which Alexander's campaign was itself an ethnographic moment, the particular point at which India and Indians came into Greek view. There can be no doubt that for *extent*, the campaign does deserve this status. But it must be conceded that the *basic features* of the Alexandrian and post-Alexandrian image of India were already present in Herodotus and Ctesias. The major exception to this is the Indian holy person, who will largely be the subject of the sixth chapter. Well before Alexander's expedition, the Achaemenid empire was a decisive context for the formation of Greek images of India. By around 300 BC, with the appearance of Megasthenes' *Indika*, the elements of Roman Indography were already established.

PART II

Features of a discourse

CHAPTER 2

India described

> So far as I am able to judge, nothing has been left undone, either by man or Nature, to make India the most extraordinary country that the sun visits on his round. Nothing seems to have been forgotten, nothing overlooked. Always, when you think you have come to the end of her tremendous specialties and have finished hanging tags upon her . . . another specialty crops up and another tag is required . . . Perhaps it will be simplest to throw away the tags and generalize her with one all-comprehensive name, as the Land of Wonders.
>
> Mark Twain (1897)[1]

Marvels and monsters characterised Hellenistic accounts of India, even more so than the earliest Greek accounts, as the first chapter has shown. Furthermore, it is clear that this marvel-based view of India was typical of Greek descriptions of the ends of the earth generally, and in many respects was not unique to India. We also identified there the doxographic problem: the phenomenon whereby our knowledge of an earlier text is contingent on the context and purposes of its preservation within a later (sometimes much later) text. This is particularly true of Megasthenes, who is usually regarded as a privileged witness, though his work is transmitted purely in fragments. Whereas, in Chapter 1, the emphasis was on the earlier texts, reconstructed as plausibly as possible, here it is necessary to concentrate instead on texts of Rome's early to high imperial periods, many of which preserve those very fragments. At issue here is the reception of the earlier texts, and their relation to newly acquired knowledge. Focusing on Diodorus Siculus, Strabo, Pliny the Elder, Arrian and others, we must still be attuned to specific themes of Indography; but now, in particular, we are in a position to consider the larger contexts within which India featured in Roman thinking. This chapter will thus involve close literary analysis of Indographic passages in the contexts of their reception. The main question here is: what are the literary devices used for describing India and its inhabitants? As we attempt a detailed

1 *Following the Equator: a journey around the world*, 2 vols. (New York: Harper, 1897), vol. II, p. 243.

answer, one issue to be borne continually in mind is that of sources, and of the ways in which various kinds of topographic information can be juxtaposed, indeed of the relation between ethnography, topography and geography within these particular texts.

In the larger contexts of Indography, an important distinction should be made at the start, even if it is merely an analytical one. On the one hand there are works in which specific consideration of India takes centre-stage, even if that is only for a limited part of a work. Thus, for example, both Strabo and Pliny discuss India at some length in the course of their surveys of world chorography; likewise, in briefer compass, Pomponius Mela. It is in fact Pliny who mentions the younger Seneca's now lost treatise on India.[2] The significance of this text stretches beyond an Indographic perspective:[3] for one thing, as a fully fledged ethnographic treatise it would have predated Tacitus' *Germania*, the oldest surviving example of this genre in Latin.

On the other hand, far outweighing these sources in bulk, are works that merely contain passing references to India, works on any variety of topics.[4] In fact, the digression was the most common literary form for conveying ethnographic information.[5] This practice was well established by the time of Herodotus, and it was so common by the time of Polybius that he regards it with critical distance.[6] For current purposes the distinction may be summed up as follows: either India is described in its own right, or in ways that make it subordinate to the larger concerns of the work. In order to assess this distinction and its implications, we shall begin by considering some of the authors for whom India features prominently, concentrating on those from the first category.

[2] At 6.60 he says, *Seneca etiam apud nos temptata Indiae commentatione* . . . This and other sources are collected in F. Haase's edition of Seneca's fragments (Leipzig: Teubner, 1903), frr. 9–12. Seneca is also supposed to have written a treatise *de situ et sacris Aegyptiorum* (Serv. *ad Aen.* 6.154).

[3] *Pace* Dieter Flach, 'Die Germania des Tacitus in ihrem literaturgeschichtlichen Zusammenhang', in *Beiträge zum Verständnis der Germania des Tacitus*, ed. Herbert Jankuhn and Dieter Timpe (Göttingen: Vandenhoeck & Ruprecht, 1989), pp. 27–58, who follows the dismissive attitude of earlier scholars. Allan A. Lund, 'Versuch einer Gesamtinterpretation der Germania des Tacitus', *ANRW* II.33.3 (1991), pp. 1858–988, esp. 1860, stresses the uniqueness of the *Germania*.

[4] In the collection of André and Filliozat, *L'Inde vue de Rome*, this latter category predominates by far. The distinction is of course somewhat unfair, given the imbalance between them. Tacitus' *Germania* stands out for its degree of engagement with a foreign people, its social life and mindset.

[5] Allan A. Lund, *Zum Germanenbild der Römer* (Heidelberg: Winter, 1990), p. 19.

[6] Note the apologetic tone of 3.57. In this respect compare *Iug.* 17.1–2. Sallust says that his excursus on African ethnogeography is occasioned by the fact that few know about such a remote place, and begs his reader's indulgence by claiming to be as brief as possible: *sed quae loca et nationes ob calorem aut asperitatem, item solitudines minus frequentata sunt, de iis haud facile compertum narrauerim. cetera quam paucissimis absoluam.* 'But, concerning those places and groups that are less often visited on account of the heat or harsh conditions or desert, I have recounted what I have found out not without difficulty. As for the rest, let me dispense with them in as few words as possible.'

I. CONTEXTS OF INDOGRAPHY

I.1. Historiography

Within the genre of historiography the Alexander historians bulk large. Partly overlapping with them is the universal history of Diodorus Siculus (fl. c. 60–30 BC). The forty books of his *Bibliothêkê* took the history of the Mediterranean world from mythological times down to Caesar.[7] Less than half survives in its original form, though further parts were quoted or paraphrased by later writers. Of his life little is known.[8] A major part of Diodorus' project, being a universal history, is to integrate the narratives of Greek and Roman events. India features mainly in the light of Alexander's expedition (2.35–42). Compared with other historians writing about Alexander, Diodorus stands out for the amount of detail he gives, including the fullest surviving Greek account of Indian social divisions.[9] It is in Diodorus that we find an account of Iambulus' journey to the Island of the Sun, and thence to the coast of India and to the city of Pataliputra (Palibothra) on the Ganges.[10]

Of the historians that devoted entire works to Alexander, Quintus Curtius Rufus will occur frequently in the pages that follow. He is of special interest, not only as someone writing in Latin about Alexander, but also because the highly wrought rhetorical style of his work reflects the influence of the schools.[11] But none demands as much attention as Arrian (Flavius Arrianus of Nicomedia, d. in or after 170).[12] His monograph on the Alans, an Iranian tribe, is lost, and so are the histories of his native Bithynia and of the Parthian empire. Arrian's public career brought him a number of

[7] In so far as this is a universal history it is considered also in Chapter 5 below.

[8] Sacks, *Diodorus Siculus*.

[9] Note especially the passage attributed by Jacoby to Megasthenes, Chapter 1, section II.2 above.

[10] Diod. 2.55–60, inviting comparison with the brief reference at Lucian's *Ver. hist.* 1.3. This is likely an abbreviated account, especially since it is in the third person, whereas Iambulus wrote originally in the first person. See further Diskin Clay and Andrea Purvis, *Four island utopias* (Newburyport, MA: Focus, 1999), pp. 107–14.

[11] The question of his dates is not easily put to rest, though a general consensus has emerged in recent decades: arguments for dating, coming down on the early reign of Claudius, are assessed by John E. Atkinson, 'Q. Curtius Rufus' *Historiae Alexandri Magni*', *ANRW* II.34.4 (1998), 3447–83. The author was, in all probability, identical with the rhetor mentioned by Suetonius in his *Rhet.* Even if there is some argument for a slightly later dating, that would have no discernible impact on the current topic.

[12] For a general discussion, see Philip A. Stadter, *Arrian of Nicomedia* (Chapel Hill: University of North Carolina Press, 1980), pp. 115–32. Christian Jacob presents Arrian's Alexander as a traveller: 'Alexandre et la maitrise de l'espace. L'Art du voyage dans l'<<Anabase>> d'Arrien', *Quaderni di Storia* 34 (1991), 5–40.

administrative and military posts in various parts of the empire. If it is true that Trajan's military programme and his imitation of Alexander gave special significance to any contemporary history of Alexander's campaigns,[13] it will be important to be alert to possible resonances between Arrian's and Trajan's interests in India.

In the *Indica*, the work sometimes counted the eighth book of the *Anabasis*, Arrian makes good his promise to discuss India's ethnographic and geographic details in greater detail than the narrative frame of the main work allowed (5.5.1–2).[14] In effect, he narrates Nearchus' return voyage. Only the first seventeen chapters, strictly speaking, are devoted to the description of places and people, but the remaining twenty-six chapters, continuing the story of Nearchus' and Alexander's campaign, reveal a concern for topographical detail.[15] Whereas the *Anabasis* is written in Attic, the *Indica* is written in Ionic, a fact that may express Arrian's homage to the Herodotean tradition of ethnography, if not to Herodotus himself.[16] By virtue of its focus on Alexander, the *Indica* 'is in no sense an account of India in Roman times'.[17]

Arrian indicates his debt to both Nearchus and Megasthenes, 'two esteemed authors' (17.6), to lend authority to his own work by valorising his sources.[18] In the introductory, scientific-geographical chapters of the *Indica* it is, however, to Eratosthenes that he appeals (3.1). Arrian has not been to India himself, but his closest point of contact with his material is his personal knowledge of two tributaries of the Ister, namely the Enus and the Saus: the context is his claim that the Ister and the Nile are comparable with the Indus and the Ganges (4.9).[19] This represents a coming together of two different sources of authority: those of autopsy and of book learning.

I.2. Geography

The most substantial topographical work to survive from antiquity is the *Geography* of Strabo of Amaseia in Galatia (64/63 BC to *c.* AD 21), which also contains the lengthiest description of India in any ancient text. For its

13 Albrecht Dihle, *Greek and Latin literature of the Roman empire* (London: Routledge, 1994), p. 243.

14 In so far as this should be regarded as an independent work, it defies the view that Tacitus' *Germania* is the only surviving ancient ethnographic monograph (Lund, *Germanenbild*, p. 19).

15 Examples are the descriptions of the Ichthyophagi (29) and of Carmania (32).

16 Albin Lesky, *A history of Greek literature* (London: Routledge, 1966), p. 848; Stadter, *Arrian*, p. 116.

17 Stadter, *Arrian*, p. 117.

18 Yet Arrian's praise for Megasthenes is elsewhere qualified: he did not see much of India, nonetheless more so than Alexander's companions did (5.3).

19 Stadter, *Arrian*, p. 120.

author, who was a Stoic by training, geography was a branch of philosophy: he says he aimed to provide a work that would be useful and helpful. Despite his own sojourn in Rome after 44 BC, he chose to write in Greek rather than Latin: it was not only his native tongue but also the language of intellectual discourse. Given the global scale of Strabo's *Geography*, it is important to compare that text with contemporary and earlier universal histories.[20] India makes two major appearances within the seventeen books of Strabo: first at the beginning of his second book, while he discusses his own methodology and those of his predecessors, including Eratosthenes, as well as issues involving the size of the earth;[21] and secondly, in the course of a lengthy description of Asia (15.1.1–73 C685–720). Asia (books 11–16) comes between Europe (3–10) and Africa (17) as Strabo moves clockwise around the Mediterranean.[22]

A Latin Strabo of lesser technical sophistication and on a more modest scale is Pomponius Mela, whose *Chorographia* comprises three books and can be dated to the middle of the first century AD.[23] The first two books are devoted to parts of the Mediterranean coastline and their adjacent interior; it is in the third book that we find India, one of the regions overlooked in this basic schema. Mela diverges from the Greek pattern by proceeding anti-clockwise from the Straits of Gibraltar, i.e. beginning with Mauretania and Numidia, rather than clockwise, with Spain.[24] India, including the Ganges valley, and its adjoining islands receive brief mention at 3.61–71.[25] Even making provision for the much smaller scale of Mela's work, it is clear that Asia receives a much lesser degree of coverage in comparison with Strabo. Mela's *orbis terrarum* centers on the Mediterranean world in narrower compass, and so it is not surprising that India receives so little attention. While Mela's text might seem at first to command little interest, it was in fact to prove a major conduit of geographical information between antiquity and the western Middle Ages, in view of texts such as Solinus and Pseudo-Aethicus, considered below.

[20] J. M. Alonso-Núñez, 'An Augustan world history: the *Historiae Philippicae* of Pompeius Trogus', *G&R* 34 (1987), 56–72.

[21] He mentions Megasthenes and Deimachus (e.g., 2.1.4 C69), Nearchus and Onesicritus (2.1.9 C70).

[22] Katherine Clarke, 'In search of the author of Strabo's *Geography*', *JRS* 87 (1997), 92–110. R. Syme, *Anatolica: studies in Strabo* (Oxford: Clarendon, 1995), esp. pp. 256–67.

[23] The *terminus post quem* of the work is Claudius' invasion of Britain in AD 43–4 (3.49–53). It is quoted as a source by the elder Pliny, who mentions it several times in the first book of his *Natural history*.

[24] On the Greek pattern visible in Strabo, see Jacoby, *FGrH* IIC 48–9.

[25] On the textual tradition see C. M. Gormley, M. A. Rouse and R. H. Rouse, 'The medieval circulation of the "de chorographia" of Pomponius Mela', *Medieval Studies* 46 (1984), 266–320; and in summary form R. H. Rouse in Reynolds (ed.), *Texts and transmission*, pp. 290–2.

Roughly contemporary with Pomponius Mela is the anonymous *Periplus of the Erythraean Sea*. Written in *koine* Greek, this work has been dated to the decades AD 40 to 70, making it roughly contemporary with Mela and Pliny.[26] This is a practical rather than a literary work, offering advice to persons sailing two different routes: from the north eastern Red Sea, round the Horn of Africa and down the east coast of Africa, to around Zanzibar; and (in greater detail) from the same area, round the Gulf of Aden, across the Arabian Sea and ultimately to the west coast of India.[27] Both of these routes involved sailing with the monsoon winds. Given the kinds of information offered in this text, and its style, this appears to have been written by a merchant for others plying the same route. It focuses on the commodities that can be obtained or exchanged at individual ports en route, and advice on sailing and trading conditions at those ports. Indeed, in view both of its content and style, it gives the impression of a conversation overheard; its very survival, via a tenth-century codex now at Heidelberg, seems particularly fortuitous. This work is of central importance in assessing the exchange of commodities between India and the Roman world.

Claudius Ptolemy lived around AD 90–168, and is today best known for his astronomical treatise *Almagest*. His *Geography* lists more than 8,000 places in Europe, Africa and Asia, according to their latitude and longitude. Ptolemy himself distinguishes his large-scale geography, which is scientific and mathematical, from the more detail-bound chorography, what would in Latin be called topography (I.I). This was essentially a Greek tradition, ardently pursued in Hellenistic times by Eratosthenes and others, though Pliny and other Latin writers show some awareness of it. Ptolemy's *Geography* may be regarded as the culmination of this tradition.[28] As important as Ptolemy's text was for the long-term history of cartography, it had little impact on most of the Indographic authors in the period discussed in this book. Whereas Strabo is dismissive of geographical information gleaned by traders, Ptolemy makes it clear that both he and his predecessor

[26] Lionel Casson (ed.), *The Periplus Maris Erythraei* (Princeton: Princeton University Press, 1989), p. 6.

[27] To compare this text with modern printed sources of nautical information shows changes and varieties of travel, even as it reiterates some of the same routes: in the early days of the Suez Canal, Britain's Hydrographic Office published *The Red Sea pilot* (London, 1873), with an equally practical bent. At a time when seaborne commerce relies on different (electronic) media for such information, would-be yachtsmen can still consult the book by Elaine Morgan and Stephen Davies, *Red Sea pilot: Aden to Cyprus*, 2nd edn (Huntingdon: Imray, 2002).

[28] *History of cartography*, ed. Harley and Woodward, vol. I, pp. 177–200; Wolfgang Hübner, 'The Ptolemaic view of the universe', *GRBS* 41 (2000), 59–93.

Marinus set great store by the astronomical observations of those plying the routes of the Erythraean Sea.[29]

Ptolemy's India deserves special consideration here, given the importance of his *Geography* in the history of maps.[30] Together with the more distant east, India occurs in the seventh and last book of the *Geography*, and is divided into four sections (7.1.1). First, India this side of the Ganges; second, beyond the Ganges; third, the location of Sinai (whose inhabitants include *Aithiopes ichthyphagi*),[31] and whose eastern side borders with unknown lands); and fourth, Taprobane and other islands. The remainder of the work is devoted to a descriptive summary of world maps, of the armillary sphere and to a general summary by way of concluding the work as a whole. It is clear, from any analysis of the geographical co-ordinates specified in the text, that Ptolemy's India is not a subcontinent or even peninsula at all; instead it has a fairly straight coastline running from east to west.[32] For Ptolemy, the Ganges represents the key dividing line. The Indus, by contrast, is a valley supporting considerable settlement, rather than a boundary of any kind. Thus the name 'Indoscythia' for one of the Indus areas suggests, in Ptolemy's view, an area whose cultural traditions combine those of both the Iranian plateau and the Indus Valley. 'Gymnosophists' are mentioned as an ethnic group living toward the eastern side, near the Ganges (7.1.51). With the partial exception of rivers, which are prominent in this section of the *Geography* (e.g., 7.1.29–41), there is nothing that substantively differentiates India from other parts of the world described by Ptolemy. Within this scheme, India, no less so than the Mediterranean, has

[29] Note for example chs. 7 (Diodorus the Samian); 9 (one Diogenes) and 17 (where the traders' information about India is balanced against that of local inhabitants); cf. J. Lennart Berggren and Alexander Jones, *Ptolemy's* Geography: *an annotated translation of the theoretical chapters* (Princeton University Press, 2000), p. 25. Contrast Strabo 15.1.4 C686.

[30] Louis Renou (ed.), *La Géographie de Ptolémée, L'Inde (VII, 1–4)* (Paris: Champion, 1925). Ptolemy's description of these parts provided the basis for an extensive work of topography and ethnography: G. E. Gerini, *Researches on Ptolemy's geography of Eastern Asia (Farther India and Indo-Malay Peninsula)* (London: Royal Asiatic Society, 1909). Cf. J. R. Sinnatamby, *Sri Lanka in Ptolemy's* Geography (Colombo: n.p., 1968). The *Geography* is currently in the process of systematic editing: Alfred Stückelberger, 'Ptolemy and the problem of scientific perception of space', in *Space in the Roman world*, ed. Talbert and Brodersen, pp. 27–40, at 31.

[31] Nicholas Purcell, 'Eating fish: the paradoxes of seafood', in *Food in antiquity*, ed. John Wilkins *et al.* (University of Exeter Press, 1995), pp. 132–49, shows that fish-eating can be the hallmark of barbarian customs. Cf. Gerini, *Researches*, pp. 255–6, on Ichthyophagoi Aithiopes.

[32] This geographical framework, buoyed by a resurgence of interest in Ptolemy, endured until after Vasco da Gama's expedition of 1498. Ananda Abeydeera, 'The geographical perceptions of India and Ceylon in the *Periplus Maris Erythraei* and in Ptolemy's *Geography*', *Terrae Cognitae* 30 (1998), 1–25, reports this anomaly, as well as the absence of any apparent explanation for it. For a reconstruction of Ptolemy's map on the basis of the co-ordinates he gives, see E. H. Bunbury, *A history of ancient geography*, 2nd edn (New York: Dover, 1959), opposite p. 578.

definite places that can be mapped by co-ordinates. It abounds with cities (*poleis*). What does, however, mark this part of the world as exotic is the nudity of some of its inhabitants, such as the Nangalogai (7.2.18) and the island-dwelling Aginnatai (7.2.26).

Ptolemy himself was largely forgotten by the medieval world, both eastern and western; but later Byzantine manuscripts reveal revived interest in him,[33] a revival that spread to Italy with the migration of Byzantine scholars in the late fourteenth and fifteenth centuries.[34] In 1406 the *Geography* was translated into Latin by Jacopo Angeli da Scarperia, and this brought the work a much wider readership in the west. The rediscovery of Ptolemy was to have a major impact on cartography and seafaring in the early modern period, and the history of editions of Ptolemy closely matches the path of cartographic innovation: for example, the world maps produced by Martin Waldseemüller in the early 1500s reflect a dialogue between Ptolemy's text and the new territorial discoveries.[35] One of the critical questions in the history of cartography was whether the Indian Ocean was an inland sea, in other words, whether it was possible to sail round the Cape of Good Hope and reach South Asia by that route. This was proven when Vasco da Gama arrived in Goa in 1497, but it took several years for this new information to be reflected in European maps. The Ptolemaic and the Plinian traditions emerged very differently in the history of European mapmaking: the one becoming the basis for maps in the early modern period, the other informing the marvel tradition of the western Middle Ages.[36]

Though, as Chapter 1 shows, the story of Dionysus' invasion of India goes back to Alexander's expedition,[37] it is in the *Dionysiaca* of Nonnus of Panopolis (fl. 450–70) that the relevant section is found. Thus it is not till

33 Maximus Planudes in late thirteenth-century Byzantium played a major role in the rediscovery of Ptolemy: O. A. W. Dilke, 'Cartography in the Byzantine empire', in *History of cartography*, ed. Harley and Woodward, vol. I, pp. 258–75 at 258–59.

34 The most significant manuscript of Ptolemy's *Geography*, Urb. gr. 82, travelled to Florence in 1397 with Chrysoloras, its probable owner: see further N. G. Wilson, *From Byzantium to Italy: Greek studies in the Italian Renaissance* (Baltimore: Johns Hopkins University Press, 1992), p. 9; Grafton, *New worlds*, p. 49.

35 E.g. O. A. W. Dilke, 'The culmination of Greek cartography in Ptolemy', in *History of cartography*, ed. Harley and Woodward, vol. I, pp. 177–200 at 177; Shankar Raman, *Framing 'India': the colonial imaginary in early modern culture* (Stanford University Press, 2002), esp. pp. 108–21. Columbus possessed a 1478 Latin translation, annotating it in the section on the circumference of the earth: Alfred Stückelberger, 'Kolumbus und die antiken Wissenschaften', *Archiv für Kulturgeschichte* 69 (1987), 331–40.

36 Abeydeera, 'Geographical perceptions', and Tony Campbell, *The earliest printed maps, 1472–1500* (Berkeley: University of California Press, 1987), esp. pp. 122–6.

37 See Chapter 1, section II.1; and see especially Bosworth, *Alexander and the East*, pp. 98–132. In addition, according to Pierre Chuvin, Nonnus' fictional India incorporates elements of the Iranian world of the late second century AD (drawn from a lost source posited by Chuvin): 'Local traditions

the fifth century that the fullest ancient version of the story was recounted, in books 13–48 of elaborate Greek hexameter. This episode makes up the bulk of the poem, which consists of forty-eight books.[38]

If Ptolemy's text had a distinctive history in antiquity and beyond, then the *Christian topography* of Cosmas Indicopleustes stands awkwardly, even eccentrically, in the history of Indography. Dating from the mid-sixth century, this text combines theological and geographical discussions. Cosmas' eleventh book includes a detailed description of the island of Taprobane, modern Sri Lanka. Of the many works that we know Cosmas to have written, the *Christian topography* is the only one to survive in more than fragments. But in fact the work in its current form does not sit easily between two covers: the longer of the two prologues to survive discusses the contents of the first five books only, and this suggests that the work may have originally ended at that point. The remaining seven books involve a high degree of repetition, not only between each other but also with the first six books. The differences between the two surviving prefaces suggest that the fuller version was the product of a second edition. When we get to the eleventh book, where Sri Lanka and to some extent India and Ethiopia are discussed at length, the focus of the work has moved considerably from the theoretical geography of the first few books to topography and natural history: several animals and plants are recounted in detail. For the present, it is sufficient to notice the variety within the work, and the possibility that the work in its current form preserves excerpts from Cosmas' other works, now lost.

Cosmas argues for a rectangular universe, in the shape of a vault, and matching that of the Tabernacle. His literal interpretation of the scriptures is in keeping with the Nestorian group based at Nisibis.[39] This cosmological vision brought him into conflict with the Aristotelian philosopher John Philoponus, a clash that emerges most clearly from Philoponus' subsequent

and classical mythology in the *Dionysiaca*', in *Studies in the* Dionysiaca *of Nonnus*, ed. Neil Hopkinson (Cambridge: Cambridge Philological Society, 1994), pp. 167–76.

[38] This number matches the *Iliad* and *Odyssey* combined, in keeping with Nonnus' aim of matching Homer, and even surpassing him in the dignity of his divine (as opposed to human) theme. In a sketch of Dionysus' Roman career, Glen Bowersock suggests that by Nonnus' time Dionysus had 'become, for pagans and Christians alike, a powerful universalising god of salvation, whose career brought together, in a common aretalogy the diverse legends and topographies of the far-flung countries where Greek was, however imperfectly, understood': 'Dionysus as an epic hero', in Hopkinson, *Studies*, pp. 156–66, at 162.

[39] Cosmas omits mention of Nestorians when he lists a number of 'heresies' (5.178–79). Cf. the invectives of 6.25–27 and 30–32, which illustrate his tendency to repetition. The Three Chapters controversy brought him into conflict with John Philoponus, the contemporary Christian Aristotelian.

De opificio mundi (557–60).[40] The use of first-person narrative, in which the monk Cosmas recalls his past trading ventures, invites comparison with another work in which authority derives not from books but from personal experience: the *Periplus of the Erythraean Sea* of some five centuries earlier, though of course that work lacks Cosmas' religious-philosophical content and its polemical tone.[41]

I.3. Natural history

Geography was a part of the encyclopaedic project of Pliny the Elder (AD 23/24–79), but merely one among many presenting themselves under the rubric of Nature (*Natura*). Despite a busy career in Roman administration and the military, Pliny wrote copiously in various genres, to judge from the biographical information preserved by his adoptive son.[42] Born at Comum to an equestrian family, he held senior posts in various parts of the empire until his death by suffocation during an eruption of Vesuvius. Of his numerous works, only the encyclopaedic *Natural history* remains today, having been much read in western Europe of the Middle Ages and beyond. Books 3–6 cover the physical geography of the 'known world' (*orbis terrarum*), area by area;[43] within this frame, book 6.21–80 deals with India and 6.81–90 Sri Lanka (*Taprobane*). Furthermore, in the seventh, anthropological book, a brief section is devoted to the monstrous creatures and strange practices of India and Ethiopia (7.21–32). In its brevity, this amounts to a rapid-fire summary of the detailed descriptions in book 6, though even here Pliny does not neglect to mention his sources.[44]

Though it cannot be claimed that India stands at the middle of his writing, it is worth mentioning Aelian here (Claudius Aelianus, *c.* 172–235),

40 Wanda Wolska, *La Topographie chretienne de Cosmas Indicopleustès: théologie et science au VIe siècle* (Paris: Presses Universitaires, 1962), pp. 147–271, on Cosmas' cosmology.

41 Cosmas will receive further attention in Chapter 3, section I.4 below, in relation to the illustrations he added to the *Christian topography*.

42 Letters 3.5; 6.16 and 6.20 (the last two being addressed to Tacitus). For a reading of the relevant letters, stressing the variety of narrative frames and readers constructed, see Umberto Eco, 'A portrait of the Elder as a Young Pliny: how to build fame', in *On signs*, ed. Marshall Blonsky (Baltimore: Johns Hopkins University Press, 1985).

43 A recent analysis of books 3–6 emphasises its triumphalist politics: Murphy, *Pliny the Elder's* Natural History, pp. 129–64.

44 Among a recent resurgence of interest in Pliny, the following also deserve mention: K. G. Sallmann, *Die Geographie des älteren Plinius in ihrem Verhältnis zu Varro* (Berlin: de Gruyter, 1971); G. E. R. Lloyd, *Science, folklore and ideology* (Cambridge University Press, 1983), esp. pp. 140–52; Andrew Wallace-Hadrill, 'The elder Pliny and man's unnatural history', *G* & *R* 37 (1990), 80–96; Mary Beagon, *Roman nature: the thought of Pliny the Elder* (Clarendon, 1992); Sorcha Carey, *Pliny's catalogue of culture: art and empire in the* Natural history (Oxford University Press, 2003).

as a reminder that a concern with India in Roman literature is not restricted to geographical and historical sources. Of his two miscellanies, his collection of information about animals, the περὶ ζῴων ἰδιότητος in seventeen books, frequently presents India as a place of zoological wonder.[45] While curiosities generally interest Aelian, it is striking that many of these are linked to an Indian location, not unlike the pseudo-Aristotelian *De mirabilibus auscultationibus* discussed in Chapter 1. Thus the satyr-like creatures of 16.21 are specifically linked with the Indian region of Kolounda. In keeping with the Stoic undercurrent of the work, this is attributed to the wisdom of Nature. Indeed, one of the larger issues to deserve special attention is the extent to which India is invoked as a way of emphasising the extremes, if not the glories of Nature. Born in Praeneste, Aelian was a native speaker of Latin; his choice to write in Greek reflects the cachet attached to the Greek language under the influence of the Second Sophistic movement.

An extension of this catalogue into the early Middle Ages would reveal a lively and varied tradition of Pliny's *Natural history*. This emerges, in fact, as the text to have an ongoing impact on European perceptions of India. In terms of the textual transmission of the work, different sections were to have very different fates.[46] The textual reconstruction of Pliny's Indographic section is hampered by the fact that the prime manuscript for the geographical books breaks off a few chapters short of the section on India, with the result that editors must rely on the *recentiores*, which are of varying quality.[47]

But this is only part of the story. Pliny's text was one of many to undergo excerption and anthologising in the course of the second and third centuries. The process by which anthologies were created out of larger works reflects the creation of canons of text and the resultant desire to codify; it owes something to the changing technologies of the ancient book, with the increased use of the parchment codex as opposed to the papyrus roll.[48] Along with Mela, Pliny's geographical books were to provide the core of

[45] The other work, the *Varia historia* or 'historical miscellany', is mentioned below, Chapter 4, section I.5.

[46] L. D. Reynolds, 'The elder Pliny', in *Texts and transmission*, pp. 307–16, esp. 307.

[47] See also Jan-Mayhoff (eds.), vi, on the *Leidensis Vossianus*, known as A. Of book 6 it has only 6.41–51. The surviving manuscript is the descendant of a tradition different to and seemingly better than that circulating in Europe.

[48] Arno Borst, *Das Buch in der Naturgeschichte. Plinius und seine Leser im Zeitalter des Pergaments* (Heidelberg: Winter, 1984); cf. Colin H. Roberts and T. C. Skeat, *The birth of the codex* (London: British Academy, 1983), pp. 67–73; L. D. Reynolds and N. G. Wilson (eds.), *Scribes and scholars: a guide to the transmission of Greek and Latin literature*, 3rd edn (Oxford: Clarendon, 1991), pp. 31–6.

Solinus' *Collectanea*.[49] Here the abbreviated version omits Pliny's source criticism, however limited that may have been in the first instance.[50] It was with Isidore of Seville's *Etymologiae* or *Origines* that this tradition, which we might call 'Plinian', was transmitted to the Latin Middle Ages, and helped create a language for the description of distant people. In concrete terms, it provided a framework and even a vocabulary for talking about the ends of the earth and their inhabitants. The *Cosmographia* transmitted under the name of 'Aethicus Ister' is a prime case of the overlap in Latin topographical writers after Mela and Pliny.[51] High medieval instances of this tradition are Robert Cricklade and Vincent of Beauvais (*Speculum mundi*);[52] even the cartographic tradition seen in the Hereford map (*mappamundi*) and the Ebstorf world map reveals a debt to the contents and language of this Plinian tradition.[53] These maps, together with other visual sources of the Middle Ages, offer visual expression of the marvel tradition, as Chapter 3 below will show.

I.4. Romance and mime

The Greek novels make considerable use of exotic settings, particularly in the eastern Mediterranean and southwest Asia. So prominent are places such as Ephesus, Babylonia and Ethiopia that earlier scholars posited an eastern origin of such stories, if not the genre as a whole.[54] While such an approach is no longer in favour, there remains the undeniable fact of locale. It is here that India makes an inevitable, if limited appearance, in several romances. Thus, in the case of Xenophon of Ephesus' *Ephesian tale*, the heroine Anthia is bought by an Indian king and narrowly escapes being shipped to India as a slave. Heliodorus' *Aithiopian tale* contains a few references to Indian commodities. Thus there are 'herbs and roots that

[49] The verdict that Solinus was 'Pliny's ape' is overstated, stemming from anachronistic assumptions about authorial originality. At all events, the textual tradition of Solinus shows the degree of overlap with other Latin writers touching on geographic themes, such as Augustine, Isidore and later Aldhelm and Bede: R. H. Rouse in *Texts and transmission*, ed. L. D. Reynolds, pp. 391–3.

[50] See, e.g., Marjorie Chibnall, 'Pliny's *Natural history* and the Middle Ages', in *Empire and aftermath*, ed. T. A. Dorey (London: Routledge and Kegan Paul, 1975), pp. 57–78 at 59.

[51] This text, which by its content and phrasing clearly belongs to a line of continuity between Pliny and the late medieval world maps, begins with the well-known threefold division of continents. See *Geographi Latini Minores*, ed. Alexander Riese (Heilbronn: Henning, 1878), pp. 71–103; also Reeve in Reynolds, *Texts and transmission*, pp. 255–6, and Rouse in *ibid.*, p. 290.

[52] Chibnall, 'Pliny'; cf. Reynolds 'The elder Pliny', in *Texts and transmission*, p. 313.

[53] It has been suggested that Orosius and Isidore were the key sources for these maps: von den Brincken, *Kartographische Quellen*; cf. Lozovsky, *The earth*, pp. 69–78 on Orosius.

[54] Ben Edwin Perry, *The ancient romances* (Berkeley: University of California Press, 1967).

grow in India, Ethiopia and Egypt' (2.30.2); 'precious necklaces and priceless gems from India and Ethiopia' (8.11.8); and the 'phoenix that comes from Ethiopia or India' (6.3.3).[55] In both works, the relevant scenes take place in the Nile valley: whether the delta or Upper Egypt, this zone linking the Indian Ocean and the Mediterranean offers considerable narrative possibilities. The playing out of these possibilities will occupy us in due course.

Atypically of the genre, Longus' *Daphnis and Chloe* has a pastoral setting and does not involve long-distance travel. But it does contain a reference to the triumph of Dionysus, a literary reference to Alexander's propaganda concerning India's past (4.3). In the middle point of the garden (*paradeisos*) that Longus describes at length is a temple and altar dedicated to Dionysus. Inside the temple are paintings on subjects related to the god: alongside the conquest of Indians (*Indoi nikômenoi*) are scenes such as his birth, the flaying of Pentheus, and the metamorphosis of the Etruscans.

This may be a brief and passing reference to India, but it is significant in several ways. India occurs at the intersection of the verbal and the visual, as if Longus is reminding us of the visual appeal of an Indian theme. Indeed, the scene described is that which survives on sarcophagus reliefs such as that in the Walters Gallery in Baltimore.[56] Prominent in this ekphrasis is the harmonious collaboration of art and nature. Again, India reflects the glories of nature.

It is generally difficult to attach a date to the 'famous five' Greek novels, and the three concerned are no exception: Xenophon of Ephesus' *Ephesian tale* and Longus' *Daphnis and Chloe* both tend to be placed in the second century AD, making them texts of the Second Sophistic, whereas the greater complexity of Heliodorus' lengthy *Aithiopian tale* suggests a later date, perhaps between the mid-third and mid-fourth centuries AD.

India features also in a dramatic text (first or second century AD) that survives in a fragmentary state among the Oxyrhynchus papyri.[57] In it, the young Greek woman Charition is held captive by the Indian king. A priestess of Selene, she takes refuge in the goddess' shrine. Her brother, arriving with a party of Greeks, brings about her escape by plying the Indians with unmixed wine. This plot is reminiscent of the Greek novels

55 Philostr. *VA* 3.49 speaks of India as the origin of the phoenix; more usually its locale is Arabia, e.g. Hdt. 2.73; or Ethiopia, e.g. Ach. Tat. 3.25.

56 Notably the Walters Gallery sarcophagus, described in Chapter 3, section I.2 below.

57 *Charition Liberata (P. Oxy. 413)*, ed. Stefania Santelia (Bari: Levante, 1991); discussed as a kind of 'pulp fiction' by Mario Andreassi, 'Il mimo tra "consumo" e "letteratura": *Charition* e *Moicheutria*', *Ancient Narrative* 2 (2002), 30–46.

and contains parallels, beyond that, with Euripides' *Iphigenia among the Taurians*. The Indians are characterised by unintelligible speech, which presumably adds to the coarse humour of the drama. India is presented, in this brief text, as a more vivid location than we find in the novels, and the prominence of language is unmatched. Yet, in keeping with the genre of mime, much more so than the novels, ethnic difference is exaggerated for humorous effect. The drunken revels of the Indians, which allow the protagonists to escape, again evoke the triumph of Dionysus.

II. 'HANGING TAGS': TOPICS OF THOUGHT

Any survey of ethnographic excursuses in Roman literature reveals a high degree of overlap in the topics described, and the manner of their presentation. Standard topics include the following: mythic or historical origins, populousness, somatic features, warfare, clothing, conditions of living (including eating and accommodation), social structure and political organisation, religious practice, gender relations and marriage. The recurrence of these has been observed in a variety of specific and general studies.[58] In the case of excursuses in historical works, there is every justification for speaking of the ethnographic set piece. It is easy to see that a set number of such criteria engage a writer in discussing any given people, as if in answer to a questionnaire. Broadly speaking, the questions recur even though the order differs. While the term 'questionnaire' is used here in a notional sense, there are important hints of its more concrete origins at an early stage in the formation of classical ethnography. The Hippocratic *Airs waters places* was written for a medical practitioner; in his travels he needed to find out particular information about any place he reached before being able to treat its inhabitants. This was based on the assumption that there was an intrinsic relation of local conditions on the one hand and physiology and psychology on the other.[59] It is here, when the Hippocratic author prescribes what geographic and human features the physician should seek out, that we see an ethnographic questionnaire in its most concrete form. This illustrates vividly what we find implied in later instances of the ethnographic tradition, one which is attuned to many of the same features and tends also to assume a fixed relation of locality to human character. But what were those criteria?

[58] On the continuity of historiographic tradition in this respect, e. g., Müller, *Ethnographie*, vol. I, pp. 104–6; *Cornelii Taciti* De Vita Agricolae, ed. R. M. Ogilvie and Sir Ian Richmond (Oxford: Clarendon, 1967), p. 164, on Tacitus' excursus on the Britons at *Agr.* 10–12.

[59] Thomas, *Herodotus in context*.

II.1. Indian pasts

Origins constitute one of the most persistent themes in ancient ethnography generally,[60] and a convenient point at which to begin surveying descriptions of India. The main lines can be summarised as follows: Indians led an uncouth, nomadic existence before being conquered in the military campaigns of Dionysus and Heracles, who brought with them the blessings of civilisation.[61] These two installed rulers, with whom India's royal succession began. On Dionysus' departure from India, says Arrian, he appointed as king Spatembas, 'the most Bacchically inclined of his Companions'.[62] He ruled for fifty-two years, and was succeeded by his son Budyas for twenty, and he in turn by his son Cradeuas. Heracles' solitary daughter was to become India's only sovereign queen, ruling the Pandae in the area beyond the Indus.[63]

For Arrian, Heracles is an indigenous figure even though he came to India as a conqueror and civiliser: there are several versions of Heracles, and Indians have a version that they call their own.[64] In this way Arrian grafts a Greek foundation myth onto Indian tradition. Heracles, like Dionysus, thus makes it possible for Alexander's troops to find their bearings in this strange land, according to Arrian. In reality, however, these myths were likely fabricated by Alexander's own officers.[65] By this reckoning, the same deity supposedly existed in various, geographically distinct forms. One effect of this perceived similarity of deities is to minimise the cultural distance between India and the Greek world. Significantly, though, this occurs at the very time the military narrative is predicated on a sense of distance between them, and with that the magnitude of Alexander's achievement.[66]

Pliny, moving his focus westwards from the Ganges to the Indus Valley, offers an explicit localisation of Dionysus:

Furthermore, people generally include in India the city of Nysa and mount Merus, which is sacred to father Bacchus, for this is the source of the tale that he was born

[60] Trüdinger, *Ethnographie*, esp. 130–1, laid the groundwork for much subsequent work on this topic; cf., more recently, Lund, *Germanenbild*, and Hartog, *Memories of Odysseus*.

[61] The same is implied, for example, in Tacitus' vague report of the story that Hercules had visited Germany (*Germ.* 2).

[62] των ἑταίρων ἕνα τὸν βακχωδέστατον, 8.1.

[63] Pliny *HN* 6.76.

[64] παρ' αὐτοῖσιν 'Ινδοῖσι γηγενέα λέγεσθαι, *Ind.* 8.4. It is clear from Herodotus 2.43 and Arrian, *Anab.* 2.16.4, both of them discussing native Egyptian forms of Heracles, that he was seen as a multiple rather than single figure. Arrian applies this same principle to Dionysus.

[65] See Chapter 1, section II.1 above.

[66] For a comparable case of the surprising similarity of cultures, see Philostr. *VA* 3.12, at the point when Apollonius is recognised by name and addressed in Greek by the messenger of the wise men.

from Jupiter's thigh; and likewise the Aspagani, a people abundant in vines, laurel trees and all fruit that grows in Greece. (6.79)[67]

In this way, Pliny ends his description of India as it began (6.61), by referring to the theme that runs through it: Alexander's expedition. In particular, the flora mentioned in this passage effectively connect India with the Mediterranean.

In their most obvious aspect, there is no difficulty in making sense of such stories. Arrian gives a clear hint of what is at stake, though his comment does contain a mark of caution: he suggests it is part of the Greco-Macedonian rhetoric of empire, a 'boast'.[68] This 'mythmaking' seems to have had its roots in the propaganda circulating at the time of Alexander's conquests.[69] Both Heracles and Dionysus were important to Alexander's self-presentation as a culture-hero; both were famous for their exploits at the very fringes of the *oikoumenê*. Heracles was otherwise more often linked with the far western Mediterranean, such as the island of Erytheia, the abode of Geryon;[70] at the very western end of the Mediterranean stood the Pillars of Heracles. Dionysus, on the other hand, whose own origins are usually thought to be Thracian, was specifically linked with the eastern Mediterranean and with Asia as far as India. Dionysus was one of the most frequently depicted deities, and his triumphal return from India was a favourite motif on Roman sarcophagi.[71] Dionysus' connection with India is suggested first in Euripides' *Bacchae*;[72] but only much later, by the time the story had been strongly tinged by the Alexander narrative, was this part of the Dionysus myth to receive its fullest expression, in Nonnus' lengthy *Dionysiaca*.[73]

It is one thing to identify the specific Alexandrian or late-antique context for the Heracles and Dionysus stories. But, more importantly for present purposes, what do they tell us about Greco-Roman ideas concerning India's

67 *nec non et Nysam urbem plerique Indiae adscribunt montemque Merum, Libero Patri sacrum, unde origo fabulae, Iouis femine editum; item Aspaganos gentem, uitis et lauri et buxi pomorumque omnium in Graecia nascentium fertilem.*

68 Μακεδονικὸν δοκέει μοί τι κόμπασμα (*Ind.* 5.10), where the last word quoted has a decidedly negative edge. It is usually used in the plural, with the same effect: e.g. Ar. *Ran.* 940.

69 *Alexander and the East* (Oxford: Clarendon, 1996), esp. ch. 4, 'The creation of belief.' On origins as retrojection, more generally, see Edward W. Said, *Beginnings: intention and method*, 2nd edn (New York: Basic, 1997).

70 Galinsky, *Herakles theme*. Among his labours, the girdle of the Amazon, Cerberus and the apples of the Hesperides were the others specifically to involve the edges of the earth.

71 Discussed in Chapter 3, section I.2.

72 James Diggle, *Euripidea: collected essays* (Oxford: Clarendon, 1994), pp. 444–53.

73 Bowersock, 'Dionysus', in Hopkinson, *Studies*, pp. 156–66; cf. his *Hellenism in late antiquity* (Ann Arbor: University of Michigan Press, 1990).

past? On the one hand, they do give India a certain historical depth: Pliny mentions that Indian history entails 153 kings over 6,451 years and 3 months, to count from Dionysus to Alexander (6.59). This number is of course suspiciously high and precise; but then Pliny's comment about these and other numbers suggests a note of caution on his own part. The number of India's kings is the measure of its antiquity. At one level this invites comparison with Herodotus' Egypt, of which it is possible to say the same thing.[74] On the other hand, there is a very different principle at work here: the use of Dionysus as a defining point of Indian history has the effect of predicating India's past on that of the Greek world; of implying, in effect, that Greece is more ancient than India. If we were to compare this comment with the time-depth accorded other eastern societies, it is curiously hesitant. In Pliny's India there is nothing to match, for example, the story of Psammetichos' experiment to test the relative antiquity of Phrygians and Egyptians (2.2) or the extended narrative supposedly based on the priests' king-lists, dominating the second part of the book. Within the discourse of cultural priority, Indian history is abbreviated in a way that brings credit to the Greeks. Consequently it would be no exaggeration to detect the tone of imperial conquest in the tales about Heracles and Dionysus as bringers of civilisation. The version of ethnographic time we see here is what Johannes Fabian has called the 'denial of coevalness'.[75]

Whereas literacy and urbanism are central to Greek and Roman descriptions of eastern lands, especially Egypt, those criteria are scarcely visible in Roman Indography. The best explanation for this relative absence involves a return to the Achaemenid empire, emphasised in the first chapter. There is no reason to suppose that Persian accounts of India were particularly concerned with its antiquity. This is, admittedly, an argument from silence, but it does explain Herodotus' lack of comment on the subject. While it is true that the urban settlements of Harappa and Mohenjo-Daro were only a few centuries younger than Mesopotamian civilisation, that relative chronology does not appear to be reflected in Persian sources. And if Hellenistic Greeks

[74] Egyptian kings as an index of that land's antiquity: Vasunia, *Gift of the Nile*, ch. 3; Stadter, *Arrian*, pp. 116–17, makes the comparison between India and Egypt here. And cf. Philostr. *VA* 2.19.

[75] *Time and the Other: how anthropology makes its object* (New York: Columbia University Press, 1983); cf. Vasunia, *Gift of the Nile*, pp. 110–35. One may compare here Walter D. Mignolo's comments, in a New World context, about 'literacy and the colonization of memory: writing history of people without history:' *The darker side of the Renaissance: literacy, territoriality and colonization* (Ann Arbor: University of Michigan Press, 1995), pp. 127–35. The notion that colonialism determines who does and who does not 'have history' was memorably expressed by Eric R. Wolf, in *Europe and the people without history* (Berkeley: University of California Press, 1982).

and subsequently Romans were heir to a basically Achaemenid image of India, it stands to reason that antiquity will not have been a major feature. Certainly the myths of Heracles and Dionysus appear to be later, post-Herodotean additions. There is every reason to sense, with Bosworth, that they formed part of Alexander's self-presentation.

If Greek and Roman views of India's past had a military context, then it is also true that the subject of warfare involves some degree of contradiction, within Strabo's *Geography* alone. At one point he claims that Indians are unwarlike (15.1.6 C686),[76] yet elsewhere that they are well behaved when at war (15.1.53 C709). Before Alexander's campaign, he says, Indians had neither suffered invasion nor dispatched an invading army. Arrian says that the Indians had not even been attacked, barring two unsuccessful attempts;[77] but later he speaks of the Indians' war equipment. Diodorus, while discussing India's fertility, says that agricultural workers are left undisturbed even if hostilities take place in their immediate proximity; this diverges from the normal practice whereby enemies destroy land (2.36.6–7). The contradiction implicit here suggests that both Strabo and Arrian were using a variety of sources, or that the sources they were using, such as Megasthenes, were themselves compilations of diverse information. On the face of it, this would seem like a prime case of Nissen's law.[78] Lying behind the assertion of peacefulness, however directly contradicted elsewhere, is a certain idealisation: the point is less an absence of war in itself than the ideal, so central to Aristotle's *Politics*, of αὐταρκεία (self-sufficiency).[79] Some of this subject matter will return in the discussion of utopianism below.

II.2. Profusion

The next topic to consider is India's populousness. Diodorus speaks of ἔθνη πολλά (2.38.1). The recurrence of this topic in various ancient Indographies, and something that continues to be remarked by travellers up to the present day, suggests that it was part of the earliest descriptions.[80] This is reflected in Pliny's comment on 'peoples and cities beyond number', which

76 Cf. Arr. *Ind.* 5.4.

77 *Ind.* 5.5–7: 'Sesostris the Egyptian' and Semiramis the Assyrian queen. Both of these figures featured prominently in the Greek romances: Giovanni Pettinato, *Semiramide* (Milan: Rusconi, 1985).

78 See e.g. Hornblower's comment that Diodorus 'used one main source at a time', in 'Sources and their uses', *CAH*, 2nd edn. (1994), vol. VI, pp. 1–23 at 9; and cf. Brent D. Shaw, 'The Elder Pliny's African geography', *Historia* 30 (1981), 424–71.

79 For self-sufficiency as a goal in human associations, see e.g. Arist. *Pol.* 1252b27–1253a1; cf. [Plato] *Def.* 412b6. From the viewpoint of historical ecology, Peregrine Horden and Nicholas Purcell, *The corrupting sea: a study of Mediterranean history* (Oxford: Blackwell, 2000), pp. 112–15, contrast this goal with practice; cf, Chapter 6, section II.1 below.

80 Compare Chapter 1, section II above.

he notes with some exasperation while paying lip service to the goal of systematic coverage.[81] Arrian cites Megasthenes in saying that there are 118 ἔθνεα, but he questions how Megasthenes could have known this, given that he visited only a limited part of India, and that various groups do not necessarily mix with each other (*Ind.* 7.1). This suggests that Arrian, like Pliny, was acutely aware of the link between descriptive numbers and claims of grandeur. This talk about populousness is part of the discourse of abundance and profusion that goes back to an early stage of Greco-Roman ethnographic writing, and would prove especially persistent in the case of India. This is sometimes connected with attention to India's rivers (e.g., Diodorus 2.35.2).

On the strength of such passages, one scholar has claimed that India is, in classical literature, a marvel of inner space, not outer.[82] But this cannot be upheld in view of other parts of the same descriptions: much is said in the texts under consideration by way of outlining the organisation of outer space as well. For example, Arrian devotes the second and third chapters of his *Indica* to describing the geographical shape of India, as if on a diagrammatic map.[83] He is careful to define it in terms of borders: to its west is the Indus, to its north Mount Taurus or Caucasus, to its south the Great Sea; about the east there is no clarity.[84] Arrian's approach here in outlining the shape of India is typical of those writers who were familiar with the Greek tradition of mathematical geography: pre-eminently Strabo and later Ptolemy, and even to a lesser extent Pliny. This mathematical aspect is absent, however, from Mela and the later Plinian tradition of Solinus and others. In this respect it is helpful to invoke the distinction Strabo and Ptolemy make between geography and chorography: the first is fundamentally on a global scale, whereas the second is articulated in regional and more detailed maps and tracts.[85]

II.3. Social divisions

Indian society consisted of groups, *merê* or *genea*. Diodorus and other Greek sources present a seven-fold division, consisting of philosophers, farmers,

[81] *gentes urbesque innumerae*, 6.58 (cf. 6.59).
[82] Romm, *Edges*, p. 83.
[83] Cf. even Curt. 8.9.2–3, as the brief start to a lengthy digression.
[84] Alexander did not go beyond the Hyphasis, and therefore no good information about it exists (cf. *Ind.* 4.1 and 6.1). Some writers have ventured as far as the Ganges, and seen India's largest city, Palibothra. Pliny also (6.56–69) begins his section on India by describing its outer proportions.
[85] On the distinction, see Claude Nicolet, *Space, geography, and politics in the early Roman empire* (Ann Arbor: University of Michigan Press, 1991), pp. 4, 100 and 171–2. Tellingly, this was an issue mostly for the Greek tradition, which nurtured both, whereas the Latin tradition was much more largely limited to chorography.

shepherds, artisans, soldiers, overseers and councillors. On the other hand, Pliny offers a different division of the 'more civilised' Indians (*mitiores populi*, 6.66): cultivators, soldiers, long-distance traders, statesmen, wise men and elephant-keepers.[86] The difference between the two lists, not least the fact that they are listed in a different order, suggests that Diodorus and Pliny have used divergent sources on this topic.

Indian sources, on the other hand, refer to a fourfold division of society. The famous *Purusha-sukta* ('Hymn of man'), dated to around 500 BC, recounts the creation of the world from the dismemberment of the primeval giant Purusa (*Rig Veda* 10.90.12). This is a key foundational text of ancient Indian religion, but the social reality it constructs is considerably complicated by later texts. For example, the *Arthashastra* tells of eighteen different kinds of high official (*mahamtras*), including a chancellor (*samahrtr*) and treasurer (*samnidhatr*).[87] The purpose of mentioning this is to show that further subdivisions were very likely.

How the many contradictions should be resolved is unclear, and this is not the place to make the attempt, especially since the fourfold Vedic division mentioned above does not preclude the possibility of further subdivisions.[88] But it is not stretching a point to suggest that the key to understanding Diodorus' division is Herodotus, who offers an identical analysis of Egyptian society in the book of his *Histories*.[89] The fact that Strabo cites Herodotus explicitly (15.1.16 C691), though in a different connection, makes such a comparison all the more plausible.

Greek and Roman Indography contains a number of explicit statements that there were no slaves in India. Thus Diodorus:

[86] *(1) tellurem exercent, (2) militiam alii capessunt, (3) merces alii suas euehunt, externas inuehunt, (4) res publicas optumi ditissimique temperant, iudicia reddunt, regibus adsident. (5) quintum genus, celebratae ibi et prope in religionem uersae sapientiae deditum, uoluntaria semper morte uitam accenso prius rogo finit. (6) unum super haec est semiferum ac plenum laboris inmensi . . . uenandi elephantos domandique.* 'One group works the land; a second hunts; a third exports and imports goods; a fourth, the most eminent and wealthy, takes care of public administration, judges legal cases and constitutes the king's advisors. A fifth group, dedicated to wisdom that is celebrated there and virtually regarded as religion, always finishes their lives with suicide on a pyre that is lit in advance. Beyond these, one group is half savage and fully engaged in the onerous task of hunting and taming elephants.'

It is striking to what extent suicide is a distinctive mark of the holy people, the fifth group mentioned. Murphy, *Pliny*, 120–5, tellingly compares Pliny's account of the suicide practised by the Hyperboreans – at the far end of the *orbis terrarum* compared to the Indians – with an 'early imperial ideology of suicide' (122).

[87] Kautilya, *The Arthashastra*, tr. L. N. Rangarajan (Oxford University Press, 1992), p. 208.

[88] Romila Thapar, *Cultural pasts: essays in early Indian history* (Oxford University Press, 2000), pp. 488–512. For earlier attempts to make sense of the social structure implied here see Chapter 1, section II.2 above.

[89] Hdt. 1.56, 101; 2.164

Concerning the customs of the Indians which are unique to them, one may consider that which was drawn up by their ancient sages to be the most remarkable; for it has been decreed that under no circumstances shall anyone among them be a slave, but that everyone shall be free and honour the equal status of all persons. (2.39.5)[90]

Here, what might otherwise have been presented in ethnographic rhetoric as an absence, or as a cultural deficit,[91] is listed as a positive attribute: the lack of slavery. Many scholars have taken this to be an idealising note.[92] The moralistic tone of Diodorus' comment makes clear that this is, from his point of view, something positive, in other words, that he is exercising the most positive connotations of the polyvalent adjective θαυμάσιος.

The strangeness of this passage comes into full relief when it is realised that slavery is seldom presented in such abstract terms, as an institution; it is much more common for ancient writers to talk about slaves as individuals or groups.[93] Two passages in Philo may be the key to understanding the sentiment expressed: *Every good man is free* 79 and *On the contemplative life* 70, concerning the Essenes and Therapeutae respectively.[94] In evidence, in both cases, are groups who are viewed en bloc as philosophers. The passages in Philo make it clear that the absence of slaves is the hallmark of a nation of philosophers; it seems that India too must be understood in this light, as we shall discuss in detail in Chapter 6.

Beyond philosophers, India rates highly in another sphere of special knowledge, namely the medical. Thus Indian doctors, unlike their Greek counterparts, are able to cure snake-bites, says Arrian citing Nearchus as his source (*Ind.* 15.11–12). As mentioned by Arrian, these doctors (ἰητροί) are a subset of the philosophers. Since the seasons are so temperate, there are few diseases, and hence little need for doctors. Strabo also speaks of Indian medicine, at 15.1.45 C706 and 15.1.60 C713, citing Nearchus and Megasthenes.

The spectacular suicide of Calanus, as we have already seen, is one feature that made him the Indian holy man par excellence in Greek and Roman sources. In fact, to judge from Josephus, suicide is the distinguishing mark of

90 νομίμων δ' ὄντων παρὰ τοῖς Ἰνδοῖς ἐνίων ἐξηλλαγμένων θαυμασιώτατον ἄν τις ἡγήσαιτο τὸ καταδειχθὲν ὑπὸ τῶν ἀρχαίων παρ' αὐτοῖς φιλοσόφων· νενομοθέτηται γὰρ παρ' αὐτοῖς δοῦλον μὲν μηδένα εἶναι τὸ παράπαν, ἐλευθέρους δ' ὑπάρχοντας τὴν ἰσότητα τιμᾶν ἐν πᾶσι.

91 See below in this chapter.

92 Thapar, *Cultural pasts*, p. 510, stresses that Helots in Spartan society are the particular point of comparison here, and that such statements should be understood in a generalised way.

93 Thomas Wiedemann, *Greek and Roman slavery* (London: Routledge, 1981).

94 The comparison is made by P. D. A. Garnsey, *Ideas of slavery in antiquity* (Cambridge University Press, 1998), p. 78.

a more generalised use of 'Calani'.[95] Its importance to the Indian philosophers merits detailed discussion in Chapter 6 below, where the holiness they represent emerges as a distinctively male affair. But in this survey of Indography, it is important to examine a distinctively feminine context for suicide, by which we may consider it to be very differently gendered.[96]

II.4. Gender relations

If gender was a staple of ethnographic visions beginning at least with Herodotus, then India reveals some particular phenomena.[97] The custom of *sati*, whereby the wives of a dead man voluntarily burn themselves on his funeral pyre, was first mentioned in Cicero among western sources (*Tusc.* 5.77–78). For Cicero in this passage, India *per se* is of less concern than Rome itself. Though India is a barbarous country, it does show some remarkable signs of virtue: its philosophers can endure the most trying physical conditions, and its women compete with one another in showing loyalty to their deceased husbands.[98] He invokes Spartans and Egyptians also in this passage. The larger question in the book is whether virtue is enough for the happy life; specifically in this passage, the point is that to feel pain must always be natural.[99] The important feature about Cicero's reference to *sati*, then, is that it furnishes the rhetorical material of proof, as part of a larger argument to which it is only tangentially linked. In terms of the distinction made at the start of this chapter, this is a classic case of a passing reference to India made within a different context.

By the same token, when Propertius speaks about *sati* he too projects virtues onto a distant place, away from morally decayed Rome to chaste India. The poem reveals much about why India should have interested Propertius:

There is a uniquely felicitous custom of funerals among eastern husbands, whom the red dawn tinges with her own horses. For when the last torch has been thrown

95 Joseph. *Ap.* 1.179; cf. Chapter 1, section II and Chapter 6, section III.

96 The topos is documented in W. Heckel and J. Yardley, 'Roman writers and the Indian practice of suttee', *Philol.* 125 (1981), 305–11. The practice lives on in India today.

97 E.g. Trüdinger, *Ethnographie*, pp. 13, 25; Balsdon, *Romans and aliens*, pp. 234–5.

98 Plut. *Mor.* 499C, in his essay 'Can vice cause unhappiness', also stresses that the element of competition between the widows, before proceeding to the male equivalent of the virtuous death: the suicide of the Indian philosophers (*sophoi*) while still healthy.

99 Earlier, at 2.40, India is also mentioned by way of an example to illustrate the point that people can be trained to endure pain. The baldness of Cicero's comment – *uri se patiuntur Indi* – shows that the story to which it refers, namely the suicide of Calanus, is readily understood, and needs no explanation.

onto the funeral pyre, the dutiful crowd of widows stands with flowing hair, and hold a deadly competition as to which of them will, living, follow her husband: it is a source of shame not to have had the chance to die . . . But we have a faithless race of brides, and among us no girl will be a faithful Evadne or a devout Penelope. (3.13.15–20, 23–24)[100]

On the one hand, the passage quoted offers a line of thought familiar from Cicero: faithful Indian women are contrasted with venal Roman women, and there is an implied contrast also between the marital status of the Indian wives and the learned young women (*doctae puellae*) represented by Cynthia, although she is not named in this poem.[101] On this account Indian *sati* is the hypertrophe of idealised female fidelity. However, such an analysis is complicated by any consideration of the Propertian corpus, or even of the elegy itself. It begins with a harangue about how Roman women have become corrupted by luxuries from the east, in a tone reminiscent of the elder Pliny.[102] Propertius moves from this to a general attack on the decline of religion and the rise of corrupting luxury in Rome. In several of Propertius' poems silk is emblematic of luxury, with all its attendant moral dangers.[103] The irony of poem 3.13 is that within its complex movement the east is seen both as the origin of morally corrupting luxuries and as the place of the most desirable Roman *fides*.[104]

Even if this poem is yet another case of Propertius' intellectual adventurousness, an important point remains: the ostensible focus on India cloaks a concern with morality, a concern firmly centred on Rome itself. By this

100 *felix Eois lex funeris una maritis,*
quos Aurora suis rubra colorat equis!
namque ubi mortifero iactast fax ultima lecto,
uxorum fusis stat pia turba comis,
et certamen habent leti, quae uiua sequatur
coniugium: pudor est non licuisse mori. . . .
hoc genus infidum nuptarum, hic nulla puella
nec fida Euadne nec pia Penelope.

101 The thought underlying Indian polygamy can be understood with reference to *Germ.* 17, where Tacitus describes the Germans as being 'virtually the only foreign people to be content with one wife apiece'.

102 See further Chapter 4, section II.

103 See Jasper Griffin, 'Augustan poetry and the life of luxury', [illegible] (Chapel Hill: University of North Carolina Press, 1986), pp. 1–31. That silk in elegy comes from Cos rather than the east is not an issue here, given that the east is very specifically linked with luxury goods in the first four couplets: thus Indian gold (line 5), shells from the Red Sea (6), dyes from Tyre (7), and aromatics from Arabia (8). Also, it must be admitted that the practice of *sati* alluded to in the quotation does not explicitly mention India, but in practice there can be no question about this identification.

104 An added complication within the poem is that the ideal of female virtue is identified with two heroines of *Greek* mythology, Evadne and Penelope.

reckoning Propertius' India, like Cicero's, constitutes very much the mirror of Rome.[105] Furthermore, it well illustrates the contradictions implicit in what might be called, by an umbrella term, a single ethnographic discourse. Though Cicero is writing a philosophical treatise, and Propertius an elegy, the use they both make of India is reminiscent of the rhetorical schools, where exempla would be used to add force to a point.[106] It is no accident that luxury is such a major theme in Curtius Rufus' excursus on India, given that his work too has been shown to owe much to the rhetorical tradition of declamation: luxury was one of the topics to recur in rhetorical exercises, and India provided an obvious pretext.

There is a hint of moral language in Arrian's preliminary description of Indians, narrated at the point when Alexander and his troops reached the Indus. According to Arrian, new reports came back to the effect that the Indians had no gold and were 'in no way extravagant in their way of life' (5.4.4).[107] The comment about their lacking gold seems to be revisionist in its tone, and this is not surprising in view of passages referring to gold dust.[108] Curtius makes pointed reference to the luxurious living of the Indians, especially their kings (8.9), and this may be the kind of reference Arrian had in mind. Also, Pliny, in describing Taprobane (6.79–91), complains that the island is beset with vices, despite its remoteness:

> But not even Taprobane, though consigned by nature outside the world, lacks our vices: there too gold and silver have commercial value, marble is considered similar to tortoise-shell, and pearls and gems have high prestige. Their entire mass of luxury is greater than ours. (6.89)[109]

Negative though the tone of these comments may be, Pliny nonetheless proceeds directly to a list of features which single Taprobane out for a higher moral status, for Romans surpass the Sri Lankans in their use of wealth: its people have no slaves, they do not sleep into the daytime, their houses are moderate and low in height, they have no litigation, they worship Hercules and they choose their king on the basis of merit and childlessness.

Pliny distinguishes luxury goods and their use, separating origin and consumption, with the result that, by turns, he casts aspersions on both

105 The use of this concept is borrowed from Hartog, *Mirror of Herodotus*.

106 Cf. *L'Inde*, ed. André and Filliozat, for comparable cases in the declamations of the elder Seneca and Pseudo-Quintilian. The exempla encapsulate moral ideals: H. I. Marrou, *A history of education in antiquity* (Madison: University of Wisconsin Press, 1956), p. 235.

107 ἥκιστα χλιδῶντας κατὰ τὴν δίαιταν.

108 Strabo 15.1.47 C707 and 15.1.69 C718.

109 *sed ne Taprobane quidem, quamuis extra orbem a natura relagata, nostris uitiis caret: aurum argentum et ibi in pretio, marmor testudinis simile, margaritae gemmaeque in honore; multo praestantior est totus luxuriae nostra cumulus.*

Sri Lankans and Romans. Both deserve criticism, by Pliny's way of thinking, by their association with such commodities. But in the process a contradiction arises. Such contradictions arise when ethnographic discourse turns precipitously towards its own society, to be held up as a mirror.[110]

II.5. Space and race

Indographers reveal some interest in somatic features. In some cases, Ethiopians, the original 'burnt-faces', arise by way of comparison. Proximity to the sun, greater in the south than the north, accounts for this and also for woolly hair.[111] Pliny presents this phenomenon as a variable factor within India: the faces of those living south of the Ganges are especially burnt, yet even they are not as black as the Ethiopians (6.70). The closer to the Indus they live, he says, switching from the one major river to the other, the darker their skin-colour (also 6.70). Arrian too presents a gradation between north and south (*Ind.* 6.9). The linen they wear is brighter than any other, or else the darkness of their skins makes it seem brighter (16.1). But skin-colour is not the only somatic feature mentioned by Roman writers: Strabo speaks of a predilection for dyeing beards and hair (15.1.30 C699);[112] Arrian's Indians are lean, tall and light in their movement (6.17).[113]

Do the features described here merit the label of race? The working definition of race used here is of the 'essentialising of groups of people which are held then to display inherent, persistent or predictive characteristics, and which thus had a biological or quasi-biological basis'.[114] Certainly, it is clear from the texts above that Pliny, Arrian and others identified Indians in terms of a particular somatic profile, one that emphasized darkness of skin-colour. What is less clear is the significance of these somatic features within the broader picture of Indography. Indeed, it is one thing to point to the existence of somatic difference in Roman thinking, and it is another to explore the social meanings of such difference. Taken together with

110 On the gendered vision of India in seventeenth-century Britain, see Kate Teltscher, *India inscribed: European and British writing on India, 1600–1800* (Oxford University Press, 1995), pp. 37–73.

111 Dihle, 'Der fruchtbare Osten', in *Antike und Orient* (1984); Schneider, L'Éthiopie et l'Inde, pp. 88–95.

112 Arr. *Ind.* 16.4, following Nearchus.

113 In Chapter 6, section II.2 we shall see the emphasis placed on the characteristic beards and esp. gestures of Indian holy men.

114 Peter Robb, 'South Asia and the concept of race', in *The concept of race in South Asia*, ed. Peter Robb (Oxford University Press, 1995), p. 1; cf. Mark Harrison, *Climates and constitutions* (Oxford University Press, 1999), p. 12. On the relation of race and ethnicity in studying Mediterranean antiquity, see Denise Eileen McCoskey, 'By any other name? Ethnicity and the study of ancient identity', *Classical Bulletin* 79 (2003), 93–109.

the visual representations of these features, such passages are few and far between, in their extent far outweighed by passages emphasising the social life of Indians. Indography offers nothing to match Aeschylus' linking of black skins, death and sexual desire in the *Suppliants*.[115] A further problem concerns the 'biological basis' of these somatic references. Generally speaking, the idea of environmental determinism, articulated in the Hippocratic *Airs waters places*, was well known in the world of Pliny and Arrian, and this could, in principle, provide a framework for comprehending distant India. It is not clear, however, whether or to what extent this framework was actually applied to India (on which, more below). In sum, then, race is indeed an issue in passages such as those mentioned. Yet, equally, it is clear that Roman Indography dwelled far more on cultural rather than somatic features of identity, and this would suggest the predominance of an ethnic over a racial vision of India.[116]

II.6. Catalogue or system?

The features sketched above, taken together, bear testimony to the organisational power of the ethnographic questionnaire, as described by Trüdinger and Müller – one form of the intellectual activity that Mark Twain called 'hanging tags'. Yet, in two important respects they fail to do justice to descriptions of India: plants and especially animals serve to mark India as a region; by virtue of its rivers, too, India is distinctive.[117] The link of place and people in ancient ethnographic thought cautions us to bear these topographic criteria in mind alongside the purely ethnographic.

Arrian's only mention of snakes is at *Indica* 15.11, in the context of Indian medicine: unlike the Greek doctors, the Indians had a cure for snakebite, so much so that ὅσοι ἰητρικὴν σοφώτατοι were assembled by Alexander for consultation in case of such an emergency. These doctors are thus presented as a case of specialised local knowledge. Elsewhere too snakes receive some degree of attention.[118] At 15.2.7 C723, Strabo speaks of them

[115] Vasunia, *Gift of the Nile*, pp. 47–53.

[116] An underlying problem in identifying racial difference in antiquity may be articulated as another question: what is at stake in identifying somatic difference here? Such a question might help transcend the polarised terms of debate around race in antiquity, e.g., Frank M. Snowden, Jr, 'Bernal's "Blacks" and the Afrocentrists', in *Black Athena revisited*, ed. Mary R. Lefkowitz and Guy MacLean Rogers (Chapel Hill: University of North Carolina Press, 1996), pp. 112–28; and Martin Bernal, *Black Athena writes back* (Durham, NC: Duke University Press, 2002), pp. 66–9.

[117] In fairness, though, it should be remembered that Trüdinger's work focuses on ethnography, at the expense (for example here) of geographical questions. In this chapter I interpret ethnography a little more broadly, so as to capture the link between people and place that is very much part of Indography.

[118] Strabo 15.1.28, 45 (Onescritus and Aristobulos).

as one of the soldiers' greatest fears.[119] Such passages suggest that fear itself played some part in Alexander's campaign. Uniquely, Philostratus' India is beset by dragons, which may be a novelistic expansion of the same idea.[120]

Whereas animals and plants underline the similarities between India and Africa generally, rivers suggest comparison with Egypt in particular. Certainly, rivers feature large in descriptions of India. They have already been considered in the context of Alexander history as borders of knowledge.[121] Diodorus mentions first the Ganges: this is the largest in size and in number of elephants, so much so that Alexander's troops took fright and mutinied once they had reached that point. It is worth noting, in passing, the misconception that Alexander did in fact arrive at the Ganges with his entire army, following his conquest of the other Indian peoples:

> For when he had reached the river Ganges with his entire army, having subdued the rest of the Indians . . . (2.37.3)[122]

In fact, Alexander's expedition did not reach the Ganges but turned back at the River Hyphasis or Hypanis. At all events, Diodorus continues by describing the Indus and its main tributaries, the Hypanis, the Hydaspes and the Acesinus, then the multitude of other rivers (2.37.5).

Taken as a whole, the ethnographic profile of India to emerge here presents a potential problem of interpretation: is there any contradiction in the coexistence in the same texts of well-organised social groupings on the one hand and marvellous creatures on the other? In other words, how are we to reconcile the India of Breloer and Timmer with that of Wittkower and Romm? If we are to judge from the one complete Indography that exists, namely Arrian's *Indica*, it appears that there was no such contradiction in the minds of Greco-Roman authors. Arrian is concerned with the accuracy of his information, it is true, yet this does not preclude his own inclusion of marvels.[123] This reflects a variegated picture of India, one in which phenomena are wilder the farther out you move. Such an analysis is of some help, in a general way: for all its limitations in modern studies, the model of centre and periphery does reflect something of ancient spatial thinking. The idea is implicit in the overall geography sketched by Arrian

[119] Cf. Diod. 17.90 = Clitarchus F18. [120] Philostr. *VA* 3.6–8.

[121] Strabo 15.1.27 C697–698; Arr. *Ind.* 4.1 and 6.1 on the Hyphasis. Cf. Dihle, 'Conception', on the significance of rivers in Indography.

[122] καταντήσας γὰρ ἐπὶ τὸν Γάγγην ποταμὸν μετὰ πάσης τῆς δυνάμεως, καὶ τοὺς ἄλλους Ἰνδοὺς καταπολεμήσας.

[123] At the very point at which Arrian says he will not be tempted into talking about India *beyond* the Hyphasis, he mentions the story of the river Silas, in which nothing can float (6.1 3, following Megasthenes).

at the beginning of his *Indica*, and corresponds to other ethnographic texts. The same feature can be found in both the *Periplus of the Erythraean Sea* and in Tacitus' *Germania*; the differences between these two texts suggests how deep the feature lies in ethnographic thought.

To end this section, it is as well to return to the ancient theory mentioned at its start. The Hippocratic notion of environmental determinism, seen most obviously in *Airs waters places*, is common currency in ancient ethnographic texts. Those describing India are no exception. Yet there is an important caveat to bear in mind here: though the overall system thus described makes provision for India, the region itself is not explicitly mentioned in the work. The farthest east the Hippocratic text goes is Lake Maeotis (17); India is thus, strictly speaking, off the map. Thus Arrian says that the 'Indians suffer few diseases, because the seasons are temperate' (*Ind.* 15.12).[124]

This theory is less important in itself than in relation to the concept of nature as it emerges in several of our texts. We should not forget that Stoicism, even if merely a loose version, left its mark on Aelian and Pliny. Arrian too came from a Stoic milieu, even if its philosophical system did not affect him particularly strongly. With Pliny, however, we are on a firmer footing. At a key point in his seventh book he says that 'nature produced all such things, games to itself but marvels to us' (7.32).[125] Casual though such a remark may seem, its placing is important: within his anthropological book there is a passage on strange human phenomena, in which India makes a second major appearance in his work. Whereas books 3 to 6 offered a chorographical conspectus of the world, including India, this seventh book effectively offers a précis of the description of India. It is tempting to assert that this different context emphasises what India really means to Pliny, and indeed to several Roman writers: a place of marvels, both human and animal, which redound to the glory of nature.

Implicit in this catalogue is a working definition of ethnicity as defined from outside: the questions informing the 'questionnaire' are the effective criteria of ethnic identity. But, it must be remembered, this is the ethnic identity of a distant people, and it is one that is etically attributed rather than emically claimed. Such names do not necessarily reflect the practices of the people described.[126] Given the radical otherness of Indians, it is unclear what purpose is served by invoking the terms of ethnicity at all. If

124 οὐ πολλὰ δὲ ἐν Ἰνδοῖσι πάθεα γίνεται, ὅτι αἱ ὧραι σύμμετροί εἰσιν αὐτόθι.

125 *haec atque talia ex hominum genere ludibria sibi, nobis miracula, ingeniosa fecit natura.*

126 Countless examples could be given of the tendency whereby a group of people is known by a name conferred on them by their immediate neighbours. Sometimes this name is 'loaded', e.g., Tzvetan

we are to understand ethnicity as an ongoing, complex negotiation between ascribed and asserted identities,[127] then Roman sources leave us well short of the goals of analysis. It is a telescopic vision. Vedic and other ancient Sanskrit literature gives us considerable insight to Indian society of the first five centuries of the common era; but attempts to integrate Indian and Greco-Roman accounts have met difficulties, if not outright resistance.[128] There is little we can know about what Indians thought about themselves in relation to foreigners, or *mlecchas*, such as Romans and Greeks, and as a result, a full-scale examination of ethnicity would be seriously hampered from the outset. Certainly, the recent flood of scholarly attention to ancient ethnic identities offers many insights to the present project: foremost among these is the insistence that ethnicity should be perceived in an aggregative manner, involving a set range of criteria, variously combined.[129] But this only helps us so far and no further, since the current project does not focus on groups of people within the Mediterranean, but one far removed from it. Consequently, the approach adopted here has been to restrict the investigation largely to the Roman discourse about India.

III. LITERARY FEATURES: MODES OF DESCRIPTION

At this point it is necessary to step back from the details of the texts described and focus on the manner in which those descriptions are made. This involves consideration of some of the literary tropes that occur in Indographic texts. Important among them, and linked to the recurrent figure of profusion that is so central to this chapter, inclusion and omission are a major issue for the writers under discussion. Thus an author occasionally apologises for providing detailed description, or even for omission of the same. Pliny's programmatic comment about 'following in the footsteps of Alexander' is significant (6.61), as a reaction to difficulties brought by the scale of his project of describing the entire universe.[130] Clearly, the statement cannot be taken literally, in view of the twists and turns of Alexander's

Todorov, *The conquest of America: the question of the other*, tr. Richard Howard (New York: Harper and Row, 1997), pp. 25–8.

127 Richard Jenkins, 'Rethinking ethnicity: identity, categorization and power', *Ethnic and Racial Studies* 17 (1994), 199–223, esp. 217–18; cf. Fredrik Barth's editorial introduction to *Ethnic groups and boundaries* (Baltimore: Johns Hopkins University Press, 1982).

128 Romila Thapar, 'Historical consciousness in early India', in *Cultural pasts* (2000 [1995]), pp. 155–72, on the tendency of colonial scholars, including William Jones, to present India as 'ahistorical'.

129 Jonathan M. Hall, *Ethnic identity in Greek antiquity* (Cambridge University Press, 1997), and *Hellenicity: between ethnicity and culture* (University of Chicago Press, 2002), emphasises perceived linguistic differences within the Greek world.

130 Cf. Chapter 1, section II.4.

itinerary; rather it suggests that the figure of Alexander provided a structuring principle. Marking-off devices, such as the adverb to indicate 'thus far' (*hactenus*),[131] illustrate the way in which an ethnographic excursus can be bracketed off. Much of what follows may be regarded as the use of a special metalanguage by which ancient authors organised writing about foreign peoples.

III.1. The Periplus *form*

As a literary technique the *periplus* made it possible to describe large expanses of coastline, and goes back to Hecataeus and other early Ionian writers of prose.[132] By the first century BC it had become a well-established literary genre, as Pliny's list of sources in book 1 shows. Among its many advantages was its ability to bring the reader along as it proceeded in serial fashion down a coastline. As such, it reflected the fact that sea-travel was throughout antiquity the quickest and cheapest means of long-distance travel and transportation. It was most commonly pursued in the form of hugging a coastline, even though open-sea travel now appears more common than was earlier supposed.[133] But the link between genre and travel was to prove restrictive in the case of any land far from the Mediterranean: it was not intended in the first instance to describe inland areas or open sea. It was, however, well suited to any substantial body of water that provided, in the form of its coastline, a major organising principle.[134]

As a literary form re-enacting the journey described, the *periplus* lies behind the broader structure of chorography, going back to Greek history's Ionian origins and particularly to Hecataeus' *periegesis*; even then, this feature is visible in the *Odyssey* and other early Greek epic.[135] There is something inevitable about this when the observer himself has done the travelling, or

[131] Notably also at 6.220, concluding the five geographical books; cf. also, from that part of the *Natural history*, 2.102; 3.1; 3.94; 4.68; 5.73; 6.84; 6.219.

[132] On Hecataeus and the *periplus* form, cf. Chapter 1, section I.2 above. Also, Lesky, *Greek literature*, pp. 219–20, on the experiences of sea-travel underlying the literary form of the periplus.

[133] A. J. Parker, *Ancient shipwrecks of the Mediterranean and the Roman provinces* (Oxford: Tempus reparatum, 1992); and Lionel Casson, *Ships and seafaring in the ancient times* (Austin: University of Texas Press, 1994).

[134] The *Periplus* of Hanno, Arrian's early *Periplus of the Black Sea* and the *Periplus of the Erythraean Sea* (which involves a certain amount of open sea, but in the special circumstances of the monsoon) show that the Mediterranean had no absolute monopoly on the genre.

[135] Jacoby has divided fragments of Hecataeus' work by area: *FGrH* 1 frr. 37–359. The comparison with Homer is of course only a limited one: the prose tradition differs crucially in its loss of the heroic or romance elements. For Karl Meuli, the *Odyssey* reflects an earlier epic tradition about Jason and the Argonauts: *Odyssee und Argonautika. Untersuchungen zur griechischen Sagengeschichte und zum Epos* (Berlin: Weidmann, 1921).

claims to have done so.[136] The *periplus* of Hanno begins in the third person, but within the space of a few sentences adopts the first person (plural), travelogue-style.[137] But by the time we get to Pliny the *periplus* is deeply ingrained as a paradigm for chorography, so much so that the writer's own journey is no longer relevant. Earlier in Pliny's lifetime (*c.* AD 43), Pomponius Mela's *Chorographia* had revealed the same principle in a different way. He uses third-person narration throughout the work, thereby implying a travelling focaliser without explicitly creating the character of a traveller. Mela brings his work to an end where the Atlantic meets the Mediterranean, sealing it with a strong closural gesture that is also a kind of homecoming (*nostos*):

Farther along are the colony of Zilia, the river Zilia, and Ampelusia, namely the point from which we began [i.e. 1.26], which turns here into our Strait [of Gibraltar]: this is the terminus both of the present work and of the Atlantic coast. (3.107)[138]

Coming even later in the tradition, Pausanias is an extreme case in so far as the journey itself may be detected in the text, even though the author himself does not make the claim.[139] Of course, the fact that he confines himself to mainland Greece, with its extensive coastline, makes such a journey all the more practicable: and it has been suggested that all his chorographic material could have been observed in person, with only the historical sections deriving from written sources. Indeed a striking feature of Pausanias is the way in which physical places and objects, such as statues, serve for him as a pretext to launch into historical material, which may include biography or the history of religious practice. This procedure in geographic writing may be contrasted with Valerius Maximus' *Facta et dicta*

[136] E.g., Hecataeus, and Herodotus in Egypt, esp. 2.99.1. The veracity of Herodotus' claims is strictly irrelevant to the present discussion, *pace* Fehling, *Herodotus*, pp. 240–3, esp. 241).

[137] 'The Carthaginians decided that Hanno should set sail . . .' (Ἔδοξε Καρχηδονίοις . . .). Principally on grounds of language, Blomqvist has dated the work to the classical period rather than the Hellenistic. He shows how it fits in with early periegetical literature, probably pre-400, linked with the heyday of Greek colonisation in the Mediterranean and Black Sea; the genre was linked at first with the practical tales of sailors and merchants, but later developed a literary character (esp. 55–6). Contrast Romm, *Edges*, pp. 19–20, who assumes a Hellenistic date for the Greek translation.

[138] *ultra est colonia et fluvius Gna et unde initium fecimus Ampelusia in nostrum iam fretum vergens promunturium, operis huius atque Atlantici litoris terminus.*

[139] Jaś Elsner, 'Pausanias: a Greek pilgrim in the Roman world', *Past and Present* 135 (1992), 3–29 has shown how Pausanias constructs his own identity through his travels; yet it is still worth emphasising that Pausanias appears more implicitly than explicitly in the work, and there is remarkably little first-person narration compared with a modern travelogue. See *Pausanias: travel and memory in Roman Greece*, ed. Susan E. Alcock, John F. Cherry and Jaś Elsner (Cambridge University Press, 2001), esp. part 1.

memorabilia: here is also a catalogue of cultural phenomena, but one that is thematically rather than spatially organised.[140]

The *periplus* is thus one response, and a limited one at that, to a residual problem of ethnographic writing: that of establishing order amid a variety of material. Where to start, how to proceed, where to end? What to include and what to leave out? These questions are not easily solved for writers seeking to integrate new material into well-established genres. The *periplus* was of limited use in describing India: the *Periplus of the Erythraean Sea* does indeed make use of the form, but it is limited to the coastline, and does little to go beyond the immediate and limited concerns of commercial travellers. Let us consider some of the other tropes to arise in Indography.

III.2. Omission and abbreviation

Omission and its twin, inclusion, are recurrent themes in the metalanguage of Indography. Pliny at various points of the *Natural history* consistently speaks of omission as something to avoid.[141] At the beginning of book 7 he says there are too many human *mores* to cover in detail, and much has already been said in the preceding books; but some are 'not to be overlooked' (*haud omittenda*), particularly those further from the sea, and he knows some will find these far-fetched (7.6). When Pliny concludes his section on Sri Lanka by saying 'These things have been established concerning Sri Lanka' (*haec conperta de Taprobane*, 6.91), we may well wonder whether the adjective for 'all' (*omnia*) should be understood as part of the sentence. At all events, this is a way by which Pliny marks the end of a description, so the author can move to a different topic, in this case northeastern Iran. After a lengthy digression on the sea-route between Egypt and India, Pliny reins himself in with the comment, 'we will return now to our theme' (6.106).[142] But essentially the nature of the encyclopaedia is such that digressions are possible within the broader rubric of the subject under discussion. Pliny's paratactic style lends itself to inclusivity, at the expense of the critical use of sources.

The following comment on the seven parallels as a system for dividing up the world offers a comparandum, coming as it does after a different, tri-continental system:

140 Nikolaus Thurn, 'Der Aufbau der Exemplasammlung des Valerius Maximus', *Hermes* 129 (2001), 79–94.

141 Of Pliny's thirty-one instances of *omittendum*, the gerundive of obligation, the negative *non* or *haut* is used on each occasion: e.g., 4.93; 10.128; 11.239.

142 *nunc revertemur ad propositum*.

To these, furthermore, we shall add another theory of Greek discovery exhibiting the most recherché acuteness, so that nothing may be lacking in our survey of the geography of the world. (6.211)[143]

Pliny's much-vaunted desire for comprehensiveness is one reason he proceeds with this passage; another is that he finds it intellectually impressive, as he says emphatically, and he invites his reader to be equally impressed.

The following may be noted as a rare instance of Pliny's admission to having omitted something, on grounds of similarity to what is already discussed:

There are many similar facts besides, which I take care to omit in my account of the several kinds of birds, to avoid [the reader's] aversion: for example, Theophrastus states that doves, peacocks and ravens are not indigenous to Asia, nor are croaking frogs to Cyrenaica. (10.79)[144]

Yet even here, where he claims to omit comparable stories concerning unusual bird behaviour, he cannot resist mentioning a brief tale from Theophrastus, so much so that the statement functions as something of a *praeteritio*.[145]

A notable Plinian *praeteritio*, on the other hand, is the famous praise of Italy, *laus Italiae* (3.38–42).[146] He apologises for the brevity with which he describes the peninsula, and particularly the city of Rome, the 'world capital', *Roma terrarum caput* (3.38). Italy he must pass over quickly for the sake of his work as a whole, and it is for this reason that he begs his readers' forgiveness.[147] But in fact the *praeteritio* proceeds at a leisurely pace, and in its course Pliny gives much attention to the beauty of Italy. It is the nurturing parent of all lands, it gathers, tames and civilises disparate peoples:

I am mindful that I may justly be thought ungrateful and apathetic if I describe so casually and cursorily a land which is both the fosterling and the mother of all lands, chosen by the providence of the gods to make heaven itself more glorious, to unite scattered empires, to moderate manners, to assemble in converse through common

[143] *his addemus etiamnum unam Graeciae inventionis sententiam (scientiam* pars codd.*) vel exquisitissimae subtilitatis ut nihil desit in spectando terrarum situ.*

[144] *multa praeterea similia, quae prudens subinde omitto in singulis generibus [avium], fastidio parcens, quippe cum Theophrastus tradat invecticias esse in Asia etiam columbas et pavones et corvos et in Cyrenaica vocales ranas.*

[145] Cf. 28.151, where he does not bother to list a remedy involving a particular animal since it has become extinct; at 28.180 he passes over a certain kind of lichen because it is pernicious and not medically useful.

[146] On this passage compare Jacques André, 'La conception de l'État et de l'Empire dans la pénsée gréco-romaine des deux premiers siècles de notre ère', *ANRW* II.30.1 (1981), 3–73, at 57.

[147] *legentes tantum quaeso meminerint ad singula toto urbe edissertanda festinari* (3.42).

language the jarring and rude tongues of so many peoples, to give humankind civilisation, and in short to become the single fatherland of all peoples throughout the world. But what am I to do? The great distinction of all its places – and who could touch on them all? – and the great renown of the various phenomena and peoples detain me. (3.40)[148]

The two parts of the *laus Italiae* are Italy's importance, resulting in part from its central location in the Mediterranean, and its beauty. A list of its ideal features is given in breathless asyndeton. Saying this after the rhetorical question, 'But what am I to do?' (*sed quid faciam?*), Pliny here feigns helplessness: though unable to go into the level of detail deserved, he is compelled to mention the kinds of thing he could have described:

Such life-giving and enduring healthiness, such mildness of climate, such fertile fields, such sunny hills, such safe pastures, such shady groves, such bountiful kinds of forests, so many mountain breezes, such abundance of fruit, vines and olives. (3.41)[149]

And so Pliny proceeds for the same length again. We may note the importance of a mild climate, again a sense of Aristotelian 'middleness' in this context.[150] The renown (*nobilitas*) of Italy lies here in the qualities that make it a *locus amoenus*, rather than in its marvels;[151] later on, in book 36, the marvels of Rome are mentioned in the context of architecture rather

[148] *nec ignoro ingrati ac segnis animi existimari posse merito si obiter atque in transcursu ad hunc modum dicatur terra omnium terrarum alumna eadem et parens, numine deum electa quae caelum ipsum clarius faceret, sparsa congregaret imperia ritusque molliret et tot populorum discordes ferasque linguas sermonis commercio contraheret ad colloquia et humanitatem homini daret, breviterque una cunctarum gentium in toto orbe patria fieret. (3.39) sed quid agam? tanta nobilitas omnium locorum, – quos quis attigerit? – tanta rerum singularum populorumque claritas tenet.*

[149] *iam vero tanta e vitalis ac perennis salubritas, talis caeli temperies, tam fertiles campi, tam aprici colles, tam innoxii saltus, tam opaca nemora, tam munifica silvarum genera, tot montium adflatus, tanta frugum vitiumque et olearum fertilitas.*

[150] E.g., in the seventh book of the *Politics* (1327b18–38) Aristotle reflects the widely current idea that natural character (φύσις) is determined by climate and locale. People inhabiting Europe and other cold areas are plucky but lacking in intelligence and skill; as a result, though themselves living relatively free, they are unable to rule and organise their neighbours. On the other hand (δέ) Asians are intelligent and skilful in temperament but lack spirit, so much so that they are always prone to subjection and slavery. Occupying a middle position geographically (μεσεύει), the *genos* of Hellenes is both spirited and intelligent. As a result it is free and possessed of good political institutions, and in fact capable of ruling all humanity if it attained political unity. It is clear, however, that Aristotle takes the old connection between locale and character a step further, by exploring the political implications of middleness, esp. ability to rule others. Geographical location and climate are thus a rationale for the 'natural' Asian servility, ungrudgingly accepted, that Aristotle mentions elsewhere (notably 1285a in the discussion of different types of kingship).

[151] A counter-example is provided by Lucan's description of 'godforsaken' Libya, 9.435: *temperies uitalis abest, et nulla sub illa/ cura Iovis terra est.* On the virtues of *temperies* see further Richard F. Thomas, *Lands and peoples in Roman poetry: the ethnographic tradition* (Cambridge: Cambridge Philological Society, 1982), pp. 11–12.

than natural history narrowly defined. Like the *praeteritiones* in Cicero's speeches, matters supposedly omitted are in fact emphatically brought to the reader's or listener's attention.[152] In this way, Italy and Rome receive textual prominence, but in a different key compared with the marvels of the edges of the earth. And it is for this reason that Pliny can, in fact must, pass over the chance to give an Italian ethnography:[153] by virtue of its marvel element, his ethnographic style is suited more for people of the edges of the earth than for those of Italy. Yet even here we may detect the submerged question of perspective in ethnography, Italy as perceived by the Greeks. A small fraction of Italy was significant enough to merit the name Magna Graecia from the Greeks, smug though they were: 'the Greeks themselves, a people hugely given to self-regard, have passed judgment on the land by giving the name Great Greece to merely a small portion of it' (3.42).[154] This disarmingly candid reflection on Greek culture is in effect a reminder of Pliny's Hellenistic background, and of the degree to which he is conscious of it.

Related to omission is abbreviation. Mela's brief passage on India (3.61–71) shows what happens when such a description is abbreviated: within individual items described, the marvel remains as the guiding principle, but the critique of sources and its debate over truth and fiction are lost in the process of compression. This is largely the fate of late-antique excerpts such as we find in Solinus and Isidore: the marvellous elements continue, while the debates around them have long since fallen by the wayside. The reasons for this process are varied, whether the familiarity of the material, the practical needs for concision, or the dynamics of transmission.

III.3. Authors and authority

A certain kind of authorial presence shines through the accounts of India. It is not autopsy in the direct sense that has been studied with regard to Herodotus and Thucydides in Greek historiography.[155] Of the writers described earlier in this chapter, only the anonymous author of the *Periplus*

[152] Heinrich Lausberg, *Handbuch der literarischen Rhetorik*, 2nd edn (Munich: Beck, 1973), pp. 436–7.

[153] *neque ingenia ritusque ac viros et lingua manuque superatas commemoro gentes* (3.42).

[154] *ipsi de ea iudicauere Grai, genus in gloriam suam effusissimum, quotam partem ex ea appellando Graeciam Magnam* (3.42). This adoption of a Greek perspective on Rome is in keeping with the Hellenistic framework of imperial geographies: Clarke, *Between geography and history*. It is interesting also to observe, on these lines, that the earliest Latin use of the word *barbarus* is of the Romans themselves: Plautus, e.g. *Curc.* 150, *Mil.* 211, *Mostell.* 828. See further *TLL* II.1735.53–68 and 1740.40–58. This designation is articulated in Paulus Festus p. 36 Müller.

[155] Clarke, 'Author of Strabo'; cf. Schepens, *'Autopsie'*.

of the Erythraean Sea and Cosmas claim to have visited India, and then those claims are muted.[156] It is significant that both of these two exceptions are traders.[157] Far more common, for the texts discussed here, is a sense of authority implicit in literary sources cited, notably Onesicritus, Megasthenes and Nearchus. As Chapter 1 showed, this may be considered a kind of deflected autopsy, namely the phenomenon whereby texts based on earlier autopsy carry special authority. Ctesias is a notable absence from this list: indeed, the fact that he never visited India is one of the main grounds for his consistently negative reputation.[158] In this way, autopsy is a key criterion for the ranking of sources. A few instances will suffice to prove the point.

Strabo tells us that Megasthenes saw tigers (15.1.37 C703). But other travellers were less fortunate. According to Arrian, Nearchus by his own account saw tiger skins only rather than the live animal (15.1), a remark that is matched by his having seen the skins only of the gold-digging ants brought into the Macedonian camp.[159] The point here is not the veracity or otherwise of the original sources; rather, the extent to which autopsy is an issue for later authors. What the texts preserve is thus not autopsy itself but the next best thing available: the sense that their sources have seen phenomena first-hand. Such statements may be taken as a nod toward the power of autopsy as a source of authority, the creation of a kind of autopsy at one remove. It could well be that autopsy was so familiar by the time of Strabo and Arrian that variations of the theme could be entertained to similar effect. In Arrian, the phenomenon is doubly deferred: first, neither a tiger not a gold-digging ant was seen: the skins of dead animals function as witnesses. Secondly and more importantly, Indian objects were seen not by the authors but their sources, by Nearchus rather than Arrian himself. The ideal of autopsy may be hard to realise in the case of India, but it remains within the purview of writers seeking to validate their accounts with reference to authorities. In so far as autopsy was an issue for ancient writers, its authority went unchallenged.

The theme of autopsy takes an unusual turn in Cosmas' *Christian topography*. Given the stigma attached to the mercantile travel in antiquity, it comes as something of a surprise that Cosmas confidently identifies himself

156 Pliny makes remarkably little of his own visits to those parts of the Mediterranean world that he did in fact visit while on military duty.

157 On the *Periplus* author and on Cosmas, see section I above, Cosmas being a former trader.

158 Cf. Chapter 1, section 1.4.

159 For a comparandum for this phenomenon in a work that is not easily dated, Hanno the Carthaginian supposedly brought back from his African voyage skins of the 'gorilla': in both cases the hides are tokens of proof.

as a trader, especially when he has given up commercial travel in order to become a monk. This he does explicitly at 2.54 and 2.56, and implicitly at several points when he speaks of his own travels.[160] What is more, in describing the natural historical details of book 11, he evaluates most phenomena in light of his own experience. Thus he has seen a giraffe and a rhinoceros, both dead and alive. Of the hog-deer, he says bluntly that he has not only seen but eaten it.[161] Here, in an adaptation of the usual theme, human interaction with an unfamiliar phenomenon takes place through eating rather than merely sight.[162] Cosmas admits, on the other hand, that he has seen neither a unicorn nor a hippopotamus, though he has seen and sold some of its large teeth.[163] Whereas autopsy is part of Cosmas' description of India, a much greater source of authority looms over the *Christian topography*, namely that of the Jewish and Christian Bibles.[164] While he does mention Christian missions to the Indian subcontinent, he freely admits that they have not been entirely successful.

Not until much later, with the preface to al Biruni's *Indica* from the first decades of the eleventh century, do we find an explicit attack on autopsy in favour of oral sources and especially of written tradition.[165] From a certain point of view, al Biruni's attack on autopsy, so prominently made in that work, reveals the tenacity of the tradition against which he argues. But already among Indographers of the Augustan age the dictates of autopsy are broadly interpreted, and necessarily so in the case of distant India.

III.4. Utopianism and barbarism

Commodities coming from India inspired considerable moral comment in Rome, as Chapter 4 will show. To what extent do Roman writers view India generally through a moralising lens? There is a certain amount of moral

[160] He identifies himself as a business traveller when referring to his companion as ἄλλον ἕνα πραγματευτήν (2.56). Note also the use of the first person in the description of Adulis: ἔνθα καὶ τὴν ἐμπορίαν ποιούμεθα οἱ ἀπὸ Ἀλεξανδρείας καὶ ἀπὸ Ἐλᾶ ἐμπορευόμενοι (2.54). Not only do we hear of Cosmas the trader but also of other traders, Roman and Iranian; however, no Indian traders are explicitly mentioned. See Chapter 4, section III.

[161] τὸν δὲ χοιρέλαφον καὶ εἶδον καὶ ἔφαγον.

[162] On the importance of autopsy in classical Greek historiography, not least in Herodotus, see esp. Schepens, *'Autopsie'*.

[163] By the same token there is a vivid sense of place, namely Alexandria, as Cosmas' base. This is clearest in the first prologue to the work; when he says that he has sold hippopotamus' teeth 'here' (ἐνταῦθα), we may well understand him to mean Alexandria.

[164] On Cosmas' bibliocentrism see esp. Wolska, *Topographie chrétienne*.

[165] *Alberuni's India*, ed. Edward C. Sachau (Delhi: D. K. Publications, 1910), pp. 3–4.

comment, but nothing to match, say, the overtly anti-Egyptian sentiment evidenced in Juvenal's satire on Egyptian cannibalism (*Satire* 15).[166] The mime, P. Oxy. 413, is arguably unmatched in its negative view of Indians, if we may draw that conclusion from their language and behaviour. It is no accident that this is also the only Indographic text that is palpably of a lower social class than the rest. When, by contrast, Cicero underlines the barbarity of India – 'What savage land is more uncouth or unrefined than India?' – he does so in order to praise the courageousness of Indian sages and widows.[167] It seems here that the rhetoric of barbarism and civilisation is employed not in its own right but as a rhetorical strategy, a means of using India as a mirror whereby to contemplate Roman failings.

Equally, there are a number of references to Indian *paideia*, which, seen in context, both prove and disprove the barbarity of India.[168] Dio Chrysostom's 53rd discourse, on the subject of Homer, makes the intriguing statement that Indians have translated Homer's poetry into their native language and perform it in that fashion:

> It is said that Homer's poetry is sung even in India, where people have translated it into their own speech and tongue. (53.6)[169]

Even though the people of India do not know the stars of our part of the world, say Dio, they are acquainted with the sufferings of Priam, Hecuba and Andromache, and the bravery of Achilles and Hector (53.7). In recounting praise for Homer on the part of the philosophers, Dio is in effect praising Homer himself in this discourse, not least his quality as a teacher. His poems delight and instruct not merely Greek speakers, but are known (in translation) even to those living far afield, who know nothing else of Greek society. At issue for Dio is not India *per se*, but the greatest cultural capital of the Greek world, the Homeric poems; India, by virtue of the considerable distance it evokes, signifies the power of Homer, and ultimately of Greek *paideia* itself.[170]

Aelian (*Var. hist.* 12.48), who makes an interesting comparison with 'Persians', succinctly makes the same point:

166 E. Courtney, *A Commentary on the* Satires *of Juvenal* (London: Athlone, 1980), pp. 590–1.

167 *quae barbaria India uastior aut agrestior?* (*Tusc.* 5.77–78).

168 Another indirect reference to India's *paideia* is found at Curt. 8.9.15, where a certain tree-bark is seen as useful for writing.

169 ὁπότε καὶ παρ' Ἰνδοῖς φασιν ᾄδεσθαι τὴν Ὁμήρου ποίησιν, μεταβαλόντων αὐτὴν εἰς τὴν σφετέραν διάλεκτόν τε καὶ φωνήν.

170 Froma I. Zeitlin, 'Visions and revisions of Homer', in *Being Greek under Rome: cultural identity, the Second Sophistic and the development of empire*, ed. Simon Goldhill (Cambridge University Press, 2001), pp. 195–266, esp. 203.

The Indians rewrite the poems of Homer into their own language and recite them. They are not alone, for the Persian kings do so as well, if we are to believe those writing on these topics.[171]

It is difficult to know what to make out of this story: certainly, this asserts the diffusion of what is perhaps the most revered of Hellenic cultural capitals, namely Homer, and with it the breadth of the Greek cultural sphere. In this respect, Philostratus' *Life of Apollonius of Tyana* bears comparison. But beyond that, analysis becomes harder, and we are left wondering whether this reflects some consciousness, however distorted, of the Sanskrit epic tradition represented by the *Mahabharata* and the *Ramayana*, so central to Indian historical consciousness.[172] Such a suggestion would carry greater weight if it were substantiated elsewhere. At all events, what emerges in these two passages is the sense that India's spatial distance implies a priori a cultural distance, and it reflects the magnitude of Homer's achievement that his poems bridge that distance.

But moral comment has another side too: again we come to the problem of utopianism.[173] On the face of it, there is no denying the idealising force of a passage such the following, in which Strabo draws on Megasthenes:

All Indians eat simply, particularly while on campaign. They take no pleasure in large mobs, and thus keep good order. They abstain for the most part from theft. Megasthenes claims, at any rate, that while he was in the camp of Chandragupta, though in an encampment of forty thousand he did not on any day see reports of thefts worth more than two hundred drachmae – this among people who use only unwritten laws. For, he says, they do not know writing, but manage all their affairs from memory: they thrive on account of their simplicity and thrift. They drink no wine except at sacrifices, and then their drink is made from rice rather than barley. Their meals consist mainly of rice porridge. Their simplicity is attested also in their laws and contracts, given that they are not litigious. They have no lawsuits concerning mortgages or deposits, and have no need for witnesses or seals, but trust their associates. Also, their leave they domestic property unguarded. (15.1.53 C709)[174]

171 ὅτι Ἰνδοὶ τῇ παρά σφισιν ἐπιχωρίῳ φωνῇ τὰ Ὁμήρου μεταγράψαντες ᾄδουσιν οὐ μόνοι ἀλλὰ καὶ οἱ Περσῶν βασιλεῖς, εἴ τι χρὴ πιστεύειν τοῖς ὑπὲρ τούτων ἱστοροῦσιν.

172 On the role of epic tradition, see for example, Thapar, *Cultural pasts*, pp. 195–212 and 647–79.

173 See Chapter 1, section III above.

174 Εὐτελεῖς δὲ κατὰ τὴν δίαιταν Ἰνδοὶ πάντες, μᾶλλον δ᾽ ἐν ταῖς στρατείαις· οὐδ᾽ ὄχλῳ περιττῷ χαίρουσι, διόπερ εὐκοσμοῦσι. πλείστη δ᾽ ἐκεχειρία περὶ τὰς κλοπάς· γενόμενος γοῦν ἐν τῷ Σανδροκόττου στρατοπέδῳ φησὶν ὁ Μεγασθένης, τετταράκοντα μυριάδων πλήθους ἱδρυμένου μηδεμίαν ἡμέραν ἰδεῖν ἀνηνεγμένα κλέμματα πλειόνων ἢ διακοσίων δραχμῶν ἄξια, ἀγράφοις καὶ ταῦτα νόμοις χρωμένοις. οὐδὲ γὰρ γράμματα εἰδέναι αὐτούς, ἀλλ᾽ ἀπὸ μνήμης ἕκαστα διοικεῖσθας· εὐπραγεῖν δ᾽ ὅμωι διὰ τὴν ἁπλότητα καὶ τὴν εὐτέλειαν· οἶνον τε γὰρ οὐ πίνειν

A number of ethnographic themes are presented here in an idealising manner: simplicity, frugality and self-restraint in their life-style generally, not least in their diet; the avoidance of crime, at least serious crime; ignorance of writing; the consequent reliance on memory in their social interactions. But Strabo's idealisation is followed directly by some qualifiers indicating disparagement. Now Indian customs are contrasted with the communal meals of Greek citizens, which are held up as the norm:

> Such behaviour [i.e. described in the previous passage] is indeed self-controlled. But nobody could commend their other practices, of always eating on their own and of not having one standard hour for dinner and breakfast rather than eating as each one pleases. For eating in the former manner better promotes social and political life. (15.1.53 C709)[175]

It should be remembered here that the Athenian symposium and the Spartan mess meal (*syssition*) were archetypes of social exchange in the Greek world, at least among male citizens.[176] It is clear, then, that Strabo's idealisation is limited in scope, applying to some spheres of social life, but not others. This alone may be regarded as an indication of the problem of utopias: they do not stand up well to scrutiny; they are utopias in so far as they are distant visions, and on closer inspection they quickly become problematic.

Do the features of Strabo's India qualify it for the status of a utopia? On the one hand, there is no mistaking a tendency to idealise within various kinds of ethnographic discourse. Two utopian texts of the early modern period underline the connection between social ideal and distant place: the main speaker of More's *Utopia*, Raphael Hythlodaeus, supposedly accompanied Vespucci on his voyage to the New World. Tomaso Campanella's *City of the sun* has its geographical location in the Indian Ocean. Obvious here are the ethnographic contexts of utopian thought, especially when a utopian tradition is considered in a broader span. Yet, on the other hand, it would be misleading to overemphasise these elements, and to assume that

ἀλλ' ἐν θυσίαι μόνον, πίνειν δ' ἀπ' ὀρύξης ἀντὶ κριθίνων συντιθέντας· καὶ σιτία δὲ τὸ πλέον ὄρυξαν εἶναι ῥοφητήν. καὶ ἐν τοῖς νόμοις δὲ καὶ συμβολαίοις τὴν ἁπλότητα ἐλέγχεσθαι ἐκ του μὴ πολυδίκους εἶναι· οὔτε γὰρ ὑποθήκης οὔτε παρακαταθήκης εἶναι δίκας, οὐδὲ μαρτύρων οὐδὲ σφραγίδων αὐτοῖς δεῖν, ἀλλὰ πιστεύειν παραβαλλομένους· καὶ τὰ οἴκοι δὲ τὸ πλέον ἀφρουρεῖν.

175 ταῦτα μὲν δὴ σωφρονικά, τἆλλα δ' οὐκ ἄν τις ἀποδέξαιτο, τὸ μόνους διαιτᾶσθαι ἀεὶ καὶ τὸ μὴ μίαν εἶναι πᾶσιν ὥραν κοινὴν δείπνου τε καὶ ἀρίστου, ἀλλ' ὅπως ἑκάστῳ φίλον· πρὸς γὰρ τὸν κοινωνικὸν καὶ τὸν πολιτικὸν βίον ἐκείνωι κρεῖττον.

176 *Sympotica: a symposium on the symposium*, ed. Oswyn Murray (Oxford: Clarendon, 1990); Nick Fisher, 'Drink, hybris and the promotion of harmony in Sparta', in *Classical Sparta: techniques behind her success*, ed. Anton Powell (London: Routledge, 1989), pp. 26–50.

every ethnography has its idealising side. Strabo's India is, as we have seen, a utopia up to a certain point only; and More's and Campanella's utopias are far from being utopian in all respects.[177]

Moving away from India momentarily, it is hard to read Tacitus' *Germania* without giving some weight to the glowing terms with which he describes German *libertas* (esp. ch. 37). If this was a major concept in Roman politics and social life,[178] then Germany too is evaluated according to this criterion, and presented in glowing terms. In describing the long combat between Romans and Germans, Tacitus mentions that there have been heavy losses on both sides, and this leads him to compare other nations with whom Rome has fought:

> Neither the Samnites, the Phoenicians, the Spaniards, the Gauls nor even the Parthians have chastened us more frequently: the freedom of the Germans is more dangerous than Arsaces' monarchy. (37)[179]

Ethnography, on these lines, carries the potential of social criticism of home. That does not mean that lands and people described should constitute an integrated utopia.

A recent account offers a four-part typology: retrospective utopias (e.g., Golden Age myths); utopias of discovery (e.g., Euhemerus' Panchaia and Iamboulos' Islands of the Sun); utopias of foundation (e.g., Plato's *Republic*); and those of the inaccessible present (e.g., the Isles of the Blest or the Hyperboreans). Faced with such categories, India's utopian status is at best tenuous. It is not retrospective, for India's antiquity receives limited recognition only; and India is too distantly located to be foundational. Instead, Strabo's description quoted above, particularly his emphasis on Indian simplicity, resonates with the kind of utopia of the inaccessible present found in the descriptions of the Aithiopians.[180] Yet, even in Strabo's account there is a much weaker utopian element than in, say, Diodorus Siculus description of Aithiopians (3.2.1–4).

From the above discussion it emerges that utopianism in this ethnographic context has its limits. Utopias, it appears, can have that status as

[177] The definition of utopia discussed by Clay and Purvis, *Four island utopias*, p. 2, stresses that they are not 'models of unrealistic perfection' but rather 'alternatives to the familiar . . . norms by which to judge existing societies'.

[178] Chaim Wirzubski, *Libertas as a political idea at Rome during the late Republic and early Principate* (Cambridge University Press, 1950). On the phenomenon of presenting a distant land as 'the location of Roman virtues' (in this case *libertas* in Britain), see Katherine Clarke, 'An island nation: re-reading Tacitus' *Agricola*', *JRS* 91 (2001), 94–112, esp. 106–9.

[179] *non Samnis, non Poeni, non Hispaniae Galliaeue, ne Parthi quidem saepius admonuere: quippe regno Arsacis acrior est Germanorum libertas.*

[180] Clay and Purvis, *Four island utopias*, pp. 168–75.

long as they are out of reach: though India had at an early stage of Greek history the makings of a utopia, that status was compromised by various developments (including the writing of texts) that brought it closer and made it more familiar. Certainly, there are elements that can be called utopian, but that does not mean we can readily describe Strabo's or Pliny's India as a utopia. Rather, we remain on safer ground by stressing the radical difference of India – a difference informed by its spatial difference, its overall difficulty of access to the Mediterranean world. If religious travel was, in the first instance, travel elsewhere,[181] then India was a destination par excellence. In practice, this is the case less often in the religious than in the commercial sphere. India's utopianism, then is a limited thing; to identify it in ancient accounts such as that of Strabo is useful mostly in so far as it emphasises India's inaccessibility, a phenomenon that kept open the possibility of implicit comparison between it and the Roman world.

III.5. Narrative space

India has already emerged as a space onto which Mediterranean people could project thought-experiments that sometimes merit the term utopia. In addition, India was good to narrate, in the sense that made possible certain turns of event in the Greek novel. Travel was central to Iambulus' account of the Islands of the Sun, islands apparently situated on the sea-route between Aithiopia and India. But the pre-eminent case occurs in Xenophon of Ephesus' *Ephesian tale*.

At one point the heroine, Anthia, is captured by pirates and taken to Alexandria. Here she is bought as a slave by the Indian king, Psammis (3.11.2). He intends to ravish her but desists once told that she is a priestess of Isis and must maintain her virginity until she reaches a marriageable age. It is because 'barbarians are superstitious by nature' (3.11.4) that he acquiesces. Soon thereafter, the bandit Hippothous heads up the Nile, though bypassing Alexandria (4.1.5). In Upper Egypt, 'near to Ethiopia', he and his five hundred companions have a field day because 'there was a large group of traders passing through en route to Ethiopia and India' (4.1.5).

Anthia is on the verge of being shipped from Upper Egypt to India, at the behest of Psammis (4.3.3). She prays to Isis to intervene, to prevent her from being taken to India, 'far from the land of Ephesus, far from the remains of Habrocomes' (the hero, whom she mistakenly thinks has died).

181 Elsner, 'Greek pilgrim', 9.

As if in answer to her prayer, Hippothous apprehends and kills Psammis, and thus obviates her journey to India and ultimately makes it possible for Anthia and Habrocomes to reunite.

Heliodorus' references to luxury goods are in many ways clichéd and typical of Roman imperial references to luxury goods. But even here, the Nile connects the Mediterranean and the Indian Ocean. When India occurs in Xenophon of Ephesus, again it is the Nile which pushes and pulls in each direction. In this story India serves to maximise narrative space. In the *Ephesian tale* the mere mention of India invests the story with further, unspecified possibilities, and hence contributes to its suspense.[182] In this way India provides the Greek novel with narrative space.

III.6. Analogy

The issue of translation has many aspects. While those related to (or absent from) the practicalities of commercial travel will be considered in Chapter 4, there is another, broader sense in which translation demands our attention, namely translation between different cultures. More often than not, this is implicit rather than explicit.[183] The principle is a simple but rich one: the less known becomes intelligible through the better known. In other words, this is a negotiation of the familiar and the unfamiliar, of the known and the strange (the marvel being an extreme case of the strange). Given this definition, the ethnographic tropes of inversion and comparison may thus be considered subspecies of the principle of translation. We see in these modes a number of ways in which writers communicate with their audiences, working within the limits imposed by literary genres and their attendant horizons of expectation.

A few examples will suffice to illustrate the principle at work within Indographic traditions. Strabo's description of India is striking for its persistent comparison with Egypt and Aithiopia, the point of comparison being the Nile valley. By Strabo's time there was a long-standing precedent for the transference of features between India and Africa, so this should in principle come as no surprise. But what is striking is the persistence of the scheme, as if it provides Strabo with a framework of explanation.

182 These possibilities are consonant with the kind of monsoon travel described in Chapter 4, section III.2 below. Both the *hydreumata* in the Eastern Desert and the Muziris papyrus are reminders of the dangers facing a merchant bringing goods from India to the Mediterranean.

183 For example, James Clifford, *Routes: travel and translation in the late twentieth century* (Cambridge, MA: Harvard University Press, 1997), p. 11, 'assumes that all broadly meaningful concepts, terms such as "travel", are translations, built from imperfect equivalences'.

Another point of ethnographic comparison that has already come up in this chapter has been between Indians and Scythians. This too can be easily understood, given the geographical proximity of the two peoples. In the texts examined Scythians are invoked as a way of showing that Indian society has changed, with the help of Heracles and Dionysus, from nomadism to sedentary pastoralism. The Scythians are thus presented as the archetypal nomads, whose lifestyle precedes that of agriculture in a schema of progress;[184] in this context their lifestyle represents the antithesis of civilisation as brought by Alexander:

> Long ago the Indians, [Megasthenes says], were nomads, like the non-agricultural Scythians, who wander in their waggons and decamp from one part of Scythia to another, neither dwelling in cities nor reverencing the gods' shrines. (Arr. *Ind.* 7.1)[185]

This comparison turns on a negative mode of description. In fact many negatives are found in descriptions, on the lines of the following: 'There are no X among the Indians,' where X corresponds to some familiar aspect of Greco-Roman life, such as agriculture or slavery. It is standard practice for pastoral nomads to be described in the rhetoric of lack.[186] The background to this is a Roman sense of its own empire as consisting, in the first instance, of cities. Thus, when the second-century sophist Aelius Aristides gives a speech *To Rome*, he reveals a provincial's admiration for the empire's urban culture.[187]

The following comment by Curtius shows that inversion is a possible mode of ethnographic understanding too: here India inverts nature's known and normal pattern. But, oddly, Curtius stresses not the explanatory power of this principle, but its inexplicability:

> But in that region the earth so inverts the regular order of seasons that when other parts become hot with the sun's heat, snow covers India; and conversely, when

184 Hartog, *Mirror of Herodotus*; Arthur O. Lovejoy and George Boas, *Primitivism and related ideas in antiquity* (Baltimore: Johns Hopkins University Press, 1935), pp. 287–367; and Brent D. Shaw, '"Eaters of flesh, drinkers of milk": the ancient Mediterranean ideology of the pastoral nomad', *Ancient Society* 13–14 (1982–3), 5–31, on Scythians as 'typical' nomads.

185 πάλαι μὲν δὴ νομάδας εἶναι Ἰνδούς, καθάπερ Σκυθέων τοὺς οὐκ ἀροτηρας, οἳ ἐπὶ τῇσιν ἁμάξῃσι πλανώμενοι ἄλλοτε ἄλλην τῆς Σκυθίης ἀμείβουσιν, οὔτε πόληας οἰκέοντες οὔτε ἱερὰ θεῶν σέβοντες.

186 Hartog, *Mirror of Herodotus*; Shaw, 'Eaters of flesh'; cf. John Matthews, *The Roman Empire of Ammianus* (London: Duckworth, 1989), pp. 333–42 on the Huns.

187 On towns and cities as the 'sinews of empire', Brent D. Shaw, 'Rebels and outsiders', *CAH*, 2nd edn (2000), vol. XI, pp. 361–403, at 362. Clifford Ando, *Imperial ideology and provincial loyalty in the Roman empire* (Berkeley: University of California Press, 2000), presents *consensus* as crucial to the stability of the empire.

other parts become cold, unbearable heat prevails there. There is no reason for this inversion of nature. (8.9.13)[188]

Curtius appeals to nature as the norm, in order to show the extent of India's divergence. Immediately after this balancing of the known and the unknown, he proceeds to reassure readers that at least the surrounding sea is like other seas, and despite its name is not unusual in its colour.[189] Again, we see here a delicate negotiation between the known, determined by set patterns of language and literary genre, and the unknown – which is, after all, the quality that assures the interest-value of a story, even as familiar a story as that of Alexander's expedition.

III.7. Fragments

Throughout this chapter and the former, fragments have loomed so large as a literary form that they demand detailed consideration. This is opportune, given that the focus here is on points of reception rather than of origin for many of the pieces of information about India. Certainly there is a tendency in accounts of India towards excerption and towards critical comment about truth and fiction.[190] Strabo and Pliny, in particular, refer to earlier writers whom they claim to be quoting or paraphrasing, often with evaluative comment. Notoriously, Diodorus is the counter-example here, as one who avoids discussing or even mentioning his sources.[191] In this, doxography is used as a means of conveying opinions – as if concern with supposed source-criticism leads to a process whereby an author divides up the information he has to hand. In some cases we see a tension between the protracted narrative description and the curious detail, the marvel, which is often subjected to source-criticism – what we might call the doxographic habit. Even this phenomenon is complex: it can by turns allow both critical evaluation and it can make it possible for a writer to hide behind 'authorities'.

In the purely formal sense, in keeping with Jacoby's *Fragmente der griechischen Historiker*, there is no difficulty in identifying a fragment. By this way of thinking, a fragment is something the scholar recognises on sight or by instinct. Yet, on closer examination, things are not so simple as they might seem. For one thing, Jacoby's own magnum opus has recently come under

188 *sed adeo in illa plaga mundus statas temporum uices mutat, ut, cum alia feruore solis exaestuant, Indiam niues obruant, rursusque, ubi cetera rigent, illic intolerandus aestus existat. nec, cur uerterit se natura, causa.*

189 'Indeed, the sea that washes it does not differ from others with regard to its colour.' (8.9.14)

190 Gabba, 'True history'; cf. Romm, *Edges*, pp. 95–103.

191 Sacks, *Diodorus Siculus*; cf. Hornblower's introduction to *Greek historiography*, ed. Hornblower.

fire for its at times deceptively facile reconstruction of lost historians.[192] What is more, if we allow ourselves to think in broader terms about the concept of the fragment, we can detect in it some conflicting tendencies. For one thing, we can identify its importance to source-criticism. To follow the lines of Greenblatt's analysis of medieval travel-writing,[193] one might say that the source-criticism here reflects the author's desire to strengthen his position as an 'authorizing self', as a dependable source in writing about material that defies credibility. Yet, in trying to strengthen their own position by this means, Strabo and Pliny in fact reduce their own texts to a collection of fragments, and in so doing effectively fragment and hence reduce the unity of their own writing. Diodorus is the odd one out in this: while his own work draws heavily on earlier sources, he seldom identifies them as such, and in the process he tends not to disrupt his own narrative with an evaluation of sources.

In his essay, translated as 'A lover's discourse: fragments,' Roland Barthes offers a sophisticated analysis of the fragment as a unit of language and thought. In utterances about the erotic, it is, for Barthes, not so much a matter of individual authors creating their own texts, but more a discourse collectively created over a period of time. There is, on this analysis, a lover's discourse that pre-exists any individual love-poet, a discourse prone to infinite fragmentation and reassembly.[194]

Even making provision for obvious and major differences in context, there might be something to gain here in identifying an ethnographer's discourse on the same lines. As for love, so for the ends of the earth, and not least India: in each case, there is a significant degree of repetition of the same *kinds* of phenomenon. The marvel is a prime example: familiar already by the time of Ctesias, it was to be much written about in Hellenistic times, and will have been clichéd by the time of Strabo and Pliny. Given the folkloric nature of the marvellous creatures, they might seem to constitute exactly the kind of discourse that lacks an original author and allows for repeated borrowing and reworking. In these ways the ethnographic discourse about India has a striking degree of openness, of iterability and malleability. Its resilience over many centuries comes, then, as no surprise. The fact that

[192] See esp. the essays by G. W. Bowersock, 'Jacoby's fragments and two Greek historians of pre-Islamic Arabia', and Guido Schepens, 'Jacoby's *FGrHist*: problems, methods, prospects', in *Collecting fragments*, ed. Most, pp. 173–85 and 144–72; cf. Chapter 1, section III.7 above.

[193] Stephen Greenblatt, *Marvelous possessions: the wonder of the New World* (University of Chicago Press, 1991), pp. 48–9, following de Man, on Mandeville: 'There is no original, no authorizing self, no authentic text; all texts are translations of/ fragments that are themselves translations.'

[194] This approach has been adopted in a recent study of Latin love-elegy: Duncan F. Kennedy, *The arts of love: five studies in the discourse of Roman love elegy* (Cambridge University Press, 1993).

Indographic discourse overlaps to such an extent with descriptions of other remote places, especially Aithiopia and to a lesser extent Egypt (thus Strabo), made it both more flexible and durable, and more intelligible to its audience, especially when accompanied by discursive comparisons.

Pliny's account is an extreme but not a unique case of inclusivity as a principle: it is as if there were no limits on what might be included in the *Natural history*, given its enormous scope, and no limits to what might be included on any one topic discussed. He himself sounds an apologetic note in the preface, admitting that much more could have been added on any given topic.[195] Pliny's tendency to criticise sources must thus be seen as an author's attempt to gain some purchase on this inclusive principle. Thus for Pliny it was more important to repeat Ctesias' judgements than to agree or disagree with its substance, to approve or disapprove of its source. The reliability of any item of information seems outweighed by the need to invoke an authority. In such cases it seems better to include bad information than to omit it entirely.

The *Natural history* is a mish-mash of material, composed from within and for a learned milieu already familiar with some degree of the material discussed (at least some of the names invoked as authorities), and alert to critical debate. It is obvious then that the work should be understood in terms of the learned culture that produced it, where, contrary to modern expectations, book-learning was more valued than autopsy.[196] The copying of earlier writers serves a useful purpose: in a society where the copying of literary texts was a laboursome and expensive business, the encyclopaedia served an important function in ensuring the survival of such information and making it more widely available. The same is true in later antiquity for the compendium and epitome.

To see only the limitations of the fragment would be to overlook its creative potentialities. Most importantly, we should see the fragment as a rhetorical mode, one that offered a number of possibilities: the chance to reshape geographical discourse into new forms, the chance to offer critique of earlier writers on any given subject.

If we bear in mind Pliny's text particularly, the history of reception speaks volumes for the power of these possibilities. Pliny's *Natural history* itself a compilation of *doxae* from a huge number of sources, as the lists of sources making up his first book make plain. Yet the fate of the work was, as we saw above, to be transmitted differently between one section and the next,

195 'I freely admit that my work is open to considerable elaboration': praef. 28, cf. 12.

196 Lloyd, *Science, folklore and ideology*, pp. 140–52; Murphy, *Pliny*, p. 53.

and to be excerpted. As we trace the metamorphoses of the same kinds of material over the centuries, the fragment emerges as the highest common denominator, a unit for the transmission of information. In the case of Pliny, the subsequent history of textual reception bears out the essentially fragmentary quality of the work.

Why should Pliny be so concerned to debate with authorities? In principle, two explanations may be offered: one stressing the power of existing tradition, and the other stressing his need to establish his own place among learned authorities. The two need not clash. Certainly there is no denying that Pliny was aware of the power wielded by scholarly tradition on any of his topics, as is shown by his care in providing the list of sources (*auctoritates*) for each of his 36 books. Yet this does not preclude a sense of his own novelty and enterprise in writing a work as compendious as the *Natural history*. Given the popularity of *Antiquitates rerum humanarum et divinarum*, Varro alone among Latin writers may have cast a powerful shadow over Pliny's enterprise, but other than that it is hard to imagine that any other Latin work matched the breadth and scale of the *Natural history*.

III.8. Closure

The question of closure in classical literature has most often been examined in relation to verse, yet it is an interesting feature of the texts under discussion.[197] In chorography it is significant to observe, in particular, instances where a description ends at a geographical point which marks a border of knowledge, a point at which nothing more is known definitely or at all. In Chapter 1, Alexander's campaign emerged, more in analytical hindsight than in actuality, as central to the creation of just such a supposed border of knowledge. Strabo speaks of the Hypanis as a frontier of knowledge, while admitting that after Alexander Greeks travelled farther east (15.1.27 C698).[198] Later he even says that the land beyond the Hypanis is generally agreed to be the best (15.1.37 C702).

This principle of ethnographic closure can be paralleled in Mela and in Tacitus.[199] In an Indian context, we need look no farther than a work that does not participate in the learned tradition of Pliny and Strabo, the *Periplus of the Erythraean Sea*. Its end is markedly indeterminate: 'What lies beyond this area, because of extremes of storm, bitter cold, and difficult terrain and

[197] Deborah H. Roberts, Frances M. Dunn and Don P. Fowler (eds.), *Classical closure: reading the end in Greek and Latin literature* (Princeton University Press, 1997).

[198] Cf. Arrian *Ind.* 4.1 and 6.1.

[199] Mela, see section I above.

also because of some divine power of the gods, has remained unexplored (ἀνερεύνητα)' (66). The text does retail information about India's southwest coast beyond Nelkynda and about the east coast, but it does so briefly and with less detail. Characteristic of the work's pragmatism, it says little about parts that were hardly known to its author, and presumably of little direct relevance to its primary audience. The basic closural gesture bears comparison with that of Tacitus' *Germania* (46):

> The rest is fabulous: that the Hellusii and Oxiones have the mouths and faces of humans but the bodies and limbs of animals. But I shall leave undecided that which is unknown.[200]

Moving ever farther north, Tacitus describes Suebia, then the wild Fenni, characterised by 'remarkable barbarism and appalling poverty', before reaching this ending. In the endings of both the *Periplus* and the *Germania* this concluding suspension of comment is all the more significant for the amount of detail that precedes them.[201]

IV. CONCLUSION

In the first chapter we surveyed two phases of Mediterranean Indography – a first, pre-Alexander and particularly an Achaemenid phase, in which the *elements* of a Greek discourse about India as a place of marvellous phenomena took shape; and a second a phase from Alexander's expedition to Megasthenes, when the *amount* of information about India increased considerably. In this chapter we have seen a third, imperial phase, examined with regard to the contexts in which Romans thought, spoke and wrote about India, and the rhetorical tropes which they employed in doing so. Even if provision is made for the potential optical illusion whereby Roman-period texts are now hard to distinguish from their Hellenistic sources, there does appear to be a considerable degree of overlap in content between these second and third phases of Indography.

The recurrence of the marvel, that hallmark of Hellenistic literature, in sources of the Augustan period and beyond is a major theme in this

200 *cetera iam fabulosa: Hellusios et Oxionas ora hominum voltusque, corpora atque artus ferarum gerere: quod ego ut incompertum in medio relinquam.*

201 To take a further example, Mela's comments on Africa also equate the periphery with barbarism (1.46–47): the shores are inhabited by people who live by Roman customs; moving on, one comes to the antisocial Gamphasantes, then finally to the headless Blemmyes. This movement inland, within only the small section of a work, it must be admitted, reveals a variation on the theme of the *periplus*. It also alerts us to the fact that closure must be seen as a principle within individual sections of composite topographic works, not just within works as a whole.

Indographic discourse. Its implications were enormous. Most notably, it stimulated the need for proof and refutation, and for frequent recourse to literary authorities. The constant appeal to authorities had the effect of making otherwise lengthy texts like Strabo's and Pliny's into collections of fragments. Indeed the fragment is a major feature of Indographic literature, representing a kind of lowest common denominator of information, ever open to being recycled and reused in new contexts. Pliny himself emerges as a nodal point in the history of ideas: he drew on an enormous variety of sources, mostly but not only Hellenistic, and later suffered the same fate of being excerpted and epitomised. Pliny is an author that illustrates the tenacity of the literary tradition, and its imperviousness to new information. As Chapter 6 will show, Buddhism is a topic which shows that Greco-Roman sources were slow to recognise historical change: it does not appear in Greek and Latin texts until several centuries after its spread. This tenacity of a canon of information has been shown to rest on written sources. But that conclusion cannot obscure the fact that Roman authors did in fact add some new information, even if somewhat grudgingly. Strabo may have echoed an old prejudice against commercial traders as sources of topographical information, but he does reveal an awareness of them. Claudius Ptolemy, composing his *Geography* some 150 years later, is even more open to commercially obtained information, and in fact his fuller topography of the Bay of Bengal would not have been possible without information gleaned from traders.

In conclusion, then, an overarching question may help to make sense of the many smaller questions discussed along the way: was knowledge about India gathered as a product or a process? There are in Pliny's text a few suggestions of *how* information was gathered, so that, for all its reliance on written sources, there is an element of process within that composite text. It has been suggested that Pliny is an eminent case of an author for whom knowledge generally is static,[202] and to an extent this is undoubtedly true. But at the same time there are hints of Pliny's receptiveness to new information, not least in the context of commercial travel. This comes as a surprise, given the low prestige of traders, and given the prominence of bookish *auctoritas*; but nonetheless there are traces that deserve serious consideration. We might say, by way of conclusion, that despite all it *was* a process, though a slow one.

[202] Gian Biagio Conte, *Genres and readers: Lucretius, love elegy, Pliny's encyclopedia*, tr. Glenn W. Most (Baltimore: Johns Hopkins University Press, 1994).

It would be true to say that the marvel, so important to this chapter as to the foregoing, is visually conceived in the first instance, though of course verbally conveyed. The tropes of comparison and inversion are its variants: they offer modes of understanding, of relating known to unknown, whereas marvel in its purest form marks the inability to comprehend. To the extent that the marvel invited criticism, proof and refutation, it also spawned the doxographic habit, whereby textual authorities are cited, sometimes in competition. This makes large texts like Strabo's or Pliny's effectively into collections of fragments: despite the conceptual unity of those texts, they retain by virtue of the doxographic habit a certain mosaic quality which in its later reception was to prove both a strength and a weakness. In the case of Strabo, the tendency to link pieces of information with individual authors also gave a certain amount of room for the authorial persona to be present in the text: Strabo himself, or the 'author function' in Barthes' term, is cited as a rival source of authority. Even Strabo, when he dismisses the reliability of traders as sources of information, makes reference to contemporary sources. On the whole, the authority of literary texts is paramount, and clearly predominant over autopsy; yet, oddly enough, when an earlier author has himself engaged in autopsy, his own trustworthiness increases thereby. If Megasthenes is controversial in his Roman imperial afterlife, that is because his trustworthiness is subject to doubt by the remoteness of his theme and the prominence of the marvel within it. Yet his travels to India were a source of credibility. Ctesias, on the other hand, is easily dismissed on the grounds, explicit or otherwise, that he has not visited India himself.

We have seen to what extent Pliny is a nodal point in the history of ideas. He himself excerpted earlier works, even his own, if we can consider the passage 7.21–32 as a summary of his own lengthier treatment in the foregoing book. Excerption was to be the fate of his own *Natural history* in later centuries. This is shown both by the variegated textual tradition of the work and by its openness to being excerpted and epitomised. To a large degree, his own procedure prefigured the fate of his work. And this fate was to prove typical of marvel-based ethnography in the Roman west.

For Mark Twain in the epigraph to this chapter, India's 'extraordinary' qualities made it difficult to describe. For Roman writers, the ethnographic questionnaire was a powerful grid by which to comprehend a foreign group and its locale. But it is also true that the process of 'hanging tags' illustrates the limits of representation. Such tropes as comparison and inversion are only helpful up to a certain point. The *periplus* as a form is best suited to coastlines in or bordering the Mediterranean. The marvel, shared also with other distant places, implies India's abundance but also emphasizes its strangeness. By such means, certain aspects of India come to the fore. Pliny and Ptolemy, with their onomastic enthusiasms, by which they devote much effort to the naming of settlements and natural features, present certain kinds of information at the expense of others; indications of antiquity that attempt to subsume Indian history into Greek. Other aspects of Indography, including references to *sati*, involve social critique of Rome itself, particularly among authors that merely mention India in passing. Such attempted alignments are acts of translation, in the broader sense of that term, and provided more ambitious though still limited ways of representing India and Indians to Roman audiences. But there were different kinds of Roman audience, at different social levels and with different degrees of learning. If this survey of ethnographic traditions has presented a varied set of Indias, that is because of the varied registers of spatial knowledge operating within the Roman empire.

CHAPTER 3

India depicted

> So geographers in Africk maps with savage pictures fill their gaps, and o'er unhabitable downs place elephants for want of towns.
>
> Jonathan Swift, from 'Poetry, a rhapsody'

If the contours of the literary India have received much attention recently, there has been much less discussion about visual traditions for representing it. Whereas the compendious *Lexicon Iconographicum Mythologiae Classicae*, offers only one image under the rubric 'India', it is more than a century ago, in an article by Hans Graeven, that a full-scale attempt was last made to survey all artifacts representing India.[1] The aim of this chapter is to revisit the material studied by Graeven, and to reconsider how India was represented in Greek and Roman art. Here, even more so than in the previous chapter, it is necessary to treat the end of antiquity in a somewhat elastic fashion: a central problem to emerge will be the belated appearance of visual representations to match literary references that were long known in antiquity.

The artifacts that may be thought to represent India offer two difficulties of a methodological nature, and it is worth considering these at the outset. First, there is the very practical problem of identification. What are the criteria by which any given artifact may be thought to represent *India* specifically? There is a danger of circularity: we do not know what India is until we have found it, and only once we have found it do we know what we were looking for in the first place. This calls for a provisional, working solution: what are the distinguishing features of India when it occurs in Greco-Roman art? Second, in dealing with artistic representations of foreign peoples, there is the strategic question of cultural boundaries. Within which visual tradition or traditions should we analyse those representations?

[1] Jean Ch. Balty, 'India', *Lexicon Iconographicum Mythologiae Classicae* (Zurich: Artemis, 1981–99), vol. V.1, cols. 654–5; Hans Graeven, 'Darstellungen der Inder in antiken Kunstwerken', *JDAI(B)* 15 (1900), 195–218; see now also Whittaker, *Rome and its frontiers*, pp. 123–6.

The problem arises when art-historical analysis takes the linear, 'vertical' approach of positing traditions that are unities over time, effectively closed to the outside world, except, at most, in special and discernible circumstances. Rather, the approach here will be to try to explain the images largely within the artistic traditions of Greece and Rome. This is undertaken as a conscious strategy, without precluding the possibility that some features of these artifacts may be understood within the traditions of India. I specifically avoid speaking of cultural 'influence'.[2] This is not to deny the possibility that the Greco-Roman artifacts might have been responding to visual traditions already existing in the subcontinent. Rather, here there is the attempt, or even experiment, to see what eventuates when the Greco-Roman artifacts are studied from within the artistic traditions they most obviously share. Such an analysis does not preclude others.

The following pages begin with an outline of four groups of evidence, divided thematically. Section II answers the need to step back from these groups in search of a broader-based analysis, including a typology.

I. VARIETIES OF IMAGE

I.1. Marvel

The most obvious category with which to begin is that of the marvel. This has emerged in the earliest Greek accounts, particularly those of Scylax of Caryanda (Herodotus 4.44). Whereas Herodotus makes little reference to monsters in his account of India, they are the distinctive feature of his later contemporary, Ctesias of Cnidos. Ctesias claims to have seen a manticore (*martikhora*) at the Achaemenid court of Artaxerxes, once it had been brought there as a gift for the King of Kings.[3] Indeed, when the word occurs in Greek it is as a loanword from the Old Persian.[4] This creature was destined to have a particularly long life in western tales of marvel, for example in the manticore of medieval bestiaries, or in particular the thirteenth-century travel writings of Marco Polo and Sir John Mandeville.[5]

[2] Though Derrett speaks about a literary tradition, the same basic principles can be applied to the visual, notably by Boardman, *The Diffusion of classical art*; likewise Daniel Schlumberger, *L'Orient hellénisé. L'Art grec et ses héritiers dans l'Asie non méditerranéenne* (Paris: Michel, 1970). For a critique of such approaches, with reference to Gandharan art, see S. Abe, 'Wonder house'.

[3] Ael. *NA* 4.21 (= F45dβ) on this passage compare Chapter 1, section I.4 above.

[4] The Greek *martikhora* appears to be a loanword from Old Persian, corresponding to a reconstructed compound, **martiya-khvara* ('man-eater'): Calvert Watkins, *The American Heritage dictionary of Indo-European roots*, 2nd edn (Boston: Houghton Mifflin, 2000), s.v. *mer-*[2] and *swel-*[1].

[5] See, for example, the anthology compiled by Joe Nigg, *The book of fabulous beasts: a treasury of writings from ancient times to the present* (Oxford University Press, 1999), where the manticore emerges as a

For a society centred on the 'pond' of the Mediterranean, to use Plato's term (*Phaedo* 109b), marvels provided a ready conception of the edges of the earth. It is therefore not surprising that, in the wider Greek world postdating Alexander's conquests, the marvel became a major part of the ethnographic imagination. The persistence of the marvellous was further assured by the prominence it attained in Roman geographies and ethnographies of the early empire, especially Pliny the Elder's *Natural history*. In keeping with the popularity of this work in the western Middle Ages, it is basically a Plinian worldview that we find in the early medieval encyclopaedia of Isidore of Seville, though one with Christian elements.[6]

These monstrous races are a conflation of human and animal: they usually lack human speech, and in many cases they share features with animals. The background against which we must understand this is that the distinction between human, divine and animal was central to ancient Greek worldviews.[7] Marvels thus have a transgressive quality in so far as they depart from conventional categories of Greek thought. Further, it is worth emphasising the remarkable persistence of these monsters over time. In the words of their major scholar, Rudolf Wittkower,

> 'Marvels of the east' determined the western idea of India for 2000 years, and made their way into natural science and geography, encyclopaedias and cosmographies, romances and history, into maps, miniatures and sculpture. They gradually became stock features of occidental mentality . . . their power of survival was such that they did not die altogether with the geographical discoveries and better knowledge of the East, but lived on in pseudo-scientific dress right into the 17th and 18th centuries.[8]

fabulous beast *par excellence*. Illustrated bestiaries, in which Christian moral teachings are extracted from the animal world, are known from the twelfth and thirteenth centuries: T. H. White, *The book of beasts, being a translation from a Latin bestiary of the twelfth century* (London: Cape, 1954). Joyce E. Salisbury, 'Human beasts and bestial humans in the Middle Ages', in *Animal acts: configuring the human in western history*, ed. Jennifer Ham and Matthew Senior (London: Routledge, 1997), pp. 9–22, shows the philosophical problems they posed. The anonymous Greek text, *Physiologus* (second century AD or perhaps somewhat later) combines the Hellenistic tradition of natural history with Christian interpretation, and is a major part of this tradition. On the use of the *Physiologus* in medieval sermons, see Ron Baxter, 'Learning from nature: lessons in virtue and vice in the *Physiologus* and bestiaries', in *Virtue and vice: the personifications in the Index of Christian Art*, ed. Colum Hourihane (Princeton University Press, 2000), pp. 29–41; more generally, Nikolaus Henkel, *Studien zum Physiologus im Mittelalter* (Tübingen: Niemeyer, 1976) and U. Treu, 'The Greek Physiologus', in *Ancient history in a modern university*, ed. T. W. Hillard *et al.* (North Ryde, NSW: Macquarie University Press, 1998), vol. II, pp. 426–32.

6 Borst, *Naturgeschichte*.

7 Jean-Pierre Vernant, *Myth and society in ancient Greece*, tr. Janet Lloyd (New York: Zone, 1990), pp. 143–82.

8 Rudolf Wittkower, 'Marvels of the East: a study in the history of monsters', *JWI* 6 (1943), 159–97, at 159.

der werlt Blat XII

Von mancherlay gestaltnus der menschen schreibē
Plinius: Augustinus vnd ysidorus die hernachge
meltē ding. In dem land india sind menschē myt hunds
köpffen vnd reden pellēde. nerē sich mit fogelgefeng vñ
klaiden sich mit thierhewtten. Item etlich haben allain
ein aug an der stirñ ob der nasen vnnd essen allain thier
fleisch. Item in dem land libia werden etlich on hawbt
gepoin vnd haben mund vnd augen. Etlich sind beder
lay geslechts. die recht prust ist in manlich vnd die lingk
weibisch vnd vermischen sich vnderemand vñ gepern.
Item gegen dem paradis bey dem fluss Ganges sind et
lich menschen die essen nichts. dann sie haben so klainen
mund das sie das getranck mit einē halm einflössen vnd
leben vom gesmack der öpffel vnd plumen. vnd sterben
pald von bössem gesmack. Daselbst sind auch lewt an
nasen eins ebnen angesichts. Etlich haben vnden so
groß lebssitzen das sie das gantz angesicht damit bedeckē
Item etlich an zungen. die deudten einander ir maynūg
mit wincken als die closterlewt. Item in dem land Sici
lia haben etlich so grosse orñ das sie den gantzen leib da
mit bedecken. Item in dem land ethiopia wandern etlich
nidergebogen als das vih. vnd etlich lebē vierhundert
iar. Item etlich haben hörner. lang nasen vnd gayßfüse
das findest du in sand Anthonius gantzer legēd. Itez in
ethiopia gein dem nidergang sind lewt mit einem pray
ten fuss. vnd so schnell das sie die wilden thier erfolgen.
Item in dem land Scithia haben sie menschē gestalt vñ
pferds füess. Item alda sind auch lewt fünff elnpogen
langk vnd werden nicht kranck bis zum tod. Item in dē
geschichtē des grossen Alexanders liset man das in india
menschen seyen mit sechs henden. Item etlich nacket vñ
rawh in den flüssen wonend. etlich die an henden vnd
füssen sechs finger haben. etlich in den wassern wonēde
halb menschen vnd halbs pferds gestalt habende. Itez
weiber mit perten bis auff die prust auff dē hawbt eben
vnd an har. Item in ethiopia gegen dem nidergang ha
ben etlich vier awgē. So sind in Eripia schön lewt mit
kranchßhelsen vnnd snebeln. Doch ist als Augustinus
schreibt nit zuglawben das etliche menschē an dem ort
der erden gegen vns da die sunn auff geet. so sie wider n
der geet die versen gegent vnsern füssen kerē. Doch ist ein
grosser streyt in der schrifft wider den wone des gemay
nen volcks. das geringßumb allenthalben menschē auff
der erden seyen. vnd die füß gegen einander kerende dar
auff steen. vnnd doch alle menschen ir schayttel gem hi
mel keren. in verwunderūg warumb doch wir oder die
die ir fersen gegen vnns wennden nit fallen. Aber das
kombt auß der natur. dann gleicherweis als der stul des
fewrs nyndert ist denn in den fewern. der wasser nyndert
denn in den wassern. vnnd des gaysts nyndert denn in
dem gayst. also auch der stul der erden nyndert anderß
wo denn in irselbs.

Figure 2 Monstrous people in the *Nuremberg chronicle* (Hartmann von Schedel, 1493). Courtesy of Parkins Library, Duke University.

Oddly enough, though these monsters stretch all the way into the eighteenth century, their visual (as opposed to verbal) depictions do not go particularly far back, in fact no further than the early Middle Ages, it seems. If this is true, then the early medieval manuscripts of, say, the *Alexander romance*, are belated representations of phenomena already known from the early fifth century BC, a full millennium earlier. If one compares the preponderance of monsters in Hellenistic literature, or in the *Natural history* of Pliny the Elder, then their absence in contemporary Greco-Roman art is really striking. Hence, in order to find the implicit visuality of Pliny's ethnography realised, we need to look at medieval works, such as the thirteenth-century Hereford (world) map. Monsters are clearly central to this monastic, classicising view of India.

To take an even later example of the same phenomenon, Hartman von Schedel's *Nuremberg chronicle* of 1493 exhibits shadow-feet, one-eyed monsters and the like. In both these cases, we see not only the continuity of monsters but also how easily they can be transferred from one edge of the earth to another: they are a marker of India, but also of other distant places, such as Africa or Ethiopia. The Hereford map and the *Nuremberg chronicle* are, in their different ways, realisations of the visuality implicit in the monsters of Scylax of Caryanda and others. In both instances, the principle seen here is not far from that enunciated by Jonathan Swift, writing about eighteenth-century maps, in the passage quoted as the epigraph to this chapter. In maps particularly, monsters serve as 'place holders' for exotic locations: they are a response to *horror vacui*. The quotation is itself testament to the durability of the monsters into and beyond the early modern period.

In a major study concentrating on the early modern through the colonial period, monsters feature as a major part of the western artistic response to Indian religious art.[9] It emerges that in Greco-Roman antiquity monsters were even more than that: to a significant degree, they may be regarded as a Mediterranean reaction to India *tout court*.

I.2. Triumph of Bacchus

Second, there are a number of sarcophagus reliefs, in which India is represented as part of the so-called triumph of Bacchus. This was a favourite topic in Antonine and Severan times, that is, from around the mid-second

[9] Partha Mitter, *Much maligned monsters: history of European reactions to Indian art* (Oxford: Clarendon, 1977).

Figure 3 Triumph of Bacchus, second or third century AD: Roman sarcophagus, Walters Gallery, Baltimore. Courtesy of the Walters Gallery.

through the early third century AD, though there are several literary references already in the Augustan age.[10] These depict a celebratory procession of the god Bacchus or Dionysus, returning after his conquest of the Indians. In some cases, male Indian prisoners are included; typically, elephants and tigers or panthers pull his chariot. In perhaps the most famous instance, the sarcophagus at the Walters Gallery in Baltimore, there is even a giraffe. This god is linked with the generative powers of nature, and hence the exotic animals; his saving powers are such that his retinue (*thiasos*) includes people from the earth's imagined corners.

While Dionysus is one of the most frequently depicted of the gods in Greek ceramics, the theme of his triumphal return from the east is distinctive of the Roman empire. In particular, it was in vogue in the second and third centuries AD.[11] At least two emperors from the earlier part of this period, Trajan and Lucius Verus, conducted extensive campaigns to the east of the Mediterranean, so that, by extension, this 'far eastern' motif had an immediate military context, as we shall discuss in Chapter 5.

The scene combines African motifs with Indian: as a species, the giraffe of the Baltimore relief lives solely in sub-Saharan Africa and not in India. The same piece includes two young boys, accompanied by a satyr, who are presented as young followers of the god. The corkscrew-curl design of their hair is a regular feature for the depiction of Africans in Greek and Roman art. On a fragment at the Metropolitan Museum, likewise from a Bacchic triumph scene, African features are even more apparent: here thick lips and a broad nose strengthen the ethnic identification.[12]

Elephants are a problem here. The two separate genera of elephants, the Indian and the African, differ considerably in appearance. Apart from being substantially smaller, the Indian has smaller ears and a flatter head, and a differently curved back. On this basis, it would seem feasible to try

10 Prop. 3.17.21–22; Verg. *Ecl.* 5.29–31; and *Aen.* 6.804–5; Ov. *Ars am.* 1.549–50; and somewhat later, Sil. *Pun.* 17.645–48. Bacchic processions were already mentioned by Catull. 64.251–64; cf. Ov. *Met.* 4.25–27. The yoking of tigers referred to in several of these texts seems to have symbolised civilising power, and in the case of the Virgil texts mentioned may have been linked with the public image of Augustus (at Hor. *Carm.* 3.3.13–15 the link is explicitly made).

11 The compendious work of Friedrich Matz, *Die Dionysischen Sarkophage*, 4 vols. (Berlin: Mann, 1968–75), shows a marked centre of gravity in the empire. The conquest of the Indians is presented in vol. III, pp. 422–33. As in the case of other polytheist mythology, Dionysian themes largely ceased to be deployed around the time of Constantine's Edict of Milan in AD 312/313: Guntram Koch, *Frühchristliche Sarkophage* (Munich: Beck, 2000), p. 346. On vase paintings of the earlier period, see esp. Thomas H. Carpenter, *Dionysian imagery in Archaic Greek art* (Oxford: Clarendon, 1997).

12 Anna Marguerite McCann, *Roman sarcophagi in the Metropolitan Museum of Art* (New York: Metropolitan Museum of Art, 1978), p. 87.

to distinguish the two in their artistic representations.[13] In certain instances of ancient art it is possible to distinguish one of these from the other, but even in such cases we cannot assume that the artist had seen the beasts in the flesh, had grasped and could convey the differences between the genera.

A remarkable class of evidence is provided by a number of marble heads, of which the finest and best known is now at the Galleria Borghese in Rome. Others are in smaller galleries in Rome, and in Madrid and Copenhagen. In each case there is a bearded man with a contemplative expression. A cirrus knot on the top creates the effect of an Indian hairstyle on what would otherwise be unexceptional marble heads from the Severan age or somewhat earlier.[14] In the case of the Galleria Borghese bust, the use of coloured marble (*bigio morato*) distinctively indicates the dark complexion of certain foreigners.[15] The connection with South Asia is easily established by a similarity to the Boddhisatva figures of Gandharan art. These may be considered a generic ethnic type (*Volkstypus*) rather than representing individuals; the earlier dating of the busts would align them with the barbarians commonly represented in Trajanic reliefs. One scholar has gone so far as to link this ethnic type with the spate of foreign ambassadors received by Trajan after his return to Rome in AD 107, since we know that Indians were among their number.[16] It is also tempting to link these hairstyles with the late-antique importation of 'Indian hair' (*capilli Indici*) mentioned in the *Digest*.[17]

The Barberini ivory is another work of art in which India is represented. This carved ivory panel, housed at the Louvre, is now firmly linked with the emperor Justinian I (r. AD 527–65). The mounted emperor occupies the central panel, below the figure of Christ and two angels in the upper panel. At his feet is the bountiful earth, personified as a woman in an attitude of supplication. A general bringing a small figure of *Nikê* (Victory) to the emperor occupies the left-hand panel, the right panel being lost. The

[13] H. H. Scullard, *The elephant in the Greek and Roman world* (London: Thames and Hudson, 1974), e.g. pp. 23–4.

[14] Piotr Bienkowski, *Les Celtes dans les arts mineurs gréco-romains* (Cracow: Polish Academy, 1928), pp. 228–42, and Rolf Michael Schneider, *Bunte Barbaren: Orientalenstatuen aus farbigem Marmor in der römischen Repräsentationskunst* (Worms: Werner, 1986), pp. 156–8. On the Trajanic connection, Erika Simon, 'Barbarenkopf', in *Führer durch die öffentlichen Sammlungen klassischer Altertümer in Rom*, vol. II, ed. Wolfgang Helbig, 4th edn (Tübingen: Wasmuth, 1966), p. 718 no. 1957; cf. *Ancient Rome and India*, ed. Rosa Maria Cimino (Delhi: Munshiram Manoharlal, 1994), pp. 126–8. For cirrus knots on Boddhisatva figures see, e.g., *The crossroads of Asia: transformations in image and symbol in the art of ancient Afghanistan and Pakistan*, ed. Elizabeth Errington and Joe Cribb (Cambridge: Ancient India and Iran Trust, 1992), pp. 199–229.

[15] Schneider, *Bunte Barbaren*, p. 156

[16] Simon, 'Barbarenkopf', 718, referring to Cass. Dio 68.15.1.

[17] See Chapter 4, section I.4.

Figure 4 Marble head with cirrus knot, Trajanic. Villa Borghese, Rome.

Figure 5 Barberini ivory, sixth century AD. Louvre, Paris.

lowest panel contains a number of well-known motifs from Roman art. At the bottom right there are two men stooped in gestures of obeisance, their legs covered and upper bodies naked; the heads of both are covered with fabric, and in each case two horn-like objects stand erect from the front of the head. One of them carries a large elephant tusk over his left shoulder. They alternate with an elephant, its trunk pointed upward as if to honour the emperor, and a panther or tiger. Together these features suggest that Indians are being represented. They are balanced in the lower panel with two other 'barbarian' men, who also approach the emperor in reverence, but the difference is that these are trousered and wear Phrygian-style caps, which would link them with the Mesopotamian world, i.e. western rather than southern Asia.[18] If the men at the lowest panel do indeed represent Indians, then there is a coincidence of subject-matter (which includes an ivory tusk being offered to the emperor, and an elephant) and artistic medium. In both the sarcophagi and the ivory, humans are in close proximity to animals, but distinct from them.[19] The animals themselves are exotic but realistic, without being monsters in the Plinian sense.

I.3. Personification

Third, India is presented as a personification. The two instances here, if the identification is correct, are the great hunt mosaic of the Villa Filosofiana near Piazza Armerina in Sicily, and a silver platter from Lampsacus now at the National Museum in Istanbul. These date from the early fourth and the sixth centuries respectively.

The mosaic at the Villa Filosofiana contains a dark-skinned woman reclining or sitting on a rock, half-naked and unshod.[20] She holds an elephant tusk in her left hand, and in her right hand a bouquet. A common feature in personifications of this type is the cornucopia, the horn of plenty, which the tusk in this mosaic effectively replaces.[21] On her right is an elephant (again, whether African or Indian is a matter for debate), and on her left a tiger; above the elephant is a phoenix. This bird presents a difficulty, for in Greek and Roman thinking the phoenix was usually linked with Egypt, where Pharaonic art had long since represented it;[22] on the other hand,

[18] See Anthony Cutler's article, 'Barberini ivory', in *Oxford dictionary of Byzantium* (Oxford: Clarendon, 1991), with further bibliography; cf. Thomas F. Matthews, *Byzantium from antiquity to the Renaissance* (New York: Abrams, 1998), p. 42.

[19] The same is true, of course, for other ivory representations of elephants. Whether they were thought to come from Africa or India, they still connote the expanse of empire, and hence the universal reach of imperial power. Thus, the ivory diptych (probably fifth century), sometimes linked with the Symmachus, shows the emperor, on his way to apotheosis, drawn in a carriage by four elephants.

[20] Andrea Carandini *et al.*, *Filosofiana, the villa of Piazza Armerina: the image of a Roman aristocrat at the time of Constantine* (Palermo: Flaccovio, 1982), esp. p. 230, arguing that the woman represents India.

[21] Marcel le Glay, 'Africa', *LIMC* I.1 (1981), 250–5, at 254 (arguing for the identification of the figure as Africa).

[22] Both Pliny (*HN* 10.4) and Tacitus (*Ann.* 6.28) show the link in Roman thought between the phoenix and the sun. See further Rainer Vollkommer , 'Phoinix III', *LIMC* VIII.1 (1997), 987–9, and R. van den Broek, *The myth of the Phoenix, according to classical and early Christian traditions* (Leiden: Brill, 1972).

Figure 6 Personification of India, apse of Great Hunt mosaic, Villa Filosofiana, Piazza Armerina, Sicily, fourth century AD.

the elephant most immediately evokes a link with the Roman province of Africa, as distinct from Egypt.[23] It is possible that the wealthy owner of the villa was involved in the hunting of big game on the nearby African continent and its importation to Rome, and it is in this way that the theme of the great hunt mosaic (and the smaller hunt mosaic) has been explained. But, in the case of the female figure adjoining the great hunt mosaic, the identification with Africa is not convincing, given that the characteristic feature of personifications of Africa was the presence of an elephant tusk, horns or ears on the head of the female figure.[24] Here we do have a tusk, but it is cradled rather than worn on the head. Further, the tiger as a species is not to be found in any part of Africa, and in Roman art was typically associated with India and other parts.[25] It seems then that the elements of the mosaic point in different directions within the eastern Mediterranean and beyond. Against such a background and with these qualifications, it is quite plausible to link the female figure with India.

[23] Le Glay, 'Africa', gives several such instances; cf. Scullard, *Elephant*.

[24] Le Glay, 'Africa'.

[25] On the geographic distribution of the tiger, see *DNP*, 'Tiger'. Again, an Achaemenid link is visible when Ael. (*NA* 15.14) speaks of tigers as royal gifts.

Figure 7 Personification of India, silver platter, Istanbul, sixth century AD. Courtesy of the Deutsches Archäologisches Institut, Berlin.

The silver platter presents similar difficulties. It was found in Lampsacus, in a basement together with several silver spoons carrying the inscription *Hagiou Georgiou* ('belonging to [the church of] Saint George'), so that we may imagine that the silverware once belonged to a church by that name. It depicts a female figure leaning or seated on elephant tusks. In her left hand she holds a bow, and her right is raised, the palm opened outward. Over curled hair she wears a turban, from which two sharp objects protrude.[26]

[26] The turban, at least, can be explained with reference to an ancient Roman text. Curtius says the following of Indian clothing: *corpora usque ad pedes carbaso uelant, soleis pedes, capita linteis uinciunt* ('They cover their bodies down to the feet with fabric, and wear sandals on their feet and linen

She wears a richly embroidered robe that leaves her right breast uncovered, a necklace, and bracelets on her arms and wrists. Surrounding her are a parrot and a guinea-fowl, two monkeys (both of which have neck-bands, suggesting domestication), and at the bottom two men accompanied by large cats on leashes. These men are themselves wearing loose-fitting robes, turbans with two antenna-like objects sticking upward from them.[27]

The substance of the platter is richly varied: a gold rim surrounds the platter, and each of the surrounding images is gilded, except for the guinea-fowl that is gilded merely in his feet and head. The woman's body is covered with finely worked black enamel; some of the enamel has come off the arms, revealing the original silver, roughened so that the enamel would hold fast. Her robes, jewellery, footwear and headwear are gilded, as are the tusks and her bow.

The Indianness of this artifact has never been disputed since it came to the attention of scholars, not least on the grounds of the animals. The parrot is linked with India; the monkeys could be Indian; so too the cats, which have been identified as a tiger and a panther respectively, by their coats and the shape of their heads. Aelian in fact speaks of tamed monkeys and panthers in India (*Historia animalium* 15.14), and the tiger is generally associated with the subcontinent. The one anomaly is the guinea-fowl, which as a species is unique to Africa; but on this platter its African provenance is overshadowed by its Indian connections.[28] Part of the problem in making the identification stems from the fact that personification in Roman art was commonly used for provinces:[29] if it is indeed India that is represented here, that would make it an exception, the consequences of which will require explanation below.

One reason for stressing the Indian connections of these personifications is their thematic resonance with Indian art. A particularly widespread motif in Kushan art is that of the woman and tree, known as the Salabhanjika (named in part for the sal tree).[30] An example of this is the Vedika pillar with Yaksini, found at Bharhut in Madhya Pradesh and dating to the Sunga

on their heads': 8.9.21). *Carbasus* is the general word for fine fabric, and here may be used in contradistinction to linen to indicate a cotton fabric: Graeven, 'Darstellungen', 206, with reference to Strabo 15.1.71 C719.

27 These protruding objects invite comparison with the two men at the bottom of the Barberini ivory.

28 In so far as the figure suggests fertility, it recalls Bacchus' status as an agricultural divinity in early Italian religion: it shows nature at its most fecund, in ways that the elder Pliny or Strabo would have understood.

29 J. M. C. Toynbee, *The Hadrianic school: a chapter in the history of Greek art* (Cambridge University Press, 1934).

30 Ananda K. Coomaraswamy, *Yaksas* (New Delhi: Munshiram Manoharlal, 1971), pp. 32–6.

period, roughly 100–80 BC.[31] Yakshi (or yaksinis), like their male counterparts called yaksas, are localised, lesser tutelary divinities, nature spirits that were part of early Indic cults and later incorporated into Buddhism. Their features are linked with fertility and abundance and 'may connote both their own procreativity and that of nature in general'.[32] In this case, the tree-touching gesture awakens nature from its dormant state and makes the tree bloom.[33] Typically, these voluptuous female figures wear heavy earrings, bangles, armlets and necklaces.

Both of the Roman artifacts exhibit some of the features of the Salabhanjika. The Piazza Armerina mosaic has the woman beneath two trees, grasping one with her right hand. On the platter, the woman's left hand is entwined with the long bow, which may here be serving the same function as a tree; the palm of her right hand is pointed outward, in a gesture similar to that of the Yaksini holding the branch. Both of the women are wearing necklaces and bangles. Coincidences of this kind may be small in themselves but their aggregative effect is substantial, especially when the two personifications have been thought on other grounds to denote India.

I.4. Christian topography

A tradition that stands out from the three above is that linked with the *Christian topography* of Cosmas Indicopleustes. The text survives in three manuscripts, which contain some striking illustrations of South Asian animals. The unusual quality of these miniatures matches the strangeness of the text itself, a text arguing that the earth is in the shape of the Tabernacle mentioned in the book of *Genesis*.[34] In this respect it is an early and striking example of what has been called 'Mosaic ethnology'.[35]

The manuscripts by which Cosmas' text is reconstructed are three in number, one from the ninth century and two from the eleventh century. All three contain illustrations, though they differ as to what is illustrated;

[31] This artifact of reddish-brown sandstone is now to be found at the Indian Museum in Calcutta: Susan L. Huntington, *The art of ancient India: Buddhist, Hindu, Jain* (New York: Weatherhill, 1985), p. 69; cf. Coomaraswamy, *Yaksas*, pp. 5–6.

[32] Huntington, *Art of ancient India*, p. 68.

[33] Stanistaw J. Czuma, *Kushan sculpture: images from early India*, with Rekha Morris (Cleveland: Cleveland Museum of Art, 1985), p. 99.

[34] For a scholarly edition of the work, including reproductions of the miniatures, see Wanda Wolska-Conus (ed.), Cosmas Indicopleustes, *Topographie chrétienne*, 3 vols. (Paris: Presses Universitaires, 1968).

[35] Trautmann, *Aryans*, pp. 41–61.

Figure 8 Yakshi (female figure), red sandstone, second century AD, Victoria and Albert Museum, London.

other cycles also are contained in these manuscripts.[36] It is clear from Cosmas' references to illustrations that his original text contained images. Furthermore, there are strong grounds to see the impact of classical art on the tenth century especially, that is, in the period following the Byzantine iconoclastic movement between 717 and 842.[37] All this gives prima facie grounds for assuming that the existing illustrations reflect Cosmas' original manuscript.

Predominant among these miniatures are animals, though there are a few humans and plants as well. The pattern throughout this book of the *Christian topography* is that first there comes a miniature, then a description by Cosmas. The animals include a rhinoceros, bull-stag (*taurelaphos*), wild ox (*agriobous*), unicorn (*monoceros*) and a hog-deer (*choerelaphos*).[38] Further, there is a giraffe that is vertically challenged (11.4), and a very horse-like hippopotamus (literally 'river-horse', 11.9), both of which suggest that the artist had no personal knowledge of the animal concerned, despite Cosmas' claims to the contrary. There is a unicorn, but otherwise all the animals are recognisable creatures of the real world, rather than monsters.[39]

Apart from the animals there are also humans: one man is pictured below a coconut tree, wearing a skirt-like garment that may represent a kind of *dhoti*, and holding a scythe; another between a pepper-tree and a coconut palm; another, rather damaged illustration, shows a man shooting a musk-deer. In the case of the most clearly visible of these, the man exhibits the kind of coiled hair usually identified with Africans. Some attention is paid to social organisation: the story of the merchant Sopatrus implies an openness and accessibility of Sri Lanka, and its intelligibility to the Roman world. Cosmas also reflects an awareness of Christian missionary activity.[40] If this is true, it would not be surprising that Cosmas' description of Sri Lanka

[36] The mss are the *Codex Vaticanus Graecus* 699 (9th century); *Laurentianus Plut.* IX.28; *Sinaiticus Graecus* 1186. See Paul Huber, *Heilige Berge: Sinai, Athos, Golgota – Ikonen, Fresken, Miniaturen*, 2nd edn (Zurich: Benziger, 1982), pp. 56–115, esp. 109–12.

[37] Foremost in developing the idea of a 'Macedonian Renaissance', under the emperors Leo VI the Wise and Constantine VII Porphyrogenitus, has been the work of Kurt Weitzmann. See, e.g., his 'The classical in Byzantine art as a mode of individual expression', in *Byzantine Art, an [sic] European art: lectures*, n.e. (Athens: Department of Antiquities, 1966), pp. 148–77; and his articles in *Studies in classical and Byzantine manuscript illumination*, ed. H. L. Kessler (University of Chicago Press, 1971), esp. pp. 126–50 and 151–75. For a reconsideration of some of the same issues, see Anthony Cutler, 'Originality as a cultural phenomenon', in his *Byzantium, Italy and the north: papers on cultural relations* (London: Pindar, 2000), pp. 26–45.

[38] 11.1, 3, 5, 7, 8.

[39] It is telling that the least realistically imaginable animal described gets the careful comment that Cosmas has not seen a specimen: the μονόκερως, which we might translate as unicorn (11.7).

[40] ἐκκλησία, κληρικοί, πιστοί, 3.65.

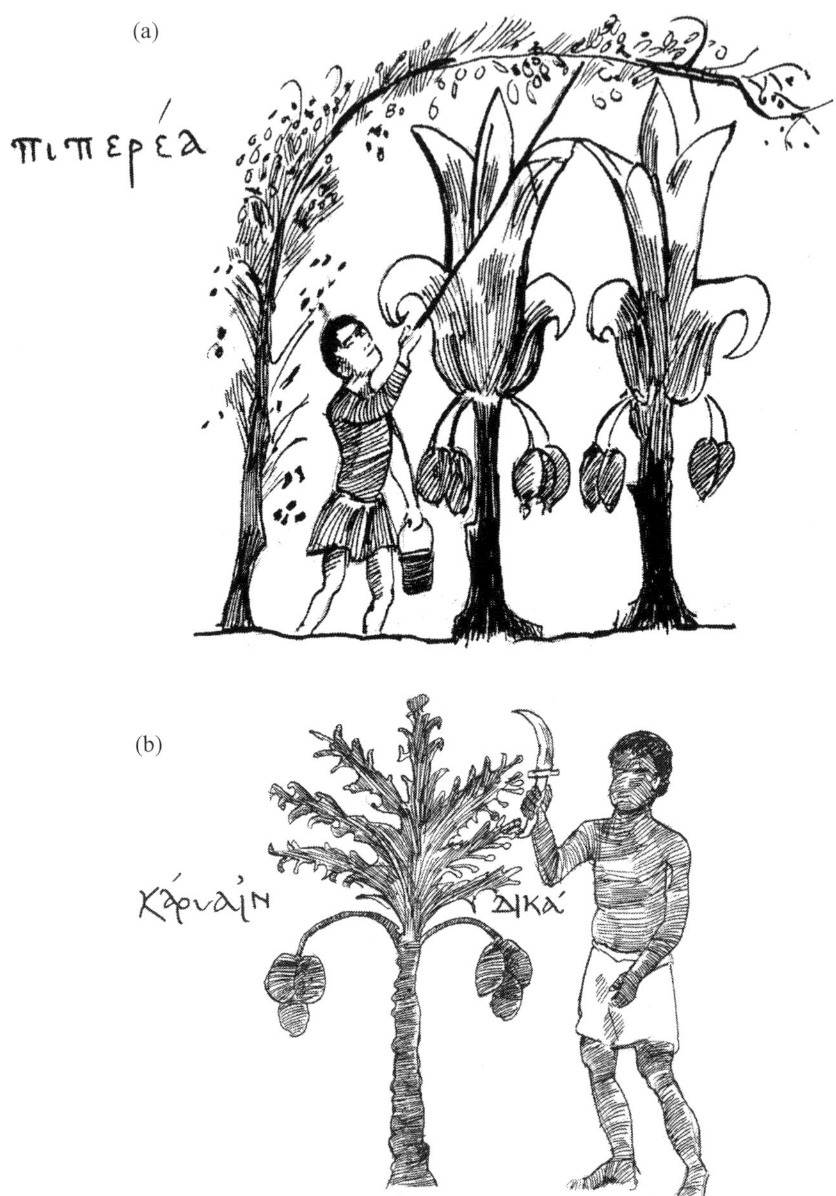

Figure 9 Cosmas Indicopleustes, manuscript miniatures, eleventh century. Sketches by Alexander Hollmann.

(c)

(d)

Figure 9 (*cont.*)

is one that emphasises and increases its familiarity to a Greek-speaking readership in the Mediterranean.

With Cosmas we are thus not talking narrowly about the subcontinent itself but about Sri Lanka; the visual tradition linked with his work focuses on animals rather than monsters particularly, but also includes some humans engaged in perfectly everyday activities.

II. A TYPOLOGY OF INDIAS

The analysis that emerges from this survey is to some extent already clear. It is possible to divide it into three categories: together, these may be understood as contexts within which India was understood by Greeks and Romans. Indeed, it appears that there was no single, canonical way of presenting Indians; rather there were several ways, each corresponding to visual codes already well established in other, non-Indian contexts. In other words, the categories offered may be considered processes of transference from the well known to the less well known, from the Mediterranean pond to vistas beyond. These categories or processes overlap, as will soon be evident, but equally they shed some light on the ways in which visual codes could and did generate meaning, and, by these familiarising processes, negotiated between artist, patron and viewer in the social sphere.

The obvious point at which to begin is the monstrous paradigm that places India on the edges of the earth. This has its origins in the earliest Greek accounts of India, indeed in some of the earliest Greek historiography, with its concern for ethnography and geography. The conflation of humans and animals is central to this paradigm. This type of visual representation is especially belated, in view of the time separating Scylax and other early Indographers on the one hand, and the many medieval images on the other.

Secondly, the mosaic and the platter point to a provincial paradigm of India. This is in some ways a surprise, given that India never was a Roman province and, given our hindsight today, never came close to becoming one (see further Chapter 5). But, for current purposes, this historical fact is less significant than the nature of imperial self-presentation. The same process of representation used for Africa in the mid-first century BC, and for other Roman provinces in the first two centuries AD, served the subcontinent in the fourth and sixth centuries. This connection goes some way towards accounting for the femaleness of the figures: the personification of lands and cities tends to be female, whereas rivers are usually represented as male figures. This is itself part of a phenomenon whereby Roman provincial conquest is symbolically represented in terms of sexual dominance, even rape.[41]

Underlying the image of India as a province is the issue of imperial ideology, and particularly the power of Alexander as a precedent.[42] As further investigation will show, it is no accident that the personifications of India, as seen on the mosaic and platter, effectively present it as a province. The principle of military conquest is implicit equally in the Barberini ivory, emphasised by the presence, in the lowest of its three panels, of adult men stooped in gestures of obeisance. In that case, the emperor Justinian, seated on his horse, has his feet touched by a woman (representing earth) and his lance by a non-Roman (thus marked by trousers and headgear), both of them in supplication. Seen against this comparandum, neither of the two personifications overtly presents India in an attitude of subjugation. In this respect these figures do not match, for example, the mid-first-century AD relief from Aphrodisias: there, the emperor Claudius, in heroic nudity, seizes the hair of Britannia as she lies on the ground, as if about to strike her with his sword. Whereas Britannia here is represented as an Amazon, India in the two images shows no explicitly martial context.[43]

Thirdly and finally, there is an eastern or Indian Ocean paradigm. The decisive point here is the overlap in elements associated with Africa and those of India. In light of histories and archaeologies on the Indian Ocean as a connected zone, it comes as no surprise that northeastern Africa or Ethiopia should be considered within the same geographic unit as the subcontinent;[44] nor indeed in light of Homer (*Odyssey* 1.22–24).[45] Indeed, we should make a virtue out of the supposed confusion or conflation of India and Africa: rather than being purely a mistake,[46] it emerges here as a means of comprehending the unfamiliar with reference to the known. On

41 Whittaker, *Rome and its frontiers*, pp. 115–43, linking the symbol and the practice of rape.

42 E.g., Trajan in Cass. Dio 68.29.1, on which see further discussion in Chapter 5, section I.5 below.

43 K. T. Erim, 'A new relief showing Claudius and Britannia from Aphrodisias', *Britannia* 13 (1982), 277–81. Several other artifacts of the second and third centuries AD, especially coins, show Britannia as a province; some of them show subjected Britannia in relation to Roman triumph, e.g., a medallion from Trier (AD 296), in which the emperor Constantius raises Britannia from her kneeling, suppliant position. See further Martin Henig, 'Britannia', *LIMC* III.1 (1986), 167–9.

44 Notably, though for a later period, K. N. Chaudhuri, *Trade and civilisation in the Indian Ocean: an economic history from the rise of Islam to 1750* (Cambridge University Press, 1985); André Wink, 'From the Mediterranean to the Indian Ocean: medieval history in geographic perspective', *CSSH* 44.3 (2002), 416–45.

45 'But the god [Apollo] had gone to the far-off Aethiopians – / the Aethiopians, remotest of people, divided asunder, / some where the sun sets, and some where he rises.' Cf. Chapter 1, section I.1 above.

46 Philip Mayerson, 'A confusion of Indias: Asian India and African India in the Byzantine sources', *JAOS* 113 (1993), 169–74. See also Schneider, *L'Éthiopie et L'Inde*.

the basis of this paradigm, there is no need to make a hard-and-fast decision between an African, Egyptian and Indian identity for the Piazza Armerina woman. When scholars do make such a choice, the decision rests merely on the emphasising of one aspect at the expense of others. More compelling than any such choice is the idea that the figure is a *mélange orientale*, her Indian features no less present than others, and thus signifying a more generalised east, a land that was distant but still comprehensible.

Within this paradigm, it is Cosmas who gives India a sense of specificity that is lacking in other writers. On the one hand, this specificity is not surprising: on theological grounds, he argues that the universe contains no antipodes, against the Aristotelian philosopher John Philoponus. It suited Cosmas' cosmological purposes to present an India that was not marvellous in the normal sense. This is underlined by the fact that he was himself a trader who travelled to the subcontinent as well as along the east coast of Africa, and he was in a position to say that he had seen, traded and even eaten some of the animals he describes. It should be remembered from the Piazza Armerina mosaic that animals were themselves objects of luxury consumption in the Roman world, most notably in public displays. Cosmas' India, like that in the *Periplus of the Erythraean Sea*, is part of a trading zone that stretched all the way to the Red Sea and the African coast.

III. CONCLUSION

It is hard to explain why visual representations of India should be so few and far between. One possible line of argument is that the canon of classical iconography was already established by the Hellenistic period, when marvellous creatures became so much a part of literature. If this is indeed the case, artifacts add a further dimension to the phenomenon identified by Dihle concerning sources of knowledge about India.[47] Just as a literary canon of information about India had been established by the Hellenistic period, and allowed no room for the new and different information from traders, so an iconographic canon had been established in the classical period, before the Hellenistic concept of marvellous India took root.

But to what extent is it possible to speak of a visual canon for representing India? It would be wrong to overestimate the coherency of such a canon. Indeed, assessment of the evidence in this chapter leads to a conclusion that distinguishes it in extent from the texts considered earlier, namely that there are significantly different Indias within the visual traditions of

[47] Dihle, 'Conception'.

Greco-Roman antiquity. No single, canonical India has emerged here, but rather a number of images that differ vastly from each other, belonging to different visual discourses. Despite the paucity of evidence, it is tempting to see in this variety a combination of positive and negative views, much like the mixture of admiration and contempt that has been seen in the highly differentiated set of Roman images of Parthians.[48] Such a conclusion prepares us to consider Roman contexts for thinking about India, contexts that relate variously to commodities, to imperial expansion or to holiness. The variety we have seen between the three paradigms here confirms the plurality that can be identified in the literary texts, between the Indus Valley region of the Alexander historians on the one hand, and the western coast known to those concerned with the monsoon trade. Given that sea-travel was quicker and cheaper than long-distance overland travel, there is every reason why Cosmas' mercantile, southern India and Sri Lanka should have a more human face and, in this sense, should more closely approximate the Mediterranean world than does the Indus valley.

By way of a coda let us dwell briefly on one aspect of the ethnographic record that seems to be entirely missing from the visual: the wise men, the Brahmans and Gymnosophists of Alexander histories and the Alexander Romance tradition. Though these made such impression on Greek and Roman minds, they evidently do not occur in their representations of the subcontinent. Again, there is a chronological issue here in the formation of visual traditions: it appears that the image of India as a place of holiness postdates that of India as a place of marvel, and hence there is no visual tradition for depicting Indian holy men. This absence is all the more striking when we compare later artifacts, such as the eighteenth-century Mughal scene illustrating the interview between Alexander and the philosophers (who here look effeminate rather than grizzled old men); or in the nineteenth-century British-made imperial monument to Warren Hastings now at Calcutta. On one side of Hastings is a Muslim and on the other a bookish Hindu, whom we might understand as a distant but direct descendant of the philosophers met by Alexander.[49] In its own way, this statue may be taken as emblematic of the contrasting dynamics of continuity and change in western visual representations of India.

48 Schneider, 'Faszination', surveying a much richer body of evidence.

49 Barbara Groseclose, 'Imag(in)ing Indians', *Art History* 13.4 (1990), 488–515.

PART III

Contexts of a discourse

CHAPTER 4

Commodities

At some point in the mid-90s AD, the poet Statius laments the death of Priscilla, wife of the emperor Domitian's courtier Abascantus. He praises her morals by showing her imperviousness to the delights of the east:

> Were you to offer her Babylonian riches or heavy Lydian treasure or alluring wealth of Indians, Chinese or Arabs, she would have preferred to die unsullied and in chaste poverty, to sacrifice her life so as to save her honour. (*Silvae* 5.1.60–63) [1]

As this passage reveals, the moral high ground was to be gained by repudiating eastern luxuries, whether they came from Babylonia, Lydia, India, China or Arabia. Statius is adapting a familiar trope: implicit in his rhetoric of praise for Priscilla is the conspicuousness of that repudiation, what might be called an inverted case of *fare lo splendido*. For all its clichéd nature, the extract is especially interesting for three related reasons. Firstly, it conflates various Asian lands, from Lydia in Asia Minor (the west coast of modern Turkey) to China, and thus informs us about mental maps of Statius' world. This tendency is paralleled in other passages and deserves our close attention. Secondly, it suggests that specific goods may be associated with specific places: thus '*Lydian* treasure', much as in other texts silk is associated with China, or pepper with India. To take another example, the elder Pliny explicitly states that perfumes are frequently named from their countries of origin (13.4), as he goes on to illustrate in detail. Thirdly, the extract points to the close embrace of economic and cultural aspects of Roman civilisation. It raises the question, can and should those aspects be kept apart?

This chapter will explore some of the problems to arise in the passage: in particular, it will interrogate commodities and the discourse about them, as one way of examining what India meant to ancient Romans. As such, this is an essay in cognitive geography much more than it is an account of trade

[1] *si Babylonos opes, Lydae si pondera gazae/Indorumque dares Serumque Arabumque potentes/diuitias, mallet cum paupertate pudica/ intemerata mori uitamque rependere famae.*

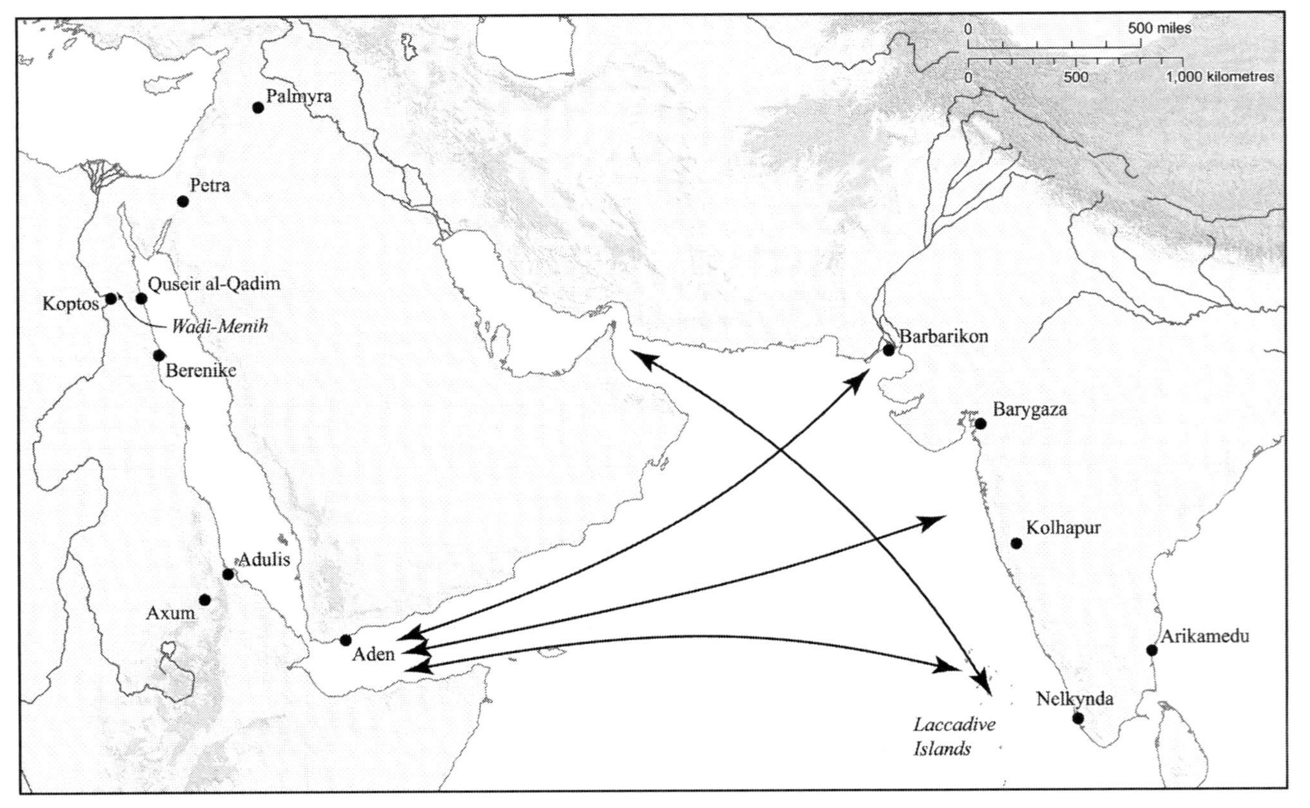

Map 3 Trade route with monsoons

between South Asia and the Mediterranean world.[2] Focusing on the period of roughly the late first century BC to the sixth century AD we shall trace the consumption of Indian goods, or rather, of *supposedly* Indian goods in the Roman world. If, as the passage from Statius suggests, Romans tended to identify goods with their supposed places of origin, the trend seems particularly strong in the case of India. On this model, we shall have to inquire how distinctive its goods were, and hence how distinctive a place it proves to be by implication. More abstractly, by what processes was it possible for Statius to group together those five lands into a generalised, undifferentiated east? It is already clear that these questions will require us to scrutinise the notion of the exotic as applied by Romans to India. Throughout this, we are dealing with an India that slips and slides on the one hand between the physical land that can today be visited or found on a modern map, and the wonderland of ancient (and modern) thought. Ultimately, through commodities linked with it, it is India's place in the *orbis terrarum* that we seek to outline more exactly.

I. OBJECTS OF EXCHANGE AND THE MATERIALITY OF DISTANCE

The emperor Justinian's *Digest*, the synthetic work of Roman law promulgated in AD 533, contains a passage which offers the following list of 'articles subject to duty' upon entry into Alexandria:

> Cinnamon, long pepper, white pepper, *folium pentasphaerum* (unidentified spice), barbary leaf, putchuk (*costum* and *costamomum*), spikenard, Turian cassia, cassia bark, myrrh, amomum, ginger, cinnamon leaf, *aroma Indicum* (unspecified Indian spice), galbanum, asafoetida, aloe-wood, barberry, astragalus, Arabian onyx, cardamom, cinnamon bark, fine linen, Babylonian furs, Parthian furs, ivory, Indian iron, raw cotton, *lapis universus* (unspecified precious stone), pearls, sardonyx, bloodstones, *hyacinthus* (precious stone, perhaps aquamarine), emeralds, diamonds, lapis lazuli, turquoise, beryls, tortoise-stone, Indian or Assyrian drugs, raw silk, garments made completely or partly from silk, painted hangings, fine linen fabrics, silk yarn, Indian eunuchs, lions and lionesses, leopards, panthers, purple cloth, cloth woven from sheep's wool, *orchil* (rouge), Indian hair. (39.4.16.7)

This list of fifty-four items is attributed to Aelius Marcianus, a jurist of the early third century; the very fact that it is quoted suggests that it still

[2] More narrowly economic aspects are now covered by Ball, *Rome in the east*, pp. 123–33; Gary K. Young, *Rome's eastern trade: international commerce and imperial policy, 31 BC – AD 305* (London: Routledge, 2001), pp. 28–32 and *passim*; Whittaker, *Rome and its frontiers*, pp. 163–80.

had some relevance in the sixth century.[3] Whereas some of the objects are specified as 'Indian', not all of these objects will have come from South Asia, by any means. Most will have come from the greater Red Sea area, including the eastern Mediterranean, the Nile Valley and Arabian peninsula. Nonetheless, the list does give an idea of the kinds of luxury objects traded via one of the Roman world's most important entrepôts, Alexandria; it also indicates the kinds of items subjected to taxation on the part of the state.

If we wish to understand both the denotative and the connotative senses of India on the strength of objects linked with it, we should begin with the objects themselves, many of them emerging in the list quoted above. Let us start in concrete fashion by considering those objects which we know to have come from South Asia, as well as those which ancient people thought to have originated there. Drawing substantially on archaeology, I focus here on objects found within the Mediterranean world itself, especially in Italy, rather than those found at intermediary points such as the Red Sea coast (see section III.2 below). Further, the rich material and documentary remains from ancient Bactria will be bracketed off from the present inquiry as tangential to the question at hand.[4] As will become clear in the course of these pages, there are strong reasons to begin in a minimalistic fashion and only then to broaden the focus, rather than to take too broad a view from the start.

I.1. Spices and aromatics

Spices are a major kind of commodity to emerge from Marcian's list, including pepper, ginger and other unidentified items, which may have come ultimately from India. These bring us not only to a problem of identification, but also to one of definition. In common parlance, 'spices' today typically refer to the products of tropical trees, and are typically used as condiments to fine-tune the taste of food. If we turn to the Greco-Roman world, neither is the case, or at least not predominantly so. First, as the list itself shows, there is considerable overlap in use between tropical spices in our sense, such as pepper and cinnamon, and others which do not necessarily come from tropical climates, e.g., terebinth, rue, cumin or saffron.[5] What is

[3] A. H. M. Jones, 'The Asian trade in antiquity', in *The Roman economy: studies in ancient economic and administrative history* (Oxford: Blackwell, 1974), pp. 140–50, at 140.

[4] Cf. Chapter 1, section II.3 above.

[5] These are mentioned in Roman texts, and came respectively from Syria, Greece, Egypt and Cilicia: J. Innis Miller, *The spice trade of the Roman empire* (Oxford: Clarendon, 1969), pp. 110–18.

more, we see other vegetable products that we would call herbs being used in many of the same contexts. Secondly, the ancient use of spices was by no means limited to cuisine, especially if we are to give them their inclusive, ancient sense. This is not the place for a history of spices in antiquity, but nonetheless several familiar points need to be raised as we stick closely to the ancient uses of spices.[6]

Sources for the existence and use of spices in the Mediterranean are richly varied, and texts such as this are only one kind. Most spectacularly, shipwrecks from the Bronze Age show that pepper was being imported into the Mediterranean as early as the second millennium BC, probably by the Phoenicians originally. Greek literary texts beginning with Homer reveal the use of aromatics in offering sacrifices to the gods.[7] The earliest Greek works to mention pepper are the gynaecological treatises attributed to Hippocrates: at one point the author glosses the spice as an 'Indian drug' (*On women's diseases* 1.81). Its typical use in these medical texts is for disorders of the eyes, mixed into an ointment. Theophrastus' work *On odours* makes it clear that pepper was among the spices known and used in the later fourth/early third centuries. Though he uses the loanword in naming it (*peperi*), he makes no explicit mention of its Indian origin, in which respect he differs from the Hippocratic text. Theophrastus' treatise is in fact central to any analysis of the social meaning of spices in the ancient world: it makes clear that they were used for perfume-powders (*aromata*), cosmetics, incense (*thumiamata*), and antidotes to poison (*theriaca*).

But it is in three very different texts of the first century AD that we have the most extensive evidence for the use of spices. These begin with the army physician Dioscorides, whose *Materia medica* (*c.* AD 65), written in Greek, illustrates the pharmacological uses. Secondly, Apicius, who lived under Augustus and Tiberius, composed a series of gourmet recipes: texts continued to be collected around his name until late antiquity. Of 478 recipes contained in the Apician corpus, almost all require some kind of spicing; so did certain preparations of wine. It mentions nine spices which

6 An important history of spices in Greco-Roman antiquity is Miller's *Spice trade*, especially the survey of pages 1–26. A problem with the later, more detailed part of the book is that it places too much emphasis on the identification of ancient literary references with modern botanical classification (on which, compare section V.2 below). See also Alfred Schmidt, 'Drogen', *RE* suppl. V (1931), pp. 172–82; Andrew Dalby, *Siren feasts: a history of food and gastronomy in Greece* (London: Routledge, 1996), pp. 137–42 and Dalby, *Empire of pleasures: luxury and indulgence in the Roman world* (London: Routledge, 2000), pp. 178–200.

7 Marcel Detienne, *The gardens of Adonis: spices in Greek mythology* (Hassocks: Harvester, 1977); Marcel Detienne and Jean-Pierre Vernant, *The cuisine of sacrifice among the Greeks* (Chicago: University of Chicago Press, 1989).

likely came from south or south-east Asia, namely pepper, ginger, putchuk (*costum*), *folium* (nard-leaf?), *malabathrum* (cinnamon leaves or their oil), spikenard, asafoetida, sesame seed and turmeric; the rest, a much longer list, probably came from within the bounds of the empire, or at least from less far afield. Pepper is by far the favoured spice, being used even in sweet dishes.[8] Thirdly, the elder Pliny devotes books 12 and 13 of his *Natural history* to trees, many of which are spice-bearing. Proceeding region by region, he categorises spices and aromatics according to their provenance. Thus, whereas Theophrastus speaks in general terms about spices, Pliny provides a geography of them, however tentatively; as I shall argue below, this difference should be explained with reference to the increased map-mindedness of Pliny's age.[9]

It is thus very likely that many of the spices consumed in the Roman world came from India: the most eminent case is provided by pepper, both long pepper and black pepper, *Piper longum* and *Piper nigrum*, which are native to northern and southern India respectively. Beyond pepper, an Indian origin is likely also for other spices, such as aloe-wood (*Aquilaria agallocha*, native to the Himalayan region of modern Bhutan) turmeric (*Curcuma domestica*, southeast Asian), and cardamom (*Elettaria cardamomum*, native to Kerala and Tamil Nadu). But in most cases, neither modern botany nor ancient texts allow any easy geography of spices: thus the ginger taxed at Alexandria or served at Trimalchio's dinner-party might come just as easily from Java or Thailand as from India, or in fact from a combination of those, if transported via the subcontinent.[10] It is impossible to make the distinction, nor is it necessarily important to do so: what matters, for current purposes, is to establish that such a commodity was known and valued in the Roman world.

In some cases it is not easy to distinguish between spices of Indian origin from those coming from Arabia or east Africa or southeast Asia. Notoriously, cinnamon is a case in point: Herodotus says it came from Dionysus' birthplace, by which he might mean India or else a more generalised east (3.111). At all events, he discusses it in relation to the Arabs, who are said to have obtained it from the Phoenicians. On the other hand, archaeobotanical evidence shows that it was native to Indonesia and Madagascar, perhaps even before it grew in South Asia.[11]

[8] Miller, *Spice trade*, pp. 6–10. [9] Cf. Nicolet, *Space, geography*. [10] Miller, *Spice trade*, pp. 53–7.

[11] Miller's discussion of this (*Spice trade*, pp. 153–72), emphasising far-flung commercial links, is suggestive but should be treated with caution. See Marie-François Boussac and Jean-François Salles (eds.), *A gateway from the eastern Meditteranean to India: the Red Sea in antiquity* (Delhi: Manohar, 2004), esp. the comment of Federico de Romanis, p. 24 n. 6).

But one larger point should be emphasised amidst the problems and uncertainties here. There is every indication that in Pliny's time more spices were available in the Mediterranean than ever before, so that his work should be thought of as providing much information that will have been new to his readers. Quite apart from variety, it seems likely that this period also witnessed the increased culinary use of spices, if the admittedly tendentious evidence of Pliny, Athenaeus and Apicius is taken on board. Rome, the ancient Mediterranean's consumer city par excellence, had developed an appetite for spices by the first century AD.

It is important to emphasise that the culinary use of spices was by no means the earliest or most important in the Greco-Roman world. In addition, it could be used as incense, in the production of perfumes, of medicines, or it could be used to flavour wine. In fact, its culinary use as seasoning (*condimentum*) was relatively small, perhaps the least of the categories mentioned. The first text specifically to mention these 'condiments' in the modern sense is that of Apicius.

In some ways pepper is the most important of the spices. Unlike others, it is limited in its origins to India; it has variety within itself, between white, black and long pepper; it enjoyed a wide range of uses, especially in cooking. The late-antique recipe book attributed to Apicius mentions pepper in most cases, even for desserts. So valuable was it that attempts would be made to 'adulterate' it by secretly compounding it with dried, ground juniper berries (Pliny 12.26–28). In fact, it is a standard part of Pliny's description of any one spice to say that it can be adulterated by some particular substitute; it is fair to conclude that such manipulation was common practice. Archaeological evidence for its domestic use as condiments is provided by pepper shakers found in various parts of Italy.[12]

From some thirteen years after Pliny's death the city of Rome had its own spice quarter, the *horrea piperatoria* built by the emperor Domitian in AD 92.[13] The continuing status of pepper as a luxury item well into late antiquity is underlined by a striking statistic: in AD 408 when the city of Rome was blockaded by the Visigoths under Alaric, the Senate offered him, together with 5,000 lb of gold, 30,000 lb of silver and other gifts, no less than 3,000 lb of pepper subject to his withdrawal (Zosimus *Historia nova* 5.35–42). Such a huge quantity is hard to square with what would otherwise seem to be declining proportions in this trade.

[12] D. E. Strong, *Greek and Roman gold and silver plate* (London: Methuen, 1966), pp. 154 and 178–80.

[13] L. J. Richardson, Jr, *A new topographical dictionary of ancient Rome* (Baltimore: Johns Hopkins University Press, 1992), pp. 194–5; M. Piranomonte, 'Horrea piperatoria', in *LTVR*, vol. III, pp. 45–6.

How is the availability of spices conceptualised, more generally? Spices are perhaps the commodity that is most open to the process of abstraction. In Pliny's *Natural history* the details and mechanics of their provenance are an important topic in their own right; but this is perhaps the exception. On the other hand, the *Periplus of the Erythraean Sea* may be closer to popular thinking, since quite naturally it views spices by their places of availability, that is, the coastal entrepôts of Kerala rather than the hills of Tamil Nadu.

I.2. Precious stones

The elder Pliny (AD 23–79), discussing precious stones in the thirty-seventh book of his *Natural history*, tells of several that he associates with India. Among the stones that are explicitly marked as Indian are the diamond, emerald, sardonyx, turquoise and onyx, to take merely those also mentioned by Marcian.[14] It is significant also that there are many undifferentiated references to precious stones from India, for example when the love elegist Propertius mentions the hair of the beloved, 'which an Indian gemstone ties at the crown' (2.22.10). Curtius Rufus' *History of Alexander* speaks in general terms of Indian rivers running with gold (8.9.18); Alexander, first contemplating the conquest of India, was aware of stories of its great wealth:

> The area [of India] was considered rich, not merely for its gold but also for its precious stones and pearls, and thought to strive more for the luxurious life than for grandeur. (8.5.3)[15]

Here Curtius implies that the natural resources of India corrupt the lives of its inhabitants. On the strength of passages such as this, it is tempting to include here the pearl in our consideration, though it is not a stone but an animal product. Here Pliny's treatment stands out for its explicit moralising, but he is not alone in this.

The fourth-century text purporting to be Alexander's letter to his former teacher Aristotle speaks at length of the precious stones and metals found in India. This text has no historical value for reconstructing Alexander's expedition, but it does tell us much about popular conceptions of India in the early fourth century: here India is a wonderland of unfathomable wealth, a late Roman Eldorado that was just at or beyond the farthest

[14] A few examples of each will suffice. Diamonds: Plin. *HN* 37.56; Avienus *Ora maritima* 1320, 1364; Aug. *de civ. D.* 21.4. Emeralds: *Letter of Alexander* 9, 69; Avienus 1324. Sardonyx: Plin. *HN* 37.86–89; Mart. 4.28.4; Isid. *Etym.* 16.8.4. Turquoise: Plin. *HN* 37.110; Isid. *Etym.* 16.7.10. Onyx: Plin. *HN* 37.90–91; Isid. *Etym.* 16.8.3.

[15] *diues regio habebatur non auro modo, sed gemmis quoque margaritisque, ad luxum magis quam ad magnificentiam exculta.*

possible limit of contemporary travel. It is worth noting that the list of stones in the supposed *Letter of Alexander to Aristotle* overlaps considerably with that in Pliny's *Natural history*, and hence the openness of Pliny's text to excerption and use in very different kinds of text.

The place of precious stones in Pliny's encyclopaedic work points us to one register of geographic information; it is another that we find in passing references within a poem. A playful epigram from the end of the fourth century centres on a mock competition between two artifacts purportedly from India:

> What is this stone? Amethyst. And this? I'm a wine-goblet – both of us from India but unequal in our powers: the amethyst boasts that it exceeds the strength of my liquid, but I boast that with my wine I can make drunk anyone who drinks me. (*Epigrammata Bobiensia* 20)[16]

Light-hearted as it is, it is in such a popular reference that we see the notional presence of India at the dinner-parties of élite Romans, an impression confirmed by other accounts of Roman dinner-parties (*cenae*) and the kinds of conversations held at them. Athenaeus' *Deipnosophists* ('Philosophers at dinner', *c.* AD 200) is a special case of this, given that much of the conversation-matter concerns the very business of eating and drinking.

This link between India and gemstones is important for late-antique geographies of India, in which it is seen to adjoin the earthly paradise.[17] Thus, when in the early fifth century AD Jerome speaks of India, he glosses it with a comment about the riches to be found there, and also the fantastic creatures guarding them:

> That's where the carbuncle, emerald, shining pearl and large pearl are to be found, all of which promote female display; and mountains of gold, which humans cannot come near because of dragons, griffins and monsters with enormous bodies, so that we can be aware how well avarice is guarded. (*Letters* 125.3)[18]

This passage reveals a combination of a fairy-tale landscape, complete with dragons, on the one hand, and social criticism on the other. Jarring as this might at first seem, it is a way of emphasising the directness of the link between distant India and Jerome's (east) Mediterranean world. Given that the monsoon trade in Jerome's time is unlikely to have reached the heights

[16] *Amethystus gemma: / quis lapis hic? – amethystus – at hic? – ego potor Iacchus, / ambo Indi, uerum uiribus impariles: // ille mei laticis iactat se uincere uires, / ast ego potantes ebrificare mero.*

[17] Lozovsky, *The earth*.

[18] *ibi nascitur carbunculus et smaragdus et margarita candentia et uniones, quibus nobilium feminarum ardet ambitio; montesque aurei, quos adire propter dracones et gryphas et immensorum corporum monstra hominibus impossibile est, ut ostendatur nobis quales custodes habeat avaritia.*

it had in Pliny's, the passage shows how central were precious stones to the memory of India.

I.3. Fabrics

Thirdly, let us consider fabrics. The *Periplus* makes several references to the import of silk from the subcontinent. In fact, it was one of only two products available at all of India's four major exporting regions (the other being nard): Muziris and Nelkynda on the southwest coast offered silk cloth (ὀθόνια Σηρικά, 56); Barbarikon in the Indus delta 'Chinese pelts, cloth and yarn' (Σιρικὰ δέρματα καὶ ὀθόνιον καὶ νῆμα Σιρικόν, 39); Barygaza silk cloth and yarn (49); and the Ganges delta the same, as well as silk floss (ἔριον . . . Σηρικόν, 64). There is some evidence that India had a silk industry of its own by this point,[19] but this is not to deny that silk was predominantly imported from China.[20] The Indian ports, it seems, functioned largely as clearing-houses for Chinese goods. There is earlier evidence for the island of Cos as a source of silk, and in fact the expression *Coae vestes* carries metaphorical force in the Augustan elegists as a symbol of luxury.[21] But, if we are to go by the silence of our sources, Cos was in the imperial period superseded by Asia as a source of silk. Strictly speaking, the two products were in any case different, as the Coan variety was not spun by caterpillars, and was of a less fine texture. When Diocletian's price edict of AD 301 mentions raw silk (μέταξα), we might take that as a reference to the Chinese product, not the Coan. What is clear is that Roman writers were not particularly curious about how silk was obtained. Major questions beset the issue of silk in the Roman world, for example the specifics of its price,[22] and the existence of a 'Silk Road' across central Asia, not least its supposed termini in east Asia and the eastern Mediterranean.[23]

The picture is further complicated by the fact that India itself, apart from serving as a point of distribution of Chinese silk, was also the source of cotton, that is to say less highly valued textiles as well. Herodotus associates

[19] L. Gopal, 'Textiles in ancient India', *JESHO* 4 (1961), 42–64.

[20] Manfred G. Raschke, 'New studies in Roman commerce with the east', *ANRW* II.9.2 (1978), 604–1378; E. J. W. Barber, *Prehistoric textiles* (Princeton University Press, 1991), pp. 30–2.

[21] Griffin, *Latin poets*, 1–31; Catharine Edwards, *The politics of immorality in ancient Rome* (Cambridge University Press, 1993), pp. 176–8.

[22] Raschke, 'New studies', 624–5, 726 n. 315

[23] The Central Asian excavations of Sir Aurel Stein played into western fascination with a 'Silk Road' supposedly reaching nearly across the breadth of Asia; see now Young, *Rome's eastern trade*, pp. 190–1. More skeptical are Millar, 'Caravan cities' and Ball, *Rome in the east*, pp. 138–9.

cotton exclusively with India (3.106). This is consonant with archaeobotanical finds, since fibres of the genus *Gossypium* have been found in the Indus valley sites of Mohenjo Daro and Harappa.[24] Some five centuries later, a number of references in the *Periplus* indicate that a range of textiles was traded together. Thus, for example, the author speaks of goods brought to the port of Barygaza from its hinterland: the list ends with 'Indian garments of cotton; garments of *molochinon*; and a considerable amount of cloth of ordinary quality.'[25]

I.4. Slaves

In slave-holding societies generally there is often a tendency to name slaves after their area of origin, and this was certainly true of the Greco-Roman world. Yet a passage that makes the point explicitly emphasises that the master is free to call the slave what he liked.[26] As a result names are a highly qualified indicator of origin. This said, the available evidence for Indian slaves in the Mediterranean world is particularly scant: with the exception of the *Digest* passage above, all the references given are statements in passing.

Three suggestions of Indian slaves in the Italian world can be identified, and as it happens all three refer to male slaves.[27] First, Horace speaks of a swarthy wine-serving slave, named after one of the tributaries of the Indus: 'dusky Hydaspes emerges bearing Caecuban wines'.[28] Secondly, Martial aims a lampoon at one Caelia who, though Roman, consorts with various foreign men, whom we might feasibly regard as slaves: 'your Egyptian lover [euphemism] sails to you from Alexandria, the dark-skinned Indian one from the Red Sea'.[29] The shame of exotic promiscuousness on the part of a Roman woman is heightened if the men involved were slaves, or even freedmen. Here it is interesting to note the juxtaposition of Egyptian and

[24] Barber, *Prehistoric textiles*, pp. 32–3.

[25] Ch. 48: σινδόνες Ἰνδικαὶ καὶ μολόχιναι καὶ ἱκανὸν χυδαῖον ὀθόνιον, cf. 51. Casson, *Periplus*, p. 249, takes *molochinon* to represent cotton garments of high quality, but this is open to debate.

[26] Strabo 7.3.12 C304: 'The Athenians would either name their slaves after the peoples from whom they were imported, like *Lydos* or *Syros*, or give them names which were common in those countries, like *Manes* or *Midas* for a Phrygian, or *Tibios* for a Paphlagonian.' See further Fraser, *Ptolemaic Alexandria*, vol. II, p. 385.

[27] Compare Tiberius' disparaging comments about a demand for 'exotic' slaves (Tac. *Ann.* 3.53.4): see section II below.

[28] *Sat.* 2.8.14–15: *procedit fuscus Hydaspes / Caecuba uina ferens*. Cf. André and Filliozat, *L'Inde*, p. 341. It is possible that Tibullus is also referring to Indian slaves at *Elegies* 2.3.55–56: *illi sint comites fusci, quos India torret/ solis et admotis inficit ignis equis*. Cf. Steven E. Sidebotham, *Roman economic policy in the Erythra Thalassa, 30 BC – AD 217* (Leiden: Brill, 1986), p. 22.

[29] 7.30.3–4: *et tibi de Pharia Menphiticus urbe fututor/ nauigat, a rubris et niger Indus aquis*.

Indian; this passage and that from Horace quoted above both mention skin-colour. Thirdly, as we have seen above, Marcian mentions Indian eunuchs (*spadones Indici*) among the luxury goods from the east on which customs duties must be levied. The same passage apparently refers to Indian hair (*capilli Indici*) imported for use in wigs; and it seems that 'Indian hair' was used for the cirrus-type 'Indian' hairstyles reflected in a number of marble heads of the Severan age (on which, see below in this section).

It is clear that this trade took place in the reverse direction as well. The *Periplus* makes it clear that slaves from afar were in demand on both the Egyptian and Indian sides of the monsoon voyage. The Indian king at Barygaza was an avid purchaser of singing boys and female concubines.[30] In an episode that may have taken place some two centuries earlier, Eudoxus of Cyzicus on his third trip to India took with him a supply of young slave musicians, along with doctors and artisans.[31] Indian literature contains some references to western slaves, which may likewise have come from the Greco-Roman world.[32] There are some indications in Han Chinese sources that slaves were exported even farther east.[33] All of these instances suggest a demand for slaves in the east. When the author of the *Periplus* speaks of acquiring female slaves at the Horn of Africa (σώματα θηλυκά, 31), it is possible that those slaves were to be sold farther down the African coast or on the Indian subcontinent, rather than being returned to the Mediterranean world. It is true that Nubia was the main source of 'Ethiopian' slaves throughout antiquity, in a tradition stretching back into Egypt's Pharaonic age.[34] Hence the purchase of slaves in Adulis and to its east in the Horn should be seen as participation in a long-standing slave-trade in that area. References in the *Periplus* to the slave-trade between the Red Sea and India make it clear that slaves were traded *along with* other goods. This gives a slightly unusual picture when we compare it with other evidence on the slave-trade, which usually appears to be a separate sphere of economic activity.[35]

30 μουσικὰ καὶ παρθένοι εὐειδεῖς πρὸς παλλακείαν (49).

31 μουσικὰ παιδισκάρια καὶ ἰατροὺς καὶ ἄλλους τεχνίτας (Strabo 2.3.4 C99).

32 E. H. Warmington, *The commerce between the Roman empire and India*, 2nd edn (New York: Octagon, 1974), p. 261.

33 Ying-shih Yü, *Trade and expansion in Han China* (Berkeley: University of California Press, 1967), p. 180.

34 On the continuation of the Nubian slave trade into the sixth-century AD, see R. H. Pierce, 'A sale of an Alodian slave girl: a reexamination of Papyrus Strassburg Inv. 1404', *Symbolae Osloenses* 70 (1995), 159–64; cf. Stanley M. Burstein, *Ancient African civilizations: Kush and Axum* (Princeton: Markus Wiener, 1998), pp. 118–20.

35 On the underdeveloped topic of ancient slave trades, W. V. Harris, 'Toward a study of the Roman slave trade', *MAAR* 36 (1980), 117–40; K. R. Bradley, *Slavery and society at Rome* (Cambridge University Press, 1994), pp. 31–56.

I.5. Animals

India was identified with certain animals, but here the problem of exclusive identification is extreme. Monstrous creatures such as winnowing fan-ears (*Otoliknoi*), single-eyes (*Monophthalmoi*) and shade-feet (*Skyapods*) were central to the earliest Greek descriptions of India.[36] This element persisted in western views right into the later Middle Ages, if we consider the fantastic creatures that so define the outer edges of medieval world-maps. For the present, let us concentrate on the less fantastic animals, ones that can be understood with reference to modern zoology. A key text here is Aelian's *Historia animalium*, a work shared between fantastic and 'normal' animals without making that distinction explicitly. Taking Aelian's work as a central text in the zoology of the early empire, the key question we must ask is to what extent India emerges as a distinctive place.

Perhaps the most distinctively South Asian animal was the (Indian) elephant, *Elephas maximus*. It was much more widely diffused in antiquity than it is today, when it exists only in India, Sri Lanka and a few parts of southeast Asia. Its domestic use in the subcontinent is attested from the early Indus valley site of Harappa; from the Early Holocene period the animal was found through much of Asia, from Central China to the Syrian coast of the Mediterranean, where it survived to about the seventh century BC. The problem of identification comes when we consider the African elephant, *Loxodonta africana*, which is a separate genus, and frequently it is impossible to know which of the genera is meant in any one particular representation. In other words, elephants may be distinctively Indian from a zoological point of view, but not in the restrictive sense used in this chapter. In fact, the difference between the two genera seems to have been of little interest to ancient authors; Aristotle, who, in various works speaks in depth about elephantine topics, from behaviour to inner organs, is apparently the first clearly to refer to elephants from India.[37]

By far the predominant use of elephants in the Greco-Roman world was in the military. Their first and probably paradigmatic use was by Alexander on his campaign in the Indus Valley. Such was the military-political cachet attached to the animals that they appear on some of the coins minted by Alexander, and even more so by his successors. While it may even have been liability on the battlefield, the elephant thus became a symbol of power among Hellenistic kings claiming continuity with Alexander. The capture and use of elephants was one of the many ways in which Alexander

[36] Milns, 'Greek writers'; Romm, *Edges*, pp. 83–92.

[37] Arist. *Cael.* 298a13; *Hist. an.* 610a15 clearly refer to the military use of elephants in India; Paus. 1.12.4. On elephants in Aristotle, see Scullard, *Elephant*, pp. 37–52.

adopted and adapted the social practices he encountered on his campaign, even though he was later to be thought of as a key agent for the transmission of (Greek) culture. This latter phenomenon is central to Plutarch's essay *On the fortune of Alexander*, but the tradition is much older.[38]

The problem of identification may be summed up as follows: whereas the ancient world's most distinguished commander was associated with Indian elephants, those known first-hand in the Roman world were by the law of probability much more likely to have come from Africa, both north Africa, that is the coastal stretch from Morocco through western Libya, and the Horn of Africa. The elephants that were famously (and calamitously) taken across the Alps by the Carthaginian commander, Hannibal, in 218 BC were in all likelihood from the hinterland of his own territory.

Thus far we have been speaking of live animals. To judge from the *Periplus*, they constituted a far smaller part of the eastern trade than animal products; the text does not mention the exchange of live animals at all, whereas it does mention such objects as ivory (49) and tortoiseshell (56). When it does mention wild animals such as leopards, tigers, elephants, huge serpents and monkeys (e.g., 50), it does so as a vague space-marker, with perhaps a hint of danger, rather than with any suggestion that they should be imported back to Egypt. In distinguishing here between animals and their products, it is significant that the word *elephas* first occurs of ivory; it is only later that it is used for the animal itself.[39] This suggests that the animal initially came into Greek consciousness through its most prized product, whereas the zoological interests of Aristotle and Aelian came after the event. The use of ivory to depict elephants is common, for example in the imperial diptych, and this is itself a case of synecdoche combined with metonymy; in other words, the medium and the obvious referent of the representation together enact the theme. This is a conceit more readily associated with the *Wunderkammer* of the early modern period.[40]

Yet, we do know that various animals considered Indian were known in Rome in their living form. The city's public spectacles, so much part of a civic life from 186 BC and till the later Roman empire, produced a constant

38 Cf. Millar, 'Looking east', 515.

39 Ivory: Hom. *Il.* 4.141; *Od.* 4.73; 8.404, etc. In a sixth-century BC inscription from Aegina the word indicates an ivory statue: *Supplementum Epigraphicum Graecum* 32.356. For what seems the earliest reference to the animal, see Hdt. 4.191, where the context makes it clear that it refers to the African variety.

40 See in general Lorraine Park and Katherine Daston, *Wonders and the order of nature, 1150–1750* (New York: Zone, 1998), pp. 265–90. For the diptych, which shows either Julian or Antoninus Pius, Scullard, *Elephant*, opposite p. 161.

demand for exotic animals: in particular, staged hunts (*venationes*) held in the city's Colosseum and other amphitheatres. Fierce animals would be pitched against each other or against specialised animal-fighting gladiators (*bestiarii*). In some cases, violent scenes from classical mythology would be enacted, which might entail the devouring of a human, typically a condemned criminal, by an animal.[41] At the opening of the Flavian Amphitheatre by the emperor Titus some 5,000 wild animals (and 4,000 domesticated) lost their lives; and when the emperor Trajan celebrated his Dacian triumph in AD 107, 11,000 were killed in this way. The impressiveness of this practice in the eyes of viewers depended in large measure on their exotic quality, their size and aggression, and hence the use of elephants, bears, ostriches, crocodiles and the gamut of large cats. For many living in Rome or other major cities, public spectacles would be the typical (if not the only) way in which such wild animals could be seen in the flesh.

The 'Great hunt' mosaic at Piazza Armerina gives a vivid sense of the capture and transport of animals, for exactly such purposes, we can reasonably suppose. Close to the centre is the depiction of an elephant being coaxed onto a ship. However, given the proximity of Sicily to North Africa, we can safely assume that this was an African elephant from 'Libya' rather than an Indian. Indeed, there is no trace that elephants were transported with the monsoon trade, and it is hard to imagine the practical difficulties involved in such an operation.[42]

More practicable for domestic consumption were birds. There are several hints of a demand for parrots at Rome, and of the idea that they came from India. The opening line of Ovid's playful lament is typical: 'Parrot, avian imitator from India in the east, has died' . . .[43] From the earliest classical references to parrots to late antiquity, the birds are consistently and almost exclusively linked with India.[44] They, too, conferred luxury status on their owners, and it was a function of the emperor Elagabalus' depravity that he would eat parrots and feed them to the lions.[45]

41 Cf. K. M. Coleman, 'Fatal charades: Roman executions staged as mythological enactments', *JRS* 80 (1990), 44–73.

42 On the comparable difficulties of transporting an elephant to the early sixteenth-century Papal court, see Silvio A. Bedini, *The Pope's elephant* (New York: Penguin, 2000).

43 *Am.* 2.6.1–2 *Psittacus, Eois imitatrix ales ab Indis,/ occidit*; for other laments, Stat. *Silv.* 2.4 and *Corpus Inscriptiorum Graecarum* III, p. 1076. See also Petron. fr. 31.1–2; Plin. *HN* 10.117; Apul. *Flor.* 12.1–4, etc.

44 The earliest reference is Ctesias, preserved in Phot. *Bibl.* 45a34.

45 SHA *Heliogab.* 20.4; 21.1; cf. D. W. Thompson, *A glossary of Greek birds* (Oxford: Clarendon, 1895), pp. 335–42; O. Keller, *Die antike Tierwelt*, 2 vols. (Leipzig: Teubner, 1920), vol. II, pp. 45–50; G. Jennison, *Animals for show and pleasure in ancient Rome* (Manchester University Press, 1937), pp. 15–20, 107–12.

Figure 10 Ivory statuette found at Pompeii, first century BC, Museo Nazionale, Naples.

Wild animals especially give the impression that it is much easier to know about their consumption at Rome, while details of their capture and importation are largely murky. That this should be so is due partly to the fact that their social impact was greater the farther afield their origins were deemed to be. In addition, when so many animals were required for a single event, this impact was surely aggregative rather dependent on any one of them. It is likely that *some* of the larger animals came from India, but certainly nowhere near as many as will have come from 'Libya', the Horn of Africa and the eastern Mediterranean. With parrots we are *a priori* on safer ground in asserting both that there was a demand for them in Rome and that long-distance networks responded to this demand. Nonetheless, the problems of evidence presented here in no way deny the fact that India was associated with wild animals in the minds of Romans.

I.6. Craft goods

Lastly, we come to Indian craft goods found in the Roman world. The pickings are meagre, for there is apparently only one artifact that can be brought to the discussion. The fourth-century epigram mentioned above does refer to a wine-goblet made in India, but for that there seems to be no corroborating material evidence.

An ivory statuette depicting a young woman was found at Pompeii in 1938, and is now in the Museo Nazionale, Naples (see Figure 10). She stands naked, her head, neck, arms and legs richly adorned. Her raised arms indicate that she is arranging her hair. On each side she is flanked by a smaller, child-like figure: these we may consider attendants, for they appear to be carrying items for her to use in her toilet. A protrusion extends from the left side of her head, as if a continuation of her hairstyle, and this is presumably a key to any understanding of the purpose this artifact may have served. Earlier scholars saw this as the handle of a mirror, but more recently it has been considered instead to have been the leg of a small piece of furniture. This is plausible, and better explains the fact that, apparently, it was intended to be viewed from three angles, if we take into account the two smaller figures; and the vertical hole that extends from the top of her head to the waist. It was found in one of the most densely populated areas of Pompeii, the Via dell'Abbondanza, in a cache of fine craft goods. The house in which it was found could easily have been that of a wealthy merchant involved in long-distance trade, to judge from its architectural plan.

At 24 cm this is a small item, but distinguished by its fine craftsmanship; the head was delicately carved, so that it exudes a sense of composure. The earlier identification of the woman with Lakshmi, goddess of good luck, fertility and prosperity, can now be dismissed as groundless.[46] But about its Indian origins there can be no dispute, as its style closely matches the statuary of the Satavahanas (first century BC to the third AD); in fact, two closely comparable ivory statuettes have been found at Ter (Tagara) and Bhokardan (Bhogavardhana) in India, and a brief inscription in Kharoshti is found in the base. Nor can anyone doubt that it was brought to the Italian peninsula by AD 79, the year in which an eruption of Vesuvius buried the city of Pompeii and others.

Mary Helms' comparative work, emphasising as it does craft goods over raw materials,[47] might have led us to expect Romans to have had a vivid sense of and even appetite for artifacts produced in distant places. But given the nature of our evidence the phenomenon does not seem to apply to Roman ideas about India. Clearly, no argument from silence here can be strong, in light of the scattershot material record; nonetheless, the observation does resonate when we compare the very strong Roman predilection for things Egyptian, both in the importation of Egyptian obelisks to metropolitan Rome's most central civic spaces and a clear tendency to recreate elements of Egyptian style in its own art.[48] On the other hand, many craft goods from the Mediterranean have been found on the subcontinent (described in section III below). These have been the subject of intensive investigation, much of which struggles with the issue of whether goods were imported in their current form or produced locally, whether from local or imported materials. In most of these cases we can merely speculate as to the life-histories of individual artifacts.[49]

This survey has consistently pointed to the power of rare commodities to connote distance. Beyond that, India emerges as an origin of choice: it would be no exaggeration to say, in general, that Indian origins of any

46 R. E. M. Wheeler, *Rome beyond the imperial frontiers* (Harmondsworth: Penguin, 1954), p. 135, lists some of the various explanations that have been offered for the lengthy protrusion from her head; cf. Sahai, *Iconography of minor Hindu and Buddhist deities* (Delhi: Abhinav, 1975), pp. 157–79.

47 Mary W. Helms, *Craft and the kingly ideal: art, trade, and power* (Austin: University of Texas Press, 1993).

48 E.g., James Stevens Curl, *Egyptomania: the Egyptian revival, a recurring theme in the history of taste* (Manchester University Press, 1994); W. A. Macdonald and J. A. Pinto, *Hadrian's Villa and its legacy* (New Haven: Yale University Press, 1995).

49 Cf. Arjun Appadurai (ed.), *The social life of things: commodities in cultural perspective* (Cambridge University Press, 1986), with especially the articles by Appadurai and Igor Kopytoff; also Chris Gosden and Yvonne Marshall, 'The cultural biography of objects', *World Archaeology* 31 (1999), 169–78.

particular item, whether real or imagined, added value to it in Roman eyes. In very few cases can we say for certain that something would definitely have come from the subcontinent, on the empirical grounds that it could not have come from anywhere else. Pepper is the major exception here, and it is an important one. In most cases what we see in practice is a variety of origins, if we are cognizant of the botanical and other evidence. This conclusion must impact on any attempt to see India through the lens of commodities, and acts as a sober reminder of the indivisibility of the imaginary and the real Indias. In sum, it is clear that the goods regarded by Romans as distinctively Indian carried with them a sense of the exotic. Not all of them were necessarily luxury goods in the normal sense of consumption, though, if we consider the presence of cotton in the monsoon trade and the medical and religious uses of spices and aromatics.

II. THE RHETORIC OF EXCESS

It is one thing to describe those goods that were considered 'Indian' by Romans; it is another to assess the social meanings of these objects. It is this second task that has taken on some urgency in anthropological work in the past twenty years or so: significant recent work has emphasised the material quality of symbols, and conversely the symbolic aspects of material culture.[50] It is to the consideration of social meaning that we must now turn.

The most important point to make is the resilience of a moral discourse around economic issues in the Roman world. As early as the fifth century BC, the Twelve Tables, the earliest codification of law in the still small-scale Roman state, included steps to restrict the power of a 'prodigal' (*prodigus*) over his property, as we know from a much later source (*Digest* 27.10.1 pr. Ulpian, early third century AD). The so-called sumptuary laws of the mid-second century BC limited the amount that could be spent on a dinner-party, stipulating the kinds of food offered and the number of guests allowed.[51] The question of luxury engaged Hellenistic ethics, and we do know that it was the topic of philosophical treatises that are now lost.[52]

Of more immediate concern, we must note that luxury was part of a well-developed philosophy of the past, as is found in the historical monographs of Sallust and in Livy's *History*. Writing in the late republic and the principate,

[50] Apart from the essays in Appadurai, *Social life*, eminent archaeological studies are Ian Hodder (ed.), *The meaning of things: material culture and symbolic expression* (London: Unwin Hyman, 1989).

[51] The *lex Fannia* (161 BC), extended and revised by the *lex Didia* (143) and the *lex Licinia* (after 143).

[52] Griffin, *Latin poets*, pp. 1–31.

these writers particularly saw the progression of Roman history as a decline from a glorious past, which valued good Roman virtues, the 'custom of the ancestors' (*mos maiorum*). They were writing at the time when Rome had greater power over the Mediterranean than ever before, and when the supply of luxury goods was larger than ever. For Sallust, it was the external threat from the Carthaginians in the western Mediterranean that had constantly honed Roman morality in the third and second centuries BC. This process ended with Rome's victory over Carthage in 146 BC, upon which that city was destroyed: the date thus heralded the increasing hold of luxury and avarice on their lives, and constituted a turning point in the tradition of moral historiography that is seen in both Sallust and Livy.[53] For Livy as for others, it was the presence of Roman troops in the eastern Mediterranean that caused the rot to set in; the celebration of triumphs in the city brought home foreign goods and values. Thus when Manlius Vulso celebrated a triumph in 186 BC, 'the beginnings of foreign luxury were brought to the city by the army from the east'.[54] By a variation on this, Pliny dated the onset of luxury in Rome to the conquest of Asia Minor.[55]

The details of these analyses, which differ in the various texts, are less important than a basic premise: that external military threat had a salutary effect on the Romans, and that Rome's ascendancy had instead brought about moral decline; or alternatively, that Roman troops in the eastern Mediterranean world brought back with them a taste for luxury goods. In either case the increase of luxury at Rome was viewed as an outside-inward dynamic, whether that movement involved Roman soldiers on campaign or commodities themselves.

This phenomenon can be understood in part by a figure that stood in opposition to it, and came to epitomise Roman republican virtue. One of the earliest works of Latin prose is the elder Cato's treatise on farming, *De agri cultura*: here farming represented the steadfast, old-fashioned Roman values to which the later onset of luxury seemed profoundly antithetical. The notoriously anti-Greek attitudes of Cato the Censor (234–149 BC) were in part an act of opposition to the effeminacy (*mollitia*) associated with Greek culture: this is, however, not specifically a matter of commodities.[56] We have already seen that the Italic herbs mentioned here by Cato

[53] Donald C. Earl, *The moral and political tradition of Rome* (Ithaca: Cornell University Press, 1967).

[54] Livy 39.6.7: *luxuriae . . . peregrinae origo ab exercitu Asiatico inuecta in urbem est.* It is no coincidence that this coincides broadly with Rome's success over the Carthaginians.

[55] 33.148–49; cf. A. W. Lintott, 'Imperial expansion and moral decline in the Roman Republic', *Historia* 21 (1972), 626–38, at 628.

[56] Edwards, *Politics of immorality*, pp. 92–7.

formed the background against which imported, tropical spices seemed like luxury goods; more generally, farming, with its emphasis on cereals and other staples, formed the backdrop of the long-distance trade in luxury goods altogether.[57] At a time when Rome's dominance spread throughout the Mediterranean and made the metropolis more cosmopolitan, Cato continued to stand for the republican ideal of good morals, grounded in agriculture. In these terms, there is a temporal aspect to luxury goods; they marked the modernity of the new cosmopolitan city and emerging world empire; they distinguished the city of Rome from its golden age of hazy memory, they are what made Rome's past a 'foreign country' in the eyes of a Sallust or a Seneca.[58] Not only does the Roman imperial discourse about luxury thus have a long heritage, but that discourse involves the creation of a very particularised view of Rome's past.

There is an aggregative aspect in Roman responses to commodities: part of their social meaning comes, if not from their quantity, then from the fact that they are densely combined. This emerges even from the lines of Statius' *Silvae* with which this chapter began, and can be illustrated in all the moralists. In effect, this is how an Apician recipe might also be read, even though of course the fact of combination has special reasons in a context of cooking. This aggregative aspect is perhaps analogous to the social meaning of a metropolis: a description of Rome, for example, by Juvenal presents not one but several of its distinctive features closely combined, with several of the senses engaged at the same time.[59]

There was in Greek and Roman texts a long tradition of talking about luxury from the east. The first case concerns eastern Greeks of Asia Minor, that is the Greek-speaking inhabitants of what is now the western coast of Turkey.[60] From the archaic Greek world, then, Lydia and its surrounding area had connotations of vice and decadence. This applied not so much to goods from Asia Minor as to its inhabitants' lives. For the purposes of this chapter, it might be said that this implied the construction of Asia Minor as a place of luxury. The key point is that this projected the practice of luxury in an eastward direction, something that can be traced throughout the rest of antiquity and even beyond. This tendency was never absolute,

[57] Indeed, this is one reason that a balanced view of the Roman economy requires a reasonable assessment of the proportional amounts involved between agriculture and trade, especially luxury trade: see section IV below.

[58] Cf. David Lowenthal, *The past is a foreign country* (Cambridge University Press, 1985).

[59] See Nicholas Purcell's twin articles, 'The city of Rome and the *plebs urbana* in the late Republic', *CAH*, 2nd edn (1994), vol. IX, pp. 644–88; and 'Rome and its development under Augustus and his successors', *CAH*, 2nd edn (1996), vol. X, pp. 782–811.

[60] Leslie Kurke, 'The politics of *habrosune* in archaic Greece', *Cl. Ant.* 11 (1992), 81–120.

when for example the Italian (i.e. western) colony of Sybaris became for Greeks a byword for decadence (e.g., Plutarch *Life of Crassus* 32); and when Trimalchio's poem thematising the indulgence of his dinner-party mentions Carthaginian jewels and 'Numidian bird' (i.e. guinea-fowl), alongside Babylonian gold and Indian pearls, North Africa fulfils the same role (Petronius *Satyrica* 55, written before AD 66).

It is worthwhile to dwell for a moment on one of the Roman empire's most conspicuous consumers, the freedman Trimalchio. At his lavish dinner-party he presents only the most exotic delights from various parts of the world. As one of the more experienced guests tells the naïve narrator, Trimalchio serves only foodstuffs from his own estates:

> You mustn't think that he buys anything: everything grows on his own estates. Wool, citrus, pepper; you can even have cock's milk if you like. To crown it all, his wool was not growing finely enough, so he bought rams from Tarentum sent them to his flocks with a smack on the rear. He ordered bees to be imported from Athens so Attic honey could be produced at his own home; and, by the way, Italian bees will be improved by the Greek ones. And these last few days, in fact, he gave instructions for mushroom-seed to be sent from India. (38.1)[61]

It is significant to notice that in this passage the mushrooms are not strictly speaking from Trimalchio's estate, but imported from beyond it. The distinction is strictly beside the point when, for example, 'cock's milk' is clearly exaggeration for comic effect. Nonetheless, they are deeply caught up in a system of value where geographical distance brings social prestige, something alluded to also in the reference to the Athenian bees. The passage is central to the concerns of this chapter also because the consumption involved is in the private sphere, and centred on the sumptuous dinner-party. The cultural politics are heightened by the fact that Trimalchio is presented as the upstart, the crude social climber, who tries to compensate for his low-prestige, freedman status by the most conspicuous kinds of consumption.

Of the commodities discussed above, we should examine two extreme cases in greater detail, moving beyond a description of their existence in the Mediterranean world to an analysis of their social meaning. Firstly, spices. In section I, we have already noted the readiness of Roman literary sources to use a moralising lens in considering pepper. A case in point is Pliny's comments about the consumption of pepper (12.14). We must now step

[61] *nec est quod putes illum quicquam emere. omnia domi nascuntur: lana, citrea, piper; lacte gallinaceum si quaesieris, invenies. ad summam, parum illi bona lana nascebatur: arietes a Tarento emit et eos culavit in gregem. mel Atticum ut domi nasceretur, apes ab Athenis iussit afferri; obiter et vernaculae quae sunt, meliusculae a Graeculis fient. ecce intra hos dies scripsit, ut illi ex India semen boletorum mitteretur.*

back and assess that bias in broader frame. What happens when we read such passages against the grain?

Pliny says that the mixing of odorific forest substances to make the very first scent in time immemorial was done for the sake of *luxuria* (13.1). However, it appears that, in his haste to criticise, Pliny seems to have got it wrong: overwhelming evidence suggests that the earliest use of spices was for incense and hence for the sake of worshipping the gods rather than decadence. Any comparison with Theophrastus' more dispassionate *On odours* shows the prominence Pliny gives to his own concerns. As the comments earlier in this section suggest, Pliny's position can be understood in terms of Rome's new status in the Mediterranean world: a cosmopolitan city at the centre of a world empire.

An implicit contrast should be detected in the rhetoric about spices: that with the earlier Roman cuisine as described by Cato in *De agri cultura*. Here there is no reference to pepper or other imported spices, though Cato does mention myrtle berries as flavouring (101.1). These we would call herbs rather than spices: they were domestic rather than imported, and carried no connotations of luxury. The difference between the world of Cato and that of Apicius was, in part, one between modest Italian-grown herbs on the one hand and exotic eastern spices on the other, or so Pliny would have us believe. This latter, more commodity-conscious world of the early empire is vividly presented by Petronius in the form of Trimalchio's dinner table, not least the host's insistence that the gourmet delicacies served come from his own estates.

One feature in Pliny's books on spices may offer a clue to their social meaning in his world, namely the consumption of spices by Persian kings. As we have seen, there is a long tradition in Greek thought of Persian luxury, going back to Herodotus' *Histories*, but the key point here is Pliny's emphasis on the fact that the Achaemenid court received a huge amount of spices from Arabia annually (12.80). In this way, Pliny's 'east' harboured both the production and the consumption of spices, and for that matter the distribution also. And this meant, by implication, that any Roman to indulge in spices would be partaking in the morally dubious ways of the east.

Let us take a moment to consider the idiomatic uses of spice.[62] When one Safinius is referred to in Petronius' *Satyrica* as 'pepper rather than a person' (44.7: *piper non homo*), we see that the sharpness of the spice

[62] Here it can be noted that Christian idioms and moralistic vocabulary are not substantially different to polytheist; in other words, there seems no specifically Christian concept of spices: Lallemand and Dittmann, 'Gewürz', *RAC*, vol. X.1201–7.

gave it idiomatic force: 'wherever he went, the earth caught fire'. Here it is interesting, in passing, to compare the idiomatic uses of salt: this sometimes serves as a spice when it is a condiment used for flavouring the good, though its potential utility goes far beyond that, and in modern times it is customary to refer to salt and pepper as a pair. Some recipes attributed to Apicius require salt in order to season meat (e.g. 1.5.1; 1.9.1), and this reveals its use in Roman cuisine. The interesting point about it, however, is that the word is related to the Latin word for health, *salus*. The word for salt occurs also in idioms, not unlike pepper, but its metaphorical use is more deeply embedded in the Latin language than that of pepper.[63] This difference between the rhetoric of the two seasonings may be taken as symptomatic of the fact that salt was used in the Mediterranean since prehistoric times, long before pepper.

Secondly, silk too deserves special consideration. This was the luxury fabric par excellence, and we find it referred to in morally coded and often gendered language. The Latin name for silk in love elegy, 'Coan robes', is virtually a byword for hedonism, notably in Propertius.[64] Another elegist, Tibullus, speaks of silk from Cos together with shell from the Red Sea as the causes of greed on the part of young women (2.4.29). The fact that in some cases silk is in such cases referred to merely as 'the Coan garment' or even 'the Coan thing' is an indication of the extent with which product had become synonymous with place of production. Thus Ovid can advise the would-be lover to be charmed with 'Coan products' if that is what he finds the beloved wearing.[65] In these cases silk is explicitly worn by women; later references tell us about silk being worn by men, often with connotations of sexual transgression. Under the emperor Tiberius the Senate in AD 16 forbade men from wearing silk (Tacitus *Annals* 2.33; Cassius Dio *Roman history* 57.15), a stipulation ignored by Tiberius' successor Gaius (Caligula), according to the biographer Suetonius (*Life of Gaius* 52.1). The flamboyant later emperor Elegabalus (AD 218–22) is said to have worn only silk, which helped make him a kind of Liberace figure.[66] In fact, several of the emperors represented in the biographies of the *Historia Augusta* (probably from the late fourth century AD) are said to have worn silk: in the case of Commodus, in order to hide a tumor in his groin from public

[63] A. Otto, *Die Sprichwörter und sprichwörtlichen Redensarten der Römer* (Leipzig: Teubner, 1890).

[64] The term *Coae uestes* is used either in the singular or in the plural, as for example at Prop. 1.2.2; 2.3.53; 4.5.57.

[65] *Ars am.* 2.298 *sive erit in Cois, Coa decere puta*; cf. Hor. *Carm.* 4.13.13.

[66] SHA *Heliogab.* 26.1; cf. David S. Potter, 'Odor and power in the Roman empire', in *Constructions of the classical body*, ed. J. I. Porter (Ann Arbor: University of Michigan Press, 1999), pp. 169–89, at 178–9.

view (13.1). Given the negative disposition and gossipy nature of this work, silk functions as an unambiguous marker of vice. It is no accident that all three rulers mentioned here, Caligula, Elegabalus and Commodus, were remembered as 'bad emperors', a status that typically carried with it tales of sexual misconduct.

Silk is thus an object lesson in the problems involved in linking product with its supposed place of origin: there was, it is clear, a particular social meaning attached to the product involved; and there was a tendency to link it with a place or places of origin. But this link remained vague, when the elegists and other Augustan age writers associated it with the Greek island of Cos; when its later name was closely tied with the name of China; and when some texts, such as Pliny and the *Periplus*, do indeed link it with India. In fact, we do know from the *Periplus* that several Indian ports served as entrepôts at which Roman merchants could acquire silk, so this should certainly be considered a factor in the inability of Romans back in the Mediterranean, on the consumer side of these transactions, to retain a clear sense of provenance.

III. TRADE NETWORKS AND THE *LONGUE DURÉE*

III.1. Varieties of evidence

Now that we have seen a number of specific goods and the rhetoric with which they are represented, it is necessary to step back to consider the mechanics of exchange whereby they were conveyed from South Asia to the Mediterranean. Thus far, consumption has been foregrounded: different perspectives arise when we consider the productive and distributive parts of economic practice.

The evidence to be considered in an overview of Roman trade with Asia is necessarily varied in nature. First, the largest single class of evidence comes from literary texts, of the kinds described above: as we have seen, they are very much the products of their own thought worlds and therefore of limited use in grasping the mechanics of exchange. Pliny's *Natural history* looms large among these texts, but there is also much to be gained from the geographical texts of Strabo (*c.* 64 BC to after AD 21) and Claudius Ptolemy (fl. AD 146–70). While geography and natural history provide the most obvious genres for such study, texts in which 'Indian' goods are mentioned in passing are also of enormous importance, not least for their lesser degree of self-consciousness on this specific topic. Expanding from the issue of consumption for the moment, what of literary sources for larger patterns of exchange? Apart from Pliny (6.104–6 and 12.84) mentioned below, there is information to be gleaned from Diodorus Siculus (*Bibliothêkê* 5.22–23) and Strabo (*Geography* 2.5.12 C118 and 17.1.13 C686). It may be noticed that, with the partial exception of Diodorus, the Alexander historians are notable by their silence on this subject. Claudius Ptolemy in his *Geography* mentions several locations on the subcontinent, among them emporia, both on the near and the far side of the Ganges (7.1 and 7.2 respectively). For the later period, Cosmas Indicopleustes' *Christian topography* shows us that the Indian trade was pursued by Byzantines in the sixth century.[67]

To adhere in a formal way to the category of literary sources, we come to a work of the greatest significance: the *Periplus of the Erythraean Sea*. The work survives in a single manuscript, now in Heidelberg, from the beginning of the tenth century.[68] Opinions about the date of this work have varied from about AD 40 to as late as 240. However, scholarly opinion is now largely united in dating the work to the period AD 40 to 70: the decisive issue is the reference to the Nabataean king Malichus, who may now safely be identified as Malichus II (reigned 40–70).[69] We know that the anonymous author was an Egyptian Greek.[70] It is tempting to conclude that the dating of the document to this period suggests that in these decades the seaborne trade with India was still a relative novelty.

The value of the *Periplus* to our understanding of Roman long-distance trade generally and of the India trade in particular is enormous. When literary sources so consistently denigrate the merchant as a social type, or even social class, it is refreshing to have this insight into the perspective of a trader. On any reading, the enormously practical perspective of its author shines through. Whereas Pliny speaks in generalising and moralising terms, the *Periplus* author is centrally concerned with specific objects of trade at specific places, and with the conditions of engaging in trade. From the text

67 See N. Pigulewskaja, *Byzanz auf den Wegen nach Indien* (Berlin: Akademie, 1969), pp. 110–29, on Cosmas. Note evidence of the demand for silk in fifth- and sixth-century Byzantium, pp. 80–91.

68 This is Cod. Pal. Gr. 398. On the other hand, B. M. Add. 19391 fols. 9r–12r, of the fourteenth or fifteenth century is merely a copy of the Palatine ms, adding no independent witness. It is accompanied by other geographical works. The work has often been printed, first in 1533: see Wilfred Schoff (ed.), *The Periplus of the Erythraean Sea: travel and trade in the Indian Ocean* (New York: Longmans, 1912), pp. 17–19, with Casson, *Periplus*, pp. 5–6, for details.

69 These dates are secure from Nabataean king-lists, and may be taken as the termini of the Periplus. On the dating see Raschke, 'New studies', 979–81 nn. 1342–6; with G. W. Bowersock, *Roman Arabia* (Cambridge, MA: Harvard University Press, 1983), pp. 70–2, for the Nabataean context, followed by Casson, *Periplus*, pp. 6–7. Furthermore, a first-century dating seems now to be confirmed by Indian history: P. J. Turner and J. E. Cribb, 'Numismatic evidence for the Roman trade with ancient India', in *The Indian Ocean in antiquity*, ed. Julian Reade (London: Kegan Paul, 1996), pp. 309–20.

70 At section 29 he speaks of 'the trees we have in Egypt'; consistently he offers Egyptian equivalents for Roman months. See Casson, *Periplus*, pp. 7–10.

we get an acute sense of the dangers involved, e.g. pirates, winds, hostile competitors. The plain, sometimes repetitious language used is yet another indication of its pragmatism, free of stylistic considerations. Reading it is much like overhearing a conversation between sea-captains and merchants.

Literary evidence from the south of India has much light to shed on this topic. The presence of 'Yavanas', which would seem at first blush to refer to 'Greeks' specifically, is attested in Tamil poetry:

> Here lies the thriving town of Muchiri (sc. Muziris), where the beautiful large ships of the Yavana come, bringing gold, splashing the white foam on the waters of the Periyar, and then return laden with pepper. Here the music of the surging sea never ceases, and the great king presents to visitors the rare products of sea and mountain.

Another poem mentions the 'cool and fragrant wine brought by the Yavana in their good ships'. In both cases, the *Periplus* would seem to receive outside verification as regards the cargo of Greek ships. There are, however, two problems here: first, it is not certain that the 'Yavanas' are Greeks rather than 'westerners' in a more general sense.[71] There is no mistaking the terminological link with 'Ionians': one can compare the term 'Yonas' in Ashoka's inscriptions.[72] But some doubt still looms over the specificity with which the term was applied, as if in the same way as the term *Firangi* was used by Arabs in the high Middle Ages to refer to all (western) Europeans, not merely Franks.[73] Then there is the problem of dating the work. Subject to a lengthy oral tradition, it is possible that the work goes back to the first century AD, but it is impossible to say so with any certainty: it might equally well have been written several centuries later.

Secondly, there are a number of documentary sources. The so-called Muziris papyrus (*P. Vind.* G40822 of the mid-second century AD, now in Vienna) was not published till the 1980s.[74] It presupposes a contract that had been concluded between two parties concerning the transport

[71] Wheeler, *Imperial frontiers*, p. 178, for one, suggests that the term may have been used also for Arab traders, about which the poems otherwise have nothing to say.

[72] For various compounds with *yona-* in the Rock and Pillar edicts, see A. C. Woolner, *Asoka: text and glossary* (Oxford University Press, 1924), p. 126. *Yavana* is a back formation from the Prakrit *Yona*, and came to be used for various trading peoples from western Asia, including Arabs in subsequent centuries: Thapar, 'Asokan India and the Gupta age', in *A cultural history of India*, ed. A. L. Basham (Oxford University Press, 1975), pp. 38–51, at 44. Further comparisons may be drawn for loanwords for 'Greeks' in other languages: Hebrew *yavan* (pl. *yavanim*); Old Persian *yauna*; Assyrian *iamanu* (or *iavanu*); Egyptian *Y^{e}-v^{a}n-(n)a*. A Jewish source probably from the early sixth century BC speaks of Greeks (*Yavan*) as traders: *Ezek.* 27:13, in the lamentation over the fall of Tyre.

[73] A. Miquel (ed.), *Usâma Ibn Mundiqh, des enseignements de la vie* (Paris: Colin, 1983), pp. 57–65.

[74] H. Harrauer and P. Sijpesteijn, 'Ein neues Dokument zu Roms Indienhandel, P. Vindob. G40822', *Anzeiger der Österreichischen Akademie der Wissenschaften, phil.-hist. Kl.* 122 (1985), 124–55.

of goods from Muziris (probably modern Cranganore) to Myos Hormos on the north-eastern coast of the Red Sea (perhaps Quseir al-Qadim),[75] in particular a loan to be paid back on the return voyage: the papyrus itself sets out the consequences of non-repayment. Whereas the *Periplus* suggests that traders would mix low-cost everyday items within its cargo of predominantly luxury goods, the Muziris papyrus is limited to expensive articles. In fact, the extremely high value of the cargo here described is something to which we shall have to return in section IV below.

In addition, a number of inscriptions survive testifying to the kind of trade mentioned by Pliny. Annius Plocamus' freedman left two inscriptions at the Wadi Menih on the Berenike-Koptos road, both of them dating to the year AD 6: 'I, Lysas, freedman of Publius Annius Plocamus, came here on 2 July (5 July), AD 6.'[76]

Excavations at Quseir al-Qadim beginning in the late 1970s turned up two ostraka inscribed in the southern India's Tamil-Brahmi script. These, which contain the names *Kanan* and *Catan*, have been dated to the first century AD. Amidst a find of pottery that can be dated to AD 60–70, the Berenike excavation has also produced two ostraka inscribed in Tamil-Brahmi.[77]

Archaeological finds constitute the third and most problematic category of evidence. South Asia itself has produced a variety of evidence, particularly from the southwest coast (known variously as Limyrike, the Malabar Coast and Kerala), and the southeast coast (the Coromandel coast or Tamil Nadu); likewise the Red Sea coast, and especially the Egyptian port of Berenike.[78]

[75] Myos Hormos used to be located at Abu-Sha 'ar until excavations (1987–93) suggested that it was not settled until the third century AD, thus invalidating the identification: Talbert, *Barrington atlas* map 78 D3 and 80 E1, with Young, *Rome's eastern trade*, pp. 40–4, and Donald Whitcomb, 'Quseir al-Qadim and the location of Myos Hormos', *Topoi* 6 (1996), 747–72.

[76] Λυσᾶς Ποπλίου Ἀννίου Πλοκάμου ἥκω Λλε Καίσαρος ἐπεὶφ η̄ (2 July), and *Lysa P. Anni Plocami veni anno XXXVIII non. Iul.* (5 July). The twin inscriptions were initially published by D. Meredith, 'Annius Plocamus: two inscriptions from the Berenice road', *JRS* 43 (1953), 38–40; cf. Federico de Romanis, *Cassia cinnamomo ossidiana. Uomini e merci tra Oceano indiano e Mediterraneo* (Rome: Bretschneider, 1996), pp. 211–12. The term *kaisaros* in the Greek version points to Augustus, hence the dating. As it happens, this Lysa(s) corresponds with the freedman of Annius Plocamus, who is mentioned at Pliny 6.84 as a collector of taxes along the Red Sea coast. See further Federico de Romanis, 'Graffiti greci da Wadi Menih el-Her. Un Vestorius tra Coptos e Berenice', *Topoi* 6 (1996), 731–45.

[77] I. Mahadevan, 'Tamil-Brahmi graffito', in *Berenike 1995: preliminary report of the 1995 excavations at Berenike (Egyptian Red Sea coast)*, ed. S. E. Sidebotham and W. Z. Wendrich (Leiden: CNWS, 1996), pp. 206–8.

[78] For a recent summary, see W. Z. Wendrich *et al.*, 'Berenike crossroads: the integration of information', *JESHO* 46.1 (2003), 46–87. Site reports have been published regularly, beginning with S. E. Sidebotham and W. Z. Wendrich (eds.), *Berenike 1994: preliminary report of the 1994 excavations at Berenike (Egyptian Red Sea coast)* (Leiden: CNWS, 1995).

By contrast, the Nile Valley itself has almost nothing to offer;[79] and, as we have seen above, the archaeological yield from Italy itself has been extremely scant.[80] Various kinds of material have been found: pots and amphorae, bronzeware, and coins. The best-known Indian site is that of Arikamedu, in part because it was excavated by the British archaeologist Mortimer Wheeler in the years 1944–48; but more recent work has challenged his analysis that this may be viewed as a Roman settlement.[81]

It is in respect to glassware that archaeology and the *Periplus* are most closely compatible. In the *Periplus* we hear of three different sorts: coloured or millefiori-type glass (6, 7, 17), glass vessels (39) and unworked glass (49, 56).[82] Many different kinds of glass beads were found in the 1967 excavations at Ter (Tagara of the *Periplus*), and many of its items have been dated to the first century AD. Glass vessels tended to be imported to the northwest of the subcontinent, whereas southern India received a greater proportion of raw glass, in the form of ingots. Much of this was destined for Indian bead industries in the Deccan and in the south of India,[83] but some may have found its way farther east to China. Finds at Arikamedu reveal a specialised glassworking industry there.[84]

Predictably, the most plentiful Greco-Roman material remains to be found on the subcontinent have been amphorae. The majority of those found at Arikamedu carried wine, others olive oil or the fish-sauce called garum.[85] On a recent assessment these are thought to be of the first century

79 Richard Alston, 'Trade and the city in Roman Egypt', in *Trade, traders and the ancient city*, ed. Helen Parkins and Christopher Smith (London: Routledge, 1998), pp. 168–202, at 194.

80 It is striking how little of obviously Indian origin has been found in the Mediterranean world, compared with Greco-Roman finds in India and Egypt. One factor to be taken into account is that archaeologists who have worked in the subcontinent (e.g., Mortimer Wheeler and John Marshall) came to their Indian work with a background in classical archaeology, and were thus quick to recognise Greco-Roman artifacts when they encountered them; not so the reverse. On Wheeler in India see Jacquetta Hawkes, *Adventurer in archaeology: the biography of Sir Mortimer Wheeler* (New York: St Martin's, 1982), with reference also to his memoirs.

81 M. P. Charlesworth, *Trade routes and commerce of the Roman Empire*, 2nd edn (New York: Cooper Square, 1970), p. 131; Vimala Begley, *The ancient port of Arikamedu: new excavations and researches, 1989–1992* (Pondichéry: École française d'Extrême-Orient, 1996), p. 6.

82 For a comparable range of glass material found on the African side of the Periplus trade, see E. M. Stern, 'The glass from Heis', in *Sur les routes antiques de l'Azanie et de l'Inde. Le fonds Révoil du Músee de l'Homme (Heïs et Damo, en Somalie)*, ed. J. Desanges, E. M. Stern and P. Ballet (Paris: MAI, 1993), pp. 21–61.

83 E. M. Stern, 'Early Roman glass from Heis on the north Somali coast', in *Annales du 10e Congrès de l'Association pour l'Histoire du Verre* (Amsterdam: AHIV, 1985), pp. 23–36, at 33.

84 E. M. Stern, 'Early Roman export glass in India', in *Rome and India: the ancient sea trade*, ed. Vimala Begley and Richard D. De Puma (Madison: University of Wisconsin Press, 1991), pp. 113–24.

85 E. Will, *Les Palmyréniens. Venise des sables* (Paris: Colin, 1992), p. 150. A detailed recent study of terra sigillata at Arikamedu concludes that its remains originated in different production centres in

AD, though they had earlier been considered somewhat later in date.[86] The same can be said for Berenike, where pots have been shown to come from as far west as Spain. In addition, several terracotta oil lamps of the early imperial period have come to light at Arikamedu and Ter in the Indian interior.

A somewhat different picture emerges from Begley's study of Indian ceramics on the subcontinent,[87] and this is introduced here to complicate an otherwise clear picture. On the basis of two types of ceramic finds, namely rouletted ware from the northwestern coast and mouldmade ware from the southeast,[88] she suggests that the Coromandel coast traded with the Mediterranean as early as the second century BC, that is some two hundred years before the *Periplus*. But this must be taken with some caution, as the only apparent grounds for viewing these ceramics as evidence for Greco-Roman trade is that they 'show clear influence of classical ceramic techniques and styles'.[89]

The inland site of Kolhapur has yielded a cache of 102 bronzes.[90] This is a great windfall: the value of bronze is such that it is prone to melting down and reuse. At least ten are Roman imports, including mirrors, stands and lamps, whereas the rest are more likely Indian in origin. Most famous is the statuette of Poseidon, 12.8 cm high and finely crafted.[91] The Kolhapur museum alone offers also jugs (Millingen-type oinochoe), basins, strainers, mirrors and a delicate calithiscus (cup) made of bronze. But just how much of this was imported from the Greco-Roman world, and how much produced locally?[92] In the case of artifacts such as the Poseidon, the emblema

the Mediterranean world: Howard Comfort, 'Terra sigillata at Arikamedu', in *Rome and India*, ed. Begley and De Puma, pp. 134–50.

86 Will, *Palmyréniens*, pp. 154–5, places the ceramic finds in the first century BC and the first AD, whereas since Wheeler it has been customary to date them to the first two centuries AD. She has found no clear evidence pointing to the second century.

87 Vimala Begley, 'Ceramic evidence for pre-periplus trade on the Indian coasts', in *Rome and India*, ed. Begley and De Puma, pp. 157–96.

88 The best examples of these ceramics are stamped bowls, footed cups and dishes from Arikamedu, and they differ markedly with finds from the northwest. The ceramic types of the two groups are not related to each other, hence Begley's conclusion that, while both regions traded with the Mediterranean world, they did not have contact with each other.

89 Begley, 'Ceramic evidence', in *Rome and India*, ed. Begley and De Puma, p. 157.

90 On the problems of identifying this site, see Richard Daniel De Puma, 'The Roman bronzes from Kolhapur', in *Rome and India*, ed. Begley and De Puma, pp. 82–112, at 82.

91 Kolhapur Museum inv. 932. It may be considered a copy of a lost original by Lysippus (*c.* 340 BC), and can itself not be exactly dated, nor can we exclude the possibility that it came to the subcontinent much later.

92 De Puma, 'Roman bronzes', in *Rome and India*, ed. Begley and De Puma. It might be noted here, in passing and by comparison, that a substantial number of Roman bronze statuettes have been unearthed in Frisia, another region 'beyond the imperial frontiers' (Wheeler, *Imperial frontiers*, p. 52). This may be taken as a reminder of the problem of the diffusion of artifacts.

with Perseus and Andromeda, and the distinctive jug-handles, importation seems probable, *a priori*, given the degree of similarity to artifacts in the Mediterranean world itself. But not so for all the bronze finds. An interesting case is presented by the three mirrors, which despite overall similarity exhibit features not matched in any Roman mirrors thus far found.[93] In general, the bronzes point to the Satavahana period (first to third centuries AD) but do not suggest any more specific a date for trade contact.

Coins are the final and most complex class of Greco-Roman goods to be found in India.[94] Hoards have been found at an astonishing variety of locations throughout the subcontinent, particularly but not exclusively in the south. In the 1980s coins were found on the Laccadive Islands: this appears to be a first 'shipwreck' hoard, i.e. one reflecting the kinds of coin in the condition in which they were imported from the west, and as such particularly valuable. These finds are still being examined, but initial indications are that this hoard contains a much higher percentage of Republican coins than anything yet found on the subcontinent.[95]

The known hoards have usefully been classed into three sections.[96] First, the early Julio-Claudian silver hoards, e.g. those found in the Coimbatore district. These exhibit only a small number of types, and are in fair to good condition, suggesting that they were carefully selected and quickly buried near centres of trade. Most of these date to the reigns of Augustus and Tiberius.[97] Secondly, there are Julio-Claudian gold hoards. These reveal greater diversity of types, and their state of wear depends on the composition of the hoards: they vary in condition between worn (that is, much used) and new. Tiberian and Claudian types predominate, thus making them slightly later. Thirdly, there are second-century gold hoards, which are mostly in good condition. Antoninus Pius and Septimius Severus feature large.[98]

The relative absence of Republican coins is accentuated by a sudden influx of Augustan and Tiberian *denarii*: this suggests a sudden surge in trade

93 De Puma, 'Roman bronzes', in *Rome and India*, ed. Begley and de Puma, pp. 98–100.

94 A general problem in the use of coins as historical evidence is germane here: how long had the coins been in circulation before being buried in hoards? Given that we are dealing with a region outside the Roman world, it is a genuine question, for that matter, whether coins were used at all.

95 Ball, *Rome in the east*, p. 127.

96 P. J. Turner, *Roman coins from India* (London: Royal Numismatic Society, 1989).

97 For the Tiberian context, see Cosmo Rodewald, *Money in the age of Tiberius* (Manchester University Press, 1976), esp. pp. 29–51.

98 A staggering number of Roman coins have been found in Sri Lanka, perhaps many times the number of finds on the subcontinent itself. But they are far from fully published and have thus far received relatively little attention from scholars, the exceptions being Weerakkody, *Taprobane*, pp. 151–70; Osmund Bopearachchi and Wilfried Pieper, *Ancient coins from Sri Lanka* (Turnhout: Brepols, 1998); Kenneth W. Harl, *Coinage in the Roman economy* (Baltimore: Johns Hopkins University Press, 1996), pp. 290–314.

in the latter part of Augustus' reign. This at least has been the orthodoxy for some time, and may be revised in the light of the new Laccadive islands, which reveal both a greater number of Republican coins and a wider variety of Augustan types than had hitherto been seen. About this there remain many questions. What is clear is that the Julio-Claudian period saw a transition from silver to gold. It is possible that local traders lost confidence in the *denarius*.[99] What is puzzling is that this switch took place before Nero's debasement of the currency in AD 64, so that it does not seem as if the switch was occasioned by the debasement.[100] At any rate, gold replaced silver, which is not found after that point.

A feature of the Roman coins found in India is that many have been slashed, whereas others have two punch-marks. This is true for two silver hoards, namely those at Akenpalle and Nasthullapur. Punch-marks are to be found also on the terracotta figures resembling coins, which were most likely produced locally as imitations.[101] It is not easy to explain why they have received this treatment. Given the locality of the finds, Buddhist practices may have played a part, it has been argued. Possibly, the punch-marks suggest use as jewellery.[102] Economic explanations have also been advanced, namely that the silver coins were marked so as not to interfere with the new Indian coinage, the Satavahana silver of around AD 70–90; or to disqualify them from returning to the Mediterranean. This complex issue has been subject to much speculation and is far from resolved.

III.2. Chronologies, personnel and routes

How are we to understand the dating of these exchanges? The literary sources discussed above point overwhelmingly to the first and second centuries AD as the high point of commerce. The key documents bear this out, namely the *Periplus* of the mid-first century AD and the Muzuris papyrus of the mid-second. The archaeological record presents many complications of detail, but even here it is possible to detect a similar centre of gravity. For one thing, finds of Roman coins have generally reflected this pattern, though new finds tend to give increasing prominence to Republican coins.

99 By contrast, Sidebotham, *Roman economic policy*, p. 30, suggests that the Roman government may have restricted silver exports but not gold.

100 Nero reduced the aureus from 1/42 to 1/45 of a pound, and the denarius from 1/84 to 1/96 the amount of silver.

101 See, e.g., Wheeler, *Imperial frontiers*, plates xxviii and xxix for Tiberian examples.

102 Certainly the practice of turning coins into jewellery was known in the Roman world, as was its reverse: see Christopher Howgego, 'The supply and use of money in the Roman world 200 BC to AD 300', *JRS* 82 (1992), 1–32, at 9.

There are obvious reasons why we should be faced with this basic chronology. The Pax Romana that began with Augustus' victory over the forces of Antony at Actium in 31 BC brought an end to decades of civil war and made possible an ease of long-distance commerce that had earlier been impossible. But it was even earlier, in 65 BC, that Pompey quashed piracy in the eastern Mediterranean, and turned Nabataea into a client state of Rome. This fact serves as a reminder of the economic implications, if not impetus, of military initiatives. It does not, of course, tell us anything about state initiatives *per se*. To take a later instance, we might consider L. Aelius Gallus was prefect of Egypt about 25–24 BC.[103] The story of his ill-fated expedition into Arabia recorded by Strabo, who claims he was misdirected and otherwise deceived by the *epitropos* Sullaios.[104] Strabo suggests that there are economic motives to the expedition, stemming from tales of wealth of Arabia and this has, plausibly, won acceptance from modern scholars.[105] From the early third century, we have Herodian's account (4.10.4) of a remarkable proposal of the emperor Caracalla to the Parthian king, Artabanus V: the unity of our two empires, he says in a letter that proves to be a ruse, would be a great boost for the exchange and consumption of luxury goods. There is no reason to take this remarkable episode at face value, and it is perhaps no accident that the Roman emperor involved is known to have been a keen imitator of Alexander.[106] All of these accounts give a political-military edge to the story of long-distance exchange, particularly around the time of Augustus. While their relevance cannot be denied, it is important to put them into perspective by emphasising traces of such exchange before and after the Pax Romana.

The Ptolemies may have taken measures to control the Red Sea itself, including the establishment of Berenike and other ports, but they do not appear to have developed long-distance trade of the scale involved here. This at least is the orthodoxy, and it is not entirely wide of the mark. But a few qualifications must be aired. As early as the second century BC we hear of commercially motivated travel to 'spice lands', which may be India.[107] The picture is considerably complicated by the possibility that Arab and

[103] *Prosopographia Imperii Romani*[2] A 179.

[104] 16.4.22–24 C780–782. Gallus receives brief mention also at 2.5.12 C118 for 'opening up' Arabia to Roman geographical knowledge through military conquest.

[105] Cf. Cass. Dio 53.29.3–4; Bowersock, *Roman Arabia*, pp. 46–9.

[106] For a discussion of Herodian's anecdote, Otto Kurz, 'Cultural relations between Parthia and Rome', in *Cambridge History of Iran*, ed. Ehsan Yarshater (Cambridge University Press, 1983), vol. III.1, pp. 559–60; Malcolm A. R. Colledge, *The Parthians* (New York: Praeger, 1967), pp. 171–2. On imitation of Alexander on the part of Roman emperors, see Chapter 5, sections I.5–6 below.

[107] Ulrich Wilcken, 'Punt-Fahrten in der Ptolemäerzeit', *Zeitschrift für ägyptische Sprache und Altertumskunde* 60 (1925), 86–102.

Indian traders acted as intermediaries.[108] Furthermore, among the various theories advanced in antiquity about the 'discovery' of the monsoon route between the Red Sea and India, two point to the Ptolemaic period (see section V.1 below).

The issue of continuities between the Hellenistic and Roman periods is an important one. In the most obvious sense, the port of Berenike was a Ptolemaic foundation.[109] Yet it seems that the initiatives of the Ptolemaic period were aimed at control of the Red Sea (in the narrow modern sense), rather than of the Indian Ocean trade.[110] The *Periplus* offers a revealing comment on the port of Eudaimon Arabia, modern-day Aden, which had fallen on evil days by the time he was writing:

> Eudaimon Arabia, previously a fully-fledged city, was called Eudaimon ('prosperous') when it used to receive the cargoes of both India and Egypt, since ships from India did not venture as far as Egypt and those from Egypt did not dare sail to farther destinations but came only this far, just as Alexandria receives goods from distant lands as well as from Egypt. (26)[111]

The suggestion here that there was trade activity predating the *Periplus* is a significant one, and one that adds resonance to Strabo's comment at 2.5.12 C118, that the Roman takeover of Egypt boosted trade with India. It is important to note the *Periplus* author's reference to 'vessels from India': it is quite possible that these were Arabian or Indian vessels rather than ones from Egypt.

The picture becomes even more complicated when we consider the other large Hellenistic kingdom, that of the Seleucids. Now there are a number of signs that the Seleucid empire pursued some trade contact with India, and this points us toward alternatives to the monsoon route. It is after all true that the *Periplus* shows no more than a most rudimentary knowledge of the Gulf. Seleucid commercial exploitation of Failaka and of Dilmun had roots in earlier trading patterns involving Mesopotamian peoples.[112] In fact, this is the point at which we must consider trade in the Arabian Gulf in

108 Raschke, 'New studies', 637–50, accords a prominent role to intermediaries.

109 Pliny (6.168) tells us that Ptolemy II Philadelphus founded Berenike in his mother's honour.

110 Sidebotham, *Roman economic policy*.

111 εὐδαίμων δὲ ἐπεκλήθη, πρότερον οὖσα πόλις, ὅτε, μήπω ἀπὸ τῆς Ἰνδικῆς εἰς τὴν Αἴγυπτον ἐρχομένων μηδὲ ἀπὸ Αἰγύπτου τολμώντων εἰς τοὺς ἔσω τόπους διαίρειν ἀλλ᾽ ἄχρι ταύτης παραγινομένων, τοὺς παρὰ ἀμφοτέρων φόρτους ἀπεδέχετο, ὥσπερ Ἀλεξάνδρεια καὶ τῶν ἔξωθεν καὶ τῶν ἀπὸ τῆς Αἰγύπτου φερομένων ἀποδέχεται. Compare this passage with Plin. *HN* 12.82–88.

112 Jean-François Salles, 'The Arab-Persian Gulf under the Seleucids', in *Hellenism in the East*, ed. Amélie Kuhrt and Susan Sherwin-White (Berkeley: University of California Press, 1987), pp. 75–108.

a slightly broader compass. This is something that helps put the monsoon trade in perspective, but not without adding problems of its own. Excavations undertaken since the 1950s in Bahrain (Dilmun of ancient Sumerian sources) suggest that trade activity in the Arabian Gulf reached a high point in the period around 3300–2200 BC. The island acted as a clearing house for exchange involving the Mesopotamian and Indus valley civilisations, a role it lost only with the decline of India's Harappan civilisation in the early second millennium BC.[113]

The first centuries of the first millennium BC saw expansion of trade activity in the Gulf: there had been active trade links between India and Mesopotamia or southern Iran under the Neoassyrians and Neobabylonians, lasting at least through the Achaemenid empire.[114] Later still, the Achaemenids and Seleucids maintained a naval presence in the Gulf to support their entrepôts. Rather than establishing a colonial settlement in the usual sense, the Seleucids seem to have pursued a deliberate policy with commercial objectives.[115]

It is important here to see Seleucid commerce as a continuation of earlier activity in the Gulf. Its continued use into Roman times is something to keep in mind, and prevents us from seeing the *Periplus* trade in isolation. The *Parthian stations* of Isidore of Charax (early first century AD), not to mention the archaeological record of sites such as Palmyra, must keep us mindful that overland transport in the very period of the *Periplus* continued to be an important alternative. The Gulf, together with the Euphrates (for someone sailing upstream) provided an alternative route that then led overland from Palmyra. This settlement in modern-day Syria is the only definite 'caravan city' for whom trade represents an entire raison d'être.[116] There can be no doubt that it was a major commercial centre with various trade-routes passing through it. Appian provides an instructive reference to Palmyra in narrating the events of 41 BC (*Civil wars* 5.9). Antonius sends troops to plunder Palmyra: his motives are the enrichment of his soldiers,

113 R. H. Brunswig, A. Parpola and D. Potts, 'New Indus type and related seals from the Near East', in *Dilmun: new studies in the archaeology and early history of Bahrain*, ed. D. T. Potts (Berlin: Reimer, 1983), pp. 101–15; Michael Rice, *Search for the paradise island* (London: Longman, 1984), p. 8; Harriet Crawford, *Dilmun and its Gulf neighbours* (Cambridge University Press, 1998), p. 141.

114 Michael Rice, *The archaeology of the Arabian Gulf, c. 5000–323 BC* (London: Routledge, 1994); cf. H. Schiwek, 'Das Persische Golf als Schiffahrts- und Seehandelsroute in Achämenidischer Zeit und in der Zeit Alexanders des Grossen', *Bonner Jahrbücher* 162 (1962), 4–97.

115 Salles, 'Arab-Persian Gulf', p. 98.

116 M. Rostovtseff, *Caravan cities* (Oxford University Press, 1932), had written in broadly similar terms also of Petra and Gerasa (Jerash) in Jordan, and Dura-Europos on the Euphrates. This is subject to critique by Millar, 'Caravan cities'; cf. Will, *Palmyréniens*, pp. 57–102, esp. 78–81, and Young, *Rome's eastern trade*, pp. 136–86.

says Appian, though he invents a pretext for the attack. But in the event, the Palmyrenes, forewarned, transported themselves and their goods to the far side of the river, and from there protected themselves with their archery. Of significance to us here is Appian's gloss on the Palmyrenes, who 'being traders, bring Indian and Arabian goods from the Persians and distribute them in Roman territory'.[117] Pliny (5.88) speaks of Palmyra as preserving its own fortunes, given its economic role and its location in an interstitial zone between the Roman and Parthian empires. It should thus be stressed that the extensive use of the monsoon from the Augustan period onward brought about a partial, not complete, change of trade-routes.

In late antiquity, Greco-Roman seaborne trade with India was to be eclipsed by Axumite trade. It is the *Periplus* that offers the earliest reference in Greek literature to the city of Axum, at a stage when it had not yet acquired its subsequent prominence:

On this section of the coast, facing [the island of] Oreine, the moderately sized village of Adulis is located twenty stades inland. From Adulis it is a three-day journey to Koloe,[118] an inland city that is the first trading post for ivory, and from there another five days to the metropolis itself, which is called Axum; all the ivory from beyond the Nile is brought into it through what is called Kyeneion, and from there down to Adulis. The large number of elephants and rhinoceroses slaughtered all inhabit the upland regions, though very occasionally they are also seen on the coast around Adulis itself. (4)[119]

The city of Axum emerges from the *Periplus* as the main commercial centre of the Southern Red Sea basin.[120] From the later third to the seventh century AD its power was to expand to such an extent that we can talk about an Axumite kingdom. The fact that Axum began to mint its own coins from the third century may well indicate its increasing economic self-determination.[121] Its high point came in the mid-fourth century following the conquest of Meroe.[122] Central to its power as an empire would be its

[117] ἔμποροι γὰρ ὄντες κομίζουσι μὲν ἐκ Περσῶν τὰ Ἰνδικὰ ἢ Ἀράβια, διατίθενται δ' ἐν τῇ Ῥωμαίων.

[118] This location does not fit well with Ptolemy's reference to the city of Koloe (4.7.25): see further Casson, *Periplus*, p. 106.

[119] καὶ κατ' αὐτὴν τὴν ἐν τῇ Ὀρεινῇ ἤπειρον ἀπὸ σταδίων εἴκοσι τῆς θαλάσσης ἐστὶν ἡ Ἄδουλι, κώμη σύμμετρος, ἀφ' ἧς εἰς μὲν Κολόην μεσόγειον πόλιν καὶ πρῶτον ἐμπόριον τοῦ ἐλέφαντος ὁδός ἐστιν ἡμερῶν τριῶν· ἀπὸ δὲ ταύτης εἰς αὐτὴν τὴν μητρόπολιν τὸν Ἀξωμίτην λεγόμενον ἄλλων ἡμέρων πέντε, εἰς ὃν ὁ πᾶς ἐλέφας ἀπὸ τοῦ πέραν τοῦ Νείλου φέρεται διὰ τοῦ λεγομένου Κυηνείου, ἐκεῖθεν δὲ εἰς Ἄδουλι. τὸ μὲν οὖν ὅλον πλῆθος τῶν φονευομένων ἐλεφάντων καὶ ῥινοκερώτων περὶ τοὺς ἄνω νέμεται τόπους, σπανίως δέ ποτε καὶ ἐν τῷ παρὰ θάλασσαν περὶ αὐτὴν τὴν Ἄδουλι θεωροῦνται.

[120] Burstein, *Ancient African civilizations*, p. 18.

[121] Sidebotham, *Roman economic policy*, p. 47 n. 94.

[122] Once Axum first circulated coins, in the third century, they used Greek as well as Sabaean and Ethiopic, thus suggesting some degree of Hellenic influence.

role in the Red Sea trade, a role it was finally to lose with the Arab conquest of Egypt and the Near East. Kushite civilisation reached its apogee at much the same time as the *Periplus* trade, that is in the first and second centuries AD, as we gather from the archaeological record of its cult monuments and royal pyramids.[123] It was thus not till somewhat later than the *Periplus* that Axumite trade rises, stepping into the breach left by the decline in direct Greco-Roman commerce.

This consideration of chronology shows that the first two centuries AD indeed seem to have been a high point of commercial contact, but in the limited sense of the monsoon trade only, and in so far as traders from Roman Egypt were undertaking the entire journey on their own. However, every effort should be made to keep this in perspective, both by being aware of traces of the participation of Arab and Indian traders, and particularly of the phenomenon of 'tramp trading' (for which the *Periplus* itself gives extensive evidence).[124] Furthermore, the monsoon should be seen in terms of much larger trade networks also, especially the Arabian Gulf route which flourished in the third millennium BC and was also known to Romans, though not obviously to the *Periplus* author. Significant new work has shown the degree of commerce between the subcontinent and southeast Asia, something on which the Greco-Roman sources have relatively little to say.[125] The broader context of the eastern trade has implications for any attempt to assess Roman experiences of the subcontinent, direct or indirect (section V.1 below).

IV. COUNTING COMMODITIES, OR HOW TO LIE WITH STATISTICS

The two best-known passages concerning Roman trade with the east are to be found in Pliny's *Natural history*. The first comes in the context of his topographic discussion of the parts of the inhabited world, at a point when he is discussing the Indian Ocean:

And it will not be inappropriate to set out the entire route from Egypt, now that reliable information of it is available for the first time. It is an important topic, given that in no year does India drain off less than fifty million sesterces of our

[123] Derek A. Welsby, *The kingdom of Kush: the Napatan and Meroitic empires* (Princeton: Markus Wiener, 1998), esp. p. 199.

[124] *Pace* Miller, *Spice trade*, p. 241, who claims that 'most of the Indian trade by sea was direct'.

[125] *Indian Ocean*, ed. Reade; but see section V below for ancient information on the Bay of Bengal.

empire's wealth, sending back goods to be sold among us at a hundred times their original cost. (6.101)[126]

Pliny proceeds, after this passage, to describe the route taken by traders on the way to India, on much the same lines as described in section III above: they would sail down the Nile from Alexandria, cross the Eastern Desert, then embark at one of two ports on Egypt's Red Sea coast (6.104–6). The tone of this passage is neutral, and the reference to commercial activity serves to underline the importance of the topic rather than undermine it; but in a comparable passage elsewhere Pliny sounds a moralising note.[127] Here the discussion is about spices and their origin. Proceeding regionally, Pliny is here covering 'Happy Arabia' (*Arabia Felix*, where the adjective in the name carries connotations of fertility and prosperity too):

But the title 'happy' is still more appropriate to the Arabian Sea, for it is the source of the pearls which that country sends us. And by the lowest count India, China and the Arabian peninsula remove 100 million sesterces from our empire each year – that is what our luxuries and our women cost us. For what fraction of these, I ask you, now goes to the gods or to the underworld deities? (12.84)[128]

Moral rectitude again emerges as the all-important lens through which Pliny visualises the issues at hand. Nonetheless, this obvious insight cannot exonerate us from considering in more strictly economic terms the implications of luxury consumption. Both passages contain numbers which are potentially valuable evidence; in fact they have been used to support the most divergent kinds of analysis. They have been dismissed as ideological projections.[129] As a hypothesis, we might nonetheless still want to ask what these figures, and indeed the undoubted reality of the trade as a whole, mean for the Roman economy. Such a question obviously has implications for any understanding of Pliny's statements above; can they in any way be used to write an economic history of Rome? The larger question concerns the place of trade in the economy, long-distance trade in non-essential items

126 *nec pigebit totum cursum ab Aegypto exponere, nunc primum certa notitia patescente: digna res, nullo anno minus HS.|D| [milia] imperii nostri exhauriente India et merces remittente, quae apud nos centiplicato veneant.*

127 Wallace-Hadrill, 'The elder Pliny', and Beagon, *Roman nature*. In the case of the second passage Pliny's negative attitude to the emperor Nero accounts for some of the animus shown: Beagon, *Roman nature*, p. 191.

128 *verum Arabiae etiamnum felicius mare est; ex illo namque margaritas mittit. minimaque computatione miliens centena milia sestertium annis omnibus India et Seres et paeninsula illa imperio nostro adimunt: tanti nobis deliciae et feminae constant. quota enim portio ex illis ad deos, quaeso, iam vel ad inferos pertinet?*

129 Thus Moses I. Finley, *The ancient economy*, 2nd edn (Berkeley: University of California Press, 1985), p. 132, influentially.

being one subsection of trade *tout court*. It is worth stating the obvious here: of the goods discussed in section I above, none is a subsistence item, and there is every indication that high-value items predominated by far in the eastern trade. Yet, one complication arises when we bear in mind that this trade passed through Egypt, the breadbasket of imperial Rome. Within the Mediterranean itself, the distribution of these luxury items will not have been as easily distinguished from the bulk transport of staple products as would have been the case in the Red Sea and the Indian Ocean.

There are several senses in which Pliny's figures are a problem. One is that the current archaeological record on the subcontinent provides nowhere near the quantity of gold (or silver) coins suggested. Of course no great conclusions can be placed on this fact in itself, especially when, as shown above, some coin hoards have indeed been found and many still await scholarly examination. Secondly, it is clear from the *Periplus* that coins are among the items exchanged in the eastern trade. Thus the major port of Barygaza in the northwestern province of Gujarat offers a market for 'Roman money, gold and silver, which commands an exchange at some profit against the local currency' (49): these are listed among several items for import and export. Further, the port of Bakare farther south is also listed as a major importer of money, this being one of the items for which pepper and malabathron would be obtained (56). As indicated above, it is possible that gold and silver coins were melted down or otherwise used as bullion outside of their original area of exchange; the fact that hoards were frequently slashed or punched suggests they could have been disqualified from reintroduction into the narrower Roman economy of the Mediterranean.

Perhaps the greatest pitfall in the attempt to make economic sense of this trade is the error of enthusiasm, the tendency to overestimate its extent.[130] Reasons for such enthusiasm are not hard to find, when it suggests a model of commercial activity much more glamorous than the exchange of the staples, such as the 'Mediterranean triad' of wine, olive oil and wheat, the first two of which are especially well attested archaeologically. So the extent of the luxury trade has enormous implications for any understanding of the Roman economy: to emphasise the trade in commodities, at the expense of staples, is to give ancient trade a modern aspect. How much was the supply of luxury goods driven by the demand at home? Did the state promote and regulate the trade, or was it entirely in the hands of entrepreneurs working in their own interest? When modern western economic practices have been so intensively studied, with so much more evidence to hand,

[130] Whittaker, 'To reach out', 20.

there are both advantages and dangers in adopting modern analyses in order to understand premodern. All of these subsidiary questions impact on the way in which we characterise ancient economic practices generally. In sum, we are faced with two distinct questions: can we, and should we separate ancient moralising from economics?

Self-evidently, it is impossible to make sense out of statistics such as Pliny's without a broader context. The most recent comprehensive assessment of the Roman imperial economy estimates the mint production at around 170–200 million sesterces per annum, reaching about one-quarter of the total budget of around 800 million sesterces.[131] By this reckoning, fully one-eighth of the total budget of the early empire was being siphoned off to the greater Red Sea region – an improbably high percentage. But here the Muziris papyrus offers valuable evidence, for the loan agreement to which it refers states its total value at 1,154 talents and 2,852 drachmae of silver, which would have amounted to a massive 7 million sesterces.[132] Strabo says, on the basis of his own experience, that 120 ships per year would sail from the Red Sea port of Myos Hormos to India (2.5.12 C118), a number that presumably would have increased hugely if other Red Sea ports were included. Thus, even if these figures are not adjusted considerably, they suggest that Pliny's numbers at the start of this section are still within the bounds of the possible.

Further, if the average annual income per head in the Roman empire around Pliny's time has been calculated at somewhat below 400 HS, then the figures mentioned by Pliny are astronomical. On the other hand, the same study emphasises the high degree to which wealth was concentrated in the hands of a very small group: 600 senatorial families received some 0.6 per cent of the total personal income, and the top 3 per cent received between 20 and 25 per cent.[133] If we can thus conclude that a small number of Romans were extremely wealthy, then Pliny's numbers are not so unbelievable. His high figures may thus be explained by the wealth of the richest Romans both in having the spare resources for such purchases, and their use for them in maintaining the luxurious lifestyle.

A further general consideration keeps Pliny's figures within the limits of credibility. It seems likely that a very high percentage of the Roman empire's gross national product was materialised in the form of gold and

131 R. Duncan-Jones, *Money and government in the Roman Empire* (Cambridge University Press, 1994).

132 Millar, 'Looking east', 531.

133 R. W. Goldsmith, 'An estimate of the size and structure of the national product of the early Roman empire', *Review of Income and Wealth* 30 (1984), 263–88.

silver coinage, and was thus in circulation.[134] This feature is of course in stark contrast to the modern American economy, in which only a very small fraction of the GNP is in circulation at any one time. As a result, though this was a huge sum of money, it would not have affected the Roman economy to the extent Pliny implies. Again this would mean that Pliny's statistics for the supposed haemorrhage are not impossible a priori. This conclusion comes as something of a surprise when there has already been so much evidence for Pliny's ethical concerns. Certainly, the moralistic edge of Pliny's comments are no guarantee that they make bad economic sense.

The demand side of the eastern trade is easily established and needs little clarification. The city of Rome was in the late Republic more of a consumer city than the Mediterranean world had ever seen before; this meant, among other things, the ever increasing need for grain to be imported from far afield to satisfy the needs of its population.[135] Its population may have been as high as 500,000 around the turn of the millennium, making it by far the Mediterranean's largest city. Its cosmopolitanism is seen in many sources, not least Juvenal's *Satires* and Martial's *Epigrams*. Popular entertainments were more important than ever before in securing the goodwill of the Roman *plebs*, and these alone created a demand for the wild animals mentioned in section I.5 above. Whereas they played an important role in the political rivalries that marked the middle decades of the first centuries BC, under the Principate of Octavian/Augustus they continued to be a sign of imperial beneficence. The description of the spectacles given above already made it clear that, at least in contemporary descriptions to survive, there was a politics of numbers: the greater the number of animals that were killed, the more impressive, and hence the more effective, the spectacle.

But there was, in addition, a private aspect to this. The legendary wealth of Lucullus and Pompey, both obtained on military campaigns in the eastern Mediterranean, provided the benchmark for conspicuous consumption. The area of the Bay of Naples, archaeologically well preserved as a result of the eruption of Vesuvius in AD 79, contained élite areas with villa complexes. It is here that the social practices and attitudes of the Roman élite have been well studied, especially through architectural remains.[136]

[134] Duncan-Jones, *Money and government*.

[135] Purcell, 'The city of Rome and the *plebs urbana*', pp. 644–88.

[136] John H. D'Arms, *Romans on the Bay of Naples* (Cambridge, MA: Harvard University Press, 1970); Andrew Wallace-Hadrill, *Houses and society in Pompeii and Herculaneum* (Princeton University Press, 1994); Paul Zanker, *Pompeii: public and private life* (Cambridge, MA: Harvard University Press, 1998).

The younger Seneca takes a grim view of this world of pleasures: in aphoristic fashion he says that 'people eat to vomit and vomit to eat. Their dishes are brought from every corner of the earth, but they do not even bother to digest them.'[137] Trimalchio's dinner-party, with its eminently lavish fare, is exactly the kind of gathering Seneca will have had in mind, all the more so in light of the host's upstart social status. And when Pliny tells of individual fish that cost the price of three cooks (9.67), or Juvenal of a mullet that cost 6,000 sesterces (*Sat.* 4), there is moral outrage, but there is also a note of fascination underlying the account. It is to a later account that we must turn to see both competitiveness of consumption and its hold over an author's imagination. Macrobius, writing around AD 400, tells the story of rivalry between Mark Antony and Cleopatra in the 30s BC. So greedy had Antony become for the delights of the east that he had conquered Egypt; but his wife Cleopatra, 'since she could not endure being outdone in luxury by Romans' (*quae uinci a Romanis nec luxuria dignaretur*), took a bet with him that she could consume 10 million sesterces at a single dinner. This she won by drinking a large pearl that she had dissolved in vinegar.[138] In this admittedly extreme example, in which the passage of four centuries had made Antony and Cleopatra into *bons vivants* of legendary proportions, the rhetoric of numbers is a means of one-upmanship.

Thus far we have seen large numbers but there are numbers on a smaller scale too. Pliny's account of eastern spices in book 12 makes consistent reference to the price fetched at Rome in each case. Thus, for example, long pepper sells at fifteen denarii per pound, white pepper at seven, black at four.[139] This is in itself a reminder that we cannot expect Pliny's work to be in any sense 'pure' natural history, a concept against which Foucault argued with regard to eighteenth-century encyclopaedias.[140] In effect, when Pliny's text does reflect the information from contemporary traders (admittedly, less so than the authority of texts), it is in some ways closer than one might have expected to the *Periplus*. Without denying the utilitarian nature of this text, it is also striking that here too we find information, both historical and natural historical, which would be of no apparent value to a trader. Nobody would deny the power of textual authority in Pliny's *Natural history*, as has been made evident by contrast with other forms of authority on any one topic.[141] But a comparison with the *Periplus* allows us to glimpse an unexpected facet of the making of this important work.

137 *Helv.* 10.3; cf. *Ep.* 95.42. And see Edwards, *Politics of immortality*, pp. 186–7.
138 *Sat.* 3.17.15; cf. Plin. *HN* 9.120–21.
139 12.28; cf. Miller, *Spice trade*, pp. 26–8.
140 Foucault, *Discipline and punish*.
141 Lloyd, *Science, folklore*, pp. 139–45.

To conclude this section, we are left with the problem of numbers, both the large numbers for the trade as a whole, and the smaller ones for individual commodities. Nobody will deny their usefulness for certain kinds of economic history, yet there are serious difficulties in using them; but they should not be used uncritically when they appear in historical sources.[142] Certainly, it is appropriate to say that Pliny's statistics are suspect: they are suspiciously rounded, and in any case, it is unclear what source could possibly have given him the information he claims to have. So Pliny himself may have been lying with statistics, using them to reinforce points motivated by concerns with morality. But at all events their purely econometric function is of limited use to us in the present inquiry. Invaluable statistical analyses have been done on the Roman economy, and with justification these continue to be used; however, when we are speaking of the wider region of the eastern trade, the margin for error escalates in undertaking such analyses, and the available evidence may simply not be adequate. Cultural factors should be considered relative not only to the Greco-Roman world, but also the Indian or other areas, including the Arabian peninsula and north Africa. It is much the safest option to make a virtue out of the biases in sources for the social meaning of Indian goods, since this is what is attested abundantly.

V. MAPPING COMMODITIES

'Brazil, where the nuts come from' (Brandon Thomas, *Charley's Aunt*)

To what extent was Roman geographical knowledge about India generated by trade activity? (This question is deliberately posed in such a way as to maintain the view from Rome.) It is worth noting that many of the passages discussed in section I above are not formally and explicitly geographical but are drawn from other literary genres. This alone is a reminder that popular thinking linked commodities and the particular place called India. So when an Apician recipe specifies that *spica Indica* should be used, that can be said to constitute a popular conception of India, whether the specification *Indica* in any such case emphasises that the product supposedly comes from India, or that the Indian variety rather than any other should be used. We should try to get beyond this limited though widespread link of product and place.

Scrutiny of geographical treatises, especially those of Strabo and Ptolemy, add new dimensions to the question, and they make clear that the practice

[142] D. Huff, *How to lie with statistics*, 2nd edn (New York: Norton, 1993).

of trade did much to make India known, beyond the limited sense mentioned above. Most obviously, Ptolemy in his *Geography* devotes considerable attention to India's east coast and to other parts of the Bay of Bengal. In his seventh book Ptolemy describes the western side of the Ganges, then the eastern (chapters 1 and 2), before proceeding to describe the island of Taprobane or Sri Lanka (3) and to delineate the inhabited world more generally (4). Thus it is the Ganges, at the north of the Bay of Bengal, that acts as the key divider of India. It should also be noted that these are the last of the world's regions given in Ptolemy's rationalisation of space. Like Ptolemy's other 'descriptions' this is very statistical: that is, particular points are plotted with their co-ordinates; in the case of these regions, the points which Ptolemy maps are settlements, river mouths and mountains. He provides almost double the amount of information for India on the near side of the Ganges than beyond, giving the impression of a marked difference of available geographical knowledge. Two striking features of Ptolemy's South Asia is that India is greatly flattened, in other words it has nowhere near the character of a subcontinent so familiar from modern maps; and that the size of Sri Lanka is much exaggerated. Both features are still reflected in fifteenth-century maps of the India Ocean. However, the crucial point here is that it can only have been through merchants, one way or another, that Ptolemy obtained the information revealed in this part of his work.[143]

In order to gauge the significance of this, we should bear in mind that the Alexander histories present almost exclusively the Indus Valley; Pliny and the *Periplus* focuses on the west coast, though it does briefly mention the east. The pattern is thus clear: it is the western part of India, and particularly the Indus Valley, that is best represented in Greek and Roman literary texts of high prestige; the east coast, on the other hand, receives little attention at all, and then only in the lower-status texts linked with trade. We have already seen that long-distance traders were looked down upon.[144] It appears that this had a direct impact on the social value of the topographical information associated with them. As regards India, Strabo says as much in a telling passage for the sociology of geographical knowledge:

As for the merchants who nowadays sail from Egypt via the Nile and Arabian Gulf as far as India, few have sailed as far as the Ganges, and even these are merely

[143] For merchants among Ptolemy's sources see O. A. W. Dilke, 'The culmination of Greek cartography in Ptolemy', in *History of cartography*, ed. Harley and Woodward, vol. I, pp. 177–200, at 178.

[144] John H. D'Arms, *Commerce and social standing in ancient Rome* (Cambridge, MA: Harvard University Press, 1981).

private individuals and are useless with regard to accounts of the places visited. (15.1.4 C686)[145]

The context of this remark is the difficulty of obtaining any information about India, and the importance of Alexander in doing so for certain parts of it. Strabo strongly implies that the cachet of geographical knowledge is in direct proportion to that of the person identified with it. It is also in this regard that we see the relative prestige value of the various texts discussed in the view of contemporary Romans: at the high end are the Alexander historians, with Strabo's *Geography* close behind; Pliny's *Natural history* and Ptolemy's *Geography* seem to be considerably lower. Certainly, Pliny's learned encyclopaedia is based on thousands of earlier works, as he is at pains to stress; yet he admits the presence of more everyday, lower prestige kinds of information, not least when discussing the geography of South Asia: 'now that reliable information is available for the first time'.[146] Ptolemy's text is in many ways the most scientific geographic text produced in Greco-Roman antiquity, yet its technical nature associated it more with merchants than *literati*; in the end it is hard to judge the contemporary status of and responses to this work, however important it was to prove in the Renaissance.

It would, however, appear that differences of social status among the users of spatial information influenced or even created different registers of geographical thought. In the rest of this section, this thesis will be developed in two directions, namely the issue of experience in the acquisition of knowledge about India, and the specificity of India relative to a more generalised 'east'.

V.1. Experience and mediation

It would be possible to hold that supposedly Indian goods were linked with various kinds of lived experience on the part of ancient Greeks and Romans: most commonly, direct experience of pepper and other luxuries; direct experience of a small number of merchantmen; less direct experience is available to ordinary persons via the accounts of others. The ultimate authorising experience, on this model, is that of Alexander on his eastern campaign; the same things that are being tasted and smelled in the Rome

145 Καὶ οἱ νῦν δὲ ἐξ Αἰγύπτου πλέοντες ἐμπορικοὶ τῷ Νείλῳ καὶ τῷ Ἀραβίῳ κόλπῳ μέχρι τῆς Ἰνδικῆς σπάνιοι μὲν καὶ περιπεπλεύκασι μέχρι τοῦ Γάγγου, καὶ οὗτοι δ' ἰδιῶται καὶ οὐδὲν πρὸς ἱστορίαν τῶν τόπων χρήσιμοι.

146 6.101 *nunc primum certa notitia patescente.*

of Pliny's time receive in the *Natural history* their foundation myth in the person of Alexander (e.g., book 12). It is thus typical, for example, that when his survey of trees reaches India, Alexander is the focaliser:

Now we will present those trees at which Alexander the Great's conquest marvelled once that part of the universe was first revealed.[147]

The *Pala* tree is the marker of the campaign's farthest point, and another is remembered for having caused diarrhoea among the troops (12.24). By way of comparison, even the *Periplus*, which seems so much like a functional text without literary embellishment, lives in the memory of Alexander:

Alexander, setting out from these parts, penetrated as far as the Ganges but did not get to Limyrike and the south of India. For this reason, one can find on the market in Barygaza even today old drachmas engraved with the inscriptions, in Greek letters, of Apollodotus and Menander, rulers who came after Alexander. (47)[148]

The past plays no major role in the work, but it is no coincidence that such a sense of the past as there is centres on Alexander. Elsewhere the *Periplus* author speaks of a place on India's northwest coast as 'preserving to this very day signs of Alexander's expedition, ancient shrines and the foundations of encampments and huge wells' (41).[149]

Perfumes were first used by the Persians, according to Pliny: when Alexander defeated King Darius he captured a chest of them, and this is how they came to the Greek world. From there it was a short step to their use among Romans as part of the elegant life (13.2). Alexander is thus presented not exactly as the first inventor of the practice, but as the agent of its transmission from the east to the Mediterranean, a role attributed to Pompey in other instances (see section II above).

The figure of Alexander is crucial, once again, as a lens by which India exists in Roman minds. And, though there is a superficial attractiveness to using experience as a criterion for assessing his and other responses to India, it is ultimately unsatisfactory. To speak in an unproblematic way of experience is to imply that there is some authentic, originary quality,

[147] 12.21 *nunc eas exponemus quas mirata est Alexandri magni victoria orbe eo patefacto*. By something of a stretch of syntax, the subject of the first subordinate clause is not Alexander himself but his conquest, *victoria*.

[148] Καὶ Ἀλέξανδρος ὁρμηθεὶς ἀπὸ τῶν μερῶν τούτων ἄχρι τοῦ Γάγγους διῆλθε, καταλιπὼν τήν τε Λιμυρικὴν καὶ τὰ νότια τῆς Ἰνδικῆς· ἀφ' οὗ μέχρι νῦν ἐν βαρυγάζοις παλαιαὶ προχωροῦσι δραχμαί, γράμμασιν Ἑλληνικοῖς ἐγκεχαραγμέναι ἐπίσημα τῶν μετ' Ἀλέξανδρον βεβασιλευκότων Ἀπολλοδότου καὶ Μενάνδρου.

[149] Σώζεται δὲ ἔτι καὶ νῦν τῆς Ἀλεξάνδρου στρατιᾶς σημεῖα περὶ τοὺς τόπους, ἱερά τε ἀρχαῖα καὶ θεμέλιοι παρεμβολῶν καὶ φρέατα μέγιστα.

which merely awaits uncovering from under layers of discourse.[150] Given how unsatisfactory this assumption is, it is better to concentrate on those layers in their own right, to focus on what we might call different tenors of mediation. This also allows us to write Roman subjects themselves into the account. In these terms, Alexander's expedition is highly mediated for a Roman in the first century AD, by a complex tissue of social memory and history. There were other journeys too, mediated by different forms of discourse, just as 'Indian' objects themselves provided kinds of mediation. At this point we should consider other journeys to India that provided, in one way or another, a certain kind of authorising experience in Roman minds.

An important foundation myth in this story concerns the supposed discovery of the monsoon, and it is worth brief consideration here for the way in which it writes individual heroes into history. There are four candidates. First and foremost, there is the figure of shadowy Hippalos: the *Periplus* states that the monsoon was thus named after its discoverer (57). It gives no date, though it has been suggested that he was steersman of Eudoxus.[151] It is from Strabo, secondly, that we hear about this Eudoxus of Cyzicus who, towards the end of the reign of Ptolemy VIII Euergetes II (*c.* 117 BC), was sent from Alexandria to explore sea-trading routes along the African coast. As a guide Eudoxus used an Indian sailor who had narrowly survived a shipwreck. Eudoxus was blown off course while sailing down the African coast; on a subsequent voyage he set out from Alexandria in order to circumnavigate Africa.[152] Thirdly, one Iambulos is mentioned in Theophrastus (*Research on plants* 9.7.2), Diodorus Siculus (2.55.2; 2.60.1–4) and Pliny (12.135; 13.18). While engaged in the spice trade off the Somali coast, he was blown off course to an island, perhaps Sri Lanka. There he spent several years, before visiting Palibothra and returning overland.[153] Lastly, one story about the discovery of the monsoon centres on the unnamed freedman of

150 For problems with the category of experience as a foundation of historical inquiry, see, e.g., Joan W. Scott, 'Experience', in *Feminists theorize the political*, ed. Judith Butler and Joan W. Scott (New York: Routledge, 1992), pp. 71–96.

151 E.g., Dihle, *Antike und Orient*, p. 120; Casson, *Periplus*, p. 224. The suggestion that it represents some kind of 'submarine' wind, i.e. sea-current (ὕφαλος), does not persuade, ingenious though it may be: Santo Mazzarino, 'On the name of the *Hipalus* (*Hippalus*) wind in Pliny', in *Crossings: early Mediterranean contact with India*, ed. F. de Romanis and A. Tchernia (Delhi: Manohar, 1997), pp. 72–9.

152 Strabo 2.3.4–6 C98–102, based on Poseidonius (= *FGrH* 87 F 28); cf. also Pomponius Mela 3.90 and 92, and Pliny 2.169, both of them based on a lost geographical work of Nepos (cf. 6.188). Among modern scholars see J. H. Thiel, *Eudoxus of Cyzicus: a chapter in the history of the sea-route to India and the route around the Cape in ancient times* (Groningen: Wolters, 1967), though the extent of Eudoxus' travels may be exaggerated.

153 Widu-Wolfgang Ehlers, 'Mit dem Monsunwind nach Indien', *WJA* 11 (1984), 73–84.

Annius Plocamus, and is found also in Pliny (6.84–85 and 12.30 instead). Carried astray by winds, the unnamed freedman reached the island of Sri Lanka after a fortnight. (In Pliny's version 'Hippuros' is not a person but a place in Sri Lanka.) He is entertained by the king, who is so impressed by the consistent weight of Roman *denarii* that he sends an embassy back to Rome.[154] The intriguing possibility is that this is the same person who is attested in the bilingual inscription mentioned in section III.1 above.

Self-evidently, these stories have several features in common: 'discovery' by someone engaged in commercial activity; chance arrival on the southern part of the subcontinent, or alternatively in Taprobane. All of them have, to some degree, the character of an episode from the Greek novel, and this alone is grounds for suspicion about their empirical value. What we can conclude from the evidence discussed is that there was some debate on the timing involved, as if it required to be discovered more than once. This is not the place to adjudicate between the different claims: rather, the various stories are attempts to identify the origins of the *Periplus* trade, and are thus foundation myths of a kind. We can see this as part of a subjective history of Rome, even if the ethnocentric concept of 'discovery' is particularly awkward here. In a sense it is true that 'there was little to discover, since the Arabs knew of it earlier'.[155] Yet we must be mindful of the above stories as ways by which Romans made sense of the monsoon to themselves.

There are many interesting aspects to these stories, not least the fortuitous accident. In fact, the English word 'serendipity' comes from a medieval Arabic version of such a story of the discovery of Sri Lanka (Serendib in Arabic). What is more, the Greek novel provides several parallels to several of the stories recounted above: here again we see the nameless, low-prestige merchants receiving names for the purposes of fictional narration.[156] It must be remembered that the novel was itself not a canonical genre in antiquity, and was thus freer to reflect more of the lower social strata than the 'higher' genres such as epic and tragedy.

On the other hand, it is possible to detect instances of direct experience that have no authorising function in Roman society. Here we are speaking of people such as the author of the *Periplus*: such people are written out of the literary record, most explicitly by Strabo, even though he and Ptolemy almost certainly made use of information stemming from their journeys. The mime (Chapter 2, section I.4) may be considered an oblique

154 Weerakkody, *Taprobane*, p. 45.

155 Romila Thapar, *A history of India*, 2nd edn (London: Penguin, 1990), vol. I, p. 107.

156 Take, for example, the pirates in Xenophon of Ephesus' *Ephesian Tale*, who kidnap the heroine Anthia: cf. Chapter 2, section I.4 above.

pointer to such travel. Furthermore, we know of some people from the Mediterranean who actually were in India at some time. A census register from Arsinoe in Egypt from AD 72–73 mentions a 32-year-old male who is absent 'in India'.[157] Like the author of the *Periplus*, he is nameless today.

There is one other figure of apparently the same social status whose name has lived on vividly: Thomas the Christian missionary. While this is not the place to consider this history of missionary activity in detail,[158] it is nonetheless striking that this figure, widely remembered as the first and most important of his kind, travelled to India as an artisan. The main source on him, the apocryphal *Acts of Saint Thomas*, speak of him not as a merchant, but as a carpenter: it is in this role that he was bought by an agent of the Indian king Gundaphar. And this is how he is initially occupied once in India, giving his earnings to the poor. If the source, which on textual grounds may be dated to the late second or early third century AD, can be trusted on this point, that would make him effectively one of the Yavanas referred to in the Tamil poems. According to tradition, this Thomas was the same person referred to in the Gospels as 'doubting Thomas', and so the story is set around the middle of the first century AD, even though the earliest remaining evidence for it is more than a century later. By any reckoning Thomas has special significance when he continues to be commemorated today as the founding father of Christianity in India.[159] Among the many aspects of the Thomas story that deserve consideration, it is important to recognise here that it constitutes independent evidence for the presence of Yavanas in south India in the first and second centuries AD.

Stories about both the discovery of the monsoon and Thomas' mission may be seen as attempts to add Roman faces to long-term history. They construct experiences which mediated India for Romans who did not themselves travel to the subcontinent. They act as a reminder to us to concentrate on the tenors of mediation themselves rather than the supposed experiences. This is particularly so when that group which experienced India most directly, the traders, were regarded with such disdain in the literary sources.[160] Items of long-distance trade, being geographically encoded, also offered a kind of experience of distant places.

157 P. Lond. 2.260 = Stud. Pal. 4.72–79 at p. 74, line 749.

158 Compare Chapter 6, section V below.

159 L. W. Brown, *The Indian Christians of Saint Thomas* (Cambridge University Press, 1956).

160 D'Arms, *Commerce*. For merchants in Christian tradition the *Apocalypse* is indicative, when it foretells the destruction of the city of Babylon, 'the whore', which may be considered an allegory of Rome: 'the merchants of the earth are waxed rich through the abundance of her delicacies' (18:3).

V.2. Specificity and identification

A central aspect of Edward Said's concept of orientalism is the tendency to generalise about 'the east'. If this chapter has shown that commodities themselves can construct mental maps, then we may well inquire into the applicability of the orientalist model to ancient Greece and Rome. On the face of it, the fit is snug, in light of what we have already seen. With regard to the Indian trade discussed above, there are three possible kinds of generalisation we might hypothetically pursue here, under the sign of orientalism. First, it is possible to construct a generalised 'East' beginning in Asia Minor, the area of Herodotus' Lydians, through the eastern Mediterranean, Arabia, Mesopotamia and extending by extrapolation as far as South Asia. This approach has the advantage of emphasising the fact that, with the possible exception of Lydia, all the lands mentioned produced goods that were marked as distinctive. This may be a gross generalisation, but it is true that all these eastern lands provided the Roman world with high-value commodities to an extent far exceeding that of, say, northern Europe, and hence they do share this feature in common. There was a high-value item from Rome's far northern frontier, namely amber or pine-resin (*sucina*), but this had nowhere near the same impact in quantity and cachet.[161] Broadly speaking, however, topographies of far western and northern lands place much less emphasis on commodities. The contrast serves to clump together the eastern lands all the more tightly.

Secondly, a generalised east can act as a reminder to consider the coexistence of land and sea-routes in long-distance trade. As we have seen in section III above, this is especially important when Greek and Latin sources tend to emphasise the monsoon route at the expense of the Arabian Gulf route, which was no less important; and to emphasise direct trade over indirect. Tramp trading via the Gulf was just as much part of the Asian trade as the monsoon route, over an even longer span of time. In any evaluation of these networks it is necessary to take intermediaries into account, not least the Parthians.

Thirdly, the concept of orientalism can make it easier to see the Indian Ocean writ large as a unified zone of exchange. The exotic element of the Indian Ocean expresses the difference between Mediterranean and more tropical products: spices are an extreme case of distinctiveness, when their Italian equivalents were so different.[162] The effect of the monsoon winds is

161 Barry Cunliffe, *The extraordinary voyage of Pytheas the Greek* (London: Penguin, 2001), pp. 134–50; Dalby, *Empire of pleasures*, p. 207.

162 On large-scale geophysical differences, see most strikingly Jared M. Diamond, *Guns, germs, and steel: the fates of human societies* (New York: Norton, 1997).

such that they facilitate travel not only from Arabia to India but in a series of routes that spanned the entire ocean as far east as Indonesia. It is only relatively recently that a more holistic approach to the Indian Ocean has won its supporters; though it does not seem to exhibit the same unitariness as has recently been shown for the Mediterranean, there is certainly much to be said for viewing the Indian Ocean as a wider zone of contact.[163] In these respects, there can be no doubt that *Orientalism* offers important insights to the present study, not least the entanglement of representations and power relations.

For current purposes, we are still left with difficulties surrounding the specificity of origins. Among the many topics broached by Pliny in his *Natural history* there is a pervasive concern, or perhaps lip-service, to the question of origins. The underlying thought, we might say, is that an object is known by knowing its origin, whether topographical or personal, in the case of an inventor (the sense in which the monsoon was 'invented' or 'discovered'). Consequently, it might be said that he offers a series of geographies of objects: for example, when he discusses trees or marble he organises his material partly by provenance. Certainly, the attempt to pin down the provenance of specific long-distance goods has occupied a great deal of scholarship. However, in its empirical form that is a problem more for conventional archaeology than for intellectual history, or for cognitive archaeologies that seek access to the minds of ancient people. As we have seen, the system quickly breaks down when, for example, the *Periplus* says that 'Indian cinnabar' can be obtained on the island of Dioscorides (modern Suqutra, ch. 30). The emphasis here has been on the *responses* of Romans to Indian goods, which is a side-stepping of the empirical question of origins. If this line of analysis is valid, then it is possible to speak of a foreshortened east seen from the point of view of Roman consumers: it would not have mattered much whether a luxury item came from the Arabian peninsula or south Asia or the horn of Africa, for they would have arrived in the same vessels and caravans. This would be true both of seaborne and overland commerce, viewed from the consumption end.

In the discussion of spices above, we have already touched on the problems in distinguishing origins (botanically determined) from points of distribution. The *Periplus*, with its practical edge, essentially gives us centres of distribution rather than production: in the case of the Indian ports, goods are gathered from the hinterland (e.g., chs. 51, 55). Closer to Italy, there is an object lesson to be learned from a study of Black Sea fish in classical

[163] E.g., Chaudhuri, *Trade and civilisation*; Reade, *Indian Ocean*; Ray, *Archaeology of seafaring* (2003); and Himanshu P. Ray (ed.), *Archaeology of seafaring: the Indian Ocean in the ancient period* (Delhi: Pragati, 1999).

sources. It is now clear that several parts of the Black Sea provided these fish, yet ancient texts consistently give the impression that they came from Byzantium: this was a Greek-built city, the product of colonisation, amidst an area that was considered a wilderness. By the necessities of sea-travel, fish imported from the Black Sea to the Mediterranean would have had to pass through Byzantium on its way to the Aegean. The obvious conclusion is that cultural factors cloud any notion of the provenance of commodities, and this is certainly something to bear in mind regarding Indian goods.[164]

Origins of commodities relate typically to their production, and by extension to their distribution; but consumption plays a major role in this also. From the earliest reference to eastern people, including the Lydians, we see them referred to in Greek sources as consumers, almost by stereotype; the wealth of Croesus is perhaps the most famous example of this. Other examples too can be found. A telling instance is given by Pliny with regard to spices, when he quotes Herodotus to say that the Arabs would pay an annual tribute of one thousand talents of incense to the king of the Persians (12.80, referring to Herodotus 3.97). The point here is as much the practice itself as the fact that Pliny repeats it with a sense of amazement. What we see here is that eastern peoples are both producers and consumers of luxury items, in this case incense produced by Arabs and consumed by the Persian kings. This combined sense of production and consumption emerges as one explanation for the process of generalising about the east in antiquity. It was the Persians that invented perfume; this was introduced to the Greco-Roman world when Alexander found a chest of it among Darius' goods.[165] To look outside of Persia, Cleopatra's supposed drinking of the expensive pearl is an eminent case of conspicuous consumption from Egypt (see section IV above).

VI. CONCLUSION: FRAGMENTS AND BIG MEN

This has been a story of, among other things, fragments and big men. In the most obvious sense, archaeologists deal concretely with the fragments of material remains, which physically or mentally they try to reconstruct into original wholes, a process that is emblematic of the larger attempts

164 David Braund, 'Fish from the Black Sea: classical Byzantium and the Greekness of trade', in *Food in antiquity*, ed. John Wilks *et al.* (University of Exeter Press, 1995), pp. 162–70. On the Black Sea as 'preserve of Constantinople' in the sixteenth century, see Fernand Braudel, *The Mediterranean and the Mediterranean world in the age of Philip II*, tr. Siân Reynolds, 2 vols. (London: Collins, 1972), vol. I, pp. 110–13.

165 Plin. *HN* 13.3; and we should remember that, for Pliny, perfume was the ultimate luxury item, because it could not be reused (13.20).

to reconstruct past societies from pieces of disparate evidence. Both kinds of reconstruction are central to the foregoing pages: they make much use of processes of extrapolation. It might be added that non-archaeological evidence also falls into the larger sense of reconstruction, especially when authors such as Pliny and Athenaeus preserve 'fragments' of earlier authors that are today otherwise lost to us. Further, when a comment is extracted from its original context, for example an Apician recipe is adduced to tell us about the geography of spices, that too functions as a fragment, even when there is no talk of a lost author. In short, the entire exercise here involves the piecing together of (usually small) pieces of data as part of a larger argument in a new context, one that is focused on Roman society. Perhaps the most arresting fragment is the ivory statuette from Pompeii: at first blush, that has a certain integrity to it, and certainly the body is unbroken, yet apparently the thin piece extending from her head is meaningful only if we understand it to have been part of a larger artifact, perhaps a small table. While we can draw some conclusions from the context of its provenance (not least that it was buried at the time of the eruption in AD 79), we know precious little about its social meaning to anyone who might have owned or otherwise interacted with it. If this object had a social biography, it is one of which we have only limited knowledge in the light of present evidence. Rather than deplore the incomplete nature of such understandings, it is useful to recognise fragments as such, for this better attunes us to the dynamics of reception and the nuances of social context.

On the other hand, the twin issues of experience and mediation have also emerged variously and at key points in this chapter. Ancient sources tend to valorise the experience of heroes in recounting the patterns of trade: the biggest man of all, Alexander, looms large in Pliny's account of several of the commodities recounted.[166] Alexander himself, and sometimes others participating in his expedition, are in several instances presented as the first from the Greco-Roman world to experience some particular plant or tree, and indeed the Indus valley itself. In this way he and his entourage answer to Greco-Roman needs for the originator of a custom (*ktistês*), a need which we saw in the mutually contradictory stories about the discovery of the monsoon. Our analysis of the monsoon showed that the entire notion of discovery needs to be reconsidered, as in fact has been the case with the discovery of the Americas. It shows a tension in this account between

[166] It is perhaps Braudel and the *Annales* school that have offered the most compelling critiques and alternatives to the (more Germanic) history of great men and of events: consider, in classical studies, Bruce Hitchner, 'The merits and challenges of an *Annaliste* approach to archaeology', *JRA* 7 (1994), 408–17, with Horden and Purcell, *Corrupting sea*, pp. 36–9.

heroes of the literary sources and the ordinary people, especially traders, about whom we read between the lines: this makes for a kind of tug-of-war between big men and little men. The gendered term is not inappropriate here, given that the only occasions in which women have come into this story has been as metropolitan consumers par excellence (as presented in Propertius) or as commodities themselves (slaves for the Indian king's harem in the *Periplus*). I have suggested that it is not possible to talk about experience without considering the processes whereby those experiences are mediated: by seeing manifestations of the memory of Alexander or of the monsoon discovery, for example, as kinds of discourse constituting tenors of mediation. It is important, through the use of this concept, to bear in mind both that India was, variously, part of the lived experience of ancient Roman and Greek people, and that it is not possible for us today to do more than grasp some sense of what those experiences were like.

But material objects too were a kind of mediation between India and Romans. In so far as, say, pepper was considered an Indian commodity, it afforded any Roman encountering it in cuisine or elsewhere with a 'taste of India'. Such considerations suggest that the tendency to identify objects with places may be strong, but it is vague, almost by definition. This may be true in general, and should not be regarded as a surprise in any sense. It does, however, inject a useful note of caution in considering scholarship on the spice trade. In the case of India, we must emphasise especially the network of trade routes within which the monsoon trade took place, including its coexistence with land routes. As regards the tendency to generalise about *eastern* luxury, it may be important to bear in mind the near Eastern precedents: Mesopotamian and Iranian courts had themselves engaged in considerable trade with South Asia, and (at least in the case of the Achaemenid court) developed their own senses of the *Indian* exotic, if the important evidence of Herodotus and Ctesias is to be given full weight. Rome of the late Republic became heir to that tradition, especially from the time of Pompey's victories in the eastern Mediterranean, and especially in light of Antony's Egyptian links. The clichéd character of this kind of language by the age of Augustus may be seen in this context.

The best explanation for the Roman tendency to generalise about eastern luxury is provided by the more wide-ranging analyses of Asian trade networks.[167] Whereas Said in *Orientalism* saw the degree of western generalisation about 'the east' in a negative light, I have tried to show the

[167] E.g., the older classics by Jones, 'Asian trade', and Wheeler, *Imperial frontiers*, though outdated: see now esp. Young, *Rome's eastern trade*, pp. 27–89.

positive side of this: undoubtedly there was a generalising tendency among Romans, but it reflects the long-term patterns of trade existing from at least the third millennium BC; further, it reflects the realities of tramp trading, and the fact that no one object could easily be mapped in an exact manner.

We began with the observation that the Romans showed a strong tendency to identify distinctive goods with distinctive places, and used this as a means to think of specifically 'Indian' goods in the Roman world. The subsequent discussion of specificity raises a possibility concerning the feasibility of this approach: a modest conclusion then would hold that the objects discussed can help us only in the most limited sense to identify the specifically 'Indian' aspects of Roman society, whereas what does emerge strongly is a vivid Roman sense of the exotic based on material objects.

Whatever the difficulties of writing the economic history of ancient societies, those aspects of ancient lives that are relatively available to modern study fall under the rubric of consumption. This is where 'India' is examined at a point of reception, and what we have is not a fuller account of Rome's trade with South Asia, but a sense of India-in-Rome. That sense is provided by a variety of objects, most of which carry the cachet of luxury, not least by persons exchanged as objects: what these shared is the capacity to connote India in Roman minds.

What has emerged in these pages is the strength of the link made by many Latin and Greek authors between India and luxury goods, whether those goods in fact came from the subcontinent or not. In this respect we may regard India as an imagined place in Roman worldviews. To scrutinise the connection between goods and place with reference to archaeology and archaeobotany is to underline the actual existence of that imagined place. But in a certain sense that is beside the point. To Roman consumers, the actual existence of so distant a place, directly visited by so few people of note, was far less important than its impact on the imagination.

At a number of points in this chapter, the conception of spices and other goods has been referred to as a process of 'mapping'. This looser use of the term is in keeping with the comments of Christian Jacob: 'The production of a world map always implies a centripetal dynamic, collecting data from the periphery at a centre, and translating empirical and field data into a network of measured distances, defining mathematical positions easily handled and combined within the geometrical frame of the map.'[168]

[168] Christian Jacob, 'Mapping the mind: the earth from ancient Alexandria', in *Mappings*, ed. D. Cosgrove (London: Consortium, 1999), pp. 24–49.

The crucial point here is the centripetal dynamic: it is in this way also that luxury goods came to Rome from India and elsewhere. To put it differently, commodities helped map the world at a time when the Roman empire was at an extent it had never had before, when the city of Rome was more of a cosmopolitan city than ever before. The mapping of India that took place through commodities was thus the mapping of Rome.

CHAPTER 5

Empire

> Our own section of the earth, about which I am writing, swims as it were in the ocean which, as we have said, surrounds it; its greatest extent is from east to west, namely from India to the Pillars consecrated to Hercules at Cadiz, a distance of 8568 miles.
>
> (Pliny, *Natural history* 2.242)

With these words, the elder Pliny introduces the topographical survey that occupies books 3 to 6 of his *Natural history*. He proceeds to measure the distance involved by two routes (2.243–44), beginning in each case with the Ganges in the east. The significance of this passage lies in the use of India, in the form of a river situated at its farthest corner, in measuring the earth. To gain perspective on this, it is necessary to revisit Plato's supposed quotation of Socrates:

> I believe, he said that [the earth] is vast in size, and that we who live between the Pillars of Hercules and the river Phasis inhabit only a tiny portion of it: we live around the sea like ants or frogs around a pond, and there are many others inhabiting similar regions. (*Phaedo* 109b1–5)[1]

In this familiar passage, Socrates (or Plato) stresses the size and complexity of the earth, which is spherical; he raises the possibility that other parts also are inhabited. The key point of contrast here is that, unlike Pliny's passage above, it conveys the sense of an entire social world focused on the Mediterranean, a kind of epigram contrasting with the epic scale of Braudel's or Horden and Purcell's works.[2]

To a certain degree, however, Socrates' statement makes provision for Pliny's, in that Socrates insists on a distinction between the great size of the

[1] ἔτι τοίνυν, ἔφη, πάμμεγά τι εἶναι αὐτό, καὶ ἡμᾶς οἰκεῖν τοὺς μέχρι Ἡρακλείων στηλῶν ἀπὸ Φάσιδος ἐν σμίκρῷ τινι μορίῳ, ὥσπερ περὶ τέλμα μύρμηκας ἢ βατράχους περὶ τὴν θάλατταν οἰκοῦντας, καὶ ἄλλους ἄλλοθι πολλοὺς ἐν πολλοῖσι τοιούτοις τόποις οἰκεῖν. On ancient conceptualisations of the Mediterranean, see Horden and Purcell, *Corrupting sea*, pp. 10–12 and 530.

[2] Braudel, *Mediterranean*; Horden and Purcell, *Corrupting sea*.

earth as a whole and the small size of the part *inhabited*. Still, the difference between the two quotations is indicative of changes in the Mediterranean world in the space of five centuries. The striking thing about the Platonic passage is that India, though already discussed by contemporary writers, is in a sense 'off the map'. By contrast, both Strabo and Isidore, to take representatives of the start and end of the period under discussion, devote a certain amount of attention to India in their very different descriptions of the *oikoumenê* or *orbis terrarum*. It is in a sense ironic that the Greek world of Socrates and Plato lies to the east of Italy, thus serving as a reminder of the geographical expanse of the Roman empire.

The idea that India marked the ends of the world should not cause any alarm, as the nearly clichéd quality of the epigraph suggests. As we shall see in the pages that follow, this sentiment abounds in texts from the Augustan age, as well as those from the later empire. Indeed, it is in the age of Augustus that we shall seek the creation of the cliché. But the deceptive ease of the proposition masks an intricate set of questions focused on just what that world was: the inhabited world or the Roman Empire specifically? What is more, we can expect this question to be answered differently for different periods of Roman history, if we were to take Augustus and Isidore as book-ends: the first because his reign marked a high point of imperial unity following the Battle of Actium, the second because his writings codify so much of ancient *paideia*, and defined much of its afterlife in the medieval west. This is a period of monarchy, and one theme of this chapter will be the relationship between conceptions of space and the (often symbolic) self-presentation of emperors who claim to rule that space.[3]

The borders of empire are, in the period discussed, not easily distinguished from the ends of the earth, and this is a problem which must engage us centrally if we are to consider what India meant as a marker of the distant periphery. What is the nature and degree of the overlap between the two? To borrow the titles of two recent studies, we are inquiring here into the degree to which the limits of empire coincide with the edges of the earth.[4] As we shall see at various points in this chapter, this question of coincidence can be traced back to the details of Alexander's expedition: on the one hand, the Indus valley was conquered by Alexander when he defeated King Porus at the river Hydaspes (Jhelam). In this sense 'India'

[3] Carsten Colpe, 'Von Alexander dem Grossen zum Grossmongul Gehangir. Die Frage nach einer indischen Enthellenisierung des Weltherrschaftsgedankens', in *Philanthropia kai Eusebeia*, ed. Glenn W. Most *et al.* (Göttingen: Vandenhoeck & Ruprecht, 1993), pp. 46–73, and esp. 47–62.

[4] Ben Isaac, *The limits of empire* (Oxford: Clarendon, 1992) and Romm, *Edges*.

came to be linked with Alexander, as a marker of the ultimate military conquest. On the other hand, India was never added to Alexander's empire in the sense of governance. We must remember here that military conquest was only one limited part of a Roman sense of empire: administration was another, in fact something much more important in the practical workings of hegemony.[5]

If the definition of empire were not difficult enough, there is the particular problem raised by the notion of imperialism.[6] As an explicit concept and term, it goes back no further than the late nineteenth century:[7] its applicability to the Rome of the first centuries raises questions of its own.[8] There is an irony here, given the explicit and implicit comparisons that have been made between the Roman empire of Augustus and the British empire of the eighteenth and nineteenth centuries:[9] whereas the concept of imperialism has often centred on the British presence in South Asia, India never was part of the Roman empire in the most obvious sense, nor perhaps in any sense at all.

There are important ways, then, in which we can use India to tease out the question of what 'empire' meant over a certain period of Roman history. Empire is effectively defined by 'governmental superstructure' according to one account.[10] The 'mental maps' emphasised in other accounts should in no way be thought to compete with this administrative sense

[5] Mommsen's landmark work, *Das römische Staatsrecht*, 3rd edn (Leipzig: Hirzel, 1877), emphasised a legalistic definition of empire, in terms of *imperium*: more recently surveyed by Georg Klingenberg, 'Imperium', *RAC* XVII (1996), cols. 1121–42. By contrast, a recent study pointedly emphasises economic over political senses of empire, with particular reference to the contemporary world (and the spatial practices that distinguish it from ancient societies): Michael Hardt and Antonio Negri, *Empire* (Cambridge, MA: Harvard University Press, 2000).

[6] On the difficulties of defining empire, see e.g. Kathleen D. Morrison, 'Sources, approaches, definitions', in *Empires: perspectives from archaeology and history*, ed. Susan E. Alcock *et al.* (Cambridge University Press, 2001), pp. 1–9; Anthony Pagden, *Empires and peoples: Europeans and the rest of the world, from antiquity to the present* (London: Weidenfeld and Nicolson, 2001), pp. 7–12.

[7] For a restatement of Marx's definition of imperialism – as opposed to empire – as a modern phenomenon, tied to capitalism, see E. J. Hobsbawm, *The age of empire, 1875–1914* (New York: Pantheon, 1987), p. 60.

[8] New approaches to the issue of Roman imperialism are to be found in *Dialogues*, ed. Mattingly (1997), and *Roman imperialism: readings and sources*, ed. Craige B. Champion (Oxford: Blackwell, 2004). Susan E. Alcock fruitfully considers empire in terms of collective memory: 'The reconfiguration of memory in the eastern Roman empire', in *Empires*, ed. Alcock *et al.*, pp. 323–50.

[9] Peter Brunt, 'British and Roman imperialism', *CSSH* 7 (1965), 267–88, repr. in his *Roman imperial themes* (Oxford: Clarendon, 1990), is one notable example among many. The same topic has been taken up, more recently, by Javed Majeed, 'Comparativism and references to Rome in British imperial attitudes to India', in *Roman presences: receptions of Rome in European culture, 1798–1945*, ed. Catharine Edwards (Cambridge University Press, 1999), pp. 88–109, and Vasunia, 'Hellenism and empire'.

[10] Fergus Millar *et al.*, *The Roman empire and its neighbours* (New York: Homes and Meier, *et al.* 1981), p. 10.

of empire, but rather be viewed as complementing and modifying it.[11] It is important to consider technical and ideological aspects in tandem, and in this respect a recent work by Claude Nicolet is exemplary; India remains, however, largely outside of his purview.[12] In this chapter, I share Nicolet's view that the Augustan period was crucial to the formation of a discourse about empire;[13] but I go well beyond that period to trace changes and continuities of that discourse in late antiquity and early Middle Ages.

The name 'Rome' initially denoted an agricultural village settlement from the end of the Bronze Age, around 1000 BC.[14] To recall this is to recognize the magnitude of the process that had brought it control first of Italy and then, by the mid-second century BC, of the entire Mediterranean. We detect some sense of the weight of the Roman past, grandly conceived, in Livy's *History*. For Diodorus, Rome provided both the physical circumstances to write and also, by virtue of its expansion (he implies), the occasion for writing:[15]

> For this city's pre-eminence, which stretches in its power to the edges of the inhabited world, has provided us during our lengthy sojourn there with the most readily available and plentiful resources. (1.4.3)[16]

There was a high premium on expressions of universal power: such was the nature of the political revolution that saw Octavian end the protracted civil conflict by wresting sole power, and then present his rule in the frame of republican democracy. In the late Republic, such assertions of power, usually with reference to Alexander, involved claims to political sovereignty, and so were part of the clashes between 'strong men'. But if it was a

[11] An influential work is that by Peter Gould and Rodney White, *Mental maps*, 2nd edn (Boston: Houghton Mifflin, 1986); see also Mark Monmonier, *How to lie with maps*, 2nd edn (Chicago: University of Chicago Press, 1996). Ideological aspects of constructing spatial distance are well explored by Martin W. Lewis and Kären E. Wigen, *The myth of continents: a critique of metageography* (Berkeley: University of California Press, 1997).

[12] Thus, most significantly, Nicolet, *Space, geography*: its only reference to India is on p. 21, in passing. More recently, Ando, *Imperial ideology*, emphasises the role of *consensus* in the creation and maintenance of political unity within the empire.

[13] Cf., for example, Roger Dion, *Aspects politiques de la géographie antique* (Paris: Belles Lettres, 1977), pp. 175–222; but note the scepticism of Nicholas Purcell, 'Maps, lists, money, order and power', *JRS* 80 (1990), 178–82.

[14] T. J. Cornell, *The beginnings of Rome: Italy and Rome from the Bronze Age to the Punic Wars, c. 1000–264 BC* (London: Routledge, 1995), pp. 48–80.

[15] In both counts, we must remember the Diodorus as a Sicilian was himself not a natural member of Rome's ruling élite; like other writers of universal history, or in fact large-scale geography, he came from the peripheries: Alonso-Nuñez, 'Augustan world history'.

[16] ἡ γὰρ ταύτης τῆς πόλεως ὑπεροχή, διατείνουσα τῇ δυνάμει πρὸς τὰ πέρατα τῆς οἰκουμένης, ἑτοιμοτάτας καὶ πλείστας ἡμῖν ἀφορμὰς παρέσχετο παρεπιδημήσασιν ἐν αὐτῇ πλείω χρόνον.

feature of Augustus' rule to maintain the trappings of republicanism, the pretence was to wear thin and in many respects disappear in the decades after his death in AD 14. His rule had seen the Roman state reach military ascendancy on a scale it had not known before. This was to provide the basis for an empire that lasted till the late fifth century in the west and mid-fifteenth in the east. Self-evidently, Rome's imperial identity evolved slowly. The more wide-ranging analyses of this process stress the role of the army, and the dual processes of political unification and decentralisation of power.[17] Imperial authority and war are both part of the equation. The birth of the name Romania in the fourth century testifies to the need to distinguish between the City and what had by now become a world empire.[18] It is no coincidence that this came into use only once the city of Rome ceased to hold the monopoly of power it did at the time of Augustus.

In the current framework we have to restrict ourselves to selected but representative points, to what has in the context of a different ethnography been described as 'sightings'.[19] These are chosen for a number of reasons: merely that they are accessible to us; that they are in some manner indicative of an evolving history; and that they shed light on the perceptions of India over an extended period.

I. *PAX ROMANA* AND PEOPLE OF THE DAWN

The ekphrasis of Roman history on Aeneas' Shield begins with Romulus and Remus and culminates, after various episodes, with the 'fanfare' representing Augustus' victory at Actium. The following extracts together offer us a key passage for grasping Augustus' discourse about empire, and for the place of India in that discourse:

Next came Antonius with outlandish wealth and multifarious arms, victorious from people of the Dawn and the Red Sea, leading the power of the East, of Egypt, even of remote Bactra . . . Actian Apollo, looking on from above, began to pull

[17] Millar *et al.*, *Roman empire*, 1–12; Garth Fowden, *Empire to commonwealth* (Princeton University Press, 1993), pp. 57–8.

[18] Johannes Irmscher, 'Sulle origine del concetto Romania', in *Populi e Spazio Romano tra Diritto e Profezia* (Naples: Edizione Scientifiche, 1986), pp. 421–9, on Romania as a designation of *imperium Romanum*, as opposed to Rome the city. This is first attested in Athanasius, *Historia Arianorum* 35 (AD 358).

[19] Jonathan D. Spence, *The Chan's great continent: China in western minds* (New York: Norton, 1998).

his bow. All the Egyptians, Indians, Arabians and Sabaeans, terrified at this sight, turned in flight. (Virgil, *Aeneid* 8.685–88 and 704–6)[20]

It is difficult to overlook in this extract a totalising sense of 'the east'. This is conveyed by a number of means: among them one might mention the building up within the passage as a whole the drama of a warlike lining-up of opposing deities, Roman and eastern; the use of the generalising term *oriens* (literally 'of the dawn', i.e. eastern);[21] and the joined naming of various peoples from the east, Egyptians, Indians and Arabians ('Sabaeans').[22] It is in this limited sense that we can talk about one aspect of Said's Orientalism: the tendency to conceive of the east as a totality. To a certain degree this fits the circumstances of the Battle of Actium; more compellingly, perhaps, it was played up in the subsequent propaganda of Octavian/Augustus.[23]

Here is triumphalist rhetoric, in which India played a part, if a limited and predictable one. But it is another matter entirely to consider what this

20
hinc ope barbarica uariisque Antonius armis,
uictor ab Aurorae populis et litore rubro,
Aegyptum uirisque Orientis et ultima secum
Bactra uenit . . .
Actius haec cernens arcum intendebat Apollo
desuper: omnis eo terrore Aegyptus et Indi,
omnis Arabs, omnes uertebant terga Sabaei.

Philip R. Hardie has analysed the shield of Aeneas as a 'cosmic icon', and indeed the centrepiece of the *Aeneid*: *Virgil's* Aeneid: *cosmos and imperium* (Oxford: Clarendon, 1986), pp. 336–76; cf. Ando, *Imperial ideology*, pp. 278–92.

21 *TLL* IX.2.1003.24, s.v. *oriens*, for this passage; but note also Hor. *Carm.* 1.12.55–56, with *TLL* IX.2.1002.76–79. In light of the ostensibly generalised use of this word, it is unclear why Whittaker, *Rome and its frontiers*, pp. 144, should take this to indicate India in a restrictive sense. Alexander is a figure around whom the idea of the east crystalised, especially its farthermost points: he set out to conquer Asia and the outermost parts of the east: *ad subigendam Asiam atque ultima orientis* (Curt. 3.10.4; cf. 5.5.14). These parts are contrasted with 'Europa'. Curtius speaks of India's inhabitants as *ultimi orientis* (6.2.18; cf. 9.10.12 also on Indians). Apart from Alexander, two others to be linked with 'the east' in a comparably generalised sense are Pompey (Solin. 1.121) and Antony (Serv. auct. *ad Verg. Aen.* 8.686). In his world history, Pompeius Trogus speaks of Rome and Parthia as being the two rival world empires, Parthia ruling the east: *Parthi, penes quos uelut diuisione orbis cum Romanis facta nunc Orientis imperium est, Scytharum exules fuere* (41.1.1). For discussion of this passage, see Alonso-Núñez, 'Augustan world history', at 64. In other instances the term *oriens* is used of Syria (*Schol. Juv.* 3.64; 4.108).

The senior military office of *comes orientis*, introduced by Constantine, came, by the middle of the fourth century, to have special significance in light of conflict on the Iranian frontier. Given the expanding field of this officer's power, the title proved to be suitably vague. See *RE* IV.1 (1900) 659–62 (Seeck); A. H. M. Jones, *Later Roman empire*, pp. 104–6.

22 With regard to this list and esp. lines 705–6, Katharine Toll, 'Making Roman-ness and the *Aeneid*', *Cl. Ant.* 16 (1997), 34–56, at 46, exaggerates somewhat when she claims that 'half of the peoples mentioned simply were not there'. I do agree with the observation that the foreign peoples on the shield of Aeneas are 'misrepresented' so as to appear more foreign; but I offer a different explanation in this chapter.

23 On the contrast between Octavian/Augustus' initially exuberant self-presentation with his later restraint, and the role of Actium in that process, Paul Zanker, *Power of images in the age of Augustus* (Ann Arbor: University of Michigan Press, 1988); and Robert Alan Gurval, *Actium and Augustus* (Ann Arbor: University of Michigan Press, 1995).

meant in the *Realpolitik* of Roman political-military strategy. To create a provisional distinction, then, for analytical purposes: we must be alert both to the rhetoric of empire and to the political and military realities linked with it, in other words both to the propaganda and the lived experience of Rome's empire. The complexities of the situation begin to emerge when we avoid a narrowly representational approach: India in Pliny or Strabo not only mirrors political reality, but it also creates or at least reinforces it in Roman minds. The issue of the social reality of literary texts has been most often considered with regard to Augustan poetry, but should not be limited to it.[24] There is a self-reproducing quality to this kind of rhetoric; to adapt Clifford Geertz's famous phrase, we are dealing with models of and for thinking about empire.[25] Certainly the tralatician element is clearly seen in the late Roman period, when there was less actual contact, and India was presented with basically literary images. The question that is harder to ask is whether the same processes are true for earlier periods too, such as the Augustan age. There can be no doubt that the authority of written texts prevailed in significant ways well before the late-antique periods also: Pliny's *Natural history* is an eminent case in point.[26] We are justified in speaking of this phenomenon as a discourse, where that term is used to emphasise the complexity and self-fulfilling quality of representations.

I.1. Orbis terrarum imperio populi Romani subiecta[27]

If statements about the grandeur of empire proliferated in the Augustan age, they were in essence no novelty.[28] The second century BC was a key period in the evolution of the discourse of empire, especially the successful conclusion of hostilities with Carthage in 146 BC.[29] Polybius is a key witness

[24] In the light of recent work on Roman poetry, it cannot now be maintained that the political element of Augustan poetry was one-way traffic from the state to writers, on the lines outlined by Ronald Syme, *Roman revolution* (Oxford: Clarendon, 1939), esp. pp. 459–75: more recently e.g. Karl Galinsky, *Augustan culture: an interpretative introduction* (Princeton University Press, 1996); Matthew S. Santirocco, 'Horace and Augustan ideology', *Arethusa* 28 (1995), 225–43, esp. 227; Thomas Habinek, *The politics of Roman poetry* (Princeton University Press, 1998), present literature as an 'intervention' in social practice.

[25] Geertz, *Interpretation of cultures*, pp. 93–4, on models of and for society.

[26] Lloyd, *Science, folklore.*

[27] This is a slight adaptation of the title of the *Res gestae.*

[28] The significant Republican background to Augustan imperialism is one absence with which Edward N. Luttwak's provocative *The grand strategy of the Roman empire from the first century* AD *to the third* (Baltimore: Johns Hopkins University Press, 1974) has been charged, with justification. For a more nuanced treatment, Susan P. Mattern, *Rome and the enemy: imperial strategy in the Principate* (Berkeley: University of California Press, 1999), esp. pp. 81–122.

[29] Peter White, *Promised verse* (Cambridge, MA: Harvard University Press, 1993), p. 61; more generally, Erich S. Gruen, *The Hellenistic world and the coming of Rome* (Berkeley: University of California Press, 1984).

on this topic: if his work as a whole documents Rome's rise to the power of world empire, then his sixth book in particular offers an explanation of the socio-political background.[30] He stands out for the clarity with which he was able to see Roman history as process as opposed to a mere sequence of events.[31]

Cicero's speeches are another rich source for thinking about the edges of the earth.[32] Such passages testify to the importance of this theme during the mid-first century BC, at a time when conflicts between rival leaders were determined as much on the fringes of the Mediterranean world as in the city of Rome.[33] As a rhetorical technique, they illustrate how an orator could appeal to (and manipulate) commonly held views, such as those of the 'perfidy of the Gauls', in communicating with his audience.

In identifying the roots of Augustus' sense of empire, we should be especially alert to Crassus' and Pompey's activities in the eastern Mediterranean. That may have been a different 'east', but it was a politically significant east nonetheless, and one that contributed to the conceptual frame for subsequent thinking. And the paradigm of Alexander, so important to Pompey, always contained the potential for the 'east' to stretch yet farther in that direction, even if this was never to be realised in practice.

In analysing Augustan discourse, it is as well to start with a text that can be linked most directly to Augustus himself, the *Res gestae*:

> Embassies were often sent to me from kings in India; never before had they been seen in the presence of any Roman commander. The Bastarnae, Scythians and the kings of the Sarmatians on either side of the river Don, as well as the kings of the Albanians, Iberians and Medes sought our friendship by means of embassies. (31.1–2)[34]

In particular, what we must notice in the passage quoted is the pointed use of 'friendship' (*amicitia*): the wide range of its connotations is exploited so that Augustus can convey both his military supremacy and his clemency at the

[30] Frank Walbank, 'A Greek looks at Rome: Polybius VI revisited', *Scripta Classica Israelica* 17 (1998), 45–59; Clarke, *Between geography and history*, pp. 77–128.

[31] Indeed, if we define imperialism as a process, we are left with Polybius, a Greek writer not a Roman, as the only one to take a general view of Roman imperialism: Gruen, *Hellenistic world*, p. 278.

[32] Ann Vasaly, *Representations: images of the earth in Ciceronian oratory* (Berkeley: University of California Press, 1993), shows how Cicero in his speeches relies on stereotypes linked to particular places. The implications of this for the current study are considerable, as will be made clear in the conclusion.

[33] This is certainly true at least from the time of the First Triumvirate of 60 BC, with Crassus, Caesar and Pompey all campaigning extensively in far-flung parts of the Mediterranean.

[34] *ad me ex India regum legationes saepe missae sunt non uisae ante id tempus apud quemquam Romanorum ducem. nostram amicitiam appetiuerunt per legatos Bastarnae Scythaeque et Sarmatarum qui sunt citra flumen Tanaim et ultra reges, Albanorumque rex et Hiberorum et Medorum.* (31.1–2)

same time.[35] The unequal power relations between Rome and its 'friends' are understood, to the degree that they can be casually glossed over in this manner. In understanding the exercise of power that lies behind these assertions it is again important to remember their Iranian background.[36] In the choice of terminology, Augustus carefully presents himself as a statesman in the Republican tradition, rather than a despot;[37] nonetheless, both precedents of Darius' and Xerxes' inscriptions are hard to overlook, when they too emphasise foreigners paying tribute.[38] In general, the passage is typical of the chapters (26–33) in which the spatial expanse of the empire is indicated: by its cool, self-assured tone it describes the borders of Roman governance in such a way as to stipulate its extent for future time. In Nicolet's words, it 'is not a text with symbolic or astrological inclinations; rather, it is a factual exposé of great sobriety' (17). And if the *Res gestae* substantiates Augustus' claim to have extended the empire's influence to the limits of the known world, we shall have to consider to what extent the texts of Strabo, Mela and Pliny come in the wake of Roman imperial expansion; to what extent they too may be regarded as texts of the *pax Romana*.

By the time of Propertius' second book of *Elegies* (28–25 BC) we find variations on the theme of the grandeur of Rome's conquests:

> No longer does the Euphrates allow Parthian cavalry to glance behind their backs, and regrets retaining possession of Crassus' men: even India presents its neck to your triumph, Augustus, and the house of virgin Arabia trembles before you; and hereafter if any land retreats to the world's end, let it be captured and feel your wrath! (2.10.13–18)[39]

35 On the pointed variation implicit in the term *amicitia*, see Ulrike Asche, *Roms Weltherrschaftsidee und Aussenpolitik in der Spätantike im Spiegel der Panegyrici Latini* (Bonn: Habelt, 1983), esp. pp. 48–65 and 130–8, well illustrates the careful balance between triumphalism and *clementia* in late Latin panegyric. On the balancing of elements in imperial self-presentation, see esp. Sabine G. MacCormack, *Art and ceremony in late antiquity* (Berkeley: University of California Press, 1981).

36 The use of Aramaic in Asoka's inscriptions shows the influence of Achaemenid monumental writing: Millar, 'Looking east', 518; cf. Thapar, *Early India*, p. 182.

37 Zvi Yavetz, 'The *Res Gestae* and Augustus' public image', in *Caesar Augustus: seven aspects* (Oxford: Clarendon, 1984), pp. 1–36; with different emphasis, Brian Bosworth, 'Augustus, the *Res Gestae* and hellenistic theories of kingship', *JRS* 89 (1999), 1–18.

38 See Chapter 1, section I above. The provenance of the surviving copy and fragments of this inscription – Ancyra, Apollonia and Antioch – further suggests continuity between the Achaemenid epigraphic habit and Augustus' self-presentation in this case.

39 *iam negat Euphrates equitem post terga tueri*
Parthorum et Crassos se tenuisse dolet:
India quin, Auguste, tuo dat colla triumpho,
et domus intactae te tremit Arabiae;
et si qua extremis tellus se subtrahit oris,
sentiat illa tuas postmodo capta manus!

It will be noticed that the passage quoted promotes the illusion that India is already conquered by Augustus. Still with Propertius we find:

> Divine Caesar is contemplating war on the Indians, planning to cleave the waters of the gem-laden ocean with his fleet. The pickings are [will be?] handsome, citizens: the ends of the earth prepare triumphs for you; the Tigris and Euphrates will flow under your jurisdiction. (3.4.1–4)[40]

The poet goes on to recall Crassus' loss of the standards, and the need for this blot on Roman history to be expiated. The pointed use of the future tense occurs also at *Elegies* 3.1. Here Propertius foretells conquest up to Bactria, which will from that point be the edge of empire:

> Many, Rome, will add your praises to their annals, singing one day of Bactra as the boundary of your rule. (3.1.15–16)[41]

By focusing on the future aspect of (yet more) military victories to come, Propertius is in effect offering an additional reason for his refusal to bow to supposed pressure to write grand epic in praise of the emperor. The idea is this: others will sing of you in the future, just as you will make further conquests in the future. While there are several levels of complexity in the *recusatio*, and indeed in the poetry of public praise generally, it is as well to note one particular aspect here: the use of the future tense as a means of deflecting expectations, its compatibility with the *recusatio*. This literary consideration is something to keep in mind in assessing the Augustan poets as possible sources for supposed expansionism.

There is no missing the poem's matter-of-fact tone, as if leaving no room for doubt that Augustus will in fact set out to conquer India. It is this casual tone of assertions about the inevitability of Roman conquest that calls for explanation. In translating the passage above, it is debatable how we should translate the ostensibly simple present-tense verbs *meditatur* (line 1, 'is planning') and *parat* (3, 'prepare'): how strong a sense of future time do they convey?[42] The military-strategic side of this leads the discussion in

40 *arma deus Caesar ditis meditatur ad Indos*
et freta gemmiferi findere classe maris.
magna, Quiris, merces: parat ultima terra triumphos;
Tigris et Euphrates sub tua iura fluent.

41 *multi, Roma, tuas laudes annalibus addent,*
qui finem imperii Bactra futura canent.

Bactria is, strictly, to the northwest of India; but in context it clearly has the same function.

42 On the Latin present tense used with forward-looking force, see Raphael Kühner and Carl Stegmann, *Ausführliche Grammatik der lateinischen Sprache*, 5th edn (Hannover: Hahn, 1976), vol. II.1, pp. 120–1. For the counter-intuitive but powerful point that the present tense in Indo-European languages bears little relation to the 'time that now is', see Andrew L. Sihler, *New comparative grammar of Greek and Latin* (Oxford: Clarendon, 1995), pp. 442–3.

a different direction, to be considered later in this chapter. For the present, as we consider the discourse about empire, let us limit ourselves to noting that in this passage, and in fact in the poem as a whole, the combination of the military and the economic elements: the first couplet moves directly from the *arma* to the economic implications of conquest, as if these were readily concomitant. Later on, he expresses the wish that Mars grant him, in his lifetime, the chance to see the day 'when I'll see Caesar's chariots weighed down with plunder' (3.5.13).[43]

Elsewhere Propertius poses Cynthia a rhetorical question, 'What would you do if I were to be kept by military service in faraway India, or if my ship were to stand still in Ocean?'[44] When so much in love elegy hinges on the physical proximity of lovers, India stands for an extreme case of distance; military service underlines that physical absence, and plays on the common elegiac trope of *militia amoris*, 'love's warfare'.[45]

Horace, in at least two passages, shows the same principles at work. First:

> May [Augustus] defeat the Parthians who threaten Latium, or else the Chinese and Indians situated alongside the eastern border, subduing them in a deserving triumph. (Horace, *Odes* 1.12.53–57)[46]

And, second, this is how Horace ends a poem commemorating fifteen years[47] of Augustus' sovereignty:

> At you the previously invincible Cantabrian marvels, the Mede marvels, and so do the Indian and the fleeing Scythian, O propitious keeper of Italy and of mistress Rome. You the Nile, which conceals the sources of its streams, heeds, and so does the Hister, and the speedy Tigris, and monster-bearing Ocean that bellows at the distant Britons; You the land of Gaul, fearless before death, and of hardy Hiberia; you the Sygambri, who rejoice in slaughter, worship, having put aside their weapons. (Horace, *Odes* 4.14.41–52)[48]

[43] *qua uideam spoliis oneratos Caesaris axes.*

[44] *quid si longinquos retinerer miles ad Indos, / aut mea si staret nauis in Oceano?* (2.9A.29–30). Goold's transposition is plausible, on the grounds that the couplet makes better sense following lines 19–20 (on Cynthia's unwillingness to be alone, *sola*) than 27–28.

[45] On the complexity of this elegiac trope, Kennedy, *Arts of love*, pp. 46–63. It may be considered characteristic of the paradoxical nature of love: cf. Anne Carson, *Eros the bittersweet* (Princeton University Press, 1986).

[46] *ille seu Parthos Latio imminentis*
egerit iusto domitos triumpho
siue subiectos Orientis orae
Seras et Indos.

[47] *tertio . . . lustro* (37).

[48] *te Cantaber non ante domabilis*
Medusque et Indus, te profugus Scythes
miratur, o tutela praesens
Italiae dominaeque Romae;

Implicit in this is a degree of wishful thinking: if an Indian ruler did send ambassadors to Rome this need not have implied any political subordination. In any case, it is not impossible that these 'ambassadors' were traders. Yet, as a marker of the ends of the earth, it was essential for a poet to imply its participation in the empire, for the purposes of glorifying that empire. By the same token, Augustus' 'victory' over the Parthians was not a full-scale military conquest, but a diplomatic deal.[49] In Horace's references to India and Indians, the subcontinent is more often than not linked with another eastern region, be that Arabia, China or Media.[50]

I.2. City and empire

Other peoples have been restricted in the territory given them, but the extent of the city of Rome matches that of the universe. (Ovid, *Fasti* 2.683–84)[51]

In this most quotable of quotes, Ovid points to a recurrent feature of the Augustan discourse we have been considering: to the expansion of the Roman polity well beyond the limits of a town settlement (*urbs*) to embrace the entire universe (*orbis terrarum*).[52] But the pun is not unique to Ovid, and did not even begin with him: it had been used earlier by Cicero and

te fontium qui celat origines
Nilusque et Hister, te rapidus Tigris,
te beluosus qui remotis
obstrepit Oceanus Britannis,
te non pauentis funera Galliae
duraeque tellus audit Hiberiae,
te caede gaudentes Sygambri
conpositis uenerantur armis.

[49] On the deal whereby the legionary standards lost by Crassus at Carrhae in 53 BC, together with the hostages captured during Antony's campaign, were regained by Augustus, see Erich S. Gruen, 'The expansion of the empire under Augustus', *CAH* IX (1996, 2nd edn), pp. 148–96, at 158–9; and J. A. Crook, 'Political history, 30 BC to AD 14', in *CAH* X, pp. 70–112, at 90.

[50] With China: *Seras et Indos* (*Carm.* 1.12.56); Arabia: *intactis opulentior / thesauris Arabum et diuitis Indiae* (3.24.1–2), *extremos Arabas . . . et Indos* (*Epist.* 1.6.6); Media: *Medus . . . et Indus* (4.14.42).

[51] *gentibus est aliis tellus data limite certo:*
Romanae spatium est urbis et orbis idem.

[52] Later in the same work, Ovid pointedly expresses the contrast between the humble rural settlement with the subsequent world empire, by focusing on the identity of place over a gap in time: *hic, ubi nunc Roma est, orbis caput, arbor et herbae / et paucae pecudes et casa rara fuit* (5.93–94). The habit of pointing to changes over time by focusing on the same locality recurs in the considerable body of later writings about Rome; here, by contrast, destruction is stressed. See, e.g., Hildebert of Lavardin in the twelfth century, and other texts collected by Bernhard Kytzler (ed.), *Roma Aeterna* (Zurich: Artemis, 1972). Cf. Nicholas Purcell, 'The city of Rome', in *The legacy of Rome: a new appraisal*, ed. Richard Jenkyns (Oxford: Clarendon, 1992), pp. 421–53; Catharine Edwards, *Writing Rome: textual approaches to the city* (Cambridge University Press, 1996), esp. pp. 69–95.

Varro.[53] It was to have a long afterlife, due at least in part to the imitability of Ovid's poetic language.[54] Be that as it may, it is the thought that is relevant here: its proverbial nature merely illustrates how familiar it was over a long period. To focus on the Augustan period, the sentiment itself comes as no great surprise when one considers the centrality of the city of Rome, and particularly its monuments, to Augustus' reign.[55] Historically speaking, this was more than wordplay: indeed, Augustus' success can be explained by a careful balancing of the interests of *orbis* and *urbs*. But what, if anything, does it imply for India, a part of the universe that was never subsumed into the Roman sphere of governance?

If any general conclusion is to be drawn from the sources discussed in this chapter, it might be said that India became more of an issue for Rome at this high point in its status world empire. In the *Res gestae*, in Virgil and in Horace we have seen a tendency to conflate empire and universe, what we might call false consciousness. We see here both a backward- and a forward-looking sense of empire: both the idea that the Roman state had already reached its grandiose limits, as Augustus would imply in his *Res gestae*, and the forward-looking aspect of outward expansion, most clearly seen later in Cassius Dio's account of Trajan (subsection I.5 below). In general, we might say that imperial expansion is best understood in a purely notional way, rather than being in any sense a literal plan to conquer. In other words, India is an issue in so far as the edges of empire were thought and spoken about at its centre(s) of empire. One might say, following Ovid, that Rome was part of the *orbis* in so far as it could be seen in the *urbs*.

In the political register at least, Augustan poetry produces an enormous range of interpretive problems, more than bear discussion here. In particular, scholars have debated how seriously to take the adulatory aspect, especially given that some passages within the same authors sound a more subversive note. Simple choices are unhelpful in this regard. The approach taken in this chapter has been to assume that, even if the discourse of imperial grandeur was sometimes subverted (especially by Ovid), it made sense only in light of an already existing non-subversive context. It is in this non-subversive sense, most reliably inferred from the *Res gestae*, that we can indeed analyse an 'imperial discourse' here. Such analysis should not be taken to deny that, at certain points, the same language might be

[53] *Parad.* 18 and *Ling.* 5.143 respectively. See *TLL* IX.2.916.15–30, s.v. *orbis*; cf. Otto, *Sprichwörter und sprichwörtliche*, no. 1834.

[54] E.g., Ven. Fort. *Carm.* 8.1.14; Arator *Act.* 2.1232. Cf. Oros. *Hist.* 1.1.14 (repeated in the same paragraph), and Isid. *Etym.* 9.4.3. Ovid's elegiac style proved imitable in his own lifetime, if we are to judge from supposed replies to his *Heroides*: *Am.* 2.18.27–34.

[55] Diane Favro, *The urban image of Augustan Rome* (Cambridge University Press, 1996); Zanker, *Power of images*.

used in subversive ways, however easy or hard it might be to identify those points now.[56]

By the time we see the discourse of empire occurring in the Augustan age it is already full-blown, complete with the force of cliché, if we are to judge from the tone of the comments in the poets cited above. This might cause surprise initially, but it need not do so: there are pointers to it in earlier literature, so much so that we might regard the Augustan references as an appropriation of existing tropes. A striking passage in Catullus clearly shows the force of hyperbole in references to the ends of the earth:

> Furius and Aurelius, Catullus' fellow-travellers, whether he makes his way even to far-flung India, where the coast is pounded by the far-resounding eastern wave, or to Hyrcania and soft Arabia, or to the Sacae and arrow-bearing Parthians, or the plains which sevenfold Nile tinges, or whether he will trudge across the lofty Alps, to visit the memorials of great Caesar, the Gaulish Rhine, the formidable Britons, furthermost of people. (Catullus 11.1–12)[57]

For the purposes of this poem the *extremos Indos* (2) are set against the *ultimos . . . Britannos* (11–12),[58] who have the added feature of being *horribiles*. The extract testifies to the kind of ethnographic shorthand that is so much part of Augustan poetry: the use of a recurring set of adjectives, e.g. *Arabas . . . molles* (5) and *sagittiferos Parthos* (6). Of course phrases such as these are not limited to poetry, but it is also true that their recurrence in verse may be related to the creation of a poetic language, and even to

[56] Alessandro Barchiesi, *The poet and the prince: Ovid and Augustan discourse* (Berkeley: University of California Press, 1997), brings out well the multifaceted nature of Ovid's poetry, to take perhaps the most ludic of the poets here discussed. See also Duncan F. Kennedy, '"Augustan" and "anti-Augustan": reflections on terms of reference', in *Roman poetry and propaganda in the age of Augustus*, ed. Anton Powell (London: Routledge, 1992), pp. 26–58; Thomas Habinek, 'Ovid and empire', in *The Cambridge companion to Ovid*, ed. Philip Hardie (Cambridge University Press, 2002), pp. 46–61.

[57] *Furi et Aureli, comites Catulli,*
siue in extremos penetrabit Indos,
litus ut longe resonante Eoa
tunditur unda;
siue in Hyrcanos, Arabasque molles,
seu Sacas, sagittiferos Parthos,
siue qua septemgeminus colorat
aequora Nilus;
siue trans altas gradietur Alpes,
Caesaris uisens monimenta magni,
Gallicum Rhenum, horribilesque ulti–
mosque Britannos

[58] See *TLL* II.2195.73–77 for the juxtaposition (mostly in poetry) of Britain and Britons with other people, such as Parthians and Scythians. See esp. Hor. *Carm.* 1.35.30 and 4.14.48.

the constraints of metre.[59] It is in this way that Catullus is central to the creation and refinement of a Latin poetic language.[60] Another feature of Catullus' poem to note, for the purposes of comparison with later verse, is the interplay of the private with the public: Furius and Aurelius are friends in the private domain in the first instance, as we may safely assume, but it is by accompanying him to faraway places that they prove their friendship. It is only once he has recounted their 'world-scale' companionship that he asks his friends to deliver a message to his beloved, and it is this message that takes up the second half of the poem. The distant parts of the world are described as *Caesaris . . . monimenta magni* (10): the distant parts redound to Caesar's credit, for they are mentioned as a means of praising him as their conqueror. It is on this basis that we can understand references in imperial panegyric: 'India' as a geographic topic is subject to an escalation of rhetoric, as we shall see below.

I.3. The production of imperial space: Strabo and Pliny

In a telling passage, Polybius draws an explicit link between the imperial conquests of Alexander and the Romans on the one hand, and the increase of topographical knowledge on the other (3.58–59).[61] He contrasts his own times with those of early Greek writers, unnamed but presumably Hecataeus, Herodotus and other Ionians (3.58.5). Military conquests have opened greater possibilities than ever before of knowing the world. This contrast, which goes some way toward vindicating the two quotations which began this chapter, is all very well as a general principle; but, specifically, what relevance does it have to India during the Augustan age? For one thing, this sense of military conquest as stimulating geographical knowledge brought with it an ongoing admiration for Alexander's conquests, not least because he achieved with regard to the east what no Roman commander was later to do.[62]

59 André and Filliozat, *L'Inde*, p. 17, point to the *'banalité'* of formulae such as *India tosta* (Catull. 45.6), *ebur Indicum* (Hor. *Carm.* 1.31.6), and *Indiae conchae* (Prop. 1.8.39).

60 Gordon Williams, *Tradition and originality in Roman poetry* (Oxford: Clarendon, 1968), pp. 701–2; Gian Biagio Conte, *Latin literature: a history* (Baltimore: Johns Hopkins University Press, 1994), pp. 142–52.

61 This passage may have been written for a second edition: F. W. Walbank, *A historical commentary on Polybius* (Oxford: Clarendon, 1957), vol. I, pp. 393–4 ad loc.; see also Clarke, *Between geography and history*, p. 111.

62 Johannes Engels, 'Die Geschichte des Alexanderzuges und das Bild Alexanders des Grossen in Strabons Geographika – Zur Interpretation der augusteischen Kulturgeographie Strabons als Quelle seiner historischen Auffassungen', in *Alexander der Grosse*, ed. Wolfgang Will (1998), pp. 131–71.

We should consider Strabo, Pomponius Mela and Pliny to assess to what degree their geographies are texts of the Roman empire, on the lines suggested by Polybius. In taking the *oikoumenê* as his subject, Strabo's project matches the world histories of his contemporaries Pompeius Trogus, Nicolaus of Damascus and Diodorus Siculus.[63] The profusion of such intellectual projects around this time cannot be considered a coincidence, but rather suggests that the discourse of empire at this time gained new force. Furthermore, Pliny, writing several decades later, is manifestly aware of Alexander's precedent, hence the comment about 'following in his footsteps' in order to describe India (Chapter 1 above). So much of the descriptions of India and Indians themselves concern matters that are of military interest: the location of rivers, mountains and settlements; among fauna the elephant was an important aspect of warfare in India, in the Hellenistic period at least.[64] What is more, recent scholarship on the *Natural history* have tended to view Pliny's geographical books as an intellectual project in its own right, rather than an accumulation of details that are more or less accurate: he is 'providing a general picture of the world as a whole'.[65] While Strabo and Pliny focus, in the first instance, on the 'world' at large, there is a subtext of empire that runs through them; both works are unthinkable for, say, the early first century BC. At the very least, it cannot be denied that Rome's political ascendancy in the Mediterranean breathed new life into world-scale geographical and historical writing.[66]

The point here is clear, but how far does it take us in trying to understand texts of such magnitude as Strabo's *Geography* and Pliny's *Natural history*?[67] Certainly, nobody will deny that they are both texts of their time, and articulations of long traditions of scholarship. When they survey the *orbis terrarum* or *oikoumenê*, it is the inhabited world rather than merely the Roman empire. There seems to be, at some level, a false consciousness in this, as if one is speciously passed off for the other. Whatever the physical

63 Alonso-Núñez, 'Augustan world history', 56; more generally, Katherine Clarke, 'Universal perspectives in historiography', in *The limits of historiography: genre and narrative in ancient historical texts*, ed. Christina Shuttleworth Kraus (Leiden: Brill, 1999), pp. 249–79.

64 Scullard, *Elephant*.

65 Sallmann, *Geographie*, p. 191; Beagon, *Roman nature*, esp. p. 189 n. 50. The older approach is exemplified by J. Oliver Thomson, *History of ancient geography* (Cambridge University Press, 1948), pp. 226–8; for more recent scholarship on Pliny, see Chapter 2, section I.3 above.

66 To the question of the connection between empire and geography we shall return at the end of this book.

67 Conte, 'Inventory of the world', in *Genres and readers*, esp. p. 74: but the essay offers surprisingly little to justify his title. Beagon, *Roman nature*, pp. 187–90, offers good evidence for the link between Pliny's scholarship and Rome's political ascendancy; cf. Purcell, 'Maps'.

form of Agrippa's map, it does seem to have expressed the full sweep of the *orbis terrarum*, well beyond the formal limits of empire.

On the face of it, there is no problem in connecting Roman geography with the interests and practice of empire. Both Strabo and Pliny played a role in the Roman military, and both of them travelled far and wide in the course of military service.[68] Certainly Pliny was well aware of Agrippa as a source of topographical information, and in fact the *Natural history* is one of the main sources in reconstructing Agrippa's supposed map.[69] Both Pliny and Strabo speak of Alexander as a military figure whose conquests 'opened up' a wider world for inquiries such as theirs.[70] These are important and obvious senses of empire embedded in their texts. Yet, that said, the texts themselves are less than helpful in clarifying the explicit connection between science and military activity. For all the travelling that we know him to have done, Pliny relies much more on the authority of book-learning than on his own experience.[71]

I.4. Policy and propaganda

Thus far we have considered the rhetoric of empire at the time of Augustus, and the role of India within that rhetoric. At this point, we should take a moment to consider more broadly the political and military realities to which it relates. There is a larger historical question we cannot escape: how seriously are we to take the assertions of future conquest? Quite seriously, Brunt would have us believe, in a provocative article that reopened the question of Roman expansionism and continues to be cited with regularity.[72] Earlier scholars, notably Mommsen, strenuously maintained that

[68] From the *Natural history* itself we do know that Pliny saw service at the source of the Danube (31.25), near the mouth of the Rhine, *extremoque in margine imperii* (12.98), and elsewhere; see also 31.20 and 16.2 (territory of the Chauci). It has generally been thought that Pliny's lost work on Germany formed the source for Tacitus' *Germania* (Syme, *Tacitus*, p. 127). If this is so, then Tacitus' Pliny is completely lost to us. (Subsequent service also took him as far afield as Judaea, Syria, Gallia Narbonensis, Africa, Hispania Tarraconensis and Gallia Belgica. Yet autopsy, and the first person in general, play very little part in the *HN*: Beagon, *Roman nature*, pp. 2–6.) Pliny's life is discussed in Chapter 2, section I.3 above.

[69] Kai Brodersen, *Terra Cognita. Studien zur römischen Raumerfassung*, 2nd edn (Hildesheim: Olms, 2003), pp. 268–85, argues that this was an epigraphic monument; for the more conventional interpretation, giving greater significance to the visual dimension, see Nicolet, *Space, geography*, pp. 95–122, and Dilke, *Greek and Roman maps*, pp. 41–52.

[70] Cf. Chapter 1, section II.

[71] Shaw, 'Elder Pliny', 431–2, and Sallmann, *Geographie*, esp. pp. 27–34 on Pliny's *Mosaikstil.*

[72] Peter Brunt, 'Roman imperialism', in his *Roman imperial themes*, pp. 96–109, a review of Hans D. Meyer, *Die Aussenpolitik des Augustus*, reprinted from *JRS* 53 (1963), 170–6.

Augustus' goals were limited.[73] This has been questioned by a number of scholars in the latter part of this century.[74] Isaac's influential study of the Roman presence in the eastern Mediterranean in the first centuries AD presupposes a degree of military aggression, and may be regarded as typical of more recent approaches to the topic.

That said, it is difficult to point to any indication of Roman military interest in India. The kind of references we have seen, and those we shall see later in this chapter, tend to be very much on the level of the ideological rather than the strategic. By the same token, the few representations of India in maps and in geographical literature are on the large scale, on world maps, rather than regional or municipal.[75] No serious thought about military topographies of India can be entertained. Indeed it would be perverse to view the geographical and cartographic material on India in a strictly military light. If the question of 'military maps' is a difficult one in any case, and prone to a prioristic exaggeration on the part of modern scholars,[76] then it is not so much an issue with regard to India. The closest we come to seeing India on a Roman military map is in the Peutinger map. This survives in a Colmar manuscript from the thirteenth century, but shows strong evidence of a fourth-century original, and even deeper roots.[77] It is unlikely, however, that a military context can account for all the features of the existing map; rather, it is possible that other kinds of travel, not least commercial, may have played their part as well in determining the places, routes, natural features and distances indicated. Despite these caveats, it is important to note that it does stretch as far as India and Taprobane on its far right-hand side: whatever the constituent parts, the final product in its thirteenth-century form does indicate a universe stretching from the Straits

73 On similar lines, E. Badian, *Roman imperialism in the late republic*, 2nd edn (Ithaca: Cornell University Press, 1968). On the other hand, W. V. Harris, *War and imperialism in republican Rome, 327–70 BC* (Oxford: Clarendon, 1979), argues for the fundamental expansiveness of the Roman state. Cf. Josiah Ober, 'Tiberius and the political testament of Augustus', *Historia* 31 (1982), 306–28.

74 It is in no sense surprising that the postwar period, not least the period of decolonisation, has seen such a strong move to re-evaluate Roman 'imperialism': from a variety of perspectives, *Dialogues*, ed. Mattingly, and Majeed, 'Comparativism', update Brunt's 1963 article. The considerable history of scholarship on this subject is very substantial and cannot be considered here in any detail.

75 Brodersen, *Terra Cognita*, helpfully divides Roman spatial thinking into these three registers.

76 See A. C. Bertrand, 'Stumbling through Gaul: maps, intelligence and Caesar's *Bellum Gallicum*', *AHB* 11 (1997), 107–22; cf. N. J. E. Austin and Boris Rankov, *Exploratio: military and political intelligence in the Roman world from the second Punic War to the Battle of Adrianople* (London: Routledge, 1995).

77 The edition of Konrad Miller, *Itineraria Romana. Römische Reisewege an der Hand der Tabula Peutingeriana* (Stuttgart: Strecker und Schröder, 1916), though often reprinted, is unreliable: Richard Talbert, 'Cartography and taste in Peutinger's Roman map', in *Space in the Roman world: its perception and presentation*, ed. Richard Talbert and Kai Brodersen (Münster: Lit, 2004), pp. 113–41, including bibliography.

of Gibraltar in the west to India in the east.[78] In this respect it matches the expanse plotted out in the Pliny passage at the start of this chapter.

In sum, no military context can be detected here; we are dealing instead with imperial discourse that is somewhat removed from practice. It cannot be seriously maintained that the military conquest of India was a practicable possibility: the sheer distance between it and Italy, with the many attendant issues of transportation, makes this hard to imagine except in the most fanciful way. Even if there were some degree of Roman military presence in the Arabian peninsula and especially in the Nile valley from the end of the first century BC through the end of antiquity,[79] it does not follow that troops in sufficient numbers could have been transported to the Indian subcontinent.

We pass now to a case, some one hundred years after Augustus, which clearly shows the paradox we have already seen: that the prospect of conquering India militarily was as desirable in principle as it was unrealistic in practice.

I.5. Trajan's Parthian campaign

Cassius Dio offers the evocative picture of an ageing emperor having arrived at the head of the Persian Gulf, watching a ship sail to India, and regretting that his ambitions of conquest were now thwarted by the onset of old age and illness:

> Then he arrived at the ocean itself, and having found out about its nature and having caught sight of a ship setting sail for India, he said he would definitely have crossed over to the Indians, were he still young. He began to cogitate the Indians and inquired into their affairs, and he deemed Alexander blessed. (Cassius Dio 68.29.1)[80]

This episode is part of Trajan's Parthian campaign, dating to the summer of 116, just over a year before his death while returning to Rome. Whether or not we should take this anecdote at face value, there is no doubt that the

[78] 'Did indicate' is the more accurate expression in this case, given that the furthest segment(s) on the left (the Iberian west of the map) has/have been lost: Ekkehard Weber (ed.), *Tabula Peutingeriana. Codex Vindobonensis 324*, 2 vols. (Graz: Akademische Druck- und Verlaganstalt, 1976), vol. II, p. 40, with Talbert, 'Cartography and taste', pp. 119–20.

[79] Bowersock, *Roman Arabia*; Fergus Millar, *The Roman Near East, 31 BC–AD 337* (Cambridge, MA: Harvard University Press, 1993), ch. 11.

[80] Κἀντεῦθεν ἐπ' αὐτὸν τὸν ὠκεανὸν ἐλθών, τήν τε φύσιν αὐτοῦ καταμαθὼν καὶ πλοῖόν τι ἐς Ἰνδίαν πλέον ἰδών, εἶπεν ὅτι πάντως ἂν καὶ ἐπὶ τοὺς Ἰνδούς, εἰ νέος ἔτι ἦν, ἐπεραιώθην. Ἰνδούς τε γὰρ ἐνενόει, καὶ τὰ ἐκείνων πράγματα ἐπολυπραγμόνει, τόν τε Ἀλέξανδρον ἐμακάριζε. Cf. Millar, 'Looking east', 507.

emperor, known in his own reign as *optimus princeps*, was a keen emulator of Alexander.[81] Before turning westwards, Trajan in fact first travelled up the Euphrates to Babylon, to visit the tomb of Semiramis and to make a sacrifice at the house where Alexander died.[82] It is no accident that Trajan was the first Roman emperor to have been born outside of Italy, in southern Spain: this fact alone goes some way towards explaining the geographic extent of Trajan's activities. Apart from anything else, Dio's anecdote, written a century after the event, strikingly combines commercial and military interests.

Two texts from the later fourth century suggest more strongly, if less poignantly, that Trajan's plans extended as far as India. Rufus Festus says that Trajan, having secured the finest part of Persia, Seleucia, Ctesiphon and Babylonia, 'advanced as far as the boundary of India, in Alexander's footsteps' (*Breuiarium* 20).[83] Festus' contemporary Eutropius says much the same thing, though without mentioning Alexander (8.3.2). To these authors we shall return in section I.6 below, but for the present we should note their impact on later writing. When the sixth-century historian Jordanes produces his own version, based in part on these writers, he explicitly imputes Indian ambitions to Trajan: he set up a fleet 'from which to conquer Indian lands' (*Romana* 268).[84]

The extent of Trajan's motives is less at issue here than the rhetoric involved in the campaign and its subsequent representation. What such stories do show is that eastern campaigns in the imperial period are readily connected with India, even if the exaggeration involved is conscious. Thus, when Lucian in his treatise, *How to write history* (section 31), scorns contemporary historians for their haste to narrate Lucius Verus' Parthian campaign of AD 162–66, he complains that they have already written of future events, such as the capture of the Parthian king Vologeses III (section 31).[85] The preface to an *Indica* has already been completed. The details of the campaign require authentication, but this they are about to receive in

81 See F. A. Lepper, *Trajan's Parthian war* (Oxford: Clarendon, 1948), pp. 34–9, on the chronology of his use of titles. On his *Oriens* coins, Harold Mattingly, *Coins of the Roman empire in the British Museum*. Vol. III, *Nerva to Hadrian* (London: British Museum, 1936), p. lxxxxvi. His presentation of himself as Hercules may imply a link with Alexander: Julian Bennett, *Trajan, optimus princeps*, 2nd edn (Bloomington: Indiana University Press, 2001), p. 72.

82 Bennett, *Trajan*, p. 199.

83 *usque ad Indiae fines post Alexandrum accessit*. Festus proceeds to say that Trajan set up a fleet, on which point scholars have disagreed: J. W. Eadie, *The* Breviarium *of Festus: a critical edition with historical commentary* (London: Athlone, 1967), pp. 139–40.

84 *nec non et in mari rubro classem, unde Indiae fines uastaret, instituit ibique suam statuam dedicauit*. The statue Trajan erected there was apparently still standing by the late sixth century: *The Roman empire: Augustus to Hadrian*, ed. Robert K. Sherk (Cambridge University Press, 1988), p. 138.

85 On the war, A. R. Birley, 'Hadrian to the Antonines', *CAH* XI, 2nd edn, pp. 132–94, at 160–5.

the form of letters received from Muziris and the Oxydraci in India. With mention of these letters Lucian sounds a novelistic note, comparable with the many letters woven into the *Alexander Romance*.[86]

An interesting element of Lucian's comments is their temporality: part of the offence caused by these historians is that, in their enthusiasm to flatter the emperor, they get ahead of themselves. The thinly veiled allusion to Alexander is assured by the reference to the circumnavigation of the outer sea (31). The implication is that these historians are flattering the emperor, not unlike the way in which Alexander was flattered by several contemporaries (5).[87] Part of the background to this is that contemporary history was subject to more stringent tests than were accounts of the more remote past.[88]

As the case of Trajan shows, the imperial sense of India is intensely concerned with Alexander's conquests. But then the focus is less on the exact details of the empire actually created by Alexander; what matters here is that its distant location brings glory to a great man. The near absence of the Indo-Greeks in the later literary records may be regarded as proof of this.[89] It suited the rhetoric of empire much better that India was radically other than that Ai Khanum had a theatre and a gymnasium. India is here less important in its own right than as the crowning glory of success against the Parthians, or later Sasanians. For Lucian in *How to write history*, the precedent of Alexander makes India effectively the *reductio ad absurdum* of history written to flatter the emperor.

I.6. Itinerarium Alexandri

The case of Trajan's Parthian campaign shows that Alexander provided a lens through which to consider India. In this regard, Trajan provides a strong link into later antiquity. Both Rufus Festus and Eutropius were writing around 369–70, at a time when the emperor Valens was contemplating an eastern campaign. This was in fact to prove his undoing, culminating with the massive defeat at the hands of the Goths at Adrianople (378). Noel Lenski's recent study suggests that these works were written not merely to provide incitement for the emperor to proceed, but also 'practical guides to Rome's historical claims to the territories of the east'.[90] In this light,

86 Patricia A. Rosenmeyer, *Ancient epistolary fictions: the letter in Greek literature* (Cambridge University Press, 2001), pp. 169–92.

87 Cf. Chapter 1, section II.1 above.

88 Luce, 'Bias'.

89 The meagre literary sources given by Holt, *Thundering Zeus*, pp. 174–84, constitute the exception.

90 *Failure of empire: Valens and the Roman state in the fourth century* AD (Berkeley: University of California Press, 2002), p. 192.

the references to India by Rufus Festus and Eutropius, though brief and arguably fanciful, cry out to be seen in the light of the politics of their authors' time.

It was the figure of Trajan that had been invoked, in another historical work a few decades earlier, again with an implied connection to India. The *Itinerarium Alexandri* was written by the courtier Flavius Polemius, and dedicated to the emperor Constantius II. The year, 340, is significant, since it was the very time Constantius was preparing for war against the Sasanians. Despite the initial promise of a geographical account (*itinerarium*), the work is in fact a potted twofold biography of Alexander and Trajan, of which the Trajanic narrative is now lost. It begins:

> My lord Constantius, who is better even than good emperors, I, thinking it particularly beneficial, both as an omen for you and as an incentive for future people, if I were to compose a *Persian campaign*, a glorious account of emperors engaged in the same undertaking, but now already favourably undertaken and dispatched, namely of Alexander the Great and Trajan, [I] acceded most willingly, desirous of the task, because indeed it demands that I wish this, and because the successes of rulers encourage others to match them. (1)[91]

There is some evidence to suggest that this text enjoyed renewed interest in 362/3, to encourage the young emperor Julian on his eastward expedition. Even if Julian's attitude to Alexander, as expressed in his writings, was ambiguous, it does appear that from this time he became preoccupied with Alexander's eastern conquests, to the degree that it cut him off from reality.[92]

It is true that, in the late republic, imitation of Alexander had been something of a mixed blessing. As Augustus was well aware, its political implications required caution in manipulating.[93] It is also true that there was a negative element to the manner in which philosophers such as Seneca

[91] *dextrum admodum sciens et omine tibi et magisterio futurorum, domine Constanti, bonis melior imperator, si orso feliciter iam accinctoque Persicam expeditionem itinerarium principum eodem opere gloriosum, Alexandri scilicet Magni Traianique, componerem, libens sane et laboris cum amore succubui, quod quidem meum uelle enim id et exigit sui pensique est, quodque regentium prospera in partem subditos uocant.* Ed. Raffaella Tabacco (Città di Castello: Olschki, 2000).

[92] Polymnia Athanassiadi, *Julian and Hellenism* (Oxford: Clarendon, 1981), pp. 224–5; R. J. Lane Fox, 'The itinerary of Alexander: Constantius to Julian', *CQ* 47 (1997), 239–52.

[93] Peter Green, 'Caesar and Alexander: *aemulatio, imitatio, comparatio*', *AJAH* 3 (1978), 1–26; and E. Gruen, 'Rome and the image of Alexander', in *Ancient history in a modern university*, ed. T. W. Hillard *et al.* (North Ryde, NSW: Macquarie University Press, 1998), pp. 178–91, aptly warn against overestimating the extent of *imitatio Alexandri* in the late Republic, but they cannot explain away all the evidence for Augustus: Dietmar Kienast, 'Augustus und Alexander', *Gymnasium* 76 (1969), 43–56. Still fundamental is A. Heuss, 'Alexander der Grosse und die politische Ideologie des Altertums', *A&A* 4 (1954), 65–104.

viewed Alexander, an *exemplum* of excessive ambition.[94] What we see in later antiquity is a whitewashed Alexander, the philosopher-king of the *Alexander Romance* rather than Seneca's drunken megalomaniac. It is this later Roman memory of Alexander that is expressed in the Peutinger map, where one of the farthermost eastern places is designated as Alexander's turning point and marked as such by an oracle.[95] This is, in any case, a distended India that blends into Scythian territory. If the Peutinger map harbours various sources from the late Republic into the mid-fourth century, this particular feature reflects, in the first instance, the late-antique memory of Alexander. Medieval versions of Alexander's interview with the Brahmans gave later authors the opportunity to show the conqueror learning humility, and on this basis he was sometimes presented as a pilgrim in search of wisdom.[96] The figure of Alexander was thus a bridge between the learned cultures of antiquity and the western Middle Ages, but one that underwent considerable metamorphosis in the process.

To this we might add the lively folk traditions of Alexander elsewhere, in a wide variety of regions. These can be most readily substantiated in the case of the western Middle Ages,[97] with the enormously wide diffusion of the *Alexander Romance* in a number of languages of the Mediterranean basin.[98] Beyond the classical canon, we find substantial Alexander traditions in the Iranian world;[99] and the Midrash attests to his presence in medieval Jewish tradition.[100] However varied this range of texts and traditions, the point

94 Notably Sen. *ep.* 53.10; 59.12; 83.19. Richard Stoneman, 'The legacy of Alexander in ancient philosophy', in *Brill's companion to Alexander the Great*, ed. Joseph Roisman (Leiden: Brill, 2003), pp. 325–45, illustrates the varied uses of Alexander as a philosophic or rhetorical *exemplum*. Cf. Diana Spencer, *The Roman Alexander*, pp. 89–93.

95 *hic Alexander responsum accepit: 'Usque quo Alexander?'* 'Here Alexander received the [oracular] reply: "How far are you going, Alexander?"' The oracular saying, found also in the Ravenna Cosmography, is part of later tradition: Miller, *Itineraria Romana*, p. 838.

96 See further Chapter 6, section III.2.

97 George Cary, *The medieval Alexander* (Cambridge University Press, 1956); C. Frugoni, *La fortuna di Alessandro magno dall' Antichita al Medioevo* (Florence: La nuova Italia, 1978); D. J. A. Ross, *Alexander historiatus: a guide to medieval illustrated Alexander literature* (Frankfurt am Main: Lang, 1988); Danielle Lecoq, 'L'image d'Alexandre à travers les mappemondes médievales (XIIe–XIIIe)', *Geographia antiqua* 2 (1993), 63–103.

98 Fraser, *Cities of Alexander*, pp. 205–26, on the genealogy of the *Alexander Romance* up to the earliest surviving Greek text.

99 John H. Marks, *Visions of one world: legacy of Alexander* (Guilford, CT: Four Quarters, 1985). In Persian versions of the *Alexander romance*, Alexander is usually but not always positively portrayed. In some instances, he is identified with Du'l-Qarnayn, the 'two-horned' prophet of the Koran (16:84). For further discussion, William L. Hanaway, 'Eskanar-nama', *Encyclopaedia Iranica* (1998); Faustina C. W. Doufikar-Aerts, 'A legacy of the *Alexander Romance* in Arab writings: Al-Iskandar, founder of Alexandria', in *The search for the ancient novel*, ed. Tatum, pp. 323–43.

100 To take an example from late-antique Judaism, Alexander as judge is sympathetic to the Jews: *The Babylonian Talmud: Seder Nezikin*, four vols., ed. Isidore Epstein *et al.* (London: Soncino, 1935), vol. III, pp. 608–10.

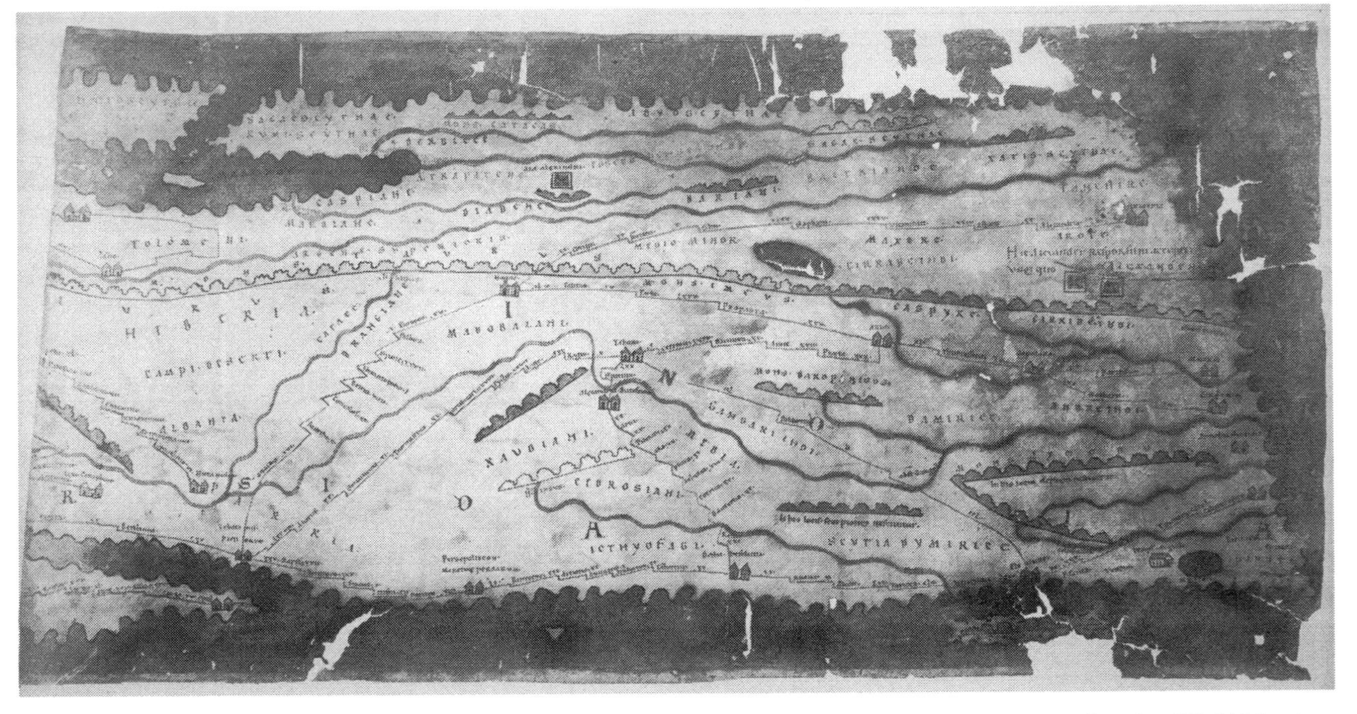

Figure 11 Peutinger map, thirteenth century, easternmost segment, Kunsthistorisches Museum, Vienna. Courtesy of Ancient World Mapping Center, University of North Carolina, Chapel Hill.

is clear: if neither the Alexander histories nor the Greco-Roman *Alexander Romance* tradition had any monopoly on the Macedonian king, then it is unfair to expect that imitation of Alexander was pursued by Roman leaders as a kind of 'package deal'. We are dealing with someone who intensely manipulated his own public image, and hence it is important to emphasise the variety of tones with which Alexander resonated in Roman imperial history. If India was often part of the memory of Alexander in the Middle Ages, then that changed form commensurately.

II. CHRISTIAN TOPOGRAPHY, CHRISTIAN EMPIRE

Now that we have seen representations of world empire in the Augustan age and somewhat later, we are well placed to consider the same set of features at a later point in Roman history. We are dealing with the later Roman period, in a series of Christian texts: now if the 'Christianisation of time' has been well described, the corresponding Christianisation of space has not received equal attention, beyond the smaller scale of holy places in Palestine and elsewhere.[101] But this is worth considering in similarly broad terms, if we are to try to grasp what India meant to Romans of the later empire.

The T-O map is most readily associated with Isidore: in this schema, the inhabited earth is represented as a T-shape within a circle ('O') representing the surrounding Ocean; Europe and Africa fill up the lower quadrants, together matching the extent of Asia, represented by the upper semicircle. First, Isidore in his *Etymologiae* or *Origines* describes an *orbis terrarum* that can be pictorially represented in this fashion; secondly, manuscripts of his work from the eighth and ninth centuries actually include such diagrams, many of them extremely schematic and simple. While Isidore is extremely important to our story, not least for the proximity of India to the earthly paradise in the western medieval tradition, we must consider earlier manifestations of this worldview, including Orosius, another author much read and copied in the western Middle Ages.

In what we may regard as a key text of the period immediately after the conversion of Constantine, Eusebius of Caesarea offers a history of the world, stretching back into the distant past and culminating in the triumphal present. There is a breadth of vision implicit in Eusebius'

[101] E.g., E. D. Hunt, *Holy land pilgrimage in the later Roman empire* (Oxford: Clarendon, 1982); Peter Brown, *The cult of the saints* (University of Chicago Press, 1981); Béatrice Caseau, 'Sacred landscapes', in G. W. Bowersock *et al.* (eds.), *Late antiquity: a guide to the postclassical world* (Cambridge, MA: Harvard University Press, 1998), pp. 21–59.

scheme, and a confident tone of its formulation. In this respect he must be considered alongside the earlier Christian chronographer Julius Africanus (*c.* 160–*c.* 240).[102] But it was Eusebius' work that was translated by Jerome into Latin, and would in that form reach many readers in the west. Some earlier Christian writers had shown a certain ambivalence, or even cautious optimism about the Roman empire as a political unit; perhaps the majority had been openly hostile.[103] For Eusebius, the conversion of the Roman empire under Constantine was the result of divine providence. In the course of this narrative he offers, in effect, a Christianisation of history, by writing a history that embraced both Judaeo-Christian and Greco-Roman pasts. This is a key moment in the creation of a Christian discourse, a key step in the gaining of 'power over the past'.[104] Several decades later Augustine in his *City of God* shows himself heir to this conception of human history, however much that may have been refracted by the military threats now facing the empire.[105] Beyond the fourth century this model was to prove strikingly resilient, with a long history in the medieval west, as is shown, for example, in the thirteenth-century Hereford map. But it is less to Augustine than to his pupil Orosius that we must turn if we wish to grasp the place of world empire, geographically understood, in this new Christian schema. At this broadest level, the Christianisation of space in Orosius and others requires consideration, parallel to the 'Christianisation of time'.[106]

What we shall see here in the fourth and early fifth centuries is the tendency of Christians to appropriate the language of Roman (and especially Augustan) public life, not least their military and political symbols of success, in asserting their own achievement following Constantine's conversion to Christianity. However much the political circumstances of the western Roman empire may have differed by the time of Isidore, the cosmological paradigm had already been established, and was in essence to remain

[102] Africanus survives only in the fragments preserved in George Syncellus' eighth-century *Ecloga chronographia*. For a consideration of Africanus, together with Eusebius, in the light of the problem of 'primordial history', see William Adler, *Time immemorial: archaic history and its sources in Christian chronography from Julius Africanus to George Syncellus* (Washington: Dumbarton Oaks, 1989), pp. 43–71.

[103] Theodor E. Mommsen, *Medieval and Renaissance studies* (Ithaca: Cornell University Press, 1959), pp. 267–9.

[104] Averil Cameron, *Christianity and the rhetoric of empire* (Berkeley: University of California Press, 1991), pp. 120–54. The book is much influenced by Michel Foucault's concept of a 'totalising discourse', though it is concerned more with society than with individuals.

[105] Peter Brown, *Augustine of Hippo* (London: Faber, 1967), pp. 299–312; Noel Lenski, '*Initium mali Romano populo*: contemporary reactions to the Battle of Adrianople', *TAPhA* 127 (1997), 129–68.

[106] R. A. Markus, *The end of ancient Christianity* (Cambridge University Press, 1990), pp. 85–135.

thus to the later Middle Ages, in fact up to the time of the New World discoveries.[107]

II.1. The western tradition of Orosius and Isidore

Born in Spain around 390, Orosius wrote *Historiae adversus paganos* in seven books, embracing the entire sweep of human history: the first six books range from Adam, i.e. the beginnings, to the birth of Christ, and the seventh takes the story down to AD 417, which we may regard as the work's immediate *terminus post quem*. We see here a providential conception of history, valorising divine intervention at the expense of individual human agency (esp. 2.2.4). Unlike Augustine, he regarded the Roman empire, the last of the four world empires, as being part of God's plan, for it facilitated Christian missionary activity.[108] The fact that Christ was born at a time when peace reigned in the world, and Augustus ruled most of it, was auspicious. And unlike Salvian of Marseilles, writing his *De gubernatione Dei* some thirty-five years later, Orosius was optimistic about the 'barbarian threat': he was hopeful that these foreigners would yet be integrated into Roman society.[109] This is a true universal history in its self-conscious adoption of a series of different scenes of historical narration, taking into account the perspective of both Romans and non-Romans.[110] This was a major work in the creation of Christian history, especially if we consider the enormous influence it was to exercise in the medieval west.[111] But it is primarily to the geographical aspects of his work that we must turn our attention.

Orosius' universe is tripartite: of the three continents, Asia, Africa and Europe, Asia matches the other two for extent.[112] This opening articulation

[107] Anthony Pagden, *The fall of natural man: the American Indian and the origins of comparative ethnology* (Cambridge University Press, 1982). Grafton, *New worlds*; Romm, *Edges*.

[108] The three world empires before the Romans were those of the Babylonians, Macedonians and Africans (Carthaginians). The scheme of four world empires, articulated in heightened expectation of a decisive fifth, can be traced back to the mid-second century and the Jewish struggle against Antiochus IV (*Daniel* 2:31–45 and 7:1–14): see Joseph Ward Swain, 'The theory of the four monarchies', *Cl. Phil.* 35 (1940), 1–21, 20–1 on Orosius.

[109] For a consideration of Orosius and Salvian side by side, see François Paschoud, *Roma Aeterna. Études sur le patriotisme romain dans l'occident latin à l'époque des grandes invasions* (Rome: Institut suisse, 1967), pp. 276–310.

[110] Explicitly articulated at 5.1.3. See further, T. E. Mommsen, *Medieval and Renaissance Studies*, p. 334.

[111] On Orosius' impact on medieval mapmaking, David Woodward, 'Medieval *Mappaemundi*', in *History of cartography*, ed. Harley and Woodward, vol. I, pp. 286–370, at 300–1; Evelyn Edson, *Mapping time and space: how medieval mapmakers viewed their world* (London: British Library, 1997), pp. 32–5.

[112] At 1.2.1. For the same idea expressed some two centuries later Isid., *Orig.* 14.3.3.

of universal space leads up to an account of the 'local disasters of individual nations that arose in an unending stream from the beginning'. They arose from Original Sin, as he goes on to explain right away in 1.3: in fact, it is no exaggeration that the description of the world brings home the point of Original Sin as a central theological concept in his history. In this respect Orosius closely follows Augustine.[113]

India, which is part of Asia, is bounded by the Indus on the west, the Caucasus on the north; the Eastern and Indian oceans on the other sides. It contains forty-four peoples, not including those living in Taprobane or on the other densely populated islands:

In this territory [of Asia] lies India, whose western boundary is the Indus River, which empties into the Red Sea, and whose northern boundary is constituted by the Caucasian mountain; the other sides . . . are bounded by the Eastern and the Indian oceans. This land has forty-four groups, excluding both those who dwell on the island of Taprobane, which has ten cities, and those who live on the very many other inhabited islands. (1.2.15)[114]

As such India is for Orosius literally at the ends of the earth, and as we shall see below it is later to be contrasted with the western Mediterranean world. Even in this briefest of surveys, its populousness is mentioned,[115] and indeed extended to Taprobane and the other surrounding islands as well.

India enters the stage of world history when the Assyrian queen Semiramis invaded it. 'Nobody had ever entered India' except Semiramis herself and Alexander.[116] This detail is subject to an intensely moralistic interpretation:

At that time it was an even more cruel and serious matter to persecute and massacre peoples living peacefully than it is today; for in those days there were no such passions for warfare abroad nor was there such practice of lusts at home. (1.4.6)[117]

As if extracting full value from his narrative of Semiramis' and later Bacchus' bloody conquests (1.9), Orosius emphasises that the Indians were themselves peace-loving and non-aggressive. What had begun as propaganda

[113] Brown, *Augustine*, pp. 388–90.

[114] *in his [sc. Asiae] finibus India est, quae habet ab occidente flumen Indum, quod Rubro mari accipitur, a septentrione montem Caucasum; reliqua, a Eoo et Indico oceano terminatur. haec habet gentes XLIIII, absque insula Taprobane, quae habet decem ciuitates, et absque reliquis insulis habitabilibus plurimis.*

[115] For populousness as a feature of descriptions of India, see also Chapter 2, section II.2.

[116] *Indis quoque bellum intulit, quos praeter illam et Alexandrum Magnum nullus intrauit.* (1.4.5)

[117] *quod eo tempore ideo crudelius grauiusque erat quam nunc est, persequi et trucidare populos in pace uiuentes, quia tunc apud illos nec foris erant ulla incendia bellorum, nec domi tanta exercitia cupiditatum.*

around the time of Alexander's conquests[118] was now to win a fixed place in the Christian master-narrative of world history.

Bacchus' subjugation of India is seen alongside the plagues and wars suffered by Ethiopians (1.9.3) and Egyptians (1.10.1–18). Again, by the law of Original Sin all people deserve punishment, though the Indians themselves are peaceful and lacking in aggression:

> Father Bacchus subdued India and drenched it with blood, filled it with carnage and violated it with lusts – even though the people of India never offended others, and were contented merely with the quiet lives of slaves. (1.9.4)[119]

Orosius makes no mention of Brahmans and other holy people, but they may well be implied in these comments about peacefulness. Such an interpretation gains weight if we remember the tendency of Augustine and other Christians to speak about Brahmans as the archetypal Indians (Chapter 6 below).

In describing Alexander's expedition to the east, his cruelty and ambition come to the forefront, in moralising terms (3.19). For Orosius, as for other epitomators of late antiquity, Alexander's expedition did in fact take him to the eastern Ocean, to the edge of the world: 'he drove his chariot round the turning post and entered Indus from Ocean and returned to Babylon' (3.20.1).[120] Accordingly, there is no mention of the decisive mutiny that forced Alexander to turn back at the Hyphasis.[121]

Alexander, the 'acknowledged leader of the most distant east', receives embassies:[122] ambassadors from the Spaniards and Morini 'seek him throughout Assyria and India, visiting ends of the earth and getting to know both oceans'.[123] In this far-fetched tale we should remember Orosius' own

[118] Bosworth, *Alexander and the east*; cf. Chapter 1, section II.1 above.

[119] *subactam Indiam Liber pater sanguine madefecit, caedibus oppleuit, libidinibus polluit, gentem utique nulli umquam hominum obnoxiam, uernacula tantum quiete contentam.*

[120] *post quasi circumacta meta de Oceano Indum flumen ingressus, Babylonam celeriter rediit.*

[121] To cite another example of the tendency of later sources to speak of Alexander as actually having reached the ends of the earth, we may compare Malalas (8.3 = 194–95 Dindorf): 'Alexander also captured all the regions of India and their empires, taking prisoner Poros, emperor of the Indians; he also captured all the other empires of the barbarian peoples, except the empire of the widow Kandake'; a little later he is baldly said to have 'conquered the world'. But it is clear that Malalas is working with a vague sense of India, one which stretches both to Arabia (18.16 = 435) and Ethiopia (18.5 = 457).

[122] The claim that Mithridates VI extended Parthian control to India (5.4) need not be taken as historical fact; rather, it reflects a scrambling of details about 'the east'.

[123] *Hispanus et Morinus ad supplicandum Alexandro Babyloniam adiit cruentumque ultro dominum, ne hostem exciperet, per Assyriam Indiamque quaesiuit, terrarum metas lustrans et utrique infeliciter notus Oceano* (3.20.8).

Spanish origins as he matches the eastern and western edges of the earth.[124] The Morini are easily identified in Orosius' intellectual background: they were the Gallo-Belgic tribe mentioned at the end of the ekphrasis of the shield of Aeneas as 'farthermost of people'.[125] Their geographic location, close to the Channel, thus puts them close to the 'remotest Britons'.[126]

This episode is later explicitly recalled in the context of a later world conqueror. At 6.21 Orosius tells of embassies from Indians and Scythians that travelled all the way to Tarraco in Hither Spain to seek out Augustus: 'farther they could not have gone'.[127] As suppliants they begged for his military intervention, reminding him of Alexander the Great, just as Gauls and Spaniards had come after Alexander. In each case, we see an embassy that attests the expanse of political power. In the broader scheme of the work, the twin stories function as reminders that mankind everywhere, even at these very corners of earth, is tainted with Original Sin.

By the time we get to the *Etymologies* of Isidore of Seville (*c.* 602–36), the tripartite *orbis* has become orthodoxy, as the extended description at 14.3.1–3 shows. In this passage in the fourteenth book on Asia, India is described immediately after the earthly Paradise. It is important to see here that Paradise has a specific geographical location (14.3.2–4), something that was to have a profound effect on later medieval worldviews.[128] The juxtaposition of India and Paradise is not explicitly stated, it is true, but it is directly implied by the framework and order of Isidore's composition. The actual content of Isidore's description of India offers little of interest in its own right (14.3.5–7): it is very much in the Plinian tradition and predicts the western medieval tradition of subsequent world maps. Though the specific details of Isidore's India are unimportant, they do mark the transition from a verbal to a visual mode of Indography.

Isidore's encyclopaedia as a whole incorporates several elements of Jewish cosmology; the matter of paradise, however, is something that he transforms

[124] For the prominence of the western Mediterranean in Orosius, see J. M. Alonso-Núñez, 'Orosius on contemporary Spain', in *Studies in Latin literature and Roman history*, ed. Carl Deroux (Brussels: Collection Latomus, 1989), vol. V, pp. 491–507; and note p. 495 for the parallelism of the two episodes.

[125] *extremique hominum* (Verg. *Aen.* 8.727).

[126] Orosius' clichéd reference to *ultimi Britanni* has direct precedent in Catull. 11.12 and Hor., *Carm.* 1.35.30 (further references at *TLL* II.2195.67–77).

[127] *interea Caesarem apud Tarraconem citerioris Hispaniae urbem legati Indorum et Scytharum, toto Orbe transmisso tandem ibi inuenerunt, ultra quod iam quaerere non possent.*

[128] Note especially 14.3.2: *Paradisus est locus in orientis partibus constitutus, cuius uocabulum ex Graeco in Latinum uertitur hortus: porro Hebraice Eden dicitur, quod in nostra lingua delicae interpretatur.* On the 'swift and extensive' diffusion of the *Etymologiae*, with its substantial Spanish, Italian and French traditions, see P. K. Marshall, 'Isidore', in *Texts and transmission*, ed. L. D. Reynolds (Oxford: Clarendon, 1983), pp. 194–6. Isidore is explicitly mentioned in the Hereford map, as is Orosius.

from Persian-Greek tradition into Christian discourse. His so-called T-O scheme of world maps is in fact closer to a 'Y-O' pattern, especially if we consider the angle at which the Nile is often placed, beginning at the delta and heading off towards one o'clock. The same can be said of many maps, including the three major *mappaemundi* of the later Middle Ages, namely the Hereford, Ebstorf and Vercelli world maps. This points to the influence of Jewish maps, which are shaped in a Y-pattern.[129] The implications of this were enormous. For one thing, the centring of the world on Jerusalem meant that there was more of Asia to fill up. We sense this in the difference in the sizes of illustrations between Europe and the outer fringes of the *orbis terrarum*.[130]

To understand the Christian tradition reflected in Orosius and Isidore we must look back not merely to the classical sources we have already considered, but also to some key texts of Jewish tradition. Of the various cosmologies implicit in the Old Testament, the one that would have the most profound effect in the medieval west was that of Noah and his sons. This foundation text, which accounts for the peopling of the earth after the new world order brought about by the flood, is an obvious place to start.

Genesis 10 lists Noah's sons, Shem, Ham and Japheth, and their descendants at some length. The genealogy that concerns us as we consider medieval conceptions of 'Asia' begins with Shem, and proceeds through Arpachshad, Shelah, Eber, Joktan. Of the thirteen sons of Joktan named, who 'occupied a stretch of country from Mesha in the direction of Sephar, the eastern mountain range' (10:30),[131] Ophir and Havilah are the ones that have been at various times linked with India. The precise geographical location of the place Ophir has caused controversy over a long period: it is sometimes thought to be in India, sometimes in the southern Arabian peninsula.[132]

[129] Philip S. Alexander, 'Notes on the *imago mundi* of the Book of Jubilees', *Journal of Jewish Studies* 33 (1982), 197–213; more generally his 'Early Jewish geography', *Anchor Bible dictionary*, vol. II, pp. 977–88; and Francis Schmidt, 'Naissance d'une géographie juive', in *Moïse Géographe*, ed. Alain Desreumaux and Francis Schmidt (Paris: Vrin, 1988), pp. 13–30.

[130] For example, in the Hereford map the details for Europe are given much more finely and in greater detail, whereas, say, the sizeable representation of tower of Babylon, or indeed the 'monstrous races' obviates the need for fine topographic detail, textual or visual, in the more peripheral areas. Even the holy land of Palestine, which receives a large expanse by virtue of its relation to Jerusalem, the central point, is not accorded a great deal of detail. See further, e.g., Scott D. Westrem, *The Hereford map: a transcription of the legends with commentary* (Turnhout: Brepols, 2001).

[131] Tr. *Jerusalem Bible*, ed. Alexander Jones.

[132] Cf. *ABD* V 26–27, s.v. 'Ophir' (David W. Baker), on the puzzle of location. David M. Goldenberg, *The curse of Ham: race and slavery in early Judaism, Christianity and Islam* (Princeton University Press, 2003), esp. pp. 43, 241, puts this in a wider context while discussing the question, 'how did ancient Jewish society look at the black African?' (10).

Two different sources lie behind this passage, a Priestly (P) and a Yahwist (J) tradition. Of these, the P-Table has been dated to the seventh century BC,[133] whereas the J-Table is older. It accounts for Shelah, Eber, Joktan and his thirteen sons, and offered a geographical schema to match the genealogy.

Another passage that was to have paradigmatic force for centuries of medieval mapmaking was the description of Paradise, in the second account of creation (*Genesis* 2). After the creation of mankind, Yahweh 'planted a garden in Eden which is in the east, and there he put the man he had fashioned' (2:8). This garden contained all kinds of tree, including the tree of life and the tree of the knowledge of good and evil. The description of its rivers is worth close attention, for they were to provide readers with the ostensible possibility of fixing a locality for Eden:

> A river flowed from Eden to water the garden, and from there it divided to make four streams. (2:10) The first is named the Pishon, and this encircles the whole land of Havilah where there is gold. (2:11) The gold of this land is pure; bdellium and onyx stone are found there. (2:12) The second river is named the Gihon, and this encircles the whole land of Cush. (2:13) The third river is named the Tigris, and this flows to the east of Ashur. The fourth river is the Euphrates. (2:14)

The Hebrew river-names *Perat* and *Hiddeqel* correspond without any difficulty to the Euphrates and Tigris, as they have been translated above; but the other two rivers emerging in the garden, the Gihon and Pishon, are less easily located. As a broad region, nonetheless, this region of the 'east' (*Gen.* 2:8) seems to be Armenia, which we might therefore identify with the eastern edge of the world. In so far as precious stones occur here, this presentation of Paradise emphasises commodities.

Taken together the two passages quoted above, though 'they reflect first and foremost the world of the west, and only indirectly external geographical space',[134] cannot be overemphasised in tracing medieval worldviews, within a chronological sweep that includes both Orosius and the Hereford map. These may be the closest the Old Testament itself comes to offering an explicit set of geographic co-ordinates on a large scale.

An expanded reworking of the Table of Nations in *Genesis* 10 was made around 100 BC by the anonymous author of the *Book of Jubilees* (chapters 8–10).[135] The work survives in Ethiopic, into which it was translated

133 E. A. Speiser (ed.), *The Anchor Bible I: Genesis* (Garden City, NY: Doubleday, 1964), pp. 64–72; Alexander, *ABD* I 980; cf. Oxford Study Bible.

134 Alexander, 'Early Jewish geography', p. 978.

135 In what follows I rely on James H. Charlesworth, *The Old Testament Pseudepigrapha* (Garden City, NY: Doubleday, 1983), pp. 1–7.

from Greek, though it was probably written originally in Hebrew. Some fragments survive in Hebrew and Latin. It stands out among the Jewish apocrypha for the prominence it devotes to chronology. When compared to the *Genesis-Exodus* narrative, its augmentations can be identified as coming from Jewish folklore. It was known to fourth-century Christians, for example to Jerome (*Epist.* 78.20), who speaks of it as the 'little *Genesis*'. The form known to Jerome was probably the Greek translation, whose date is unknown; this was also the form read by the eighth-century Byzantine chroniclers Syncellus and Cedrenus.[136] This Greek version provided the basis also for the Latin version, which was translated no later than the sixth century AD,[137] but possibly as early as the mid-fifth century.

The following passage contains an explicit reference to India, and comes after it is already mentioned as being among Noah's bequest to Shem (8.21):[138]

> And Shem also divided his land among his sons; and the first share fell to Elam and his sons – what lies east of the river Tigris till it reaches the east, the whole land of India, and the Red Sea coast, and the waters of Dedan, and all the mountains of Mebri and Ela, and all the land of Susa, and all that is on the side of Pharnak to the Red Sea and the river Tina. (9.2)

The tripartite scheme of *Genesis* is in *Jubilees* matched with that of the Ionian geography. This fact might go some way to explaining its resilience for so many centuries during the Middle Ages.

We come next to Josephus, another author to interpret the Table of Nations for his own purposes. Like *Jubilees*, Josephus begins by outlining the territory of Shem, Ham and Japheth before speaking of their descendants (*Ant. Iud.* 1.122–147).

The composite text now known as I *Enoch*, 'a thesaurus of early Jewish lore on astronomy, meteorology, botany and geography', dating to the late first century AD, makes no explicit reference to India. Yet the journeys of Enoch, described in the section known as the *Book of the Watchers*, are highly suggestive: on his tour of the east Enoch saw, among other things in the desert, trees looking like those of frankincense and myrrh (29:2), and

[136] Syncellus (ed. A. E. Mosshamer [Leipzig: Teubner, 1984]) makes only a few passing references to India explicitly. Chronographic tradition embraced several Indias, and Syncellus appears to entertain both an Arabian and an Ethiopian 'India'. This is hardly surprising in view of the early Jewish tradition concerning Kush: Goldenberg, *Curse of Ham*, p. 211.

[137] Some substantial fragments survive in a sixth-century MS containing also the Assumption of Moses.

[138] It should be mentioned, as we think back on Isidore, that Eden is mentioned here in the same breath (8.21).

others fragrant like mastic and cinnamon (30:2–3). Various other trees are mentioned, including the almond (31):

> And after (experiencing) this fragrant odour, while looking toward the northeast over the mountains, I saw seven mountains full of excellent nard, fragrant trees, cinnamon trees, and pepper. (32:1) From there I went over the summits of the mountains, far toward the east of the earth. I (then) passed over the Erythraean Sea and went far from it, and passed over the head of angel Zutu'el. (32:2) And I came to the garden of righteousness and saw beyond those trees many (other) large (ones) growing there – their fragrance sweet, large ones, with much elegance, and glorious. And the tree of wisdom, of which one eats and knows great wisdom, (was among them). (32:3) (tr. Charlesworth, *Old Testament Pseudepigrapha*, 50)

It will be noticed that the paradise of righteousness lies on the northeast edge of the world, in the region of outer darkness beyond Ocean. The journeys elsewhere in the book are, likewise, without explicit topographical referent and yet highly suggestive of an exotic, even mystical location.

Josephus' version of the Table of Nations (*Ant. Iud.* 1.122–47) also adds topographical specificity to the *Genesis* text. His major concern in this is to provide onomastic correspondences: thus, for example, Arphaxades gave his name to the Arphaxadaeans, 'who are called Chaldaeans today'.[139] The sons of Shem rule 'Asia as far as the Indian Ocean, starting at the Euphrates' (143). He claims he has Hellenised the Hebrew names for the pleasure of his readers; elsewhere he claims to have omitted names which might cause offence by their non-Greek sound.[140]

II.2. The eastern tradition of Cosmas Indicopleustes

Orosius and Isidore emerge from this analysis as nodal points in the history of ideas, as key points of connection between antiquity on the one hand, in its overlapping Judaeao-Christian and Greco-Roman aspects, and medieval Europe on the other. But we come now to an east Mediterranean author who was also writing in a discernibly Judaeo-Christian tradition; who was heir to much of the same material as Orosius and Isidore, but responded in different ways, and certainly with different emphases. But whereas the classical tradition in Orosius and Isidore is Roman, refracted by Pliny's *Natural history*, that tradition in Cosmas is Greek: among Cosmas' sources

[139] τοὺς νῦν Χαλδαίους καλουμένους (144): exotic place-names are 'unscrambled' through identification with better known localities.

[140] 1.129, cf. 7.369; 11.68, 152; 12.57. On this point we might compare Pliny's apologetic tone in mentioning the 'strange names' (*barbarae appellationes*) of foreign peoples, in this case of Hither Spain (3.29); the north-east Adriatic coast produces 'a few names of people that merit or allow repetition' (*populorum pauca effatu digna aut facilia nomina*, 3.139).

are Ephorus and other classical writers, but these are far outweighed by biblical texts.[141]

In keeping with Nestorian exegesis, Cosmas' world was in the shape of square building, representing Moses' tabernacle of *Genesis* 10. He strives in his work to refute both the astronomy of Claudius Ptolemy and contemporary Christian Aristotelian thought, as represented by John Philoponus in the Three Chapters controversy;[142] in his arguments he favours literal acceptance of scripture, and quotes profusely from both Testaments throughout the work. In particular, Cosmas attacks views about the sphericity of the earth and the existence of Antipodes (esp. book 1). As much as Cosmas' worldview differed from, say, Orosius' or Isidore's, all three share a debt to Jewish cosmology.[143]

Thus, for example, when Cosmas in his second book offers his own to Aristotelian and Ptolemaic geography we return to the by now familiar first principles of Judaeo-Christian geography. From his exegesis of the Table of Nations, the following section is relevant to the east:

> *The sons of Shem, Elam and Ashur* (*Gen.* 10:21), that is the Elamites and Assyrians and remaining nations, and as many of these as were spread far and wide over Asia and the East – the nations of the Persians, Huns, Baktrians, Indians, onwards to the ocean. (2.27)[144]

The phrasing of the end of the extracts shows that the list of regions listed is not exclusive. Nonetheless, India marks the ends of the (inhabited) earth.

Yet Cosmas' sources demonstrably include not only biblical but also polytheist works. Such is the nature of his sources, as we can now imply them from his text, that he has been characterised by his most recent editor as a kind of low- to middlebrow autodidact: such is his watered-down coverage of scientific topics.[145] Book 12, which is not found in all the manuscripts, stands out also in the extent of its similarity of content and language to Hellenistic and early imperial texts such as those of Berossus, Manetho and Josephus.[146] Any implications that might be drawn from this

141 Ephorus (2.79–80) and Hyperides (quoted at 5.26) are referred to in detail, whereas others such as Homer (12.9) and Pytheas of Marseilles (2.80) are referred to only in a very general way.

142 Philoponus, *On creation* 3.9 explicitly claims that Cosmas followed Theodore of Mopsuestia in interpreting the scriptures.

143 See further M. V. Anastos, 'The Alexandrian origin of the *Christian Topography* of Cosmas Indicopleustes', *DOP* 3 (1946), 73–80; Kunio Kitamura, 'Cosmas Indicopleustès et la figure de la terre', in *Moïse Géographe*, ed. Desreumaux and Schmidt, pp. 79–98.

144 υἱοὶ δὲ Σὴμ, Ἐλὰμ καὶ Ἀσοὺρ, τουτέστιν Ἐλαμίτας καὶ Ἀσυρίους, καὶ τὰ λοιπὰ ἔθνη καὶ ὅσα ἐξ αὐτῶν ἐπεξετάθησαν ἕως Ἀσίας καὶ ἐπὶ ἀνατολὴν, Περσῶν, Οὕννων, Βάκτρων, Ἰνδῶν ἕως τοῦ Ὠκεανοῦ.

145 'Cosmas représente la science abâtardie qui caractérise certains milieux chrétiens et païens de la fin de l'antiquité' (Wolska, *Topographie chrétienne*, p. 16).

146 Wolska, *Topographie chrétienne*, p. 57.

about his intended audience must take into account that he aims the main thrust of his attack at those Christians who have taken pagan beliefs on board, and no doubt we must understand this group to encompass a wide range of learning: not only the likes of John Philoponus but also those less learned.

A few words might be said about Cosmas' conception of the world in purely geographical terms. Paradise lies to the east: before the flood it was inhabited by humans (2.78–79). He locates the river Phison of *Genesis* in India, though refusing to choose between the Indus and the Ganges:

> Of these [rivers originating in Paradise] the Phison is the India river, which some call Indus or Ganges. It flows down from regions in the interior, and flows by many mouths into the Indian Sea. (2.81)[147]

It is interesting to note that at this very point Cosmas proceeds to compare the Phison with the Nile; and then to describe the river Gihon as flowing through Ethiopia.[148] This rapid code-switching vividly shows Cosmas' multiple debts: to Greek learning, however indirectly gleaned, and to scripture. As such, it may be regarded as one of the many, often conflicting attempts of late-antique Christians to engender a new *paideia* that they could call their own.

One of the main targets of Cosmas' polemic is the notion of the antipodes. This he attacks by ridiculing the idea that people walk upside down.[149] In mentioning Taprobane, India and Ethiopia, together with their flora and fauna and even to some extent their peoples, he comes to those regions that are generally described as antipodean in the Hellenistic or Plinian tradition of ethnography. A few humans are mentioned in these accounts, e.g. 11.11. On no occasion do we encounter in Cosmas the monstrous races so familiar in the Plinian tradition. In mentioning what he

[147] ὁ μὲν Φεισὼν ἐν τῇ Ἰνδικῇ χώρᾳ, ὃν καλοῦσί τινες Ἰνδὸν ἢ Γάγγην, ἐκ τῶν μεσογείων που κατερχόμενος, πολλὰς ἐκροίας ἔχει ἐν τῷ Ἰνδικῷ πελάγει.

It is characteristic of Cosmas' Christian *paideia* that this passage comes immediately after an appeal to the authority of the pagan writers, Ephorus, Pytheas of Marseilles and Xenophanes of Colophon, who are cited because they supposedly accord with holy scripture (i.e. in supposedly opposing the idea of the earth's sphericity): καὶ ταῦτα μὲν οἱ ἔξωθεν συμφωνοῦντες τῇ θείᾳ Γραφῇ εὑρίσκονται εἰρηκότες.

[148] The roughly contemporary version of the Table of Nations, by the Byzantine chronicler John Malalas, makes explicit mention of India: 'The tribe of Shem took as the length of its territory the land from Persia and Bactria as far as India and, as for the breadth, as far as Rhinokourouroi, that is, from the East as far as the region of the South, including Syria and Media and the river called the Euphrates' 1.6 (ch. 10 Dindorf) tr. Jeffreys, Jeffreys and Scott (Melbourne: Australian Association for Byzantine Studies, 1986), p. 5.

[149] The term 'antipodes' implies strict symmetry across the equatorial plain, a one-to-one correspondence of north and south, and is thus used by Eratosthenes; on the other hand 'antichthones' assumes asymmetry and dissymmetry.

has seen on his own travels, he is making India and Taprobane seem more accessible to travellers from the Roman world. In the process he might be emphasising that the subcontinent was ready to receive missionaries. Despite the autobiographic element in the work, there is no hint of danger in travelling to and in India.[150]

Autobiography is indeed one of the unusual features of the *Christian topography*, and one that deserves special consideration. Since so much stigma was attached to the profession of trading, in the classical period at least,[151] it comes as something of a surprise that Cosmas so confidently identifies himself as a trader. This he does explicitly at 2.54 and 56,[152] and implicitly at several points when he speaks of his own travels. Not only do we hear of Cosmas the trader but also of other traders, Roman and Persian; however, no Indian traders are explicitly mentioned. What is more, in describing the natural historical details of book 11, he evaluates almost every item against his own experience. Thus, for example, in discussing individual animals in turn, he mentions that he has seen a giraffe, a rhinoceros (both dead and alive). Of the hog-deer (*taurelaphos*), he says bluntly, in a variation on the theme of autopsy, that he has 'both seen and eaten it'.[153] On the other hand, he has not seen a unicorn; nor a hippopotamus, though he has seen (and in fact sold) some of its large teeth (11.9). These two features of first-person narration invite comparison with a work in which there is no authority of books: *Periplus of the Erythraean Sea*, though of course the earlier work lacks Cosmas' insistent polemical edge.

There is more than one source of authority implicit within the *Christian topography*, both his own experience of the present time, complete with autopsy,[154] and that of the book – *the* book, one might say from Cosmas' perspective, namely the Old and New Testaments. While he does mention Christian missions to the Indian subcontinent, he freely admits that they

[150] The *Periplus* on the other hand has much to say about the practical dangers of travelling, e.g., ch. 20 on the Arabian Red Sea coastline and ch. 40 on the Indian. The dangers of travel, at the hands of bandits, is acknowledged in Roman law as a possible cause of death, e.g., *Digest* 13.6.5.4: Ray Laurence, 'Afterword: travel and empire', in *Travel and geography in the Roman empire*, ed. Colin Adams and Ray Laurence (London: Routledge, 2001), pp. 167–76 at 172.

[151] Andrea Giardina, 'The merchant', in *The Romans*, ed. Andrea Giardina, tr. Lydia G. Cochrane (University of Chicago Press, 1993), pp. 245–71; and cf. Chapter 4, section II above.

[152] He identifies himself as a business traveller when referring to his companion as ἄλλον ἕνα πραγματευτήν (2.56). Note also the use of the first person in the description of Adulis: ἔνθα καὶ *τὴν ἐμπορίαν ποιούμεθα* οἱ ἀπὸ Ἀλεξανδρείας καὶ ἀπὸ Ἐλᾶ ἐμπορευόμενοι (2.54).

[153] τὸν δὲ χοιρέλαφον καὶ εἶδον καὶ ἔφαγόν.

[154] By the same token there is a vivid sense of place, namely Alexandria, as Cosmas' base. This is clearest in the first prologue to the work; when he says that he has sold hippopotamus' teeth 'here' (ἐνταῦθα), we may well understand him to mean Alexandria.

have not been entirely successful. This seems to be a function of his commercial perspective, which is based on a close-up view of the subcontinent and its social relations.

The animals he describes and draws owe something to the marvel tradition, but are much closer than Pliny's *Natural history* to identifiable non-mythical animals. Thus the first chapters of book 11 are devoted to a variety of Indian fauna and flora: the rhinoceros, buffalo (*taurelaphos*), giraffe (*kamelopardalis*), wild cattle (*agriobous*), musk (*moskhos*), unicorn (*monokeros*), wild boar (*khoirelaphos*), hippopotamus (all 11.1–9); pepper and coconut (*piperea* and *karua indika*, 10.10); the seal, dolphin and turtle (*phoke, delphinos* and *khelone*). These animals may be unusual from a Mediterranean perspective, but they are not completely outlandish in the way that invokes, say, Ctesias' mantichores.[155] On the other hand, the description of humans owes nothing to the marvel tradition: where they are mentioned it is with no sense of the 'marvellous people' but with some attention to social organisation. The story of the merchant Sopatrus reflects well on the king of Taprobane, for he is able to distinguish the equitably minted Roman coins from the dishonest Persian ones.[156] The story implies an openness and accessibility of that land, and conversely its intelligibility to the Roman world. Most importantly, there is an awareness of Christian missionary activity. That activity may not always be successful, by Cosmas' own admission, but it is nonetheless in evidence. Taprobane has a church, clergy and its band of the faithful;[157] but Cosmas is unsure whether the same can be said for regions beyond it. Given the humanising description of the local inhabitants, it thus seems that Cosmas' description of the subcontinent is imbued with the implicit idea of Christian mission. If this is true, it would not be surprising that Cosmas describes Taprobane in terms that emphasise its comprehensibility over its strangeness.

III. THE RHETORICAL BACKGROUND: IMPERIAL PANEGYRIC

The discussion above has illustrated two related phenomena: geographical generalisation by which a mental category of 'the east' is created; and the false consciousness of imperial rhetoric in which empire is presented as coterminous with the edges of the earth. In seeking to understand the link

155 It is telling that the least realistically imaginable animal described gets the careful comment that Cosmas has not seen a specimen: the μονόκερως, which we might translate as unicorn.

156 11.17–19. In a detailed study of this episode, F. F. Schwarz presents Sopatrus as Cosmas' source: 'Kosmas und Sielediba', *Ziva Antika* 25 (1975), 469–90.

157 ἐκκλησία, κληρικοί, πιστοί, 3.65.

between these, we should turn to the extravagances of imperial panegyric. In particular, the 'amplifications' described by Menander Rhetor give a compelling reason for the resulting vagueness about the (eastern) edges of the earth.[158]

The principle can be illustrated with regard to India from a considerable range of panegyrics. Thus the anonymous panegyric of 297/8 mentions fear inspired by the emperor Constantius I among 'Aethiopians and Indians':

> May the Nile trophies under which the Ethiopian and the Indian trembled pardon me. May the recent destruction of the Carpi likewise be satisfied with a mention of its glory. (8[5].5.2)[159]

The speech in fact celebrates Constantius' victory over the Britons in 297. Though India is the farthest point from Britain, it may have special relevance here in view of his keenness to imitate Alexander.[160]

At Trier in 310 the anonymous panegyrist had this to say in honour of Constantine:

> Beneficent gods, why is it that new divinities, destined to be worshipped the whole world over, always come from some very remote part of the earth? Thus Mercury from the river Nile, whose source is unknown, and Liber [Bacchus] from the land of the Indians, who are nearly privy to the sunrise, have shown themselves to mankind as gods manifest. (6[7].9.4)[161]

The panegyrist goes on to claim, by way of an answer to his question here posed, that regions adjoining heaven are holier than Mediterranean ones; 'it is closer for an emperor to be sent by the gods from where the land ends'.[162]

158 αὐξήσεις, 368.22. On this kind of phenomenon, called *amplificatio* in Latin, see Marincola, *Authority and tradition*, pp. 35–7, as applied to the histories of individual rulers.

159 *dent ueniam trophaea Niliaca sub quibus Aethiops et Indus intremuit. contenta sit uoce gloriae suae etiam proxima illa ruina Carporum.*

C. E. V. Nixon and Barbara Saylor Rodgers, *In praise of later Roman emperors* (Berkeley: University of California Press, 1996), pp. 115–16 ad loc., discuss the question of what this might mean: if the 'Nile trophies' indeed refer to the suppression of the revolt in Busiris and Coptos, then the 'Aithiopian and Indian' may denote the peoples of southern Egypt. Even if this is so, it does not diminish the evocative force of 'Indian' as an expression of the broad spread of imperial power.

160 Lane Fox, 'Itinerary of Alexander'.

161 *di boni, quod hoc est quod semper ex aliquo supremo fine mundi noua deum numina uniuerso orbi colenda descendunt? sic Mercurius a Nilo, cuius fluminis origo nescitur, sic Liber ab Indis prope consciis solis orientis deos se gentibus ostendere praesentes.*

For an analysis of geographical space in the panegyrics, and of this passage in particular, see Nicola Baglivi, 'Osservazioni su paneg. VII(6).9', *Orpheus* n.s. 7 (1986), 329–37, esp. 332.

162 *Sacratiora sunt profecto mediterraneis loca uicina caelo, et inde propius a dis mittitur imperator ubi terra finitur.* The phrase describing India as 'almost privy to the sunrise' is matched by 10(2).2.1, where the western side of the Ocean, near the river Ebro, is *conscio occidui solis* ('witness of the

Later, when Pacatus addresses Theodosius in 389, we sense some slippage between the descriptive and the normative: the question of just how far Roman power has spread is complicated by the supposed extent of the emperor's own fame.

For your guidance, Emperor, has frightened not only those peoples divided from our world by swathes of forest or rivers or mountains, but those which Nature has separated, made inaccessible by perpetual heat, set apart by unending winter, or cut off by intervening seas. The Indian is not protected by Ocean, nor the man from Bosphorus by the cold, nor the Arab by the equatorial sun. Your power reaches places that the name of Rome had hardly reached before. (2[12].22.2)[163]

Despite their enormous distance, these peoples have heard the name of Rome, and live under the immediate shadow of its political might. Even if Roman power has not reached India and other distant corners in the formal sense of governance, the emperor is known and feared there. In this case, India stands for areas under Roman influence though not administrative control, and this respect reflects on the emperor's personal charisma.

When Hercules and Dionysus are invoked by way of comparison,[164] the emperor's wide geographic range is graphically illustrated. Artists can forget their depictions of those gods' triumphs, says Pacatus, for his panegyric provides sufficient material for artists and historians:[165]

Artists, to whom favourable fate has granted the power to give fame to events, you too should despise those clichéd themes of ancient tales, the labours of Hercules and the Indian triumphs of Bacchus, and the wars with snake-footed monsters. (2[12].44.5)[166]

To see the phenomenon of generalising about India within the rhetorical tradition, we must turn to the treatises attributed to Menander Rhetor, to

setting sun'). Again a god's wide geographical range provides the material for praising an emperor, and in this case Hercules is invoked in honour of Maximian.

[163] *tua enim, Imperator, auspicia non hae tantum gentes tremunt quas ab orbe nostro siluarum interualla uel flumina montesue distinguunt, sed quas aeternis ardoribus inaccessas aut continua hieme separatas aut interfusis aequoribus abiunctas Natura disterminat. non Oceano Indus, non frigore Bosphoranus, non Arabs medio sole securus est; quo uix peruenerat nomen ante Romanum, accedit imperium.* This passage is discussed by Asche, *Weltherrschaftsidee*, pp. 11–18.

[164] Elsewhere the labours of Hercules are celebrated, and at 10(2).4.2–4 Pacatus develops the double comparison of 'divine' assistance, suggesting that Maximian is to Diocletian as Hercules is to Jove. In fact, Hercules recurs in monuments and coins of the Tetrarchic period, often in connection with the gigantomachy. Dionysus' Indian conquest was also open to explicitly negative interpretation, as something morally degenerate: Prudent. *C. Symm.* 122–8.

[165] For an historical evaluation of panegyric, Sabine MacCormack, 'Latin prose panegyrics', in *Empire and aftermath: Silver Latin*, ed. T. A. Dorey (London: Routledge and Kegan Paul, 1975), vol. II, pp. 143–205, and MacCormack, *Art and ceremony*, pp. 1–14.

[166] *uos quoque quibus secunda sors cessit dare famam rebus, artifices, uulgata illa ueterum fabularum argumenta despicite, Herculeos labores et Indicos Liberi triumphos et anguipedum bella monstrorum.*

the sections devoted to the *epibaterios logos*, or speech on arrival (387.17–28). The author speaks of *thesis* or praising the 'position' of a country:

> our fathers did not rule over a small area like the Peloponnese, but reigned over Lydia and then subdued Caria and proceeded to conquer all the east; Egyptians, Blemmyes and the tribes of the Erembi claimed they were our subjects – they who in recent times appear to have been obedient to us, in the alliances and assemblies. (ref. in Menander Rhet.)[167]

There are textual problems in and around this passage.[168] But, for our purposes, there is no mistaking a central point: the ends of the earth could be used in praising a ruler with whom it might be associated, at whatever stretch of the imagination. In the passage quoted it should be noted that Menander moves between particular lands (such as Lydia, Caria and Egypt) and a generalising idea of 'the entire east': τὴν ἑώιαν ἅπασαν (387.24). In the context of the work,[169] we can safely assume that 'the east' here is the eastern Mediterranean.

Among his plentiful verbal conjurings, the panegyrist here exhibits a special sleight of hand, which might be analysed as follows in a slow-motion replay: in former times the *father* of the ruler conquered various 'eastern people' (an implicit vagueness here being important); those eastern people have sent ambassadors to the ruler in the present; therefore we in the present have dominion over people from the east. This paraphrase is clearly exaggerated, but an important principle emerges here. While we should bear in mind that the panegyrics are very much rooted in the occasion of their initial delivery,[170] we have seen a theme that is common to a range of them: of a generalised east, and of India specifically, bringing glory to the emperor, whether by virtue of the supposed extent of his rule, or by comparison with the ever-recurrent Hercules and Dionysus. This we may regard as an important link, chronologically at the very least, between the Roman Empire of Augustus and Trajan and that of Constantine and Theodosius.

167 οἱ πατέρες ἡμῶν ἦρξαν . . . οὐδὲ περιγεγραμμένων τόπων, καθάπερ ἡ Πελοπόννησος, ἀλλ' ἦρξαν μὲν Λυδίας, ἐπῆρξαν δὲ Καρίας, καὶ προῆλθον τὴν ἑώιαν ἅπασαν καταστρεφόμενοι, καὶ ὡμολόγησαν ἡμῖν δουλεύειν Αἰγύπτιοι καὶ Βλέμμυες καὶ Ἐρεμβῶν γένη, εἴπερ αὐτοὶ καὶ ἐν τοῖς τελευταίοις χρόνοις φαίνονται ὑπακούοντες ἡμῖν ἐν ταῖς συμμαχίαις καὶ κλήσεσιν.

168 See D. A. Russell and N. G. Wilson (eds.), *Menander Rhetor* (Oxford: Clarendon, 1981), pp. 291–3 ad loc.

169 On the authorship of the work(s) attributed to Menander Rhetor, as well as their social milieu, see Russell and Wilson, *Menander*, pp. xi–xii.

170 MacCormack, 'Latin prose panegyrics', p. 151. In this regard Robin Seager, 'Some imperial virtues in the Latin prose panegyrics: the demands of propaganda and the dynamics of literary composition', *PLLS* 4 (1983), 129–66, leaves little room to perceive differences between the panegyrics, useful as the article may be as a descriptive catalogue of topoi.

IV. *ORBIS TERRARUM URBI SPECTANDUS*: THE MECHANICS OF REPRESENTATION

We have already seen wordplay on *urbs/orbis* by Ovid and others: now the same pun used by Pliny in discussing Agrippa's map (3.17) alerts us to the issue of reception.[171] The central question for us to consider in this final section of the chapter is by what means India was represented. Given the centrality of maps in modern conceptions of space, it is tempting to retroject the visual element onto Greco-Roman antiquity, but it is not clear that this is justified. What is more, we are faced with real questions about the reconstruction of Augustan 'maps': any attempt to reconstruct them, as in the case of Bunbury, must rely on a combination of literary evidence and on retrojection from later medieval maps. In contrast to earlier studies, Kai Brodersen has recently argued for the predominance of written over visual representations of space in the Roman empire. By this reckoning, even when images do exist, they tend to be less important afterthoughts, serving more of a decorative than a utilitarian function.[172] Of greater practical utility, and indeed significance, were itineraries, which more closely reflect actual routes, and make it possible for others to replicate particular journeys. Inscriptions play a vital role here.[173] Such a view is a useful corrective to the work of earlier scholars, who assumed similarities between ancient and contemporary uses and categories of maps. Yet it may be overstated: Brodersen's definition of scale, a key component for a map as opposed to a cartogram, seems needlessly stringent, with the result that no candidate for a Roman scale-map can pass muster.[174]

[171] For the pun, see section I.2 above. In the case of Pliny the reading is in some doubt, it must be admitted, since *urbi* was printed by old editions up to Harduin's Paris edition of 1685; Detlefsen, followed by Jan-Mayhoff, preferred the rather flat reading, *orbi*. The conjecture does however receive the blessing of the *TLL*, which adduces 3.67 from the same book of the *HN* as a comparable case of paronomasia (vol. IX.2.916.24).

[172] Brodersen, *Terra cognita*, cf. Bunbury, *History of ancient geography*, and now Carey, *Pliny's catalogue*, pp. 61–74, tracing links between Pliny's text and Augustan monuments.

[173] Janni, *Mappa*, is fundamental in its emphasis on itineraries, an approach recently reaffirmed by C. R. Whittaker, 'Mental maps and frontiers: seeing like a Roman', reprinted in his *Rome and its frontiers*, pp. 63–87 (orig. 2002). Against this, R. J. A. Talbert has argued for the importance of provinces as units: 'Rome's provinces as framework for world-view', in *Roman rule and civic life: regional perspectives (first to fourth centuries AD)* ed. L.de Ligt, A. Hemelrijk and H. W. Singor (Amsterdam: Gieben, 2004), pp. 21–37. See also Benet Salway, 'Travel, *itineraria* and *tabellaria*', in *Travel and geography*, ed. Adams and Laurence (2001), pp. 22–66.

[174] Brodersen, 'The presentation of geographical knowledge for travel and transport in the Roman world: *itineraria non tantum adnotata sed etiam picta*', in *Travel and geography*, ed. Adams and Laurence (2001), pp. 7–21; and his 'Neue Entdeckungen zu antiken Karten', *Gymnasium* 108 (2001), 137–48.

One reason this question has not been easy to resolve is the elusive nature of the 'map' of Agrippa, by any account a key instance of map-mindedness in Augustan Rome. One reason this question has been difficult to adjudicate is that the term 'map' has been made to bear too much weight, combining utility with symbolism. In the practice of Romans, the variety of terms used suggests a variety of ways in which space could be represented, and a variety of uses for those representations. It is therefore with due caution about undue assumptions about ancient 'maps' that we should proceed to consider some of the visual means by which India was represented.

An obvious place to start is the extensive *Geography* of Claudius Ptolemy, which has with justification been viewed as the culmination of the Greek scientific-mathematical tradition of cartography. The *Geography* may be regarded as a 'how-to' text, intended to inform those wishing to make their own maps of particular areas. It is unclear whether or not the work itself included its own diagrams.[175] The relevance of Cosmas' *Christian topography* is puzzling on this very question: that text itself makes reference to illustrations, and these have been reconstructed on the basis of three manuscripts of the ninth to eleventh centuries.[176] It is unclear to what extent Ptolemy's text can be compared to Cosmas' in this respect.

The issue of Roman map-mindedness now gains intriguing if frustrating new evidence in the form of a papyrus from Antaiopolis in Upper Egypt and dated to the first century BC.[177] Its drawn map, sharing the papyrus with a geographic text of Artemidorus of Ephesus (fl. 100 BC) and various sketches of animals, might constitute a precedent for the Peutinger map, particularly if its zig-zag lines represent routes. This possibility remains somewhat speculative, given that the map on the papyrus (thus far inaccessible and not yet fully published) seems to be incomplete. Nonetheless, the implications of the map for the present study are considerable since Artemidorus' geographical work is known to have covered not only Spain but the farthest extreme, Taprobane (e.g., Plin. *HN* 7.30).[178]

175 O. A. W. Dilke, 'The culmination of Greek cartography in Ptolemy', in *History of cartography*, ed. Harley and Woodward, vol. I, pp. 189–90. For bibliography on this question, see Dilke, *Greek and Roman maps* (Ithaca: Cornell University Press, 1985), p. 207 n. 28, updated by Stückelberger, 'Ptolemy'.

176 Huber, *Heilige Berge*, pp. 109–12.

177 C. Gallazzi and B. Kramer, 'Artemidor im Zeichensaal', *Archiv für Papyrusforschung* 44 (1998), 189–208, and B. Kramer, 'The earliest known map of Spain (?) and the geography of Artemidorus of Ephesus on papyrus', *Imago Mundi* 53 (2001), 115–20.

178 Bunbury, *History of ancient geography*, pp. 61–8; Weerakkody, *Taprobane*, pp. 223–4; Geus, *Eratosthenes*, pp. 286–7.

Of the visual representations presented in Chapter 3 above, two different kinds point to an imperial context: scenes of the triumph of Dionysus, on the Baltimore sarcophagus; and the late-antique personifications of India of the Piazza Armerina mosaic and the silver plate. The personifications aligned India with provinces ruled by the Romans, even though India never came close to political subjection to Rome. The provincial paradigm for representing India (Chapter 3, section II.2 above) needs emphasis here for its obvious imperial framework.

On what scale of geographical conception did India feature in Roman thinking? A tripartite scheme is usefully outlined by Brodersen, and let us briefly apply it to India: world maps, regional *itineraria* and local land-surveying. Of these, there can be no doubt that India registered on the largest of these scales, as we saw in connection with the Greek scientific tradition of geography in Chapter 1 above. On the smallest scale, we have no evidence for cadastral surveys of the subcontinent conducted by Romans in the way they were conducted for settlements of the Mediterranean world.[179] On the other hand, it is less clear whether India fitted into the mid-scale of geography. Strabo's *Geography* and Pliny's *Natural history* even more so exhibit a confluence of different kinds of topographic information, and resist simplifying attempts to pigeon-hole them. To take another key witness, the Peutinger map allows no easy assumptions about military use.[180] We might assume a priori that a map of such a scale was useful in a military context; yet military establishments such as forts account for less of the actual place-markings in India than they do to its west. Such practical considerations may well be subordinated to the overall impression created by public display. Recent scholarship has pointed to the complexity and sophistication of the map, and we might aptly see in it the combining of various kinds of topographic information. A striking feature of India in the Peutinger map is its profusion of roads, some along the coast, all of which suggest much more land travel than the *Periplus* would lead us to expect. We can hardly imagine that these are Roman-built roads; yet they are presented within the symbolic frame of universal Roman power.[181] The Indian roads, complete with distances, and the temple of Augustus close to Muziris are a means of naturalising the subcontinent as part of the extended Mediterranean world, and thus by implication subject to Roman power.

[179] Brian Campbell, *The writings of the Roman land surveyors: introduction, text, translation and commentary to the* Agrimensores (London: Society for the Promotion of Roman Studies, 2000).
[180] Talbert, 'Cartography and taste', 127–8.
[181] Ibid., 131; cf. Whittaker, *Rome and its frontiers*, p. 126.

V. CONCLUSION

That governance should be the first criterion by which to characterise the Roman empire cannot be questioned.[182] But much would be lost if we failed to consider the more subjective senses that constitute 'mental maps'. By such a definition, it would not be extravagant to claim that India *was* in fact part of the Roman empire. By the same token, 'imperialism' has been discussed here in a restrictive sense of the perceived limits of empire, and the propaganda constructing India as a region that could and would be conquered. Strictly speaking, it was of course a false consciousness that allowed Augustan poets to claim or imply that India *was* in fact already part of the Roman empire;[183] by the same token, several histories of Alexander, exaggerated the easternmost point reached by him – for Diodorus, the Ganges, and for the romance tradition, the eastern edge of the world itself. The origin of this misapprehension may be traced back to Alexander's own manipulation of myth, and the continuing appeal he held for later leaders of the late Republic and empire. For the later period, there is also a tendency to view Hellenism, what might now be thought of as the diffusion of culture, in political terms: hence the exaggerations about Alexander's geographical turning point may be seen as a kind of political-military encoding of the cultural realities of the Indo-Greek empires.

Comparison of this chapter with the previous one highlights some distinguishing criteria between different kinds of geographical information, namely those from the commercial and the military spheres. Information linked explicitly with imperial conquest had a certain cachet attached to it, particularly in so far as it invoked the memory of Alexander's conquests. The converse of this holds too, namely that information linked with commercial enterprise has distinctly less prestige, as Strabo openly says at one point (15.1.4 C686, cf. Chapter 4, section V above). But this distinction is not absolute, for even Strabo, in dismissing the traders as unreliable witnesses, acknowledges that they are indeed sources; there is every chance that, unheralded, information linked with commercial enterprises is embedded within Strabo's and Pliny's texts. Ptolemy's *Geography*, is on the other hand, explicit that merchants, who are in fact named, were sources for Marinus' account of India, and by implication for his own.

In general, there are two major senses in which an imperial context of geographical information can be identified. First, it is undeniable that the

[182] Among such studies note esp. Millar *et al.*, *Roman empire*; Andrew Lintott, *Imperium Romanum: politics and administration* (London: Routledge, 1993); and Nicolet, *World of the citizen*.

[183] India was among the *uictae longo ordine gentes* mentioned in the Shield of Aeneas (Verg. *Aen.* 8.722).

military and administrative realities of the Roman empire went some way towards stimulating the tremendous surge of interest in, and engagement with issues of spatial distance evidenced in the Augustan age and early empire. Not all such journeys made an impression on literary Indography. To take a later example, we hear of one Aurelius Gaius (d. AD 299), whose considerable travels while on military service included India, which is mentioned on his funerary inscription after Palestine, Egypt and Alexandria.[184] Secondly, maps and related texts made possible the symbolic expression of imperial power, many of those expressions centring on the emperor himself. It is in this second, imaginative sphere rather than in the first that we see the significance of India in the Roman discourse of empire. The persistence of references to Alexander's expedition, often in distorted and popular versions, historiographically far inferior to Arrian in accuracy and detail, goes some way towards underlining the extent to which India could indeed mark the ends of the world. In this way, India represented the ultimate goal of military achievement. It is no accident that universal history and large-scale geographical writing flourishes in the Augustan age.[185]

India as a marker of empire is something that needs to be taken seriously: though India shares with other 'eastern' nations (e.g., Egypt, Arabia and Mesopotamia) features such as antiquity and specialised priesthoods, it is distinct from them in that it marks the edges of the earth. It was Alexander's expedition that secured for India an imperial context, even if that was much more symbolic than administrative, a cognitive rather than a political geography. In considering Christian empire, we are dealing with some of the same features, but in a different context. In the coalescing of Jewish and Greco-Roman traditions of geography, India retained a place in the tripartite scheme, marking the extreme eastern edges.

Though Alexander was never to colonise it, India marked the end of his empire: for the emperor Trajan, notably, it was a good to think with. This chapter, like the first, gives the impression that whenever Alexander was spoken about, India was never far from the mind of the person speaking. If there is a vagueness about the exact location of India, that is because it was probably not possible and certainly not easy to delimit a world empire conceptually. This we might regard as a paradox in its own right. It is

184 Thomas Drew-Bear, 'Les voyages d'Aurélius Gaius, soldat de Dioclétien', in *La Géographie administrative et politique d'Alexandre à Mahomet* (Strasbourg: Centre de recherche, 1981), pp. 93–141; cf. *l'Année epigraphique* 1981.777.

185 W. Schmitthenner, 'Rome and India: aspects of universal history during the Principate', *JRS* 69 (1979), 90–106; Franz Ferdinand Schwarz, 'Magna India Pliniana', *WS* (1995), 439–65.

certainly easier to locate 'Roman' India on mental maps rather than with the mathematically precise co-ordinates of Claudius Ptolemy.

To judge from accounts of Alexander's expedition itself, it seems that the issue of the ends of the earth became deeply imbued with that of military conquest. The same issue would arise in different ways later. But, in so far as Alexander was central to the self-fashioning of Roman strong men of the late Republic and the empire, it was impossible to consider the extent of the empire without considering India. It was India, more than anything, that could remind Romans that 'Rome' had expanded from agricultural village to world empire.

In a recent article, Erich Gruen has injected a note of scepticism on the actual extent of *imitatio Alexandri*. He suggests, persuasively, that the evidence on this has been exaggerated and too readily generalised; and he emphasises the ways in which Alexander was a model to be avoided, for his *pothos* and excessive behaviour. This is without doubt a valuable note of caution. But two objections may be raised, and both have important implications for this chapter. First, Gruen's chronological span goes up to Augustus and does not consider emperors such as Trajan or Caracalla.[186] This later, more autocratic era of Roman history, provides ample and perhaps less problematic evidence that some leaders did use the more appealing side of Alexander in order to assert proximity to an ideal type. Secondly, it would seem inappropriate to expect imitation of Alexander to be available only as a package deal of imperial self-presentation, as Gruen seems to imply: rather, Alexander provided a set of symbols which offered a wide variety of uses, less an ultimate and abiding meaning than a tenacious adaptability. It may be significant that India is not mentioned in the article, for any emphasis given to it might have produced a different picture. Writers mentioning India as a place conquered or to be conquered tend to imply the desirability of world conquest, and hence the positive sides of Alexander's image. It would be hard to imagine Trajan's later reputation as *optimus princeps* without his conscious manipulation of the Alexander image.

Authors and especially poets of the Augustan period tended to give the impression that the borders of the empire coincided with the ends of the earth. The hyperbolic language of poetry allowed this false consciousness to be easily maintained. The *Res gestae* and later imperial panegyric in their own ways illustrate the centrality of such hyperbole to imperial

[186] This in itself is not decisive, given the largely negative image of him among philosophers of the empire: Stoneman, 'Legacy of Alexander'. On Caracalla, cf. Chapter 4, section III.2.

self-presentation. It must be stressed that this operates at the level of rhetoric and propaganda, without carrying any connotations about actual military strategy. Indeed, India may be regarded as a good test-case which proves the slippage between propaganda and policy. Much the same scenario can be detected when Christians appropriate the Augustan language of world conquest in the fourth century, following the conversion of Constantine. In both cases, talk about India suggests the interwoven possibilities that India has been conquered and that it can be conquered.

The resilience of this paradigm, solidly crystallised by Isidore, is tellingly shown by the Hereford map and other world maps of the late Middle Ages: it was a paradigm that was to last till the momentous coincidences of the early modern period. It was only with the introduction in the west of Ptolemy's map, and later with the voyages of discovery, that the old paradigm for perceiving the world eventually gave way to something substantially different.

To end this chapter, let us return to the five-century gap between Socrates and Pliny with which it began. Whatever else had happened in between, worthy of recounting in universal histories, two facts must be regarded as central to thoughts about India: first, Alexander had visited the ends of the earth; secondly, Rome had expanded into a world empire. In this chapter I have attempted to show how these two elements are related, for Alexander gave Romans, and indeed the western Middle Ages, eminently reusable ways of thinking about that expansion.

CHAPTER 6

Wisdom

I. WRITING WISDOM

Holiness is one of the main spheres to be considered in any survey of Greek and Roman ideas about India. Closely related and, as we shall see, just as culturally specific, is the concept of wisdom.[1] By way of a working definition, we may posit that Indian wisdom (typically of wisdom in general) is a kind of mystified knowledge;[2] this mystification is central to the concept of the holiness of certain Indians. We shall have to consider how, if at all, the distance implicit in specifically Indian sages is an extension of the separation that in so many instances marks off the sacred as such.[3] To be sure, the Indian sages identified as Brahmans and Gymnosophists made a major impression on the Alexander historians, and for a long time were considered the bearers of Indian holiness. Indeed, as we saw in Chapter 1, Alexander's encounter with them is a feature of all the major witnesses of his expedition. Such an assertion is supported by the considerable degree of overlap in the Alexander historians, and also the *Alexander romance* tradition. From that time onward the Brahmans were to become an important feature of Greco-Roman Indography. Now the Brahmans do not appear to have featured in accounts predating Alexander, if we are to judge from the apparent silence of Herodotus and Ctesias. This chapter therefore proceeds from a conclusion reached in Chapter 1: that Greeks became aware of Indians before they developed an interest in Indian wisdom. This provides an instructive contrast with, say, Jews or Babylonians in Greek perceptions,

[1] It is no accident that both the religious and philosophical sides of Greco-Roman Indography are taken into account in the standard collection of texts discussed here: Bernhard Breloer and Franz Bömer (eds.), *Fontes Historiae Religionum Indicarum* (Bonn: Röhrscheid, 1939).

[2] The connection between wisdom and knowledge is unproblematic if one considers, for example, *Stoicorum Veterum Fragmenta* 1.216. More difficult is the question of what kind of knowledge is at stake: see G. B. Kerferd, 'What does the wise man know?' in *The Stoics*, ed. John M. Rist (Berkeley: University of California Press, 1978), pp. 125–36.

[3] Mary Douglas, *Purity and danger: an analysis of the concept of pollution and taboo*, rev. edn (London: Routledge, 2002), e.g. pp. 8, 11.

cases in which the wisdom of a foreign society was among the first and most enduring part of its ethnographic image.

In this chapter we shall seek out the Indian sages amongst various kinds of Greek and Latin texts, measuring them up, where appropriate, against the picture to emerge from other (Sanskrit and Chinese) sources. If we are to understand them as bearers of holiness, we must compare them with other holy people, such as Magi, Chaldaeans and Druids. The history of Alexander's expedition is central here, not only among the authors mentioned above, but also in alternative traditions, including the brief text *On the life of the Brahmans* linked with the *Alexander romance*. Such texts in the 'popular' Alexander tradition present Alexander as a scholar, eager for knowledge about the curiosities of the strange world he encounters, or even as a pilgrim, seeking out the Indian sages once he finds out about them and then reverencing them. A more obvious kind of pilgrim is Apollonius, whose travels to India are described in Philostratus' hagiography of him.

Apart from the Brahmans, another part of Indian religion to be noticed by Greeks and Romans was Buddhism. It is not until Clement of Alexandria (*Stromateis* 1.305) in the late second or early third century that Buddhism is explicitly mentioned in a Greek text.[4] Clement speaks of the Buddha merely as one revered for his piety. For Jerome, the Buddha was the founder (*princeps*) of the Gymnosophists; he was borne from the side of his mother, who was a virgin:

> Among the Gymnosophists of India, as it were through adherents of this folly, the view is handed down that a virgin gave birth to the Buddha, the originator of their sect, out of her side. This is nothing unusual for barbarians, when the Greeks in all their learning suppose that Minerva was born from Jupiter's head and Father Bacchus from his father's thigh. (*Against Jovinianus* 1.42)[5]

Jerome's concern with virginity in the treatise as a whole goes some way towards explaining the Buddha's supposed virgin birth, a detail which is not otherwise attested. In fact, Jerome soon goes on to talk about the marital piety of Indian women, as expressed in *sati* (1.44). However, the birth from

[4] It is possible, however, that the term Σαρμάναι refers to Buddhists: Grigorij M. Bongard-Levin and Sergei Karpyuk, 'Nachrichten über den Buddhismus in der antiken und frühchristlichen Literatur', in *Hellenismus*, ed. Bernd Funck (Tübingen: Mohr Siebeck, 1996), pp. 701–12. Predating Greek and Latin literary references to Buddhism, a Kushan coin of around AD 100 presents a standing Buddha and the Greek legend ΒΟΔΔΟ: see further Errington and Cribb, *Crossroads*, pp. 46–8, with Millar, 'Looking east', 519.

[5] *apud gymnosophistas Indiae quasi per manus huius opinionis auctoritas traditur, quod Buddham principem dogmatis eorum a latere suo uirgo generarit. nec hoc mirum de barbaris, cum Mineruam quoque de capite Iouis et Liberum Patrem de femore eius procreatos doctissima finxerit Graecia.*

A. Dihle, analysing this passage, suggests that Jerome's source was Egyptian, perhaps Clement himself: 'Buddha und Hieronymus', in *Antike und Orient*, pp. 98–101.

his mother's side does tally with Buddhist scriptures. Here, Jerome's explicit comparison with Dionysus is a matter of presenting two different kinds of foreigners, both the 'most learned' Greeks and Indians: in the process a kind of *consensus barbarorum* is presented. Given that the life of Gautama Buddha, the earliest historical figure in Indian history, dates back to the fifth century BC,[6] this represents a remarkable time-lag, one that deserves consideration in its own right. In this passage, India and Greece are on the opposite ends of the scale between learning and its opposite (which is harder to label: a special kind of *barbaries*). Something to consider in this chapter is the extent to which learning, *paideia* or *doctrina*, was a criterion with which to evaluate Indian sages.

A major theme examined here is that of India as a destination of religious travel. In fact, the varying role of travel as a phenomenon in all of this will demand our attention. The travellers mentioned above came from the west; others would come from the east. Towards the end of the period covered here, we do know of one Fa-Hsien,[7] a Chinese pilgrim who visited India's Buddhist sites during the years AD 399–414. In their different ways these descriptions reflect India's status as a site of spirituality.[8] This chapter must also set the scene for an account of another kind of religious travel, namely Christian missionary activity. This will involve, however cursorily, the figures of the apostle Thomas and Pantaenus, separated by almost two centuries. For all their differences in motive and circumstance, all these instances reflect the journeys of specific individuals, and the very fact of individuality is worth noting.

It is therefore important to consider consultation with the Brahmans as a kind of traffic in wisdom, a traffic that crossed cultural boundaries. Arnaldo Momigliano's landmark study, *Alien wisdom*,[9] continues

[6] On the dating of the historical Buddha see, e.g., Hermann Kulke and Dietmar Rothermund, *A history of India*, 3rd edn (London: Routledge, 1998), p. 52.

[7] Also known in Roman transliteration as Fa Hian or Fa Hien or Fa Xian. Among the various translations available see Fa-Hsien, *A record of Buddhistic kingdoms: being an account by the Chinese monk Fa-Hien of his travels in India and Ceylon (AD 399–414) in search of the Buddhist books of discipline*, trans. James Legge (Oxford: Clarendon, 1886). Fa-Hsien was the first, and perhaps the most famous, of several Chinese Buddhist missionaries to India: see I-ching, *Chinese monks in India: biography of eminent monks who went to the western world in search of the law during the great T'ang dynasty*, tr. Latika Lahiri (Delhi: Motilal Benarsidass, 1986), p. 12 n. 3. Cf. Jack Finegan, *An archaeological history of religions of Indian Asia* (New York: Paragon, 1989), esp. pp. 120–2 and 318–19.

[8] One substantial work traces the early history of Buddhism in the northern part of the subcontinent, informed partly by Carl Jung's interest in eastern religions: Peter Lindegger, *Griechische und römische Quellen zum peripharen Tibet*, 3 vols. (Zurich: Libresso, 1979–93).

[9] *Alien wisdom: the limits of Hellenization* (Cambridge University Press, 1975). In a sense the book is misleadingly titled, given that its main concern is the broader one of 'the cultural connections between Greeks, Romans, Celts, Jews and Iranians in the Hellenistic period' (6). Cf. Guy Stroumsa, *Barbarian philosophy: the religious revolution of early Christianity* (Tübingen: Mohr Siebeck, 1999), esp. p. 58.

to offer questions for the study of knowledge at the intersection of cultures. Yet India does not feature in the book. There is no reference to India as a place of wisdom, as it would later be for Apollonius, nor to the Indian sages who made such an impression on the historians of Alexander.

But there is a general difficulty in considering India's wisdom, as there is in considering that of any foreign peoples: to what extent are we justified in talking about wisdom *per se*, given the difficulties in defining ancient notions of wisdom? Any attempt to tell the full story of Greco-Roman wisdom would have to pace itself against a major history of Greek philosophy, and would have to take into account the iconography of the intellectual (itself a hard human category to pin down), histories of Gnosticism, and much else besides. Such a task is clearly impracticable.[10] Yet again, any approach to the issue of Greek and Roman travel to India has to deal with the related issues of holiness and wisdom, however provisionally. At the very least, if we want to examine a particular instance of *alien* wisdom, it is necessary to see it also in light of the non-alien.

II. WISDOMS ALIEN AND OTHER

It might be worthwhile to outline at this point some features of wisdom, as attested in a variety of other sources, as a control against which to test the Indian material.[11] These criteria are offered in the understanding that no single wise person is likely to exhibit all of them. For reasons that will become clear in the course of this chapter, the philosopher Pythagoras recurs as a point of comparison.

II.1. Metamorphoses of sophia

But the prehistory of religious travel proceeds even Pythagoras. Though Odysseus supposedly 'knew the minds' of the peoples he encountered,[12] he was no religious traveller: such things as he observed, e.g., the harbour

[10] W. K. C. Guthrie, *A history of Greek philosophy*, 6 vols. (Cambridge University Press, 1962–81); Paul Zanker, *The mask of Socrates: the image of the intellectual in antiquity* (Berkeley: University of California Press, 1995).

[11] The concept of wisdom *per se* occurs rarely in the standard works of reference, whereas it arises often in connection with particular persons, notably the Seven Sages; and of particular travellers, in Hartog, *Memories of Odysseus*.

[12] πολλῶν δ' ἀνθρώπων ἴδεν ἄστεα καὶ νόον ἔγνω (νόμον Zenodotus). Odysseus' intelligence raises questions of ethical ambiguity: W. B. Stanford, *The Ulysses theme*, 2nd edn (Ann Arbor: University of Michigan Press, 1968); Hartog, *Memories of Odysseus*, pp. 15–39.

at Scheria, most famously, are viewed and described with a view to their practical viability for shipping and agriculture.[13] This has been seen as a colonist's perspective, articulated at the time of Greek expansion into Magna Graecia. On the other hand, religion is a major part of Herodotus' ethnographic vision.[14] As we saw in Chapter 1, Herodotus makes little of the religious or intellectual world of the Indians, being concerned instead with the more practical elements of social life. Though Herodotus does not use the terms Brahman and Gymnosophist, there is one passage in which he describes an ascetic kind of lifestyle:

> However, there is another Indian group with different customs: they neither kill any being nor plant crops nor build houses: instead they eat vegetables, and they collect, cook and eat – complete with pod – a certain kind of seed, which is about the size of a millet-seed and grows without being planted. If anyone takes ill, he goes to a remote area and lies down, and nobody is concerned whether he is dead or sick. (3.100)[15]

Though this passage refers to an ethnic group rather than a social class, it has sometimes been thought to point to the Brahmans.[16] We may note here that Herodotus identifies this as an 'alternative' lifestyle among Indians, these comments coming in the course of a description of the various groups of Indians. Given the importance of religion in Herodotean ethnography, this silence about Brahmans comes as a surprise.

At all events, it is not until the Alexander historians that Brahmans and Gymnosophists, literally 'naked philosophers', come to the forefront of Indography. (Sometimes the two terms are used more or less interchangeably, sometimes they refer to different groups.[17] In some cases the term is used to refer to Egyptian priests, as in Philostratus.)

[13] Note, e.g., 6.262–72 and 9.131–141. Cf. Carol Dougherty, *The poetics of colonization: from city to text in Archaic Greece* (Oxford University Press, 1993), p. 21; cf. now her *The raft of Odysseus: the ethnographic imagination of Homer's* Odyssey (Oxford University Press, 2001).

[14] Walter Burkert, 'Herodot als Historiker fremder Religionen', in *Hérodote et les peuples non grecs* (Vandoeuvres: Fondation Hardt, 1988), pp. 1–32.

[15] Ἑτέρων δέ ἐστι Ἰνδῶν ὅδε ἄλλος τρόπος· οὔτε κτείνουσι οὐδὲν ἔμψυχον οὔτε τι σπείρουσι οὔτε οἰκίας νομίζουσι ἐκτῆσθαι ποιηφαγέουσί τε, καὶ αὐτοῖσι <ὄσπριόν τι> ἔστι ὅσον κέγχρος τὸ μέγαθος ἐν κάλυκι, αὐτόματον ἐκ τῆς γῆς γινόμενον, τὸ συλλέγοντες αὐτῇ τῇ κάλυκι ἕψουσί τε καὶ σιτέονται. Ὃς δ᾽ ἂν ἐς νοῦσον αὐτῶν πέσῃ, ἐλθῶν ἐς τὴν ἔρημον κεῖται· φροντίζει δὲ οὐδεὶς οὔτε ἀποθανόντος οὔτε κάμνοντος.

[16] See section III.1 below for the vacillation between Brahmans as a priestly caste and ethnic, geographically distinct group.

[17] Christian[us] Lassen, 'De nominibus, quibus a veteribus appellantur Indorum philosophi,' *Rheinisches Museum* 1 (1833), 171–90, documents the varied use of *Gymnosophista, Bragmanus* and other terms such as *Sarmanus/Samanaeus*. The pointed distinction between these groups is one reason that Buddhists may be indicated by the last term: see n. 4 above.

Though Brahmans and Gymnosophists do not appear in Greek sources till Hellenistic times, there is already a pre-existing framework within which they can be understood, a framework which can be substantiated from Herodotean ethnography alone:[18] the *Histories* say much about the priests of Egypt and Babylonia; as we have seen, one part of Indian society was thought to follow ascetic practices.

How far in grasping the history of wisdom will a word-study of *sophia* and *sophos* bring us? We would want to know, for one thing, in what sphere it is that *sophia* prevails, that someone is *sophos*. From a number of studies that have been undertaken on these lines some clear lines of development can be identified.[19] In Homer, it means expertise in a technical sphere, as for example in the case of a shipbuilder (*Iliad* 15.412), and so the use of the word is to remain through the archaic period.[20] It is only with the references to the Seven Sages, beginning with Plato (*Protagoras* 343a), that the term takes on its central modern sense, given the variety of skills they embodied, especially in statecraft.[21]

It is with the Seven that expert knowledge (varying, it is true, in degrees of specificity) becomes mystified knowledge. A key step in this transition was the sphere of statesmanship: it is in this sphere that their general skills had a very specific, socially significant role to play, and a civic aspect involving moral virtue. This process of mystification depended, in part, on physical distance. Travel is a standard part of the sage's repertoire, if not a major feature: either he came from outside the polis, e.g., Anacharsis, or he was a local citizen who would go abroad for a spell, as in the case of Solon.[22]

For Plato's time, Socrates of the *Apology* and the *Crito* may be regarded as the sage par excellence, as the embodiment of *sophia*.[23] His commitment

18 Following Murray, 'Herodotus', much has been made in Chapter 1 above of the ways in which Herodotus set the terms of Hellenistic ethnography, though this is true for India to only a limited extent.

19 E.g., W. K. C. Guthrie, *The Sophists* (Cambridge University Press, 1971), pp. 27–9.

20 Guthrie, *Sophists*, p. 27.

21 For an example of this intermediate stage, see Plut. *Them.* 2 on Mnesiphilus, whom Themistocles admired: 'This man was neither an orator nor one of the so-called natural philosophers, but had made a special study of what at that time went by the name of "wisdom". This was really a combination of political acumen and practical intelligence, which had been formulated and handed down in unbroken succession from Solon, as though it were a set of philosophical principles.' Cf. G. B. Kerferd, 'The first Greek sophists', *CR* 64 (1950), 8–10, at 9, on the use of *sophistês* here and elsewhere.

22 Such variations within an identifiable tradition have been illustrated by Andrew Szegedy-Maszak, 'Legends of the Greek lawgivers', *GRBS* 19 (1978), 199–211; and Karl-J. Höhlkeskamp, 'Arbitrators, lawgivers and the codification of law in Archaic Greece: problems and perspectives', *Mètis* 7 (1992), 49–81.

23 Cf. *Kleiner Pauly* s.v. 'Sophia' (Heinrich Dörrie); now *DNP* s.v. 'Weisheit' (Franco Volpi *et al.*) points the way to comparative approaches.

to that cause is proven by his semi-voluntary martyrdom.[24] Socrates may himself have followed the Pythagorean principle of *striving* for wisdom, and it is probably Plato who first used the term 'philosophy' in this modern sense.[25] It is no coincidence that the one explicit story about Indian sages to precede Alexander's expedition adheres to the name of Socrates. Aristoxenus of Tarentum (fl. 320–300 BC) tells the tale that in 399, the year of his death, Socrates encounters a visiting Indian sage in Athens. Scornfully, the sage tells Socrates that knowledge of human affairs is not possible without knowledge of the divine:

> Aristoxenus the musician says that the Indians' version is as follows. One of their number happened to encounter Socrates in Athens and asked him, 'How do you pursue philosophy?' When Socrates answered that he did so by inquiring into human life, the Indian laughed, saying that nobody can contemplate human affairs without knowing the divine.[26]

The question over the historicity of this anecdote need not detain us here.[27] At all events we can note that we see here, unusually, an Indian interlocutor to Socrates, who by the time of Eusebius had long since come to embody polytheist thought.

By Aristotle's time, several changes will have taken place, partly due to the specialisation and systematisation of knowledge that characterised the Lyceum. Well before this time, the emergence of the Sophists would be one factor in the specialisation of knowledge. The controversy surrounding the Sophists was itself, in an important sense, a crisis over the nature of wisdom, and one implicit, for example, in debates over the gods and over the relative status of *nomos* and *physis*.[28] Though we cannot regard the Sophists

[24] Tessa Rajak, by identifying parallels between Socrates' death and that of Eleazar in IV *Maccabees*, alerts us to a possible Socratic paradigm at work in Hellenistic Judaism: 'Dying for the law: the martyr's portrait in Jewish-Greek literature', in *Portraits: biographical representation in the Greek and Latin literature of the Roman empire*, ed. M. J. Edwards and Simon Swain (Oxford: Clarendon, 1997), pp. 39–68, at 58–60.

[25] Walter Burkert, *Greek religion* (Cambridge, MA: Harvard University Press, 1985), p. 306; cf. 'Platon oder Pythagoras? Zum Ursprung des Wortes Philosophie', *Hermes* 88 (1960), 159–77.

[26] φησὶ δ᾿Ἀριστόξενος ὁ μουσικὸς Ἰνδῶν εἶναι τὸν λόγον τοῦτον. Ἀθήνησι γὰρ ἐντυχεῖν Σωκράτει τῶν ἀνδρῶν ἐκείνων ἕνα τινά, κἄπειτα αὐτοῦ πυνθάνεσθαι, τί ποιῶν φιλοσοφοίη. τοῦ δ᾿ εἰπόντος, ὅτι ζητῶν περὶ τοῦ ἀνθρωπίνου βίου, καταγελάσαι τὸν Ἰνδόν, λέγοντα μὴ δύνασθαί τινα τὰ ἀνθρώπινα κατιδεῖν ἀγνοοῦντά γε τὰ θεῖα. Fr. 53 (= Eus. *PE* 11.3), *Die Schule des Aristoteles II. Aristoxenos*, ed. Fritz Wehrli, 2nd edn (Basel: Schwabe, 1967), pp. 25 and 67–8. Cf. Wilhelm Halbfass, *India and Europe: an essay in understanding* (Albany: SUNY Press, 1988), p. 9.

[27] Filliozat, 'Valeur des connaissances', 99–100, may be alone in advocating its historicity, finding similarities between this fragment and the teachings of the *Upanishad* on *atman* and *brahman*. (The more usual, sceptical line on this is seen in Jaeger, Festugière and earlier scholars there cited.)

[28] On the Sophists as a challenge to conventional thought and morality, see, e.g., Burkert, *Greek religion*, pp. 311–17. It is typical of the nature of the conflict that Socrates was seen by some as a

as a philosophical movement, it is true, in general, that they tended to be 'philosophical relativists, sceptical about the possibility of knowledge of universal truth'.[29] The professional status of the Sophists and its attendant suspicions of venality were to prove politically dangerous in the classical polis.[30] The very term 'Sophist' came to carry negative connotations by the time of Plato. The pejorative sense was well established by the time Diogenes Laertius was writing in the second century AD (see 1.12). Though the Sophists went by the specialised name *sophistai* rather than *sophoi*; yet it is clear that the bad reputation they had gained gave a bad name to wisdom generally. As symptoms of the crisis over wisdom we may mention two very different instances: the execution in 399 BC of Socrates, though so pious and wise as portrayed by his pupils Plato and Xenophon; and the explicit problematisation of wisdom (and piety) when Pentheus is killed, despite having defended the rational order.[31]

These changes in the commonly perceived status of wisdom may be considered a pendant to the increasing specialisation in scientific and philosophical thought in Aristotle's age, a process which was to develop further in the Hellenistic age. The Museum in Alexandria focused on research, an activity which attracted the patronage of the Ptolemies, whereas the Academy and Lyceum had been first and foremost institutions of teaching.[32] It was in this context of increased specialisation and professionalisation that the third and second centuries BC witnessed major changes in astronomy, biology and other spheres of what we might today call science.[33]

Later in the Stoic school of Hellenistic philosophy, one that would prove so important in late Republican and subsequent Roman thought, great emphasis came to be placed in the sage (*sophos* or *sapiens*) as a bearer of wisdom. The Stoic conception of wisdom borrowed from the Platonic/Socratic paradigm the idea that a series of steps had to be taken on the road to

Sophist (notably in Aristophanes' *Clouds*), though he himself seems to have been hostile towards them (note, e.g., Pl. *Hp. mai.* 282b–283b).

29 George Kennedy, *A new history of classical rhetoric* (Princeton University Press, 1994), p. 7.

30 See, e.g., Josiah Ober, *Mass and elite: rhetoric, ideology and the power of the people* (Princeton University Press, 1989), on the explosive power of oratory in the classical polis.

31 Pointedly expressed at Eur. *Bacch.* 395; cf. Burkert, *Greek religion*, p. 317 and E. R. Dodds, *Euripides Bacchae, edited with introduction and commentary* (Oxford: Clarendon, 1960) ad loc.

32 G. E. R. Lloyd, *Greek science after Aristotle* (New York: Norton, 1973), p. 3; cf. Fraser, *Ptolemaic Alexandria*, esp. vol. 1, pp. 305–35; and *Library of Alexandria*, ed. Macleod.

33 'Two key methodological principles, the application of mathematics to the investigation of natural phenomena, and the notion of deliberate empirical research, go back to the earlier period which culminates in Aristotle. What the later period . . . provides is, above all, examples of the application of these principles in practice.' Cf. Lloyd, *Greek science*, p. 177 and Fraser, *Ptolemaic Alexandria*, pp. 376–446.

wisdom; to this it added the concept of self-sufficiency.[34] With the possible exception of Marcus Porcius Cato, this goal could not be attained.[35]

Later still, in the second century AD, the Second Sophistic, represented in this chapter by the biographer Philostratus, would be an age which saw the reinvention of the sophist-as-rhetorician. With this cultural ideal a specific, rhetorical concept of *sophia* became rejuvenated.[36] Typically of his times, Philostratus '[saw] sophistry as a philosophical movement embracing Hellenic wisdom and eloquence in a Neoplatonic synthesis'.[37] *Paideia* as a shared ideal, bonding members of local élites to each other or collectively to the emperor, was focused most intensely on these philosophers of the later Roman empire in the east.[38] One might say it fostered the creation of an 'imagined community' of learned men based on a selective view of the earlier history of rhetoric.[39] In this late-antique world, Greek philosophers became symbols of a common culture among aristocrats over a wide geographical area. It is against this background that we must consider, on the basis of Philostratus' *Life of Apollonius of Tyana*, how and why Indian sages captured the imagination.

If this diachronic survey has achieved nothing else, it shows the vastly changing conceptions of wisdom (implied by the changing word-history),

[34] On self-sufficiency as an ethical ideal, see Diels-Kranz 86 A1 and 12. Cf. also Glenn W. Most, 'The stranger's stratagem: self-disclosure and self-sufficiency in Greek culture', *JHS* 109 (1989), 114–33, and Chapter 2, section II.2 above.

[35] Dörrie, 'Sophia', *DKP* V. 270-1. On Cato's exemplarity for later generations, see A. E. Astin, *Cato the Censor* (Oxford: Clarendon, 1978).

[36] For a pointed reminder of the dynamic interface between philosophy and rhetoric during the Second Sophistic, we do well to recall the career of Dio of Prusa: expelled from Italy and his native Bithynia, he consulted the Delphic oracle about what he should do. He was told to continue doing what he had done till he reached the ends of the earth, and took this to mean he should follow the life of an itinerant, mendicant Cynic sage. See J. L. Moles, 'The career and conversion of Dio Chrysostom', *JHS* 98 (1978), 79–100, and C. P. Jones, *The Roman world of Dio Chrysostom* (Cambridge, MA: Harvard University Press, 1978); Swain, *Hellenism*, pp. 187–241.

[37] George A. Kennedy, *Greek rhetoric under Christian emperors* (Princeton University Press, 1983), p. 137. On their cultural world, see Glen W. Bowersock, *Greek sophists in the Roman empire* (Oxford: Clarendon, 1969). On archaism and a general obsession with the past, E. L. Bowie, 'Greeks and their past in the Second Sophistic', *P&P* 46 (1970), 3–41. The skepsis about any supposed 'Greek renaissance', articulated by P. A. Brunt, 'The bubble of the Second Sophistic', *BICS* 39 (1995), 25–52, is now answered by Bowersock, 'Philosophy and the Second Sophistic', in *Philosophy and power in the Greco-Roman world: essays in honour of Miriam Griffin*, ed. Gillian Clark and Tessa Rajak (Oxford: Clarendon, 2002), pp. 157–70.

[38] See Peter Brown, *Power and persuasion in late antiquity: towards a Christian empire* (Madison: University of Wisconsin Press, 1992), pp. 35–41 and *passim*; Swain, *Hellenism and empire*.

[39] The term is from Benedict Anderson, *Imagined communities: reflections on the origins and spread of nationalism*, rev. edn (New York: Verso, 1991), who examines the role of printed texts and maps in creating fellow-feeling in a later, industrialised age. By virtue of its selectivity, this phenomenon might also be regarded as an instance of the 'invention of tradition', to follow Hobsbawm's essay by that title.

and its sensitivity to the specific issues of the day. The political and intellectual crisis surrounding the Sophists of the fourth century BC is something we must particularly bear in mind as a key point in the reinvention of wisdom. It provided not only the need, but also some of the means by which such conceptions could be constructed. In this sense, as I shall suggest, the Brahmans were *ben trovati* as bearers of wisdom at a time when existing notions of wisdom had been destabilised.

II.2. Elements of wisdom

From these very general considerations a few features of wisdom deserve to be isolated.[40] The first is that it tends to be individualised, by which I mean the degree to which it is identified with individual persons.[41] This we see most obviously and importantly in references to the Seven Sages. However much membership of this group might have varied, its total number remained constant.[42] The phenomenon of writing philosophic biographies, attested in the works of Diogenes Laertius, Philostratus and Eunapius from later antiquity, exemplify this tendency. Broadly speaking, this habit should be understood in terms of the habit of attaching sayings to a particular person (sayings which may originally have been orally transmitted), with the result that a legend concerning that person springs up. In the case of Pythagoras, a legend had arisen within a hundred years of his death (around 570 BC), and Aristotle talks about Pythagoreans rather than a putative person Pythagoras.[43]

[40] In so far as the following criteria are chosen by individuals for themselves rather than ascribed to them by others (and that distinction is a difficult one), this may be called self-fashioning, to follow an oft-cited study: Stephen Greenblatt, *Renaissance self-fashioning from More to Shakespeare* (University of Chicago Press, 1980). While the instances we are here dealing with are in the first instance representations, we should not pretend that there is no element of choice, manipulation on the part of subjects themselves.

[41] This sense of individuality must be distinguished from the tendency to *personify* wisdom as a character, as we see in the 'wisdom writings' of the Old Testament: *Job, Proverbs, Ecclesiastes, Ecclesiasticus* and *Wisdom*. Much here may be called practical wisdom, with precepts for successful living. Taken together, these and related books reflect much of the Near East's wisdom tradition, some of which was later taken over by strands of Christianity. For Gnostics, Sophia was one of the Aeons, bearer of the female principle, which in various forms could be counterpart to the Father, Christ or the Saviour: see J. Meyendorff, 'Wisdom-Sophia: contrasting approaches to a complex theme', *DOP* 41 (1987), 391–401; Deirdre Joy Good, *Reconstructing the tradition of Sophia in Gnostic literature* (Atlanta: Scholars Press, 1987).

[42] See the important article by Richard P. Martin, 'The Seven Sages as performers of wisdom', in *Cultural poetics in archaic Greece*, ed. Carol Dougherty and Leslie Kurke (Cambridge University Press, 1993), pp. 108–28.

[43] J. A. Philip, *Pythagoras and early Pythagoreanism* (Toronto: University of Toronto Press, 1966); Walter Burkert, *Lore and science in ancient Pythagoreanism* (Cambridge University Press, 1972).

These legends in turn can articulate cultural ideals, as happens both in the philosophical biographies and in late-antique saints' lives.[44] *Imitatio Christi*, so important a feature of Christian hagiography, is either tacitly or overtly held up as something that invites further emulation on the part of the reader.[45] Just as the saint imitated Christ's life of self-sacrifice, so is the saint her- or himself to be imitated. In this way, the written form of a Christian life is not merely a celebration but an active inducement on the part of its author. Out of a Christian context, exemplarity adheres to classical learning itself, the *paideia* celebrated in the philosophers' lives of Eunapius, Philostratus and others.[46] Especially in so far as they contain *doxai* (i.e. the distinctive sound-bytes of individual philosophers),[47] these biographies are themselves performances of *paideia*. Let us take a moment to consider what features the lives exhibit, in so far as they represent the features of wisdom.

The aphorism is the favoured unit for the retailing of wisdom, and it frequently involves a paradox. According to Diogenes Laertius, the aphorism is the rhetorical feature that characterises both Druids and Gymnosophists (1.6). Now if paradox is central to many ascetic traditions,[48] then it should come as no surprise that the distinctive forms of discourse show much of the rhetorical paradox. Historically speaking, this feature can be traced back to the earliest surviving archaic Greek literature.[49] Theognis' precepts on statecraft would certainly seem to fit Aristotle's definition of a general statement.[50] It is here that statecraft emerges as a province of wisdom in the Greek world, one that changed over time into a kind of social criticism

44 Peter Brown, 'The saint as exemplar in late antiquity', *Representations* 1 (1983), 1–25 on the paradigmatic function of the saints' lives. For a general reflection on the dynamics of exemplarity, see Bruce Lincoln, *Authority* (University of Chicago Press, 1994).

45 An obvious example is Sulp. Sev. *Vita Martini* 1. The enjoined imitation of the saint's life is in effect imitatio Christi, in so far as the saint himself followed Christ's example. Christ's injunction to renounce the world (Matth. 19:21) would prove to be paradigmatic, as we see, e.g., in the *Vita Antonii* 2. Compare the comments of Simon Swain ('In a tightly controlled system like the Church the biographic was never simply celebration, but was also part of the disciplinary, normalizing process'), 'Biography and the biographic in the literature of the Roman empire', in *Portraits*, ed. Edwards and Swain, pp. 1–38 at 33.

46 I. Sevcenko, 'A shadow outline of virtue: the classical heritage of Greek Christian literature', in *The age of spirituality*, ed. K. Weitzmann (Princeton University Press, 1980), pp. 53–73.

47 The element of personalisation certainly looms large in doxography: see, e.g., André Laks, 'Du témoignage comme fragment', in *Fragmente sammeln*, ed. Most, pp. 237–72.

48 Elizabeth A. Clark, 'The ascetic impulse in religious life: a general response', in *Asceticism*, ed. Richard Valantasis and Vincent A. Wimbush (Oxford: Clarendon, 1995), pp. 505–10.

49 André Lardinois, 'The wisdom and wit of many: the orality of Greek proverbial expressions', in *Speaking volumes: orality and literacy in the Greek and Roman world*, ed. Janet Watson (Leiden: Brill, 2001), pp. 93–108; and Jan Fredrik Kindstrand, 'The Greek concept of proverbs', *Eranos* 76 (1978), pp. 71–85.

50 On Theognis as a *sophistês* in the sense of teacher see Guthrie, *Sophists*, p. 29.

articulated by the lawgivers. Looking much further back in time and farther east, it is indeed tempting to see continuities between Greco-Roman aphorisms and those of the Near Eastern wisdom tradition;[51] for one thing, the *Apophthegmata patrum* should be viewed as a late, Christianised instance of that Near Eastern tradition.[52] Many of these are in the form of injunctions. Indeed these early didactic roots may go some way towards accounting for the persistence of the aphorism or sententia as the expression of wisdom.

In terms of physical appearance, there is a language of gesture that requires special attention in understanding ancient wisdom.[53] We shall have to attend to gesture in discussing the Brahmans and Gymnosophists. As Zanker has illustrated amply, beards are a distinctive mark of the philosopher, and hence of wisdom.[54] Here again, Socrates is an important exemplar, though of course the practice predates him significantly.[55] While there is to this some consistency over time, it is true that the imperial age witnessed many philosophical diatribes about the removal of facial (and bodily) hair.[56]

Most significantly perhaps, social marginality shines through many of the cases that can be considered. If we take Diogenes Laertius' life of Diogenes as paradigmatic of a particular kind of wise person, we see that the Cynic philosopher was from the outset a marginal figure, reacting against social convention, and also against the more conventional approach of the philosophical schools. By the same token, St Anthony, so central a figure in early Christian monasticism, inhabited the fringes of society. The harshness of the Egyptian desert exaggerated not only his personal sufferings but also his marginal position in relation to society, thereby setting extreme

51 W. G. Lambert, *Babylonian wisdom literature* (Oxford: Clarendon, 1960); cf. M. L. West, *East of Helicon* (Oxford: Clarendon, 1997).

52 Peter Brown, *The making of late antiquity* (Cambridge, MA: Harvard University Press, 1978), pp. 82–3. On this work see Owen Chadwick, *Western asceticism* (Philadelphia: Westminster, 1958).

53 On gesture as index of a person's moral or intellectual life see Jan Bremmer, 'Walking, standing, and sitting in ancient Greek culture', in *A cultural history of gesture*, ed. Jan Bremmer and H. Roodenburg (Ithaca: Cornell University Press, 1992), pp. 15–35; and Patricia L. Cox, *Biography in late antiquity* (Berkeley: University of California Press, 1983), page xi.

54 In the case of Cynic philosophers they suggest proximity to animals: Michel Onfray, *Cynismes. Portrait du philosophe en chien* (Paris: Grasset, 1990), pp. 25–32.

55 A. A. Long, 'Socrates in Hellenistic philosophy,' *CQ* 38 (1988), 150–71, has shown that Socrates' reputation dropped off somewhat among Hellenistic philosophers. But note continued awareness of and interest in him on the part of Cynics.

56 A. C. van Geytenbeek, *Musonius Rufus and Greek diatribe* (Assen: Van Gorcum, 1963), pp. 119–23, with references; cf. Jaap-Jan Flinterman, *Power, paideia and Pythagoreanism* (Amsterdam: Gieben, 1995), p. 93.

standards for Christian ascetic practice.[57] It has been shown that with the passage of time (and in particular the rise of Christendom) the pagan holy man of late antiquity drifted into an increasingly marginal position.[58] The sage's capacity to articulate social criticism was a direct result of this.

The activity that many of these wise individuals pursue, that which in some cases actually *brings* them wisdom, is travel.[59] This is something shared by other types, particularly poets, and lawgivers.[60] Travel to India may be relatively rare in the stories of philosophers, but Egypt features more prominently. Solon is supposed to have spent ten years travelling after implementing his reforms,[61] and this may be echoed in the travels of Herodotus and Plato themselves.[62] According to Isocrates (*Busiris* 28–29), Pythagoras travelled to Egypt, where, naturally enough, he consulted with priests. Plutarch, after recounting Lycurgus' travels to Crete and 'Asia', goes on to speak of his supposed travels farther east: the Egyptians claim Lycurgus visited them too, a claim supported by 'some' Greek writers (4.5). But Plutarch backs off from the claim that he visited India and there held conversations with the Gymnosophists (and that he visited Libya and Spain as well): the authority for this claim rests solely with Aristocrates the Spartan, son of Hipparchus, says Plutarch with a note of caution:

57 Peter Brown, 'The rise and function of the holy man', in *Society and the holy in late antiquity* (Berkeley: University of California Press, 1982), has shown that this marginality played out differently in Egypt and Syria, given the differences in those landscapes, particularly the harshness of the Egyptian desert as opposed to the lesser climatic austerity of Syria.

58 The increasing marginality of the pagan holy man has been shown by Garth Fowden, 'The pagan holy man in late antique society', *JRS* 102 (1982), 33–59, esp. pp. 51–4, with qualifications by Elsner, 'Hagiographic geography', 34–5.

59 For a survey of Pythagoras' travels, see Isidore Lévy, *La légende de Pythagore en Grèce en Palestine* (Paris: Champion, 1927), pp. 20–6.

60 Poets: Mary R. Lefkowitz, *Lives of the Greek poets* (London: Duckworth, 1981). Lawgivers (a category which overlaps with sages and even poets): Szegedy-Maszak, 'Legends'. On this branch of biographical traditions see J. A. Fairweather, 'Fiction in the biographies of ancient writers', *Ancient Society* 5 (1974), 231–75, where many of the 'fanciful deductions' unmasked involve travel. Diogenes Laertius alone has these to offer (the list is not exhaustive): Thales visits Egyptian priests (1.27); Plato goes with Euripides to Egypt (3.6); Pythagoras visits Egypt, and speaks with Chaldaeans and Magi (8.3); Eudoxus visits Egypt (8.87); Democritus visits Egypt, Chaldaeans, Persia, perhaps India and Ethiopia (9.34–35); Pyrrho visits Indian Gymnosophists and Magi (9.61). See further G. S. Kirk and J. E. Raven, *The Presocratic philosophers* (Cambridge University Press, 1957), 77; and Fairweather, 'Fiction', 268. The pattern is clear, and can be summed up in two parts: it suits the lives of philosophers to have travelled; eastern lands provide the destinations of choice.

61 *Ath. pol.* 12; Plut. *Sol.* 26. Solon's own elegies mention the Nile and Cyprus (Anth. lyr. [3] 6.7D). Some of these travels actually took place before his reforms. There is a certain amount of flexibility in the tradition: present at all events is the element of travel.

62 On the travels of Herodotus, compare Chapter 1, section I.3 above; by the same token, Fehling expresses radical scepsis concerning the sages, *Die sieben Weisen und die griechische Chronologie* (Bern: Lang, 1985). On Plato, Paul Friedländer, *Plato* (New York: Meridian, 1958).

Concerning his travels to Libya and Spain and his discussions with the Gymnosophists in India, I find, on investigation, no source other than Aristocrates the Spartan, son of Hipparchus. (Plutarch, *Life of Lycurgus* 4.6)[63]

There can be no doubt that this grand tour owes something to Alexander's itinerary.[64] About this Aristocrates, Plutarch's source, we know little beyond a handful of references elsewhere in the *Lives* and in Athenaeus. A prose writer of the first centuries BC/AD, he seems to have gone beyond the norm in sensationalising and glamorising Spartan antiquity.[65] The veracity or otherwise of Lycurgus' travels need not trouble us here, in the way that it troubled Plutarch in writing the above sentence. The point remains, and underlines a major thesis of this chapter: a claim such as this proceeds from the assumption that travels bring wisdom, particularly travels to an ancient land of the east.[66] There is no doubt about the journey to India by Pyrrho of Elis. Diogenes Lartius, following Antigonus of Carystus (a contemporary source) and Ascanius of Abdera, says that it is here that Pyrrho acquired his sceptical philosophy (9.69, cf. 9.62–63).[67]

II.3. Jews, Chaldaeans and Indians

Having reached this point, we are in a better position to consider the alienness of alien wisdom for a moment. For one thing, it adds a note of mystification. It is clear that a number of features mark out the Near Eastern cultures in the minds of Greeks and Romans. First, their sheer antiquity counted for a great deal, if we are to consider Solon's interview with Egyptian priests (Plato *Tim.* 22b) or Hecataeus' visit to that land (Hdt.

[63] ὅτι δὲ καὶ Λιβύην καὶ Ἰβηρίαν ἐπῆλθεν ὁ Λυκοῦργος καὶ περὶ τὴν Ἰνδικὴν πλανηθεὶς τοῖς Γυμνοσοφισταῖς ὡμίλησεν, οὐδένα πλὴν Ἀριστοκράτη τὸν Ἱππάρχου Σπαρτιάτην εἰρηκότα γινώσκομεν.

[64] Elizabeth Rawson, *The Spartan tradition in European thought* (Oxford: Clarendon, 1969), p. 94.

[65] For the little available information on Aristocrates see *FGrH* IIIB 591, cf. *RE* 2.1 (1895) 941 s.v. Aristokrates 25 (Schwartz) and *DNP* 1 (1996) 1112 s.v. Arist. 4 (M. Meier).

[66] For further instances see Elsner, 'Hagiographic geography', 26 n. 25; esp. Porph. *Vita Plotini* 3 for a philosopher's (failed) visit to Babylon and India.

[67] Everard Flintoff, 'Pyrrho and India', *Phronesis* 25 (1980), 88–108, ratifies this theory of transmission, on the basis of detailed comparison with Indian texts. The argument runs very roughly as follows: similarities can be found between Pyrrho's and Indian thought; Pyrrho travelled to India (as a contemporary source indicates); therefore Pyrrho was influenced by Indian thought. I offer this analysis, at the risk of reductionism, not to caricature what may well be a careful evaluation of the available evidence, but to show the persistence of an ancient paradigm of thought about religious-philosophical travel. Less directly than this, M. L. West, *Early Greek philosophy and the Orient* (Oxford: Clarendon, 1971), sees the Iranian Magi as transmitting Indian (and of course Iranian) thought to the Greek world. On the question of looking eastwards to explain features of Greek philosophy, the pointedly critical comments of A. H. Armstrong, 'Plotinus and India', *CQ* 30 (1936), pp. 22–8, have not lost their resonance; cf. Momigliano, *Alien wisdom*, pp. 126–9.

2.143).[68] The whole of Josephus' *Contra Apionem* is devoted polemically to this question, focused on the 'antiquity' (*archaiologia* or *archaiotês*) of the Jews. Secondly, their use of writing *per se*, particularly in religious contexts, what has been described as 'sacral graphocentricism'.[69] Jewish society may have been the most extreme case of this.[70] In the case of Egyptian and particularly Babylonian culture, literacy was partnered by highly developed scientific and mathematical skills.

Thirdly and perhaps most importantly, we must consider the ongoing dependence of these cultures on a priestly class. An important innovation of the Hellenistic world, according to Bickerman,[71] was that the onus of studying the law was for the first time placed on individual citizens, lay people rather than specialists. This change has its roots in Platonic and especially in universalising Stoic thought; it was adopted by some strands of Judaism, as we see most obviously in Josephus. On the other hand, Babylonia,[72] Egypt and seemingly also the populations of Syria and Iran resisted this development, retaining its reliance on the priestly class. The retention of archaic languages underscored the inaccessibility of legal texts to lay people: thus Akkadian, written in cuneiform, continued to be used by Babylonian priests, and likewise Egyptian, written in hieroglyphics, for the copying of sacred texts. This is at a time when Aramaic and demotic respectively, and also Greek would have been the languages of everyday intercourse. What is more, the sophistication attained by Near Eastern cultures in the 'exact sciences', particularly in the astronomy and mathematics of Babylonia and Egypt,[73] was certainly noticed in the Greco-Roman world. To be sure, in

[68] E. Bickerman, 'Origines gentium', *Cl. Phil.* 47 (1952), 65–81; Louis H. Feldman, *Jew and gentile in the ancient world* (Princeton University Press, 1993), pp. 177–8; Erich S. Gruen, 'Cultural fictions and cultural identity', *TAPhA* 123 (1993), 1–14.

[69] Alan K. Bowman and Greg Woolf, 'Literacy and power in the ancient world,' p. 13, in their *Literacy and power in the ancient world* (Cambridge University Press, 1994). In the same volume, Martin Goodman ('Texts, scribes and power in Roman Judaea', pp. 99–108) makes the intriguing suggestion, contrary to what one might expect from modern society, that Romans did not view a society's ability to write as a badge of its civilisation. This may be true, but perhaps a more pertinent problem for consideration here is whether this mattered to Romans, or whether it is more a matter of modern retrojection.

[70] For Goodman '[n]o ancient society was more blatantly dominated by a written text than that of Jews in the Roman period' in 'Texts, scribes', in *Literacy and power*, p. 99.

[71] E. J. Bickerman, *The Jews in the Greek age* (Cambridge, MA: Harvard University Press, 1988), pp. 172–3.

[72] It so happens that Greco-Roman ideas about Babylonian antiquity are matched by the tendency of Babylonian scholars to ascribe great antiquity to astronomical and other texts: cf. William W. Hallo, 'On the antiquity of Sumerian literature', *JAOS* 83 (1963), pp. 167–76; Stanley M. Burstein, 'Callisthenes and Babylonian astronomy', *EMC* 28 (1984), pp. 71–4.

[73] O. Neugebauer, *The exact sciences in antiquity*, 2nd edn (Providence, RI: Brown University Press, 1957).

the double spheres of astrology and astronomy (to use a predominantly modern distinction) Greeks and Romans continued to hold eastern practitioners in a certain degree of awe.[74] One might go as far as saying that they particularly respected eastern cultures for their scientific skills. Related to this was the tendency to use the ethnikon *Chaldaeus* to designate, in principle, *any* person able to foretell or manipulate the future. On the strength of such cases we see one feature of eastern cultures that continued to fascinate Greeks and Romans: the authority of priests as guardians of special knowledge.[75] This role may be considered linked with that of being arbiters of the sacred.[76] The fact that this special knowledge often verged on magic both heightened the marginality with which its guardians were regarded and added to its mystique.

Of the Near Eastern groups mentioned, the Jews were perhaps the most graphocentric of all.[77] In fact the Jews deserve special attention, not least because of their supposed link with Indian philosophers.[78] In a passage well-known for the fact that it represents one of the very earliest Greek references to Jews, Clearchus of Soli in Cyprus speaks of the Jews as being descended from Indian Gymnosophists:

> These people (i.e. Jews) are descended from the Indian philosophers. The philosophers, they say, are in India called Calani, in Syria they go by the territorial name of Jews; for the region in which they live is called Judaea.[79]

This passage is quoted by Josephus in his diatribe asserting the antiquity of the Jews. He attributes it to Clearchus, who in turn claims to be quoting his teacher Aristotle word-for-word. Of significance here is not so much the veracity of the claims made, or of the reliability of the various levels of doxography involved, but the fact of the tendency to see Jews as philosophers, in which regard they are descended from the Indian Gymnosophists. Now if Greco-Roman notions of origins tended in general to be very

[74] See Tamsyn Barton, *Ancient astrology* (London: Routledge, 1994), p. 9, on the ancient controversy over whether astrology came originally from Egypt or Mesopotamia.

[75] For his comments about Egypt in Homer as a 'repository of unusual knowledge', see Momigliano, *Alien wisdom*, p. 3.

[76] For magic viewed as special knowledge, see e.g. Fritz Graf, *Magic in the ancient world* (Cambridge, MA: Harvard University Press, 1997), pp. 220–1.

[77] Goodman, 'Texts, scribes', in *Literacy and power*, ed. Bowman and Woolf, p. 99.

[78] On what follows see Emilio Gabba, *Greek knowledge of Jews up to Hecataeus of Abdera* (Berkeley: Center for Hermeneutical Studies in Hellenistic and Modern Culture, 1981), esp. pp. 6–7.

[79] οὗτοι δέ εἰσιν ἀπόγονοι τῶν ἐν Ἰνδοῖς φιλοσόφων, καλοῦνται δέ, ὥς φασιν, οἱ φιλόσοφοι παρὰ μὲν Ἰνδοῖς Καλανοί, παρὰ δὲ Σύροις Ἰουδαῖοι τοὔνομα λαβόντες ἀπὸ τοῦ τόπου· προσαγορεύεται γὰρ ὃν κατοικοῦσι τόπον Ἰουδαία. (Contra Apionem 1.179 = fr. 6 Wehrli). See further Momigliano, *Alien wisdom*, p. 75.

loaded,[80] then all the more in this case, where they indicate descent.[81] Specifically, it should be noted that there is here no simple parallel between Indians and Jews *tout court*: rather the correspondence may be summed up as follows: Jews are to Coele Syria as Gymnosophists are to India. In other words, each represents the special philosophical elite of a distant ethnic group. As it stands, the passage suggests a need on the part of Clearchus to qualify the statement of who the Jews are, i.e. that Greeks did not know about them before.[82] In this passage it appears that the less familiar Jews are presented with reference to the more familiar Indians. This link between Jews and Gymnosophists is made also in the course of Megasthenes' detailed discussion of Indian society, as reported by Clement of Alexandria.[83] However, Megasthenes merely mentions them together rather than asserting descent.

In fact, Clearchus' interest in the east is attested by an inscription: he is mentioned as the one who erected the 147 Delphic maxims on a stele found in 1966 at Ai Khanum, the Bactrian city in what is now northern Afghanistan.[84] There seems no reason to doubt that the Clearchus there mentioned as having travelled to that point and set up the stele was in fact this same person, and this identity has been accepted by Louis Robert.[85] It must, however, be admitted that we have no independent evidence for the supposed eastern travels of this Clearchus. The provenance of these inscriptions has been interpreted as an indication of the diffusion of Hellenism in the aftermath of Alexander's expedition.[86]

80 See G. E. R. Lloyd, *Revolutions in wisdom* (Berkeley: University of California Press, 1987), pp. 51–2 on 'first discoverers': typically, a supposed originator (mythical or legendary) is invoked to explain the nature of an object or a custom. More generally, Said, *Beginnings*, explores the extent to which supposed origins are retrojections.

81 As inscriptions from the Hellenistic Near East amply attest, the language of parentage (and with it, common ancestry) was used to describe the relation between poleis: Christopher P. Jones, *Kinship diplomacy in the ancient world* (Cambridge, MA: Harvard University Press, 1999), and Claude Orrieux, 'La "parenté" entre Juifs et Spartiates,' in *L'Etranger dans le monde grec*, ed. Raoul Lonis (Nancy: Presses Universitaires, 1988), vol. I, pp. 169–91.

82 Thus Gabba, *Greek knowledge*, p. 34, arguing against the interpretation that Jews were overlooked as powerless. We must, however, be chastened by the 'doxographic problem' before pushing this too far: the possibility of distortion on Josephus' part cannot be ruled out.

83 *FGrH* 715 F3 = Clem. Alex. *Strom.* 1.72.4: 'All opinions expressed by the ancients about nature may be found also in philosophers outside Greece, some in India by the Brahmans and others in Syria by those called Jews' (tr. Gabba, ibid., 7).

84 L. Robert, 'De Delphes à l'Oxus. Inscriptions grecques nouvelles de la Bactriana', *CRAI* (1968), 416–57 = *Opera minora selecta* 5 (Amsterdam: Gieben, 1989), pp. 510–51. On Ai Khanum see Chapter 1, section II.3.

85 It may be assumed that the inscriptions appeared too late to permit mention in Wehrli's second edition.

86 E.g., Sherwin-White and Kuhrt, *Samarkhand to Sardis*; Green, *Alexander to Actium*, pp. 332–4.

It is striking that in this passage the plural 'Kalanoi' is used in this passage. At a certain level it is clear what is happening here: the name of the Brahman Calanus, known from the Alexander historians, is generalised in its plural form, as if the process of individualisation is taken further, or even inverted. The surprise, or indeed 'misunderstanding',[87] is that the use of this term is imputed to the Indians themselves. What is more, there may be some chronological awkwardness here:[88] Aristotle, to whom the comment is attributed, died in 322 BC; Clearchus wrote relatively soon after Alexander's expedition. That a generalising plural should have come into currency so soon seems unlikely. Thus it would seem unlikely that Aristotle himself would have made this comment, as the fragment claims him to have done. If chronology is indeed a problem, then Josephus' reliability is at issue here.

Diogenes Laertius, in the context of discussing a much broader issue, preserves another fragment of Clearchus:

> Clearchus of Soli in his book *On education* claims that the Gymnosophists are descended from the Magi, and some trace the Jews to the same origin.[89]

Here the Magi are brought into the picture, but the claim is the same as regards Jews and Gymnosophists. Again philosophy is a distinctive ethnographic feature, to the extent that it suggests genealogical descent. It is no accident, furthermore, that the work of Clearchus cited is on *paideia*.

This is a fitting point at which to think more about Diogenes' conception of wisdom as something to be learned from an older culture. Much of the prologue to his work is devoted to a sustained argument against the view that philosophy began with the barbarians:

> Some people say that the pursuit of philosophy began with the barbarians. They claim that the Persians have had their Magi, the Babylonians or Assyrians their Chaldaeans, the Indians their Gymnosophists, the Celts or Gauls those called Druids or holy ones . . . They also claim that Ochus was a Phoenician, Zamolxis a Thracian and Atlas a Libyan. (1.1)[90]

The tendency to speak of Gymnosophists in the same breath as Magi and Chaldaeans may be regarded as typical in Greek and Roman texts.[91]

87 Thus Gabba, *Greek knowledge*, p. 6.

88 This appears not to be seen as a problem by Gabba or Feldman, *Jew and gentile*, pp. 5 and 204.

89 Κλέαρχος δὲ ὁ Σολεὺς ἐν τῷ Περὶ παιδείας καὶ τοὺς γυμνοσοφιστὰς ἀπογόνους εἶναι τῶν Μάγων φησίν· (Diogenes Laertius 1.9 = Wehrli fr. 13).

90 Τὸ τῆς φιλοσοφίας ἔργον ἔνιοί φασιν ἀπὸ βαρβάρων ἄρξαι. γεγενῆσθαι γὰρ παρὰ μὲν Πέρσαις Μάγους, παρὰ δὲ Βαβυλωνίοις ἢ Ἀσσυρίοις Χαλδαίους, καὶ γυμνοσοφιστὰς παρ' Ἰνδοῖς, παράτε Κελτοῖς καὶ Γαλάταις τοὺς καλουμένους Δρυίδας καὶ Σεμνοθέους . . . Φοίνικά τε γενέσθαι, Ὦχον, καὶ Θρᾷκα Ζάμολξιν, καὶ Λίβυν Ἄλαντα.

91 Cf. Halbfass, *India and Europe*, p. 3, on this passage.

For Diogenes, rival claims to the origins of philosophy involve claims to antiquity itself: 'These authors forget that the achievements which they attribute to the barbarians belong to the Greeks, with whom not merely philosophy but the human race itself began' (1.3). According to Diogenes, Hermodorus the Platonist and Xanthus the Lydian both speak of a long, transcultural succession of philosophers: for Hermodorus this goes back to Zoroaster the Persian, five millennia before the fall of Troy; for Xanthus there were six millennia between Zoroaster and the expedition of Xerxes (1.3). In fact the word Diogenes uses here to indicate succession, *diadochê*, recurs in the prologue and later throughout the biographies as a technical term.

With the help of the epitaph of 'Theban Linus', Diogenes claims to have proven that philosophy originated with the Greeks. Its very name resists translation into a foreign language:

> Thus it was from the Greeks that philosophy arose. Even its name resists translation into a foreign language. (1.4)[92]

This is a striking instance of untranslatability:[93] the phenomenon by which cultural capital is valued in such a way that it appears specific to its (Greek) milieu and thus resistant to translation. This alleged specificity is part of the process by which wisdom is mystified. Diogenes challenges Orpheus' status as a founder of philosopher by questioning not his ethnic origins, but his claim to the title of philosopher (1.5). In this context where the concept of philosophy is ethnically loaded, it comes as something of a contradiction that Diogenes should include the Scythian Anacharsis among his list of Seven Sages.[94]

So central to this inquiry is the notion that philosophy began with the barbarians that we should pause to consider two variants of it, both of which involve the Brahmans explicitly. First, Lucian in his *Fugitivi* shows how clichéd it had already become by the late second century AD. In this parody of a Platonic dialogue, Philosophy in its personified form tells her father Zeus of the ills she has suffered at the hands of bogus philosophers, who turn out to be the Cynics. Recalling her reception by humans after being sent by Zeus, Philosophy has this to say:

92 καὶ ὧδε μὲν ἀφ' Ἑλλήνων ἦρξε φιλοσοφία, ἧς καὶ αὐτὸ τὸ ὄνομα τὴν βάρβαρον ἀπέστραπται προσηγορίαν.

93 Jan Assmann, 'Translating gods: religion as a factor of cultural (un)translatability', in *The translatability of cultures*, ed. Sanford Budick and Wolfgang Iser (Stanford University Press, 1996), pp. 25–36.

94 On Anacharsis see Richard P. Martin, 'The Scythian accent: Anacharsis and the Cynics', in *The Cynics*, ed. Branham and Goulet-Cazé, pp. 136–55.

> When I darted off, father, I did not head directly for the Greeks; but, since it seemed to me the harder part of my task to educate and teach foreigners, I resolved to do that first. . . Heading initially for the Indians, the most populous nation in existence, I had no trouble in persuading them to descend from their elephants and converse with me. As a result the Brahmans, an entire tribe bordering on the Nechraei and the Oxudracae, are all recruited under my command: they not only live in accordance with my tenets, revered by all their neighbours, but die a spectacular kind of death. (*Runaways* 6)[95]

Much of this dialogue is devoted to comment on the death of Peregrinus, and will be discussed in this connection. Some room must of course be made for ethnographic caricature, typical of Lucian's parodic modes and seen here especially in the reference to elephants. Here the idea of the barbarian origins of philosophy is first *inverted* (at first she expected the Greeks to be amenable to her), only to be explicitly *restated.* From the Brahmans she went to Ethiopia, then to priests and prophets of Egypt, then to the Chaldaeans and Magi of Babylon, then to Scythia and Thrace (para. 8); and only then to the Greeks, who gave her no more than a cool welcome (9). In this work Lucian is able to use an already well-worn idea in order to scorn a particular branch of Greek 'philosophers', namely the Cynics.

Secondly, Clement of Alexandria (c. AD 215) offers a slightly later variant which reveals the generally more positive Christian attitude to Brahmans. In a passage already referred to for its juxtaposition of Brahmans and Jews, Clement is favourably disposed to the Brahmans because their study of nature has brought them the outlines of Greek philosophy.[96] Elsewhere he is, however, critical of the Brahmans for their exhibitionism in death (*Strom.* 3.7).

A significant feature of alien wisdom to be brought out might be called its ambivalence. We have already seen a Greco-Roman tendency to link astronomy and mathematics with Mesopotamians (Babylonians, Magians and Chaldaeans) and to a lesser extent Egyptians. This connection could be

[95] Ἠιξα μέν, ὦ πάτερ, οὐκ ἐπὶ τοὺς Ἕλληνας εὐθύς, ἀλλ᾽ ὅπερ ἐδόκει μοι χαλεπώτερον τοῦ ἔργου εἶναι, τὸ βαρβάρους παιδεύειν καὶ διδάσκειν, τοῦτο πρῶτον ἠξίουν ἐργάσασθαι· . . . ὁρμήσασα δὲ εἰς Ἰνδοὺς τὸ πρῶτον, ἔθνος μέγιστον τῶν ἐν τῷ βίῳ, οὐ χαλεπῶς ἔπεισα καταβάντας ἀπὸ τῶν ἐλεφάντων ἐμοὶ συνεῖναι, ὥστε καὶ γένος ὅλον, οἱ Βραχμᾶνες, τοῖς Νεχραίοις καὶ Ὀξυδράκαις ὅμορον, οὗτοι τοῖς Νεχραίοις καὶ Ὀξυδράκαις ὅμορον, οὗτοι πάντες ὑπ᾽ ἐμοὶ τάττονται καὶ βιοῦσίν τε κατὰ τὰ ἡμῖν δοκοῦντα, τιμώμενοι πρὸς τῶν περιοίκων ἁπάντων, καὶ ἀποθνήσκουσι παράδοξόν τινα τοῦ θανάτου τρόπον.

[96] On *barbaros philosophia* see A. Dihle, 'Indische Philosophie bei Clemens Alexandrinus,' in Dihle, *Antike und Orient*, pp. 78–88, at 78, and cf. 219.

made in a neutral or even complimentary way.[97] On the other hand there was a dark side to this too,[98] perhaps inevitably, if we consider that the strict modern division between astronomy and astrology was not made till relatively late (Ptolemy makes this point polemically in the introduction to his *Tetrabiblos*). Terms such as *magus*, *mathematicus* and *Chaldaeus* each have a range of valences, which at their most negative speak volumes for the pariah status of 'magicians' and 'quacks'.[99] The miracle-working element of the Christian holy man has emerged as one of his most important features, but it is certainly not limited to him.[100]

These various elements lead us to validate the working definition of wisdom as knowledge that is mystified.[101] We must, above all, be alert to a politics of knowledge in which secrecy, exoticism, authority and paideia play their part.[102] Mystification in this sense is a means of establishing authority, a way that differs, say, from the systematisation of knowledge in the corpus of medical writings attributed to Galen.[103] Above all, we should note from the foregoing discussion that, in so far as wisdom is the preserve of foreign peoples, it has an inaccessible quality, one that might even make it impossible to be known: this is part of its status as special knowledge. The secrecy incumbent on initiates to Pythagoreanism, though not necessarily a foreign wisdom in the first instance, may be taken as a Greek case of this phenomenon.

So much for the features of wisdom, and particularly of 'alien wisdom', that can be isolated in theory. It is time for us to consider Brahmans, and to ask in what ways Brahmans fit the mould outlined, and to what extent the literary image of them combines on the one hand this mystified knowledge we have been calling wisdom and on the other hand the features of holiness.

97 Strictly speaking, the Chaldaeans were originally an ethnic group, which arrived in Babylonia around the ninth century BC: Amélie Kuhrt, *The ancient Near East* (London: Routledge, 1994), p. 399. Greek and Latin uses of the term exhibit massive generalisation, with the inevitable loss of its original ethnic referent. The same process is at work with the *Magi*.

98 A notable case comes when Cato forbids the *uilicus* (overseer) to consult with fortune-tellers: *aruspicem, augurem, hariolum, Chaldaeum nequem consuluisse uelet* (*Agr*. 7.4). In this context xenophobia coalesces with prejudice against magic.

99 Note, e.g., Graf, *Magic*, ch. 2; W. J. W. Koster, 'Chaldäer', *RAC* II.1006–21, esp. 1019.

100 R. Reitzenstein, *Hellenistische Wundererzählungen* (Leipzig: Teubner, 1906), examining the theme of miracle-working in a wide variety of texts, among holy men, magicians, thaumaturges and others.

101 On the concept of mystification (and its attempted reversal on the part of modern scholars) see, e.g., G. E. R. Lloyd, *Demystifying mentalities* (Cambridge University Press, 1990).

102 On the politics of special knowledge see the important study of Marie-Therese Fögen, *Die Enteignung der Wahrsage. Studien zum kaiserlichen Wissensmonopol in der Spätantike* (Freiburg: Suhrkamp, 1993).

103 Dale B. Martin, *Inventing superstition: from the Hippocratics to the Christians* (Cambridge, MA: Harvard University Press, 2004).

It will become clear that Brahmans and Gymnosophists emerged substantially after Alexander's expedition.

III. BRAHMANS AND GYMNOSOPHISTS

III.1. Social hierarchy

In order to consider the Brahmans, the Indian ascetics par excellence, we need a historical context. In sketching this we must draw on a wider range of sources before focusing on Palladius himself. Just who were these Brahmans that made such an impression on Greek and later Roman writers?

Turning first to Indian sources, we hear of Brahmans spoken of unequivocally as a social group, i.e. as a 'caste' in terms of the *varna* system. The *Purusa-sukta* (Hymn of man) is one of the hymns dealing with the creation, and it is here that we find classical Indian literature's most significant reference to Brahmans: the gods create the world by dismembering the primeval giant Purusa:

> His mouth was the Brahman,
> his two feet were made the warrior,[104]
> his two thighs the Vaisya;
> from his two feet the Sudra was born.
> (*Rig Veda* 10.90.12)

By linguistic evidence it is known to be one of the last of the Rig Veda to be composed, and it can be dated to as late as around 500 BC. This is the earliest Indian reference to the system of four social classes or *varnas*, and the only one in the Vedas.[105] (The historical problem that this refers to four castes, compared to the seven in Greco-Roman sources, need not concern us here: see Chapter 2.) The term *brahmana* originally applied to one possessing the mystical force, *brahman*. Its earliest use was for the priest overseeing the entire sacrificial ritual, and who could by his magical spells counteract the evil influence eventuating from minor errors of ritual. By the end of the Vedic period its use had been broadened to

[104] *rajan-ya* ('royal' or 'warrior'), the name given to the second caste, is related to word *raj*, 'rule' (cf. Latin *reg-*). After the Vedic period the term *ksatriya* was used instead for this group: A. L. Basham, *The wonder that was India*, rev. edn (New York: Hawthorn: 1963), p. 141.

[105] Arthur A. Macdonell (ed.), *A Vedic reader for students* (Oxford: Clarendon, 1917), p. 201; Wendy Doniger O' Flaherty (ed. and tr.), *The Rig Veda* (Harmondsworth: Penguin, 1981), p. 30. On the interpretation of this passage in terms of Indian historical consciousness, see Romila Thapar, 'Society and historical consciousness: the Itihasa-Purana tradition', in *Situating Indian history: for Sarvapalli Gopal*, ed. Sabyasachi Bhattacharya and Romila Thapar (Oxford University Press, 1986), pp. 353–83, at 356–7.

refer to all members of the priestly class. After the Vedic period the Brahman class, already split into septs (*gotra*), divided further into branches (*sakha*), determined by the choice of which recension of the Vedic texts was honoured.

In terms of the social structure that transpires from texts such as the *Laws of Manu* (though much later, round the turn of the millennium, in its extant form, it reflects an already old tradition), we know of various further subdivisions.[106] Among these were the semi-legendary *rshis*, who combined the roles of seer and composer of the sacred Vedic texts.[107] For the performance of sacrificial duties there were a number of priests (*rtvij*): invokers (*hotr*), cantors (*adgatr*) and those carrying out the rituals by hand (*adhvaryu*).

By virtue of this priestly capacity, the Brahmans may be regarded India's arbiters of the sacred par excellence. Most of the Brahman class lived off royal patronage, but some owned land which was worked by peasants. That they are socially distinct from other groups may be deduced from Manu's injunction (4.84) that Brahmans do not accept gifts from members of the *ksatriya* class. Serving as the king's council, those brahmans in the *purohita* class had great influence.[108] These would appear to match Megasthenes' group of 'councillors' (*FGrH* 715 F4 = Diod. 2.41.4).

There is ample Indian evidence for Brahmans leading lives devoted to religious observance, remote from the rest of society. Kalidasa's *Sakuntala* gives an almost utopian picture of communities of Brahman hermits living in forests, supported by gifts of the king and of nearby peasants. However, the *Laws of Manu* and other Smrti texts suggest that most Brahmans are likely to have lived less idyllic lives, if we are to take into account stipulations about their involvement in loans and trade. There was certainly a stigma attached to professional activity on the part of Brahmans, and this was sometimes expressed in the form of satire at their expense.

The key passages on Indian society generally have been traced by Jacoby back to Megasthenes; so too those on the Brahmans.[109] In a lengthy

[106] For what follows I am indebted to Basham, *The wonder*, pp. 139–41.

[107] The coincidence in number between the Seven *Rshis* of Indian mythology with the Seven Sages of the Greek tradition does not mean we should see a connection through Indo-European roots: Martin, 'Seven sages', p. 121, and John E. Mitchiner, *Traditions of the Seven Rsis* (Delhi: Motilal Benarsidass, 1982).

[108] Basham, *The wonder*, p. 100.

[109] Jacoby's grounds for identifying Megasthenes as the source for Diodorus' long Indographic passage 2.35–42 are more tenuous than might initially appear: Chapter 1, section II.2 above.

description of Indian social organisation, we read the following about the group[110] of 'philosophers':

(1) The entire population of India is divided into seven castes (*merê*), the first of which comprises the tribe of philosophers – outnumbered by the other castes but exceeding them in pre-eminence. Being exempt from all public duties, they are neither anyone's masters or servants. (2) However, they are called upon by private citizens to offer all the sacrifices due in their lifetimes and to hold rites for those who have died, for they are considered to have shown themselves dearest to the gods and especially adept in matters concerning Hades, and for this service they receive gifts and honours. To the population of India as a whole they perform enormous services: assembling in a huge gathering at the start of the year, they tell the populace about droughts, rains, favourable winds, diseases, and whatever is useful to those listening. (3) . . . [Both king and ordinary people make provisions accordingly.] . . . The philosopher who goes astray in his forecast receives no punishment other than criticism and spends the rest of his life in silence. (*FGrH* 715 F4 = Diod. 2.40.1–3)[111]

We must note that these 'philosophers' serve priestly functions (note paragraph 2 above): this combination is not characteristic of the Greco-Roman world's pagan priesthoods.[112] The fact that they preside over sacrifices marks them out as 'pagan priests', ones whose priesthood is further sanctified by their status as philosophers.[113]

In Diodorus' long passage this, however, not the only *meros* with which we can identify the historical Brahman. Of the seventh caste Diodorus has the following to say:

The seventh caste is that of deliberators and councillors, whose concern is with the decisions affecting shared interests. Numerically this group is the smallest, but in nobility of birth and in prudence it is the most deserving of admiration, for the

[110] On problems surrounding the use of the term 'caste', see Chapter 1, section II.2.

[111] τὸ δὲ πᾶν πλῆθος τῶν Ἰνδῶν εἰς ἑπτὰ μέρη διῄρηται, ὧν ἐστι τὸ μὲν πρῶτον σύστημα φιλοσόφων, πλήθει μὲν τῶν ἄλλων μερῶν λειπόμενον, τῇ δ' ἐπιφανείᾳ πάντων πρωτεῦον. ἀλειτούργητοι γὰρ ὄντες οἱ φιλόσοφοι πάσης ὑπουργίας οὔθ' ἑτέρων κυριεύουσιν οὔθ' ὑφ' ἑτέρων δεσπόζονται. παραλαμβάνονται δ' ὑπὸ μὲν τῶν ἰδιωτῶν εἴς τε τὰς ἐν τῷ βίῳ θυσίας καὶ εἰς τὰς τῶν τετελευτηκότων ἐπιμελείας, ὡς θεοῖς γεγονότες προσφιλέστατοι καὶ περὶ τῶν ἐν ᾅδου μάλιστ' ἐμπείρως ἔχοντες, ταύτης τε τῆς ὑπουργίας δῶρά τε καὶ τιμὰς λαμβάνουσιν ἀξιολόγους· τῷ δὲ κοινῷ τῶν Ἰνδῶν μεγάλας παρέχονται χρείας παραλαμβανόμενοι μὲν κατὰ τὸ νέον ἔτος ἐπὶ τὴν μεγάλην σύνοδον, προλέγοντες δὲ τοῖς πλήθεσι περὶ αὐχμῶν καὶ ἐπομλέγοντες δὲ τοῖς πλήθεσι περὶ αὐχμῶν καὶ ἐπομβρίας, ἔτι δ' ἀνέμων εὐπνοίας καὶ νόσων καὶ τῶν ἄλλων τῶν δυναμένων τοὺς ἀκούοντας ὠφελῆσαι. . . . ὁ δ' ἀποτυχῶν τῶν φιλοσόφων ἐν ταῖς προρρήσεσιν ἄλλην μὲν οὐδεμίαν ἀναδέχεται τιμωρίαν ἢ βλασφημίαν, ἄφωνος δὲ διατελεῖ τὸν λοιπὸν βίον.

[112] *Pagan priests: religion and power in the ancient world*, ed. Mary Beard and John North (London: Duckworth, 1990).

[113] E.g., ibid., pp. 8–9; John Scheid, 'The priest', in *The Romans*, ed. Andrea Giardina (University of Chicago Press, 1993), pp. 55–84, at 57–9.

king's advisors and the administrators of the affairs of state and judges of disputes are drawn from among them, and generally speaking they take their leaders and magistrates from among these people. (2.41.4)[114]

Within Arrian, for one, there is some degree of confusion as to whether the Brahmans are a tribe or a class. In most cases he talks about them as a tribe, but at *anab.* 6.16.5 he seems to be referring to them as a sect rather than a tribe, as instigators of a rebellion against Alexander's conquest (cf. 6.17.2). At this point Arrian, in a curious remark, promises that later in his *Indica* he will tell more about the wisdom of the Brahmans, 'if that is what it is', a promise that is not realised in the surviving work.[115] It is worth noticing here that as soon as Arrian refers to the group, 'the sages of India', he refers to their wisdom, yet he seems to question the nature of that wisdom. If this interpretation is correct, we might take it to be a reminder of the fragility of 'alien wisdom'.

Pliny in his *Natural history* (6.64) speaks of the Brahmans as follows, as an umbrella ethnic group:

The races that deserve mention as we leave the Hemodi mountains . . . are the Isari, Cosiri, Izi, and spread across the mountains the Chirotosagi and several tribes with the name of Bragmanae, among them the Mactocalingae.[116]

This is part of Pliny's geographical survey of northern India, and he mentions Brahmans here in order to characterise the region. In fact, they will have been found much farther south than Pliny indicates, so that his geographical accuracy on this score is poor.

A short while later, speaking of the social divisions of the Indians of the Ganges valley, Pliny states that there are five groups or *genera*, to which a further one of half-wild people is added at the end. The fifth of these has the features we *expect* to identify with the Brahmans, yet nowhere does Pliny make such a connection:

114 ἕβδομον δ᾽ ἐστὶ μέρος τὸ βουλεῦον μὲν καὶ συνεδρεῦον τοῖς ὑπὲρ τῶν κοινῶν βουλευομένοις, πλήθει μὲν ἐλάχιστον, εὐγενείᾳ δὲ καὶ φρονήσει μάλιστα θαυμαζόμενον· ἐκ τούτων γὰρ οἵ τε σύμβουλοι τοῖς βασιλεῦσίν εἰσιν οἵ τε διοικηταὶ τῶν κοινῶν καὶ οἱ δικασταὶ τῶν ἀμφισβητουμένων, καὶ καθόλου τοὺς ἡγεμόνας καὶ τοὺς ἄρχοντας ἐκ τούτων ἔχουσι.

115 ὑπὲρ ὧν (sc. Βραχμάνων) ἐγῶ τῆς σοφίας, εἰ δή τίς ἐστιν, ἐν τῇ ᾿Ινδικῇ ξυγγραφῇ δηλώσω. This is not enough to sustain the idea that the second section of Palladius' text is indeed Arrian's, as it claims to be (1.15): for one thing, it is not in his style to indulge in such long speeches as characterise that part of the work. See William H. Willis and Klaus Maresch, 'The encounter of Alexander with the Brahmans,' *ZPE* 74 (1988), 59–83, at 61–2, with refs.

116 *gentes, quas memorare non pigeat a montibus Hemodis, . . . Isari, Cosiri, Izi et per iuga Chirotosagi multarumque gentium cognomen Bragmanae, quorum Mactocalingae.*
Stoneman, 'Naked philosophers: the Brahmans in the Alexander historians and the *Alexander Romance*', *JHS* 115 (1995), 115–29 at 101–2 compares Strabo 15.1.66 C716.

There is a fifth class of persons devoted to wisdom, a group highly esteemed by them and nearly raised into a religion; they always end their life by suicide upon a pyre that is already set aflame. (6.66)[117]

Somewhat surprising here is that, in emphasising the respect that the Brahmans command as practitioners of wisdom, Pliny implies that they are themselves nearly honoured as gods. We may also notice that self-immolation is given as one of their features. Presumably this is an extrapolation from the story of Calanus.[118]

Several of the Greek and Roman references to Brahmans present them as teachers. Thus Apuleius, in speaking of the education of Pythagoras (*flor.* 15.11–13), mentions lessons among the Indian sages, both Brahmans – *hi sapientes uiri sunt, Indiae gens est* – and Gymnosophists. In the same breath he mentions mathematical lore taught by the Egyptian priests and the astrology taught by the Chaldaeans. In this group the Brahmans stand out for their ability to withstand bodily hardships:

The Brahmans have combined the general principles of Pythagoras' philosophy: physical and mental discipline, the number of parts of the soul, and stages of life, the torments and rewards everyone's spirit receives according to merit. (15.13)[119]

It is also in their role as teachers that Ammianus mentions them, following on his excursus on the 'land of the Magi' (23.6.33). In this case their pupil is Zoroaster, presented as a Bactrian sage.[120] Apollonius pays homage to them also as a pupil reverences a teacher.[121] It is this didactic role that we should bear in mind when Alexander meets the Brahman Dandamis.

In Chapter 1 we caught a glimpse of Calanus the renegade, the subject of Dandamis' harsh words. Here and in the Palladius text discussed below he emerges as a complex figure, especially when we measure up the various texts against each other.[122] Arrian (*Anab.* 7.2–3) speaks of Calanus' lack

117 *quintum genus celebratae illis* (Mayhoff, *illi[c]* tradd.) *et prope in religionem uersae sapientiae deditum uoluntaria semper morte uitam accenso prius rogo finit.*

118 The practice of *sati* among Indian widows is discussed separately in Chapter 2, section II.5.

119 *Bracmani autem pleraque philosophiae eius contulerunt, quae mentium documenta, quae corporum exercitamenta, quot partes animi, quot uices uitae, quae diis manibus pro merito suo cuique tormenta uel praemia.*
On this passage see the lengthy note by André and Filliozat, *L'Inde*, pp. 379–81.

120 Joseph Bidez and Franz Cumont, *Les mages hellenisés. Zoroastre, Ostanès et Hystaspe d'après la tradition grecque* (Paris: Belles Lettres, 1938), vol. I, p. 27 and vol. II, p. 96 n. 2, write this reference off as too late to be trustworthy. Certainly Ammianus uses poetic, evocative language in his brief description. An unusual feature of this passage is his reference to the astrological observation of the Brahmans – *rationes mundani motus et siderum* – which may be explained by their supposed link with the Magi.

121 Jer. *Ep.* 53.1; Sid. Apoll. *Epist.* 8.3.4.

122 R. Stoneman, 'Who are the Brahmans? Indian lore and Cynic doctrine in Palladius' *de bragmanibus* and its models,' *CQ* 44 (1994), pp. 500–10, at 505.

of self-control, thereby echoing the negative side of what Strabo describes as a dispute in the sources (15.1.68 C718). But when Plutarch has him reciting a parable (*Alex.* 8.65) there is no hint of a negative attitude on the author's part, nor presumably that of his source. In Philo he receives an outstandingly good press: he is praised for his exemplary, truly philosophic attitude, and, by implication, for his denial of the flesh in taking his life.[123] It is possible that Philo is well disposed to the Indians in view of the supposed link between Jews and Indians we have seen in Josephus.[124] On the other hand, several fathers of the church are negative towards the Brahmans: when Tertullian claims that Christians do indeed help to support the state, he does so by contrasting them to the socially aberrant Indian sages: 'for we are not Indian Brahmans or Gymnosophists, forest-dwellers and exiles from life'.[125] The point of comparison is, properly, with Indians in general, but the reference to the Brahmans and Gymnosophists tacitly reaffirms the Christians' own status as philosophers of a kind.[126] This is taken further by Augustine, who opposes the notion of salvation for the Indians and scorns their marginal status relative to society and their distance from the Christian faith:

> The gymnosophists of India, also, who are said to practise philosophy in the jungles of India without clothing, are citizens of that [earthly] city, and yet they abstain from procreation. For such continence is good only when it takes place in keeping with faith in the highest good, which is God. (*City of God* 15.20)[127]

Clearly we are dealing with a wide range of opinions, among Christian writers and others. Of these, it was to be the positive one that would predominate in the medieval west.[128]

Within Indian texts there is also a substantial degree of variation in the presentation of Brahmans.[129] Much of Sanskrit literature was actually produced, or at least written down, by Brahmans, and tends consequently to represent their perspectives and interests. On the other hand, Buddhist texts

[123] In the *quod omnis probus liber est* 14.92–96 he is among the ἀνδρῶν ἀγαθῶν; cf. the general comment at *vita Abraham* 33.181–82 on the praiseworthiness of the Gymnosophists and their wives in readiness to face death.

[124] Cf. section II.3 above.

[125] *neque enim Brachmanae aut Indorum gymnosophistae sumus, sylvicolae et exules vitae* (*apol.* 42.1).

[126] Cf. section II.3 above.

[127] *et Indorum Gymnosophistae, qui nudi perhibentur philosophari in solitudinibus Indiae, ciues eius mundi sunt, et a generando se cohibent. non est enim hoc bonum nisi cum fit secundum fidem summi boni, qui Deus est.*

[128] This was partly as a result of the strength of the Alexander legend: Thomas Hahn, 'The Indian tradition in western medieval intellectual history', *Viator* 9 (1978), 213–34.

[129] On Sanskrit representations of Brahmans see Basham, *The wonder*, pp. 139–41.

generally exalt the *ksatriya* class over the Brahman. This is usually done with reverence for the Brahmans. These sources portray very different kinds of Brahman, and in so doing offer very different attitudes to priestly practices performed by members of the class. Here we find both learned Brahmans, performing rituals and receiving due reverence; but also village Brahmans, who live by fortune-telling and sorcery, and are less honoured. In fact, the fool (*vidusaka*) in Sanskrit drama is typically presented as a Brahman; just as he is gluttonous, so bibulousness is sometimes linked with Brahmans. Sanskrit sources portray the Oxudrakai group, who are admittedly on the fringes of Brahman society, as one of the many disorderly people of the Punjab.[130]

III.2. Alexander's interview: Palladius and others

It is against this complex background that we must turn to a late-antique story about Brahmans. In Chapter 1 we saw that the Brahmans came into view during Alexander's campaign. Indeed, they might be considered, together with the details of Indian social structure, to be the major addition to Greek Indography to emerge from the campaign. Thus it is that an account of Alexander's journey now occupies us: not one of the earliest, certainly, but a text that describes them in vivid detail.[131] This is the treatise *On the life of the Brahmans*, attributed to Palladius and transmitted on the fringes of the *Alexander romance* tradition. It survives in both a Greek version and in a Latin translation erroneously ascribed to Ambrose. Because of the obscurity of this work and its importance to this chapter, I shall summarise it before embarking on an analysis. The summary in itself will bring to light various aspects of wisdom touched on above, and these aspects will be further teased out in what follows.

As it now stands, the work falls into two disparate sections. In the first, the primary narrator tells what he has learned about the Brahmans and how. He has not been to this distant and dangerous place, having fallen ill and had to turn back on his travels in that direction (1.1). He did, however, find

[130] O. Stein, *RE* 36.2024–32, at 2031, s.v. Oxudrakai; Karttunen, *Hellenistic world*, pp. 216–18, 226–8; Bosworth, *Commentary*, vol. II, p. 219.

[131] The role of Brahmans in the Alexander historians has been touched on above in the introduction, so that text of Palladius is offered to indicate a different and perhaps more complicated strand in an alternative tradition. It is for two reasons that I choose this text over the much more widely disseminated *Alexander romance*: first, it was composed by a Christian bishop, of whom we have other writings; secondly, the *Alexander romance* has already received comprehensive treatment by Stoneman, 'Naked philosophers'. The first of these reasons makes it possible for us to set the work in a Christian milieu.

out much from a Theban scholar who travelled there of his own accord, was captured and used the opportunity to study the Indians. This Theban, who becomes the secondary narrator for much of the rest of section 1, sails first to Adule and Axum in his quest for the island of Taprobane. Here in Axum, ruled by a local Indian king,[132] he joins some local Indian traders who are setting out for the land of the big-headed Bedsades. Once among the Bedsades, he is taken captive and charged with trespassing, and taken to the leader. He can neither understand what is being said to him, nor make himself understood, in the absence of a translator. He is convicted to work in the royal bakery, where he remains six years, long enough to learn the language and find out about the way of life of the residents (1.9). He gains his release during a clash between the local potentate and another: the great king forces the ruler of Bedsades to release the traveller to avoid slighting the powerful Roman state (this results from the intervention of the opposing potentate, 1.10).

At this point the primary narrator resumes, recounting various details about the Brahmans: they are set aside by divine dispensation, they keep no animals and don't farm, they eat only what the earth produces of its own accord; they pray unceasingly, gazing at the sky rather than eastward, though they have only little knowledge of God and of Providence (1.12–13). They live on the far side of the Ganges, their wives on the near side; they meet only a short period every year for the purpose of procreation, and only produce up to two children – the reason their race is not numerous. The river Ganges is hard to cross in view of the very long Odontotyrannus, big enough to swallow an elephant whole. Near the rivers are very large serpents, of which I have seen only the skin. The primary narrator ends off by saying that he is enclosing a work by Epictetus' student Arrian, one that provides the recipient with a moral code worth following (1.15).

The second section begins by presenting itself as the comments of Dandamis, teacher of the Brahmans.[133] Alexander was dissatisfied with Macedonia and desired to rule our part of the world as well, on the false pretext that his father was Ammon (2.1). He prayed to Wisdom, mother of Providence, for a meeting with the Brahmans, having heard about them from Calanus (2.2). The Brahmans and Indians spoke to Alexander as follows: you have come to us in search of wisdom, which we gained and which rules our lives.

[132] Again we have here the conflation of Ethiopia and India. When Taprobane is described as the place where the great Indian king rules over minor potentates 'as over satraps', the comparison with Persia is striking.

[133] This introduction varies in the different manuscripts; its authenticity is brought into question by the switch to the third person at 2.12.

We philosophers are not subject to worldly rulers (2.3). Calanus, through whom you came to know about us, was a wicked man, for he pursued wealth, and the riches which he obtained made a backslider out of him, though he had drunk the Tiberoboam's waters of self-control (*sôphrosunê*, 2.4). We are by nature without riches, and death is our companion; wearing nothing, in accordance with nature, and see no virtue in killing other people, but have conquered our inner warfare and regard the demands of desire our enemy (2.5–7). Your definition of a philosopher, on the other hand, is one who talks too much, and even pursues luxury, wealth and power (2.8). (There is a fair degree of repetition here, in which Dandamis pointedly contrasts the Brahmans' renunciation of worldly goods with the Macedonians' desire for the same.)

Calanus left the fold, having fallen prey to avarice and become unworthy of God's love (2.10). But there is among our number a man who lives in the forest, Dandamis: it is to him that Alexander is taken when he asks to speak to their leader (2.11–12). Because he could not see him lying in the forest he sends Onesicritus,[134] who at first tries to lure Dandamis with a mixture of death-threats and promises of gifts (2.13–14). Dandamis' response is that Alexander is not immortal and hence in no position to threaten; he disdains the gifts, because his simple life suffices, and ignores the threats (2.15–17). Alexander will have to come to him if he wishes an interview (2.18).

Intrigued by Onesicritus' report, Alexander goes to the forest with fifteen soldiers to meet Dandamis. When he says he wishes to learn God's wisdom, he is told that his worldly desires have left no room in his heart for this: his geographical ambitions are singled out (2.20–21). Dandamis' cross-questioning of Alexander culminates with his central, paradoxical creed: desire nothing, and everything will be yours; desire (*epithumia*) is the mother of penury, and never finds what it seeks (2.23). He invites Alexander to join him as a pupil in the life of renunciation, sustained by Providence (*pronoia*); he extols the benefits of his own life, being able to foretell the works of God and to intercede with God's Providence (2.24–25). Killing is criticised and contrasted with the life of pacifism and tranquillity: ultimately Alexander cannot avoid God's justice, however aggressive he might be. He is told to live the life allotted him by God rather than killing others, which is presented as greed. (2.26–30). The speech ends with the promise that Alexander's failure to obey will be met with punishment, at a future time when his success in war will not help him (2.30).

[134] The unusual –κρατ– of the name is transmitted in the majority of the manuscripts, and is matched by a corresponding -a- in the Latin.

Alexander is both struck and pleased by what he hears, 'for there was in fact a divine spirit in him but one which had, by an evil demon, been perverted into murder' (2.31). He salutes Dandamis for his greatness, beyond what Calanus had led him to expect; struck by the blessings of the tranquil life, he contrasts his own life of fear, especially at night-time, even of his friends (2.32–33). In practice, though, he cannot repudiate his own actions, and would in any case be prevented by his soldiers from living in the wilderness (2.34). To honour Dandamis he orders slaves to bring gifts of gold and silver coins, of clothing, bread and oil, for 'it is a good deed to honour wisdom'.[135] Dandamis refuses the gifts, inveighs against luxurious living, for he feeds on air and the water of the river, and all his needs are supplied by God. But he does accept the oil, 'in order not to dishonour one honouring wisdom', pours it on a pile of wood, sets it alight and prays to God (2.37–39).

Alexander, moved by these 'wise and true words', takes back the gifts refused, whereupon Dandamis launches on a further exposition of his doctrine (2.41–57). In fact the rest of the work is taken up with a further speech of Dandamis, much of it echoing earlier sound-bytes, much of it contrasting Brahmans with Macedonians and Greeks. Calanus is criticised for learning Brahmans' secrets under false pretences, only to abscond to the Greeks: it is he who has instigated Alexander's killing of Brahmans, despite their peacefulness and lack of materialism (2.41–42). Much is said about eating and appetites, now in terms of slavery and freedom (2.44); this leads to attacks on the eating of meat, and also on the drinking of wine and on castration (2.45, 47–48, 54). Epicurean, Stoic and Peripatetic philosophers are all scorned, the first two for their effeminacy and their desire for money respectively (2.53). Dandamis ends his speech by saying that the Brahmans pity the Macedonians, and indeed all of humankind, and will play no part in the hostilities that beset them; again he offers Alexander the possibility of staying with them in the wilderness, following a peaceful life, imitating God (2.55–57). It is on this note that the work ends.

Self-evidently, the story shows many of the features sketched earlier in this chapter: for example, they speak in paradoxes, their gestures are accentuated, their social position marginal. There are so many of these features in evidence in this text that we may regard its main characters, the Brahmans, as figures of wisdom. Let us consider some aspects of this in greater detail.

[135] ἐγὼ γὰρ εὐεργετοῦμαι σοφίαν τιμῶν (2.35–36).

Significantly, they do not themselves travel,[136] but they are the objects of religious travel.

In general, the story may be said to represent an element present in the other Alexander histories: Alexander's *pothos*. The very fact of Alexander's presence at the edges of the earth shows this. In fact, the drama implicit in this confrontation over the nature of knowledge is heightened for its being at the same time a cross-cultural encounter. The tendency to think of the conqueror in moralistic terms is of course not new, and apparent in Plutarch's rhetorical treatise *On the fortune of Alexander*. This may be regarded as typical of the ancient habit of focusing on the personality of a 'great man'.[137]

There is in fact a contradiction in the presentation of Alexander here. On the one hand, he is supreme representative of the world, and particularly of its desires and lusts. As we have seen, he is the figure of worldly authority,[138] the sounding board against which the Brahmans can advertise themselves. At stake here is nothing less than the question about the nature of true knowledge: the worldly or geographical knowledge of Alexander, with its implicit proximity to power (e.g., 2.21), is contrasted with knowledge of the divinity. On the other hand, his own search for the Brahmans is in itself a search for wisdom (e.g., 2.39). The scholarly side of Alexander is brought out more clearly in the western medieval tradition.[139]

In its basic outline the story-pattern is a familiar one from the realm of folklore: a sage's encounter with a king, whom he outwits.[140] But it is more than that. Much of the first part reads like an ancient novel: the almost picaresque story of travel, capture and release, and there is some complexity of narrative frames. A rationalising element is seen, for example, at 1.13 on the procreative habits of the Brahmans, as if in answer to the question, how else would their tribe increase? (The issue is complicated by the hostility to marriage exhibited in the work, a feature that has

136 Except, perhaps, in so far as Calanus accompanies Alexander's retinue up till his spectacular death. This occurs not here but in other versions, notably Arrian *Anab.* 7.2–3. This is presented not as travel in search of wisdom but as a result of his loss of self-control and consequent estrangement from the Brahmans.

137 For Alexander as a prime target of the Cynic project of subverting authority, see Anthony A. Long, 'The Socratic tradition: Diogenes, Crates and hellenistic ethics', in *The Cynics*, ed. Branham and Goulet-Cazé, pp. 28–46, at pp. 29 and 35 n. 20: 'Even if the encounters between Diogenes and Alexander the Great are spurious, they became the favourite Cynic illustration of ethical opposition to political kingship.'

138 On Alexander (like Plato) as a figure of authority against which Cynics react, see *The Cynics*, ed. Branham and Goulet-Cazé.

139 See Chapter 5, section I.6.

140 E.g., Stoneman, 'Naked philosophers', 114, adduces the *Life of Aesop* and the Jewish stories of Esther and Daniel, among others.

been taken to betray Gnostic links.) The presence in the text of learned digressions is also in keeping with the Greek novel, if one compares, say, Heliodorus' excursus on the hippopotamus, and indeed Philostratus' *Life of Apollonius*.[141]

On the other hand, the second part is characterised by maxims or gnomai of a moralising nature. Much space is devoted to the arguments in favour of vegetarianism.[142] This is merely one of several ways in which accepted social practices are questioned, in a manner and tone reminiscent of the Cynic diatribe. We have seen earlier in this chapter the tendency, common to Greco-Roman and several other cultures, to give maxims or paradoxes a special status as rhetorical units of wisdom.

The language of gesture as it occurs in this story accentuates difference in both social status and in worldview: it is no coincidence that Alexander is standing while they are lying on the ground.[143] We might sense here an implicit comparison with the striding of a commander in the *Iliad*, eager to assert himself on the battlefield.[144] More specifically, the presentation of this episode in the *Alexander romance* invites comparison with the ritual prostration (*proskynêsis*) required by Persian kings and, controversially, in 327 BC by Alexander himself.[145] The gesture is spoken of by Aristotle as a specifically barbarian mark of honour (*Rhetorica* 1361a36).

It has been pointed out, in a cultural history of ancient gesture, that 'sitting or lying on the ground is part of a complex of gestures which all aim at a total self-abasement of the subject';[146] and that '[t]he presentation of the self in public . . . was often acted out according to the contrast of high (upright carriage) and low (sitting, prostration)'; in the process hierarchies of prosperity and power were enacted.[147] The Brahmans are then very notable for the extent of their self-abasement.

That this self-abasement should not be taken for obeisance towards authority is made clear in the response of the Brahmans to Alexander. This is reminiscent of Diogenes the Cynic's famous response to Alexander's question of what he desired from him: 'Get out of my sunlight.'[148] In so far as body-language defies the norms of social hierarchy, Palladius' Brahmans can very easily have been taken for Cynic sages.

[141] Shadi Bartsch, *Decoding the ancient novel* (Princeton University Press, 1989).

[142] Stoneman, 'Brahmans', 504–9.

[143] On gesture as a central aspect of self-presentation in Roman society which places such a high premium on public rhetoric, see, e.g., Cox, *Biography*, xi; Brown, *Power and persuasion*, p. 57; Maud Gleason, *Making men* (Princeton University Press, 1995).

[144] Bremmer, 'Walking, standing', pp. 16–17.

[145] Bosworth, *Conquest and empire*, pp. 284–7, narrates the crisis this sparked in Alexander's camp.

[146] Bremmer, 'Walking, standing', p. 26. [147] Bremmer, ibid. [148] Arr. *Anab.* 7.2.1.

The emphasis placed in the tale of Calanus on suicide by fire has invited several scholars to seek parallels in Indian society, but such attempts have borne little fruit. For example, in Jain asceticism starvation rather than fire is the preferred method of suicide.[149] It appears, at any rate, that this form of suicide elicited two different lines of response. First, there were those who admired the control of the self it expressed, hence the many references to the fact that Calanus went calmly into the fire without protesting or flinching, as, for example, we saw in Philo above. On the other hand, the calculated exhibitionism involved could cause irritation, as it does in the case of the (admittedly fictional) speaker of Lucian's *On the death of Peregrinus*. We should bear in mind that for Greeks and Romans self-immolation was never regarded as an acceptable form of death, and remained a marker of foreignness.[150]

Perhaps the most important figure for us to notice is the Brahmans' distance from human culture, their marginality, already touched on in connection with Tertullian and Augustine. In fact, 'India' is in this text the shorthand expression for the wilderness (*erêmia*) of that region, which is set up as a utopia, at the expense of 'the world' as represented by Alexander.

> Dandamis . . . was lying among the woods, resting peacefully on leaves, close by a spring from which he drank as if milking the breast of mother earth.[151]

As Dandamis is reported to say later, 'in the wilderness, the soul is tempted towards virtue'.[152] This utopian vision relies heavily on the idea of nature as a refuge from human culture, which comes across as the activities of money-seeking, warfare, meat-eating and the drinking of alcohol – all of which come under the rubric of desire. Underlying this is a view of nature as radically distanced from culture. Whereas other holy persons, for example in Syria and Egypt, assumed positions which were marginal to their own societies, 'India' here emerges as being itself marginal to the Greco-Roman world embodied in Alexander. This may be considered a geographical variant on the theme of social marginality that we noticed in the case of the Christian holy person.

Stepping back a moment from these features of the story, what are we to make of its curious textual history? The authorship of Palladius is now

149 Stoneman, 'Brahmans', 505–6.

150 Anton J. L. van Hooff, *From autothanasia to suicide* (London: Routledge, 1990), pp. 57–9.

151 Δάνδαμις . . . ἐν ὕλῃ ἀνάκειται ἐπὶ φύλλοις ἐαρινοῖς ἐγγὺς ἔχων πηγὴν ὡς μαζὸν ἀκέραιον ἀμέλγων μητρός (2.12).

152 πειράζεται γὰρ εἰς ἀρετὴν ἐν ἐρημίᾳ ψυχή (2.28).

generally accepted,[153] the first part being the safer bet.[154] It is easy to see how part of the work can have got caught up in Alexander legends.[155] It was written by Palladius of Helenopolis (b. 363/364), who served as bishop first in Bithynia (c. 400–406) and later in his native Galatia (*c.* 412–*c.* 431). His support for John Chrysostom earned him exile from Bithynia in 406, as well as suspicion of sympathy towards Origenism; after being expelled from Bithynia he travelled within Egypt before assuming his new see. The *Lausiac history*, which he composed around 419, remains, along with Athanasius' *Life of Anthony*, a key witness to early Egyptian monasticism. His treatise 'On the life of the Brahmans' gained currency in the west through its translation into Latin by Pseudo-Ambrose.[156] A textual tradition in the east nearly matching that of the *Alexander romance* for complexity is an indication of its widespread popularity. It was in Egypt that the *Romance* was much read, and it is probably here that the text was composed.

If, then, we can safely assume authenticity, it is intriguing to consider the work alongside two other aspects of its author's life. First, what connections can be drawn between this work and the more famous *Lausiac history* (which does not mention it, or in fact Brahmans at all)? Certainly the first-person narration of the first section of the life of the Brahmans can be paralleled in the *Lausiac history*, where he makes constant reference to his own travels in Egypt. It can be no coincidence that, at a time when Christian ascetic theory and practice reached new heights in the Mediterranean world, Indian ascetics should have attracted attention. Even if the monastic movement had by the early fifth century spread well beyond its Egyptian desert origins (witness Syria), then Anthony's Egypt continued its exemplary status. If it could be shown that Brahmans too participated in the world of ascetic piety, then their spectacular achievements would redound to the glory of Christian asceticism. In this way, the Brahmans, already familiar from stories about Alexander, would offer Christians some exotic and eminent comrades.

153 The arguments of P. R. Coleman-Norton, 'The authorship of the *Epistola de Indicis gentibus et de Bragmanibus*', *Cl. Phil.* 21 (1926), pp. 154–60, still hold firm, however tenuous his grounds for claiming that Palladius himself travelled to the east (itself perhaps another instance of the 'biographical fallacy' noted above in connection with the Greek lyric poets). More recent scholarship on the subject heavily favours Palladian authorship: J. D. M. Derrett, 'The history of "Palladius on the races of India and the Brahmans"' *C&M* 21 (1960), 64–35; Beverley Berg, 'The letter of Palladius on India', *Byzantion* 44 (1974), pp. 5–16; Wilhelm Berghoff, *Palladius, de gentibus Indiae et Bragmanibus* (Meisenheim: Hain, 1967); Richard Stoneman, *Legends of Alexander the Great* (London: Everyman, 1994).

154 For discussion see Derrett, 'Palladius', 64–135.

155 Partly because it narrates the journey of an Egyptian scholar. Berg, 'Letter of Palladius', 5–16.

156 Latin tr. ed. Berghoff, *Palladius*.

This line of interpretation gains strength if we take into account Jerome's claim of Palladius' complicity with the Origenist controversy. The notion that all people, not merely Christians, would be saved effectively gives greater room for the Brahmans within Christian thought: at the very least, Origenism redirects emphasis from conversion to the ascetic ideal itself. In the light of Origenism it is easy to see why the Brahmans could, in such a brand of Christianity gain sanctity by their ascetic achievements, and could in so doing effectively become a non-Christian holy people.[157]

III.3. Christians and Cynics

The Cynic connection has already been brought out in earlier scholarship.[158] This is an important line of inquiry, and one that gains huge importance if we remember that, as we have seen, Arrian, for one, speaks of Calanus and Diogenes in the same breath (*Anab.* 7.2–3).[159] We should not forget that the earliest Greek name associated with the interview, apart from Alexander himself, is Onesicritus, whom we know to have been a pupil of Diogenes of Sinope.[160] But if we consider the authorship of the work we must be mindful also of a different context, that of Christian asceticism. The main question we have to consider is, what is it about the Brahmans that appealed to Christians?

To be sure, the work has many features in common with Christian asceticism. But the problem comes when similar features are identified in other brands of ascetic behaviour. Thus we have the conquest of inner warfare (reminiscent of Anthony's fight with his own sexuality, presented in Athanasius' *vita* in very physical terms),[161] submission to the divine, renunciation of the world. But then, as a recent collection richly illustrates,[162] there are non-Christian traditions of renunciation too.

157 However, Berg, 'Letter of Palladius', sees the text as Gnostic with Encratite elements; Pénélope Photiadès, 'Les diatribes cyniques du papyrus de Genève 271, leurs traductions et élaborations successives', *MH* 16 (1959), 116–39, esp. 126, as Arrian.

158 E.g. Victor Martin, 'Un recueil de diatribes cyniques Pap. Genev. inv. 271', *MH* 16 (1959), 77–115. Stoneman, 'Brahmans', takes this further with a valuable critique of earlier analyses, but see also Willis and Maresch, 'Encounter of Alexander', concerning recently found papyrus fragments.

159 Diog. Laert. (6.76, 79) tells us that Diogenes the Cynic died the same day as Alexander, at the age of eighty, that is on 13 June 323. Such a coincidence must be regarded as improbable, and it might be best to interpret the story as expressing a pointed juxtaposition between authority and subversion: Long, 'Socratic tradition', in *The Cynics*, ed. Branham and Goulet-Cazé, pp. 28–46, at 45. While the historical arguments for Alexander's meeting with the Brahmans are stronger, we must here too make provision for pointed exaggeration.

160 Brown, *Onesicritus*; and Pearson, *Lost histories*.

161 Peter Brown, *The body and society* (New York: Columbia University Press, 1988).

162 Vincent L. Wimbush and Richard Valantasis, (eds.) *Asceticism* (Oxford: Clarendon, 1995).

Why should Christians have taken an interest in the Brahmans? It is after all a bishop of Caesarea, Eusebius (*PE* 11.3), who tells the story of a visit paid to Socrates by an Indian, following Aristotle's pupil Aristoxenus.[163] For Clement, barbarian wisdom in general 'becomes a means of criticizing the Greek confidence in human reason, the uniqueness of the Hellenic tradition, and their proud proclamation of philosophy and theory';[164] as such, it was part of the idea of 'original wisdom' invoked against Greek philosophy in its rationalising mould. These cases, taken alongside Palladius' text, show us that the Brahmans, by their very lack of *paideia*, offered Christians like Clement unexpected allies, and a way of chipping away at the imposing edifice of polytheist philosophy.

Various scholars have grappled with a possible connection between this work and Cynic philosophy.[165] Is it possible that this story was a folktale circulating in Alexandria's philosophical milieu? Certainly, as Chapter 3 shows, it is true that trade activity did bring Indian merchants to Alexandria, and Greeks and Romans to the Indian subcontinent. So it is a priori likely that Alexandria, as a major international centre with not only regular trade activity but also a scholarly hubbub since the third century BC, would have been a place where such stories could be exchanged. But we must guard here against too readily speaking about 'folktale', when this obviates the need to think about points of contact with the 'real' world.

A more profitable way to interpret this material is one which makes us recognise the prominence and changing fortunes of holy men and of Cynic sages; and, further, explore features those holy men shared with other types of sages, such as wandering Cynics and even Brahmans.[166] It is in the sphere of *perceptions* that we must seek the possibility of overlap between holy men and Cynics of the Mediterranean world on the one hand, and the Brahmans of India on the other. There is no underestimating the significance of contemporary perceptions of such people. The room for slippage within such perceptions is attested in an important study of Jesus' contemporary reception.[167]

[163] See section II.1 above. [164] Halbfass, *India and Europe*, p. 9.

[165] Beverley Berg, 'Dandamis: an early Christian portrait of Indian ascetism', *C&M* 1970 (31), 269–305, has seen Dandamis as an entirely Cynic figure; more moderately, Stoneman in 'Brahmans' and 'Naked philosophers' agrees in essence but looks to earlier roots, e.g. Hdt. 3.100 on the non-violence of the Indians. Brown, *Onesicritus*, has argued both that Cynic doctrine originates in India *and* that Dandamis is a projection of the Cynic – seemingly contradictory positions.

[166] This is already to some extent implicit in Reitzenstein's study on wonder-working, though Brahmans themselves do not come under the spotlight: *Hellenistische Wundererzählungen*.

[167] Morton Smith, *Jesus the magician* (San Francisco: Harper and Row, 1978), focusing on exorcism, 'nature miracles' and healing; cf. Fögen, *Enteignung*, pp. 189–92.

This apparent confluence of elements brings us to a problem of analysis which we may term comparative asceticism. There is in general the risk of overinterpreting similarities of ascetic practice that may not necessarily be related; in fact there are many other ascetic practices throughout the world, and the same features tend to recur, such as mortification of the flesh and vegetarianism. Yet it would seem worthwhile here to consider the possibility that all three had some effect on each other. Similarities between Christians and Cynics were asserted by Lucian and Aelius Aristides,[168] and much of the recent research on the historical Jesus, at least in the eyes of contemporaries, as a Cynic sage.[169] Certainly, Dandamis exhibits many of the features of Diogenes of Sinope in Diogenes Laertius' *Vita*. There too we must be conscious of projection, given the time-lag of some 500 years between them; and Cynicism had had a varied career by the time Diogenes Laertius was writing.[170] After having low prestige it gained greatly when in the high empire the Stoics claimed them as their philosophical ancestors; qua philosophers they were to get the approval of Julian the Apostate, who nonetheless criticises their exhibitionism.[171]

It is also true that neither Dandamis nor Diogenes of Sinope exhibit all the features of the holy man, especially his functions as arbitrator in non-religious contexts; but both share his histrionics (particularly in the Syrian version), and his place on society's margins. If holy people such as Symeon the Stylite appeared in the Byzantine world at a time of Christianisation,[172] then it would not seem unfair to see the Brahman (or for that matter the Cynic sage) as answers to the same area of religious need – all of this in a period of heightened religious conflict.

IV. THE DIFFUSION OF *PAIDEIA*: APOLLONIUS OF TYANA

We turn now to the testimony of Indian holiness given by the writer of a very different text: the life of Apollonius of Tyana by Philostratus, composed probably around AD 222–35.[173] In the most obvious sense, Philostratus'

168 Derek Krueger, 'The bawdy and society', in *The Cynics*, ed. Branham and Goulet-Cazé, pp. 222–39.

169 Smith, *Jesus*.

170 Branham and Goulet-Cazé, *The Cynics*, introduction.

171 Or. 6, 'to the uneducated Cynics'; elsewhere (esp. or. 7) Julian tries to breathe new life into the Cynic movement, and to show the unity of their philosophy. At issue in both, to an extent, is their degree of *paideia*. Like several contemporaries, Julian reveals admiration for the 'classical' Cynicism of Diogenes while attacking their contemporary followers as charlatans: G. W. Bowersock, *Julian the Apostate* (Cambridge, MA: Harvard University Press, 1978), pp. 81–2; Athanassiadi, *Julian and Hellenism*, pp. 128–31.

172 Derek Krueger, *Symeon the holy fool* (Berkeley: University of California Press, 1996).

173 Elsner, 'Hagiographic geography', 22, following E. L. Bowie, 'Apollonius of Tyana: tradition and reality', *ANRW* II.16.2 (1978), 1652–99.

life of Apollonius exhibits the same features that we have already seen. His eastward journey has the form, at first glance at least, of a pilgrimage to the wise teachers of ancient societies, inviting comparison with Herodotus' visit to the Egyptian priests, and it is in this light that we see the Brahmans (note esp. 1.2). Yet, as Elsner has made clear in a recent article, the hagiography harbours different modalities of travel: on this score alone, its complexities are considerable. In the course of this discussion, we shall have to consider the judgement that 'Philostratus presents Pythagoras as a recipient and transmitter of Egyptian and, ultimately, Indian wisdom'.[174]

Most of what we know about Apollonius comes, in fact, from Philostratus, a fact that brings difficulties if we are searching for the historical Apollonius, given the nature of Philostratus' own agenda, as we are able to reconstruct it from his other works. The work itself is more hagiography than biography.[175] To complicate matters, when Apollonius attracts interest again in the fourth century, it is in a highly polemical context: at issue is the comparison of him with Christ. This topic is brought out polemically in Eusebius' *Against Hierocles*, at a time when the debate over Apollonius heated up amidst conflict between polytheists and Christians.[176] But, before we concern ourselves with the complexities of Apollonius' story, let us first outline the Indian leg of his travels, as told by Philostratus.[177]

Having remained twenty months at the court of the Parthian king Bardanes or Vardanes at Babylon, Apollonius sets out with Damis and some other servants. He has received from his host the necessary camels and guide. They cross the Hindu Kush and reach the Indus. Here they are amicably received by the local satrap, who heeds Vardanes' letter of introduction and aids their river-crossing. This satrap intercedes with his own king, who rules the land between the Indus and the Hydraotes (Ravi), for

[174] Halbfass, *India and Europe*, p. 9. [175] Edwards in *Portraits*, ed. Edwards and Swain, p. 233.

[176] Eusebius' authorship has been impugned by Tomas Hägg, 'Hierocles the lover of truth and Eusebius the Sophist', *SO* 67 (1992), 138–50. *Contra*: Timothy D. Barnes, *Constantine and Eusebius* (Cambridge, MA: Harvard University Press, 1981), pp. 164–7, who dates its composition to shortly before 303. What is more, the *VA* shows certain parallels to Christian hagiography, and these may in fact betray influences from Christian texts: Smith, *Jesus the magician*, pp. 84–93; Swain in *Portraits*, ed. Edwards and Swain, p. 28.

[177] For an older generation of scholarship concerned primarily with the historicity of the journey, see the analysis of Vincent A. Smith, 'The Indian travels of Apollonius of Tyana', *ZDMG* 68 (1914), 329–44, with ample reference to earlier work; cf. Christopher P. Jones, 'Apollonius of Tyana's passage to India', *GRBS* 42 (2001), 185–99. It is striking that Eusebius never denies that Apollonius visited India, though he does ridicule the travellers' tales he brings back. More specifically, the historicity of Apollonius' companion Damis has been doubted by Barnes, *Constantine and Eusebius*, p. 166; Bowie, 'Apollonius', sees him as an invention of Philostratus.

safe passage. Having crossed the Indus, they reach Taxila,[178] where they are received for three days by an Indian philosopher-king, known by the Parthian name of Phraotes (2.19–20). Their lengthy conversations span various topics, including the nature of philosophical training, of rulership, and Apollonius advises the king on a legal dispute (2.39). From here the travellers set out to find the Indian sages, taking with them fresh camels and a letter of introduction from the king. Two days from Taxila they come upon the battlefield where Alexander defeated Porus. They cross the Hydraotes and then the Hyphasis. Still thirty stadia from the Hyphasis they catch sight of monuments marking the limit of Alexander's expedition (2.43).

They then cross that part of the Hindu Kush which stretches down to the Arabian Sea, coming to a plain irrigated by channels from the Ganges. Here they hunt dragons. Having heard of a great city called Parax or Paraka, situated at the foot of an unspecified mountain, they proceed for four days through fertile countryside until they arrive at the castle of the sages, placed atop a hill.

Here Apollonius stays for four months as a guest of the philosophers, with whom he converses regularly in Greek.[179] Among others, he meets Iarchas, chief of the sages. Supplied again with a guide and fresh camels he travels for ten days before reaching the sea.[180] He reaches an unnamed port where passenger ships lay at anchor, and sends the camels home with a letter addressed to Iarchas. He embarks one of the ships, encouraged by a gentle breeze; but soon sailing conditions become much less favourable at the mouth of the Hyphasis. He sails past the mouth of the Indus, along the Makran to the mouth of the Euphrates, following the route taken by Nearchus (3.53). He returns to Babylon and visits king Vardanes. From there he travels by land to Seleucia via Nineveh, then by ship to Cyprus, and thence to Ionia. (Book four is devoted to his travels in Ionia, the Greek mainland and Italy.)

Apollonius' own status as a sage is assured at the start by his own stated search for wisdom: such is his piety that he exceeds Pythagoras in *sophia*

[178] Though there might be archaeological evidence for Taxila as a 'university city' (Smith, 'Indian travels', 336), this diagnosis cannot be made of Philostratus' chapter: the grandeur of the royal palace includes Greek reliefs, and the city is compared with Nineveh, but it would be going too far to speak of this as a site of Greek *paideia* in the text: Dani, *Taxila*.

[179] We may note that, in keeping with the ancient (mostly historiographic) discourse on autopsy, Philostratus actually meets the Brahmans in person. Just as Onesicritus is an intermediary in the Alexander histories, so the Indian messenger fulfils that function here.

[180] Philostratus claims at this point that he kept the Ganges on his right and the Hyphasis on his left, a geographical possibility.

(1.2). This search for wisdom is explained by the author as a series of interviews with the Babylonian Magi, Indian Brahmans and Egyptian Gymnosophists. At the same time, as the author concedes, these very visits made him subject to accusations of quackery, accusations which Philostratus is at pains to counter from the outset. Some praised him, but for others these visits were grounds for suspicion:

> Because he was in contact with the wizards of Babylon, the Brahmans of India, and the naked philosophers of Egypt, some dismissed him as a charlatan, and alleged that he was a wizard, passing a negative judgment on him. (1.2)[181]

Again we see the fragility of wisdom: journeys of the kind that conferred wisdom on the Seven Sages are the very ones that elicit criticisms of Apollonius' quackery. Philostratus' defends Apollonius by comparing him with Empedocles, Pythagoras and Democritus, who spoke with Magians though themselves never resorted to magic. Even Plato, whose reputation for wisdom is beyond reproach, visited Egypt to speak with its prophets and priests. And so Philostratus' apologia continues. Philostratus does not suggest that the eastern sages are in themselves dubious: at issue is the acceptability of consorting with them on the part of Greeks. The polemical note of these comments is matched by many of the earliest references to Apollonius, on the part of both Christians and polytheists.[182]

One feature that marks this text from other ancient ethnographies is the attention given to language. A striking case comes at 3.12, when Apollonius meets the Brahmans' messenger. 'He ran up to Apollonius and spoke to him in Greek. In itself this did not seem remarkable, for the inhabitants of the village spoke Greek.'[183] The surprise comes when the messenger addresses the visitors by name. For Apollonius, this is a sign of the Indians' foreknowledge and hence their 'true wisdom', and as such marks the success of their journey. This he says to Damis:

> 'We have reached men,' he said, 'who are absolutely wise, for they seem to have the gift of premonition.' (3.12)[184]

[181] οἱ δέ, ἐπειδὴ μάγοις Βαβυλωνίων καὶ Ἰνδῶν Βραχμᾶσι καὶ τοῖς ἐν Αἰγύπτῳ Γυμνοῖς συνεγένετο, μάγον ἡγοῦνται αὐτὸν καὶ διαβάλλουσιν ὡς βιαίως σοφόν, κακῶς γιγνώσκοντες·

[182] See the testimonia collected by G. Petzke, *The Traditionen über Apollonius von Tyana und das Neue Testament* (Leiden: Brill, 1970), pp. 19–45.

[183] προσδραμόντα δὲ τῷ Ἀπολλωνίῳ φωνῇ Ἑλλάδι προσειπεῖν αὐτόν, καὶ τοῦτο μὲν οὔπω θαυμαστὸν δόξαι διὰ τὸ καὶ τοὺς ἐν τῇ κώμῃ πάντας ἀπὸ Ἑλλήνων φθέγγεσθαι.

[184] παρὰ ἄνδρας, ἔφη, σοφοὺς ἀτεχνῶς ἥκομεν, ἐοίκασι γὰρ προγιγνώσκειν

The emphasis on Greek language as a cultural index may be regarded as typical of the work as a whole.[185] It is part of Philostratus' particularly Hellenising view of India.

It is already clear that Philostratus' India emphasises the diffusion of *paideia*. Beyond this, if we ask what role it plays in the text, two answers can be given. The first, more obvious, one involves travel as a source of authority. It is his journey to India that empowers Apollonius, from a certain point of view, to confront the Roman emperors. His two very different interviews with the Indian kings prepare the way for those with two Roman emperors, namely Vespasian at Alexandria (5.27–38) and particularly Domitian at Rome (7.32–33 and 8.1–5). The last of these is in the form of a legal trial, from which Apollonius is acquitted and departs miraculously. There are important differences between the Indian rulers, differences whose significance becomes even more apparent in hindsight. On the one hand, the philosopher-king Phraotes, advocates the simple life free of war, as well as vegetarianism, and speaks fluent Greek (2.25–29); he tells of strict rules restricting admission to the status of philosopher (2.30). On the other, the unnamed Indian king dismisses philosophy as foolishness and is contemptuous of the Greeks generally (3.28–29). Though Apollonius successfully refutes the king's insult of the Greeks as 'slaves', he refuses his invitation. This second king in his boastfulness comes close to Aristotle's idea that India contains despots, and contrasts with the philosopher-king.[186] Later in the hagiography, Apollonius clashes with both Nero and Domitian, whereas Vespasian seeks his guidance. The difference between these two models of rulership has already emerged in India.

Even if the second king's comments on the Greeks reflect badly on himself, India in this work is nonetheless the place that makes critique possible. The philosopher Iarchus criticises the Greeks as hypocritical in their lip-service to justice (*dikaiosune*, 3.25). In his encounters with the Roman emperors, it is Apollonius' travels that make it possible for him to speak truth to power; in so far as this is especially true of the Indian leg of his

185 Apollonius' impeccable Greek is without any tinge of a Cappadocian accent (1.7). See the discussion of Flinterman, *Power, paideia*, pp. 90–100. In general, on the role of language in the construction of Hellenic culture (though focusing on an earlier period and on differences between Greek groups), see Hall, *Ethnic identity* and *Hellenicity*.

186 The unnamed king's accusation that the Greeks were the 'slaves of Xerxes' resonates with Aristotle's comment on Indian despotism, which he attributes to Scylax: cf. Chapter 1, section I.1 above. This view contrasts with Aristotle's positive image of the philosopher-king: Malcolm Schofield, *Saving the city: philosopher-kings and other classical paradigms* (London: Routledge, 1999).

journey, by implication India itself is the space of critique. This is true of India in a way that does not apply to Egypt, that part of Apollonius' journey described in book 6. Apollonius' lengthy speech in his own defence against Domitian's accusations contains praise of Indian philosophers, distinguished from Egyptian, as his teachers (8.7).

Second, less obviously but no less significantly, India invokes the memory of Alexander in a particular way. References to Alexander are relatively few, yet he is a profound presence in the text, not only by means of his own itinerary but also that of his general Nearchus (2.17 and 3.53). What is more, India's sacred geography is mapped in relation to Dionysus and Heracles, themselves linked with Alexander's expedition. The invocation of Alexander is no simple matter, and is certainly not adulatory in an uncomplicated way; rather, it contains a strong sense of revisionism. Thus the party visits the shrine of Dionysus at Mount Nysa (2.9). In describing this episode, Philostratus enters into discussion about whether Alexander did in fact ascend or whether, according to local tradition, he refrained from doing so in order to spare his troops the temptations of grapes available there. The tone of the chapter is defensive, as if Philostratus is aware of controversy on the subject. In this way Alexander is the subject of ongoing debate. By the same token, the travellers' refusal to visit Mount Aornus shows both awareness of the campaign and a willingness to diverge from its path (2.10).

The memory of Alexander lives also in relation to monuments. His combat with Porus is commemorated in several ways in book 2. One of Porus's elephants, by the name of Ajax, still lives at Taxila. Enjoying celebrity status well into its fourth century of life, it wore golden rings on its tusks, to which Alexander had added a dedicatory inscription to the Sun (2.12). The temple of the Sun was adorned with golden images of Alexander, whereas those of Porus were of black bronze (2.24, cf. 2.20). Such references to Porus emphasise his subjugation to Alexander, and one even suggests affectionate loyalty (2.20–21). The most remarkable monument to Alexander comes, however, at the point where Apollonius and his party cross the river Hyphasis, and thus proceed farther into India than Alexander's troops had allowed. Near the river they found altars inscribed as follows:

'To father Ammon and his brother Heracles and Athena Pronoia and Olympian Zeus and the Kabeiri of Samothrace and the Indian Sun and Apollo of Delphi.' They say that a bronze stele was also dedicated, and on it was inscribed: 'Alexander reached this point.' We may imagine that the altars were the work of Alexander, who thus acknowledged the extent of his empire, but I suspect, on the other hand, that the stele was put up by the Indians beyond the Hyphasis, so as to express their pride that Alexander had gone no farther. (2.43)[187]

This location is presented as a very distinctive landmark within Philostratus' cultural geography of Hellenism. Its placing at the end of the second book merely heightens its impact. The sentiment expressed, containing as it does a hint of resistance to Alexander, is somewhat at odds with Porus' adulation of him. Given the nature of Alexander in the text, however, this is no serious contradiction; it merely points to a variety of responses inspired by his campaign. Philostratus' gloss in this extract certainly differs from the more laudatory responses to Alexander's campaign.

The possibility of varied responses to Alexander's campaign is analogous to the complexity of India itself in the *Life of Apollonius*. On the one hand it shows the diffusion of Hellenism, particularly in light of the attention given to the Greek language; on the other, it is also a source of wisdom, and of authority. In this respect, India in this text, is distinctly superior to Egypt. It is thus not surprising that Apollonius is both a pilgrim, going to learn from the Indian sages, and also a teacher. The clearest example of this is the counsel he gives Phraotes in a legal dispute (2.39). Philostratus, it is true, devotes some attention to the topography and natural history of India. Much of this, however, is highly stylised. It would be more accurate to say that it occupies a complicated place in Philostratus' 'hagiographic geography': by virtue of its remoteness, it symbolises the diffusion of Greek culture, and is thus a place-marker of sorts.[188]

V. MODALITIES OF TRAVEL

Again we are faced with the simple question: what is the geographical area described by Greeks and Romans as India? Naturally enough, the Brahmans of the Alexander histories are a feature of the Indus Valley. Indeed Alexander's 'India' was very much the Indus Valley. Philostratus' story of Apollonius, which can be closely mapped, adheres narrowly to the route taken by Alexander and, finally, by his officer Nearchus. All of this is unsurprising, in the light of Chapter 1. Indian history, on the other hand, shows

[187] ΠΑΤΡΙ ΑΜΜΩΝΙ ΚΑΙ ΗΡΑΚΛΕΙ ΑΔΕΛΦΩΙ ΚΑΙ ΑΘΗΝΑΙ ΠΡΟΝΟΙΑΙ ΚΑΙ ΔΙΙ ΟΛΥΜΠΙΩΙ ΚΑΙ ΣΑΜΟΘΡΑΙΞΙ ΚΑΒΕΙΡΟΙΣ ΚΑΙ ΙΝΔΩΙ ΗΛΙΩΙ ΚΑΙ ΔΕΛΦΩΙ ΑΠΟΛΛΩΝΙ, φασὶ δὲ καὶ στήλην ἀνακεῖσθαι χαλκῆν, ᾗ ἐπιγεγράφθαι ΑΛΕΞΑΝΔΡΟΣ ΕΝΤΑΥΘΑ ΕΣΤΗ. τοὺς μὲν δὴ βωμοὺς Ἀλεξάνδρου ἡγώμεθα τὸ τῆς ἑαυτοῦ ἀρχῆς τέρμα τιμῶντος, τὴν δὲ στήλην τοὺς μετὰ τὸν Ὕφασιν Ἰνδοὺς ἀναθεῖναι δοκῶμοι λαμπρυνομένους ἐπὶ τῷ Ἀλέξανδρον μὴ προελθεῖν πρόσω.

[188] On this, more generally, see G. W. Bowersock, *Hellenism in late antiquity* (Ann Arbor: University of Michigan Press, 1990).

us that Brahmans were by no means confined to this region, in that we do have Sanskrit texts from before the time of Alexander, speaking of Brahmans in the Ganges valley.[189] This is the best corroboration we can hope to find for the Indian king's comment to Apollonius: Alexander merely spoke to the warlike Oxydracae tribe, whereas the 'true sages'[190] live between the Hyphasis and the Ganges, in territory never reached by Alexander (2.33). It is here that the Greco-Roman field of vision shifts eastwards of Alexander's conquests. Very different still in its setting is the Thomas story, which refers more to the south of the subcontinent. These southern parts came into the Greco-Roman field of perception only later, as we see in Pliny's *Natural history* and other texts mentioning Roman trade. Though such trade, famously, had little impact on the formation of a literary image of India, it had the effect of making possible the kinds of contact that fostered the diffusion of Christianity.[191]

V.1. Pilgrimage into mission

The geographical question of north versus south is thus linked with that of modalities of travel. To be sure, much has emerged in this chapter to portray India as a site of pilgrimage, and this relates mostly to the north and northwest. The paradigm of pilgrimage was set up by Alexander's interview with the Brahmans, and underlined by his oft-described reverence toward them.[192] Historically, this may be true in retrospect only, i.e. much more the interpretation of later commentators than part of Alexander's own actions; but at all events the paradigm thus created was a strong and enduring one.[193] It was reinforced by a number of factors: the antiquity of Indian civilisation was well known, and may variously have accounted for and been strengthened by a tendency to link Brahmans with other eastern

[189] By contrast, the *Shatapatha Brahmana* (Brahmana of the hundred paths), a text of around the eighth century BC, speaks of Brahmans living in the Gangetic plains, i.e. in the northeast of the subcontinent: Kulke and Rothermund, *History of India*, pp. 48–9.

[190] οἱ δὲ ἀτεχνῶς σοφοί.

[191] Dihle, 'Conception of India' (= *Antike und Orient*, pp. 89–97, at 91), has shown that the spread of Christianity largely matches trade routes of the first and second centuries AD. Note also his comment on the different geographical conceptions of India mentioned here, pp. 89–90.

[192] With much continuity up to the present day, parts of India have also been the site of Buddhist pilgrimage: for a sample of texts reflecting this, including Fa-Hsien, see the collection edited by Molly Emma Aitken, *Meeting the Buddha: on pilgrimage in Buddhist India* (New York: Riverhead, 1995). Benares, or the modern Varanasi in the central Gangetic plain, is an example of an urban centre which has religious rather than specifically political significance.

[193] Hahn, 'The Indian tradition'.

sages, namely those of Egypt and Babylonia.[194] Furthermore, in historical terms Brahmans held a powerful and insular position in Indian society, so that Indian society may have seemed to Greeks and Romans to support a strongly institutionalised brand of holiness – one which, more than in their own societies, explicitly linked holiness and wisdom.

Of the two texts we have considered here at length, Palladius' *On the life of the Brahmans* was composed more than two centuries after Philostratus' *Life of Apollonius of Tyana*. But the Alexander tradition stretches back much further into the past (as is shown by the Berlin papyrus), and it is quite possible that Philostratus in fact knew the *Alexander romance*, for many of its features seems to be presumed by the biography, with its greater sophistication.[195] Accordingly, the kind of travel we find in Philostratus is more complicated than that in Palladius (and indeed elsewhere in the historical and romance traditions of Alexander).

What is at stake in this kind of religious travel? Travel in itself dramatises the exchange of cultural capital, as Elsner has shown.[196] The same could be said of the recurrent and variable motif of Alexander's interview with the Indian philosophers: a confrontation of political authority and social criticism. This emerges from Palladius and the *Alexander romance* tradition even more strongly than the earlier Alexander historians. We have already noted above that a sense of separation or distance tends to be implicit in the sacred; one could claim here that this sense is magnified by distance involved in travel. What is more, if priests in the Greco-Roman world are in any case a group of people set apart, then Indian priests are that much more radically set apart. Certainly there is from the fourth century AD a substantial Christian tradition of travel to a particular holy land, following Helena's discovery of the True Cross, but we must not forget that there had already been a strong precedent in Greek religion in the form of travel

194 Ultimately, as we shall discuss in the conclusion, this may have been a factor leading to a totalising Roman view of 'the east'.

195 Stoneman, 'Naked philosophers'.

196 Pilgrimage was by no means a Christian invention: Sabine MacCormack, '*Loca sancta*: the organisation of sacred topography in late antiquity', in *The blessings of pilgrimage*, ed. Robert Ousterhout (Urbana: University of Illinois Press, 1990), pp. 7–40, and R. L. Wilken, *The land called holy* (New Haven: Yale University Press, 1992), emphasise polytheist and Jewish precedents respectively. Matthew Dillon, *Pilgrims and pilgrimage in ancient Greece* (London: Routledge, 1997), esp. pp. 60–98, identifies three types of pilgrim 'seeking a solution to specific problems' (60): those visiting an oracle to secure a god's approval or advice, those seeking initiation into a mystery cult in the hope of a better afterlife, and those seeking a cure. Elsner, 'Hagiographic geography', in suggesting Christian paradigms for Apollonius' 'pilgrimage' might have made clearer that Christian pilgrimage, strictly speaking, did not occur before Helena's discovery of the True Cross: e.g., Wilken, *Land called holy*, pp. 101–25; and Hunt, *Holy Land pilgrimage*, pp. 28–9.

to shrines and oracles, and also in the post-exilic Jewish concept of the Promised Land.

To what extent do Greco-Roman ideas about India's holiness begin with Alexander? Did the earlier Greek travellers visit India as a site of holiness, in the way that Hegel diagnosed?[197] Not so, in so far as the Achaemenid context outlined in Chapter 1 was most readily understood in a military light. The Brahmans do not feature in any accounts of India preceding Alexander. Whether or not Alexander actually sought the Brahmans out as wise people is impossible to say. But it is clear that the post-Platonic period left much room for sages untainted with the negative effects of the Sophistic revolution; other eastern sages, such as Magi or Chaldaeans came into the breach in a more obvious way than did Brahmans, given that they were better known to Greeks at this time. But it is clear that the Brahmans were to some extent viewed in the same light as these other sages, by extension if nothing else.

It is one thing to speak of modalities of travel *per se* and another to talk about India as a destination of such travel. It does seem, from our survey, that India became such as a destination at a relatively late stage, if we are to think of pre-Alexander accounts. On the other hand, the principle of travel to eastern lands is well established from the lawgivers. It appears, however, that this generally means Mesopotamia and Egypt rather than India. From Herodotus and Plato alone we see that eastern lands constitute a region deserving to be visited by those seeking wisdom, but in those authors India does not get explicitly included.

But pilgrimage on these lines is not the whole story. Another kind of journey exists from much earlier, and considerably complicates the picture. The travel of Greco-Roman sages involved a degree of teaching also on their own part – something that essentially reverses the direction of cultural assimilation. It is thus important to emphasise the complexity of Philostratus' *Life of Apollonius*, as a text harbouring varied concepts of religious travel.

V.2. Thomas and tradition

Christian texts concerning India show much in common with polytheist ones, not least in their coverage of the sages. Yet there is a specifically Christian India, in which the subcontinent is a place of mission, and inspires

[197] 'Without being known too well, it has existed for millennia in the imagination of the Europeans as a wonderland. Its fame, which it has always had with regard to its treasures, both its natural ones, and in particular, its wisdom, has lured men there.' (Hegel, *Philosophie der Weltgeschichte*, quoted in translation by Halbfass, *India and Europe*, p. 2)

teaching rather than learning. Embedded within this missionary perspective is a distinction between northern (mostly northwestern) and southern India, one that reflects different travel routes.

It is the apostle Thomas that is, at least in the modern period, most widely considered the first Christian missionary to India.[198] Fifteenth-century Portuguese colonial accounts reported Christians on the southern coast who honoured Thomas as their founder. As early as Gregory of Tours in the fifth century, some Christians considered Thomas to have been martyred near Chennai (Madras).[199] By at least the fourth century Thomas was linked with peninsular India. But, as we shall see, this identification comes relatively late in the day.

The major source of this tradition is the apocryphal *Acts of Thomas*. Originally written in Syriac, as now seems likely, in the early third century AD, it was translated into Greek at an early date.[200] Through these and further translations, into Latin and most other languages of early Christianity, it became widely diffused in late antiquity. According to this text, the apostles at Jerusalem divide amongst themselves the lands for missionary travel. Thomas, to whom India falls, is unhappy:

> And India fell by lot to Judas Thomas the Apostle. And he was not willing to go, saying, 'I have not strength enough for this, because I am weak. And I am a Hebrew: how can I teach Indians?' And whilst Judas was reasoning thus, our Lord appeared to him in a vision of the night, and said to him: 'Fear not, Thomas, because my grace is with you.' But he would not be persuaded at all, saying: 'Whithersoever you will, our Lord, send me; only to India I will not go.'[201]

It is only when, by chance, an Indian merchant comes to Jerusalem that Judas is sold by Jesus as a slave and a carpenter, and thus goes to India somewhat against his will. This merchant is in the service of king Gudnaphar. Once in India, he builds a palace for the king; he is imprisoned because he donates his payment to the poor. The rest of the work consists of a series of 'acts', including the expelling of demons. In its contents the work is similar to the four other apocryphal *Acts*. His eventual martyrdom comes as a result of his success in converting various people, including the wife

[198] Brown, *Indian Christians*.

[199] Gregory of Tours, *Glor. mart.* 32 [PL 71, 733f]. This continues to be a cult site of Thomas today, along with another at Kalliene near Mumbai (Bombay). N. J. Thomas, *Die syrisch-orthodoxe Kirche der südindischen Thomas-Christen* (Würzburg: Augustinus, 1967); still fundamental is A. Mingana, 'The early spread of Christianity in India', *Bulletin of the John Rylands Library* 10 (1926), 435–96.

[200] A. F. J. Klijn, *The Acts of Thomas: introduction, text, and commentary*, 2nd edn (Leiden: Brill, 2003), pp. 3–4 and 8–9, revisited by Jan N. Bremmer, 'The Acts of Thomas: place, date and women', in *The apocryphal Acts of Thomas*, ed. Jan N. Bremmer (Leuven: Peeters, 2001), pp. 74–90; in what follows, I am indebted both to Klijn's edition and Bremmer's volume.

[201] Klijn, *Acts of Thomas*, p. 17.

of an officer of the king. Thomas preaches against marriage which, unless chaste, is a 'deed of shame' (e.g., chs. 14 and 54). The king, having ordered Thomas' execution, finally converts to Christianity after the dust from the apostle's grave cures his sick son. In the text conversion is expressed in terms of purity and abstinence from sex. The emphasis on purity and redemption from corruption has been seen in light of the encratitic strands of eastern Christianity.[202]

Compared with Philostratus' *Life of Apollonius*, there is little in this text that gives topographical specificity to India. However, what is especially interesting is Thomas' hesitation to go to India, even though he is otherwise a willing missionary. The Latin version adds an explanation:

> For that region is distant and rough, and the inhabitants of the place are evil and ignorant of the truth.[203]

The significance of this passage is that it brings the vague Christian missionary idea of India closer to the ethnographies surveyed in Chapter 2. It is thus no surprise that it is a Latin translation that adds this detail.

The tradition surrounding the *Acts* involved overland exchange networks between Mesopotamia and the Persian Gulf, and thus, in its earlier forms, points more strongly to the northwest than the south. The supposedly Indian names found in the text are identifiably Persian, an indication of northwestern links. The ruler mentioned in the text, Gundaphorus, has been identified from coin finds with Parthian dynasts of the first centuries BC and AD.[204] Thomas' itinerary from Mesopotamia to the Indus valley demonstrably coincided with the Persian Gulf sea-route. In this respect, Thomas' India occupies the same geographical space as Apollonius'.

Though the *Acts* have become well known over time, they represent only one strand of missionary history. On the other hand, some earlier strands of Christian tradition present Bartholomew as the first missionary. Eusebius reports that Pantaenus, a Stoic philosopher and Clement's teacher at Alexandria, was 'appointed to preach the gospel of Christ to the peoples of the east, and travelled as far as India'.[205] Having reached the subcontinent,

202 Y. Tissot, 'L'encratisme des Acts de Thomas', *ANRW* II.25 (1988), pp. 1415–30.

203 *De miraculis beati Thomae apostoli* 46.3: *regio enim illa longinqua et grauis est, incolae quoque loci illius iniqui et ignorantes sunt ueritatem*: Klaus Zelzer, *Die alten lateinischen Thomasakten* (Berlin: Akademie, 1977). An Arabic version goes even further: 'for they are hard men, like wild beasts, and it will be difficult for them to receive the hearing of the words of the Gospel' (*Preaching of Thomas, Arabic*, ed. Smith Lewis, p. 80). Klijn, *Acts of Thomas*, p. 19, lists examples from the Hebrew bible of rejections of the divine call.

204 Dihle, *Antike und Orient*, pp. 65–8; Raschke, 'New Studies', 1368–72.

205 *Hist. eccl.* 5.10 ὡς καὶ κήρυκα τοῦ κατὰ Χριστὸν εὐαγγελίου τοῖς ἐπ' ἀνατολῆς ἔθνεσιν ἀναδειχθῆναι, μέχρι καὶ τῆς Ἰνδῶν στειλάμενον γῆς; cf. Jer. *Ep.* 125.3.

he found that there was already a handful of Christians *in situ*. This group owed its origins to the apostle Bartholomew, who on his missionary journey to India had left behind a copy of Matthew's gospel written in Hebrew characters.[206] By contrast to the details of the apocryphal *Acts*, Eusebius has Thomas travel to Parthia, where eventually he dies a peaceful death. For Philostorgios also, writing shortly after AD 400, it was Bartholomew that brought the gospel to India (*Hist. eccl.* 18.33). The tradition concerning Bartholomew involves southern India, and is related to the monsoon route. Within that framework, a link with Alexandria is unmistakeable in the case of Pantaenus. It is in this light that we may understand a reference to Indian religion in an Egyptian papyrus of the second century AD: the mother of the Buddha is referred to as Isis (*P. Oxy.* 1380).

Related to this monsoon connection are the stories of the Indian Theophilus in the mid-fourth century. Born on the island of Dibus, he was brought to the court of Constantius II as a hostage and raised there, he later became a bishop and a counsellor to the emperor and ambassador. Whether the island of his birth should be identified with the Maldives or Socotra, it is clear that this figure also is linked with the monsoon route rather than the Persian Gulf route, and with the southern rather than the northwestern part of the subcontinent.[207]

How, then, can we explain the overlap of these traditions, whereby Thomas had become associated more with the south than the north of India?[208] How and why did Thomas come to displace Bartholomew as first missionary of the south? The change seems to have occurred in the third century, at a time when there was a clear drop in the monsoon trade. This was a period when the Roman state underwent economic and political turmoil, and the early Sassanid rulers extended their power to India via the Persian Gulf. It is thus reasonable to conclude, with Dihle and Van den Bosch, that by the end of the third century Christians in south India had stronger ties with the Syrian church of Sassanian Mesopotamia than Egypt and other parts of the eastern Roman empire.[209]

206 The language involved no doubt reflects the ancient view, current until recently, that the Gospel of Matthew was originally written in Hebrew. See further Jacob Neusner, 'The Jews east of the Euphrates', *ANRW* II.9.1 (1978), 46–69.

207 Gianfranco Fiaccadori, 'Teofilo Christiano', *SCO* 33 (1983), 295–331 and 34 (1984), 271–308; Albrecht Dihle, 'Die Sendung des Inders Theophilos', in *Antike und Orient*, pp. 102–8.

208 In one fourth-century attempt to align the diverging traditions on this score, Ephraim the Syrian refers to the moving of the relics from south to north: *carm. Nisib.* 42.

209 According to the *Chronicle of Seert*, David, bishop of Spasinou Charax (Basra) travelled to India during the years 295 and 300 (*Patrologia Orientalis* 4.236, 292). Circumstantial evidence suggests that this was more likely southern than northern India: Albrecht Dihle, 'Early Christianity in

What these divergent Christian geographies have in common is that India lies beyond easy reach, and thus represents the ultimate achievement of mission. For the Syrian tradition, a Parthian locale for Thomas would not have been far enough, and hence the tendency to associate him, more impressively, with India.

V.3. Belatedness and extrapolation

A further qualification to an unnecessarily linear model of cultural exchange is provided by those Indian sages coming to the Mediterranean world. Aristoxenus' story of Socrates' Indian interlocutor is the obvious instance to mention here. This story may be without parallel, but it serves as a salutary reminder of the ways in which modes of religious travel can coexist; and it also recalls the varieties of travel on the part of the Greek lawgivers, of whom some came originally from outside the polis, and others travelled away from their native poleis before returning.

Greek notice of Indian wisdom may begin with Alexander in so far as it focuses explicitly on Indian holy men, but it does gel with earlier ideas about Indian peacefulness (Hdt. 3.100). Brahmans made a big impression on Greeks and Romans because they represent a coming together of different strands: first, the virtue of distant people,[210] individually personalised here in the form of Dandamis; and, secondly, the wisdom of sages, especially of ancient eastern peoples, gained and reinforced by their marginal position relative to the Mediterranean world. They reflect the advantages, ambiguities and problems of both those elements: on the positive side, they had the *parrhêsia* of the Christian holy man, and yet they were also reminiscent of the Cynic sage, who was not an acceptable figure in his own right.

Perhaps, then, in characterising our eastern sages generally we must contrast them with some of their most frequent visitors from the west: the philosophers. These differed not only by their ethnic identity, but by their *paideia*. Gymnosophists and Brahmans bore wisdom, without having undergone the arduous process of learning, a process which is also important to the making of the Stoic sage, or of late antiquity's pagan holy man. It is in this sense that they offered an alternative kind of wisdom.

India' in *Ancient history*, ed. Hillard *et al.*, pp. 314–15. Also Lourens P. van den Bosch, 'India and the apostolate of St Thomas', in *The apocryphal Acts of Thomas*, ed. Jan N. Bremmer, pp. 125–48, esp. 144.

210 Notable examples are the Scythians and Germans: cf. Chapter 2, section III.4 above.

But this was not without its problems. Ultimately it is hard to get beyond the ambivalence of wisdom, especially in its alien form: whatever authority it might otherwise confer, it might still be uncomfortably close to the magical arts. The range of meanings in the word *Chaldaeus* is a case in point. In this chapter, the charges levelled against Apollonius and the consequent defensiveness they produce on the part of his hagiographer may be taken as the most obvious reminder (1.3). Yet on the other hand, we cannot forget that wisdom, perhaps by its very alienness, is potentially a source of authority: to wit the Egyptian travels of Solon as recounted in Herodotus, or Plato's own travels.

The different ways in which Calanus was presented show what kind of ambiguities we are dealing with here. As we have seen, he is explicitly praised or criticised by particular authors. His suicide was the kind of heroic action that made him memorable for Philo, for one, and for the majority of western medieval Alexander stories. If we bear in mind how much exhibitionism attended the death of Peregrinus in Lucian, or the feats of Syria's ascetic stars, we should not be surprised that this was to become his distinctive feature, and to some extent of Brahmans in general, if we are to judge from the Christian Fathers.

As we have seen, when Greeks first began to pay attention to India, it did not particularly seem to be a place of holiness. This may seem an improbable conclusion, given the importance of Brahmans and other ascetics in Hellenistic and Roman-period sources, beginning with the Alexander historians, and given the explicit presence of other 'alien wisdoms' of the east, from the time of Herodotus and Plato. If the conclusion of Chapter 1 is correct, then we would have to scrutinise the Achaemenid context within which Greeks first found out about India – a task which is beyond the limits of this book.

As a rider to this conclusion, it must be said that after Alexander's expedition, and with the raised Greek consciousness of and interest in a wider geographical world that attended it, India became largely a place of pilgrimage. From the Greek point of view, India's relative proximity to Babylonia and Mesopotamia brought with it an obvious comparison with Chaldaeans, Magians and Babylonians. These societies all shared the ability from an early period to write, and in each case the priestly caste was guardian not only of holiness but of holy texts specifically. In each case, there is in naming these groups some degree of confusion in the minds of Greeks and later Romans between the *ethnikon* and the designation of a social group. Yet ultimately, Brahmans were destined never to be as well known as Chaldaeans, or to come as much to the forefront of astrological thought as did Babylonian *mathematici*.[211] If astrology and other forms of divination were the preserve of Chaldaeans, then the most distinctive mark of Brahmans was their propensity for self-immolation. Hence the enduring fame of Calanus, however dubious his reputation as an ascetic. By the late-antique period it had become impossible to think of Brahmans without the intervening lens of Christian asceticism (and indeed of its polytheist competitors). Chaldaeans seem not to have been remembered so specifically by name, but more generally and vaguely as a group. If such terms are anything to go by (and they are no more than a vague pointer), the Brahmans never fully lost the exoticism of the unknown.

A major problem in the attempt to contextualise Roman ideas about India's holiness is the exceptionalism of Egypt. Apollonius' itinerary, which to some extent follows Alexander's, is one reason to consider the comparison; overlap in the use of the term Gymnosophist is another.[212] Certainly, some geographic features the two lands were known to have in common:[213] the enormous river(s), crocodiles, elephants, the priests and perhaps most importantly a sense of cultural antiquity. Yet Romans also had a keen sense of the ways in which Egypt was unique, particularly geographical features relating to the Nile, its flooding and its centrality to human settlement there. If we were to compare Egyptian religion with Indian, we would soon find that there is no Indian equivalent for the very monument-based Herodotean impression of Egypt. We can certainly talk about Roman Egyptomania in the aftermath of the Battle of Actium,[214] but it does not follow that there was a corresponding 'Indomania'. Nor is Indian writing an issue for Greeks and Romans. This latter fact comes as something of a surprise, given that writing was certainly known in Indian society by this time; sacred and state records were administered by Brahmans themselves. Yet this remains a blind spot in Greco-Roman ethnography of India.

To speak of the Brahmans and Gymnosophists as a Hellenistic fiction might seem unnecessarily skeptical, and to do so would be wrong in the most obvious sense. To be sure, a number of references in this chapter indicate that there is substantial independent Indian evidence to corroborate the

[211] In fact, with a few exceptions (e.g., Amm. Marc. 23.6.33 discussed above), Brahmans differ from the other groups in that they were *not* overtly linked with astrology in the eyes of Greeks and Romans, even though we know from surviving Sanskrit texts that there was an ancient tradition of Indian astrology. This factor, due perhaps to the relative lateness of their 'discovery', was probably a factor in the positive image they won among some Christians.

[212] Jer. *Ep.* 107.8.3; cf. *TLL* VI.2.2382.12ff. for supposed Ethiopian links.

[213] For Strabo's frequent references to Egypt in his description of India, compare Chapter 2, section III.6 above.

[214] See, e.g., Versluys, *Aegyptiaca Romana*; more generally, Curl, *Egyptomania*, esp. pp. 1–36.

existence of these groups. Their historical reality is beyond question, even if there are considerable difficulties in trying to distinguish the dynamics of ethnic identity or of social division. Yet on the other hand, we must be very aware of the ways in which these ascetics filled a need on the part of Greeks and Romans: the need for holy people, leading a gloriously independent existence within their own social worlds. This independence was accentuated by the spatial distance between Brahmans, as indeed of other eastern sages, from the Mediterranean world. As I have tried to suggest, this need had much to do with the 'revolutions of wisdom' (G. E. R. Lloyd's term) that accompanied the end of the classical polis; the crisis surrounding the Sophists, for one, underlined the need for a mystified kind of wisdom. Both of these features added much to the image of Brahmans as figures, symbols almost, of *parrhêsia*. Thus the question is not, in the first instance, whether texts like the *Alexander romance* and Palladius' 'reflect genuine knowledge about Indian philosophers',[215] but for what reasons Indian ascetics mattered, in so far as they did matter, to the authors and audiences of Greco-Roman works.

Not unlike Apollonius in the battle between pagans and Christians more than two centuries after his death, Brahmans came to be a screen onto which contemporary debates could be projected. In talking about Brahmans, there was not so much at stake; they were open to appropriation for the purposes of those choosing to write about them. Their inherent exoticism also meant that they were always open to being redescribed. It is in this way that they had any importance for Greeks and Romans: it is not so much a question of the Brahmans themselves, but of what underlying issues could be projected onto them. It is in order at this point to consider the image of Persians to emerge from Roman expressions of Mithraism. Cumont and other scholars of an earlier generation tended to take at face value the asserted historicity of their Persian connections. More recently, the work of Richard Gordon has cast doubt on these by stressing their cognitive value: they have emerged as an ethnic invention, answering Roman ideas of what Persian might be like. Indeed, at several points, this does coincide with historical reality; yet that does not detract from the fact of that ethnic invention.[216]

In particular, the Brahmans offered the opportunity to construct an ideal which was by turns unlikely and partly desirable: that of wisdom

[215] Stoneman, 'Brahmans', 500 (cf. 'Naked philosophers', 99).

[216] R. L. Gordon, 'The sacred geography of a *mithraeum*: the example of Sette Sfere,' *Journal of Mithraic Studies* 1 (1976), pp. 119–65, esp. 145–6; as well as his 'Reality, evocation and boundaries in the Mysteries of Mithras,' *Journal of Mithraic Studies* 3 (1980), 19–99, esp. 68. Cf. Momigliano, *Alien wisdom*, p. 141: 'What circulated in the Hellenistic world under the names of Zoroaster and of the Magi was a mixture of some genuine information with much arbitrary imagination.'

without *paideia*. In this sense we should read Philostratus' Indian sages as a counterpoint to the holy men of polytheist writers such as Eunapius and Plotinus, the distance between them lying, most pointedly, in the sphere of *paideia*. The Brahmans of Palladius' text are harder to fit into a milieu that makes them intelligible, given the complexities of that work. In the most obvious sense, they owe much to the Alexander tradition stretching back to long before the Christian period. On the other hand, if we accept that their social marginality and attendant *parrhêsia* stand out as their salient features, we see nothing so much as the overlap of different ascetic traditions. Our analysis has shown a variety of features, Christian and Cynic.

The problem of 'comparative asceticism' is in the end a difficult one, and one which militates against the formulation of sweeping theses in this conclusion.[217] If we must concede, first, that there are features of ascetic life which overlap between different cultures and religions; and, secondly, that both Philostratus' and even more so Palladius' texts were written in milieux which brought together various religious traditions, we see how hard it is to unravel. In purely historical terms, we cannot underestimate the practical difficulties involved in analysing ascetic practice across cultural boundaries. The ascetic repertoire all too often involves the same practices, such as mortification of the flesh, whatever their contextual differences may be. Whereas ethnographic writing in ancient (and indeed in modern) times often focuses on cultural difference, to the point of distortion, it is the task of the scholar to restore the balance by seeking the points of similarity between those speaking and those being spoken about. The critical problem that has emerged with Palladius' text is to diagnose its consciousness of similarity or difference.

VI. CONCLUSION

A number of important recent works have inquired into the influence of Indian culture on Greco-Roman.[218] In the religious sphere recent decades have seen, for example, Sedlar's exploration of the links and influences of Indian religion on Gnosticism.[219] The wide-ranging, valuable and more circumspect work of Halbfass also goes to some lengths in its use of

[217] For the difficulties involved in interpreting asceticism across cultural boundaries, see Wimbush and Valantasis, *Asceticism*.

[218] Representative of the tendency to interpret similarities as borrowing is David Karnos, 'On Apollonius, Pythagoras and the Jaina vision', in *Ionian philosophy*, ed. K. J. Boudouris (Athens: International Association for Greek Philosophy, 1989), pp. 211–17.

[219] Cf. E. Conze, 'Buddhism and Gnosis', in *Further Buddhist studies* (Oxford: Cassirer, 1975), pp. 15–32.

this approach. In this chapter issues of influence have been avoided as intractable, or at best speculative, in favour of a more limited scrutiny of Roman culture. While Greek and Roman sources frequently spoke of cultural influence in terms of parentage, such claims tend to be problematic and subject to specific and distorting agendas. These ancient paradigms of cultural interaction tend often to be suspiciously linear and unidirectional. Instead, the set of questions I have pursued here are more geared to those aspects of Greco-Roman culture which were addressed by 'India'. It seems more feasible to ask: What did India mean to Romans? (Again, in examining mostly sources of the Roman principate and empire, we find that the basic features go back to early Hellenistic times; again there is the doxographic problem.) In the end, the inquiry into Roman literary images of Indian wisdom or Indian holiness is an inquiry into the closely related questions, how did Roman culture react to India?; and how did Roman culture construct India?

This chapter, which set out in the first instance to examine Brahmans, has moved far and wide. Its breadth of focus has been necessary to understand the impression they made, and to outline some of the issues involved in their status as bearers of holiness. If it has been necessary to consider wisdom and holiness together, that zeugma should be seen as a feature of Greco-Roman conceptions of Indian sages. No one will deny that the Hellenistic period witnessed radical changes in the politics of knowledge. At a time of increased specialisation and professionalisation (a process going back to Aristotle and the Lyceum, and even earlier to the emergence of the Sophists), Near Eastern cultures appeared to honour special kinds of knowledge. If, to return to our earlier definition, wisdom is mystified knowledge, then these eastern kinds of wisdom remained pure for the reason that they seemed immune to the demystification that accompanied the Sophistic movement and the specialisation of Hellenistic science. Like Chaldaeans and other Near Eastern bearers of wisdom, the Brahmans offered the Hellenistic and later the Roman world the nostalgic opportunity to reinvent wisdom. But the effective failure to recognise the existence of Indian astrology saved the Brahmans from the negative Christian view of Chaldaean and Babylonian wisdom.

In an influential analysis of the Oedipus legend, J.-P. Vernant[220] speaks of the pervading ambiguity of Oedipus' character in Sophocles' *Oedipus tyrannus*: he is by turns at the lowest and highest social position, rescuer

[220] 'Ambiguity and reversal: on the enigmatic structure of *Oedipus Rex*', in Jean-Pierre Vernant and Pierre Vidal-Naquet, *Myth and tragedy in ancient Greece* (New York: Zone, 1988), pp. 113–40.

from and cause of the plague – these and other contradictions are tied up with his position, from birth, as an outsider to Thebes (though one originating, it is true, from within). After all, if spatial separation marks out something or someone as sacred, then that same separation can just as easily impart pariah status. A comparable ambiguity of the outsider can be found in differing views of the Brahmans, alien sages par excellence. The *parrhêsia* linked to their marginal status made it possible for them to express social criticism in ways which Cynic philosophers would have found commendable. In this way they were real bearers of objectivity. On the other hand, their behaviour, and particularly their propensity for suicide by fire, was dangerously close to the exhibitionism of Cynic sages. The figure of Calanus is a prime case of alien wisdom run wild, and in fact attracting varied responses: for Alexander in the *Alexander romance* this was an heroic act of endurance, whereas for Dandamis in Palladius it showed a lack of self-control, a dubious exhibitionism. Problems of this kind were, in general, very close to the ambiguity of the Cynic sage himself, if we consider their reception in late antiquity; or of the most extreme types of holy people, who were eventually to cause the church to promote monasticism as a means of exercising control over problematic would-be Anthonys. Ultimately, the behaviour of such people was both the crowning glory of the Christian faith, way beyond the time of the Great Persecution, and it was also a potential danger to society.

In sum, two features of the Brahmans should be emphasised in the profile that has emerged in the foregoing pages: first, their position on the margins of society, exaggerated by ethnic difference and geographical location; and, second, their indifference to *paideia*, in which respect they seemed to obviate a major problem faced by Christianity as it reached the higher social strata, namely the ongoing, often troubled attraction of classical *paideia* to aristocratic Christians such as Jerome and Augustine. Both of these were part of their image as social critics, and even reinforced it. In this regard they came, in late antiquity, to resemble by turns the Cynic sage and the Christian holy man. Of these ethnographic features, the second could conceivably have turned out differently, had Hellenistic Greeks shown greater interest than they did in learning the languages of their neighbours.[221]

[221] Momigliano, *Alien wisdom*, pp. 8 and 149.

Conclusion: Intersections of a discourse

1. MUTATIONS OF INDOGRAPHY

It is the imagination that has received the greatest prominence in this account. From a Roman point of view, India remained an 'oneiric horizon' (to borrow the subtitle of Jacques le Goff's classic essay), a moveable site of exotic fantasy that drifted in and out of focus at different times and in different contexts.[1] Nonetheless, four broad phases of Indography can be identified. The following periods are offered despite the abiding practical problem of distinguishing earlier authors from the contexts in which they are preserved. The first two belong, strictly speaking, to the prehistory of our topic: in these, spanning the archaic to Hellenistic periods of Greek literature, all the evidence is or originally was in Greek. But these two phases covered in Chapter 1 shaped the subsequent history of Indography.

1. In the Achaemenid phase, Greek images of India were formed in close relation to the Iranian world. This period deserves some emphasis in the history of Indography, since it has tended to be overlooked in favour of post-Achaemenid developments. We should not forget that when Scylax of Caryanda became the earliest Greek person known to have travelled to India, he travelled at the behest of Darius I. Furthermore, Herodotus' description, the earliest account to survive in a complete text, is part of a survey of Darius' satrapies. There are strong hints that the Achaemenid empire was the original setting of Indography; elements that were later embroidered and expanded upon were initially gathered here. Even if details were not filled in until later, this is where a basic framework of knowledge emerged. Starting with Ctesias, the marvel was to prove a major part of Indography, though at this stage expressed by verbal rather than visual

[1] Jacques le Goff, 'The medieval west and the Indian Ocean: an oneiric horizon', in his *Time, work and culture in the Middle Ages* (University of Chicago Press, 1980), pp. 189–200; cf. Monique Mund-Dopchie, 'L'invention de l'Inde merveilleuse. Structures de l'imaginaire et découverte de l'Autre lointain', in *Inde, Grèce ancienne*, ed. Jean-Claude Carrière *et al.* (1995), pp. 99–112.

means. The marvel, linked as it was with questions of truth and fiction, was to have special significance in historiography as well as the novel. On the other hand, Herodotus' account contains no mention of marvellous people. This contradiction suggests that there was no well worked-out discourse about India in the classical period of Greek literature; even, perhaps, that India carried no special significance to the Greek world at this time.

2. Once Alexander's expedition brought Greek and Macedonian troops to the Indus Valley, this was to change significantly. The expedition and its immediate aftermath considerably fleshed out the picture that had already emerged. But most importantly, this Hellenistic period reveals greater interest in distant lands generally, as well as greater interaction between Greek and non-Greek people of Asia. To a substantial degree, later writers were to look back on the expedition as the formative moment in Greco-Roman Indography, though in practice its elements were already familiar beforehand. The repertoire of monsters and marvellous people, already known to Ctesias, expanded considerably in this period. This was the time of Megasthenes, who, travelling just a few years after Alexander, was held up by several writers as an authority. With Megasthenes the question of truth and fiction came to be centred on autopsy. His mixed reputation in later times rested on contradictory principles: firstly, the marvellous nature of the material aroused many suspicions; secondly, the fact that he visited the court of Chandragupta Maurya lent him a high degree of credibility. This is also the period in which wisdom and holiness became key themes in Indography, stemming from Alexander's interview with the 'naked philosophers'. In one way or another, it was Alexander that was to cast a long shadow over subsequent accounts of India. In historical terms it is important here to emphasise an aspect of Alexander's expedition that the sources leave implicit: its continuities with the Achaemenid world. Indeed, it can be argued that in the geographic reach of his expedition Alexander was highly aware of the extent of the Achaemenid empire.

3. The Roman phase is characterised above all by the doxographic habit, by which writers on India appealed to their Hellenistic and even earlier predecessors. Often this was expressed amid the critical evaluation of different sources. The period of Augustus saw a substantial amount of rhetoric about empire: one of the functions of India was to provide a marker for the easternmost point of the Roman empire, just as it had marked the eastern limit of Alexander's expedition. In the eminent case of Trajan, standing at the head of the Persian Gulf, imperial ambitions were readily focused on Alexander. The rhetoric of imperial grandeur should more readily be understood in terms of the self-presentation of Roman emperors,

I have argued, than strategic military policy. Whenever Alexander was mentioned in such rhetoric, India was the most obvious symbol of his achievements.

This was also the time of heightened commercial contact, mostly through the monsoon route but also via the Persian Gulf and then across land to the Mediterranean. About the dynamics of these exchanges we can make some reconstruction from the varied evidence, archaeological, documentary and literary. It made remarkably little impact on Indography, but it was not completely without effect. Pliny's *Natural history* and even Strabo's *Geography* may rely in the first instance on book learning in their construction of authority; but they are by no means innocent of the new information brought by traders at this time, even if long-standing prejudice against traders brought disparaging comments from them on the subject. Rather, they reveal the combination of various strands of topographic and geographic knowledge. Perhaps surprisingly, it is the most technical and scientific of the imperial-age works concerning territorial space, namely Ptolemy's *Geography*, that makes the most obvious use of information only lately acquired in a commercial context. This would seem the best way to explain Ptolemy's knowledge of the Bay of Bengal. With the exception of Ptolemy, awareness of trade links with India was principally focused on the moral implications of Roman consumption, and reflected a Rome-centred perspective. But occasionally there are references to India itself as a place of luxurious consumption and its attendant immoralities (discussed below in relation to Curtius Rufus). In a few cases, this moralising view was contrasted with the mystifying sense of India as a place of wisdom and holiness.

4. The Christian phase of Indography rests heavily on an appropriation of the Augustan discourse about empire. This we see especially clearly in the early fifth-century world history by Orosius which, tellingly, begins with a description of the world. But it also contains traces of the very different discourse about Christian mission. The Macedonian's plea, 'Come and help us', in Paul's dream (*Acts* 16:10) was to have obvious implications for India, not only for its remoteness, but also for the tenacity of its religious traditions centred on Brahmans and Gymnosophists. Awareness of these charismatic individuals brought a sense that India needed more substantial and urgent missionary activity. This is expressed in the apocryphal *Acts of Thomas*. Philostratus' *Life of Apollonius* is an important work for this later phase of Indography, for its polytheist agenda apparently gives powerful evidence for Christian thinking about religious travel: it appears to be at the very edge of debates between polytheists and Christians.

The later Roman empire witnessed substantial interest in Indian wisdom. Much of this can be attributed to an ongoing fascination with Alexander, among both polytheists and Christians. But this fascination was more notional than the result of actual contact. Archaeological evidence suggests a slump in commerce in the third century AD. Though the late fifth and sixth centuries were to see something of a revival, as Cosmas Indicopleustes shows, it was never again to reach its apogee of the first two centuries AD. But by this period, nonetheless, India was already established in the mental matrix represented in the world maps of Orosius and Isidore, maps that were to have a profound influence on western medieval cartography. Its place at the far eastern edge was ensured by a number of related factors: its link with the earthly paradise, the persistence of the Alexander legend, and the need to balance the Pillars of Hercules on the western edges of the T-O schema with India on the eastern edge.

II. READERS, SPEAKERS AND POPULAR XENOLOGY

In order to give greater concreteness to the pattern described above, let us consider a passage that crystallises many of its issues, pointing both forward and backward in time. It serves also to summarise the concerns of this book as a whole.

Curtius Rufus interrupts his narrative of Alexander's campaign to offer an excursus about India (8.9.1–36). Unlike Arrian's lengthier *Indica*, this description is integrated into the history itself and shares its concerns and techniques. Assuming that Curtius was writing in the early years of Claudius' reign, we may fit him into the third, Roman phase of Indography outlined above; yet he should also be seen alongside the *Alexander romance* tradition, which was to have a textual diffusion of extraordinary complexity, involving several different languages, in the early centuries AD. Hence he looks forward, as a Latin writer about Alexander, also to the very substantial medieval tradition shared by many Christian writers.

Earlier, a distinction was made between texts in which India is central and those in which it is referred to merely in passing (introduction to Chapter 2). One of the several significant points about the Curtius passage is that it challenges that pattern: on the one hand, the Indian episode was by any account tremendously important to Alexander's expedition, and hence its significance to his narrative as a whole; on the other hand, this is merely an excursus, standing outside the narrative flow of the work, rather than a prime concern.

The passage has all the marks of a colourful and complex piece of Indography. Curtius begins with a description of the geographical orientation of India (chapters 1–2), before moving on at some length to rivers (4–11). Some natural historical details of flora and fauna are presented, some as divergences from nature (12–19). From land to people: the remaining chapters are devoted to Indian 'manners and customs', including an account of their taboo of tree-violation (34) and their astronomical pursuits (33, 35–36). A feature that marks out this description from others is the amount of attention given to the Indian king (23–30), whose lifestyle is presented in morally loaded language as a case of intentional *luxuria* exceeding the vices of all other peoples (23). A lengthy description of the king's life of luxury, which includes the conspicuous use of gold, silver, precious stones and aromatics, reaches a crescendo with his exploitation of women:

> The women cook food and pour wine, something that is copiously consumed by all Indians. Courtesans, calling on the gods of the night with a traditional incantation, take the king to bed once he is lulled by wine and sleep. (8.9.30)[2]

This is the very point at which Curtius uses strongly loaded moral language in making the transition from one kind of ethnographic language to another:

> Who would expect to find concern for wisdom among these vices? There is a wild and boorish group they call Wise Men.[3]

As in Cicero,[4] Indian virtue and Indian barbarism are mentioned in the same breath, almost as if one is dependent on the other. This we might call the paradox of alien wisdom. Both virtue and barbarism are most clearly seen at a distance, and from this point of view imply radical difference between Indians and Romans.

A number of features align this description with others. Winter and summer occur, as it were, in reverse order: here is the principle of inversion or *Verkehrte Welt*. It is a travesty of nature that brooks no explanation: 'there is no reason why nature inverts itself' (13).[5] In this way, India's profound strangeness is also a means of understanding it. By the same token, there are a number of comparisons, explicitly with the Nile of Egypt (9) and with the animals of Africa (17); implicitly perhaps with Persian hunting (28), Arabian unguents (27) and Babylonian or Chaldaean astronomy (35–36). If that were

[2] *feminae epulas parant; ab isdem uinum ministratur, cuius omnibus Indis largus est usus. regem mero somnoque sopitum in cubiculum pelices referunt patrio carmine noctium inuocantes deos.*

[3] *quis credat inter haec uitia esse sapientiae? unum agreste et horridum genus est quod Sapientes uocant.*

[4] *Tusc.* 5.77–78, discussed at Chapter 2, section II.3.

[5] *nec cur uerterit se causa natura.*

not enough, there is a hint of the question of the limits of knowledge, for the description of rivers ends with a reference to the many watercourses that are 'not known' (*ignobiles*, 11). There is an aphoristic formulation of the familiar Hippocratic idea of environmental determinism: 'in their case, as usually happens, the lie of the land shapes the talents of people' (20).[6]

All these features are familiar from the foregoing discussion. But the excursus differs from many other Indographies in one important aspect: at no point does Curtius mention his sources. This omission is, to a degree, a feature of Curtius' style, just as it is of Diodorus Siculus'. However, it does point us in the direction of a major context for the production and circulation of information about India: the rhetorical tradition, particularly as manifested in the *suasoria*. Historical topics were certainly a staple of higher training in rhetoric. But it is necessary here to understand the term historical in a loose manner: 'the imaginary themes (*plasmata*) of the declaimers are set vaguely in the classical past. Sometimes the mere addition of names turns them into a sort of rudimentary fiction.'[7] Of 350 surviving Greek declamations with historical topics, some twenty-five involve Alexander, the Persian and Peloponnesian wars being the other favourite topics. There can be no doubt that Curtius was influenced by the tradition of the Roman rhetorical schools, not merely in his speeches but in the dramatic quality of his writing generally.[8]

Nor is Curtius alone in this. In various genres, historical *exempla* were cited as a matter of course to prove a particular point. For example, the commonplace that 'nobody is without vice' is proven by the fact that Cato lacked moderation, Cicero steadfastness, and so on.[9] It is noteworthy that the first *suasoria* of the elder Seneca is addressed to Alexander, urging him not to sail the outer Ocean after traversing India. The geography implied by this is of course counter-factual when compared with the Alexander historians. Valerius Maximus also makes use of Alexander in a number of different contexts.[10] It is in cases such as these that we glimpse how ideas

6 *ingenia hominum, sicut ubique, apud illos locorum quoque situs format.*

7 D. A. Russell, *Greek declamation* (Cambridge University Press, 1983), p. 106; cf. Marrou, *History of education*, pp. 202–3; Robert A. Kaster, 'Controlling reason: declamation in rhetorical education at Rome', in *Education in Greek and Roman antiquity*, ed. Yun Lee Too (Leiden: Brill, 2001), pp. 317–37.

8 E.g., Elizabeth Baynham, *Alexander the Great: the unique history of Quintus Curtius* (Ann Arbor: University of Michigan Press, 1998), pp. 15–56.

9 Stanley F. Bonner, *Roman declamation in the late Republic and early Empire* (Liverpool University Press, 1949), pp. 61–2.

10 1.8 ext. 10 on Alexander's interview with Calanus. Otherwise India is worthy of mention on the subject of *sati* (2.6.14), for the Indians' powers of endurance (3.3 ext. 6) and their longevity (8.13 ext. 5) Valerius Maximus' work 'provided a stock of rhetorical illustrations and in its treatment of

about India were inculcated into the minds of young Romans and thereby naturalised. In this regard, it is not amiss to underline the related concepts of practice and everyday life, in view of both the breadth and the depth of their impact on Roman lives.[11]

This leads to the broader question that has all the features of the chicken and the egg: did Alexander account for Greek and Roman interest in India, or conversely was it India's enormity and remoteness that informed Alexander's reputation? This would be differently answered, depending on the kind of evidence examined. But it would seem reasonable to conclude that the reputations of Alexander and India were to some degree mutually constituting. True enough, there is much in the Indographic profile that does not necessarily have to be linked to him; but in practice much did, including the myths about Dionysus and Heracles.

Fragments emerged as a lowest common denominator in the examination of historians, geographers and natural historians, reflecting the need to appeal to authorities.[12] What we see here is a variation on the same principle, or perhaps even its antithesis. Extemporaneous public speaking on a topic such as India necessarily drew on a common fund of information shared by speaker and listener; by the same token, it provided the stimulus to fabricate material that would be appropriate to the context of any speech. Fabrication could be done on the basis also of other ethnographies, as we sense in Curtius' use of the comparative mode discussed above. The common fund of ethnographic discourse provided the material for a constant and flexible dialogue between India's strangeness and its capacity to be known. To be sure, this aspect of Roman rhetorical practice makes it difficult, or even unnecessary, to distinguish between producing and conveying information about India. In such cases, the two processes were combined in the practice of a speaker.

To focus on Roman practice is to broaden the question of map-mindedness. As we saw in Chapter 5, strong cases have variously been made that the Romans conceived of space in terms of itineraries or provinces; that they relied mainly on verbal or visual representations thereof.[13] The case of

this material demonstrated the various rhetorical shapes an *exemplum* could take and the ways to introduce, join, and conclude such stories.' Martin W. Bloomer, *Valerius Maximus and the rhetoric of the new nobility* (Chapel Hill: University of North Carolina Press, 1992), p. 2.

11 Two important articulations are Pierre Bourdieu, *Outline of a theory of practice*, tr. Richard Nice (Cambridge University Press, 1977); and Michel de Certeau, *The practice of everyday life*, tr. Steven F. Rendall (Berkeley: University of California Press, 1984).

12 Chapter 2, section III.7.

13 Thus, with markedly different emphases, Whittaker, *Rome and its frontiers*, pp. 63–87, and Talbert, 'Rome's provinces'; Brodersen, *Terra cognita*, and Talbert, 'Cartography and taste'.

Curtius' extract reminds us of the platitudinous manner in which visions of India were regenerated, with little interest in the addition of new information. Such practice of rhetoric was the means by which children learned about the *orbis terrarum* and their place in it, sometimes with the help of visual cues.[14] Nor is rhetoric purely an issue in the western Mediterranean: declamation was a major part of the Second Sophistic in the Greek east also. What we do see is that India was relevant to topics related to Alexander, to Rome's imperial grandeur, and often to the two in combination. The Peutinger map shows that such information could be represented visually, and that Alexander was sometimes part of those representations. Indicating both ports and the roads, the Peutinger map forms an obvious contrast with the *Periplus* and its coast-hugging route. Certainly Strabo, Pliny and Ptolemy give much greater prominence to coastal locations in covering peninsular India, whereas the Alexander historians present northern overland routes, but the overall point is clear: a variety of travels underlie such representations, and it is important to grasp the resulting coexistence of different kinds of geographical information underpinning any one such text or map. Ideas of India can clearly be traced in both the verbal and visual dimensions. The verbal far outweighs the visual in terms of surviving evidence, but nonetheless there are signs that the Romans did have a more developed tradition of visual maps than is sometimes supposed. To take the one example of a depiction of India, the Peutinger map, it appears that its presentation was geared more to an overall effect than to practical utility, even if actual travels ultimately underlie its production.

III. IMPERIAL MEMORIES OF ALEXANDER

The history of Indography in section I above proceeds in terms of the experience of actual travellers between the Mediterranean and the subcontinent. Yet the rhetoric discussed in section II, constituting the everyday practice of Romans, is of a different order of experience: less direct but more widely shared by the vast majority of Romans who did not themselves make the journey, but nonetheless were imaginatively engaged with the exotic effects of India. In recognising the difference between these registers of geographic information, it is useful to use a study of social memory: Wickham and Fentress draw on psychological studies to distinguish between episodic memory and semantic memory. The first of these is linked to specific learning episodes, whereas the second is tied to shared knowledge rather

14 *Panegyrici Latini* 9.20.2–9.21.3 Mynors.

than specific experiences necessarily.[15] Significantly, this distinction serves as a reminder of just how few persons would, in the course of a lifetime, make the journey from Italy, or any other part of the Mediterranean, all the way to south Asia. One such person would likely have been the *Periplus* author, to read between the lines of that text, and then even he probably started only in the Nile valley. Furthermore, there is no apparent evidence of south Asians in Rome, however cosmopolitan the city may have been by the first century AD.[16] For the vast majority, the stay-at-homes, on the other hand, representations of India would have functioned at the level of semantic memory. The shared knowledge of semantic memory was most obviously transmitted in the kind of rhetorical education discussed above.

In his varied guises, Alexander is a figure that spanned the distinction: the semantic memory of India was contingent on his supposed experience. This we have seen in each of the three contexts of Indography: most obviously in that of empire and wisdom, for it was only with his expedition that the Indian sages are reported in Greek sources. Most surprising in this regard is the context of commodities. Yet this too is clear when Pliny in his *Natural history* describes particular trees in relation to the expedition (12.21, 24; cf. 13.3). Pliny's learning certainly embraced the Alexander historians, but it is particularly striking to note the references to Alexander in two texts related to the long-distance exchange of goods: *Periplus* 41 and 47 and the briefer *Parthian stations* (as a city-founder: *FGrH* 781 F2.1).[17] Though the earliest surviving Alexander histories connect him with the sages, texts of the Second Sophistic present Alexander himself as a sage: Philostratus' *Life of Apollonius* and Plutarch's *On the fortune of Alexander*. This is part of the broadening scope of the image of Alexander in the Roman empire, and prepares the way for the medieval image of Alexander the pilgrim. In the Middle Ages his spiritual aspects come to predominate over his political and military leadership, as is evident in the Hereford map.

If we take Alexander as a symbol of empire, we quickly see that the imperial context embraces other registers of geographical knowledge: it would thus be wrong to think that the three contexts of Indography are fully parallel to each other. Beyond this consciousness of Alexander, there

15 James Fentress and Chris Wickham, *Social memory* (Oxford: Blackwell, 1992), p. 20, drawing on the work of Endel Tulving, e.g., his essay, 'Episodic and semantic memory', in *The organization of memory*, ed. Endel Tulving and Wayne Donaldson (New York: Academic Press, 1972), pp. 381–403.

16 David Noy, *Foreigners and Rome: citizens and strangers* (London: Duckworth, 2000). There is however some evidence for Indians in Alexandria: Dio Chrys. *Or.* 32.40.

17 Norbert Kramer, 'Das Itinerar Σταθμοί Παρθικοί des Isidor von Charax – Beschreibung eines Handelsweges?', *Klio* 85 (2003), 120–30 makes a strong case for a military rather than commercial route, yet the fragmentary nature of the text makes such clear-cut options implausible.

can be no doubt, at the level of a different kind of history, that the political revolution of the late first century BC made possible the much greater awareness of India in the first century AD. The *pax Romana* not only made possible the long-distance exchange of goods to a greater degree than earlier; it also heightened the demand for luxury goods in the Roman world, both in the city of Rome and in other urban centres. The ivory statuette found in Pompeii, though seemingly unmatched in the ancient Mediterranean, may be taken as representative of this.

In this broad sense, Said's model of Orientalism provides the inescapable framework of Roman Indography. It is appropriate to assert that the imperial context of geographical information deserves emphasis over others. This conclusion is in keeping with Foucault's definition of a discourse, a system of knowledge largely defined by the power relations in which it is entwined. To see empire as a transcendent context is, admittedly, to adopt an early twenty-first century view, by now several years into the Iraq War. There are however two points to be made in conclusion, both of them challenging or at least qualifying the orientalist model in its usual form.

First, the imperial context here is no simple matter of us-and-them. In a prominent position early in his work, Strabo speaks of the geographic knowledge made possible by the military successes of both the Roman and Parthian empires:

> Indeed, the ascendancy of the Romans and the Parthians have offered contemporary writers much geographical knowledge, just as Alexander's campaign did for earlier writers, as Eratosthenes points out. (1.2.1 C14)[18]

The point here is the inclusion of the Parthian empire within Strabo's purview. This is presumably linked to his Pontic origins, not far from the Parthian world at a time of its strength. Even if Strabo was writing at a time of détente between Parthia and Rome, this remains somewhat surprising – and beyond what the usual concepts of orientalism might lead one to expect.[19] To emphasise the Parthians in the economy of knowledge is thus to be alert to the funnelling effects of an intermediate people between Rome and India.

Second, Alexander in this account (especially in the first two chapters above) gives the Roman empire itself an ambiguous aspect. On the one

[18] καὶ γὰρ δὴ πολύ τι τοῖς νῦν ἡ τῶν Ῥωμαίων ἐπικράτεια καὶ τῶν Παρθυαίων τῆς τοιαύτης ἐμπειρίας προσδέδωκε, καθάπερ τοῖς μετὰ τὴν Ἀλεξάνδρου στρατείαν, ὥς φησιν ρατοσθένης.

[19] Much more crudely than Said's relational view of east and west, Samuel P. Huntington's concept of a *Clash of civilisations and the remaking of the world order* (New York: Simon and Schuster, 1996) has been embraced in the official rhetoric of the United States in the new millennium. Its essentialist tendencies are obvious.

hand, Rome became the empire *par excellence* for the west in the Middle Ages and beyond. This obvious point can hardly be disputed.[20] On the other hand, if Alexander himself was an important figure in the creation of an imperial ideology (and India a common element linking Alexander and the Roman empire), he was himself highly conscious of Achaemenid rulers. India is important here, for his desire (*pothos*) to conquer India and reach the end of the world seems very much like a desire to fulfil the achievements of the Persian kings. Alexander's concern with India seems, from this point of view, like the consummate performance of Iranian kingship. From a Roman viewpoint, India fulfilled imperial desires by virtue of the memory of Alexander, not least, as we have seen, in the case of the emperor Trajan.[21] Behind Trajan and, even more directly, behind Alexander, the Achaemenid precedent bulks large.

[20] The point has been often made, e.g. Michael W. Doyle, *Empires* (Ithaca: Cornell University Press, 1986), p. 25. Further, Thomas J. Barfield usefully distinguishes between primary and secondary empires: 'The shadow empires: imperial state formation along the Chinese-Nomad frontier', in *Empires*, ed. Alcock *et al.*, pp. 10–41. The Roman empire proper easily fits into the category of primary empire, by virtue of its diversity, communication and transportation networks, use of force and unity, and the unreality of Roman India should be seen in this light. Yet late antiquity saw the appropriation of such images by 'empires of nostalgia', i.e. secondary empires: see Chapter 5, section II.

[21] Chapter 5, section I.5.

Bibliography

ABBREVIATIONS

ANRW	*Aufstieg und Niedergang der römischen Welt*
CAH	*Cambridge Ancient History*
Cl. Phil.	*Classical Philology*
CQ	*Classical Quarterly*
DNP	*Der Neue Pauly*
FGrH	*Fragmente der griechischen Historiker, ed. F. Jacoby*
JHS	*Journal of Hellenic Studies*
JRS	*Journal of Roman Studies*
LIMC	*Lexicon Iconographicum Mythologiae Classicae*
RAC	*Reallexikon für Antike und Christentum*
RE	*Realencyclopädie der Klassischen Altertumswissenschaft*
TLL	*Thesaurus Linguae Latinae*

Abe, Stanley, 'Inside the wonder house: Buddhist art and the West', in Donald S. Lopez (ed.), *Curators of the Buddha: the study of Buddhism under colonialism*, University of Chicago Press, 1995, pp. 63–106.

Abeydeera, Ananda, 'The geographical perceptions of India and Ceylon in the *Periplus Maris Erythraei* and in Ptolemy's *Geography*', *Terrae Cognitae* 30 (1998), 1–25.

Adams, Colin, and Ray Laurence (eds.), *Travel and geography in the Roman empire*, London: Routledge, 2001.

Adler, William, *Time immemorial: archaic history and its sources in Christian chronography from Julius Africanus to George Syncellus*, Washington: Dumbarton Oaks, 1989.

Aerts, W. J., 'Alexander the Great and ancient travel stories', in Zweder von Martels (ed.), *Travel fact and travel fiction*, Leiden: Brill, 1994, pp. 30–8.

Aitken, Molly Emma (ed.), *Meeting the Buddha: on pilgrimage in Buddhist India*, New York: Riverhead, 1995.

Alcock, Susan E., 'The reconfiguration of memory in the eastern Roman empire', in Alcock *et al.* (eds.), *Empires*, 2001, pp. 323–50.

Alcock, Susan E., Terence N. D'Altroy, Kathleen D. Morrison and Carla M. Sinopoli (eds.), *Empires: perspectives from archaeology and history*, Cambridge University Press, 2001.

Alcock, Susan E., John F. Cherry and Jaś Elsner (eds.), *Pausanias: travel and memory in Roman Greece*, Cambridge University Press, 2001.

Alexander, Philip S., 'Notes on the *imago mundi* of the Book of Jubilees', *Journal of Jewish Studies* 33 (1982), 197–213.

'Early Jewish geography', in D. N. Freedman (ed.), *Anchor Bible dictionary*, vol. II, New York and London: Doubleday, 1992, pp. 977–88.

Allchin, F. R., 'Upon the antiquity and methods of gold mining in ancient India', *Journal of the Economic and Social History of the Orient* 5 (1962), 195–211.

Alonso-Núñez, J. M., 'An Augustan world history: the *Historiae Philippicae* of Pompeius Trogus', *Greece and Rome* 34 (1987), 56–72.

'Orosius on contemporary Spain', in Carl Deroux (ed.), *Studies in Latin literature and Roman history*, vol. V, Brussels: Collection Latomus, 1989, pp. 491–507.

Alston, Richard, 'Trade and the city in Roman Egypt', in Helen Parkins and Christopher Smith (eds.), *Trade, traders and the ancient city*, London: Routledge, 1998, pp. 168–202.

Anastos, M. V., 'The Alexandrian origin of the *Christian topography* of Cosmas Indicopleustes', *Dumbarton Oaks Papers* 3 (1946), 73–80.

Anderson, Benedict, *Imagined communities: reflections on the origins and spread of nationalism*, rev. edn, New York: Verso, 1991.

Anderson, Graham, *The Second Sophistic: a cultural phenomenon in the Roman Empire*, London: Routledge, 1993.

Ando, Clifford, *Imperial ideology and provincial loyalty in the Roman empire*, Berkeley: University of California Press, 2000.

André, Jacques, 'La conception de l'État et de l'Empire dans la pénsée gréco-romaine des deux premiers siècles de notre ère', *ANRW* II.30.1 (1981), 3–73.

André, Jacques, and Jean Filliozat, *L'Inde vue de Rome*, Paris: Belles Lettres, 1986.

André, Jean-Marie, and Marie-Françoise Baslez, *Voyager dans l'antiquité*, Paris: Fayard, 1993.

Andreassi, Mario, 'Il mimo tra "consumo" e "letteratura": *Charition* e *Moicheutria*', *Ancient Narrative* 2 (2002), 30–46.

Appadurai, Arjun (ed.), *The social life of things: commodities in cultural perspective*, Cambridge University Press, 1986.

Arens, William, *The man-eating myth: anthropology and anthropophagy*, Oxford University Press, 1979.

Armstrong, A. H., 'Plotinus and India', *CQ* 30 (1936), 22–28.

Asche, Ulrike, *Roms Weltherrschaftsidee und Aussenpolitik in der Spätantike im Spiegel der Panegyrici Latini*, Bonn: Habelt, 1983.

Asheri, David, and Silvio Medaglia (eds.), *Erodoto. Le storie, Libro III*, Milan: Mondadori, 1990, vol. III.

Assmann, Jan, 'Translating gods: religion as a factor of cultural (un)translatability', in Sanford Budick and Wolfgang Iser (eds.), *The translatability of cultures*, Stanford University Press, 1996, pp. 25–36.

Astin, A. E., *Cato the Censor*, Oxford: Clarendon, 1978.

Athanassiadi, Polymnia, *Julian and Hellenism: an intellectual biography*, Oxford: Clarendon, 1981.

Atkinson, John E., 'Q. Curtius Rufus' *Historiae Alexandri Magni*', *ANRW* II.34.4 (1998), 3447–83.

Auberger, Janick, 'Ctésias et l'Orient', *Topoi* 5.2 (1995), 337–52.

Austin, N. J. E., and Boris Rankov, *Exploratio: military and political intelligence in the Roman world from the second Punic War to the Battle of Adrianople*, London: Routledge, 1995.

Badian, E., *Roman imperialism in the late republic*, 2nd edn, Ithaca: Cornell University Press, 1968.

'Nearchus the Cretan', *Yale Classical Studies* 24 (1975), 147–70.

'Alexander in Iran', in *Cambridge History of Iran*, Cambridge University Press, 1985, vol. II, pp. 420–501.

'Alexander at Peucelaotis', *Classical Quarterly* 37 (1987), 117–38.

'The King's Indians', in Will (ed.), *Alexander der Grosse*, 1998, pp. 205–24.

Baglivi, Nicola, 'Osservazioni su paneg. VII(6).9', *Orpheus* n.s. 7 (1986), 329–37.

Ball, Warwick, *Rome in the east: the transformation of an empire*, London: Routledge, 2000.

Balsdon, J. P. V. D., *Romans and aliens*, Chapel Hill: University of North Carolina Press, 1979.

Barber, E. J. W., *Prehistoric textiles*, Princeton University Press, 1991.

Barchiesi, Alessandro, *The poet and the prince: Ovid and Augustan discourse*, Berkeley: University of California Press, 1997.

Barfield, Thomas J., 'The shadow empires: imperial state formation along the Chinese-Nomad frontier', in Alcock *et al.* (eds.), *Empires* (2001), pp. 10–41.

Barnes, Timothy D., *Constantine and Eusebius*, Cambridge, MA: Harvard University Press, 1981.

Barth, Fredrik (ed.), *Ethnic groups and boundaries*, Baltimore: Johns Hopkins University Press, 1982.

Barton, Tamsyn, *Ancient astrology*, London: Routledge, 1994.

Bartsch, Shadi, *Decoding the ancient novel: the reader and the role of description in Heliodorus and Achilles Tatius*, Princeton University Press, 1989.

Basham, A. L., *The wonder that was India*, rev. edn, New York: Hawthorn, 1963.

Baxter, Ron, 'Learning from nature: lessons in virtue and vice in the *Physiologus* and bestiaries', in Colum Hourihane (ed.), *Virtue and vice: the personifications in the Index of Christian Art*, Princeton University Press, 2000, pp. 29–41.

Baynham, Elizabeth, *Alexander the Great: the unique history of Quintus Curtius*, Ann Arbor: University of Michigan Press, 1998.

Beagon, Mary, *Roman nature: the thought of Pliny the Elder*, Oxford: Clarendon, 1992.

Beard, Mary and John North (eds.), *Pagan priests: religion and power in the ancient world*, London: Duckworth, 1990.

Bedini, Silvio A., *The Pope's elephant*, New York: Penguin, 2000.

Begley, Vimala, *The ancient port of Arikamedu: new excavations and researches, 1989–1992*, Pondichéry: École française d'Extrême-Orient, 1996.

Begley, Vimala and Richard D. De Puma (eds.), *Rome and India: the ancient sea trade*, Madison: University of Wisconsin Press, 1991.

Bennett, Julian, *Trajan, optimus princeps*, 2nd edn, Bloomington: Indiana University Press, 2001.

Berg, Beverley, 'Dandamis: an early Christian portrait of Indian ascetism', *Classica et Mediaevalia* 1970 (31), 269–305.

'The letter of Palladius on India', *Byzantion* 44 (1974), 5–16.

Berggren, J. Lennart, and Alexander Jones, *Ptolemy's* Geography: *an annotated translation of the theoretical chapters*, Princeton University Press, 2000.

Berghoff, Wilhelm, *Palladius, de gentibus Indiae et Bragmanibus*, Meisenheim: Hain, 1967.

Bernal, Martin, *Black Athena writes back*, Durham, NC: Duke University Press, 2002.

Bernard, Paul, 'The Greek kingdoms of central Asia', in János Harmatta (ed.), *History of civilizations of Central Asia*, vol. II: *The development of sedentary civilizations, 700 BC to AD 250*, Paris: UNESCO, 1994, pp. 99–130.

'Aï Khanoum en Afghanistan hier (1964–1978) et aujourd'hui (2001): un site en péril. Perspectives d'avenir', *Comptes rendus de l'Académie des Inscriptions et Belles-Lettres* (2001), 971–1029.

Bertrand, A. C., 'Stumbling through Gaul: maps, intelligence and Caesar's *Bellum Gallicum*', *Ancient History Bulletin* 11 (1997), 107–22.

Berve, Helmut, *Das Alexanderreich auf prosopographischer Grundlage*, 2 vols. Munich: Beck, 1926.

Bevan, E. R., 'India in early Greek and Latin literature', in E. J. Rapson (ed.), *The Cambridge history of India*, rev. Indian repr. edn, Delhi: Chand, 1962, vol. I, pp. 351–83.

Bichler, Reinhold, *Herodots Welt. Der Aufbau der Historie am Bild der fremden Länder und Völker, ihrer Zivilisation und ihrer Geschichte*, Berlin: Akademie, 2000.

Bickerman, E., 'Origines gentium', *Cl. Phil.* 47 (1952), 65–81.

Bickerman, E. J., *The Jews in the Greek age*, Cambridge, MA: Harvard University Press, 1988.

Bienkowski, Piotr, *Les Celtes dans les arts mineurs gréco-romains*, Cracow: Polish Academy, 1928.

Bidez, Joseph, and Franz Cumont, *Les mages hellenisés. Zoroastre, Ostanès et Hystaspe d'après la tradition grecque*, Paris: Belles Lettres, 1938.

Bigwood, J. M., 'Ctesias' *Indica* and Photius', *Phoenix* 43 (1989), 302–16.

'Ctesias' parrot', *CQ* 43 (1993), 321–7.

'Ctesias, his royal patrons and Indian swords', *JHS* 115 (1995), 135–40.

Bloomer, Martin W., *Valerius Maximus and the rhetoric of the new nobility*, Chapel Hill: University of North Carolina Press, 1992.

Boardman, John, *The diffusion of classical art in antiquity*, Princeton University Press, 1994.

Bongard-Levin, Grigorij M., and Sergei Karpyuk, 'Nachrichten über den Buddhismus in der antiken und frühchristlichen Literatur', in Bernd Funck (ed.), *Hellenismus: Beiträge zur Erforschung von Akkulturation und politischer Ordnung in den Staaten des hellenistischen Zeitalters*, Tübingen: Mohr Siebeck, 1996, pp. 701–12.

Bonner, Stanley F., *Roman declamation in the late Republic and early Empire*, Liverpool University Press, 1949.

Boorstin, Daniel J., *The discoverers*, New York: Random, 1983.

Bopearachchi, Osmund, and Wilfried Pieper, *Ancient coins from Sri Lanka*, Turnhout: Brepols, 1998.

Borst, Arno, *Das Buch in der Naturgeschichte. Plinius und seine Leser im Zeitalter des Pergaments*, Heidelberg: Winter, 1984.

Bosch, Lourens P. van den, 'India and the apostolate of St Thomas', in Bremmer (ed.), *The apocryphal Acts of Thomas*, 2001, pp. 125–48.

Bosworth, A. B., *A historical commentary on Arrian's* History of Alexander, 2 vols. Oxford: Clarendon, 1980–.

Conquest and empire: the reign of Alexander the Great, Cambridge University Press, 1988.

From Arrian to Alexander: studies in historical interpretation, Oxford: Clarendon, 1988.

'Aristotle, India, and the Alexander historians', *Topoi* 3 (1993), 407–24.

Alexander and the East: the tragedy of triumph, Oxford: Clarendon, 1996.

'The historical setting of Megasthenes' *Indica*', *Cl. Phil.* 91 (1996), 113–27.

'Calanus and the Brahman opposition', in Will (ed.), *Alexander der Grosse*, 1998, pp. 173–204.

'Augustus, the *Res Gestae* and Hellenistic theories of kingship', *JRS* 89 (1999), 1–18.

'*Plus ça change* . . . Ancient historians and their sources', *Classical Antiquity* 22 (2003), 167–97.

Bourdieu, Pierre, *Outline of a theory of practice*, tr. Richard Nice, Cambridge University Press, 1977.

Boussac, Marie-François, and Jean-François Salles (eds.), *A gateway from the eastern Mediterranean to India: the Red Sea in antiquity*, Delhi: Manohar, 2004.

Bové, A., 'Discourse', in Frank Lentricchia and Thomas McLaughlin (eds.), *Critical terms for literary study*, 2nd edn, University of Chicago Press, 1995, pp. 50–65.

Bowersock, Glen W., *Greek Sophists in the Roman Empire*, Oxford: Clarendon, 1969.

Julian the Apostate, Cambridge, MA: Harvard University Press, 1978.

Roman Arabia, Cambridge, MA: Harvard University Press, 1983.

'Herodotus, Alexander, and Rome', *The American Scholar* 58 (1989), 407–14.

Hellenism in late antiquity, Ann Arbor: University of Michigan Press, 1990.

'Dionysus as an epic hero', in Hopkinson (ed.), *Studies*, 1994, pp. 156–66.

'Jacoby's fragments and two Greek historians of pre-Islamic Arabia', in Most (ed.), *Collecting fragments*, 1997, pp. 173–85.

'Philosophy and the Second Sophistic', in Gilian Clark and Tessa Rajak (eds.), *Philosophy and power in the Greco-Roman world: essays in honour of Miriam Griffin*, Oxford: Clarendon, 2002, pp. 157–70.

Bowie, E. L., 'Greeks and their past in the Second Sophistic', in M. I. Finley (ed.), *Studies in ancient society*, London: Routledge and Kegan Paul, 1974, pp. 166–209, originally in *Past and Present* 46 (1970), 3–41.

'Apollonius of Tyana: tradition and reality', *ANRW* II.16.2 (1978), 1652–99.

Bowie, Ewen L. and Stephen J. Harrison, 'The romance of the novel', *JRS* 83 (1993), 159–78.

Bowman, Alan K. and Greg Woolf (eds.), *Literacy and power in the ancient world*, Cambridge University Press, 1994.

Bradley, K. R., 'On the Roman slave supply and slavebreeding', in M. I. Finley (ed.), *Classical slavery*, London: Frank Cass, 1987, pp. 42–64.

Slavery and society at Rome, Cambridge University Press, 1994.

Branham, R. Bracht and Marie-Odil Goulet-Cazé (eds.), *The Cynics*, Berkeley: University of California Press, 1996.

Braudel, Fernand, *The Mediterranean and the Mediterranean world in the age of Philip II*, tr. Siân Reynolds, 2 vols., London: Collins, 1972.

Braund, David, 'Fish from the Black Sea: classical Byzantium and the Greekness of trade', in John Wilks, David Harvey and Mike Dobson (eds.), *Food in antiquity*, University of Exeter Press, 1995, pp. 162–70.

Breckenridge, Carol, and Peter van der Veer (eds.), *Orientalism and the postcolonial predicament: perspectives on South Asia*, Philadelpia: University of Pennsylvania Press, 1993.

Breloer, Bernhard, *Kautaliya-Studien*, 2 vols. Bonn: Schroeder, 1927–8.

Breloer, Bernhard, and Franz Bömer (eds.), *Fontes Historiae Religionum Indicarum*, Bonn: Röhrscheid, 1939.

Bremmer, Jan, 'Walking, standing, and sitting in ancient Greek culture', in Jan Bremmer and H. Roodenburg (eds.), *A cultural history of gesture*, Ithaca: Cornell University Press, 1992, pp. 15–35.

Bremmer, Jan N. (ed.), *The apocryphal Acts of Thomas*, Leuven: Peeters, 2001.

Briant, Pierre, *From Cyrus to Alexander: a history of the Persian empire*, tr. Peter T. Daniels, Winona Lake, IN: Eisenbrauns, 2002.

Bridges, Margaret, and J. Christoph Bürgel (eds.), *The problematics of power: eastern and western representations of Alexander the Great*, Bern: Lang, 1996.

Brincken, Anna-Dorothee von den, *Kartographische Quellen. Welt-, See- und Regionalkarten*, Turnhout: Brepols, 1988.

Brocker, Max, *Aristoteles als Alexanders Lehrer in der Legende* (diss. Bonn 1965).

Brodersen, Kai, 'Neue Entdeckungen zu antiken Karten', *Gymnasium* 108 (2001), 137–48.

'The presentation of geographical knowledge for travel and transport in the Roman world: *itineraria non tantum adnotata sed etiam picta*', in Adams and Laurence (eds.), *Travel and geography*, 2001, pp. 7–21.

Terra cognita. Studien zur römischen Raumerfassung, 2nd edn, Hildesheim: Olms, 2003.

Brown, L. W., *The Indian Christians of Saint Thomas*, Cambridge University Press, 1956.
Brown, Peter, *Augustine of Hippo*, London: Faber, 1967.
The making of late antiquity, Cambridge, MA: Harvard University Press, 1978.
The cult of the saints, University of Chicago Press, 1981.
'The rise and function of the holy man', in *Society and the holy in late antiquity*, Berkeley: University of California Press, 1982, pp. 103–52.
'The saint as exemplar in late antiquity', *Representations* 1 (1983), 1–25.
The body and society, New York: Columbia University Press, 1988.
Power and persuasion in late antiquity: towards a Christian empire, Madison: University of Wisconsin Press, 1992.
Brown, Truesdell S., *Onesicritus*, Berkeley: University of California Press, 1949.
'The reliability of Megasthenes', *American Journal of Philology* 76 (1955), 18–33.
'The merits and weaknesses of Megasthenes', *Phoenix* 11 (1957), 12–24.
'Suggestions for a vita of Ctesias of Cnidos', *Historia* 27 (1978), 1–19.
Brunswig, R. H., A. Parpola and D. Potts, 'New Indus type and related seals from the Near East', in Daniel T. Potts (ed.), *Dilmun: new studies in the archaeology and early history of Bahrain*, Berlin: Reimer, 1983, pp. 101–15.
Brunt, P. A., 'On historical fragments and epitomes', *CQ* 30 (1980), 477–94.
(ed. and tr.), *Arrian*, 2 vols. Loeb Classical Library, Cambridge, MA: Harvard University Press, 1983.
Roman imperial themes, Oxford: Clarendon, 1990.
'The bubble of the Second Sophistic', *Bulletin of the Institute of Classical Studies* 39 (1995), 25–52.
Bunbury, E. H., *A history of ancient geography among the Greeks and Romans from the earliest ages till the fall of the Roman empire*, 2nd edn, New York: Dover, 1959 [1883].
Burkert, Walter, 'Platon oder Pythagoras? Zum Ursprung des Wortes Philosophie', *Hermes* 88 (1960), 159–77.
Lore and science in ancient Pythagoreanism, Cambridge University Press, 1972.
Greek religion, Cambridge, MA: Harvard University Press, 1985.
'Herodot als Historiker fremder Religionen', in *Hérodote et les peuples non grecs*, Vandoeuvres: Fondation Hardt, 1988, pp. 1–32.
Burn, A. R., *Persia and the Greeks*, 2nd edn, London: Duckworth, 1984.
Burstein, Stanley M., 'Callisthenes and Babylonian astronomy', *Échos du monde classique* 28 (1984), 71–4.
The Hellenistic age, Cambridge University Press, 1985.
Ancient African civilizations, Princeton: Markus Wiener, 1998.
Bynum, Caroline W., 'Wonder', *American Historical Review* 102 (1997), 1–26.
Cameron, Averil, *Christianity and the rhetoric of empire*, Berkeley: University of California Press, 1991.
Campbell, Brian, *The writings of the Roman land surveyors: introduction, text, translation and commentary to the Agrimensores*, London: Society for the Promotion of Roman Studies, 2000.

Campbell, Tony, *The earliest printed maps, 1472–1500*, Berkeley: University of California Press, 1987.

Carandini, Andrea *et al.*, *Filosofiana, the villa of Piazza Armerina: the image of a Roman aristocrat at the time of Constantine*, Palermo: Flaccovio, 1982.

Carey, Sorcha, *Pliny's catalogue of culture: art and empire in the* Natural history, Oxford University Press, 2003.

Carpenter, Edmund, *Oh, what a blow that phantom gave me!*, New York: Holt, Rinehart and Winston, 1973.

Carpenter, Thomas H., *Dionysian imagery in Archaic Greek art*, Oxford: Clarendon, 1997.

Carrier, James G. (ed.), *Occidentalism: images of the west*, Oxford: Clarendon, 1995.

Carrière, Jean-Claude, Evelyne Geny, Marie-Madeleine Mactoux and Françoise Paul-Lévy (eds.), *Inde, Grèce ancienne. Regards croisés en anthropologie de de l'espace. Actes de Colloque international, Besançon 4–5 décembre 1992*, Paris: Belles Lettres, 1995.

Carson, Anne, *Eros the bittersweet*, Princeton University Press, 1986.

Cary, George, *The medieval Alexander*, Cambridge University Press, 1956.

Cary, M., *The ancient explorers*, rev. by E. H. Warmington, Baltimore: Penguin, 1963.

Caseau, Béatrice, 'Sacred landscapes', in G. W. Bowersock *et al.* (eds.), *Late antiquity: a guide to the postclassical world*, Cambridge, MA: Harvard University Press, 1998, pp. 21–59.

Casson, Lionel (ed.), *The Periplus Maris Erythraei*, Princeton University Press, 1989.

Casson, Lionel, *Ships and seafaring in ancient times*, Austin: University of Texas Press, 1994.

de Certeau, Michel, *The practice of everyday life*, tr. Steven F. Rendall, Berkeley: University of California Press, 1984.

Chadwick, Owen, *Western asceticism*, Philadelphia: Westminster, 1958.

Champion, Craige B. (ed.), *Roman imperialism: readings and sources*, Oxford: Blackwell, 2004.

Charlesworth, J. H., *The Old Testament Pseudepigrapha*, Garden City, NY: Doubleday, 1983, pp. 1–7.

Charlesworth, M. P., *Trade routes and commerce of the Roman Empire*, 2nd edn, New York: Cooper Square, 1970.

Chaudhuri, K. N., *Trade and civilisation in the Indian Ocean: an economic history from the rise of Islam to 1750*, Cambridge University Press, 1985.

Chibnall, Marjorie, 'Pliny's *Natural history* and the Middle Ages', in T. A. Dorey (ed.), *Empire and aftermath*, London: Routledge and Kegan Paul, 1975, pp. 57–78.

Christ, Matthew R., 'Herodotean kings and historical inquiry', *Classical Antiquity* 13 (1994), 167–202.

Chuvin, Pierre, 'Local traditions and classical mythology in the *Dionysiaca*', in Hopkinson (ed.), *Studies*, 1994, pp. 167–76.

Cimino, Rosa Maria (ed.), *Ancient Rome and India: commercial and cultural contacts between the Roman world and India*, Delhi: Munshiram Manoharlal, 1994.

Clark, Elizabeth A., 'The ascetic impulse in religious life: a general response', in Richard Valantasis and Vincent A. Wimbush (eds.), *Asceticism*, Oxford: Clarendon, 1995, pp. 505–10.

Clarke, Katherine, 'In search of the author of Strabo's *Geography*', *JRS* 87 (1997), 92–110.

Between geography and history: Hellenistic constructions of the Roman world, Oxford: Clarendon, 1999.

'Universal perspectives in historiography', in Christina Shuttleworth Kraus (ed.), *The limits of historiography: genre and narrative in ancient historical texts*, Leiden: Brill, 1999, pp. 249–79.

'An island nation: re-reading Tacitus' *Agricola*', *JRS* 91 (2001), 94–112.

Clay, Diskin, and Andrea Purvis, *Four island utopias*, Newburyport, MA: Focus, 1999.

Clifford, James, *The predicament of culture: twentieth-century ethnography, literature and art*, Cambridge, MA: Harvard University Press, 1988.

Routes: travel and translation in the late twentieth century, Cambridge, MA: Harvard University Press, 1997.

Clifford, James, and George E. Marcus (eds.), *Writing culture: the poetics and politics of ethnography*, Berkeley: University of California Press, 1986.

Cohn, Bernard S., *An anthropologist among the historians and other essays*, Oxford University Press, 1987.

Coleman, K. M., 'Fatal charades: Roman executions staged as mythological enactments', *JRS* 80 (1990), 44–73.

Coleman-Norton, P. R., 'The authorship of the *Epistola de Indicis gentibus et de Bragmanibus*', *Cl. Phil.* 21 (1926), 154–60.

Colledge, Malcolm A. R., *The Parthians*, New York: Praeger, 1967.

Colpe, Carsten, 'Von Alexander dem Grossen zum Grossmongul Gehangir. Die Frage nach einer indischen Enthellenisierung des Weltherrschaftsgedankens', in Glenn W. Most *et al.* (eds.), *Philanthropia kai Eusebeia*, Göttingen: Vandenhoeck & Ruprecht, 1993, pp. 46–73.

Comfort, Anthony, Catherine Abadie-Reynal and Rifat Ergeç , 'Crossing the Euphrates in antiquity: Zeugma seen from space', *Anatolian Studies* 50 (2000), 99–126.

Comfort, Anthony, and Rifat Ergeç , 'Following the Euphrates in antiquity: north–south routes around Zeugma', *Anatolian Studies* 51 (2001), 19–49.

Conte, Gian Biagio, *Genres and readers: Lucretius, love elegy, Pliny's encyclopedia*, tr. Glenn W. Most, Baltimore: Johns Hopkins University Press, 1994.

Latin literature: a history, Baltimore: Johns Hopkins University Press, 1994.

Conze, E., 'Buddhism and Gnosis', in *Further Buddhist studies*, Oxford: Clarendon, 1975, pp. 15–32.

Coomaraswamy, Ananda K., *Yaksas*, New Delhi: Munshiram Manoharlal, 1971.

Cornell, T. J., *The beginnings of Rome: Italy and Rome from the Bronze Age to the Punic Wars (c. 1000–264 BC)*, London: Routledge, 1995.

Courtney, E., *A Commentary on the Satires of Juvenal*, London: Athlone, 1980.

Cox, Patricia L., *Biography in late antiquity*, Berkeley: University of California Press, 1983.

Craib, Raymond, 'Cartography and power in the conquest and creation of New Spain', *Latin American Research Review* 35.1 (2000), 7–36.

Crawford, Harriet, *Dilmun and its Gulf neighbours*, Cambridge University Press, 1998.

Crook, J. A., 'Political history, 30 BC to AD 14', in *CAH*, 2nd edn (1996), vol. X, 70–112.

Cunliffe, Barry, *The extraordinary voyage of Pytheas the Greek*, London: Penguin, 2001.

Curl, James Stevens, *Egyptomania: the Egyptian revival, a recurring theme in the history of taste*, Manchester University Press, 1994.

Cutler, Anthony, 'Originality as a cultural phenomenon', in his *Byzantium, Italy and the north: papers on cultural relations*, London: Pindar, 2000.

Dahlquist, Allan, *Megasthenes and Indian religion: a study in motives and types*, Stockholm: Almqvist and Wiksell, 1962.

Dalby, Andrew, *Siren feasts: a history of food and gastronomy in Greece*, London: Routledge, 1996.

Empire of pleasures: luxury and indulgence in the Roman world, London: Routledge, 2000.

Dandamaev, M. A., *A political history of the Achaemenid empire*, Leiden: Brill, 1989.

Dani, Ahmad Hasan, *The historical city of Taxila*, Tokyo: Centre for East Asian Cultural Studies, 1986.

D'Arms, John H., *Romans on the Bay of Naples*, Cambridge, MA: Harvard University Press, 1970.

Commerce and social standing in ancient Rome, Cambridge, MA: Harvard University Press, 1981.

Davidson, James, *Courtesans and fishcakes: the consuming passions of ancient Greece*, New York: St Martin's, 1997.

Derow, Peter, 'Historical explanation: Polybius and his predecessors', in Simon Hornblower (ed.), *Greek historiography*, Oxford: Clarendon, 1994, pp. 73–90.

Derrett, J. D. M., 'The history of "Palladius on the races of India and the Brahmans"', *Classica et Mediaevalia* 21 (1960), 64–135.

'Homer in India', *Journal of the Royal Asiatic Society* series III.2 (1992), 47–57.

'An Indian metaphor in St. John's Gospel', *Journal of the Royal Asiatic Society* series III.9 (1999), 271–86.

Desreumaux, Alain and Francis Schmidt (eds.), *Moîse Géographe. Recherches sur les représentations juives et chrétiennes de l'espace*, Paris: Vrin, 1988.

Detienne, Marcel, *The gardens of Adonis: spices in Greek mythology*, tr. Janet Lloyd, Hassocks: Harvester Press, 1977.

The creation of mythology, tr. Margaret Cook, University of Chicago Press, 1986.

Detienne, Marcel, and Jean-Pierre Vernant, *The cuisine of sacrifice among the Greeks*, tr. Paula Wissing, University of Chicago Press, 1989.

Diamond, Jared M., *Guns, germs, and steel: the fates of human societies*, New York: Norton, 1997.

Diggle, James, *Euripidea: collected essays*, Oxford: Clarendon, 1994.

Dihle, Albrecht, 'The conception of India in Hellenistic and Roman literature', in *Proceedings of the Cambridge Philological Society* 190 (1964), 15–23, repr. in *Antike und Orient*, pp. 89–97.

Dihle, Albrecht, *Umstrittene Daten. Untersuchungen zum Auftreten der Griechen am Roten Meer*, Köln: Westdeutscher Verlag, 1965.

Antike und Orient. Gesammelte Aufsätze, Heidelberg: Winter, 1984.

'Dionysos in Indien', in Pollet (ed.), *India and the ancient world*, 1987, pp. 47–58.

'Arabien und Indien', in *Hérodote et les peuples non grecs*, Entretiens 35, Vandoeuvres: Fondation Hardt, 1990, pp. 41–61.

'Indien und die hellenistisch-römische Welt in der neueren Forschung', *Geographia antiqua* 1 (1992), 151–9.

Greek and Latin literature of the Roman empire, London: Routledge, 1994.

'Early Christianity in India', in Hillard *et al.* (eds.), *Ancient history*, 1998, vol. II, pp. 305–16.

Dihle, Albrecht, 'Indien', *RAC* XVIII (1998), cols. 1–56.

Dilke, O. A. W., *Greek and Roman maps*, Ithaca: Cornell University Press, 1985.

'Cartography in the Byzantine empire', in Harley and Woodward (eds.), *History of cartography*, 1987, vol. I, pp. 258–75.

'The culmination of Greek cartography in Ptolemy', in Harley and Woodward (eds.), *History of cartography*, 1987, vol. I, pp. 177–200.

Dillon, Matthew, *Pilgrims and pilgrimage in ancient Greece*, London: Routledge, 1997.

Dion, Roger, *Aspects politiques de la géographie antique*, Paris: Belles Lettres, 1977.

Dirks, Nicholas B., *Castes of mind: colonialism and the making of modern India*, Princeton University Press, 2001.

Dodds, E. R., *The Greeks and the irrational*, Berkeley: University of California Press, 1951.

Dognini, Cristiano, 'Alessandro Magno e la conoscenza dell' Iliade in India', *Aevum* 71 (1997), 71–7.

Doniger O'Flaherty, Wendy (ed. and tr.), *The Rig Veda*, Harmondsworth: Penguin, 1981.

Doufikar-Aerts, Faustina C. W., 'A legacy of the *Alexander Romance* in Arab writings: Al-Iskandar, founder of Alexandria', in Tatum (ed.), *The search for the ancient novel*, 1994, pp. 323–43.

Dougherty, Carol, *The poetics of colonization: from city to text in Archaic Greece*, Oxford University Press, 1993.

The raft of Odysseus: the ethnographic imagination of Homer's Odyssey, Oxford University Press, 2001.

Douglas, Mary, *Purity and danger: an analysis of the concepts of pollution and taboo*, rev. edn, London: Routledge, 2002.

Doyle, Michael W., *Empires*, Ithaca: Cornell University Press, 1986.

Drew-Bear, Thomas, 'Les voyages d'Aurélius Gaius, soldat de Dioclétien', in *La Géographie administrative et politique d'Alexandre à Mahomet. Actes du colloque de Strasbourg, 14–16 juin 1979*, Strasbourg: Centre de recherche, 1981, pp. 93–141.

Droge, Arthur J., and James D. Tabor, *A noble death: suicide and martyrdom among Jews and Christians in the ancient world*, San Francisco: Harper, 1992.

Dueck, Daniela, *Strabo of Amasia: a Greek man of letters in Augustan Rome*, London: Routledge, 2000.

Dumont, Louis, *Homo Hierarchicus: the caste system and its implications*, University of Chicago Press, 1980.

Duncan-Jones, Richard, *Money and government in the Roman Empire*, Cambridge University Press, 1994.

Düring, Ingemar, *Aristotle in the ancient biographical tradition*, Göteborg University Press, 1957.

Eadie, J. W., *The* Breviarium *of Festus: a critical edition with historical commentary*, London: Athlone, 1967.

Earl, Donald C., *The moral and political tradition of Rome*, Ithaca: Cornell University Press, 1967.

Eck, Bernard, 'Sur la vie de Ctésias', *Révue des études grecques* 103 (1990), 409–34.

Eco, Umberto, 'A portrait of the Elder as a Young Pliny: how to build fame', in Marshall Blonsky (ed.), *On signs*, Baltimore: Johns Hopkins University Press, 1985.

Edson, Evelyn, *Mapping time and space: how medieval mapmakers viewed their world*, London: British Library, 1997.

Edwards, Catharine, *The politics of immorality in ancient Rome*, Cambridge University Press, 1993.

Writing Rome: textual approaches to the city, Cambridge University Press, 1996.

Edwards, Mark, and Simon Swain, (eds.), *Portraits: biographical representation in the Greek and Latin literature of the Roman Empire,* Oxford: Clarendon, 1997.

Eggermont, P. H. L., *Alexander's campaigns in Sind and Baluchistan,* Leuven: Peeters, 1975.

Alexander's campaigns in Southern Punjab, Leuven: Peeters, 1993.

Ehlers, Widu-Wolfgang, 'Mit dem Monsunwind nach Indien', *Würzburger Jahrbücher für Altertumswissenschaft* 11 (1984), 73–84.

Elliott, J. H., *The Old world and the new, 1492–1650*, Cambridge University Press, 1970.

Elsner, Jaś, 'Pausanias: a Greek pilgrim in the Roman world', *Past and Present* 135 (1992), 3–29.

Elsner, John, 'Hagiographic geography: travel and allegory in the *Life of Apollonius of Tyana*', *Journal of Hellenic Studies* 117 (1997), 22–37.

Engels, Johannes, 'Die Geschichte des Alexanderzuges und das Bild Alexanders des Grossen in Strabons Geographika – Zur Interpretation der augusteischen Kulturgeographie Strabons als Quelle seiner historischen Auffassungen', in Will (ed.), *Alexander der Grosse*, 1998, pp. 131–71.

Erbse, Hartmut, *Fiktion und Wahrheit im Werke Herodots*, Göttingen: Vandenhoeck & Ruprecht, 1991.

Erim, K. T., 'A new relief showing Claudius and Britannia from Aphrodisias', *Britannia* 13 (1982), 277–81.

Errington, Elizabeth, and Joe Cribb (eds.), *The crossroads of Asia: transformations in image and symbol in the art of ancient Afghanistan and Pakistan*, Cambridge: Ancient India and Iran Trust, 1992.

Euben, Roxanne L., 'The comparative politics of travel', *Parallax* 9.4 (2003), 18–28.

Fabian, Johannes, *Time and the Other: how anthropology makes its object*, New York: Columbia University Press, 1983.

Fa-Hsien, *A record of Buddhist kingdoms: being an account by the Chinese monk Fa-Hien of his travels in India and Ceylon (AD 399–414) in search of the Buddhist books of discipline*, tr. James Legge, repr. edn, San Francisco: Harper, 1975.

Fairweather, J. A., 'Fiction in the biographies of ancient writers', *Ancient Society* 5 (1974), 231–75.

Faller, Stefan, *Taprobane im Wandel der Zeit. Das Sri-Lanka-Bild in griechischen und lateinischen Quellen zwischen Alexanderzug und Spätantike*, Stuttgart: Steiner, 2000.

Favro, Diane, *The urban image of Augustan Rome*, Cambridge University Press, 1996.

Fehling, Detlev, *Die sieben Weisen und die griechische Chronologie*, Bern: Lang, 1985.

Herodotus and his 'sources', tr. J. G. Howie, Leeds: Cairns, 1989.

Feldman, Louis H., *Jew and gentile in the ancient world*, Princeton University Press, 1993.

Fentress, James and Chris Wickham, *Social memory*, Oxford: Blackwell, 1992.

Fiaccadori, Gianfranco, 'Teofilo Christiano', *Studi classici e orientali* 33 (1983), 295–331 and 34 (1984), 271–308.

Filliozat, Jean, 'La valeur des connaissances gréco-romaines sur l'Inde', *Journal des savants* (1981), 97–135.

Finegan, Jack, *An archaeological history of religions of Indian Asia*, New York: Paragon, 1989.

Finley, Moses I., *The ancient economy*, 2nd edn, Berkeley: University of California Press, 1985.

Fisher, Nick, 'Drink, hybris and the promotion of harmony in Sparta', in Anton Powell (ed.), *Classical Sparta: techniques behind her success*, London: Routledge, 1989, pp. 26–50.

Flach, Dieter, 'Die Germania des Tacitus in ihrem literaturgeschichtlichen Zusammenhang', in Herbert Jankuhn and Dieter Timpe (eds.), *Beiträge zum Verständnis der Germania des Tacitus*, Göttingen: Vandenhoeck & Ruprecht, 1989, pp. 27–58.

Flinterman, Jaap-Jan, *Power, paideia and Pythagoreanism: Greek identity, conceptions of the relationship between philosophers and monarchs and political ideas in Philostratus'* Life of Apollonius, Amsterdam: Gieben, 1995.

Flintoff, Everard, 'Pyrrho and India', *Phronesis* 25 (1980), 88–108.

Fögen, Marie-Therese, *Die Enteignung der Wahrsage. Studien zum kaiserlichen Wissensmonopol in der Spätantike*, Frankfurt: Suhrkamp, 1993.

Foucault, Michel, *The order of things: an archaeology of the human sciences*, New York: Vintage, 1973.
'What is an author?' in David Lodge (ed.), *Modern criticism and theory*, London: Longman, 1988, pp. 197–210.
Discipline and punish: the birth of the prison, tr. Alan Sheridan, 2nd edn, New York: Vintage, 1995.
Fowden, Garth, 'The pagan holy man in late antique society', *JRS* 102 (1982), 33–59.
Empire to commonwealth: consequences of monotheism in late antiquity, Princeton University Press, 1993.
Fowler, Robert, 'Herodotus and his contemporaries', *JHS* 116 (1996), 62–87.
Fraser, P. M., *Ptolemaic Alexandria*, 3 vols., Oxford: Clarendon, 1972.
Cities of Alexander the Great, Oxford: Clarendon, 1996.
Fraser, P. M., 'The world of Theophrastus', in Simon Hornblower (ed.), *Greek historiography*, Oxford: Clarendon, 1994, pp. 167–92.
Friedländer, Paul, *Plato*, New York: Meridian, 1958.
Frugoni, Chiara, *La fortuna di Alessandro magno dall' Antichita al Medioevo*, Florence: La nuova Italia, 1978.
Gabba, Emilio, *Greek knowledge of Jews up to Hecataeus of Abdera*, Berkeley: Center for Hermeneutical Studies in Hellenistic and Modern Culture, 1981.
'True history and false history in classical antiquity', *JRS* 71 (1981), 50–62.
Galinsky, G. Karl, *The Herakles theme: the adaptations of the hero in literature from Homer to the twentieth century*, Totowa: Rowman and Littlefield, 1972.
Augustan culture: an interpretative introduction, Princeton: Princeton University Press, 1996.
Gallazzi, C., and B. Kramer, 'Artemidor im Zeichensaal', *Archiv für Papyrusforschung* 44 (1998), 189–208.
Garnsey, P. D. A., *Ideas of slavery in antiquity*, Cambridge University Press, 1998.
Garnsey, Peter and Richard Saller, *The Roman empire: economy, society and culture*, Berkeley: University of California Press, 1987.
Garzetti, Albino, *From Tiberius to the Antonines*, London: Methuen, 1974.
Geertz, Clifford, *The interpretation of cultures: selected essays*, 2nd edn, New York: Basic, 2000.
Gerini, G. E., *Researches on Ptolemy's Geography of Eastern Asia (Farther India and Indo-Malay Peninsula)*, London: Royal Asiatic Society, 1909.
Geus, Klaus, *Eratosthenes von Kyrene. Studien zur hellenistischen Kultur- und Wissenschaftsgeschichte*, Munich: Beck, 2002.
van Geytenbeek, A. C., *Musonius Rufus and Greek diatribe*, Assen: Van Gorcum, 1963.
Giardina, Andrea, 'The merchant', in Andrea Giardina (ed.), *The Romans*, tr. Lydia G. Cochrane, University of Chicago Press, 1993, pp. 245–71.
Gleason, Maud, *Making men: sophists and self-presentation in ancient Rome*, Princeton University Press, 1995.
le Goff, Jacques, *Time, work and culture in the Middle Ages*, tr. Arthur Goldhammer, University of Chicago Press, 1980.

Goldenberg, David M., *The curse of Ham: race and slavery in early Judaism, Christianity and Islam*, Princeton University Press, 2003.

Goldhill, Simon (ed.), *Being Greek under Rome: cultural identity, the Second Sophistic and the development of empire*, Cambridge University Press, 2001.

Goldsmith, R. W., 'An estimate of the size and structure of the national product of the early Roman empire', *Review of Income and Wealth* 30 (1984), 263–88.

Good, Deirdre Joy, *Reconstructing the tradition of Sophia in Gnostic literature*, Atlanta: Scholars Press, 1987.

Goodman, M. D., 'Texts, scribes and power in Roman Judaea', in Bowman and Woolf, *Literacy and power*, 1994, pp. 99–108.

Gopal, L., 'Textiles in ancient India', *Journal of the Economic and Social History of the Orient* 4 (1961), 42–64.

Gordon, R. L., 'The sacred geography of a *mithraeum*: the example of Sette Sfere', *Journal of Mithraic Studies* 1 (1976), 119–65.

Gordon, R. L., 'Reality, evocation and boundaries in the Mysteries of Mithras', *Journal of Mithraic Studies* 3 (1980), 19–99.

Gould, Peter, and Rodney White, *Mental maps*, 2nd edn, Boston: Houghton Mifflin, 1986.

Gormley, C. M., M. A. Rouse and R. H. Rouse, 'The medieval circulation of the "de chorographia" of Pomponius Mela', *Medieval Studies* 46 (1984), 266–320.

Gosden, Chris and Yvonne Marshall, 'The cultural biography of objects', *World Archaeology* 31 (1999), 169–78.

Gould, John, 'Herodotus and religion', in Hornblower (ed.), *Greek historiography*, 1994, pp. 91–106.

Graeven, Hans, 'Darstellung der Inder in antiken Kunstwerken', *Jahrbuch des deutschen archäologischen Instituts (Berlin)* 15 (1900), 195–218.

Graf, Fritz, *Magic in the ancient world*, Cambridge, MA: Harvard University Press, 1997.

Grafton, Anthony, *Forgers and critics: creativity and duplicity in western scholarship*, Princeton University Press, 1990.

New worlds, ancient texts: the power of tradition and the shock of discovery, Harvard: Belknap, 1992.

Green, Peter, 'Caesar and Alexander: *aemulatio, imitatio, comparatio*', *American Journal of Ancient History* 3 (1978), 1–26.

Alexander to Actium: the historical evolution of the Hellenistic age, Berkeley: University of California Press, 1990.

Greenblatt, Stephen, *Renaissance self-fashioning from More to Shakespeare*, University of Chicago Press, 1980.

Marvelous possessions: the wonder of the New World, University of Chicago Press, 1991.

Griffin, Jasper, *Latin poets and Roman life*, Chapel Hill: University of North Carolina Press, 1986.

Groseclose, Barbara, 'Imag(in)ing Indians', *Art History* 13.4 (1990), 488–515.

Gruen, Erich S., *The Hellenistic world and the coming of Rome*, Berkeley: University of California Press, 1984.

'Cultural fictions and cultural identity', *Transactions of the American Philological Assocation* 123 (1993), 1–14.
'The expansion of the empire under Augustus', *CAH*, 2nd edn (1996), vol. IX, pp. 148–96.
'Rome and the myth of Alexander', in Hillard *et al.* (eds.), *Ancient history*, 1998, vol. I, pp. 178–91.
Güngerich, Rudolf, *Die Küstenbeschreibung in der griechischen Literatur*, Münster: Aschendorff, 1950.
Gupta, Dipankar (ed.), *Social stratification*, Oxford University Press, 1992.
Gurval, Robert Alan, *Actium and Augustus*, Ann Arbor: University of Michigan Press, 1995.
Guthrie, W. K. C., *A history of Greek philosophy*, 6 vols., Cambridge University Press, 1962–81.
The Sophists, Cambridge University Press, 1971.
Habinek, Thomas, *The politics of Roman poetry*, Princeton University Press, 1998.
'Ovid and empire', in Philip Hardie (ed.), *The Cambridge companion to Ovid*, Cambridge University Press, 2002, pp. 46–61.
Hägg, Tomas, *The novel in antiquity*, Berkeley: University of California Press, 1983.
'Callirhoe and Parthenope: the beginnings of the historical novel', *Classical Antiquity* 6 (1985), 184–204.
'Hierocles the lover of truth and Eusebius the Sophist', *Symbolae Osloenses* 67 (1992), 138–50.
Hahn, Thomas, 'The Indian tradition in western medieval intellectual history', *Viator* 9 (1978), 213–34.
Halbfass, Wilhelm, *India and Europe: an essay in understanding*, Albany: SUNY Press, 1988.
Hall, Edith, *Inventing the barbarian: Greek self-definition through tragedy*, Oxford: Clarendon, 1989.
Hall, Jonathan M., *Ethnic identity in Greek antiquity*, Cambridge University Press, 1997.
Hellenicity: between ethnicity and culture, University of Chicago Press, 2002.
Hallo, William W., 'On the antiquity of Sumerian literature', *Journal of the American Oriental Society* 83 (1963), 167–76.
Hanaway, William L., 'Eskandar-nama', *Encyclopaedia Iranica* (1998), vol. VIII, pp. 609–12.
Hänger, Christian, *Die Welt im Kopf. Raumbilder und Strategie im Römischen Kaiserreich*, Göttingen: Vandenhoeck and Ruprecht, 2001.
Hardie, Philip R., *Virgil's* Aeneid: *cosmos and imperium*, Oxford: Clarendon, 1986.
Hardt, Michael and Antonio Negri, *Empire*, Cambridge, MA: Harvard University Press, 2000.
Harl, Kenneth W., *Coinage in the Roman economy*, Baltimore: Johns Hopkins University Press, 1996.
Harley, J. B., and David Woodward (eds.), *History of cartography*, University of Chicago Press, 1987, vol. I.

Harrauer, H., and P. Sijpesteijn, 'Ein neues Dokument zu Roms Indienhandel, P. Vindob. G40822', *Anzeiger der Österreichischen Akademie der Wissenschaften, phil.-hist. Kl.* 122 (1985), 124–55.

Harris, W. V., *War and imperialism in republican Rome, 327–70 BC*, Oxford: Clarendon, 1979.

Harris, W. V., 'Toward a study of the Roman slave trade', *Memoirs of the American Academy in Rome* 36 (1980), 117–40.

Harrison, Mark, *Climates and constitutions*, Oxford University Press, 1999.

Hartog, François, *The mirror of Herodotus: the representation of the other in the writing of history*, tr. Janet Lloyd, Berkeley: University of California Press, 1988.

Hartog, François, *Memories of Odysseus: frontier tales from ancient Greece*, tr. Janet Lloyd, University of Chicago Press, 2001.

Hatzopoulos, M. B., 'Alexandre en Perse: la revanche et l'empire', *Zeitschrift für Papyrologie und Epigrafik* 116 (1997), 41–52.

Hauser, Stephan R., 'Orientalismus', *DNP* XV.1 (2001) cols. 1233–43.

Hawkes, Jacquetta, *Adventurer in archaeology: the biography of Sir Mortimer Wheeler*, New York: St Martin's, 1982.

Healy, John F., *Pliny the elder on science and technology*, Oxford: Clarendon, 1999.

Heckel, Waldemar, *The marshals of Alexander's empire*, London: Routledge, 1992.

Heckel, W. and J. Yardley, 'Roman writers and the Indian practice of suttee', *Philologus* 125 (1981), 305–11.

Henkel, Nikolaus, *Studien zum Physiologus im Mittelalter*, Tübingen: Niemeyer, 1976.

Helms, Mary W., *Craft and the kingly ideal: art, trade, and power*, Austin: University of Texas Press, 1993.

Heuss, A., 'Alexander der Grosse und die politische Ideologie des Altertums', *Antike und Abendland* 4 (1954), 65–104.

Hillard, T. W., R. A. Kearsley, C. E. V. Nixon and A. M. Nobbs (eds.), *Ancient history in a modern university*, 2 vols., North Ryde, NSW, and Grand Rapids, MI: Macquarie University Press and Eerdmans, 1998.

Hinz, Walther, 'Darius und der Suezkanal', *Archäologische Mitteilungen aus Iran* 8 (1975), 115–21.

Hitchner, Bruce, 'The merits and challenges of an *Annaliste* approach to archaeology', *Journal of Roman Archaeology* 7 (1994), 408–17.

Hobsbawm, E. J., *The age of empire, 1875–1914*, New York: Pantheon, 1987.

Hobsbawm, E. J. and Terence Ranger (eds.), *The invention of tradition*, Cambridge University Press, 1983.

Hodder, Ian (ed.), *The meaning of things: material culture and symbolic expression*, London: Unwin Hyman, 1989.

Höhlkeskamp, Karl-J., 'Arbitrators, lawgivers and the codification of law in Archaic Greece: problems and perspectives', *Mètis* 7 (1992), 49–81.

Holt, Frank L., *Thundering Zeus: the making of Hellenistic Bactria*, Berkeley: University of California Press, 1999.

Into the land of bones: Alexander the Great in Afghanistan, Berkeley: University of California Press, 2005.

van Hooff, Anton J. L., *From autothanasia to suicide: self-killing in classical antiquity*, London: Routledge, 1990.

Hopkinson, Neil (ed.), *Studies in the* Dionysiaca *of Nonnus*, Cambridge: Cambridge Philological Society, 1994.

Horden, Peregrine, and Nicholas Purcell, *The corrupting sea: a study of Mediterranean history*, Oxford: Blackwell, 2000.

Hornblower, Simon, 'Sources and their uses', *CAH*, 2nd edn (1994), vol. VI, pp. 1–23.

How, W. W., and J. Wells, *A commentary on Herodotus*, 2 vols., Oxford: Clarendon, 1912.

Howgego, Christopher, 'The supply and use of money in the Roman world 200 BC to AD 300', *Journal of Roman Studies* 82 (1992), 1–32.

Huber, Paul, *Heilige Berge: Sinai, Athos, Golgota – Ikonen, Fresken, Miniaturen*, 2nd edn, Zurich: Benziger, 1982.

Hübner, Wolfgang, 'The Ptolemaic view of the universe', *Greek, Roman and Byzantine Studies* 41 (2000), 59–93.

Huff, Darrell, *How to lie with statistics*, 2nd edn, New York: Norton, 1993.

Hughes, Diane Owen, and Thomas R. Trautmann (eds.), *Time: histories and ethnographies*, Ann Arbor: University of Michigan Press, 1995.

Humphreys, Sally, 'Law, custom and culture in Herodotus', *Arethusa* 20 (1987), 211–20.

Hunt, E. D., *Holy Land pilgrimage in the later Roman empire*, Oxford: Clarendon, 1982.

Huntington, Samuel P., *Clash of civilisations and the remaking of the world order*, New York: Simon and Schuster, 1996.

Huntington, Susan L., *The art of ancient India: Buddhist, Hindu, Jain*, New York: Weatherhill, 1985.

I-ching, *Chinese monks in India: biography of eminent monks who went to the western world in search of the law during the great T'ang dynasty*, tr. Latika Lahiri, Delhi: Motilal Benarsidass, 1986.

Inden, Ronald B., *Imagining India*, Oxford: Blackwell, 1990.

Irmscher, Johannes, 'Sulle origine del concetto Romania', in *Populi e Spazio Romano tra Diritto e Profezia*, Naples: Edizione Scientifiche, 1986, pp. 421–9.

Isaac, Benjamin H., *The limits of empire: the Roman army in the east*, rev. edn, Oxford: Clarendon, 1992.

Isaac, Benjamin H., *The invention of racism in classical antiquity*, Princeton University Press, 2004.

Jacob, Christian, 'Alexandre et la maitrise de l'espace. L'art du voyage dans l'<<Anabase>> d'Arrien', *Quaderni di Storia* 34 (1991), 5–40.

L'Empire de Cartes: approaches théoretique de la cartographie à travers l'histoire. Paris: Michel, 1992.

'Mapping the mind: the earth from ancient Alexandria', in D. Cosgrove (ed.), *Mappings*, London: Consortium, 1999, pp. 24–49.

Jacobs, Bruno, *Die Satrapienverwaltung im Perserreich zur Zeit Darius III*, TAVO Beihefte B87, Wiesbaden: Steiner, 1994.

Janni, Pietro, *La Mappa e il Periplo*, Rome: Bretschneider, 1984.

Jenkins, Richard, 'Rethinking ethnicity: identity, categorization and power', *Ethnic and Racial Studies* 17 (1994), 199–223.

Jennison, George, *Animals for show and pleasure in ancient Rome*, Manchester University Press, 1937.

Jones, A. H. M., 'The Asian trade in antiquity', in *The Roman economy: studies in ancient economic and administrative history*, Oxford: Blackwell, 1974, pp. 140–50.

Jones, A. H. M., *The later Roman empire, 284–602: a social, economic and administrative survey*, 2 vols., Oxford; Blackwell, 1964.

Jones, C. P., *The Roman world of Dio Chrysostom*, Cambridge, MA: Harvard University Press, 1978.

Kinship diplomacy in the ancient world, Cambridge, MA: Harvard University Press, 1999.

'Apollonius of Tyana's passage to India', *Greek, Roman and Byzantine Studies* 42 (2001), 185–99.

de Jong, J. W., 'The discovery of India by the Greeks', *Asiatische Studien* 27 (1973), 115–43.

Karnos, David, 'On Apollonius, Pythagoras and the Jaina vision', in K. J. Boudouris (ed.), *Ionian philosophy*, Athens: International Association for Greek Philosophy, 1989, pp. 211–17.

Karttunen, Klaus, 'The country of fabulous beasts and naked philosophers: India in classical and medieval literature', *Arctos* 21 (1987), 43–52.

India in early Greek literature, Helsinki: Finnish Oriental Society, 1989.

India and the Hellenistic world, Helsinki: Finnish Oriental Society, 1997.

'The ethnography of the fringes', in Egbert J. Bakker *et al.* (eds.), *Brill's companion to Herodotus*, Leiden: Brill, 2002, pp. 457–74.

Kaster, Robert A., 'Controlling reason: declamation in rhetorical education at Rome', in Yun Lee Too (ed.), *Education in Greek and Roman antiquity*, Leiden: Brill, 2001, pp. 317–37.

Keller, O., *Die antike Tierwelt*, 2 vols., Leipzig: Teubner, 1920.

Kennedy, David *et al.*, *The twin towns of Zeugma on the Euphrates: rescue work and historical studies*, Portsmouth, RI: *JRA* supplement 27, 1998.

Kennedy, Duncan F., '"Augustan" and "anti-Augustan": reflections on terms of reference', in Anton Powell (ed.), *Roman poetry and propaganda in the age of Augustus*, London: Routledge, 1992, pp. 26–58.

The arts of love: five studies in the discourse of Roman love elegy, Cambridge University Press, 1993.

Kennedy, George A., *Greek rhetoric under Christian emperors*, Princeton University Press, 1983.

A new history of classical rhetoric, Princeton University Press, 1994.

Kent, Roland G., *Old Persian*, 2nd edn, New Haven: AOS, 1953.

Kerferd, G. B., 'The first Greek sophists', *Classical Review* 64 (1950), 8–10.

'What does the wise man know?' in John M. Rist (ed.), *The Stoics*, Berkeley: University of California Press, 1978, pp. 125–36.

Kienast, Dietmar, 'Augustus und Alexander', *Gymnasium* 76 (1969), 43–56.

Kindstrand, Jan Fredrik, 'The Greek concept of proverbs', *Eranos* 76 (1978), 71–85.

Kirk, G. S., and J. E. Raven, *The Presocratic philosophers*, Cambridge University Press, 1957.

Kitamura, Kunio, 'Cosmas Indicopleustès et la figure de la terre', Desreumaux and Schmidt (eds.), in *Moïse Géographe*, pp. 79–98.

Klijn, A. F. J., *The Acts of Thomas: introduction, text, and commentary*, 2nd edn, Leiden: Brill, 2003.

Klingenberg, Georg, 'Imperium', *RAC* XVII (1996), cols. 1121–42.

Koch, Guntram, *Frühchristliche Sarkophage*, Munich: Beck, 2000.

Konstan, David, 'Persians, Greeks and empire', *Arethusa* 20.1–2 (1987), 59–73.

Koster, W. J. W., 'Chaldäer', *RAC* II (1954), cols. 1006–21.

Kramer, B., 'The earliest known map of Spain (?) and the geography of Artemidorus of Ephesus on papyrus', *Imago Mundi* 53 (2001), 115–20.

Kramer, Norbert, 'Das Itinerar Σταθμοὶ Παρθικοί des Isidor von Charax – Beschreibung eines Handelsweges?' *Klio* 85 (2003), 120–30.

Krueger, Derek, *Symeon the holy fool*, Berkeley: University of California Press, 1996.

'The bawdy and society: the shamelessness of Diogenes in Roman imperial culture', in Branham and Goulet-Cazé (eds.), *The Cynics*, pp. 222–39.

Kuhrt, Amélie, *The ancient Near East, c. 3000–300 BC*, 2 vols., London: Routledge, 1994.

Kulke, Hermann, and Dietmar Rothermund, *A history of India*, 3rd edn, London: Routledge, 1998.

Kurke, Leslie, 'The politics of *habrosune* in archaic Greece', *Classical Antiquity* 11 (1992), 81–120.

Kurz, Otto, 'Cultural relations between Parthia and Rome', *Cambridge History of Iran*, vol. III.1 (1983), pp. 559–67.

Kytzler, Bernhard (ed.), *Roma Aeterna*, Zurich: Artemis, 1972.

Lach, Donald F., *Asia in the making of Europe*, University of Chicago Press, 1965, vol. I.

Lambert, W. G., *Babylonian wisdom literature*, Oxford: Clarendon, 1960.

Lane Fox, R. J., 'The Itinerary of Alexander: Constantius to Julian', *CQ* 47 (1997), 239–52.

Lardinois, André, 'The wisdom and wit of many: the orality of Greek proverbial expressions', in Janet Watson (ed.), *Speaking volumes: orality and literacy in the Greek and Roman world*, Leiden: Brill, 2001, pp. 93–108.

Lassen, Christian[us], 'De nominibus, quibus a veteribus appellantur Indorum philosophi', *Rheinisches Museum* 1 (1833), 171–90.

Indische Alterthumskunde, 5 vols., Leipzig: Kittler, 1856–62.

Lateiner, Donald, *The historical method of Herodotus*, University of Toronto Press, 1989.

Lecoq, Danielle, 'L'image d'Alexandre à travers les mappemondes médievales (XIIe–XIIIe)', *Geographia antiqua* 2 (1993), 63–103.

Lefkowitz, Mary R., *Lives of the Greek poets*, London: Duckworth, 1981.
Lenfant, Dominique, 'L'Inde de Ctésias', *Topoi* 5 (1990), 309–36.
(ed. and comm.), *Ctésias de Cnide, La Perse, l'Inde*, Paris: Belles Lettres, 2004.
Lenski, Noel, '*Initium mali Romano populo*: contemporary reactions to the Battle of Adrianople', *Transactions of the American Philological Association* 127 (1997), 129–68.
Failure of empire: Valens and the Roman state in the fourth century AD, Berkeley: University of California Press, 2002.
Lepper, F. A., *Trajan's Parthian war*, Oxford: Clarendon, 1948.
Lesky, Albin, *A history of Greek literature*, London: Routledge, 1966.
Lestringant, Frank, *Cannibals: the discovery and representation of the cannibal from Columbus to Jules Verne*, tr. Rosemary Morris, Oxford: Polity, 1997.
Lévy, Isidore, *La légende de Pythagore en Grèce en Palestine*, Paris: Champion, 1927.
Lewis, Martin W. and Kären E. Wigen, *The myth of continents: a critique of meta-geography*, Berkeley: University of California Press, 1997.
Lightfoot, C. S., 'Trying to rescue Zeugma', *Journal of Roman Archaeology* 14 (2001), 643–8.
Lincoln, Bruce, *Authority: construction and corrosion*, University of Chicago Press, 1994.
Lindegger, Peter, *Griechische und römische Quellen zum peripharen Tibet*, 3 vols., Zurich: Libresso, 1979–93.
Lintott, A. W., 'Imperial expansion and moral decline in the Roman Republic', *Historia* 21 (1972), 626–38.
Imperium Romanum: politics and administration, London: Routledge, 1993.
Lloyd, A. B., *Herodotus, Book II: introduction*, Leiden: Brill, 1975.
Lloyd, G. E. R., *Polarity and analogy; two types of argumentation in early Greek thought*, Cambridge University Press, 1966.
Greek science after Aristotle, New York: Norton, 1973.
Science, folklore and ideology: studies in the life sciences in ancient Greece, Cambridge University Press, 1983.
Revolutions in wisdom, Berkeley: University of California Press, 1987.
Demystifying mentalities, Cambridge University Press, 1990.
Long, A. A., 'Socrates in Hellenistic philosophy', *CQ* 38 (1988), 150–71.
'The Socratic tradition: Diogenes, Crates and Hellenistic ethics', in Branham and Goulet-Cazé (eds.), *The Cynics*, 1994, pp. 28–46.
Lovejoy, Arthur O, and George Boas, *Primitivism and related ideas in antiquity*, Baltimore: Johns Hopkins University Press, 1935.
Lowenthal, David, *The past is a foreign country*, Cambridge University Press, 1985.
Lozovsky, Natalia, *'The earth is our book': geographical knowledge in the Latin West, ca. 400–1000*, Ann Arbor: University of Michigan Press, 2000.
Luce, T. J., 'Ancient views on the causes of bias in historical writing', *Classical Philology* 84 (1989), 16–31.
Lund, Allan A., *Zum Germanenbild der Römer. Eine Einführung in die antike Ethnographie*, Heidelberg: Winter, 1990.

Lund, Allan A., 'Versuch einer Gesamtinterpretation der Germania des Tacitus', *ANRW* II.33.3 (1991), pp. 1858–988.

Luttwak, Edward N., *The grand strategy of the Roman empire from the first century AD to the third*, Baltimore: Johns Hopkins University Press, 1974.

McCann, Anna Marguerite, *Roman sarcophagi in the Metropolitan Museum of Art*, New York: Metropolitan Museum of Art, 1978.

MacCormack, Sabine, 'Latin prose panegyrics', in T. A. Dorey (ed.), *Empire and aftermath: Silver Latin II*, London: Routledge and Kegan Paul, 1975, pp. 143–205.

Art and ceremony in late antiquity, Berkeley: University of California Press, 1981.

'*Loca sancta*: the organisation of sacred topography in late antiquity', in Robert Ousterhout (ed.), *The blessings of pilgrimage*, Urbana: University of Illinois Press, 1990, pp. 7–40.

McCoskey, Denise Eileen, 'By any other name? Ethnicity and the study of ancient identity', *Classical Bulletin* 79 (2003), 93–109.

Macdonald, W. A., and J. A. Pinto, *Hadrian's Villa and its legacy*, New Haven: Yale University Press, 1995.

Macdonnell, Arthur A. (ed.), *A Vedic reader for students*, Oxford University Press, 1917.

Macfie, Alexander Lyon (ed.), *Orientalism: a reader*, New York University Press, 2000.

MacLeod, Roy (ed.), *The Library of Alexandria: centre of learning in the ancient world*, London: Tauris, 2000.

Mahadevan, I., 'Tamil-Brahmi graffito', in S. E. Sidebotham and W. Z. Wendrich (eds.), *Berenike 1995: preliminary report of the 1995 excavations at Berenike (Egyptian Red Sea coast)*, Leiden: CNWS, 1996, pp. 206–8.

Majeed, Javed, 'Comparativism and references to Rome in British imperial attitudes to India', in Catharine Edwards (ed.), *Roman presences: receptions of Rome in European culture, 1798–1945*, Cambridge University Press, 1999.

Majumdar, Ramesh Chandra, *The classical accounts of India*, Calcutta: Mukhopadhyay, 1960.

Marcus, George E., *Anthropology as cultural critique*, University of Chicago Press, 1986.

Marincola, John, *Authority and tradition in ancient historiography*, Cambridge University Press, 1997.

Marks, John H., *Visions of one world: legacy of Alexander*, Guilford, CT: Four Quarters, 1985.

Markus, R. A., *The end of ancient Christianity*, Cambridge University Press, 1990.

Marrou, Henri Irenée, *A history of education in antiquity*, tr. George Lamb, Madison: University of Wisconsin Press, 1956.

Marshall, Sir John Hubert, *A guide to Taxila*, Cambridge University Press, 1960.

Martels, Zweder von (ed.), *Travel fact and travel fiction: studies on fiction, literary tradition, scholarly discovery and observation in travel writing*, Leiden: Brill, 1994.

Martin, Dale B., *Inventing superstition: from the Hippocratics to the Christians*, Cambridge, MA: Harvard University Press, 2004.

Martin, Richard P., 'The Seven Sages as performers of wisdom', in Carol Dougherty and Leslie Kurke (eds.), *Cultural poetics in archaic Greece*, Cambridge: Cambridge University Press, 1993, pp. 108–28.

Martin, Richard P., 'The Scythian accent: Anacharsis and the Cynics', in Branham and Goulet-Cazé (eds.), *The Cynics*, 1996, pp. 136–55.

Martin, Victor, 'Un recueil de diatribes cyniques Pap. Genev. inv. 271', *Museum Helveticum* 16 (1959), 77–115.

Mason, P., 'Notes on cormorant-fishing: Europe and its other', *Ibero-Amerikanisches Archiv* NF 13 (1987), 147–74.

Mattern, Susan P., *Rome and the enemy: imperial strategy in the Principate*, Berkeley: University of California Press, 1999.

Matthews, John, *The Roman Empire of Ammianus*, London: Duckworth, 1989.

Matthews, Thomas F., *Byzantium from antiquity to the Renaissance*, New York: Abrams, 1998.

Mattingly, D. J. (ed.), *Dialogues in Roman imperialism: power, discourse and discrepant experience in the Roman empire* (Portsmouth, RI: Journal of Roman Archaeology, Supplementary series no. 23, 1997).

Mattingly Harold, *Coins of the Roman empire in the British Museum.* Vol. III, *Nerva to Hadrian*, London: British Museum, 1936.

Matz, Friedrich, *Die Dionysischen Sarkophage*, 4 vols., Berlin: Mann, 1968–75.

Mayerson, Philip, 'A confusion of Indias: Asian India and African India in the Byzantine sources', *Journal of the American Oriental Society* 113 (1993), 169–74.

Mazzarino, Santo, 'On the name of the *Hipalus* (*Hippalus*) wind in Pliny', in F. de Romanis and A. Tchernia (eds.), *Crossings: early Mediterranean contact with India*, Delhi: Manohar, 1997, pp. 72–9.

Meredith, D., 'Annius Plocamus: two inscriptions from the Berenice road', *JRS* 43 (1953), 38–40.

Merkelbach, Reinhold, *Die Quellen des griechischen Alexanderromans*, 2nd edn, Munich: Beck, 1977.

Meuli, Karl, *Odyssee und Argonautika. Untersuchungen zur griechischen Sagengeschichte und zum Epos*, Berlin: Weidmann, 1921.

Meyendorff, J., 'Wisdom-Sophia: contrasting approaches to a complex theme', *Dumbarton Oaks Papers* 41 (1987), 391–401.

Mignolo, Walter D., *The darker side of the Renaissance: literacy, territoriality and colonization*, Ann Arbor: University of Michigan Press, 1995.

Millar, Fergus *et al.*, *The Roman empire and its neighbours*, 2nd edn, New York: Holmes and Meier, 1981.

Millar, Fergus, *The Roman Near East, 31 BC–AD 337*, Cambridge, MA: Harvard University Press, 1993.

'Caravan cities: the Roman Near East and long-distance trade by land', in Michel Austin, Jill Harries and Christopher Smith (eds.), *Modus operandi: essays in honour of Geoffrey Rickman*, London: Institute of Classical Studies, 1998, pp. 119–37.

'Looking east from the classical world', *International History Review* 20.3 (1998), 507–31.

Miller, J. Innis, *The spice trade of the Roman empire*, Oxford: Clarendon, 1969.

Miller, Konrad, *Itineraria Romana. Römische Reisewege an der hand der Tabula Peutingeriana*, Stuttgart: Strecker und Schröder, 1916.

Milns, R. D., 'Greek writers on India before Alexander', *Australian Journal of Politics and History* 35 (1989), 353–63.

Mingana, A., 'The early spread of Christianity in India', *Bulletin of the John Rylands Library* 10 (1926), 435–96.

Miquel, A. (ed.), *Usâma Ibn Mundiqh, Des Enseignements de la Vie*, Paris: Colin, 1983.

Mitchiner, John E., *Traditions of the Seven Rsis*, Delhi: Motilal Benarsidass, 1982.

Mitter, Partha, *Much maligned monsters: history of European reactions to Indian art*, Oxford: Clarendon, 1977.

Moles, J. L., 'The career and conversion of Dio Chrysostom', *JHS* 98 (1978), 79–100.

Momigliano, Arnaldo, 'Il razionalismo di Ecateo di Mileto', *Atene et Roma* n.s. 12 (1931), 15–44.

Studies in historiography, London: Weidenfeld and Nicolson, 1966.

'Fattori orientali della storiografia ebraica post-esilica e della storiografia greca', *Terzo Contributo alla Storia degli Studi classici e del Mondo antico*, Rome: Edizioni di Storia e Letteratura, 1966 [1965], vol. II, pp. 807–18.

'Tradizione e invenzione in Ctesia', in *Quarto Contributo* (Rome: Edizione di Storia e Letteratura, 1969 [1931]), pp. 181–212.

Alien wisdom: the limits of Hellenization, Cambridge University Press, 1975.

Essays in ancient and modern historiography, Oxford: Blackwell, 1977.

'The historians of the ancient world and their audiences: some suggestions', *Annali di Scuola Normale di Pisa* 8 (1978), 59–75.

Mommsen, Theodor, *Das römische Staatsrecht*, 3 vols., 3rd edn, Leipzig: Hirzel, 1877.

Mommsen, Theodor E., *Medieval and Renaissance studies*, Ithaca: Cornell University Press, 1959.

Monmonier, Mark, *How to lie with maps*, 2nd edn, University of Chicago Press, 1996.

Morgan, Elaine and Stephen Davies, *Red Sea pilot: Aden to Cyprus*, 2nd edn, Huntingdon: Imray, 2002.

Morgan, J. R., 'Make-believe and make believe: the fictionality of the Greek novels', in Christopher Gill and T. P. Wiseman (eds.), *Lies and fiction in the ancient world*, Austin: University of Texas Press, 1994, pp. 175–229.

Morrison, Kathleen D., 'Sources, approaches, definitions', in Susan E. Alcock *et al.* (eds.), *Empires*, Cambridge: Cambridge University Press, 2001, pp. 1–9.

Most, Glenn W., 'The stranger's strategem', *JHS* 109 (1989), 114–33.

Most, Glenn W. (ed.), *Collecting fragments – Fragmente sammeln*, Göttingen: Vandenhoeck & Ruprecht, 1997.

Müller, Klaus E., *Geschichte der antiken Ethnographie und ethnographischen Theoriebildung*, 2 vols., Wiesbaden: Steiner, 1972–80.

Mund-Dopchie, Monique, 'L'invention de l'Inde merveilleuse. Structures de l'imaginaire et découverte de l'Autre lointain', in Jean-Claude Carrière *et al.* (eds.), *Inde, Grèce ancienne* (1995), pp. 99–112.

Murphy, E. M., and J. P. Mallory, 'Herodotus and the cannibals', *Antiquity* 74.284 (2000), 388–94.

Murphy, Trevor, *Pliny the Elder's* Natural history*: the empire in the encyclopedia*, Oxford University Press, 2004.

Murray, Oswyn, 'Herodotus and Hellenistic culture', *CQ* 22 (1972), 200–13.

Murray, Oswyn (ed.), *Sympotica: a symposium on the symposium*, Oxford: Clarendon, 1990.

Musti, Domenico, 'Syria and the East', in *CAH*, 2nd edn (1984), vol. VII.1, pp. 175–220.

Narain, A. K., *The Indo-Greeks*, Oxford: Clarendon, 1957.

'The Greeks of Bactria and India', *CAH*, 2nd edn (1989), vol. VIII.2, pp. 388–421.

Neiman, David, 'Ethiopia and Kush: Biblical and ancient Greek geography', *Ancient World* 3 (1980), 35–42.

Nesselrath, Heinz-Günther, 'Herodot und die Enden der Erde', *Museum Helveticum* 52 (1995), 20–44.

Neugebauer, O., *The exact sciences in antiquity*, 2nd edn, Providence: Brown University Press, 1957.

Neusner, Jacob, 'The Jews east of the Euphrates', *ANRW* II.9.1 (1978), 46–69.

Nicolet, Claude, *The world of the citizen in Republican Rome*, tr. P. S. Falla, Berkeley: University of California Press, 1980.

Space, geography, and politics in the early Roman empire, Ann Arbor: University of Michigan Press, 1991.

Nigg, Joe, *The book of fabulous beasts: a treasury of writings from ancient times to the present*, Oxford University Press, 1999.

Nixon, C. E. V., and Barbara Saylor Rodgers, *In praise of later Roman emperors*, Berkeley: University of California Press, 1996.

Noy, David, *Foreigners and Rome: citizens and strangers*, London: Duckworth, 2000.

Ober, Josiah, 'Tiberius and the political testament of Augustus', *Historia* 31 (1982), 306–28.

Mass and elite: rhetoric, ideology and the power of the people, Princeton University Press, 1989.

Ogilvie, R. M., and Sir Ian Richmond (eds.), *Cornelii Taciti* De Vita Agricolae, Oxford: Clarendon, 1967.

Olmstead, A. T., *History of the Persian empire*, University of Chicago Press, 1948.

Onfray, Michel, *Cynismes. Portrait du philosophe en chien*, Paris: Grasset, 1990.

Orrieux, Claude, 'La "parenté" entre Juifs et Spartiates', in Raoul Lonis (ed.), *L'Etranger dans le monde grec*, Nancy: Presses Universitaires, 1988, pp. 169–91.

Otto, August, *Die Sprichwörter und sprichwörtlichen Redensarten der Römer*, Leipzig: Teubner, 1890.

Pagden, Anthony, *The fall of natural man: the American Indian and the origins of comparative ethnology*, Cambridge University Press, 1982.

Empires and peoples: Europeans and the rest of the world, from antiquity to the present, London: Weidenfeld and Nicolson, 2001.

Palmer, J. A. B., 'Periplus Maris Erythraei: the Indian evidence as to the date', *CQ* 41 (1947), 137–40.

Park, Lorraine, and Katherine Daston, *Wonders and the order of nature, 1150–1750* New York: Zone, 1998.

Parker, A. J., *Ancient shipwrecks of the Mediterranean and the Roman provinces*, Oxford: Tempus reparatum, 1992.

Parker, Grant, 'Porous connections: the Mediterranean and the Red Sea', *Thesis Eleven* 67 (2001), 59–79.

Paschoud, François, *Roma Aeterna. Études sur le patriotisme romain dans l'occident latin à l'époque des grandes invasions*, Rome: Institut suisse, 1967.

Pearson, Lionel, *The lost histories of Alexander the Great*, New York: American Philological Association, 1960.

Pédech, Paul, *Historiens compagnons d'Alexandre*, Paris: Belles Lettres, 1984.

Perry, Ben Edwin, *The ancient romances*, Berkeley: University of California Press, 1967.

Pettinato, Giovanni, *Semiramide*, Milan: Rusconi, 1985.

Petzke, G., *The Traditionen über Apollonius von Tyana und das Neue Testament*, Leiden: Brill, 1970.

Philip, J. A., *Pythagoras and early Pythagoreanism*, University of Toronto Press, 1966.

Photiadès, Pénélope, 'Les diatribes cyniques du papyrus de Genève 271, leurs traductions et élaborations successives', *Museum Helveticum* 16 (1959), 116–39.

Pierce, R. H., 'A sale of an Alodian slave girl: a reexamination of Papyrus Strassburg Inv. 1404', *Symbolae Osloenses* 70 (1995), 159–64.

Pigulewskaja, N., *Byzanz auf den Wegen nach Indien*, Berlin: Akademie, 1969.

Plácido, Domingo, 'L'image d'Alexandre dans la conception plutarchéenne de l'empire Romain', *Dialogues d'histoire ancienne* 21 (1995), 131–38.

Pollet, Gilbert (ed.), *India and the ancient world: history, trade and culture before* AD *650*, Leuven: Peeters, 1987.

Possehl, Gregory L., *Indus age: the beginnings*, Philadelphia: University of Pennsylvania Press, 1999.

Potter, David S., 'Odor and power in the Roman empire', in J. I. Porter (ed.), *Constructions of the classical body*, Ann Arbor: University of Michigan Press, 1999, pp. 169–89.

Potter, D. S., *Prophets and Emperors*, Cambridge, MA: Harvard University Press, 1994.

Priaulx, Osmund de Beauvoir, 'The Indian travels of Apollonius of Tyana', *Journal of the Royal Asiatic Society* 17 (1860), 70–105.

Pritchett, W. Kendrick, *The liar school of Herodotus*, Amsterdam: Gieben, 1993.

Purcell, Nicholas, 'Maps, lists, money, order and power', *JRS* 80 (1990), 178–82.

'The city of Rome', in Richard Jenkyns (ed.), *The legacy of Rome: a new appraisal*, Oxford: Clarendon, 1992, pp. 421–53.

'The city of Rome and the *plebs urbana* in the late Republic', *CAH*, 2dn edn (1994), vol. IX, pp. 644–88.

'Eating fish: the paradoxes of seafood', in John Wilkins *et al.* (eds.), *Food in antiquity*, University of Exeter Press, 1995, pp. 132–49.

'Rome and its development under Augustus and his successors', *CAH*, 2nd edn (1996), vol. X, pp. 782–811.

Rajak, Tessa, 'Dying for the law: the martyr's portrait in Jewish-Greek literature', in M. J. Edwards and Simon Swain (eds.), *Portraits: biographical representation in the Greek and Latin literature of the Roman empire*, Oxford: Clarendon, 1997, pp. 39–68.

Raman, Shankar, *Framing 'India': the colonial imaginary in early modern culture*, Stanford University Press, 2002.

Raschke, Manfred G., 'New studies in Roman commerce with the east', *ANRW* II.9.2 (1978), 604–1378.

Rawson, Elizabeth, *The Spartan tradition in European thought*, Oxford: Clarendon, 1969.

Ray, Himanshu P. (ed.), *Archaeology of seafaring: the Indian Ocean in the ancient period*, Delhi: Pragati, 1999.

The archaeology of seafaring in ancient South Asia, Cambridge University Press, 2003.

Reade, Julian (ed.), *The Indian Ocean in antiquity*, London: Kegan Paul, 1996.

Reardon, Bryan P., *The form of Greek romance*, Princeton University Press, 1991.

The Red Sea pilot, London: Hydrographic Office, 1873.

Reese, Wilhelm, *Die griechischen Nachrichten über Indien*, Leipzig: Teubner, 1914.

Reitzenstein, R., *Hellenistische Wundererzählungen*, Leipzig: Teubner, 1906.

Renou, Louis (ed.), *La Géographie de Ptolémée, L'Inde (VII, 1–4)*, Paris: Champion, 1925.

Reynolds, L. D. (ed.), *Texts and transmission*, Oxford: Clarendon, 1983.

Reynolds, L. D., and N. G. Wilson (eds.), *Scribes and scholars: a guide to the transmission of Greek and Latin literature*, 3rd edn, Oxford: Clarendon, 1991.

Rhys Davids, T. W. (tr.), *The questions of King Milinda*, 2 vols., Oxford: Clarendon, 1890–4.

Rice, Michael, *Search for the Paradise Island*, London: Longman, 1984.

The archaeology of the Arabian Gulf, c. 5000–323 BC, London: Routledge, 1994.

Richardson, L. J., Jr, *A new topographical dictionary of ancient Rome*, Baltimore: Johns Hopkins University Press, 1992.

Riese, Alexander (ed.), *Geographi Latini Minores*, Heilbronn: Henning, 1878.

Robb, Peter (ed.), *The concept of race in South Asia*, Oxford University Press, 1995.

Robert, L., 'De Delphes à l'Oxus. Inscriptions grecques nouvelles de la Bactriana', *Comptes rendus de l'Académie des Inscriptions et Belles-Lettres* (1968), 416–57 = *Opera minora selecta* 5, Amsterdam: Hakkert, 1989, 510–51.

Roberts, Colin H., and T. C. Skeat, *The birth of the codex*, London: British Academy, 1983.
Roberts, Deborah H., Frances M. Dunn and Don P. Fowler (eds.), *Classical closure: reading the end in Greek and Latin literature*, Princeton University Press, 1997.
Robinson, T. R., 'Alexander and the Ganges: the text of Diodorus 18.6.2', *Ancient History Bulletin* 7 (1993), 84–99.
Rodewald, Cosmo, *Money in the age of Tiberius*, Manchester University Press, 1976.
de Romanis, Federico, *Cassia, cinnamomo, ossidiana. Uomini e merci tra Oceano indiano e Mediterraneo*, Rome: Bretschneider, 1996.
'Graffiti greci da Wadi Menih el-Her. Un Vestorius tra Coptos e Berenice', *Topoi* 6 (1996), 731–45.
de Romanis, F. and A. Tchernia (eds.), *Crossings: early Mediterranean contact with India*, Delhi: Manohar, 1997.
Romm, James S., 'Aristotle's elephant and the myth of Alexander's scientific patronage', *American Journal of Philology* 110 (1989), 566–75.
The edges of the earth in ancient thought, Princeton University Press, 1992.
Romm, James S., 'Dog heads and noble savages: Cynicism before the Cynics?' in Branham and Goulet-Cazé (eds.), *The Cynics*, 1996, pp. 121–35.
Rosenmeyer, Patricia A., *Ancient epistolary fictions: the letter in Greek literature*, Cambridge University Press, 2001.
Ross, D. J. A., *Alexander historiatus: a guide to medieval illustrated Alexander literature*, Frankfurt am Main: Lang, 1988.
Rostovtseff, M., *Caravan cities*, Oxford University Press, 1932.
Russell, D. A., *Greek declamation*, Cambridge University Press, 1983.
Russell, D. A., and N. G. Wilson (eds.), *Menander Rhetor*, Oxford: Clarendon, 1981.
Sachau, Edward C., *Alberuni's India*, Delhi: D. K. Publications, 1910.
Sacks, Kenneth S., *Diodorus Siculus and the first century*, Princeton University Press, 1990.
Sahai, B., *Iconography of minor Hindu and Buddhist deities*, Delhi: Abhinav, 1975.
Said, Edward, *Orientalism*, New York: Vintage, 1995 with new afterword [1978].
Beginnings: intention and method, 2nd edn, New York: Basic, 1997.
de Ste Croix, G. E. M., *The class struggle in the ancient Greek world*, London: Duckworth, 1981.
Salisbury, Joyce E., 'Human beasts and bestial humans in the Middle Ages', in Jennifer Ham and Matthew Senior (eds.), *Animal acts: configuring the human in western history*, London: Routledge, 1997, pp. 9–22.
Salles, Jean-François, 'The Arab-Persian Gulf under the Seleucids', in Amélie Kuhrt and Susan Sherwin-White (eds.), *Hellenism in the East*, Berkeley: University of California Press, 1987, pp. 75–108.
Sallmann, K. G., *Die Geographie des älteren Plinius in ihrem Verhältnis zu Varro*, Berlin: De Gruyter, 1971.

Salway, Benet, 'Travel, *itineraria* and *tabellaria*', in Adams and Laurence (eds.), *Travel and geography*, 2001, pp. 22–66.

Santelia, Stefania (ed. and comm.), *Charition liberata (P. Oxy. 413)*, Bari: Levante, 1991.

Santirocco, Matthew S., 'Horace and Augustan ideology', *Arethusa* 28 (1995), 225–43.

Schachermeyr, Fritz, 'Alexander und die Ganges-Länder', *Innsbrucker Beiträge zur Kulturgeschichte* 3 (1955), 123–35.

Scheid, John, 'The priest', in Andrea Giardina (ed.), *The Romans*, University of Chicago Press, 1993, pp. 55–84.

Scheidel, Walter, and Sitta von Reden (eds.), *The ancient economy*, London: Routledge, 2002.

Schepens, Guido, *L'Autopsie' dans la méthode des historiens grecs du Ve siècle avant J.-C.*, Brussels: AWLSK, 1980.

'Jacoby's *FGrHist*: problems, methods, prospects', in Most (ed.), *Collecting fragments*, 1997, pp. 144–72.

Schepens, Guido, and Kris Delcroix, 'Ancient paradoxography: origin, evolution, production and reception', in Oronzo Pecere and Antonio Stramaglia (eds.), *La letteratura di consumo nel mondo Greco-latino*, Cassino: Università degli Studi di Cassino, 1996, pp. 373–460.

Schiwek, H., 'Das Persische Golf als Schiffahrts- und Seehandelsroute in Achämenidischer Zeit und in der Zeit Alexanders des Grossen', *Bonner Jahrbücher* 162 (1962), 4–97.

Schlumberger, Daniel, *L'Orient hellénisé. L'Art grec et ses héritiers dans l'Asie non méditerranéenne*, Paris: Michel, 1970.

Schlumberger, Daniel, Louise Robert, André Dupont-Sommer and Émile Benveniste , 'Une bilingue gréco-araméene d'Asoka', *Journal Asiatique* 246 (1958), 1–48.

Schmidt, Erich F., *Persepolis*, 3 vols., Chicago: Oriental Institute, 1953–70.

Schmidt, Francis, 'Naissance d'une géographie juive', in Desreumaux and Schmidt (eds.), *Moîse Géographe*, 1988, pp. 13–30.

Schmitt, Rüdiger, 'Ctesias', in *Encyclopaedia Iranica*, ed. Ehsan Yarshatar, 1993, vol. VI, pp. 441–6.

Schmitthenner, W. 'Rome and India: aspects of universal history during the Principate', *JRS* 69 (1979), 90–106.

Schneider, Pierre, *L'Éthiopie et L'Inde. Interférence et confusions aux extrémités du monde antique (VIIIe siècle J.-C.–VIe siècle après J.-C.)*, Rome: MEFRA, 2004.

Schneider, Rolf Michael, *Bunte Barbaren: Orientalenstatuen aus farbigem Marmor in der römischen Repräsentationskunst*, Worms: Werner, 1986.

'Die Faszination des Feindes: Bilder der Parther und des Orients in Rom', in Josef Wiesehöfer (ed.), *Das Partherreich*, 1998, pp. 95–146.

Schoff, Wilfred (ed.), *The Periplus of the Erythraean Sea: travel and trade in the Indian Ocean*, New York: Longmans, 1912.

Schofield, Malcolm, *Saving the city: philosopher-kings and other classical paradigms*, London: Routledge, 1999.

Schön, Franz, 'Fluss', in Holger Sonnabend (ed.), *Mensch und Landschaft in der Antike. Lexikon der historischen Geographie*, Stuttgart: Metzler, 1999, pp. 145–50.

Schwarz, F. F., 'Kosmas und Sielediba', *Ziva Antika* 25 (1975), 469–90.

'Magna India Pliniana', *Wiener Studien* (1995), 439–65.

Scott, Joan W., 'Experience', in Judith Butler and Joan W. Scott (eds.), *Feminists theorize the political*, New York: Routledge, 1992, pp. 71–96.

Scullard, H. H., *The elephant in the Greek and Roman world*, Ithaca: Cornell University Press, and London: Thames and Hudson, 1974.

Seager, Robin, 'Some imperial virtues in the Latin prose panegyrics: the demands of propaganda and the dynamics of literary composition', *Proceedings of the Liverpool Latin Seminar* 4 (1983), 129–66.

Searle-Chatterjee, Mary, and Ursula Sharma (eds.), *Contextualising caste: post-Dumontian perspectives*, Oxford: Clarendon, 1994.

Sedlar, Jean W., *India and the Greek world: a study in the transmission of culture*, Totowa, NJ: Rowman and Littlefield, 1980.

Seibert, Jakob, *Alexander der Grosse*, Darmstadt: Wissenschaftliche Buchgesellschaft, 1972.

Seldeslachts, Erik, 'Translated loans and loan translations as evidence of Graeco-Indian bilingualism in antiquity', *L'Antiquité classique* 67 (1998), 273–99.

Sevcenko, I., 'A shadow outline of virtue: the classical heritage of Greek Christian literature', in K. Weitzmann (ed.), *The age of spirituality*, Princeton University Press, 1980, pp. 53–73.

Shabazi, A. Sh., 'Darius Haft Kisvar', in Heidemarie Koch and D. N. Mackenzie (eds.), *Kunst, Kultur und Geschichte der Achämenidenzeit und ihr Fortleben*, ed., DAI(T) Ergbd. 10, Berlin: Reimer, 1983, pp. 239–46.

Shaw, Brent D., 'The elder Pliny's African geography', *Historia* 30 (1981), 424–71.

'"Eaters of flesh and drinkers of milk": the ancient Mediterranean ideology of the pastoral nomad', *Ancient Society* 13–14 (1982–3), 5–31.

'Rebels and outsiders', *CAH*, 2nd edn, (2000), vol. XI, pp. 361–403.

Sherk, Robert K. (ed.), *The Roman empire: Augustus to Hadrian*, Cambridge University Press, 1988.

Sherwin-White, Susan, and Amélie Kuhrt, *From Samarkhand to Sardis; a new approach to the Seleucid empire*, London: Duckworth, 1993.

Sidebotham, Steven E., *Roman economic policy in the Erythra Thalassa, 30 BC–AD 217*, Leiden: Brill, 1986.

Sidebotham, S. E., and W. Z. Wendrich (eds.), *Berenike 1994: preliminary report of the 1994 excavations at Berenike (Egyptian Red Sea coast)*, Leiden: CNWS, 1995.

Sinnatamby, J. R., *Sri Lanka in Ptolemy's* Geography, Colombo: n.p., 1968.

Smith, Morton, *Jesus the magician*, San Francisco: Harper and Row, 1978.

Smith, Vincent A., 'The Indian travels of Apollonius of Tyana', *Zeitschrift der deutschen morgenländischen Gesellschaft* 68 (1914), 329–44.

The early history of India from 600 BC to the Muhammadan conquest, 4th edn, Oxford: Clarendon, 1957.

Snowden, Frank M., Jr, *Blacks in antiquity: Ethiopians in the Greco-Roman experience*, Cambridge, MA: Harvard University Press, 1970.

'Bernal's "Blacks" and the Afrocentrists', in Mary R. Lefkowitz and Guy MacLean Rogers (eds.), *Black Athena revisited*, Chapel Hill: University of North Carolina Press, 1996, pp. 112–28.

Spence, Jonathan D., *The Chan's great continent: China in western minds*, New York: Norton, 1998.

Spencer, Diana, *The Roman Alexander: reading a cultural myth*, University of Exeter Press, 2002.

Stadter, Philip A., *Arrian of Nicomedia*, Chapel Hill: University of North Carolina Press, 1980.

Stanford, W. B., *The Ulysses theme: a study in the adaptability of a traditional hero*, 2nd edn, Ann Arbor: University of Michigan Press, 1968.

Steinby, Eva Margareta (ed.), *Lexicon Topographicum Urbis Romae*, 6 vols., Rome: Quasar, 1993–2000.

Stern, E. Marianne, 'Early Roman glass from Heis on the north Somali coast', in *Annales du 10e Congrès de l'Association pour l'Histoire du Verre*, Amsterdam: AHIV, 1985, pp. 23–36.

'Early Roman export glass in India', in Begley and De Puma (eds.), *Rome and India*, 1991, pp. 113–24.

'The glass from Heis', in J. Desanges, E. M. Stern and P. Ballet (eds.), *Sur les routes antiques de l'Azanie et de l'Inde. Le Fonds Révoil du Músee de l'Homme (Heïs et Damo, en Somalie)*, Paris: MAI, 1993, pp. 21–61.

Stoianovitch, Traian, *French historical method: the Annales paradigm*, Ithaca: Cornell University Press, 1976.

Stoneman, Richard, *Legends of Alexander the Great*, London: Everyman, 1994.

'Who are the Brahmans? Indian lore and Cynic doctrine in Palladius' *de bragmanibus* and its models', *CQ* 44 (1994), 500–10.

'Naked philosophers: the Brahmans in the Alexander historians and the *Alexander Romance*', *JHS* 115 (1995), 115–29.

'The legacy of Alexander in ancient philosophy', in Joseph Roisman (ed.), *Brill's companion to Alexander the Great*, Leiden: Brill, 2003, pp. 325–45.

Strong, D. E., *Greek and Roman gold and silver plate*, London: Methuen, 1966.

Stroumsa, Guy, *Barbarian philosophy: the religious revolution of early Christianity* Tübingen: Mohr Siebeck, 1999.

Stückelberger, Alfred, 'Kolumbus und die antiken Wissenschaften', *Archiv für Kulturgeschichte* 69 (1987), 331–40.

'Ptolemy and the problem of scientific perception of space', in Talbert and Broderson (eds.), *Space in the Roman world*, 2004, pp. 27–40.

Swain, Joseph Ward, 'The theory of the four monarchies', *Cl. Phil.* 35 (1940), 1–21.

Swain, Simon, *Hellenism and empire: language, classicism and power in the Greek world, AD 50–250*, Oxford: Clarendon, 1996.

Syme, Ronald, *The Roman revolution*, Oxford: Clarendon, 1939.

Anatolica: studies in Strabo, Oxford: Clarendon, 1995.

Szegedy-Maszak, Andrew, 'Legends of the Greek lawgivers', *Greek, Roman and Byzantine Studies* 19 (1978), 199–211.

Tabacco, Raffaella (ed.), *Itinerarium Alexandri. Testo, apparato critico, introduzione, traduzione e commento*, Città di Castello: Olschki, 2000.

Talbert, Richard J. A. (ed.), *Barrington atlas of the Greek and Roman world*, Princeton University Press, 2000.

'Cartography and taste in Peutinger's Roman map', in Talbert and Brodersen (eds.), *Space in the Roman world*, 2004, pp. 113–41.

'Rome's provinces as framework for world-view', in L. de Ligt, E. A. Hemelrijk and H. W. Singor (eds.), *Roman rule and civic life: local and regional perspectives.* Impact of Empire, vol. IV. Amsterdam: Gieben, 2004, pp. 21–37.

Talbert Richard, and Kai Brodersen (eds.), *Space in the Roman world: its perception and presentation*, Münster: Lit, 2004.

Tarn, W. W., *The Greeks in Bactria and India*, 3rd edn, rev. by F. L. Holt and M. C. J. Miller, Chicago: Ares, 1997.

Tatum, James (ed.), *The search for the ancient novel*, Baltimore: Johns Hopkins University Press, 1994.

Teltscher, Kate, *India inscribed: European and British writing on India, 1600–1800*, Oxford University Press, 1995.

Thapar, Romila, 'Asokan India and the Gupta age', in A. L. Basham (ed.), *A cultural history of India*, Oxford University Press, 1975, pp. 38–51.

'Society and historical consciousness: the Itihasa-Purana tradition', in Sabyasachi Bhattacharya and Romila Thapar (eds.), *Situating Indian history: for Sarvapalli Gopal*, Oxford University Press, 1986, pp. 353–83.

A history of India, 2nd edn, London: Penguin, 1990, vol. I.

Asoka and the decline of the Mauryas, rev. edn, Oxford University Press, 1997.

Cultural pasts: essays in early Indian history, Oxford University Press, 2000.

Early India: from the origins to AD 1300, Berkeley: University of California Press, 2002.

Thiel, J. H., *Eudoxus of Cyzicus: a chapter in the history of the sea-route to India and the route around the Cape in ancient times*, Groningen: Wolters, 1967.

Thomas, Navakatesh J., *Die syrisch-orthodoxe Kirche der südindischen Thomas-Christen*, Würzburg: Augustinus, 1967.

Thomas, Richard F., *Lands and peoples in Roman poetry: the ethnographic tradition*, Cambridge: Cambridge Philological Society, 1982.

Thomas, Rosalind, *Herodotus in context: ethnography, science, and the art of persuasion*, Cambridge University Press, 2000.

Thompson, D'Arcy Wentworth, *A glossary of Greek birds*, Oxford: Clarendon, 1895.

Thompson, Lloyd A., *Romans and blacks*, London: Routledge, 1989.

Thompson, Stith, *Motif-index of folk-literature*, 6 vols., Bloomington: Indiana University Press, 1955–8.

Thomson, J. Oliver, *History of ancient geography*, Cambridge University Press, 1948.

Thundy, Zacharias P., *Buddha and Christ: nativity stories and Indian traditions*, Leiden: Brill, 1993.

Thurn, Nikolaus, 'Der Aufbau der Exemplasammlung des Valerius Maximus', *Hermes* 129 (2001), 79–94.

Timmer, Barbara Catherina Jacoba, *Megasthenes en de Indische maatschappij*, Amsterdam: H. J. Paris, 1930.

Tissot, Y. 'L'encratisme des Acts de Thomas', *ANRW* II.25 (1988), 1415–30.

Todorov, Tzvetan, *On human diversity: nationalism, racism and exoticism in French thought*, tr. Catherine Porter, Cambridge, MA: Harvard University Press, 1993.

The conquest of America: the question of the other, tr. Richard Howard, New York: Harper and Row, 1997.

Toll, Katharine, 'Making Roman-ness and the *Aeneid*', *Classical Antiquity* 16 (1997), 34–56.

Toynbee, J. M. C., *The Hadrianic school: a chapter in the history of Greek art*, Cambridge University Press, 1934.

Trautmann, Thomas R., *Kautilya and the Arthasastra; a statistical investigation of the authorship and evolution of the text*, Leiden: Brill, 1971.

'Elephants and the Mauryas', in S. N. Mukherjee (ed.), *India: history and thought: essays in honor of A. L. Basham*, Calcutta: Subarnarekha, 1982, pp. 254–81.

Aryans and British India, Berkeley: University of California Press, 1997.

Treu, U. 'The Greek Physiologus', in Hillard *et al.* (eds.), *Ancient history in a modern university*, 1998, vol. II, pp. 426–32.

Trüdinger, Karl, *Studien zur Geschichte der griechisch-römischen Ethnographie*, Basel: Birkhäuser, 1911.

Tuan, Yi-Fu, *Space and place: the perspective of experience*, Minneapolis: University of Minnesota Press, 1977.

Tulving, Endel, 'Episodic and semantic memory', in Endel Tulving and Wayne Donaldson (eds.), *The organization of memory*, New York: Academic Press, 1972, pp. 381–403.

Tuplin, Christopher, 'Darius' Suez canal and Persian imperialism', *Achaemenid History Workshop* 6 (1991), 237–81.

Turner, Paula J., *Roman coins from India*, London: Royal Numismatic Society, 1989.

Turner, P. J., and J. E. Cribb, 'Numismatic evidence for the Roman trade with ancient India', in Julian Reade (ed.), *The Indian Ocean in antiquity*, London: Kegan Paul, 1996, pp. 309–20.

Vasaly, Ann, *Representations: images of the earth in Ciceronian oratory*, Berkeley: University of California Press, 1993.

Vasunia, Phiroze, *The gift of the Nile: Hellenizing Egypt from Aeschylus to Alexander*, Berkeley: University of California Press, 2001.

'Hellenism and empire: reading Edward Said', *Parallax* 9 (2003), 88–97.

Vernant, Jean-Pierre, 'Ambiguity and reversal: on the enigmatic structure of *Oedipus Rex*' in Jean-Pierre Vernant and Pierre Vidal-Naquet (eds.), *Myth and tragedy in ancient Greece*, tr. Janet Lloyd, New York: Zone, 1988, pp. 113–40.

Myth and society in ancient Greece, tr. Janet Lloyd, New York: Zone, 1990.

Versluys, M. J., *Aegyptiaca Romana: Nilotic scenes and the Roman views of Egypt*, Leiden: Brill, 2002.

Vidal-Naquet, Pierre, 'Flavius Arrien entre deux mondes', in Pierre Savinel (tr.), *Arrien, Histoire d'Alexandre*, Paris: Minuit, 1984.

Vogelsang, Willem, 'The Achaemenids and India', *Achaemenid History Workshop* 4 (1990), 93–110.

Vogt, Josef, 'Herodot in Ägypten', in Walter Marg (ed.), *Herodot. Eine Auswahl aus der neueren Forschung*, Darmstadt: Wissenschaftliche Buchgesellschaft, 1962 [1929], pp. 412–33.

Walbank, F. W., *A historical commentary on Polybius*, Oxford: Clarendon, 1957, vol. I.

Walbank, Frank, 'A Greek looks at Rome: Polybius VI revisited', *Scripta Classica Israelica* 17 (1998), 45–59.

Wallace-Hadrill, Andrew, 'The elder Pliny and man's unnatural history', *Greece and Rome* 37 (1990), 80–96.

Houses and society in Pompeii and Herculaneum, Princeton University Press, 1994.

Warmington, E. H., *The commerce between the Roman empire and India*, 2nd edn, New York: Octagon, 1974.

Weerakkody, D. P. M., *Taprobane: ancient Sri Lanka as known to Greeks and Romans*, Turnhout: Brepols, 1997.

Wehrli, Fritz (ed.), *Die Schule des Aristoteles II. Aristoxenos*, 2nd edn, Basel: Schwabe, 1967.

Weitzmann, Kurt, 'The classical in Byzantine art as a mode of individual expression', in *Byzantine Art, an [sic] European Art: lectures*, n.e., Athens: Department of Antiquities, 1966, pp. 148–77.

Studies in classical and Byzantine manuscript illumination, ed. H. L. Kessler, University of Chicago Press, 1971.

Welsby, Derek A., *The kingdom of Kush: the Napatan and Meroitic Empires*, Princeton: Markus Wiener, 1998.

Wendrich, W. Z., R. S. Tomber, S. E. Sidebotham, J. A. Harrell, R. T. J. Cappers and R. S. Bagnall, 'Berenike crossroads: the integration of information', *Journal of the Economic and Social History of the Orient* 46.1 (2003) 46–87.

West, M. L., *Early Greek philosophy and the Orient*, Oxford: Clarendon, 1971.

East of Helicon: west Asiatic elements in Greek poetry and myth, Oxford: Clarendon, 1997.

West, Stephanie, 'Herodotus' portrait of Hecataeus', *JHS* 111 (1991), 144–60.

Westrem, Scott D., *The Hereford map: a transcription of the legends with commentary*, Turnhout: Brepols, 2001.

Wheeler, R. E. M., *Rome beyond the imperial frontiers*, Harmondsworth: Penguin, 1954.

Whitcomb, Donald, 'Quseir al-Qadim and the location of Myos Hormos', *Topoi* 6 (1996), 747–72.

White, Peter, *Promised verse: poets in the society of Augustan Rome*, Cambridge, MA: Harvard University Press, 1993.

White, T. H., *The book of beasts, being a translation from a Latin bestiary of the twelfth century*, London: Cape, 1954.

Whitmarsh, Tim, *Greek literature and the Roman empire: the politics of imitation*, Oxford University Press, 2001.

Whittaker, C. R., *Frontiers of the Roman empire: a socio-economic study*, Baltimore: Johns Hopkins University Press, 1994.

'"To reach out to India and pursue the dawn": the Roman view of India', *Studies in History* 14.1 (1998), 1–20.

Rome and its frontiers: the dynamics of empire, Routledge: London, 2004.

Wiedemann, Thomas, *Greek and Roman slavery*, London: Routledge, 1981.

Wiesehöfer, Josef (ed.), *Das Partherreich und seine Zeugnisse. The Arsacid Empire: sources and documentation. Beiträge des internationalen Colloquiums, Eutin (27.-30. Juni 1996)*, Stuttgart: Steiner, 1998.

Wilcken, Ulrich, 'Punt-Fahrten in der Ptolemäerzeit', *Zeitschrift für ägyptische Sprache und Altertumskunde* 60 (1925), 86–102.

Wilken, Robert L., *The land called holy: Palestine in Christian history and thought*, New Haven: Yale University Press, 1992.

Will, E., *Les Palmyréniens. Venise des sables*, Paris: Colin, 1992.

Will, W., and J. Heinrichs (eds.), *Zu Alexander dem Grossen. Festschrift G. Wirth*, 2 vols., Amsterdam: Hakkert, 1988.

Will, Wolfgang (ed.), *Alexander der Grosse. Eine Welteroberung und ihr Hintergrund. Vorträge des Internationalen Bonner Alexanderkolloquiums, 19.-21.12.1996*, Bonn: Habelt, 1998.

Williams, Gordon, *Tradition and originality in Roman poetry*, Oxford: Clarendon, 1968.

Willis, William H., and Klaus Maresch, 'The encounter of Alexander with the Brahmans', *Zeitschrift für Papyrologie und Epigrafik* 74 (1988), 59–83.

Wilson, N. G., *Scholars of Byzantium*, Baltimore: Johns Hopkins University Press, 1983.

From Byzantium to Italy: Greek studies in the Italian Renaissance, Baltimore: Johns Hopkins University Press, 1992.

Wimbush, Vincent L., and Richard Valantasis (eds.), *Asceticism*, Oxford: Clarendon, 1995.

Wink, André, 'From the Mediterranean to the Indian Ocean: medieval history in geographic perspective', *Comparative Studies in Society and History* 44.3 (2002), 416–45.

Wirzubski, Chaim, *Libertas as a political idea at Rome during the late Republic and early Principate*, Cambridge University Press, 1950.

Wittkower, Rudolf, 'Marvels of the East: a study in the history of monsters', *Journal of the Warburg and Courtauld Institutes* 6 (1943), 159–97.

Wolf, Eric R., *Europe and the people without history*, Berkeley: University of California Press, 1982.

Wolska, Wanda, *La Topographie chrétienne de Cosmas Indicopleustès: théologie et science au VIe siècle*, Paris: Presses Universitaires, 1962.

Wolska-Conus, Wanda (ed.), *Cosmas Indicopleustès*, Topographie chrétienne, pref. by Paul Lemerle, 3 vols., Paris: du Cerf, 1968–73.
Wolska-Conus, Wanda, 'Geographie', *RAC* vol. X (1978), cols. 155–222.
Woodcock, George, *The Greeks in India*, London: Faber, 1966.
Woodman, A. J., *Rhetoric in classical historiography*, London: Croom Helm, 1988.
Woodward, David, 'Medieval *Mappaemundi*', in Harley and Woodward (eds.), *History of cartography*, 1987, vol. I, pp. 286–370.
Woolf, Greg, 'Monumental writing and the expansion of Roman society in the early empire', *JRS* 86 (1996), 22–39.
Woolner, A. C., *Asoka: text and glossary*, Oxford University Press, 1924.
Yavetz, Zvi, 'The *Res Gestae* and Augustus' public image', in *Caesar Augustus: seven aspects*, Oxford: Clarendon, 1984, pp. 1–36.
Young, Gary K., *Rome's eastern trade: international commerce and imperial policy, 31 BC–AD 305*, London: Routledge, 2001.
Young, T. Cuyler, Jr, 'The consolidation of the empire and its limits and growth under Darius and Xerxes', *CAH*, 2nd edn, vol. IV (1988), pp. 53–111.
Yü, Ying-shih, *Trade and expansion in Han China*, Berkeley: University of California Press, 1967.
Zambrini, Andrea, 'Gli Indika di Megastene', *Annali di Scuola Normale di Pisa* 12 (1982), 71–149 and 15 (1985), 781–853.
Zanker, Paul, *Power of images in the age of Augustus*, tr. Alan Shapiro, Ann Arbor: University of Michigan Press, 1988.
The mask of Socrates: the image of the intellectual in antiquity, Berkeley: University of California Press, 1995.
Pompeii: public and private life, Cambridge, MA: Harvard University Press, 1998.
Zeitlin, Froma I., 'Visions and revisions of Homer', in Simon Goldhill (ed.), *Being Greek under Rome: cultural identity, the Second Sophistic and the development of Empire*, Cambridge University Press, 2001, pp. 195–266.
Zelzer, Klaus, *Die alten lateinischen Thomasakten. Texte und Untersuchungen zur Geschichte der altchristlichen Literatur* 122, Berlin: Akademie, 1977.

Index